Existential Psychotherapy

Books by the Same Author

Theory and Practice of Group Psychotherapy

Every Day Gets a Little Closer: A Twice-Told Therapy
(with Ginny Elkin)

Encounter Groups: First Facts
(with Morton A. Lieberman and Matthew B. Miles)

EXISTENTIAL PSYCHOTHERAPY

Irvin D. Yalom

Basic Books, Inc., Publishers

NEW YORK

Library of Congress Cataloging in Publication Data

Yalom, Irvin D   1931–
  Existential psychotherapy.

  Includes bibliographical references and index.
  1. Existential psychotherapy.   I. Title.
RC489.E93Y34   616.89   80-50553
ISBN: 0–465–02147–6

To Marilyn, for every reason.

PART II / Freedom

PART III / Isolation

CONTENTS

Contents

ACKNOWLEDGMENTS

Many have helped me in my work, and I am unable to thank them all: this book was several years in the writing, and my debts stretch back beyond my memory. Rollo May and Dagfin Follesdal were exceptionally important teachers and guides. Many colleagues read and criticized all or parts of the manuscript: Jerome Frank, Julius Heuscher, Kent Bach, David Spiegel, Alex Comfort, James Bugental, Marguerite Lederberg, Michael Bratman, Mitchell Hall, Alberta Siegel, Alvin Rosenfeld, Herbert Leiderman, Michael Norwood, and numerous Stanford psychiatric residents. To all, my gratitude.

I am indebted to Gardner Lindzey and the Center for Advanced Study in the Behavioral Sciences for providing me with an ideal setting for scholarship during my fellowship year of 1977–78. I am deeply grateful to Stanford University, which throughout my career has generously provided me with the equipment of academic life: intellectual freedom, material support, and professional colleagues of the highest order. I am grateful, too, to Thomas Gonda, Chairman of the Department of Psychiatry, for considerately shielding me from administrative chores. And to Marjorie Crosby, for her sponsorship and encouragement. Phoebe Hoss provided magnificent editorial assistance. This is a long book, and every word of every draft from first scribblings to finished manuscript was typed by my secretary, Bea Mitchell, whose patience, exuberance, and diligence rarely flagged over the many years we worked together. My wife, Marilyn, provided not only endless sustenance but, as with all my previous books, invaluable substantive and editorial counsel.

Grateful acknowledgment is made for permission to quote from the following sources:

The Standard Edition of the Complete Psychological Works of Sigmund Freud, translated and edited by James Strachey. By permission of Sigmund Freud Copyrights Ltd., The Hogarth Press Ltd., and The Institute of Psycho-Analysis; also of Allen & Unwin Ltd. and Basic Books, Inc.

EST* 60 Hours That Transform Your Life, by Adelaide Bry. Copyright © 1976 by Adelaide Bry. Reprinted by permission of Harper & Row Publishers, Inc.

Acknowledgments

Maria Nagy, "The Child's Theories Concerning Death," *Journal of Genetic Psychology* (1948) 73:3-27. Reprinted by permission of the author and *The Journal Press*.

"Everyman," in M. Abrams, et al., eds., *The Norton Anthology of English Literature*, vol. I, pp. 281-303. Copyright © 1962. Reprinted by permission of W. W. Norton, Inc.

E. Fromm, D. Suzuki, and R. DeMartino, *Zen Buddhism and Psychoanalysis*. Copyright © 1960. Reprinted by permission of Harper & Row Publishers, Inc.

"Forgive, O Lord," from *The Poetry of Robert Frost*, edited by Edward Connery Lathem. Copyright © 1962 by Robert Frost. Copyright © 1967 by Holt, Rinehart and Winston. Reprinted by permission of Holt, Rinehart and Winston, Publishers. Four lines from "Desert Places," from *The Poetry of Robert Frost*, edited by Edward Connery Lathem. Copyright © 1936 by Robert Frost. Copyright © 1964 by Lesley Frost Ballantine. Copyright © 1969 by Holt, Rinehart and Winston. Reprinted by permission of Holt, Rinehart and Winston, Publishers.

Purpose in Life Test (PIL) by James C. Crumbaugh and Leonard T. Maholick. Reprinted with permission of James C. Crumbaugh. Published by Psychometric Affiliates, P. O. Box 3167, Munster, Indiana 46321.

V. Frankl, "Fragments from the Logotherapeutic Treatment in Four Cases," in A. Burton, ed., *Modern Psychotherapeutic Practice* (Palo Alto, Calif.: Science Behavior Book, Inc., 1965). Reprinted by permission of Arthur Burton.

Existential Psychotherapy

CHAPTER 1

Introduction

ONCE, several years ago, some friends and I enrolled in a cooking class taught by an Armenian matriarch and her aged servant. Since they spoke no English and we no Armenian, communication was not easy. She taught by demonstration; we watched (and diligently tried to quantify her recipes) as she prepared an array of marvelous eggplant and lamb dishes. But our recipes were imperfect; and, try as hard as we could, we could not duplicate her dishes. "What was it," I wondered, "that gave her cooking that special touch?" The answer eluded me until one day, when I was keeping a particularly keen watch on the kitchen proceedings, I saw our teacher, with great dignity and deliberation, prepare a dish. She handed it to her servant who wordlessly carried it into the kitchen to the oven and, without breaking stride, threw in handful after handful of assorted spices and condiments. I am convinced that those surreptitious "throw-ins" made all the difference.

That cooking class often comes to mind when I think about psychotherapy, especially when I think about the critical ingredients of successful therapy. Formal texts, journal articles, and lectures portray therapy as precise and systematic, with carefully delineated stages, strategic technical interventions, the methodical development and resolution of transference, analysis of object relations, and a careful, rational program of insight-offering interpretations. Yet I believe deeply that, when no one is looking, the therapist throws in the "real thing."

3

But what are these "throw-ins," these elusive, "off the record" extras? They exist outside of formal theory, they are not written about, they are not explicitly taught. Therapists are often unaware of them; yet every therapist knows that he or she cannot explain why many patients improve. The critical ingredients are hard to describe, even harder to define. Indeed, is it possible to define and teach such qualities as compassion, "presence," caring, extending oneself, touching the patient at a profound level, or—that most elusive one of all—wisdom?

One of the first recorded cases of modern psychotherapy is highly illustrative of how therapists selectively inattend to these extras.[1] (Later descriptions of therapy are less useful in this regard because psychiatry became so doctrinaire about the proper conduct of therapy that "off the record" maneuvers were omitted from case reports.) In 1892, Sigmund Freud successfully treated Fraulein Elisabeth von R., a young woman who was suffering from psychogenic difficulties in walking. Freud explained his therapeutic success solely by his technique of abreaction, of de-repressing certain noxious wishes and thoughts. However, in studying Freud's notes, one is struck by the vast number of his other therapeutic activities. For example, he sent Elisabeth to visit her sister's grave and to pay a call upon a young man whom she found attractive. He demonstrated a "friendly interest in her present circumstances"[2] by interacting with the family in the patient's behalf: he interviewed the patient's mother and "begged" her to provide open channels of communication with the patient and to permit the patient to unburden her mind periodically. Having learned from the mother that Elisabeth had no possibility of marrying her dead sister's husband, he conveyed that information to his patient. He helped untangle the family financial tangle. At other times Freud urged Elisabeth to face with calmness the fact that the future, for everyone, is inevitably uncertain. He repeatedly consoled her by assuring her that she was not responsible for unwanted feelings, and pointed out that her degree of guilt and remorse for these feelings was powerful evidence of her high moral character. Finally, after the termination of therapy, Freud, hearing that Elisabeth was going to a private dance, procured an invitation so he could watch her "whirl past in a lively dance." One cannot help but wonder what really helped Fraulein von R. Freud's extras, I have no doubt, constituted powerful interventions; to exclude them from theory is to court error.

It is my purpose in this book to propose and elucidate an approach to psychotherapy—a theoretical structure and a series of techniques emerging from that structure—which will provide a framework for many of the extras of therapy. The label for this approach, "existential psychotherapy," defies succinct definition, for the underpinnings of the existential orientation are not empirical but are deeply intuitive. I shall begin by offering a formal definition, and then, throughout the rest of this book, I shall elucidate that definition: *Existential psychotherapy is a dynamic approach to therapy which focuses on concerns that are rooted in the individual's existence.*

It is my belief that the vast majority of experienced therapists, regardless of their adherence to some other ideological school, employ many of the existential insights I shall describe. The majority of therapists realize, for example, that an apprehension of one's finiteness can often catalyze a major inner shift of perspective, that it is the relationship that heals, that patients are tormented by choice, that a therapist must catalyze a patient's "will" to act, and that the majority of patients are bedeviled by a lack of meaning in their lives.

But the existential approach is more than a subtle accent or an implicit perspective that therapists unwittingly employ. Over the past several years, when lecturing to psychotherapists on a variety of topics, I have asked, "Who among you consider yourselves to be existentially oriented?" A sizable proportion of the audience, generally over 50 percent, respond affirmatively. But when these therapists are asked, "What *is* the existential approach?" they find it difficult to answer. The language used by therapists to describe any therapeutic approach has never been celebrated for its crispness or simple clarity; but, of all the therapy vocabularies, none rivals the existential in vagueness and confusion. Therapists associate the existential approach with such intrinsically imprecise and apparently unrelated terms as "authenticity," "encounter," "responsibility," "choice," "humanistic," "self-actualization," "centering," "Sartrean," and "Heideggerian"; and many mental health professionals have long considered it a muddled, "soft," irrational, and romantic orientation which, rather than being an "approach," offers a license for improvisation, for undisciplined, woolly therapists to "do their thing." I hope to demonstrate that such conclusions are unwarranted, that the existential approach is a valuable, effective psychotherapeutic paradigm, as rational, as coherent, and as systematic as any other.

Existential Therapy: A Dynamic Psychotherapy

Existential psychotherapy is a form of dynamic psychotherapy. "Dynamic" is a term frequently used in the mental health field—as in "psychodynamics"; and if one is to understand one of the basic features of the existential approach, it is necessary to be clear about the meaning of dynamic therapy. "Dynamic" has both lay and technical meanings. In the lay sense "dynamic" (deriving from the Greek *dunasthi*, "to have strength or power") evokes energy and movement (a "dynamic" football player or politician, "dynamo," "dynamite"); but this is not its technical sense for, if it were, what therapist would own to being nondynamic—that is, slow, sluggish, stagnant, inert? No, the term has a specific technical use that involves the concept of "force." Freud's major contribution to the understanding of the human being is his dynamic model of mental functioning—a model that posits that there are forces in conflict within the individual, and that thought, emotion, and behavior, both adaptive and psychopathological, are the resultant of these conflicting forces. Furthermore—and this is important—*these forces exist at varying levels of awareness;* some, indeed, are entirely unconscious.

The psychodynamics of an individual thus include the various unconscious and conscious forces, motives, and fears that operate within him or her. The dynamic psychotherapies are therapies based upon this dynamic model of mental functioning.

So far, so good. Existential therapy, as I shall describe it, fits comfortably in the category of the dynamic therapies. But what if we ask, Which forces (and fears and motives) are in conflict? What is the *content* of this internal conscious and unconscious struggle? It is at this juncture that dynamic existential therapy parts company from the other dynamic therapies. Existential therapy is based on a radically different view of the specific forces, motives, and fears that interact in the individual.

The precise nature of the deepest internal conflicts is never easy to identify. The clinician working with a troubled patient is rarely able to examine primal conflicts in pristine form. Instead, the patient harbors an enormously complex set of concerns: the primary concerns are deeply buried, encrusted with layer upon layer of repression, denial, displacement, and symbolization. The clinical investigator must contend with a clinical picture of many threads so matted together that disentanglement is difficult. To identify the primary conflicts, one must use many avenues of access—deep reflection, dreams, nightmares, flashes

6

of profound experience and insight, psychotic utterances, and the study of children. I shall, in time, explore these avenues, but for now a stylized schematic presentation may be helpful. A brief review of three contrasting views of the individual's prototypic intrapsychic conflict—Freudian, neo-Freudian, and existential—illustrates by counterpoint the existential view of psychodynamics.

FREUDIAN PSYCHODYNAMICS

According to Freud, the child is governed by instinctual forces that are innate and, like a fern frond, gradually unfurl through the psychosexual developmental cycle. There are conflicts on several fronts: dual instincts (ego instincts versus libidinal instincts or, in the second theory, Eros versus Thanatos) oppose one another; the instincts collide with the demands of the environment and, later, with the demands of the internalized environment—the superego; the child is required to negotiate between the inner press for immediate gratification and the reality principle which demands delay of gratification. The instinctively driven individual is thus at war with a world that prevents satisfaction of innate aggressive and sexual appetites.

NEO-FREUDIAN (INTERPERSONAL) PSYCHODYNAMICS

The neo-Freudians—especially Harry Stack Sullivan, Karen Horney, and Erich Fromm—present another view of the individual's basic conflict. The child, rather than being instinct-powered and preprogrammed, is instead a being who, aside from innate neutral qualities like temperament and activity levels, is entirely shaped by cultural and interpersonal environment. The child's basic need is for security—for interpersonal acceptance and approval—and the quality of interaction with security-providing significant adults determines his or her* character structure. The child, though not powered by instincts, nonetheless has great innate energy, curiosity, an innocence of the body, an inherent potential for growth, and a wish for exclusive possession of loved adults. These attributes are not always consonant with the demands of surrounding significant adults, and the core conflict is between these natural growth inclinations and the child's need for security and approval. If a child is unfortunate enough to have parents so caught up in their own neurotic struggles that they can neither provide

---

* Throughout this book I have tried to avoid language with sexist connotations. Because linguistic convention lags behind social change, I have not always been successful.

security nor encourage autonomous growth, then severe conflict ensues. In such a struggle, growth is always compromised for the sake of security.

EXISTENTIAL PSYCHODYNAMICS

The existential position emphasizes a different kind of basic conflict: neither a conflict with suppressed instinctual strivings nor one with internalized significant adults, but *instead a conflict that flows from the individual's confrontation with the givens of existence.* And I mean by "givens" of existence certain ultimate concerns, certain intrinsic properties that are a part, and an inescapable part, of the human being's existence in the world.

How does one discover the nature of these givens? In one sense the task is not difficult. The method is deep personal reflection. The conditions are simple: solitude, silence, time, and freedom from the everyday distractions with which each of us fills his or her experiential world. If we can brush away or "bracket" the everyday world, if we reflect deeply upon our "situation" in the world, upon our existence, our boundaries, our possibilities, if we arrive at the ground that underlies all other ground, we invariably confront the givens of existence, the "deep structures," which I shall henceforth refer to as "ultimate concerns." This process of reflection is often catalyzed by certain urgent experiences. These "boundary" or "border" situations, as they are often referred to, include such experiences as a confrontation with one's own death, some major irreversible decision, or the collapse of some fundamental meaning-providing schema.

This book deals with four ultimate concerns: death, freedom, isolation, and meaninglessness. The individual's confrontation with each of these facts of life constitutes the content of the existential dynamic conflict.

Death. The most obvious, the most easily apprehended ultimate concern is death. We exist now, but one day we shall cease to be. Death will come, and there is no escape from it. It is a terrible truth, and we respond to it with mortal terror. "Everything," in Spinoza's words, "endeavors to persist in its own being";[3] and a core existential conflict is the tension between the awareness of the inevitability of death and the wish to continue to be.

Freedom. Another ultimate concern, a far less accessible one, is freedom. Ordinarily we think of freedom as an unequivocally positive concept. Throughout recorded history has not the human being yearned and striven for freedom? Yet freedom viewed from the perspective of ultimate ground is riveted to dread. In its existential sense "freedom" refers to the absence of external structure. Contrary to everyday experience, the human being does not enter (and leave) a well-structured universe that has an inherent design. Rather, the individual is entirely responsible for—that is, is the author of—his or her own world, life design, choices, and actions. "Freedom" in this sense, has a terrifying implication: it means that beneath us there is no ground—nothing, a void, an abyss. A key existential dynamic, then, is the clash between our confrontation with groundlessness and our wish for ground and structure.

Existential Isolation. A third ultimate concern is isolation—not *interpersonal* isolation with its attendant loneliness, or *intrapersonal* isolation (isolation from parts of oneself), but a fundamental isolation—an isolation both from creatures and from world—which cuts beneath other isolation. No matter how close each of us becomes to another, there remains a final, unbridgeable gap; each of us enters existence alone and must depart from it alone. The existential conflict is thus the tension between our awareness of our absolute isolation and our wish for contact, for protection, our wish to be part of a larger whole.

Meaninglessness. A fourth ultimate concern or given of existence is meaninglessness. If we must die, if we constitute our own world, if each is ultimately alone in an indifferent universe, then what meaning does life have? Why do we live? How shall we live? If there is no preordained design for us, then each of us must construct our own meanings in life. Yet can a meaning of one's own creation be sturdy enough to bear one's life? This existential dynamic conflict stems from the dilemma of a meaning-seeking creature who is thrown into a universe that has no meaning.

EXISTENTIAL PSYCHODYNAMICS: GENERAL CHARACTERISTICS

"Existential psychodynamics" refers, thus, to these four givens, these ultimate concerns, and to the conscious and unconscious fears and motives spawned by each. The dynamic existential approach retains the basic dynamic *structure* outlined by Freud but radically alters the *content*. The old formula of:

$$\text{DRIVE} \longrightarrow \text{ANXIETY} \longrightarrow \text{DEFENSE MECHANISM}^*$$

is replaced by

---

*Where the *anxiety* is a signal of danger—that is, if instinctual drives are permitted free rein, the organism is endangered, since the ego will be overwhelmed and retaliatory punishment (castration-abandonment) is inevitable; and the *defense mechanisms* restrict direct drive gratification but afford indirect expression—that is, in displaced, sublimated, or symbolic form.

AWARENESS OF
ULTIMATE CONCERN ⟶ ANXIETY ⟶ DEFENSE MECHANISM *

Both formulas assume that anxiety is the fuel of psychopathology; that psychic operations, some conscious and some unconscious, evolve to deal with anxiety; that these psychic operations (defense mechanisms) constitute psychopathology; and that, though they provide safety, they invariably restrict growth and experience. A major difference between these two dynamic approaches is that Freud's sequence begins with "drive," whereas an existential framework begins with awareness and fear. As Otto Rank knew,[6] the therapist has far more leverage if he or she views the individual primarily as a fearful, suffering being rather than as an instinctually driven one.

These four ultimate concerns—death, freedom, isolation, and meaninglessness—constitute the corpus of existential psychodynamics. They play an extraordinarily important role at every level of individual psychic organization and have enormous relevance to clinical work. They also provide a central organizing principle; the four sections of this book will focus on each ultimate concern in turn and explore the philosophical, psychopathological, and therapeutic implications of each.

EXISTENTIAL PSYCHODYNAMICS: THE QUESTION OF DEPTH

Another major difference between existential dynamics and Freudian and neo-Freudian dynamics involves the definition of "deep." To Freud, exploration always meant excavation. With the deliberateness and patience of an archaeologist he scraped away at the many-layered psyche until he reached bedrock, a layer of fundamental conflicts that were the psychological residue of the *earliest* events in the life of the individual. Deepest conflict meant earliest conflict. Freud's psychodynamics are thus developmentally based, and "fundamental" or "primary" are to be grasped chronologically: each is synonymous with "first." Accordingly, the "fundamental" sources of anxiety, for example, are considered to be the earliest psychosexual calamities: separation and castration.

Existential dynamics are not wedded to a developmental model. There is no compelling reason to assume that "fundamental" (that is,

---

* Where the *anxiety* springs from fear of death, groundlessness, isolation, and meaninglessness, and the *defense mechanisms* are of two types: (1) conventional mechanisms of defense, which have been described thoroughly by Freud, Anna Freud,[4] and Sullivan,[5] and which defend the individual generally against anxiety regardless of its source; and (2) specific defenses, to be discussed shortly, which arise to serve the specific function of coping with each of the primary existential fears.

important, basic) and "first" (that is, chronologically first) are identical concepts. To explore deeply from an existential perspective does not mean that one explores the past; rather, it means that one brushes away everyday concerns and thinks deeply about one's existential situation. It means to think outside of time, to think about the relationship between one's feet and the ground beneath one, between one's consciousness and the space around one; it means to think not about the way one came to be the way one is, but *that* one is. The past—that is, one's memory of the past—is important insofar as it is part of one's current existence and has contributed to one's current mode of facing one's ultimate concerns; but it is, as I shall discuss later, not the most rewarding area for therapeutic exploration. The future-becoming-present is the primary tense of existential therapy.

This distinction does not mean that one cannot explore existential factors in a developmental framework (in fact, chapter 3 explores in depth the development of the child's concept of death); but it does mean that development issues are not germane when an individual asks, "At this moment, at the deepest levels of my being, what are the most fundamental sources of dread?" The individual's earliest experiences, though undeniably important in life, do not provide the answer to this fundamental question. In fact, the residue of earliest life creates a biological static that serves to obscure the answer. The answer to the inquiry is transpersonal. It is an answer that cuts beneath any individual's personal life history. It is an answer that applies to every person: it belongs to the human being's "situation" in the world.

This distinction between the developmental, dynamic, analytic model and the immediate, ahistorical, existential one has more than theoretical interest: as I shall discuss in later chapters, it has profound implications for the technique of the therapist.

The Existential Orientation: Strange But Oddly Familiar

A great deal of my material on the ultimate concerns will appear strange yet, in an odd way, familiar to the clinician. The material will appear strange because the existential approach cuts across common categories and clusters clinical observations in a novel manner. Furthermore, much of the vocabulary is different. Even if I avoid the jargon of the professional philosopher and use common-sense terms to describe existential concepts, the clinician will find the language psychologically alien. Where is the psychotherapy lexicon that contains such terms as "choice," "responsibility," "freedom," "existential isolation," "mortality," "purpose in life," "willing"? The medical library computers snickered at me when I requested literature searches in these areas.

Yet the clinician will find in them much that is familiar. I believe that the experienced clinician often operates implicitly within an existential framework: "in his bones" he appreciates a patient's concerns and responds accordingly. That response is what I meant earlier by the crucial "throw-ins." A major task of this book is to shift the therapist's focus, to attend carefully to these vital concerns and to the therapeutic transactions that occur on the periphery of formal therapy, and to place them where they belong—in the center of the therapeutic arena.

Another familiar note is that the major existential concerns have been recognized and discussed since the beginning of written thought, and that their primacy has been recognized by an unbroken stream of philosophers, theologians, and poets. That fact may offend our sense of pride in modernism, our sense of an eternal spiral of progress; but from another perspective, we may feel reassured to travel a well-worn path trailing back into time, hewed by the wisest and the most thoughtful of individuals.

These existential sources of dread are familiar, too, in that they are the experience of the therapist as Everyman; they are by no means the exclusive province of the psychologically troubled individual. Repeatedly, I shall stress that they are part of the human condition. How then, one may ask, can a theory of psychopathology* rest on factors that are experienced by every individual? The answer, of course, is that each person experiences the stress of the human condition in highly individualized fashion. In this regard the existential model does not differ significantly from every major competing theory. Every individual passes through certain developmental stages, each with its own attendant anxiety. Everyone passes through the oedipal conflict, the disturbing emergence of aggressive and sexual feelings, castration anxiety (for males at least), the pain of individuation and separation, and many other severe developmental challenges. The only model of psychopathology that does not rest on universally experienced factors is one based on acute trauma. However, traumatic neuroses are rare. The overwhelming majority of patients suffer from stress that to differing degrees is part of every person's experience.

---

* In this discussion, as elsewhere in this text, I refer to psychologically based disturbance, not to the major psychoses with a fundamental biochemical origin.

In fact, only the universality of human suffering can account for the common observation that patienthood is ubiquitous. André Malraux, to cite one such observation, once asked a parish priest who had been taking confession for fifty years, what he had learned about mankind. The priest replied, "First of all, people are much more unhappy than one thinks . . . and then the fundamental fact is that there is no such thing as a grown up person."[7] Often it is only external circumstances that result in one person, and not another, being labeled a patient: for example, financial resources, availability of psychotherapists, personal and cultural attitudes toward therapy, or choice of profession—the majority of psychotherapists become themselves bona fide patients. The universality of stress is one of the major reasons that scholars encounter such difficulty when attempting to define and describe normality: the difference between normality and pathology is quantitative, not qualitative.

The contemporary model that seems most consistent with the evidence is analogous to a model in physical medicine that suggests that infectious disease is not simply a result of a bacterial or a viral agent invading an undefended body. Rather, disease is a result of a disequilibrium between the noxious agent and host resistance. In other words, noxious agents exist within the body at all times—just as stresses, inseparable from living, confront all individuals. Whether an individual develops clinical disease depends on the body's resistance (that is, such factors as immunological system, nutrition, and fatigue) to the agent: when resistance is lowered, disease develops, even though the toxicity and the virility of the noxious agent are unchanged. Thus, all human beings are in a quandary, but some are unable to cope with it: psychopathology depends not merely on the presence or the absence of stress but on the interaction between ubiquitous stress and the individual's mechanisms of defense.

The claim that the ultimate existential concerns never arise in therapy is entirely a function of a therapist's selective inattention: a listener tuned into the proper channel finds explicit and abundant material. A therapist may choose, however, not to attend to the existential ultimate concerns precisely because they are universal experiences, and therefore nothing constructive can come from exploring them. Indeed, I have often noted in clinical work that, when existential concerns are broached, the therapist and the patient are intensely energized for a short while; but soon the discussion becomes desultory, and the patient and therapist seem to say tacitly, "Well that's life, isn't it! Let's move on to something neurotic, something we can do something about!"

Other therapists veer away from dealing with existential concerns not only because these concerns are universal but because they are too terrible to face. After all, neurotic patients (and therapists, too) have enough to worry about without adding such cheery items as death and meaninglessness. Such therapists believe that existential issues are best ignored, since there are only two ways to deal with the brutal existential facts of life—anxious truth or denial—and either is unpalatable. Cervantes voiced this problem when his immortal Don said, "Which would you have, wise madness or foolish sanity?"

An existential therapeutic position, as I shall attempt to demonstrate in later chapters, rejects this dilemma. Wisdom does not lead to madness, nor denial to sanity: the confrontation with the givens of existence is painful but ultimately healing. Good therapeutic work is always coupled with reality testing and the search for personal enlightenment; the therapist who decides that certain aspects of reality and truth are to be eschewed is on treacherous ground. Thomas Hardy's comment, "if a way to the Better there be, it exacts a full look at the Worst,"[8] is a good frame for the therapeutic approach I shall describe.

The Field of Existential Psychotherapy

Existential psychotherapy is rather much a homeless waif. It does not really "belong" anywhere. It has no homestead, no formal school, no institution; it is not welcomed into the better academic neighborhoods. It has no formal society, no robust journal (a few sickly offspring were carried away in their infancy), no stable family, no paterfamilias. It does, however, have a genealogy, a few scattered cousins, and friends of the family, some in the old country, some in America.

EXISTENTIAL PHILOSOPHY: THE ANCESTRAL HOME

"Existentialism is not easily definable." So begins the discussion of existential philosphy in philosophy's major contemporary encyclopedia.[9] Most other reference works begin in similar fashion and underscore the fact that two philosophers both labeled "existential" may disagree on every cardinal point (aside from their shared aversion to being so labeled). Most philosophical texts resolve the problem of definition by listing a number of themes relating to existence (for example, being, choice, freedom, death, isolation, absurdity), and by proclaiming that an existential philosopher is one whose work is dedicated to exploring them. (This is, of course, the strategy I use to identify the field of existential psychotherapy).

There is an existential "tradition" in philosophy and a formal existential "school" of philosophy. Obviously the existential tradition is ageless. What great thinker has not at some point in both work and life turned his or her attention to life and death issues? The formal school of existential philosophy, however, has a clearly demarcated beginning. Some trace it to a Sunday afternoon in 1834, when a young Dane sat in a café smoking a cigar and mused upon the fact that he was on his way to becoming an old man without having made a contribution to the world. He thought about his many successful friends:

> ... benefactors of the age who know how to benefit mankind by making life easier and easier, some by railways, others by omnibuses and steamboats, others by telegraph, others by easily apprehended compendiums and short recitals of everything worth knowing, and finally the true benefactors of the age who by virtue of thought make spiritual existence systematically easier and easier.[10]

His cigar burned out. The young Dane, Sören Kierkegaard, lit another and continued musing. Suddenly there flashed in his mind this thought:

> You must do something but inasmuch as with your limited capacities it will be impossible to make anything easier than it has become, you must, with the same humanitarian enthusiasm as the others, undertake to make something harder.[11]

He reasoned that when all combine to make everything easier, then there is a danger that easiness will be excessive. Perhaps someone is needed to make things difficult again. It occurred to him that he had discovered his destiny: he was to go in search of difficulties—like a new Socrates.[12] And which difficulties? They were not hard to find. He had only to consider his own situation in existence, his own dread, his choices, his possibilities and limitations.

Kierkegaard devoted the remainder of his short life to exploring his existential situation and during the 1840s published several important existential treatises. His work remained untranslated for many years and exerted little influence until after the First World War, when it found fertile soil and was taken up by Martin Heidegger and Karl Jaspers.

The relation of existential therapy to the existential school of philosophy is much like that of clinical pharmacotherapy to biochemical bench research. I shall frequently draw upon philosophical works to explicate, corroborate, or illustrate some of the clinical issues; but it is not my intention (nor within my range of scholarship) to discuss in a comprehensive fashion the works of any philosopher or the major tenets of existential philosophy. This is a book for clinicians, and I mean it to be clinically useful. My excursions into philosophy will be brief and pragmatic; I shall limit myself to those domains that offer leverage in clinical work. I cannot blame the professional philosopher who may liken me to the Viking raider who grabbed gemstones while leaving behind their intricate and precious settings.

As the education of the great majority of psychotherapists includes little or no emphasis on philosophy, I shall not assume any philosophical background in my readers. When I do draw upon philosophical texts, I shall attempt to do so in a straightforward, jargon-free fashion—not an easy task, incidentally, since professional existential philosophers surpass even psychoanalytic theoreticians in the use of turbid, convoluted language. The single most important philosophical text in the field, Heidegger's *Being and Time*, stands alone as the undisputed champion of linguistic obfuscation.

I have never understood the reason for the impenetrable deep-sounding language. The basic existential concepts themselves are not complex, they do not need to be uncoded and meticulously analyzed as much as they need to be uncovered. Every person, at some point in life, enters a "brown study" and has some traffic with existential ultimate concerns. What is required is not formal explication: the task of the philosopher, and of the therapist as well, is to de-repress, to reacquaint the individual with something he or she has known all along. This is precisely the reason that many of the leading existential thinkers (for example, Jean-Paul Sartre, Albert Camus, Miguel de Unamuno, Martin Buber) prefer literary exposition rather than formal philosophical argument. Above all, the philosopher and the therapist must encourage the individual to look within and to attend to his or her existential situation.

THE EXISTENTIAL ANALYSTS: OLD COUNTRY COUSINS

A number of European psychiatrists took issue with many of the basic tenets of Freud's psychoanalytic approach. They objected to Freud's model of psychic functioning, to his efforts to understand the human being by way of an energy-conservation schema borrowed from the physical sciences, and suggested that such an approach resulted in an inadequate view of the human being. If one applies one schema to explain all individuals, they argued, one misses the unique experience of the particular person. They objected to Freud's reductionism (that is, tracing all human behavior to a few basic drives), to his materialism (that is, explaining the higher in terms of the lower), and to his determinism (that is, the belief that all mental functioning is caused by identifiable factors already in existence).

The various existential analysts agreed on one fundamental procedural point: the analyst must approach the patient phenomenologically; that is, he or she must enter the patient's experiential world and listen to the phenomena of that world without the presuppositions that distort understanding. As Ludwig Binswanger, one of the best known of the existential analysts, said, "There is not one space and time only, but as many spaces and times as there are subjects."[13]

Aside from their reaction against Freud's mechanistic, deterministic model of the mind and their assumption of a phenomenological approach in therapy, the existential analysts have little in common and have never been regarded as a cohesive ideological school. These thinkers—who include Ludwig Binswanger, Melard Boss, Eugene Minkowsky, V. E. Gebsattel, Roland Kuhn, G. Caruso, F. T. Buytendijk, G. Bally, and Viktor Frankl—were almost entirely unknown to the American psychotherapeutic community until Rollo May's highly influential 1958 book *Existence*—and especially his introductory essay[14]—introduced their work into this country.

However, today, more than twenty years after May's book, it is striking that these figures exert little influence upon American psychotherapeutic practice. They mean little more than the unknown faces in faded daguerreotypes in the family photo album. In part, this neglect has resulted from a language barrier: aside from some of the writings of Binswanger, Boss, and Frankl, these philosophers have been seldom translated. For the most part, however, it is due to the abstruse nature of their writing: they are steeped in a Continental philosophical *Weltanschauung* far out of synchrony with the American pragmatic tradition in therapy. Thus, the Continental existential analysts remain scattered and, for the most part, lost cousins of the existential therapy approach I intend to describe. I do not draw heavily from them here, with the single exception of Viktor Frankl, an eminently pragmatic thinker, whose work has been widely translated.

HUMANISTIC PSYCHOLOGISTS: FLASHY AMERICAN COUSINS

The European existential analytic trend arose both from a desire to apply philosophical concepts to a clinical study of the person and as a reaction to Freud's model of man. In the United States an analogous movement began to rumble in the late 1950s, it surfaced and coalesced in the 1960s, and it rode madly off in all directions at once in the 1970s.

Academic psychology had by the 1950s been long dominated by two major ideological schools. The first—and, by far, the longest dominant—was a scientific positivistic behaviorism; the second was Freudian psychoanalysis. A minor voice first heard in the late 1930s and 1940s belonged to abnormal and social psychologists who coexisted uncomfortably in the experimental psychology bastions. Gradually those personality theorists (for example, Gordon Allport, Henry Murray, and Gardner Murphy and, later, George Kelly, Abraham Maslow, Carl Rogers, and Rollo May) grew uncomfortable with the limitations of both the behavioristic and the analytic schools. They felt that both of these ideological approaches to the person excluded some of the most important qualities that make the human being human—for example, choice, values, love, creativity, self-awareness, human potential. In 1950 they formally established a new ideological school which they labeled "humanistic psychology." Humanistic psychology, sometimes referred to as the "third force" in psychology (after behaviorism and Freudian analytic psychology), became a robust organization with growing membership rolls and an annual convention attended by thousands of mental health professionals. In 1961 the American Association of Humanistic Psychology founded the *Journal of Humanistic Psychology*, which has included on its editorial board such well-known figures as Carl Rogers, Rollo May, Lewis Mumford, Kurt Goldstein, Charlotte Buhler, Abraham Maslow, Aldous Huxley, and James Bugental.

The fledgling organization made some early attempts to define itself. In 1962 it formally stated:

> Humanistic Psychology is primarily concerned with those human capacities and potentialities that have little or no systematic place, either in positivist or behaviorist theory or in classical psychoanalytic theory: e.g., love, creativity, self, growth, organism, basic need-gratification, self-actualization, higher values, being, becoming, spontaneity, play, humor, affection, naturalness, warmth, ego-transcendence, objectivity, autonomy, responsibility, meaning, fairplay, transcendental experience, psychological health, and related concepts.[15]

In 1963 the association's president, James Bugental, suggested five basic postulates:

1. *Man, as man, supersedes the sum of his parts* (that is, man cannot be understood from a scientific study of part-functions.)
2. *Man has his being in a human context* (that is, man cannot be understood by part-functions which ignore interpersonal experience.)

3. *Man is aware* (and cannot be understood by a psychology which fails to recognize man's continuous, many-layered self-awareness.)
4. *Man has choice* (man is not a bystander to his existence; he creates his own experience.)
5. *Man is intentional** (man points to the future; he has purpose, values and meaning.)[16]

Much in these early manifestos—antideterminism, the emphasis on freedom, choice, purpose, values, responsibility, the dedication to appreciating the unique experiential world of each individual—is of great importance in the existential frame of reference I present in this book. But by no means is the American field of humanistic psychology synonymous with the Continental existential tradition; there is a fundamental difference in accent. The existential tradition in Europe has always emphasized human limitations and the tragic dimensions of existence. Perhaps it has done so because Europeans have had a greater familiarity with geographic and ethnic confinement, with war, death, and uncertain existence. The United States (and the humanistic psychology it spawned) bathed in a *Zeitgeist* of expansiveness, optimism, limitless horizons, and pragmatism. Accordingly, the imported form of existential thought has been systematically altered. Each of the basic tenets has a distinct New World accent. The European focus in on limits, on facing and taking into oneself the anxiety of uncertainty and nonbeing. The humanistic psychologists, on the other hand, speak less of limits and contingency than of development of potential, less of acceptance than of awareness, less of anxiety than of peak experiences and oceanic oneness, less of life meaning than of self-realization, less of apartness and basic isolation than of I-Thou and encounter.

In the 1960s the counterculture with its attendant social phenomena—such as the free speech movement, the flower children, the drug culture, the human-potentialists, the sexual revolution—engulfed the humanistic psychological movement. Soon the association conventions developed aspects of a carnival. The big tent of humanist psychology was, if nothing else, generous and soon included a bewildering number of schools barely able to converse with one another even in an existential Esperanto. Gestalt therapy, transpersonal therapy, encounter groups, holistic medicine, psychosynthesis, Sufi, and many, many others pranced into the arena. The new trends have value orientations that bear significant implications for psychotherapy. There is an emphasis

---

* To be distinguished from the technical philosophical use of intentionality which refers to the phenomenon that consciousness is always directed toward some object: that is, consciousness is consciousness *of* something.

on hedonism ("if it feels good, do it"), on anti-intellectualism (which considers any cognitive approach as "mind-fucking"), on individual fulfillment ("doing your own thing," "peak experiences"), and on self-actualization (a belief in human perfectibility is common to most humanistic psychologists, with the major exception of Rollo May, who is more deeply grounded in the existential philosophical tradition).

These proliferating trends, especially the anti-intellectual ones, soon effected a divorce between humanistic psychology and the academic community. Humanistic psychologists in established academic positions felt uneasy about the company they were keeping and gradually disaffiliated themselves. Fritz Perls, himself far from an advocate of discipline, expressed great concern about the "turner-oners," the "anything goes," the "instant sensory awareness" approach,[17] and eventually the three figures who supplied humanistic psychology with its initial intellectual leadership—May, Rogers, and Maslow—grew deeply ambivalent about these irrational trends and gradually decreased their active sponsorship.

Existential psychotherapy, thus, has a hazy relationship with humanistic psychology. They share many basic tenets, however, and many humanistic psychologists have an existential orientation. Among them, Maslow, Perls, Bugental, Buhler, and especially Rollo May will be cited frequently in this text.

HUMANISTIC PSYCHOANALYSTS: FRIENDS OF THE FAMILY

There remains a group of relatives whom I shall refer to as "humanistic psychoanalysts," and who split off early from the genealogical branches I have described. Though they never considered themselves a clan, they closely parallel one another in their work. The major voices in this group—Otto Rank, Karen Horney, Erich Fromm, and Helmuth Kaiser—were all trained in the European Freudian psychoanalytic tradition but emigrated to America; and all, with the exception of Rank, made their major contributions while immersed in the American intellectual community. Each objected to Freud's instinct-powered model of human behavior, and each suggested important correctives. Though the work of each was far-ranging, each, for a period of time, turned his or her attention to some aspect of existential therapy. Rank, whose contributions have been brilliantly augmented by latter-day interpreter Ernest Becker, emphasized the importance of the will and of death anxiety; Horney, the crucial role of the future as an influencer of behavior (the individual is motivated by purpose, ideals, and goals rather than shaped and determined by past events); Fromm has masterfully illuminated the role and fear of freedom in behavior; while Kaiser has dealt with responsibility and isolation.

In addition to these major branches of philosophers, humanistic psychologists, and humanistically oriented psychoanalysts, the genealogical tree of existential therapy contains another important segment constituted by the great writers who, no less fully than their professional brethren, explored and explicated existential issues. Thus, the voices of Dostoevsky, Tolstoy, Kafka, Sartre, Camus, and many other distinguished teachers will be heard frequently throughout this book. Great literature survives, as Freud pointed out in his discussion of *Oedipus Rex*,[18] because something in the reader leaps out to embrace its truth. The truth of fictional characters moves us because it is our own truth. Furthermore, great works of literature teach us about ourselves because they are scorchingly honest, as honest as any clinical data: the great novelist, however his or her personality may be split among many characters, is ultimately highly self-revelatory. Thornton Wilder once wrote: "If Queen Elizabeth or Frederick the Great or Ernest Hemingway were to read their biographies, they would exclaim, 'Ah—my secret is still safe!' But if Natasha Rostov were to read *War and Peace* she would cry out, as she covered her face with her hands, 'How did he know? How did he know?' "[19]

Existential Therapy and the Academic Community

Earlier I likened existential therapy to a homeless waif who was not permitted into the better academic neighborhoods. The lack of academic support from academic psychiatry and psychology has significant implications for the field of existential therapy, since academically dominated institutions control all the vital supply routes that influence the development of the clinical disciplines: the training of clinicians and academicians, research funding, licensure, and journal publication.

It is worth taking a moment to consider why the existential approach is so quarantined by the academic establishment. The answer centers primarily on the issue of the basis of knowledge—that is, how do we know what we know? Academic psychiatry and psychology, grounded in a positivist tradition, value empirical research as the method of validating knowledge.

Consider the typical career of the academician (and I speak not only from observation but from my own twenty-year academic career): the young lecturer or assistant professor is hired because he or she displays aptitude and motivation for empirical research, and later is rewarded and promoted for carefully and methodically performed research. The crucial tenure decision is made on the basis of the amount of empirical research published in refereed scientific journals. Other factors, such as teaching skills or nonempirical books, book chapters, and essays, are given decidedly secondary consideration.

It is extraordinarily difficult for a scholar to carve out an academic career based upon an empirical investigation of existential issues. The basic tenets of existential therapy are such that empirical research methods are often inapplicable or inappropriate. For example, the empirical research method requires that the investigator study a complex organism by breaking it down into its component parts, each simple enough to permit empirical investigation. Yet this fundamental principle negates a basic existential principle. A story told by Viktor Frankl is illustrative.[20]

Two neighbors were involved in a bitter dispute. One claimed that the other's cat had eaten his butter and, accordingly, demanded compensation. Unable to resolve the problem, the two, carrying the accused cat, sought out the village wise man for a judgment. The wise man asked the accuser, "How much butter did the cat eat"? "Ten pounds" was the response. The wise man placed the cat on the scale. Lo and behold! it weighed exactly ten pounds. "Mirabile dictu!" he proclaimed. "Here we have the butter. But where is the cat?"

Where is the cat? All the parts taken together do not reconstruct the creature. A fundamental humanistic credo is that "man is greater than the sum of his parts." No matter how carefully one understands the composite parts of the mind—for example, the conscious and the unconscious, the superego, the ego, and the id—one still does not grasp the central vital agency, the person whose unconscious (or superego or id or ego) it is. Furthermore, the empirical approach never helps one to learn the *meaning* of this psychic structure to the person who possesses it. Meaning can never be obtained from a study of component parts, because meaning is never caused; it is created by a person who is supraordinate to all his parts.

But there is in the existential approach a problem for empirical research even more fundamental than the one of "Where is the cat?" Rollo May alluded to it when he defined existentialism as "the endeavor to understand man by cutting below the cleavage between subject and object which has bedeviled Western thought and science since shortly after the Renaissance."[21] The "cleavage between subject and object"—let us take a closer look at that. The existential position challenges the traditional Cartesian view of a world full of objects and of subjects who perceive those objects. Obviously, this is the basic premise of the scientific method: there are objects with a finite set of properties that can be understood through objective investigation. The existential position cuts below this subject-object cleavage and regards the person not as a subject who can, under the proper circumstances, perceive external reality but as a consciousness who participates in the construction of reality. To emphasize this point, Heidegger always spoke of the human being as *dasein. Da* ("there") refers to the fact that the person is there, is a constituted object (an "empirical ego"), but at the same time constitutes the world (that is, is a "transcendental ego"). *Dasein* is at once the meaning giver and the known. Each *dasein* therefore constitutes its own world; to study all beings with some standard instrument as though they inhabited the same objective world is to introduce monumental error into one's observations.

It is important to keep in mind, however, that the limitations of empirical psychotherapy research are not confined to an existential orientation in therapy; it is only that they are more explicit in the existential approach. Insofar as therapy is a deeply personal, human experience, the empirical study of psychotherapy of any ideological school will contain errors and be of limited value. It is common knowledge that psychotherapy research has had, in its thirty-year history, little impact upon the practice of therapy. In fact, as Carl Rogers, the founding father of empirical psychotherapy research, sadly noted, not even psychotherapy researchers take their research findings seriously enough to alter their approach to psychotherapy.[22]

It is also common knowledge that the great majority of clinicians stop doing empirical research once they finish their dissertation or earn tenure. If empirical research is a valid truth-seeking, truth-finding endeavor, why do psychologists and psychiatrists, once they have fulfilled academic requirements, put away their tables of random numbers for good? I believe that as the clinician gains maturity, he or she gradually begins to appreciate that there are staggering problems inherent in an empirical study of psychotherapy.

A personal experience may be illustrative. Several years ago two colleagues and I conducted a large research project on the process and the outcome of encounter groups. We published the results in a book, *Encounter Groups: First Facts*,[23] which has been at once hailed as a benchmark for precision in clinical work and attacked vociferously by many humanistic psychologists. In fact, an issue of the afore-mentioned *Journal of Humanistic Psychology* was devoted to a vigorous attack on this work. My two colleagues wrote robust and effective replies to the critiques, but I declined to do so. For one thing, I was entirely occupied in writing my present book. At a deeper level I had doubts about the meaning of our research—not for the reasons under public attack but for something else: I could not believe that the true experience of the participants was adequately described by our highly technical, computerized statistical approach. One finding in the methodological center of the work[24] particularly troubled me: we had used an enormous battery of psychological instruments to assess how much each encounter-group participant had changed. Outcome measures were taken from four different perspectives: (1) from the participant himself, (2) from the group leader, (3) from the participant's co-members, (4) from the participant's social network. The correlation between these four perspectives of change was zero! In other words, there was zero-order agreement between the various sources of information about who had changed and how much they had changed.

Now, of course, there are statistical ways to "handle" this finding, but the fact remains that outcome evaluation is highly relative and depends heavily on the source of information. Nor is this a problem confined to this project: it plagues every psychotherapy outcome study. The more methods used to assess outcome, the less certain is the researcher of his results!

How do researchers deal with this problem? One method is to increase reliability by asking fewer questions and to rely upon a single source of data. Another common method is to steer clear of "soft," or subjective, criteria and measure only objective criteria, such as amount of alcohol consumed, the number of times one spouse interrupts the other in some given period of time, the number of bites of food taken, galvanic skin response, or the size of penile tumescence while looking at slides of naked youths. But woe to the researcher who tries to measure the important factors, such as ability to love or care for another, zest in life, purposefulness, generosity, exuberance, autonomy, spontaneity, humor, courage, or engagement in life. Again and again one encounters a basic fact of life in psychotherapy research: the precision of the result is directly proportional to the triviality of the variables studies. A strange type of science!

What is the alternative? The proper method of understanding the inner world of another individual is the "phenomenological" one, to go directly to the phenomena themselves, to encounter the other without "standardized" instruments and presuppositions. So far as possible one must "bracket" one's own world perspective and enter the experiential world of the other. Such an approach to knowing another person is eminently feasible in psychotherapy: every good therapist tries to relate to the patient in this manner. That is what is meant by empathy, presence, genuine listening, non-judgmental acceptance, or an attitude of "disciplined naïvety"—to use May's felicitous phrase.[25] Existential therapists have always urged that the therapist attempt to understand the private world of the patient rather than to focus on the way the patient has deviated from the "norms." But this phenomenological approach, which by definition is nonempirical, raises staggering and as yet unsolved problems for the researcher who struggles to achieve high scientific standards in his or her work.

In spite of these reservations, my professional training has compelled me to consider the extant research for each of the four basic existential concerns—death, freedom, isolation, and meaninglessness. And, of course, careful research can shed light on several important areas of inquiry. For example, research can tell us how frequently patients are explicitly concerned with existential issues or how frequently therapists perceive these concerns.

For the many existential topics that have never been explicitly studied by researchers, I have examined research in tangential areas which may possibly bear upon the issue. For example, chapter 6 discusses "locus of control" research because it is relevant to the areas of responsibility and willing.

Other topics do not, for reasons discussed, permit empirical research. Researchers have accordingly selected some part-problems that are more available for study. For example, as we shall see, there exist many "death anxiety" scales which study the phenomenon of dread, but in such a superficial and norm-based manner as to offer little illumination. I am reminded of the story of the man searching at night for a lost key, not in the dark alley where he dropped it but under a lamppost where the light was better. I cite this part-problem research with appropriate caveats.

There are still other domains where knowledge must remain intuitive. Certain truths of existence are so clear and sure that logical argument or empirical research corroboration seems highly gratuitous. Karl Lashley, the neuropsychologist, is said to have once commented: "If you teach an airedale to play the violin, you don't need a string quartet to prove it."

I have attempted to write this book in a style sufficiently lucid and free of jargon that it will be intelligible to the lay reader. However, the primary audience for whom I intend it is the student and the practicing psychotherapist. It is important to note that, even though I assume for my reader no formal philosophical education, I do assume some clinical background. I do not mean this to be a "first" or a complete psychotherapy text but expect the reader to be familiar with conventional clinical explanatory systems. Hence, when I describe clinical phenomena from an existential frame of reference, I do not always offer alternate modes of explanation for them. My task, as I view it, is to describe a coherent psychotherapy approach based on existential concerns which gives an explicit place to the procedures that the majority of therapists employ implicitly.

I do not pretend to describe *the* theory of psychopathology and psychotherapy. Instead, I present a paradigm, a psychological construct, that offers the clinician a system of explanation—a system that permits him or her to make sense out of a large array of clinical data and to formulate a systematic strategy of psychotherapy. It is a paradigm that has considerable explanatory power; it is parsimonious (that is, it rests on relatively few basic assumptions) and it is accessible (that is, the assumptions rest on experiences that may be intuitively perceived by every introspective individual). Furthermore, it is a humanistically based paradigm, consonant with the deeply human nature of the therapeutic enterprise.

But it is *a* paradigm, not *the* paradigm—useful for some patients, not for all patients; employable by some therapists, not by all therapists. The existential orientation is one clinical approach among other approaches. It repatterns clinical data but, like other paradigms, has no exclusive hegemony and is not capable of explaining all behavior. The human being has too much complexity and possibility to permit that it do so.

Existence is inexorably free and, thus, uncertain. Cultural institutions and psychological constructs often obscure this state of affairs, but confrontation with one's existential situation reminds one that paradigms are self-created, wafer-thin barriers against the pain of uncertainty. The mature therapist must, in the existential theoretical approach as in any other, be able to tolerate this fundamental uncertainty.

PART I

Death

IN THE NEXT four chapters I shall explore the role played by the concept of death in psychopathology and psychotherapy. The basic postulates I describe are simple:

1. The fear of death plays a major role in our internal experience; it haunts as does nothing else; it rumbles continuously under the surface; it is a dark, unsettling presence at the rim of consciousness.
2. The child, at an early age, is pervasively preoccupied with death, and his or her major developmental task is to deal with terrifying fears of obliteration.
3. To cope with these fears, we erect defenses against death awareness, defenses that are based on denial, that shape character structure, and that, if maladaptive, result in clinical syndromes. In other words, psychopathology is the result of ineffective modes of death transcendence.

4. Lastly, a robust and effective approach to psychotherapy may be constructed on the foundation of death awareness.

Chapter 2 will provide an overview of the role of the concept of death in psychotherapy, will present relevant clinical and research evidence, and then will explore why traditional analytic thought has painstakingly omitted death from both psychotherapy theory and technique.

Chapter 3 will discuss the development of the concept of death in children and will focus on the defense mechanisms that emerge to protect the individual from death anxiety. Chapter 4 will present a paradigm of psychopathology based on these death-denying defenses; and chapter 5 will describe both the theory and the practical implementation of an approach to therapy based on death awareness.

CHAPTER 2

Life, Death, and Anxiety

D ON'T SCRATCH where it doesn't itch," the great Adolph Meyer counseled a generation of student psychiatrists.[1] Is that adage not an excellent argument against investigating patients' attitudes toward death? Do not patients have quite enough fear and quite enough dread without the therapist reminding them of the grimmest of life's horrors? Why focus on bitter and immutable reality? If the goal of therapy is to instill hope, why invoke hope-defeating death? The aim of therapy is to help the individual learn how to live. Why not leave death for the dying?

These arguments demand a response, and I shall address them in this chapter by arguing that death itches all the time, that our attitudes toward death influence the way we live and grow and the way we falter and fall ill. I shall examine two basic propositions, each of which has major implications for the practice of psychotherapy:

1. Life and death are interdependent; they exist simultaneously, not consecutively; death whirs continuously beneath the membrane of life and exerts a vast influence upon experience and conduct.
2. Death is a primordial source of anxiety and, as such, is the primary fount of psychopathology.

Life-Death Interdependence

A venerable line of thought, stretching back to the beginning of written thought, emphasizes the interdigitation of life and death. It is one
of life's most self-evident truths that everything fades, that we fear the
fading, and that we must live, nonetheless, in the face of the fading, in
the face of the fear. Death, the Stoics said, was the most important
event in life. Learning to live well is to learn to die well; and conversely, learning to die well is to learn to live well. Cicero said, "To philosophize is to prepare for death,"[2] and Seneca: "No man enjoys the true
taste of life but he who is willing and ready to quit it."[3] Saint Augustine expressed the same idea: "It is only in the face of death that man's
self is born."[4]

It is not possible to leave death to the dying. The biological life-death
boundary is relatively precise; but, psychologically, life and death
merge into one another. Death is a fact of life; a moment's reflection
tells us that death is not simply the last moment of life. "Even in birth
we die; the end is there from the start" (Manilius).[5] Montaigne, in his
penetrating essay on death, asked, "Why do you fear your last day? It
contributes no more to your death than each of the others. The last step
does not cause the fatigue, but reveals it."[6]

It would be a simple matter (and a most seductive one) to continue
citing important quotations about death. Virtually every great thinker
(generally early in life or toward its end) has thought deeply and written about death; and many have concluded that death is inextricably a
part of life, and that lifelong consideration of death enriches rather
than impoverishes life. Although the physicality of death destroys
man, the idea of death saves him.

This last thought is so important that it bears repeating: although the
physicality of death destroys man, the *idea* of death saves him. But what
precisely does this statement mean? How does the idea of death save
man? And save him from what?

A brief look at a core concept of existential philosophy may provide
clarification. Martin Heidegger, in 1926, explored the question how the
idea of death may save man, and arrived at the important insight that
the awareness of our personal death acts as a spur to shift us from one
mode of existence to a higher one. Heidegger believed that there are
two fundamental modes of existing in the world: (1) a state of forgetfulness of being or (2) a state of mindfulness of being.[7]

When one lives in a state of *forgetfulness of being*, one lives in the world of things and immerses oneself in the everyday diversions of life: One is "leveled down," absorbed in "idle chatter," lost in the "they." One surrenders oneself to the everyday world, to a concern about the *way* things are.

In the other state, the state of *mindfulness of being*, one marvels not about the *way* things are but *that* they are. To exist in this mode means to be continually aware of being. In this mode, which is often referred to as the "ontological mode" (from the Greek *ontos*, meaning "existence"), one remains mindful of being, not only mindful of the fragility of being but mindful, too (as I shall discuss in chapter 6), of one's responsibility for one's own being. Since it is only in this ontological mode that one is in touch with one's self-creation, it is only here that one can grasp the power to change oneself.

Ordinarily one lives in the first state. Forgetfulness of being is the everyday mode of existence. Heidegger refers to it as "inauthentic"—a mode in which one is unaware of one's authorship of one's life and world, in which one "flees," "falls," and is tranquilized, in which one avoids choices by being "carried along by the nobody."[8] When, however, one enters the second mode of being (mindfulness of being), one exists authentically (hence, the frequent modern use of the term "authenticity" in psychology). In this state, one becomes fully self-aware—aware of oneself as a transcendental (constituting) ego as well as an empirical (constituted) ego; one embraces one's possibilities and limits; one faces absolute freedom and nothingness—and is anxious in the face of them.

Now, what does death have to do with all this? Heidegger realized that one doesn't move from a state of forgetfulness of being to a more enlightened, anxious mindfulness of being by simple contemplation, by bearing down, by gritting one's teeth. There are certain unalterable, irremediable conditions, certain "urgent experiences" that jolt one, that tug one from the first, everyday, state of existence to the state of mindfulness of being. Of these urgent experiences (Jaspers later referred to them as "border" or "boundary" or "limit" situations[9]), death is the nonpareil: *death is the condition that makes it possible for us to live life in an authentic fashion.*

This point of view—that death makes a positive contribution to life—is not one easily accepted. Generally we view death as such an unmitigated evil that we dismiss any contrary view as an implausible joke. We can manage quite well without the plague, thank you.

But suspend judgment for a moment and imagine life without any thought of death. Life loses something of its intensity. Life shrinks

31

when death is denied. Freud who, for reasons I shall discuss shortly, spoke little of death, believed that the transience of life augments our joy in it. "Limitation in the possibility of an enjoyment raises the value of the enjoyment." Freud, writing during the First World War, said that the lure of war was that it brought death into life once again: "Life has, indeed, become interesting again; it has recovered its full content."[10] When death is excluded, when one loses sight of the stakes involved, life becomes impoverished. It is turned into something, Freud wrote, "as shallow and empty as, let us say, an American flirtation, in which it is understood from the first that nothing is to happen, as contrasted with a continental love-affair in which both partners must constantly bear its serious consequences in mind."[11]

Many have speculated that the absence of the *fact* of death, as well as of the idea of death, would result in the same blunting of one's sensibilities to life. For example, in the French playwright Jean Giraudoux's *Amphitryon 38*, there is a conversation between the immortal gods. Jupiter tells Mercury what it is like to don earthly guise to make love to a mortal woman:

> She will use little expressions and that widens the abyss between us. . . . She will say, "When I was a child"—or "When I am old"—or "Never in all my life"—This stabs me, Mercury. . . . We miss something, Mercury—the poignance of the transient—the intimation of mortality—that sweet sadness of grasping at something you cannot hold?"[12]

Similarly, Montaigne imagines a conversation in which Chiron, half-god, half-mortal, refuses immortality when his father, Saturn (the god of time and duration), describes the implications of the choice:

> Imagine honestly how much less bearable and more painful to man would be an everlasting life than the life I have given him. If you did not have death, you would curse me incessantly for having deprived you of it. I have deliberately mixed with it a little bitterness to keep you, seeing the convenience of it, from embracing it too greedily and intemperately. To lodge you in the moderate state that I ask of you, of neither fleeing life nor fleeing back from death, I have tempered both of them between sweetness and bitterness.[13]

I do not wish to participate in a necrophilic cult or to advocate a life-denying morbidity. But it must not be forgotten that our basic dilemma is that each of us is both angel and beast of the field; we are the mortal creatures who, because we are self-aware, know that we are mortal. A denial of death at any level is a denial of one's basic nature and begets an increasingly pervasive restriction of awareness and experience. The integration of the *idea* of death saves us; rather than sentence us to existences of terror or bleak pessimism, it acts as a catalyst to plunge us into more authentic life modes, and it enhances our pleasure in the living of life. As corroboration we have the testimony of individuals who have had a personal confrontation with death.

CONFRONTATION WITH DEATH: PERSONAL CHANGE

Some of our greatest literary works have portrayed the positive effects on an individual of a close encounter with death.

Tolstoy's *War and Peace* provides an excellent illustration of how death may instigate a radical personal change.[14] Pierre, the protagonist, feels deadened by the meaningless, empty life of the Russian aristocracy. A lost soul, he stumbles through the first nine hundred pages of the novel searching for some purpose in life. The pivotal point of the book occurs when Pierre is captured by Napoleon's troops and sentenced to death by firing squad. Sixth in line, he watches the execution of the five men in front of him and prepares to die—only, at the last moment, to be unexpectedly reprieved. The experience transforms Pierre, who then spends the remaining three hundred pages of the novel living his life zestfully and purposefully. He is able to give himself fully in his relationships to others, to be keenly aware of his natural surroundings, to discover a task in life that has meaning for him, and to dedicate himself to it.*

Tolstoy's story "The Death of Ivan Ilyich" contains a similar message.[15] Ivan Ilyich, a mean-spirited bureaucrat, develops a fatal illness, probably abdominal cancer, and suffers extraordinary pain. His anguish continues relentlessly until, shortly before his death, Ivan Ilyich comes upon a stunning truth: *he is dying badly because he has lived badly.* In the few days remaining to him, Ivan Ilyich undergoes a dramatic transformation that is difficult to describe in any other terms than personal growth. If Ivan Ilyich were a patient, any psychotherapist would beam with pride at the changes in him: he relates more empathically to others; his chronic bitterness, arrogance, and self-aggrandizement disappear. In short, in the last few days of his life he achieves a far higher level of integration than he has ever reached previously.

This phenomenon occurs with great frequency in the world of the clinician. For example, interviews with six of the ten would-be suicides who leaped off the Golden Gate Bridge and survived indicate that, as a

---

* In real life, Dostoevsky was reprieved at the age of twenty-nine from execution by a firing squad at the last minute—an event that crucially influenced his life and his fiction.

result of their leap into death, these six had changed their views of life.[16] One reported, "My will to live has taken over.... There is a benevolent God in heaven who permeates all things in the universe." Another: "We are all members of the Godhead—that great God humanity." Another: "I have a strong life drive now.... My whole life is reborn.... I have broken out of old pathways.... I can now sense other people's existence." Another: "I feel I love God now and wish to do something for others." Another:

> I was refilled with a new hope and purpose in being alive. It's beyond most people's comprehension. I appreciate the miracle of life—like watching a bird fly—everything is more meaningful when you come close to losing it. I experienced a feeling of unity with all things and a oneness with all people. After my psychic rebirth I also feel for everyone's pain. Everything was clear and bright.

Other clinical examples abound. Abraham Schmitt describes in detail a chronically depressed patient who made a serious suicide attempt and survived by sheer chance, and points out the "total discontinuity between the two halves of her life"—before and after her suicide attempt. Schmitt speaks of his professional contact with her not as therapy but as a monitoring of her drastic life change. To describe her, her friends use the word "vibrant," meaning "tinkling with life and enthusiasm." The therapist states that following her suicide attempt she was, "in touch with herself, her life and her husband. Her life is now lived to the fullest and is filling many other lives.... Within a year after the suicide and the transition she became pregnant with the first of several children who were born in quick succession. (She had long been barren)."[17]

Russel Noyes studied two hundred individuals who had near-death experiences (automobile accidents, drownings, mountain climbing falls, and so forth), and reported that a substantial number (23 percent) described, even years later, that as a result of their experience they possessed a

> strong sense of the shortness of life and the preciousness of it ... a greater sense of zest in life, a heightening of perception and emotional responsivity to immediate surroundings ... an ability to live in the moment and to savor each moment as it passes ... a greater awareness of life—awareness of life and living things and the urge to enjoy it now before it is too late.[18]

Many described a "reassessment of priorities," of becoming more compassionate and more human-oriented than they had been before.

2 / Life, Death, and Anxiety

Abdul Hussain and Seymour Tozman, physicians on a prison's "death row," describe, in a clinical case report, three men condemned to death, who received last-minute reprieves. All three, according to the authors, evinced a deep alteration in personality style and a "remarkable change in attitude" which persisted through the follow-up of several months.[19]

Cancer: Confrontation with Death. The Chinese pictogram for "crisis" is a combination of two symbols: "danger" and "opportunity." Over my many years of work with terminally ill cancer patients, I have been struck by how many of them use their crisis and their danger as an opportunity for change. They report startling shifts, inner changes that can be characterized in no other way than "personal growth":

- A rearrangement of life's priorities: a trivializing of the trivial
- A sense of liberation: being able to choose not to do those things that they do not wish to do
- An enhanced sense of living in the immediate present, rather than postponing life until retirement or some other point in the future
- A vivid appreciation of the elemental facts of life: the changing seasons, the wind, falling leaves, the last Christmas, and so forth
- Deeper communication with loved ones than before the crisis
- Fewer interpersonal fears, less concern about rejection, greater willingness to take risks, than before the crisis.

Senator Richard Neuberger, shortly before his death from cancer, described these changes:

> A change came over me which I believe is irreversible. Questions of prestige, of political success, of financial status, became all at once unimportant. In those first hours when I realized I had cancer, I never thought of my seat in the Senate, of my bank account, or of the destiny of the free world. . . . My wife and I have not had a quarrel since my illness was diagnosed. I used to scold her about squeezing the toothpaste from the top instead of the bottom, about not catering sufficiently to my fussy appetite, about making up guest lists without consulting me, about spending too much on clothes. Now I am either unaware of such matters, or they seem irrelevant. . . .
>
> In their stead has come a new appreciation of things I once took for granted—eating lunch with a friend, scratching Muffet's ears and listening for his purrs, the company of my wife, reading a book or magazine in the quiet cone of my bed lamp at night, raiding the refrigerator for a glass of orange juice or slice of coffee cake. For the first time I think I actually am savoring life. I realize, finally, that I am not immortal. I shudder when I remember all the occasions that I spoiled for myself—even when I was in the best of health—by false pride, synthetic values, and fancied slights.[20]

How commonly do positive personal changes follow a confrontation with death? The cancer patients I studied were a self-selected sample consisting of psychologically minded women with cancer who had elected to seek a support group for cancer patients. To examine the general prevalence of this phenomenon, my colleagues and I designed a research project to study patients in a purely medical setting.[21] We constructed a questionnaire to measure some of these personal changes and administered it to seventy consecutive patients who consulted medical oncologists for treatment of metastatic breast cancer (cancer that has spread elsewhere in the body, and for which there is no surgical or medical cure).* One part of the questionnaire consisted of seventeen personal-growth statements,† each of which patients were asked to score on a five-point scale (ranging from "hardly ever" to "always") for two time periods: "before" the onset of cancer and "now." When we examined the results, we learned that the majority of patients had rated no changes between "before" and "now." However, of those patients who did report differences between "before" and "now," the differences were almost invariably in the direction of greater growth since the onset of cancer. More patients reported positive than negative changes on fourteen of the seventeen items.‡ Some of the items

---

* The patients in the study were all outpatients: few had incapacitating physical pain or disability. They all knew their diagnosis and knew, too, that, though they might live for months or even years, they would ultimately die of their disease.

† 1. I communicate openly with my husband.
2. I appreciate the beauty of nature.
3. I have a sense of personal freedom.
4. I try to communicate openly with my children.
5. It is important to me to be liked by everyone.
6. I obtain much pleasure from life.
7. I communicate honestly and frankly.
8. I do only those things I really want to do.
9. I live in the present rather than in the past or future.
10. I have moments of deep serenity.
11. I stand up for my own personal rights.
12. I have a sense of psychological well-being.
13. I communicate openly with my friends.
14. I feel I have something of value to teach others about life.
15. I am able to choose what I want to do.
16. My life has meaning and purpose.
17. Religious/spiritual beliefs have much significance for me.

‡ The only two items that showed a reversal were item 3 ("I have a sense of personal freedom") which I believe was probably influenced by the great physical restrictions suffered by the cancer patient, and item 13 ("I communicate openly with my friends"). The explanation for the latter reversal probably lay in the fact that many of the patients' friends demonstrated extreme discomfort; patients found that while some close relationships were strengthened, many others were strained.

showed significant differences: for example, on item 14 ("I feel I have something of value to teach others about life") eighteen patients report a positive shift, three a negative one; item 11 ("I stand up for my own personal rights")—twelve positive, three negative; item 2 ("I appreciate the beauty of nature")—eleven positive, two negative. Who would suspect that terminal cancer might increase one's "moments of deep serenity" (item 10)? Yet eighteen patients reported such an increase (in contrast to eight who reported a negative shift).

Another part of the questionnaire examined changes in the intensity of common fears. Twenty-nine fears were selected from a standard fear check list,* and patients were asked to rate severity ("before" cancer and "now"). The results of this questionnaire indicated the same trend in the personal growth items, though not of the same magnitude. On nine items patients reported greater fear since the onset of cancer; on one item there was an equal shift (the same number of patients reported less fear "now" as reported more fear "now"); and on *nineteen of the twenty-nine items, more patients reported less fear "now" than "before" they had cancer.*

Though no other systematic studies of this phenomenon appear in the literature,† most therapists can supply anecdotal clinical material to illustrate it. Many therapists have worked with patients who in the midst of therapy had some confrontation with death which resulted in a rapid change in life perspective and a realignment of life's priorities.

---

* 1. Dead people
  2. Angry people
  3. Parting from friends
  4. Enclosed places
  5. Feeling rejected by others
  6. Feeling disapproved of
  7. Being ignored
  8. Darkness
  9. People with deformities
  10. Making mistakes
  11. Looking foolish
  12. Losing control
  13. Being in charge or responsible for decisions
  14. Becoming mentally ill
  15. Taking written tests
  16. Being touched by others
  17. Feeling different from others
  18. Being alone
  19. Being in a strange place
  20. Speaking in public
  21. Bad dreams
  22. Failure
  23. Entering a room where other people are already seated
  24. Looking down from high buildings
  25. Strangers
  26. Feeling angry
  27. People in authority
  28. A lull in conversation
  29. Crawling insects.

† Some studies[22] have been conducted on hospitalized patients near death and report many more negative findings than in our study; but such patients are often isolated, cachectic, and in great pain. Recently a cancer patient took Kübler-Ross to task for this very point, by emphasizing that Kübler-Ross's "stages" of dying were skewed to a cachectic hospital population and overlooked the "golden period" that occurs if a patient has time to assimilate his confrontation with death.[23]

Schmitt had a patient whom kidney failure had brought extremely close to death. After a long period of time on renal dialysis the patient had a successful kidney transplant and re-entered life with a sense of both physical and psychological rebirth. She describes her experience:

> Actually the only way I can describe myself is that I think of myself as having lived two lives. I even call them the first and the second Kathy. The first Kathy died during dialysis. She could not make it long in the face of death. A second Kathy had to be born. This is the Kathy that was born in the midst of death. . . . The first Kathy was a frivolous kid. She lived only one minute at a time. She quibbled about cold food in the cafeteria, about the boredom of surgical nursing lectures, about the unfairness of her parents. Her goal in life was to have fun on the weekends. . . . The future was far away and of little concern. She lived for trivia only.
>
> But the second Kathy—that's me now. I am infatuated with life. Look at the beauty in the sky! It's gorgeously blue! I go into a flower garden, and every flower takes on such fabulous colors that I am dazzled by their beauty. . . . One thing I do know, had I remained my first Kathy, I would have played away my whole life, and I would never have known what the real joy of living was all about. I had to face death eyeball to eyeball before I could live. I had to die in order to live.[24]

A unusual confrontation with death afforded a turning point in the life of Arthur, an alcoholic patient. The patient had had a progressive downhill course. He had been drinking heavily for several years and had had no periods of sobriety sufficiently long to permit effective psychotherapeutic contact. He entered a therapy group and one day came to the session so intoxicated that he passed out. The group, with Arthur unconscious on the couch, continued their meeting, discussed what to do with Arthur, and finally carried him bodily from the session to the hospital.

Fortunately the session was videotaped; and later, when Arthur watched the videotape, he had a profound confrontation with death. Everyone had been telling him for years he was drinking himself to death; but until he saw the videotape, he never truly allowed that possibility to register. The videotape of himself stretched out on the couch, with the group surrounding his body and talking about him, bore an uncanny resemblance to the funeral of his twin brother who had died of alcoholism a year previously. He visualized himself at his own wake stretched out on a slab and surrounded by friends talking about him. Arthur was deeply shaken by the vision, embarked on the longest period of sobriety he had had in adult life, and for the first time committed himself to therapeutic work, which was ultimately of considerable benefit to him.

My interest in existential therapy was, to a large extent, kindled by witnessing, several years ago, the impact of death upon one of my patients. Jane was a twenty-five-year-old perpetual college student who sought therapy because she was depressed, had severe functional gastric distress, and experienced a pervasive sense of helplessness and purposelessness. In her initial session she presented her problems in a diffuse manner and lamented repetitively, "I don't know what's going on." I did not understand what she meant by this statement and, since it was imbedded in a lengthy litany of self-derogation, soon forgot it. I introduced Jane into a therapy group, and in the group she again had a strong sense of not knowing what was going on. She did not understand what was happening to her, why the other members were so uninterested in her, why she developed a conversion paralysis, why she developed masochistic relationships with the other members, why she became so infatuated with the therapist. To a great extent life was a mystery, something "out there" happening to her, something raining upon her.

In the therapy group Jane was timid and boring. Her every statement was predictable; before speaking, she scanned the sea of faces in the group for clues about what others wanted, and then shaped her statements to please as many people as possible. Anything to avoid offense, to avoid driving others away. (What happened, of course, was that she drove people away, not from anger but from boredom.) It was clear that Jane was in chronic retreat from life. Everyone in the group tried to find "the real Jane" within the cocoon of compliance she had spun about herself. They tried to encourage Jane; they urged her to socialize, to study, to write the last paper she needed for graduation, to buy clothes, to pay her bills, to groom herself, to comb her hair, to prepare her résumé, to apply for jobs.

This exhortation, like most exhortation in therapy, was not successful, so the group tried another tact: they urged Jane to consider the lure and the blessing of failure. What was the payoff? Why was failure so rewarding? That line of inquiry was more productive, and we learned that the payoff was considerable. Failing kept Jane young, kept her protected, kept her from having to make choices. Idealizing and worshiping the therapist served the same purpose. Help was "out there." Her task in therapy, as she viewed it, was to enfeeble herself to the point where the therapist could not in all good conscience withhold his royal touch.

The critical event in therapy occurred when Jane developed a large, ominous, axillary lymph node. The group met on Tuesday evenings; and it happened that she had a biopsy done on a Tuesday morning and had to wait twenty-four hours before learning whether the growth was malignant. She came to the meeting that evening in terror. She had never previously contemplated her own death, and the meeting was a powerful one for her as the group helped her face and express her fears. Her paramount experience was a terrifying loneliness—a loneliness that she had always perceived on the edge of consciousness and had always dreaded. In that meeting Jane realized on a deep level that no matter what she did, no matter how she enfeebled herself, she would ultimately face death alone—no one could intercede for her, no one could die her death for her.

The following day she learned that the lymph node was benign, but nonetheless the psychological effects of the experience were profound. Many things began to fall together for Jane. She began to make decisions in a way that she had never done before, and she took over the helm of her life. At one meeting she commented, "I think I know what's going on." I had long since forgotten her initial complaint, but now I remembered and finally understood it. It had been important for her not to know what was going on. More than anything else, she had been trying to avoid the loneliness and the death that accompany adulthood. In a magical way she had tried to defeat death by staying young, by avoiding choice and responsibility, by choosing to believe the myth that there would always be someone who would choose for her, would accompany her, would be there for her. Growing up, choosing, separating oneself from others also mean facing loneliness and death.

To summarize, the concept of death plays a crucial role in psychotherapy because it plays a crucial role in the life experience of each of us. Death and life are interdependent: though the physicality of death destroys us, the *idea* of death saves us. Recognition of death contributes a sense of poignancy to life, provides a radical shift of life perspective, and can transport one from a mode of living characterized by diversions, tranquilization, and petty anxieties to a more authentic mode. There are, in the examples of individuals undergoing significant personal change after confrontation with death, obvious and important implications for psychotherapy. What is needed are techniques to allow psychotherapists to mine this therapeutic potential with all patients, rather than be dependent upon fortuitous circumstances or the advent of a terminal illness. I shall consider these issues fully in chapter 5.

Death and Anxiety

Anxiety plays such a central and obvious role in psychotherapy that there is little need to belabor the point. The unique position of anxiety is apparent from traditional psychiatric nosology, in which the major psychiatric syndromes are called "reactions"—psychotic reactions, neurotic reactions, psychophysiological reactions. We consider these conditions *reactions to anxiety*. They are efforts, albeit maladaptive ones, to cope with anxiety. Psychopathology is a vector—the resultant of anxiety and the individual's anxiety-combatting defenses, both neurotic and characterological. Therapists generally begin work with a patient by focusing on manifest anxiety, anxiety equivalents, or the defenses that the individual sets up in an attempt to protect himself or herself from anxiety. Though therapeutic work extends in many directions, therapists continue to use anxiety as a beacon or compass point: they work toward anxiety, uncover its fundamental sources, and attempt as their final goal to uproot and dismantle these sources.

DEATH ANXIETY: AN INFLUENTIAL DETERMINANT OF HUMAN
EXPERIENCE AND BEHAVIOR

The terror of death is ubiquitous and of such magnitude that a considerable portion of one's life energy is consumed in the denial of death. Death transcendence is a major motif in human experience—from the most deeply personal internal phenomena, our defenses, our motivations, our dreams and nightmares, to the most public macro-societal structures, our monuments, theologies, ideologies, slumber cemeteries, embalmings, our stretch into space, indeed our entire way of life—our filling time, our addiction to diversions, our unfaltering belief in the myth of progress, our drive to "get ahead," our yearning for lasting fame.

The basic human group, the molecules of social life were, as Freud speculated, formed out of the fear of death: the first humans huddled together out of a fear of separateness and a fear of what lurked in the dark. We perpetuate the group in order to perpetuate ourselves, and history-taking of the group is a symbolic quest for mediated immortality. Indeed, as Hegel postulated, history itself is what man does with death. Robert Jay Lifton has described several modes by which man attempts to achieve symbolic immortality. Consider their pervasive cultural implications: (1) the biological mode—living on through one's progeny, through an endless chain of biological attachments; (2) the theological mode—living on in a different, higher plane of existence; (3) the creative mode—living on through one's works, through the enduring impact of one's personal creation or impact on others (Lifton suggests that the therapist draws personal sustenance from this fount: by helping his patient, he initiates an endless chain as the patient's children and associates pass on his spore); (4) the theme of eternal nature—one survives through rejoining the swirling life forces of nature; (5) the experiential transcendent mode—through "losing oneself" in a state so intense that time and death disappear and one lives in the "continuous present."[25]

These social ramifications of the fear of death and the quest for immortality are so widespread that they extend far beyond the range of this book. Among those who have written of these issues, Norman Brown, Ernest Becker, and Robert Jay Lifton, in particular, have brilliantly demonstrated how the fear of death has permeated the fabric of our social structure. Here I am concerned with the effects of death anxiety on the internal dynamics of the individual. I shall argue that the fear of death is a primal source of anxiety. Although this position is simple and consonant with everyday intuition, its ramifications for theory and clinical practice are, as we shall see, extensive.

DEATH ANXIETY: DEFINITION

First, let me examine the meaning of "death anxiety." I shall use several terms interchangeably: "death anxiety," "fear of death," "mortal terror," "fear of finitude." Philosophers speak of the awareness of the "fragility of being" (Jaspers), of dread of "non-being" (Kierkegaard), of the "impossibility of further possibility" (Heidegger), or of ontological anxiety (Tillich). Many of these phrases imply a difference in emphasis, for individuals may experience the fear of death in very different ways. Can we be more precise? What exactly is it that we fear about death?

Researchers investigating this issue have suggested that the fear is a composite of a number of smaller discrete fears. For example, James Diggory and Doreen Rothman asked a large sample (N=563) drawn from the general population to rank-order several consequences of death. In order of descending frequency, these were the common fears about death:

1. My death would cause grief to my relatives and friends.
2. All my plans and projects would come to an end.
3. The process of dying might be painful.
4. I could no longer have any experiences.

5. I would no longer be able to care for my dependents.
6. I am afraid of what might happen to me if there is a life after death.
7. I am afraid of what might happen to my body after death.[26]

Of these fears, several seem tangential to personal death. Fears about pain obviously lie on this side of death; fears about an afterlife beg the question by changing death into a nonterminal event; fears about others are obviously not fears about oneself. The fear of personal extinction seems to be at the vortex of concern: "my plans and projects would come to an end," and "I could no longer have any experiences."

Jacques Choron, in a review of major philosophic views about death, arrives at a similar analysis. He distinguishes three types of death fear: (1) what comes after death, (2) the "event" of dying, and (3) ceasing to be.[27] Of these, the first two are, as Robert Kastenbaum points out, fears *related to* death.[28] It is the third, "ceasing to be" (obliteration, extinction, annihilation), that seems more centrally the fear of death; and it is this fear to which I refer in these chapters.

Kierkegaard was the first to make a clear distinction between fear and anxiety (dread); he contrasted fear that is fear of *some* thing with dread that is a fear of *no* thing—"not," as he wryly noted, "a nothing with which the individual has nothing to do."[29] One dreads (or is anxious about) losing oneself and becoming nothingness. This anxiety cannot be located. As Rollo May says, "it attacks us from all sides at once."[30] A fear that can neither be understood nor located cannot be confronted and becomes more terrible still: it begets a feeling of helplessness which invariably generates further anxiety. (Freud felt that anxiety was a reaction to helplessness; anxiety, he wrote, "is a signal which announces that there is danger" and the individual is "expecting a situation of helplessness to set in."[31]

How can we combat anxiety? *By displacing it from nothing to something.* This is what Kierkegaard meant by "the nothing which is the object of dread becomes, as it were, more and more a something."[32] It is what Rollo May means by "anxiety seeks to become fear."[33] If we can transform a fear of nothing to a fear of something, we can mount some self-protective campaign—that is, we can either avoid the thing we fear, seek allies against it, develop magical rituals to placate it, or plan a systematic campaign to detoxify it.

DEATH ANXIETY: CLINICAL MANIFESTATIONS

The fact that anxiety seeks to become fear confounds the clinician's attempt to identify the primal source of anxiety. Primal death anxiety is rarely encountered in its original form in clinical work. Like nascent oxygen, it is rapidly transformed to another state. To ward off death anxiety, the young child develops protective mechanisms which, as I shall discuss in the next chapter, are denial-based, pass through several stages, and eventually consist of a highly complex set of mental operations that repress naked death anxiety and bury it under layers of such defensive operations as displacement, sublimation, and conversion. Occasionally some jolting experience in life tears a rent in the curtain of defenses and permits raw death anxiety to erupt into consciousness. Rapidly, however, the unconscious ego repairs the tear and conceals once again the nature of the anxiety.

I can provide an illustration from my personal experience. While I was engaged in writing this book, I was involved in a head-on automobile collision. Driving along a peaceful suburban street, I suddenly saw, looming before me, a car out of control and heading directly at me. Though the crash was of sufficient force to demolish both automobiles, and though the other driver suffered severe lacerations, I was fortunate and suffered no significant physical injury. I caught a plane two hours later and was able that evening to deliver a lecture in another city. Yet, without question, I was severely shaken, I felt dazed, was tremulous, and could not eat or sleep. The next evening I was unwise enough to see a frightening movie (*Carrie*) which thoroughly terrified me, and I left before its end. I returned home a couple of days later with no obvious psychological sequellae aside from occasional insomnia and anxiety dreams.

Yet a strange problem arose. At the time I was spending a year as a fellow at the Center for Advanced Study in the Behavioral Sciences in Palo Alto, California. I enjoyed my colleagues and especially looked forward to the daily leisurely luncheon discussions of scholarly issues. Immediately after the accident I developed intense anxiety around these lunches. Would I have anything of significance to say? How would my colleagues regard me? Would I make a fool of myself? After a few days the anxiety was so extreme that I began to search for excuses to lunch elsewhere by myself.

I also began, however, to analyze my predicament, and one fact was abundantly clear: the luncheon anxiety appeared for the first time following the automobile accident. Furthermore, explicit anxiety about the accident, about so nearly losing my life, had, within a day or two, entirely vanished. It was clear that anxiety had succeeded in becoming fear. Considerable death anxiety had erupted immediately following the accident, and I had "handled" it primarily by displacement—by splitting it from its true source and riveting it to a convenient specific situation. My fundamental death anxiety thus had only a brief efflorescence before being secularized to such lesser concerns as self-esteem, fear of interpersonal rejection, or humiliation.

Although I had handled, or "processed," my anxiety, I had not eradicated it; and traces were evident for months afterward. Even though I had worked through my lunch phobia, a series of other fears emerged—fears of driving a car, of bicycling. Months later when I went skiing, I found myself so cautious, so frightened of some mishap that my skiing pleasure and ability were severely compromised. Still these fears could be located in space and time and could be managed in some systematic way. Annoying as they were, they were not fundamental, they did not threaten my being.

In addition to these specific fears, I noted one other change: the world seemed precarious. It had lost, for me, its hominess: danger seemed everywhere. The nature of reality had shifted, as I experienced what Heidegger called "uncanniness" (*unheimlich*)—the experience of "not being at home in the world," which he considered (and to which I can attest) a typical consequence of death awareness.[34]

One further property of death anxiety that has often created confusion in mental health literature is that the fear of death can be experienced at many different levels. One may, as I have discussed, worry about the act of dying, fear of pain of dying, regret unfinished projects, mourn the end of personal experience, or consider death as rationally and dispassionately as the Epicureans who concluded simply that death holds no terror because "where I am, death is not; where death is, I am not. Therefore death is nothing to me" (Lucretius). Yet keep in mind that these responses are adult conscious reflections on the phenomenon of death; by no means are they identical to the primitive dread of death that resides in the unconscious—a dread that is part of the fabric of being, that is formed early in life at a time before the development of precise conceptual formulation, a dread that is chilling, uncanny, and inchoate, a dread that exists prior to and outside of language and image.

The clinician rarely encounters death anxiety in its stark form: this anxiety is handled by conventional defenses (for example, repression, displacement, rationalization) and by some defenses specific only to it (see chapter 4). Of course this situation should not overly trouble us: it prevails for every theory of anxiety. Primary anxiety is always transformed into something less toxic for the individual; that is the function of the entire system of psychological defenses. It is rare, to use a Freudian frame of reference, for a clinician to observe undisguised castration anxiety; instead, one sees some transformation of anxiety. For example, a male patient may be phobic of women, or fearful of competing with males in certain social situations, or inclined to obtain sexual gratification in some mode other than heterosexual intercourse.

A clinician who has developed the existential "set," however, will recognize the "processed" death anxiety and be astonished at the frequency and the diversity of its appearance. Let me give some clinical examples. I recently saw two patients who sought therapy not because of existential anxiety but to solve commonplace, painful relationship problems.

Joyce was a thirty-year-old university professor who was in the midst of a painful divorce. She had first dated Jack when she was fifteen and married him at twenty-one. The marriage had obviously not gone well for several years, and they had separated three years previously. Although Joyce had formed a satisfying relationship with another man, she was unable to proceed with a divorce. In fact, her chief complaint when entering therapy was her uncontrollable weeping whenever she talked to Jack. An analysis of her weeping uncovered several important factors.

First, it was of the utmost importance that Jack continue to love her. Even though she no longer loved him or wanted him, she wanted very much that he think of her often and love her as he had never loved any other woman. "Why?" I asked. "Everyone wishes to be remembered," she replied. "It's a way of putting myself into posterity." She reminded me that the Jewish Kaddish ritual is built around the assumption that, as long as one is remembered by one's children, one continues to exist. When Jack forgot her, she died a little.*

Another source of Joyce's tears was her feeling that she and Jack had shared many lovely and important experiences. Without their union, these events, she felt, would perish. The fading of the past is a vivid reminder of the relentless rush of time. As the past disappears, so does the coil of the future shorten. Joyce's husband helped her to freeze time—the future as well as the past. Though she was not conscious of it, it was clear that Joyce was frightened of using up the future. She had

---

* Allen Sharp in *A Green Tree in Geddes* describes a small Mexican cemetery that is divided into two parts: the "dead" whose graves are still adorned with flowers placed there by the living, and the "truly dead" whose grave sites are no longer maintained—they are remembered by no living soul.[35] In a sense, then, when a very old person dies, many others die also; the dead person takes them along. All those recently dead who are remembered by no one else become, at that moment, "truly" dead.

a habit, for example, of never quite completing a task: if she were doing housework, she always left one corner of the house uncleaned. She dreaded being "finished." She never started a book without another one on her night table awaiting its turn. One is reminded of Proust whose major literary corpus was devoted to escaping "the devouring jaws of time" by recapturing the past.

Still another reason why Joyce wept was her fear of failure. Life had until recently been an uninterrupted stairway of success. To fail in her marriage meant that she would be, as she often put it, "just like everyone else." Though she had considerable talent, her expectations were grandiose. She anticipated achieving international prominence, perhaps winning a Nobel prize for a research program upon which she was embarking. If that success did not occur within five years, she planned to turn her energies to fiction and write the *You Can't Go Home Again* of the 1970s—although she had never written any fiction. Yet she had reason for her sense of specialness: thus far she had not failed to accomplish every one of her goals. The failure of her marriage was the first interruption of her ascent, the first challenge to her solipsistic assumptive world. The failure of the marriage threatened her sense of specialness, which as I will discuss in chapter 4, is one of the most common and potent death-denying defenses.

Joyce's commonplace problem, then, had roots stretching back to primal death anxiety. To me, an existentially oriented therapist, these clinical phenomena—the wish to be loved and remembered eternally, the wish to freeze time, the belief in personal invulnerability, the wish to merge with another—all served the same function for Joyce: to assuage death anxiety.

As she analyzed each one and came to understand the common source of these phenomena, Joyce's clinical picture improved remarkably. Most strikingly, as she gave up her neurotic needs for Jack, and stopped using him for all the death-defying functions he served, she was able to turn toward him for the first time in a truly loving fashion and re-establish the marriage on an entirely different basis. But that is another issue, which I shall address in chapter 8.

Then there was Beth, a thirty-year-old single woman, who sought therapy because of her inability to form a gratifying relationship with a man. She had on many occasions previously "chosen poorly," as she put it, and had broken off the relationship because she lost interest in the man. While in therapy she repeated the cycle: she fell in love with a man, entered a tormented state of indecision, and finally was unable to make a commitment to him.

As we analyzed her dilemma, it became apparent that she felt pressured to form an enduring relationship: she was tired of loneliness, tired of living the singles life, and desperately eager to have children. The pressure was intensified by her concerns about growing older and passing the childbearing age.

When, however, her lover tried to discuss marriage, she panicked; and the more he pressed, the more anxious she grew. Beth likened marriage to being pinned to the wall: she would be fixed, forever, the way formaldehyde fixes a biological specimen. It was important to keep growing, to become something else, something other than what she was; and she feared her lover was too complacent, too satisfied, with himself and his life. Gradually Beth became aware of the importance of this motif in her life. She had never lived in the present. Even when eating or serving a meal, she had stayed one course ahead; when eating a main course, her thoughts were dwelling on dessert. She had often thought with horror about "settling down," which she equated with "settling in." "Is this all there is to life?" she frequently asked herself when she thought of marriage or any other form of commitment.

As Beth, in therapy, delved into these areas—her compulsion to be always ahead of herself, her fear of aging, of death and stagnation—she grew more anxious than ever before. One evening following a session in which we had probed particularly deeply, she experienced extraordinary terror. While walking her dog, she had the uncanny feeling she was being pursued by some unearthly being. She looked behind herself, on all sides, and finally broke into a run and scurried home. Later a rainstorm broke out, and she lay awake all night with an irrational terror that the roof would be torn off, or that her house would be washed away. As I will discuss in chapter 5, an augmentation of anxiety often occurs when fear of *some* thing (in Beth's case, a fear of marriage or of making the wrong choice) is understood for what it truly is—a fear of *no* thing. For Beth, both the press toward marriage and the fear of marriage were in part surface reverberations of a deeper struggle to contain death anxiety.

Many clinicians have described the presence and the transformation of death anxiety across the entire spectrum of clinical psychopathology. Chapter 4 deals with this in depth, and I need only highlight it here. R. Skoog reports that over 70 percent of patients with a severe obsessional neurosis had, at the onset of illness, a security-disturbing death experience. As the syndrome develops, patients are increasingly concerned about controlling their world and preventing the unexpected or accidental. Patients shun disorder or uncleanliness and develop rituals to ward off evil and danger.[36] Erwin Strauss notes that the obsessional patient's disgust at decay, illness, germs, and dirt was intimately related to fear of personal annihilation.[37] W. Schwidder observes that these obsessive defenses were not entirely effective in absorbing death anxiety. In a study of over a hundred obsessional-phobic patients he notes that a third feared constriction and darkness and that a somewhat larger proportion had explicit death anxiety.[38]

Herbert Lazarus and John Kostan, in an extensive study of the hyperventilation syndrome (an extremely common condition: between 5 and 10 percent of all patients consulting physicians suffer from this complaint), emphasize the underlying dynamic of death anxiety, which is transformed into a series of other phobias. An inability to bind death anxiety sufficiently results in the hyperventilation panic.[39]

D. B. Friedman describes an obsessional patient whose death anxiety took the form of an obsessive thought that he would be forgotten by everyone. Linked to this was his preoccupation that he was always missing the exciting things in the world about him: "Something really new happens only when I'm not around, before my time, or after my time, before I was born or after I'm dead."[40]

Death anxiety is only thinly disguised in the hypochondriacal patient who is continually concerned about the safety and well-being of his or her body. Hypochondriacal illness in a patient often begins after a severe illness suffered by that patient or by someone close to him or her. Early in the course of the affliction, V. Kral observes, there is a directly experienced fear of death which is later diffused among many body organs.[41]

Several clinical investigations have reported the central role of death anxiety in depersonalization syndromes.[42] Martin Roth for example, found that death or severe illness was the precipitating event in over 50 percent of patients reporting a depersonalization syndrome.[43]

These neurotic syndromes share one important common feature: though they inconvenience and restrict a patient, they all succeed in protecting him or her from overt and terrifying death anxiety.

DEATH ANXIETY: EMPIRICAL RESEARCH

Over the past three decades there has been a continuous but feeble stream of empirical social science research on death. Virtually every research article on death begins with a clarion call to research and either a lament or an indignant protest about the lack of careful investigation. After reviewing the literature, I cannot help but echo a similar complaint. Certainly the contrast between the speculative or impressionis-

49

tic writings on death and the methodical research into it is striking. For example, a bibliography on death up to 1972 listed over 2,600 books and articles; yet fewer than 2 percent report empirical research, and only a handful bear direct relevance to existential theory and therapy.

The research even remotely relevant to my present discussion attempts to investigate the following issues: the incidence of death anxiety, correlative studies of the degree of death anxiety and a number of variables—demographic (age, sex, marital status, occupation, religion, education, and so forth), personality factors (MMPI dimensions*, general anxiety or depression levels), and life experiences (early loss, institutionalization)—and the relation of death anxiety to psychopathology or to other psychological experience, especially fantasies, dreams, and nightmares.

So far, so good. However, as Robert Kastenbaum and Ruth Aisenberg point out in their thoughtful review, the studies, with few exceptions, are either severely limited in scope or severely flawed methodologically.[44] Many studies investigate death in an imprecise fashion; for example, they fail to distinguish between one's fear of one's own death, one's fear of the death of another, or one's fear of the effects of one's death on others.

An even more serious problem, however, is that most studies have measured conscious attitudes toward death or conscious manifest anxiety. To compound the problem still further, the studies use instruments that (with a couple of exceptions[45]) are hastily constructed, "home brew" scales whose reliability or validity has not been established.

One occupational study is of interest. Medical students were studied using a conscious death anxiety scale and the "authoritarian" scale (California Personality Inventory F scale). A negative relationship was found between death anxiety and authoritarianism—that is, the more authoritarianism, the less death anxiety, and vice versa). Moreover, medical students who chose to enter psychiatry had more death anxiety (and were less authoritarian) than those who entered surgery.[46] Perhaps surgeons are better defended against death anxiety, and psychiatrists more aware of death anxiety. (Perhaps, too, fledgling psychiatrists have more absolute death anxiety and enter the mental health field in search of personal relief.)

Several projects report that devoutly religious individuals have less death anxiety.[47] Students who have lost a parent have higher death anxiety.[48] Most studies show few differences related to age,[49] although

---

*Minnesota Multiple Personality Inventory.

there is a positive relationship between death concerns and nearness to death.[50] A study of the most common fears of one thousand college co-eds indicates that death-related fears are extremely important in this population group.[51]

Several projects have demonstrated, but not attempted to explain, that females have higher conscious death anxiety than males.* [53]

A consideration of conscious death anxiety, though of some interest, is of limited relevance to an understanding of personality structure and psychopathology. The cornerstone of dynamic psychology is precisely that strong anxiety does *not* remain conscious: it is repressed and "processed." One of the major steps in the processing of the anxiety source is to separate or to isolate affect from object. Thus, one can think about death with only moderate discomfort, and one can experience displaced anxiety with few clues to its true source. A few studies, to be discussed shortly, have been sensitive to the difference between conscious and unconscious death anxiety and have attempted to examine death fear at unconscious levels. They have used such instruments as the TAT,† the Rorschach, dream analysis, word-association tests, sentence-completion tests, and tachistoscopic projection and the galvanic skin response.

DEATH ANXIETY AND PSYCHOPATHOLOGY

Conscious death anxiety. A few scattered reports attempt to correlate conscious death anxiety and psychopathology. There is a positive correlation, in student volunteers, between death anxiety and neuroticism (Eysenck neuroticism scale.)[54] Prisoners incarcerated for a "minor" offense (no further details of offense given) when compared with normal controls have significantly more death anxiety, death preoccupation, and more fear of funerals and medical diseases and are more often aware of suppressing thoughts about death.[55] Conscious death anxiety correlates positively with the MMPI depression scale in aged psychiatric patients; in fact, the correlation was so strong that the investigators suggested that heightened death anxiety be considered part of the depressive syndrome in the aged. The same study revealed no correlation between death anxiety and somatic symptomatology (on the Cornell

---

*A large study (N=825) reported no male-female differences but a careful inspection of the data showed that women were less inclined than men to answer unsettling items on the questionnaire; for example, one item ("Do you vividly imagine yourself as dying or being dead") was answered by only 78 percent of the women and by 98 percent of the men.[52]

†Thematic Apperception Test.

Medical Index).[56] Possibly somatization emerges in response to, and acts as a sump for, death anxiety.

Though studies indicate a lack of overt death anxiety in the normal aged population,[57] those aged who are psychologically immature or psychiatrically disturbed show evidence of high death anxiety.[58] Adolescents tend to show higher death anxiety than other age groups; and once again we find that the individuals who give evidence of psychopathology (in this study defined as delinquent acts of significant magnitude to warrant incarceration) express more death anxiety than do the controls.[59] A study of normal and institutionalized "sub-normal adolescent girls" demonstrated that the institutionalized population was more overtly fearful about death.[60] Similarly, another researcher found that poorly achieving high school girls had considerably greater fear of death—"often so pervasive that it can be communicated only indirectly."[61]

Unconscious death anxiety. But these studies of conscious death attitudes and anxiety are of little help in understanding the role of death anxiety in psychodynamics. Several researchers have accordingly attempted to study unconscious concerns about death. Feifel and his associates have defined three levels of concern: (1) conscious (measured by scoring the response to the question, "Are you afraid of your own death?"); (2) fantasy (measured by coding the positivity or negativity of responses to the directive, "What ideas or pictures come to your mind when you think about your death?"); (3) below-level awareness (measured by mean reaction time to death words on a word-association test and a color word interference test).[62]

The investigators found that death concerns varied greatly at each of these levels. On a conscious level, the great majority (over 70 percent) of individuals denied a fear of death. On the fantasy level, 27 percent denied death fear, 62 percent answered ambivalently, and 11 percent gave considerable evidence of death anxiety. At a level below awareness, most of the subjects gave evidence of considerable aversion to death. The major difference among normals, neurotics, and psychotics was that psychotic individuals evinced more overall death anxiety than the others. On the more conscious levels, the older subjects and the more religious subjects perceived death in a "fairly positive vein, but succumbed to anxiety at the gut level."[63] Though these studies use crude instrumentation, nonetheless they do point out the necessity of studying death concerns at different levels of awareness.

In an interesting experiment, W. W. Meissner demonstrated the existence of significant unconscious anxiety.[64] He tested the galvanic skin response (GSR) of normal subjects who were presented with a series of fifty items: thirty neutral terms and twenty death symbols (for example, black, a candle burning out, a journey, a sleeping person, the silent one, crossing a bridge). The death symbols evoked a significantly greater GSR response than did the control words.

Klass Magni tested unconscious death anxiety in another way.[65] Death-relevant scenes (pictures of funerals, decayed and mutilated corpses, and so forth) were projected tachistoscopically in progressively longer exposures. Magni measured the time required by a subject to identify the scene, and demonstrated that theology students planning to enter parish priesthood required significantly less time to identify the scene (and thus presumably had significantly less unconscious death anxiety) than did students planning research or teaching careers where they would be less intimately engaged in ministering to others. Several studies using interview data[66] or TAT[67] data indicate that individuals with higher levels of neuroticism have greater death anxiety.

Studies of unconscious death anxiety in the aged using the TAT and sentence completion tests indicate that elderly individuals who are assigned separate living quarters similar to a familiar setting have significantly less death anxiety than those individuals in traditional institutions for the aged.[68] Furthermore, the aged have less unconscious death anxiety if they are involved in many life activities.[69] Death anxiety on the TAT in the aged is positively correlated with MMPI neurotic indicators (hypochondriasis, dependency, impulsivity, and depression.)[70] A study of unconscious death anxiety (a sentence-completion projective technique) in a population of middle-aged to aged adults demonstrated that the younger adults had more death anxiety than their elderly cohorts.[71]

If fear of death is a primary source of anxiety, then it should be found in dreams, where unconscious themes often appear in relatively undisguised form. A large normative study of dreams indicated that overt death anxiety was found in 29 percent of dreams.[72] An extensive study of nightmares revealed that the most common anxiety theme in the dreams of adults was either dying or being murdered. The other common themes were also death-linked: some family member or other individual dying, or the dreamer's life being threatened by an accident or by someone chasing him or her.[73] Does the amount of conscious death anxiety correlate with the number of death nightmares? The studies show conflicting results depending upon the specific death anxiety scale used. However, a subject who has suffered (especially when under the age of ten) the death of close friends and relatives is more likely to have death nightmares.[74] One study reports an intriguing finding: there is a curvilinear relationship between conscious death anxiety and death themes in dreams.[75] In other words, those individuals who have very high *or* very low conscious death anxiety tend to dream of death. Possibly high conscious anxiety reflects such high unconscious anxiety that it cannot be contained and spills over into failed dreams (nightmares) and into consciousness. Very low conscious death anxiety (less than one would expect in the average individual) may reflect strong unconscious death anxiety which in the waking state is contained by denial and repression but which in the sleeping state overwhelms the dream censor.

In summary the research literature on death anxiety offers some limited help in increasing our understanding of the role of death fear in psychopathology and psychotherapy. Most of the research consists of correlational studies of conscious death anxiety (on crudely constructed scales) and a host of demographic and psychometric variables. These studies demonstrate some positive correlation between high death anxiety and depression, early loss, lack of religious belief, and occupational choice. Other studies investigate deeper layers of consciousness and demonstrate that considerable death anxiety lies outside of awareness; that death anxiety increases as one moves from conscious to unconscious experience; that the fear of death stalks us in our dreams; that the aged fear death more if they are psychologically immature, or if they have few life activities in which to engage; and, lastly, that death anxiety, both conscious and unconscious, is related to neuroticism.

The Inattention to Death in Psychotherapy Theory and Practice

All of the foregoing perspectives on death—cultural tradition, clinical experience and empirical research—bear strong implications for psychotherapy. The incorporation of death into life enriches life; it enables individuals to extricate themselves from smothering trivialities, to live more purposefully and more authentically. The full awareness of death may promote radical personal change. Yet death is a primary source of anxiety; it permeates inner experience, and we defend against it by a number of personal dynamisms. Furthermore, as I shall discuss in chapter 4, death anxiety dealt with maladaptively results in the vast variety of signs, symptoms, and character traits we refer to as "psychopathology."

Yet despite these compelling reasons, the dialogue of psychotherapy rarely includes the concept of death. Death is overlooked, and overlooked glaringly, in almost all aspects of the mental health field: theory, basic and clinical research, clinical reports, and all forms of clinical practice. The only exception lies in the area in which death cannot be ignored—the care of a dying patient. The sporadic articles dealing with death that do appear in the psychotherapy literature are generally in second- or third-line journals and are anecdotal in form. They are curiosities that are peripheral to the mainstream of theory and practice.

CLINICAL CASE REPORTS

The omission of the fear of death in clinical case reports, to take one example, is so blatant that one is tempted to conclude that nothing less than a conspiracy of silence is at work. There are three major strategies for dealing with death in clinical case reports. First, the authors selectively inattend to the issue and report no material whatsoever pertaining to death. Second, authors may present copious clinical data related to death but ignore the material completely in their dynamic formulation of the case. This is the situation, for example, in Freud's case histories, and I shall shortly provide evidence of it. Third, authors may present death-related clinical material but, in a formulation of the case, translate "death" into a concept compatible with a particular ideological school.

In a widely cited article, "The Attitudes of Psychoneurotics toward Death," published in a leading journal, two eminent clinicians, Walter Bromberg and Paul Schilder, present several case histories in which death plays a prominent role.[76] For example, one female patient developed acute anxiety after the death of a woman friend for whom she had had some erotic longings. Although the patient stated explicitly that her personal fear of death was kindled by watching her friend die, the authors conclude that "her anxiety reaction was against the unconscious homosexual attachment with which she struggled . . . her own death meant the reunion with the homosexual beloved who had departed . . . to die means a reunion with the denied love object."

Another patient, whose father was an undertaker, described her severe anxiety: "I have always feared death. I was afraid I would wake up

55

while they were embalming me. I have these queer feelings of imminent death. My father was an undertaker. I never thought of death while I was with corpses . . . but now I feel I want to run. . . . I think of it steadily. . . . I feel as though I was fighting it off." The authors conclude that "the anxiety about death is the expression of a repressed wish to be passive and to be handled by the father-undertaker. In their view the patient's anxiety is the product of her self-defense against these dangerous wishes and of her desire for self-punishment because of her incestuous wish. The other case histories in the same article provide further examples of translations of death into what the authors consider to be more fundamental fears: "death means for this boy final sado-masochistic gratification in a homosexual reunion with the father," or "death means for him separation from the mother and an end to expression of his unconscious libidinal desires."

Obviously one cannot but wonder why there is such a press for translation. If a patient's life is curtailed by a fear, let us say, of open spaces, dogs, radioactive fallout, or if one is consumed by obsessive ruminations about cleanliness or whether doors are locked, then it seems to make sense to translate these superficial concerns into more fundamental meanings. But, *res ipsa loquitur*, a fear of death may be a fear of death and not translatable into a "deeper" fear. Perhaps, as I shall discuss later, it is not translation that the neurotic patient needs; he or she may not be out of contact with reality but instead, through failing to erect "normal" denial defenses, may be too close to the truth.

CLINICAL RESEARCH

Inattention to the concept of death has far-reaching implications for clinical research as well. To take one example, consider the field of mourning and bereavement. Although many researchers have studied in painstaking detail the adjustment of the survivors, they have consistently failed to take into consideration that the survivor has not only suffered an "object loss" but has encountered the loss of himself or herself as well. Beneath the grief for the loss of another lies the message, "If your mother (father, child, friend, spouse) dies, then you will die, too." (Shortly after a patient of mine lost his father, he had the hallucination of a voice from above booming down to him the words, "You're next.") In a heavily cited study of the first year of bereavement of widows, the researcher records statements from the subjects like, "I feel like I'm walking on the edge of a black pit," or comments to the effect that they now view the world as an insecure and potentially harmful place, or that life seems pointless and without purpose, or that they are angry but without a focus for that anger.[77] I believe that each of these reactions would, if explored in depth, lead an investigator to important conclusions about the role of loss as an experience that has the potential to facilitate the survivor's encounter with his or her personal death. However, the researcher in this study, and in each of the other extensive studies in bereavement I have read, worked from a different frame of reference and accordingly failed to till some rich soil. This failure is another sorry example of the impoverishment that ensues when behavioral science ignores intuitively evident truths. Four thousand years ago, in one of the first pieces of written literature, the Babylonian epic *Gilgamesh*, the protagonist knew well that the death of his friend, Enkidu, betokened his own death: "Now what sleep is this that has taken hold of thee? Thou hast become dark and canst not hear me. When I die shall I not be like unto Enkidu? Sorrow enters my heart, I am afraid of death."[78]

THE CLINICAL PRACTITIONER

Some therapists state that death concerns are simply not voiced by their patients. I believe, however, that the real issue is that the therapist is not prepared to hear them. A therapist who is receptive, who inquires deeply into a patient's concerns will encounter death continuously in his or her everyday work.

Patients, given the slightest encouragement, will bring in an extraordinary amount of material related to a concern about death. They discuss the deaths of parents or friends, they worry about growing old, their dreams are haunted by death, they go to class reunions and are shocked by how much everyone else has aged, they notice with an ache the ascendancy of their children, they occasionally take note, with a start, that they enjoy old people's sedentary pleasures. They are aware of many small deaths: senile plaques, liver spots on their skin, gray hairs, stiff joints, stooped posture, deepening wrinkles. Retirement approaches, children leave home, they become grandparents, their children take care of them, the life cycle envelops them. Other patients may speak of annihilation fears: the common horrifying fantasy of some murderous aggressors forcing entry into the home, or fearful reactions to television or cinematic violence. The termination work that occurs in the therapy of every patient is accompanied, if the therapist will only listen, by undercurrents of concern about death.

My personal clinical experience is highly corroborative of the ubiquity of death concerns. Throughout the writing of this book I have encountered considerable amounts of heretofore invisible clinical material. Undoubtedly to some extent I have cued patients to provide me with certain evidence. But it is my belief that, in the main, it was always there; I was simply not properly tuned in. Earlier in this chapter, for example, I presented two patients, Joyce and Beth, who had commonplace clinical problems involving the establishment and the termination of interpersonal relationships. On deeper inquiry both women evinced much concern about existential issues which I would never have been able to recognize had I not had the appropriate psychological set.

Another example of "tuning in" is offered by a psychotherapist who attended a Saturday lecture I gave on the topic of death anxiety. A few days later she wrote in a letter:

> ... I did not expect the subject to come up in my work now, since I am a counselor at Reed College and our students are usually in good physical health. But my first appointment Monday morning was with a student who had been raped two months ago. She has been suffering from many disagreeable and painful symptoms since then. She made the comment, with an embarrassed laugh, "If I'm not dying of one thing, I'm dying of another." It was probably at least in part because of your remarks that the interview turned towards her fear of dying, and that being raped and dying used to be things she thought would happen only to other people. She now feels vulnerable and flooded with anxieties that used to be suppressed. She seemed to be relieved that it was all right to talk about being afraid to die, even if no terminal illness can be found in her body.[79]

Psychotherapy sessions following even some passing encounter with death often offer much clinical data. Dreams, of course, are especially fertile sources of material. For example, one thirty-year-old woman, the night following the funeral of an old friend, dreamed: "I'm sitting there watching TV. The doctor comes over and examines my lungs with a stethoscope. I get angry and ask him what right he has to do that. He said I was smoking like a smoke house. He said I have far advanced 'hourglass' disease of my lungs." The dreamer does not smoke, but her dead friend smoked three packs a day. Her association to "hourglass" disease of the lungs was "time is running out."[80]

Denial plays a central role in a therapist's selective inattention to death in therapy. Denial is a ubiquitous and powerful defense. Like an aura, it surrounds the affect associated with death whenever it appears. (One joke from Freud's vast collection has it that a man says to his wife: "If one of us two dies before the other, I think I'll move to Paris.")[81] Denial does not spare the therapist, and in the treatment process the denial of the therapist and the denial of the patient enter into collusion. Many therapists, though they have had long years of personal analysis, have not explored and worked through their personal terror of death; they phobically avoid the area in their personal lives and selectively inattend to obvious death-linked material in their psychotherapy practice.

In addition to the denial of any single therapist, there is collective denial in the entire field of psychotherapy. This collective denial may be best understood by exploring why death has been omitted from formal theories of anxiety. Though anxiety plays an absolutely central role in both the theory and the everyday practice of dynamic psychotherapy, there is no place accorded to death in the traditional dynamic theories of anxiety. If we are to alter therapeutic practice, to harness the clinical leverage that the concept of death provides, it will be necessary to demonstrate the role of death in the genesis of anxiety. There is no better way to begin than by tracing the evolution of psychodynamic concepts of anxiety and attempting to understand the systematic exclusion of the concept of death.

Freud: Anxiety without Death

Freud's ideas have so influenced the field that to a great extent the evolution of dynamic thought is the evolution of Freud's thought. Despite his extraordinary prescience, however, I believe that in the area of death he had a persistent blind spot which obscured for him some patently obvious aspects of man's inner world. I shall present some material to illustrate the way Freud avoided death in clinical and theoretical considerations, and then suggest some of the reasons behind this avoidance.

FREUD'S AVOIDANCE OF DEATH

Freud's first significant clinical and theoretical contribution appears in *Studies in Hysteria,* which he wrote with Josef Breuer in 1895.[82] It is a fascinating work and merits attention for it illustrates strikingly a selective inattention to death, and it laid the foundation for the exclusion of death from the entire field of dynamic therapy which it spawned. The book presents five major cases, one (Anna O.) by Breuer and four by Freud. Several other cases, in fragmentary form, flit in and out of footnotes and discussion sections. Each patient begins therapy with florid symptoms which include paralysis, anesthesias, pain, tics, fatigue, obsessions, sensations of choking, loss of taste and smell, linguistic disorganization, amnesia, and so forth. From a study of these five patients Freud and Breuer postulated an etiology of hysteria and a systematic form of therapy based on that etiology.

The five patients all suffered from some important emotional trauma experienced earlier in their lives. Ordinarily, Freud notes, a trauma, though disturbing, produces no lasting effect because the emotions aroused by it are dissipated: either they are abreacted (the individual undergoes a catharsis by expressing the emotion in some effective way) or worked through in some other way (Freud states that the memory of the traumas may enter "the great complex of associations, it comes alongside other experiences" and then is "worn away" or rectified or subjected to reality testing by, for example, dealing with an insult by considering one's achievements and strengths).[83]

In these five patients the trauma did not dissipate but instead continuously haunted the victim. ("The hysteric suffers from reminiscences"[84]). Freud suggested that, in his patients, memory of the trauma and the attendant emotions were repressed from conscious thought (the first use of the concept of repression and the unconscious) and thus were not subject to the normal processes of affect dissipation. The stifled affect persisted, however, with freshness and strength in the unconscious and found some conscious expression through conversion (hence, "conversion hysteria") to physical symptoms.

The treatment implications are clear: one must enable the patient to remember the trauma and to give expression to the strangulated affect. Freud and Breuer used hypnosis, and later Freud used free association, to help patients recapture the original offending memory and express the affect verbally and behaviorally.

Freud's speculations about affect built-up and dissipation, about the formation of symptoms, and about a system of therapy resting on these assumptions are of landmark importance and adumbrate much of the dynamic theory and therapy that followed him. What is most germane to my discussion is Freud's view about the *source* of the dysphoric affect—the nature of the original trauma. The theory of symptoms and the approach to therapy remain consistent throughout the text, but Freud's descriptions of the nature of the trauma responsible for the symptoms undergo a fascinating evolution from the first patient to the last. (In his introduction he states, "I can give no better advice to anyone interested in the development of catharsis into psychoanalysis than to begin with *Studies in Hysteria* and thus follow the path which I myself have trodden.")[85]

In the first cases of the book the traumas seem trivial: it strains belief that a person's profound neurotic state could result from one's being chased by a vicious dog,[86] or being hit with a stick by an employer, or discovering a maid allowing a dog to drink water out of one's glass,[87] or being in love with one's employer and having to suffer the latter's unjust reproaches.[88] As the book progresses, Freud's explanations of precipitating traumas become ever more dazzling in their sophistication: to him, his patients were, he came to believe, bedeviled by archetypal concerns worthy of a Greek tragedian's attention—hatred of children (since they interfered with a wife's ability to minister to a dying husband),[89] incestuous activity with a parent,[90] a primal scene experience,[91] and pleasure (and ensuing guilt) at the death of a sister whose husband the woman patient loved.[92] These latter cases, the footnotes, and Freud's letters[93] all bear evidence of the inexorable direction of Freud's thinking about the source of anxiety: (1) he gradually shifted the time of the "real" trauma responsible for anxiety to a period earlier in life; and (2) he came to view the nature of the trauma as explicitly and exclusively sexual.

Freud's musings about the emotional traumas of his five patients gradually developed into a formal theory of anxiety. Anxiety was a signal of anticipated danger; the seed of anxiety was planted early in life when an important trauma occurred: the memory of the traumatic event was repressed, and its attendant affect transformed to anxiety. An expectation of the trauma's recurrence or of some analogous danger could evoke anxiety anew.

What kind of trauma? What events are so fundamentally malignant that their echoes haunt an individual's entire life? Freud's first answer stressed the importance of the affect of helplessness. "Anxiety is the original reaction to helplessness and is reproduced, later on, as a signal for help in the face of trauma."[94] Then the task is to determine which situations call forth helplessness. Since the problem of anxiety is the very heart of psychoanalytic theory, and since Freud boldly altered basic theory throughout his career, it is not surprising that his statements on anxiety are many, varied, and at times conflicting.[95] Two primary origins of anxiety survive Freud's restless sifting: loss of mother (abandonment and separation) and loss of the phallus (castration anxiety). Other major sources include superego or moral anxiety, the fear of one's own self-destructive tendencies, and the fear of ego disintegration—of being overwhelmed by the dark, irrational night forces that reside within.

Though Freud often mentioned other sources of anxiety, he placed his major emphasis on abandonment and castration. He believed that, in ever-changing guise, these two psychic Katzenjammer Kids bedevil us throughout our waking lives and, in our sleep, provide the fuel for our two common nightmares: of falling and of being chased. Always the archaeologist, always searching for more basic structures, Freud suggested that castration and separation had a common feature: loss— loss of love, loss of the ability to unite with mother. Chronologically, separation occurs first, templated in fact in the trauma of birth—the first moment of life; but Freud chose to consider castration as the generic, primary source of anxiety. The earlier separation, he suggested, primed the individual for castration anxiety which, when it develops, subsumes the earlier anxiety experiences.

When one considers the data base (the case material of the patients in *Studies in Hysteria*) from which Freud's conclusions about anxiety and trauma spring, one is struck by an astonishing discrepancy between the case histories and Freud's conclusions and formulations: *death so pervades the clinical histories of these patients that only by a supreme effort of inattention could Freud have omitted it from his discussion of precipitating traumas.* Of the five patients, two are discussed only briefly. (One patient, Katarina, Freud's waitress at a vacation resort, was treated in a single session.) The three major patients—Anna O., Frau Emmy von N., and Fraulein Elisabeth von R. (the first dynamic case reports in psychiatric literature)—are remarkable in that their clinical descriptions groan with references to death. Furthermore, it is likely that, had Freud been specifically interested in death anxiety, he would have elicited and reported even more material on the theme of death.

Anna O.'s illness, for example, first developed when her father fell ill (and succumbed to that illness ten months later). She nursed him indefatigably at first; but eventually her illness, consisting of bizarre altered states of consciousness, amnesia, linguistic disorganization, anorexia, and sensory and muscular conversion symptoms, resulted in her being removed from contact with her dying father. During the following year her condition deteriorated badly. Breuer noted Anna O's preoccupation with death. He commented, for example, that, although she had "bizarre and rapidly fluctuating disturbances in consciousness, the one thing that nevertheless seemed to remain conscious most of the time was the fact that her father had died."[96]

During Breuer's hypnotic work with Anna O., she had terrifying hallucinations associated with her father's death. While nursing him, she had once fainted when she imagined she saw him with a death's head. (During treatment she once looked in the mirror and saw not herself but her father with a death's head glaring at her.) On another occasion she hallucinated a black snake coming to attack her father. She tried to fight the snake, but her arm had fallen asleep, and she hallucinated her fingers turning to snakes and each fingernail becoming a tiny skull. Breuer considered these hallucinations emanating from her terror of death as the primal cause of her illness: "On the last day [of treatment]—by the help of rearranging the room so as to resemble her father's sick room—she reproduced the terrifying hallucinations I have described above and which constituted the root of her whole illness."[97]

Frau Emmy von N., like Anna O., developed her illness immediately following the death of the person to whom she was closest—her husband. Freud hypnotized Frau Emmy von N. and asked for important associations. She reeled off a litany of death-related memories: seeing her sister in a coffin (at age seven), being frightened by her brother dressed as a ghost and by siblings throwing dead animals at her, seeing her aunt in a coffin (at age nine), finding her mother unconscious from a stroke (age fifteen) and then (at age nineteen) finding her dead, nursing a brother dying of tuberculosis, mourning (at age nineteen) the death of her brother, witnessing the sudden death of her husband. In the first eight pages of the clinical case report there are no fewer than eleven explicit references to death, dying, or corpses. Throughout the clinical description Frau Emmy von N. explicitly discusses her pervasive fear of death.

The illness of the third patient, Fraulein Elisabeth von R., incubated during the eighteen months that she nursed her dying father and witnessed the inexorable deterioration of her family: one sister moved far away, her mother suffered a severe illness, her father died. Finally, following the death of a much-loved older sister, Fraulein Elisabeth's illness erupted in full force. In the course of therapy Freud, in order to accelerate the recall of old memories and affect, assigned the task of visiting her sister's grave (in much the same way Breuer had re-arranged his consulting room to resemble the room in which Anna O's father had died).

Freud believed that anxiety is called forth by a situation that evokes an earlier, long-forgotten situation of terror and helplessness. Surely the death-linked traumas of these patients evoked in them deep feelings of terror and helplessness. But in his dénouement of each case Freud either neglects entirely the theme of death or simply calls attention to the generalized stress caused by each patient's loss. His formulations focus on the erotic components of each patient's trauma.* Thus, when Fraulein Elisabeth's sister died, Freud helped her to recognize that, in the pit of her mind, she rejoiced (and subsequently was overcome with guilt) because her sister's husband, whom she coveted, was now free to marry her. An important discovery: the unconscious, a residue of primitive wishes buried in the cellar of the mind because they were unfit for the sunlight, escaped briefly into consciousness and caused great anxiety which was ultimately bound by conversion symptomatology.

No doubt Freud uncovered, in each of his patients, important conflicts. It is what he omitted that bears scrutiny. The death of a parent, a spouse, or some close associate is more than generalized stress; it is more than loss of an important object. It is a knock at the door of denial. If, as Freud speculated, Fraulein Elisabeth thought, even for a fleeting moment, when her sister died, "Now her husband is free again, and I can be his wife," then most certainly she also shuddered with the thought, *"If my darling sister dies, then I, too, will die."* Like Fraulein Elisabeth at her sister's death so Anna O. at her father's or Frau Emmy von N. at her husband's: each must have caught, at a deep level and just for an instant, a glimpse of her own death.

In his subsequent formulations regarding the sources of anxiety, Freud, in a most curious fashion, continued to overlook death. He settled on loss: castration and abandonment—the loss of the penis and the loss of love. His posture here is uncharacteristic. Where is the intrepid archaeological excavator? Freud always drilled for bedrock—for the earliest origins—the dawn of life—the ways of primitive man—the antediluvian primal horde—the fundamental drives and instincts. Yet before death he pulled up short. Why did he not take one more obvious step toward the common denominator of abandonment and castration? Both concepts rest on ontological bedrock. Abandonment is inextricably entangled with death: the abandoned primate always perishes; the fate of the outcast is invariably social death followed quickly by physical death. Castration, if taken in the figurative sense, is synonymous with annihilation; if taken literally (and Freud, alas, meant it literally), then it also leads to death since the castrated individual cannot thrust his seed into the future, cannot escape extinction.

---

* Robert Jay Lifton in *The Broken Connection* (New York: Simon & Schuster, 1979) makes almost precisely the same point about another of Freud's important cases, Little Hans, and concludes that libido theory "dedeathifies" death. As Lifton's book unfortunately appeared after my book was completed I was unable to assimilate his rich insights in any meaningful way. It is a thoughtful, important work which bears careful reading.

2 / Life, Death, and Anxiety

In "Inhibitions, Symptoms and Anxiety," Freud briefly considered the role of death in the etiology of the neuroses but dismissed it as superficial (I shall later discuss the topsy-turvy analytic view of what constitute "depth" and "superficiality"). In a passage that has been quoted countless times by theoreticians, Freud describes why he omits the fear of death from consideration as a primary source of anxiety.

> It would seem highly improbable that a neurosis could come into being merely because of the objective presence of danger, without any participation of the deeper levels of the mental apparatus. But the unconscious seems to contain nothing that could give any content to our concept of the annihilation of life. Castration can be pictured on the basis of the daily experience of the faeces being separated from the body or on the basis of losing the mother's breast at weaning. But nothing resembling death can ever have been experienced; or if it has, as in fainting, it has left no observable traces behind. I am therefore inclined to adhere to the view that the fear of death should be regarded as analogous to the fear of castration and that the situation to which the ego is reacting is one of being abandoned by the protecting super-ego—the powers of destiny—so that it has no longer any safeguard against all the dangers that surround it.[98]

The logic falters badly here. First, Freud insists that, since we have had no experience of death, it can have no representation in the unconscious. Have we had an experience with castration? No direct experience, Freud acknowledges; but he states that we experience other losses that are experientially equivalent: the daily separation of feces or weaning experience. Surely the feces-weaning-castration linkage is not more logically compelling than the concept of an innate, intuitive awareness of death. In fact, the argument whereby death is replaced by castration as a primary source of anxiety is so untenable that I feel uncomfortable attacking it, much as if I were fighting an obviously crippled opponent. For example, consider the obvious point that women, too, have anxiety; the gymnastic efforts required to apply castration theory to women are truly the supreme high jinks of analytic metapsychology.

Melanie Klein was explicitly critical of Freud's curious inversion of primacy. "The fear of death reinforces castration fear and is not analagous to it . . . since reproduction is the essential way of counteracting death, the loss of the genital would mean the end of the creative power which preserves and continues life." Klein also disagreed with Freud's position that there is no fear of death in the unconscious. Accepting Freud's later postulate that there is, in the deepest layers of the unconscious, a death instinct (Thanatos) she argued that "a fear of death, also residing in the unconscious, operates in opposition to this instinct."[99]

Despite the dissent of Klein, as well as of Rank and Adler and others who mounted guerrilla opposition, Freud persisted in his views and begat a cult of death denial in generations of therapists. The major analytic textbooks reflect and perpetuate this trend. Otto Fenichel states that "because the idea of death is subjectively inconceivable, every fear of death covers other unconscious ideas."[100] Robert Waelder omits a consideration of death entirely;[101] while Ralph Greenson briefly discusses death from the perspective of Thanatos, Freud's death instinct, and then dismisses it as a curiosity—a bold but unstable theory.[102] Only gradually and by workers outside the Freudian tradition (or who rapidly found themselves outside) was the necessary corrective supplied.

Why did Freud exclude death from psychodynamic theory? Why did he not consider the fear of death as a primary source of anxiety? Obviously the exclusion is not mere oversight: the fear of death is neither profound nor an elusive concept; and Freud could hardly have failed to consider (and then to dismiss deliberately) the issue. He is explicit about it in 1923: "The high-sounding phrase 'every fear is ultimately the fear of death' has hardly any meaning and at any rate cannot be justified."[103] His argument proceeds along the same unconvincing lines as before: that it is not truly possible to conceive of death—some part of the ego always remains a living spectator. Once again Freud arrives at the unsatisfying conclusion that "the fear of death, like the fear of conscience, is a development of the fear of castration."[104]

Note, too, that Freud's inattention to death is limited to discussions of the formal theory of anxiety, repression, and the unconscious: in short, to the inner workings—the cogs, bearings, and energy cell—of the mental mechanism.* Wherever he allowed himself free reign, he speculated boldly and energetically about death. For example, in a short, penetrating essay written at the end of the First World War, "Our Attitude toward Death," he discussed the denial of death and man's attempt to vanquish death through the creation of immortality myths. Earlier I cited some of his comments about how life's transience increases its poignance and richness. He was mindful of the role death plays in the shaping of life:

> Would it not be better to give death the place in reality and in our thoughts which is its due, and to give a little more prominence to the

---

* At the age of sixty-four, in *Beyond the Pleasure Principle*, Freud made a place for death in his model of the mind; but even in this formulation he spoke not of a primary dread of death but instead of a will to death—Thanatos was designated as one of the two primary drives.[105]

unconscious attitude towards death which we have hitherto so carefully suppressed. This hardly seems an advance to higher achievement, but rather in some respects a backward step—a regression; but it has the advantage of taking the truth more into account, and of making life more tolerable for us once again. To tolerate life remains, after all, the first duty of all living beings. Illusion becomes valueless if it makes this harder for us. We recall the old saying: "Si vis pacem, para bellum." If you want to preserve peace, arm for war. It would be in keeping with the times to alter it: "Si vis vitam, para mortem." If you want to endure life, prepare yourself for death.[106]

"If you want to endure life, prepare yourself for death." Freud believed that the task of a therapist was to help a patient endure life. Freud's entire therapeutic career was devoted to that end. Yet, aside from this maxim, he remained mute forever about preparing for death, about the role of the concept of death in psychotherapy. Why?

One can go only so far in pointing out what Freud overlooked, in commenting upon his blind spots, until one begins to look back uneasily over one's shoulder. Perhaps his vision was greater than ours, it was in many other respects. Perhaps the issue is so simplistic that he never felt the necessity to provide the full argument for his position. We are well advised, I believe, to consider carefully the reasons behind Freud's position. I believe he omitted death from dynamic theory for unsound reasons that flow from two sources: one, an outmoded theoretical model of behavior; and the other, a relentless quest for personal glory.

FREUD'S INATTENTION TO DEATH: THEORETICAL REASONS

When Freud was seventy-five years old, he was asked who had most influenced him. Without hesitation he answered, as he always had answered, "Brücke." Ernst Brücke had been Freud's physiology professor in medical school and his mentor during his brief research career in neurophysiology. Brücke was a forbidding man, with a Prussian iron will and steel-blue eyes, much feared by Viennese medical students. (At examination time each student was allotted several minutes for oral questioning. If a student missed the first question on an examination, Brücke would sit for the rest of the allotted time in stern silence impervious to the desperate entreaties of the student and the dean, who was present.) In Freud, Brücke finally found a student worthy of his interest, and the two worked closely together in the neurophysiological laboratory for several years.

Brücke was a primary force behind the ideological school of biology that was founded by Hermann von Helmholtz, and that dominated Western European medical and basic scientific research in the latter part of the nineteenth century. The basic Helmholtzian position, Brücke's legacy to Freud, was clearly delineated in a statement by another of the founders, Emil du-Bois Reymond:

> No other forces than the common physical-chemical ones are active within the organism; that, in those cases which cannot at the time be explained by these forces one has either to find the specific way or form of their action by means of the physical-mathematical method, or to assume new forces equal in dignity to the chemical-physical forces inherent in matter, reducible to the force of attraction and repulsion.[107]

The Helmholtzian position is thus deterministic and antivitalistic. Man is a machine activated by chemical-physical mechanisms. Brücke stated in his 1874 *Lectures in Physiology* that, though organisms differ from machines in assimilative power, they are nonetheless phenomena of the physical world, moved by forces according to the principle of the conservation of energy. The number of forces propelling the organism seems large only in the presence of ignorance. *"Progress in knowledge reduces them to two—attraction and repulsion. All this applies as well to the organism, man"* (my italics).[108]

Freud adopted this mechanistic, Helmholtzian model of the organism and applied it to constructing a model of the mind. At seventy he said, "My life has been aimed at one goal, 'to infer how the mental apparatus is constructed and how forces interplay and counteract in it.'"[109] Hence, it is apparent what Freud owed Brücke: Freudian theory, often ironically assailed as irrational, is deeply rooted in traditional biophysical-chemical doctrine. Freud's dual instinct theory, the theory of libidinal energy conservation and transformation, and his unyielding determinism antedate his decision to become a psychiatrist: all have their anlage in Brücke's mechanistic view of man.

With this background in mind, we may return, with greater understanding, to the question of Freud's exclusion of death from his formulations of human behavior. Duality—the existence of two inexorably opposed basic drives—was the bedrock upon which Freud built his metapsychological system. Helmholtzian doctrine called for duality. Recall Brücke's statement: the fundamental forces active within the organism are two—attraction and repulsion. The theory of repression, the starting point of psychoanalytic thought, calls for a dualistic system: repression requires conflict between two fundamental forces. Throughout Freud's career he attempted to identify the pair of basic antagonistic drives that propel the human organism. His first proposal was "hunger and love," as incarnated in the struggle between the preservation of the individual organism and the perpetuation of the species. Most analytic theory rests on this antithesis: the struggle between ego and libido instincts was, in Freud's earlier theory, the cause of repression and the source of anxiety. Later, for reasons not relevant to this discussion, he realized that this duality was untenable, and he espoused another dualism: a fundamental dualism grounded in life itself—between life and death, Eros and Thanatos. Freudian metapsychology and psychotherapy, however, are based on the first dual instinct theory; neither Freud nor his students (with the single exception of Norman O. Brown[110]) reformulated his work on the basis of life-death duality; and most of his followers discarded the second instinct theory because it led to a position of great therapeutic pessimism. They either remained with the first libido-ego preservation dialectic or drifted into a Jungian instinctual monism—a position that undermines the theory of repression.

Death is not yet; it is an event-to-be, an event located in the future. To imagine death, to be anxious about it, requires a complex mental activity—the planning and the projection of self into the future. In Freud's deterministic schema the unconscious forces that clash and whose vector determines our behavior are primitive and instinctual. There is no place in the psychic power cell for complex mental acts where the future is imagined and feared. Freud is close to Nietzsche's position, which considers conscious deliberation entirely superfluous to the production of behavior. Behavior, according to Nietzsche, is determined by unconscious mechanical forces: conscious consideration *follows* behavior rather than precedes it; one's sense of governing one's behavior is entirely illusion. One only imagines oneself to be choosing behavior in order to satisfy one's will to power, one's need to perceive oneself as an autonomous, deciding being.

Death, then, can play no role in Freud's formal dynamic theory. Since it is a future event that has never been experienced and cannot be truly imagined, it cannot exist in the unconscious and thus cannot influence behavior. It has no place in a view of behavior reducible to the opposition of two opposing primal instincts. Freud became a prisoner of his own deterministic system and could discuss the role that death plays in the generation of anxiety and in man's perspective on life in only one of two ways: he could work outside his formal system (in footnotes or "off the record" essays like "Thoughts for the Times on War and Death"[111] and "The Theme of the Three Caskets"[112]) or he could cram death into his system by either subsuming the fear of death under some more primal (castration) fear or by considering the will to death as one of the two fundamental drives underlying all behavior. To proclaim death a fundamental drive does not solve the problem: it fails to consider death as a *future* event, it overlooks the importance in life of death as a beacon, a destination, a final terminal that has the power either of stripping life of all meaning or of beckoning one into an authentic form of being.

FREUD'S INATTENTION TO DEATH: PERSONAL REASONS

To discover why Freud continued to cling to a theoretical system that obviously cramped his soaring intellect and forced him into contorted positions, I must turn to a brief study of Freud the man. The work of artist, mathematician, geneticist, or novelist speaks for itself; it is a luxury—often an entertaining, interesting luxury, occasionally an intellectually enlightening one—to study the personal lives and motivations of artists and scientists. But when one considers a theory that purports to lay bare the deepest levels of human behavior and motivation, and when the data supporting that theory emanate, in large part, from the self-analysis of one man, then it becomes not a luxury but a necessity to study that man as deeply as possible. Fortunately there is no scarcity of data: probably more is known about the person of Freud than about any other modern historical figure (with the possible exception of Woody Allen).

Indeed, there is so much biographical material on Freud—ranging from Ernest Jones's exhaustive three-volume, 1,450-page *The Life and Work of Sigmund Freud*,[113] to lay biographies,[114] published recollections of former patients,[115] to volume after volume of published correspondence[116]—that one may, with careful picking and choosing, defend any number of outrageous hypotheses about his character structure. Therefore, *caveat emptor*.

I believe that there is much to suggest that at the core of Freud's consuming determination was his unquenchable passion to attain greatness. Jones's biography centers on that theme. Freud was born in a caul (an unbroken amniotic sac)—an event that in folklore has always predicted fame. His family believed that he was destined for fame: his mother, who never doubted it, called him "my golden Siggy" and favored him above all her children. He wrote later: "A man who has been the indisputable favorite of his mother keeps for life the feeling of a conqueror, that confidence of success that often induces real success."[117] The belief was fanned by early prophecies: one day in a pastry shop, an elderly stranger informed Freud's mother that she had brought a great man into the world; a minstrel in an amusement park, selected Freud from among the other children and predicted that he would one day become a government minister. Freud's obvious intellectual gifts also reinforced the belief; he always stood at the head of his class at the gymnasium—in fact, according to Jones, he occupied such a privileged place that he was hardly ever questioned.[118]

It was not long before Freud ceased to question his destiny. In his adolescence he wrote a boyhood friend that he had received an outstanding grade on a composition, and continued: "You didn't know you were exchanging letters with a German stylist. You had better keep them carefully—one never knows."[119] The most interesting statement in this regard is to be found in a letter to his fiancée written when he was twenty-eight years old (*and had yet to enter the field of psychiatry!*):

> I have just carried out one resolution which one group of people, as yet unborn and fated to misfortune, will feel acutely. Since you can't guess whom I mean I will tell you: they are my biographers. I have destroyed all my diaries of the past fourteen years, with letters, scientific notes and the manuscripts of my publications. Only family letters were spared. Yours, my dear one, were never in danger. All my old friendships and associations passed again before my eyes and mutely met their doom . . . all my thoughts and feelings about the world in general, and in particular how it concerned me have been declared unworthy of survival. They must now be thought all over again. And I had jotted down a great deal. But the stuff simply enveloped me, as the sand does the Sphinx, and soon only my nostrils would show above the mass of paper. I cannot leave here and cannot die before ridding myself of the disturbing thought of who might come by the old papers. Besides, everything that fell before the decisive break in my life, before our coming together and my choice of calling, I have put behind me: it has long been dead and it shall not be denied an honorable burial. Let the biographers chaff; we won't make it too easy for them. Let each one of them believe he is right in his "Conception of the Development of the Hero": even now I enjoy the thought of how they will all go astray.[120]

In his quest for greatness Freud searched for the great discovery. His early letters describe a dizzying profusion of ideas that he entertained and discarded. He, according to Jones, just missed greatness by not pursuing his early neurohistological work to its logical conclusion: the establishment of the neurone theory. He once again missed it in his work with cocaine. Freud described this incident in a letter that begins: "I may here go back a little and explain how it was the fault of my fiancée that I was not already famous at an early age."[121] Freud continues, mentioning how one day he had casually mentioned to a physician friend, Karl Koller, his own observation of cocaine's anesthetic properties and then had left town for a long visit with his fiancée. By the time Freud returned, Koller had already conducted decisive surgical experiments and gained fame as the discoverer of local anesthesia.

Few men have been endowed with intellectual powers comparable to Freud's; he had great imagination, limitless energy, and indomitable courage. Yet as he entered full professional adulthood he found his path to success unfairly and capriciously blocked. Brücke had to inform Freud that, because of anti-Semitism in Vienna, there was virtually no hope of his having a successful academic career: university support, recognition, promotion were all closed to him. Freud, at the age of twenty-seven, was forced to abandon his research and earn his living as a practicing physician. He studied psychiatry and entered private medical practice. The "great discovery" was now his only chance of achieving fame.

Freud's sense that time and opportunity were slipping away no doubt explains his injudiciousness in the cocaine incident. He read that South American natives gained strength from chewing the cocaine plant; he introduced cocaine into his clinical practice and, in an address to the Viennese Medical Society, lauded the drug's beneficial effects on depression and fatigue. He prescribed cocaine for many of his patients and urged friends (even his fiancée) to use it. When, as they soon did, the first reports of cocaine addiction appeared, Freud's credibility before the Viennese Medical Society plummeted. (This incident accounts, at least in some small part, for the Viennese academic community's lack of responsiveness to Freud's later discoveries.)

Psychology began to absorb him completely. Unraveling the structure of the mind became, as Freud put it, his mistress. He soon generated a comprehensive theory of the psychogenesis of hysteria. His hopes for glory depended on the success of this theory; when contradictory clinical evidence appeared, he was crushed. Freud described this setback in a letter to his friend Wilhelm Fliess in 1897: "The hope of eternal fame was so beautiful, and so was that of certain wealth, complete independence . . . all that depended on whether hysteria succeeded or not."[122]

Piecemeal observations were of little import. Freud's quarry was nothing less than an all-encompassing model of the mind. In 1895 when still midway between neurophysiologist and psychiatrist, Freud felt that the discovery of a model of the mind was at hand. He wrote in a letter:

> The barriers suddenly lifted, the veils dropped, and it was possible to see from the details of neurosis all the way to the very conditioning of consciousness. Everything fell into place, the cogs meshed, the thing really

seemed to be a machine which in a moment would run of itself. The three systems of neurones, the "free" and "bound" states of quantity, the primary and secondary processes, the main trend and the compromise trend of the nervous system, the two biological rules of attention and defense, the indications of quality, reality, and thought, the state of the psychosexual group, the sexual determination of repression, and finally the factors determining consciousness as a perceptual function—the whole thing held together, and still does. I can naturally hardly contain myself with delight.[123]

For the discovery to satisfy Freud's requirements fully, two features were necessary: (1) that the model of the mind be a comprehensive one that met Helmholtzian scientific requirements; and (2) that it be an original discovery. The Freudian basic schema of the mind: the existence of repression, the relationship between conscious and unconscious, the basic biological substrate of thought and affect was a creative synthesis—not novel in its components (Schopenhauer and Nietzsche had blazed a bold trail) but novel in its thoroughness and in its applicability to many human activities, from dreaming and fantasy to behavior, symptom formation, and psychosis. (Of his predecessors Freud somewhere said, "Many people have flirted with the unconscious, but I was the first to marry it.") The energy component of Freud's model (the sexual force or libido)—a constant amount of energy that proceeds through predetermined, well-defined stages of development during infancy and childhood, that may be bound or unbound, that may be cathected onto objects, that may overflow, be dammed up, or be displaced, that is the source of thought, behavior, anxiety, and symptoms—is entirely original; it was the big discovery, and Freud clung to it fiercely. For the sake of the libido theory he sacrificed his relationships with his most promising disciples, who deviated because they refused to accept his absolute insistence on the new discovery—the central role of libido in human motivation.

Obviously the role of death in human behavior either as a source of anxiety or as a determinant of motivation had little appeal to Freud. It met none of his personal dynamic requirements: it was not an instinct (though Freud in 1920 was to postulate that it was) and did not fit into a mechanistic Helmholtzian model. Nor was it novel: it was old hat, Old Testament, in fact; and it was not Freud's aim to join a long procession of thinkers stretching back to the beginning of time. "Eternal fame," as he was wont to put it, did not lie there. Eternal fame would be his from discovering a heretofore unknown source of human motivation: the libido. There seems little question that Freud correctly delineated an important factor in human behavior. Freud's was an error of overcathexis: his fierce investment in the primacy of libido was overdetermined; he elevated one aspect of human motivation to a position of absolute primacy and exclusivity and under that aspect subsumed everything human, for all individuals and for all times.

COUNTER THEORIES

Counter theories soon appeared. Freud's most creative students took issue with libido theory; and by 1910, Carl Jung, Alfred Adler, and Otto Rank had all chosen to leave the good graces of the master rather than accept his mechanistic, dual-instinct view of human nature. Each of these defectors proposed another source of motivation. Jung posited a spiritual life-force monism. Adler emphasized the child's concern about survival and his or her smallness and helplessness in the face of a macroscopic adult world and an enveloping universe. Rank stressed the importance of death anxiety and suggested that the human being was ever twisting between two fears—the fear of life (and its intrinsic isolation) and the fear of death. These viewpoints, and the contributions of such latter-day theoreticians as Fromm, May, Tillich, Kaiser, and Becker, all supplement but do not replace the Freudian structural theory. Freud's great contribution was his formulation of a dynamic model of the mind. To introduce death, both a fear of death and an embracement of death, into Freud's dynamic model is merely to reintroduce it: death has always been there, beneath castration, beneath separation and abandonment. In this one instance Freud and the subsequent analytic tradition remained too superficial; subsequent theorists have provided a corrective force and so served to deepen our view of the human being.

CHAPTER 3

The Concept of Death in Children

O UR CONCERNS about death and our modes of dealing with death anxiety are not surface phenomena that are easy either to delineate or to apprehend. Nor do they arise *de novo* in adulthood. Rather, they are deeply rooted in the past and extensively transfigured through a lifetime preoccupied with security and survival. The study of the child provides an unparalleled opportunity to study, in pristine form, the human being's grapple with death. To study the child's confrontation with mortality, the child's recognition of death, his or her terror, evasions and fortifications, and subsequent development in the face of the fear of death is the purpose of this chapter.

There is to my mind a marked discrepancy between the importance of death to the child and the attention accorded death in child developmental scholarship. The relevant literature is meager and, when compared with the voluminous literature on other child-development issues, seems at best perfunctory. Empirical studies of the child's concept of death are particularly rare; psychoanalytically oriented clinicians have on occasion attempted to study the issue but, as we shall see, with a bias that often undermines accuracy of observation. Furthermore, much of the pertinent material is generally found in old publications often out of the mainstream of the child-development or the child psychiatric literature. We owe much to Sylvia Anthony, who so ably reviewed and analyzed the research and observational literature in her monograph *The Discovery of Death in Childhood and After.*[1]

Both my clinical work and survey of the work of others lead me to several conclusions:

1. When behavioral scientists choose to investigate the issue closely, they invariably discover that children are extraordinarily preoccupied with death. Children's concerns about death are pervasive and exert far-reaching influence on their experiential worlds. Death is a great enigma to them, and one of their major developmental tasks is to deal with fears of helplessness and obliteration, whereas sexual matters are secondary and derivative.[2]
2. Not only are children profoundly concerned with death, but these concerns begin at an earlier age than is generally thought.
3. Children go through an orderly progression of stages in awareness of death and in the methods they use to deal with their fear of death.
4. Children's coping strategies are invariably denial-based: it seems that we do not, perhaps cannot, grow up tolerating the straight facts about life and death.

Pervasiveness of Death Concern in Children

Freud believed that the silent, sexual researches, the preoccupation with the question Whence? was a pervasive concern of children and constituted the foundation of the generation gap existing between child and adult. There is ample evidence, however, that the question Whither? also intensely occupies one's mind as a child and buzzes in one's ear throughout life: one can face it, fear it, ignore it, repress it, but one cannot be free of it.

Few parents or observers of young children have not been surprised by the emergence of sudden, unexpected questions from a child about death. Once, when my five-year-old son and I were strolling silently along the beach, he suddenly turned his face up to me and said, "You know, both my grandfathers died before I ever met them." It seemed like a "tip of the iceberg" statement. I was certain that he had long pondered the issue silently. I asked him, as gently as I could, how often he thought about things like that, about death, and I was staggered when he replied, in a strangely adult voice, "I never stop thinking about it."

Another time on the occasion of his brother's departure to college he commented artlessly, "There's just three of us at home now, you and me and Mommy. I wonder who will be the first to die?"

A four-and-one-half-year-old child said suddenly to her father, "Every day I'm afraid of dying; I wish I'd never grow old for then I'd never die."[3] A three-and-one-half-year-old girl asked to have a stone put on her head so that she would stop growing and wouldn't have to grow old and die.[4] A little girl four years old wept for twenty-four hours when she learned that all living things die. Her mother was unable to calm her by any other means than a silent promise that she, the little girl, would never die.[5] A few days after the death of her paternal grandmother, a four-year-old child came into the kitchen of the family's apartment and saw on the table a dead goose whose bloody head hung down motionless from the long neck. The child, who had heard of the death of her grandmother but had shown no special reaction, now looked anxiously for a short time at the goose and said to her mother, "Is that what you call dead?"[6]

Erik Erikson reports the case of a four-year-old child whose grandmother died, and who had an epileptiform attack the night after he saw her coffin. A month later he found a dead mole, asked about death, and again had convulsions. Two months later he had a third series of convulsions after accidentally crushing a butterfly in his hand.[7]

The artless nature of a child's questions can take one's breath away. The young child asks straight out, "When are you going to die?" "How old are you?" "How old are people when they die?" The child asserts, "I want to live to be a thousand years old. I want to live to be the oldest person on earth." These are thoughts of an age of innocence and may be stimulated by a death—the death of a grandparent, an animal, perhaps even a flower or a leaf; but often they arise unprompted by any external stimulus: the child merely vents the internal concerns upon which he or she has long meditated. Later, as the child learns to see the "emperor's new clothes," he or she will also come to believe that death is a matter of no great concern.

By administering a story-completion test to ninety-eight children, ages five to ten, Anthony has provided an objective measure of children's death concern.[8] The stories were open-ended and without explicit reference to death. (Example: "When the boy went to bed at nighttime, what did he think about?" or, "A boy went to school; when playtime came, he didn't play with the others but stayed all alone in the corner. Why?") In completing the stories, the children evince considerable preoccupation with death or annihilation. Approximately 50 percent of the children referred in their story completions to death, funerals, killings, or ghosts. When slightly inferential answers were also included ("He got run over," or "She lost one of her children") the proportion rose to over 60 percent. For example, children answered the question, "When the boy went to bed at nighttime, what did he think about?" with such responses as, "Someone would come in his room and kill him," or, "Snow White. I haven't seen her but I've seen her dead in a story book," or, "Someone was coming into his house, his father died, and then he died too." One story told of a magic fairy asking a child if he wanted to be grown up or remain young for a long time, perhaps forever. Contrary to common belief that the child is impatient to grow up and become strong and effective, over 35 percent of the children expressed in their story completions a preference for staying young, since they linked growing old to death.

Concept of Death: Developmental Stages

Thus, with ample evidence of children's concern with death, I shall consider the ontogeny of the concept of death. Many investigators have noted that children's thoughts and fears about death and their methods of coping with that fear are specific to certain stages of development.

IMPEDIMENTS TO KNOWING WHAT THE CHILD KNOWS ABOUT DEATH

There is a great deal that stands in the way of our knowing what the very young child knows about death; consequently must controversy exists in the field.

Lack of Language and Capacity for Abstract Thought. The very young child's lack of language is a formidable barrier to adults' understanding the child's inner experience. Therefore, assumptions, often highly biased ones, are made by professionals about what the child knows and does not know. Another factor is that developmentalists, especially Jean Piaget, have demonstrated that very young children lack the capacity for abstract thought. Even at ten years old the child is in a stage of concrete mental operations and is just beginning to take proper account of what is "potential" or "possible."[9] Since death, one's personal death, being and nonbeing, consciousness, finality, eternity, and the future are all abstract concepts, many developmental psychologists have concluded that young children have no accurate concept of death whatsoever.

Freud's Stand. Another important factor influencing professional views about the young child's concept of death has been the strong stand of Freud, who was convinced that the young child does not grasp the true implications of death. Since Freud considered the very early years of life as the ones most instrumental in shaping character, it was precisely for this reason that he considered death as an unimportant motif in psychic development. These passages from *The Interpretation of Dreams* convey his position:

> ... the child's idea of being "dead" has nothing much in common with ours apart from the word. Children know nothing of the horrors of decay, of freezing in the ice-cold grave, of the terrors of eternal nothingness—ideas which grown-up people find it so hard to tolerate, as is proved by all myths of the future life. The fear of death has no meaning to a child; hence it is that he will play with the dreadful word and use it as a threat against a playmate: "If you do that again, you'll die like Franz!" ... it was actually possible for a child who was over eight years old at the time coming home from a visit to the Natural History Museum to say to his mother: "I'm so fond of you mummy: when you die I'll have you stuffed and I'll keep you in this room so that I can see you all the time." So little resemblance is there between a child's idea of being dead and our own, I was astonished to hear a highly intelligent boy of ten remark after the sudden death of his father: "I know father's dead, but what I can't understand is why he doesn't come home to supper."
>
> To children, who, moreover, are spared the sight of the scenes of suffering which precede death, being "dead" means approximately the same as being "gone"—not troubling the survivors anymore. A child makes no distinction as to how this absence is brought about: whether it is due to a journey, to a dismissal, to an estrangement, or to death. . . . When people are absent children do not miss them with any great intensity; many mothers learn this to their sorrow when, after being away from home for some weeks on a summer holiday, they are met on their return by the news that the children have not once asked after their mummy. If their mother does actually make the journey to that "undiscover'd country, from whose bourn no traveller returns," children seem at first to have forgotten her, and it is only later on that they begin to call their dead mother to mind.[10]

Thus, in Freud's view, the child, even at the age of eight or nine, knows little (and, hence, fears little) about death. Freud, in his formulations about the child's basic concerns, relegated death to a position relatively late in development and assigned sexual concerns an earlier and primary position. His conclusions about the role of death in personal development were highly influential and resulted in the issue being prematurely sealed off for a generation. Not only are there, as I discussed in the last chapter, personal and theoretical reasons for Freud's error, but methodological ones as well: he never worked directly with young children.

Adult Bias. Bias is another important barrier to knowing what the child knows of death. Whether the study is observational, psychometric, or projective, an adult must collect and interpret the data; and that adult's personal fear and denial of death frequently contaminate the results. Adults are reluctant to speak to children about death, they avoid the topic, they accept surface data unquestioningly because they are unwilling to probe into a child farther, they systematically misperceive a child's experience, and they always err in the direction of assuming that a child has less awareness of death, and less anguish therefrom, than is the case.

A widely cited research inquiry into children's fears by Rema Lapouse and Mary Monk is illustrative of the role of bias.[11] The authors studied an extensive sample (N=482) of normal children aged six to twelve, with the objective of determining the nature and the extent of children's fears—but, because they felt it would have been impossible to conduct hundreds of interviews of children, they interviewed the mothers instead! The mothers considered the two fear items most closely related to death ("getting sick, having an accident or dying," or "worries about health") to be of minimal concern: only 12 percent of the mothers rated the first item as an important concern, and 16 percent, the second. (By contrast, 44 percent rated "snakes" as an important concern, and 38 percent rated "school marks" similarly.)

The authors then selected a subsample (N=192) and interviewed the children as well as the mothers. The results demonstrated that in general mothers underestimated the frequency of children's fears. The two death-related items showed particularly high discrepancies: on these items mother and child agreed on their answers in only 45 percent of the cases: *of the disagreements, 90 percent were the result of a mother's underestimating the child's concerns about death.* (Mothers also underestimated, to the same degree, other items more inferentially related to death: "anyone in the family getting sick or dying," "germs," "fires.") The findings suggest that mothers tend to be unaware of the degree to which their children are concerned with death.

Another study reports the reactions in a children's hospital to the death of John F. Kennedy.[12] The researchers note that highly trained hospital staff members were unexpectedly unreliable in observing children's reactions to death. These staff members differed widely not only in their observations of these reactions but also in their opinions about how much information children should be given and how much emotional stress children could be expected to tolerate.

Piaget, who has worked with children his entire professional life, felt that psychological testing, even of a highly sophisticated genre, often yields incomplete or deceptive data, and that—and most clinicians would agree—that the most satisfactory mode of inquiry is a "general examination" (or a "clinical interview"). Yet there are precious few reports of in-depth interviews with children in the literature. One's nurturing instinct is aroused at the sight of the young of almost any mammalian species, ranging from kittens, puppies, and colts to humans. It is difficult to go against biological grain, to expose a child to the naked truth about death; and this difficulty is, I believe, the major factor behind the dearth of professional inquiry. In fact, I have serious doubts whether a research project whose design included explicit questioning of young children about death would today even obtain clearance from a human subjects research committee; without question, such a project would encounter strong opposition from parents.

Consequently, the inquiries are generally inferential and often superficial. There are only a few reports of inquiries based on direct interviews,[13] and the most thorough of these are several decades old. Maria Nagy and Sylvia Anthony reported on work done in the 1940s. Nagy (who was known as "Auntie Death" to the children at the school where she conducted her researches) asked children to draw pictures about death, to write compositions about death, and to discuss verbally their thoughts about death.[14] Anthony asked for definitions to death-linked words and used a story-completion test.[15] Paul Schilder and David Wechsler, in 1935, administered a series of death-related pictures to children and asked for their reactions.[16] Though the pictures were explicit, indeed macabre, the authors made concessions to the sensitivities of the children by accepting and reporting the reactions at face value. Had the subjects been adults, the researchers would never have condoned this procedure; instead, they would have probed, investigated, and interpreted the responses at great depth.

What the Child Is Taught. There is one other obstacle to knowing what the child knows about death. A child's state of knowing about death rarely exists long in nascent form: adults are extraordinarily anguished at the sight of a child grappling with the idea of death and rush in to spare the child. The child perceives the adult's anxiety and accordingly discovers that it is imperative to suppress death concerns: there will be little genuine relief from his or her parents. Many parents, despite considerable enlightenment and firm resolve to provide honest instruction, waver in the face of a child's distress. Anthony reports a brief illustrative conversation between a five-year-old child and his university professor mother:

> Child: "Do animals come to an end, too?"
> Mother: "Yes, animals come to an end, too. Everything that lives comes to an end."
> Child: "I don't want to come to an end. I should like to live longer than anyone on earth."
> Mother: "You need never die; you can live forever."[17]

Generally parents attempt to assuage a child's fears by offering some form of denial, either some idiosyncratic denial system or a socially sanctioned immortality myth. What an investigator often discovers, then, is not a child's natural inclination but a complex amalgam consisting of a child's awareness, anxiety, and denial intermingled with an adult's anxiety and denial defenses. What the child should and should not be told is an issue I shall discuss elsewhere, but we must understand why we choose various courses of death education. Is it for the child's benefit or the adult's? Erma Furman, who closely studied young children who had lost a parent, concluded that "concrete information about death was helpful to them at certain points and that the child's task was made more difficult when the adults in their environment wittingly or unwittingly misrepresented or obscured the objective facts."[18]

FIRST AWARENESS OF DEATH

When does the child first know about death? Several sources of data are available (all of which are inhibited by the impediments I have described): careful longitudinal observations—by parents or trained observers; psychological tests—primarily word definitions (that is, "dead," "life," "living"), story completions, TAT (Thematic Apperception Test), analysis of children's drawings; systematic observations made by staff of hospital or residential home; and case reports of child therapists or adult therapists who furnish retrospective data.

Death and the Development of Language. The more objective measures rely on the child's mastery of language. Anthony attempted to answer the question, When does the child know about death? by asking eighty-three children to define the word "dead" inserted into a test of general vocabulary. The responses of 100 percent of the children seven or older (and of two thirds of the six-year-olds) indicated comprehension of the meaning of the word (though they often included in their definitions phenomena not logically or biologically essential). Only three of the twenty-two children six or younger were totally ignorant of the meaning of the word.[19]

Another objective approach to the problem is to study the child's development of the concept of "living" or of "life." Young children seem to have much confusion about the properties of living entities. J. Sully noted in 1895 that young children consider all apparently spontaneous movements as a sign of life and, accordingly, consider such objects as fire or smoke to be alive.[20] Piaget considered that the animism of children (which, he felt, paralleled the animism of primitive man) falls into four stages. At first inanimate objects are generally considered to have life and will. At about the beginning of the seventh year the child attributes life only to things that move. From the eighth to twelfth year the child attributes life to things that move by themselves; and afterward the child's view increasingly becomes the adult view.*[21]

The child goes through a great deal of confusion in trying to understand what lives or has life and what is inanimate. For example, in one study over one third of seven- to eight-year-old children believed that a watch or a river lives; three fourths felt that the moon lives, whereas 12 percent felt that a tree does not live.[22] The confusion of the child is probably enhanced by confusing messages from the environment. The child is never educated clearly and precisely about these matters by adults. He or she is confused by dolls and mechanical toys which simulate life. Poetic license in language is another source of confusion ("clouds race across the sky," "the moon peeps in at the window," "the brook dances to the sea").

Observations of Children. These studies of linguistic development have prompted many developmentalists and clinicians to date the child's awareness of death to a time much later than is indicated by the

---

*Piaget considered the subject of death to be instrumental in the development of mature concepts of causality. In the early thought of the child, motivation is considered the source and explanation of the existence of things and every cause is coupled with a motive. When the child becomes aware of death, that system of thought undergoes an upheaval: animals and people die, and their deaths cannot be explained as a result of their motives. Gradually children begin to understand that death must be a law of nature—a law that is uniform and impersonal.

direct observations that I shall now consider. Perhaps researchers are making unnecessarily stringent evidential demands. Is there any reason that a child must be able to define "living," or, for that matter, "dead" in order to know in his bones that he, like insects, animals, or other people, will one day cease to be. Researchers who study very young children almost invariably conclude that they have considerable traffic with death. The theoretical objection that the child younger than eight to ten cannot comprehend abstract concepts begs the question. As Kastenbaum and Aisenberg point out, "between the extremes of 'no understanding' and explicit, integrated abstract thought there are many ways by which the young mind can enter into relationship with death."[23] Despite a certain vagueness, the phrase "enter into a relationship with death" is serviceable: the very young child thinks about death, is fearful of it, is curious about it, registers death-related perceptions that stay with him or her all his life, and erects magic-based defenses against death.

Kastenbaum and Aisenberg describe some observations of David, an eighteen-month-old child, who discovered a dead bird in his yard. The boy appeared stunned, and his face, according to his parents, "was set in a frozen, ritualized expression resembling nothing so much as the stylized Greek dramatic mask for tragedy."[24] David was a typical toddler who tended to pick up and examine everything he could reach; in this instance, however, he crouched closely to the bird but made no effort to touch it. A few weeks later he found another dead bird. This time he picked up the bird and insisted, through gestures, which included an imitation of a bird flying, that the bird be placed back on a tree limb. When his parents placed the dead bird in the tree, and the bird, alas! did not fly, David repeatedly insisted that the bird be placed in the tree. A few weeks later the boy's attention focused on a single fallen leaf, and he became deeply engaged in trying to place it back on the tree. When he failed to reverse the leaf's fate, he instructed his father to restore the leaf to the tree. Because David was not able to speak, one cannot be certain of the precise nature of his inner experience, but his behavior suggests that he was grappling with the concept of death. Certainly there is no question that the exposure to death elicited unprecedented and unusual behavior.

Szandor Brant, a psychologist, reports an incident involving his son Michael, aged two years three months.[25] Michael, who had been weaned from his bottle for a year, began waking up several times a night screaming hysterically for a bottle. When questioned, Michael insisted he must have a bottle or "I won't make contact," "I'll run out of gas," "My motor won't run and I'll die." His father says that, on two occasions immediately prior to Michael's night awakenings, a car had run out of gas and in the child's presence there had been much discussion of how the motor had "died" and how a battery had gone "dead." Michael seemed convinced, his father concludes, that he had to keep on drinking fluid or else he, too, would die. Michael's visible death concerns had begun even earlier in life when he saw a photograph of a dead relative and directed an endless stream of questions toward his parents about the status of this relative. Michael's story indicates that death can be a source of significant distress for the very young child. Furthermore, as was true with the previous case, Michael at a very early age recognized death as a problem—perhaps, as Kastenbaum suggests, the first vital problem and a prime stimulus to continued mental development.[26]

Gregory Rochlin, on the basis of several play sessions with a series of normal children aged three to five, concludes, too, that the child at an early age learns that life has an end, and that death will come for himself or herself as well as for those upon whom he or she depends.

> My own studies have shown that the knowledge of death, including the possibility of one's own death, is acquired at a very early age, and far sooner than is generally supposed. By the age of three years the fear of one's own death is communicable in unequivocal terms. How much earlier than three years of age this information is acquired is a matter of tenuous speculation. Communication with a younger child on the subject is unlikely. It also would be much too fragmentary. What is more important is that in a child three years old death as a fear, as a possibility, has already begun to produce significant effects.[27]

The evidence is readily available, Rochlin states, to whoever is willing to listen to children and observe their play.[28] Children the world over play games of death and resurrection. Opportunities to learn about death are abundant: a trip to the meat market tells any child more than he or she wishes to know. Possibly no experience is required; possibly, as Max Scheler claims,[29] each of us has intuitive knowledge of death. Regardless of the source of the knowledge, however, one thing is certain: the tendency is deep-seated in each of us, even in early life, to deny death. Knowledge is relinquished when desire opposes it.

When reality intrudes forcibly, the fledgling death-denial defenses falter, allowing anxiety to break through. Rochlin describes a three-and-one-half-year-old boy who for several months had been asking his parents when he or they would die.[30] He was heard to mutter that he himself would not die. Then his grandfather died. (This grandfather lived in a distant city and was barely known to the child.) The child began having frequent nightmares and regularly delayed going to sleep; he apparently equated going to sleep and death. He asked whether it hurt to die, and commented that he was afraid to die. His play indicated a preoccupation with illness, death, killing, and being killed. Though it is difficult to know with assurance what "death" means to the inner world of the preoperational child, it seemed that this child associated it with considerable anxiety: death meant being put in the sewer, being hurt, disappearing, vanishing down the drain, rotting in the graveyard.

Another child, aged four, also lost a grandfather who died on his third birthday. The boy insisted that his grandfather was not dead. Then when he was told that his grandfather had died of old age, he wanted reassurance that his mother and father were not old, and told them that he would not get older. Part of the transcription of this play session reveals clearly that this four-year-old had "entered into a relationship with death."

> D: Last night I found a dead bee.
> Dr.: Did it look dead?
> D: He got killed. Someone stepped on him and it got dead.
> Dr.: Dead like people are dead?
> D: They're dead but they're not like dead people. Nothing like dead people.
> Dr.: Is there a difference?
> D: People are dead and bees are dead. But they're put in the ground and they're no good. People.
> Dr.: Are no good?
> D: After a long time he'll get alive (the bee). But not a person. I don't want to talk about it.
> Dr.: Why?
> D: Because I have two grandfathers alive.
> Dr.: Two?
> D: One.
> Dr.: What happened to one?
> D: He died a long time ago. A hundred years ago.
> Dr.: Will you live long too?
> D: A hundred years.
> Dr.: Then what?
> D: I'll die perhaps.
> Dr.: All people die.
> D: Yes, I will have to.
> Dr.: That is sad.
> D: I have to anyway.

> Dr.: You have to?
> D: Sure. My father is going to die. That is sad.
> Dr.: Why is he?
> D: Never mind.
> Dr.: You don't want to talk about it.
> D: I want to see my mother now.
> Dr.: I'll take you to her.
> D: I know where dead people are. In cemeteries. My old grandfather is dead. He can't get out.
> Dr.: You mean where he is buried.
> D: He can't get out. Never.[31]

Melanie Klein, on the basis of her experience in analyzing children, concludes that the very young child has an intimate relationship with death—a relationship that antedates by a considerable period his or her conceptual knowledge of death. The fear of death, Klein states, is part of the infant's earliest life experience. She accepts Freud's 1923 theory that there is a universal unconscious drive toward death, but argues that, if the human being is to survive, then there must be a counterbalancing fear of loss of life. Klein considers the fear of death as the original source of anxiety; sexual and superego anxiety are thus latecomers and derivative phenomena.

> My analytic observations show that there is in the unconscious a fear of annihilation of life. I would also think that if we assume the existence of a death instinct, we must also assume that in the deepest layers of the mind there is a response to this instinct in the form of fear of annihilation of life. The danger arising from the inner working of the death instinct is the first cause of anxiety. . . . The fear of being devoured is an undisguised expression of the fear of total annihilation of the self. . . . The fear of death enters into castration fear and is not "analogous" to it. . . . Since reproduction is the essential way of counteracting death, the loss of the genital would mean the end of the creative power which preserves and continues life.[32]

Klein's argument that concern about reproduction flows from death fear is, I believe, formidable and brings into question traditional analytic views of what is "primary" in the mental life of the individual. Kurt Eissler, who early in the psychoanalytic movement thought deeply about death, arrived also at the conclusion that the child's early preoccupation with sexuality is a derivative inquiry, secondary to an earlier and terrifying awareness of death:

> Refined research into this matter might show that the child's inquiry into the generative processes (i.e. the "facts of life") is a secondary edi-

tion of an earlier and short-lasting inquiry into death. Possibly the child turns away from such a inquiry because of the accompanying horror and because of the utter hopelessness and ensuing despair about any possible progress in his investigation.[33]

Other workers, who have observed children closely, have arrived at the conclusion that the young child, regardless of whether theoretically he or she is intellectually equipped to understand death, grasps the essence of the matter. Anna Freud, working with young children in the London blitz, wrote: "It can be safely said that all the children who were over two years at the time of the London blitz realized the house will fall down when bombed and that people are often killed or get hurt in falling houses."[34] She described a four-and-one-half-year-old child who acknowledged his father's death: The child's mother wished the children to deny their father's death, but the child insisted, "I know all about my father. He has been killed and he will never come back."

Furman worked with a large number of children who had lost a parent, and she concluded that during their second year of life children could achieve a basic understanding of death. The understanding of death is enhanced by some type of earlier experience that helps the child form the necessary mental category. Furman cites the following example:

Suzie was barely three years old when her mother died. After being told this sad news, Suzie soon asked, "Where is Mommy?" Her father reminded her of the dead bird they had found and buried not too long ago. He explained that Mommy, too, had died and had to be buried. He would show her where whenever Suzie wished. One month later Suzie reported to her father, "Jimmy (the neighbor's six-year-old son) told me that my Mommy would come back soon because his mommy said so. I told him that's not true because my mommy is dead and when you're dead you can't ever come back. That's right, daddy, isn't it?"[35]

A mother reported this interaction with a child of three years and nine months:

Jane has received no religious instruction and has so far never met death in connection with any human being of her acquaintance. A few days ago she began asking questions about death. . . . The conversation began by Jane asking if people came back again in the spring like flowers. (A week or so before she had been very upset by her favorite flower dying and we had consoled her by saying they would return in the spring.) I answered that they do not return the same but different, possibly as babies. This answer obviously worried her—she hates change and people getting old—for she said, "I don't want Nan to be different, I don't want her to change and grow old." Then "Will Nan die? Shall I die too? Does everyone die?" On my saying yes, she broke into really heartbreaking tears and kept on saying, "But I don't want to die, I don't want to die. . . ." She then asked how people died, if it hurt, whether when they were dead they opened their eyes again, whether they spoke, ate and wore clothes. Suddenly in the midst of all these questions and tears she said, "Now I will go on with my tea" and the matter was temporarily forgotten.[36]

It is interesting to note the troubled uncertain responses of this mother, who a short time previously had managed with little difficulty to answer her daughter's questions about birth and where babies come from. She ended the preceding report: "It took me all unawares. Although I expected the questions about birth, etc., those about death I hadn't thought of yet and my own ideas are very hazy." Obviously a child perceives such a parent's anxiety and confusion along with any verbal comforting reassurances the parent may provide.

Other reports of conversations with parents give the flavor of the child's fear and curiosity about death. For example:

Lately at bath time Richard (5 yrs. 1 mo.) has begun to whimper and be miserable about dying. Yesterday as he swam up and down in his bath he played with the possibility of never dying, of living to a thousand. Today he said, "I might be alone when I die, will you be with me?" "But I don't want to be dead ever; I don't want to die." Some days previously when he had seemed afraid of not knowing *how* to die, his mother had told him he need not worry because she would die first so he would know how it was done. This seemed to reassure him.[37]

In a controversial essay Adah Maurer makes some intriguing speculations about the infant's early awareness of death.[38] The infant's first task, Maurer reasons, is to differentiate between self and environment—to know being as the opposite of nonbeing. As the baby wavers back and forth between consciousness and unconsciousness, between sleep and wakefulness, he or she comes to have a sense of these two states. What is the infant's mental experience during a night terror? Maurer suggests that the infant may be experiencing fear and awareness of nonbeing. Lying in a dark, quiet room and deprived of both sight and hearing, the infant may be panicked by a half-here, disembodied sensation. (Max Stern, who studied night terrors, arrived at a similar conclusion: the child is terrified of nothingness.[39])

Why does the infant delight in the game of throwing toys from a highchair? The infant who can find an accommodating partner to return the toy, will generally persist in the game until the partner retires in fatigue. Perhaps this delight stems from erotic pleasure in muscular movement; perhaps it is a manifestation of what Robert White calls the drive for "effectance"—the inherent pleasure in mastering one's environment.[40] Maurer suggests that the infant is fascinated by disappearance and reappearance which, in the thought and behavior available to the infant, are material symbols of the concepts of being and nonbeing.[41] Indeed, White's effectance drive may be a derivative of the infant's attempt to vanquish nonbeing. These speculations resonate with an enormous body of child developmental literature on "object permanence," a thorough discussion of which would take me too far afield. Briefly, though, the child cannot appreciate the disappearance of an object until he or she established its permanence. Permanence has no meaning without an appreciation of change, destruction, or disappearance; thus, the child develops the concept of permanence and change in tandem.[42] Furthermore, there is an intimate relationship between object permanence and a sense of self-permanence; the same type of oscillation, the pairing of permanence (aliveness, being) and disappearance (nonbeing, death) is essential in the development of the child.

"All gone" is one of the first phrases in the child's vocabulary, and "all gone" is a common theme in childhood fears. Children note how a chicken disappears at mealtime; or, once the plug is pulled, how the bath water becomes all gone; or how the feces is flushed away. Rare is the child who does not fear being devoured, flushed away, or sucked through the drain. Analytic literature notes the unconscious equation of feces and corpse.[43] Perhaps it is time for psychotherapists to reconsider the dynamics of the toilet training conflict, because more than anal eroticism or stubborn resistance may be involved: to the child, toilet training raises fears about physical integrity and survival.

When the child realizes that eternal recurrence of vanished objects is not the order of the day, then the child searches for other strategies to protect himself or herself from the threat of nonbeing. The child becomes the master rather than the victim of "all gone." The child pulls out the bathtub plug, flushes objects down the toilet, gleefully blows out matches, is delighted to assist mother by pressing the pedal of the garbage pail. Later the child disperses death, either symbolically in games of cowboys and Indians, or literally by extinguishing life in insects. Indeed, Karen Horney felt that the hostility and the destructiveness of a child are directly proportional to the extent to which that child feels his or her survival is endangered.

3 / The Concept of Death in Children

ONCE THE CHILD "KNOWS," WHAT HAPPENS TO THE KNOWING?

The known does not remain known. Matilda McIntire, Carol Angle, and Lorraine Struempler inquired of 598 children whether a dead pet knows that its owner misses it, and they found that seven-year-olds are far more inclined than are children of eleven and twelve to accept death's finality and irreversibility.[44] A related finding was reported by Irving Alexander and Arthur Adlerstein who tested the GSR* of a large number of children, ages five to sixteen, who were exposed to a series of death-related words interspersed among a series of neutral words.[45] They divided the children into three groups: childhood (5–8), preadolescence or latency (9–12), and adolescence (13–16). The results indicated that *the young children (and the adolescents) had a much greater emotional response to death-related words than had the latency-aged subjects.* The authors concluded that latency is a benign period, the "golden age" of childhood. "Children at this age seem to be too much involved in the routine of life and its attendant pleasures to be concerned with the concept of death."

I believe that there is a less pollyannaish way of explaining these results, that the child at an early age stumbles upon the "true facts of life," that the child's solitary researches lead him or her to the discovery of death. But the child is overwhelmed by the discovery and experiences primal anxiety. Though the child searches for reassurance, he or she must deal with death: he or she may panic in the face of it, deny it, personify it, scoff at it, repress it, displace it, but deal with it the child must. During latency the child learns (or is taught) to negate reality; and gradually, as the child develops efficient and sophisticated forms of denial, awareness of death glides into the unconscious, and the explicit fear of death abates. The carefree days of preadolescence— the "golden age" of latency—do not diminish death anxiety but result from it. Though in latency one acquires much general knowledge, at the same time one retreats from knowledge about the facts of life. And it is the awareness of death, as much as infantile sexuality, that is "latent." During adolescence, childhood denial systems are no longer effective. The introspective tendencies and the greater resources of the adolescent permit him or her to face, once again, the inevitability of death, to bear the anxiety, and to search for an alternate mode of coping with the facts of life.

---

*Galvanic skin response—a physiological measure of anxiety.

STAGES OF KNOWING

A working model of the child's subsequent development of the concept of death depends upon the open question of when he or she first "knows" about death. Either the child gradually develops an awareness and understanding of death; or, as I believe, the child is caught in a "herky-jerky" process of "knowing" too much, too early, and then finds ways to repress that knowledge, to "un-know," until, gradually, the child is prepared to accept that which he or she originally knew. There is no certainty in this matter; there exists no conclusive evidence for either viewpoint.

I consider the stages that succeed a child's first knowledge of death as based on denial. Inherent in the concept of denial is the existence of former knowledge: one can only deny that which is known. If a reader chooses not to accept the arguments I have posited in support of former knowledge, then he or she must read "approximations to knowledge" where I have written "denial."

Denial: Death Is Temporary, Diminution, Suspended Animation, or Sleep. Many children old enough to talk report that they consider death to be reversible or temporary or to be a diminution rather than a cessation of consciousness. This view receives considerable reinforcement from the ubiquitous television cartoons that show characters blown apart, flattened, crushed, or mutilated in an endless number of ways and then, finally and miraculously, reconstituted. Nagy reported some illustrative interview excerpts:

S.C. (4 yrs., 8 mos.): "It can't move because it's in the coffin."

"If it weren't in the coffin, could it move?"

"It can eat and drink."

S.J. (5 yrs., 10 mos.): "Its eyes were closed, it lay there, so dead. No matter what one does to it, it doesn't say a word."

"After ten years, will it be the same as when it was buried?"

"It will be older then, it will always be older and older. When it is 100 years old it will be exactly like a piece of wood."

"How will it be like a piece of wood?"

"That I couldn't say. My little sister will be five years old now. I wasn't alive yet when she died. She will be so big this time. She has a small coffin, but she fits in the small coffin."

"What is she doing now, do you think?"

"Lying down, always just lies there. She's still so small, she can't be like a piece of wood. Only very old people."

"What happens there under the earth?"

B.I. (4 yrs., 11 mos.): "He cries because he is dead."

"But why should he cry?"

"Because he is afraid for himself."

T.P. (4 yrs., 10 mos.): "A dead person is just as if he were asleep. Sleeps in the ground, too."

"Sleeps the same as you do at night or otherwise?"

"Well—closes his eyes. Sleeps like people at night. Sleeps like that, just like that."

"How do you know whether someone is asleep or is dead?"

"I know if they go to bed at night and don't open their eyes. If somebody goes to bed and doesn't get up, he's dead or ill."

"Will he ever wake up?"

"Never. A dead person only knows if somebody goes out to the grave or something. He feels that somebody is there, or is talking."

"He feels the flowers put on his grave. The water touches the sand. Slowly, slowly, he hears everything. Auntie, does the dead person feel it if it goes deep into the ground?" (i.e., the water).

"What do you think, wouldn't he like to come away from there?"

"He would like to come out, but the coffin is nailed down."

"If he weren't in the coffin, could he come back?"

"He couldn't root up all that sand."

H.G. (8 yrs., 5 mos.): "People think dead persons can feel."

"And can't they?"

"No, they can't feel, like sleep. Now, I sleep, I don't feel it, except when I dream."

"Do we dream when we're dead?"

"I think we don't. We never dream when we're dead. Sometimes something flashes out, but not half as long as a dream."

L.B. (5 yrs., 6 mos.): "His eyes were closed."

"Why?"

"Because he was dead."

"What is the difference between sleeping and dying?"

"Then they bring the coffin and put him in it. They put the hands like this when a person is dead."

"What happens to him in the coffin?"

"The worms eat him. They bore into the coffin."

"Why does he let them eat him?"

"He can't get up any longer, because there is sand on him. He can't get out of the coffin."

"If there weren't sand on him, could he get out?"

"Certainly, if he wasn't very badly stabbed. He would get his hand out of the sand and dig. That shows that he still wants to live."

T.D. (6 yrs., 9 mos): "My sister's godfather died and I took hold of his hand. His hand was so cold. It was green and blue. His face was all wrinkled together. He can't move. He can't clench his hands, because he is dead. And he can't breathe."

"His face?"

"It has goose-flesh, because he is cold. He is cold because he is dead and cold everywhere."

"Does he feel the cold or was it just that his skin was like that?"

"If he is dead he feels too. If he is dead he feels a tiny little bit. When he is quite dead he no longer feels anything."

G.P. (6 yrs.): "He stretched out his arms and lay down. You couldn't push down his arms. He can't speak. He can't move. Can't see. Can't open his eyes. He lies for four days."

"Why for four days?"

"Because the angels don't know yet where he is. The angels dig him out, take him with them. They give him wings and fly away."[46]

These statements are most informative. One is struck by the internal contradictions, by the shifting levels of knowing that are apparent even in these short excerpts. The dead feel, but they do not feel. The dead grow but somehow stay the same age and fit in the same-size coffin. A child buries a pet dog but leaves food on the grave because the dog may be a little hungry.[47] The child seems to believe in several stages of death. The dead can feel "a tiny little bit" (or may have dream flashes); but one who is "quite dead . . . no longer feels anything." (Incidentally, these quotations are offered by Nagy as proof that a child either considers death as temporary or denies it completely by equating it with departure or sleep. Once again, observer bias seems evident; to me, these passages indicate that the children had considerable knowledge. There is nothing temporary or incomplete about being eaten by worms, by remaining forever under the dirt, about being "quite dead" and "no longer feel[ing] anything.")

The child's equation of sleep and death is well known. The state of sleep is the child's closest experience of being nonconscious and the only clue the child has to what it is like to be dead. (In Greek mythology, death, Thanatos, and sleep, Hypnos, were twin brothers.) This association has implications for sleep disorders, and many clinicians have suggested that death fear is an important factor in insomnia both for adults and children. Many fearful chidlren regard sleep as perilous. Recall the childhood prayer:

> Now I lay me down to sleep,
> I pray the Lord my soul to keep;
> If I should die before I wake,
> I pray the Lord my soul to take.

The statements Nagy collected also make it crystal clear that children, even with imperfect knowledge, consider death dreadful and frightening. Horrifyng indeed are the ideas of being trapped in a nailed-down coffin, crying for oneself under the earth, lying buried for a hundred years and then turning into wood, being eaten by worms, feeling the cold, turning blue and green, or being unable to breathe.*

These children's views of death are sobering, especially for parents and educators who prefer to ignore the unpleasantness of the entire subject. "What they don't know won't hurt them" is the rationale behind officially sanctioned silence. Yet what children do not know, they invent; and, as we see in these examples, the inventions are more hideous than the truth. I shall have more to say about death education later, but for now it is evident that the beliefs of children about death are terrifying indeed, and that children feel compelled to find ways to set their minds at ease.

Denial: The Two Basic Bulwarks Against Death. The child has two basic defenses against the terror of death—defenses that date from the very beginning of life: deep belief both in his or her personal inviolability and in the existence of a uniquely personal, ultimate rescuer. Though

---

* These early views of death remain in the unconscious with astonishing perdurance. Elliot Jacques, for example, describes this dream of a middle-aged claustrophobic patient: "She was lying in a coffin. She had been sliced into small chunks and was dead. But there was a spider-web-thin thread of nerve running through every chunk and connected with her brain. As a result she could experience everything. She knew she was dead. She could not move or make a sound. She could only lie in the claustrophobic dark and silence of the coffin." [48]

these beliefs are abetted by explicit parental and religious instruction in afterlife myths, in an all-protecting God, and in the efficacy of personal prayer, they are also grounded in the infant's early life experience.

Specialness. Each of us, first as child and then as adult, clings to an irrational belief in our specialness. Limits, aging, death may apply to *them* but not to oneself, not to *me*. At a deep level one is convinced of one's personal invulnerability and imperishability. The origins of this primeval belief (or "ur-defense," as Jules Masserman terms it[49]) are to be found in the dawn of life. For each of us, early life is a time of intense egocentricity. One is the universe: there are no boundaries between one and other objects and beings. One's every whim is satisfied without personal effort: one's thought results in the deed. One is templated with a sense of specialness, and one summons this ready belief as a shield against death anxiety.

The Ultimate Rescuer. Hand in hand with this anthropocentric delusion (and I do not use the word in a pejorative sense, for it is a widely shared, perhaps universal, delusion) is a belief in the ultimate rescuer. This belief, too, is grounded in the dawn of life, in the time of the shadowy figures, the parents, those wondrous appendages of the child's, who are not only powerful movers but eternal servants as well. The belief in the external servant is reinforced by the parent's caring watchfulness during infancy and childhood. Time and time again the child ventures too far, encounters the cruel picket fence of reality, and is rescued by enormous maternal wings which enfold him or her in body warmth.

The beliefs in specialness and the ultimate rescuer serve the developing child well: they are the absolute foundation of the defense structure that the individual erects against death terror. Upon them are erected other secondary defenses which in the adult patient often obscure the original ur-defenses as well as the nature of the primal anxiety. These two basic defenses are deeply ingrained (witness their persistence, in terms of immortality myths and the belief in a personal god, in virtually every major religious system*) and persist into adulthood to exert a powerful influence, as I shall discuss in the next chapter, upon character structure and symptom formation.

---

* It is important to underscore that the psychodynamic value or meaning of religion does not necessarily obviate the intrinsic truth of religious views. Or, as Viktor Frankl puts it: "to satisfy precocious sexual curiosity we invent the story that storks deliver babies. But it does not follow from this that storks do not exist!"[50]

3 / The Concept of Death in Children

Denial: The Belief That Children Do Not Die.   One common solace that children avail themselves of early in life is a belief that children have an immunity from death. The young do not die; death occurs to the old, and old age is so very, very far away. Some illustrations:

> S.   (aged 5 yrs., 2 mos.): Where's your mummy?
> Mother: In heaven. She died some time ago. I think she was about 70.
> S.:   She must have been 80 or 90.
> Mother: No, only 70.
> S.:   Well, men live till they're 99. When are you going to die?
> Mother: Oh, I don't know. When I'm about 70 or 80 or 90.
> S.:   Oh (pause) when I'm grown up I shan't shave and then I will have a beard, shan't I? [In a previous conversation S. said that he knew that men grew beards when they became very, very old. Later it became clear that he proposed to abstain from shaving in an effort to delay death indefinitely!][51]

> Ruth   (4 yrs., 7 mos.): Will you die, Father?
> Father: Yes, but not before I grow old.
> Ruth: Will you grow old?
> Father: Yes, yes.
> Ruth: Shall I grow old, too?
> Father: Yes.
> Ruth: Everyday I'm afraid of dying. I wish I might never grow old for then I would never die. Would I?[52]

> Interviewer: Can a child die?
> G. M.   (age 6): No, boys don't die unless they get run over. If they go to a hospital I think they come out living.
> E. G.   (age 5): I shall not die. When you are old you die. I shall never die. When people get old they die. [Later he says he will die when he gets very old.][53]

In response to story-completion tests, most children gave a preference for staying a child a long time rather than growing up quickly. A nine-and-one-half-year-old boy stated that he wanted to stop growing in order to remain a child because "as someone grows older, there's less life in him."[54]

The actual death of a child, of course, poses severe problems for children, which they often resolve by making a distinction between dying and being killed. One boy stated, "Boys don't die unless they get stabbed or hit by a car." Another child said, "When you're ten years old I don't know how you could die unless someone kills you."[55] Another (age six): "I won't die but when you go out into the rain, you can die."[56] All of these comments assuage anxiety by reassuring the child that

97

death is not an immediate, or at least not an unavoidable, problem. Either death is relegated to old age—a time beyond imagination for the child—or else accidental death may occur, but only if one is "very, very" careless.

Denial: Personification of Death. Most children between the ages of five and nine go through a period in which they anthropomorphize death. Death is given form and will: it is the bogeyman, the grim reaper, a skeleton, a ghost, a shadow; or it is simply associated with the dead. Illustrations abound:

B.G. (4 yrs., 9 mos.): "Death does wrong."

"How does it do wrong?"

"Stabs you to death with a knife."

"What is death?"

"A man."

"What sort of a man?"

"Death-man."

"How do you know?"

"I saw him."

"Where?"

"In the grass. I was gathering flowers."

B.M. (6 yrs., 7 mos.): "Death carries off bad children. Catches them and takes them away."

"What is he like?"

"White as snow. Death is white everywhere. It's wicked. It doesn't like children."

"Why?"

"Because it's bad-hearted. Death even takes away men and women too."

"Why?"

"Because it doesn't like to see them."

"What is white about it?"

"The skeleton. The bone-skeleton."

"But in reality is it like that, or do they only say so?"

"It really is, too. Once I talked about it and at night the real death came. It has a key to everywhere, so it can open the doors. It came in, messed about everywhere. It came over to the bed and began to pull away the covers. I covered myself up well. It couldn't take them off. Afterwards it went away."

P.G. (8 yrs., 6 mos.): "Death comes when somebody dies, and comes with a scythe, cuts him down and takes him away. When death goes away, it leaves footprints behind. When the footprints disappeared, it came back and cut down more people. And then they wanted to catch it, and it disappeared."

B.T. (9 yrs., 11 mos.): "Death is a skeleton. It is so strong it could overturn a ship. Death can't be seen. Death is in a hidden place. It hides in an island."

V.P. (9 yrs., 11 mos.): "Death is very dangerous. You never know what minute he is going to carry you off with him. Death is invisible, something nobody has ever seen in all the world. But at night he comes to everybody and carries them off with him. Death is like a skeleton. All the parts are made of bone. But then when it begins to be light, when it's morning, there's not a trace of him. It's that dangerous, death."

M.I. (9 yrs., 9 mos.): "They always draw death with a skeleton and a black cloak. In reality you can't see him. In reality he's only a sort of spirit. Comes and takes people away, he doesn't care whether it's a beggar or a king. If he wants to, he makes them die."[57]

Though these accounts seem frightening, the process of death personification is an anxiety emollient. The vision of a stalking skeleton emerging nightly from graveyard humus, grim though it be, is, in contrast to the truth, reassuring. As long as a child believes that death is brought by some outside force or figure, the child is safe from the really terrible truth that death is *not* external—that, from the beginning of life, one carries within the spores of one's own death. Furthermore, if death is a sentient being, if—as the child said in the last illustration— the situation is such that *"if he wants to,* he makes them die," then perhaps Death can be influenced *not* to want to. Perhaps like the Button Maker, Ibsen's death metaphor in *Peer Gynt,* Death can be delayed, propitiated or—who knows?—even outwitted or defeated. In personifying death, the child recapitulates cultural evolution: every primitive culture anthropomorphizes the blind forces of nature in an effort to experience greater control over its own destiny.*

---

*Koocher's 1974 study of death attitudes of American children[58] does not corroborate Nagy's findings (with Hungarian children) about the personification of death. Perhaps there are marked cultural differences, but the difference in methodology of the two studies makes comparisons difficult: in the American study the interview was heavily structured with little probing or subject-interviewer interaction, whereas in the Hungarian project the interview was far more open-ended, intensive, and personal.

The anthropomorphic fear of death lingers with one all through life. Rare is the individual who does not at some level of awareness continue to harbor a fear of darkness, demons, ghosts, or some representation of the supernatural. Even a moderately well-made supernatural or ghost movie will, as filmmakers well know, strike deep chords in an audience.

Denial: Taunting of Death.   The older child attempts to assuage fear of death by confirming his or her aliveness. Nine- and ten-year-olds often taunt death; they jeer at their old enemy. A study of the language of schoolchildren revealed many death jibes that seemed hilariously funny to them; for example,

> You gonna be burned or buried.

> It's not the cough that carries you off, it's the coffin they carry you off in.

> Now I lay me down to sleep,
> A bag of bananas at my feet.
> If I should die before I wake,
> You'll know it was the tummy ache.

> The worms crawl in,
> The worms crawl out,
> You hardly know what it's all about.[59]

Many children, especially boys, engage in feats of reckless daredeviltry. (Quite possibly some male adolescent delinquent behavior may reflect a persistence of this defense against death anxiety.) Young girls do so much less commonly, either because of social role demands or because, as Maurer suggests,[60] they are less oppressed by death fears owing to their knowledge of their biological role as mothers, and hence creators.

Denial of Death Awareness in Child Psychiatric Literature.   In spite of the compelling and persuasive arguments and supporting evidence that children discover death at an early age and are pervasively concerned with it, one searches in vain for a reasoned inclusion of death fear in psychodynamic formulations of personality development or in psychopathology. Why is there a discrepancy between clinical observation and dynamic theory? There are, I believe, a "how" and a "why" to consider.

How? I believe that death is excluded from psychodynamic theory by a simple mechanism: death is translated into "separation," which assumes death's role in dynamic theory. John Bowlby, in his monumental work on separation,[61] presents convincing ethological, experimental, and observational evidence, too extensive to be considered here, that indicates that separation from the mother is a catastrophic event for the infant, and that separation anxiety is clearly evident during the ages of six to thirty months. Bowlby concludes—and this conclusion is widely accepted by clinicians—that separation is the primal experience in the formation of anxiety: separation anxiety is the fundamental anxiety; and other sources of anxiety, including the fear of death, acquire emotional significance by equation with separation anxiety. In other words, death is fearful because it re-evokes separation anxiety.

Bowlby's work, for the most part, is elegantly argued. Yet in his consideration of death anxiety his imagination seems curiously curtailed. For example, he cites Jersild's research in which four hundred children were asked about their fears.[62] Jersild found that specific fears of becoming ill or dying were conspicuous for their infrequency: they were mentioned by none of the two hundred children under nine years of age and by only six of the two hundred from nine to twelve. Bowlby concludes from these data that fear of death in children under ten is absent, that it is a later and learned fear, and that it is important because it is equated with separation.[63] Jersild's research shows that what children do fear are animals, darkness, heights, or being attacked in the dark by such creatures as ghosts or kidnapers. What is not asked is the obvious question, What is the significance to children of darkness or ghosts or ferocious animals or being attacked in the dark? In other words, what is the underlying *meaning*, the mental representation, of these fears.

Rollo May in his lucid book on anxiety argues that Jersild's study merely demonstrates that anxiety is converted into fear.[64] The child's fears are often unpredictable and shifting and unrelated to reality (the child is more likely, for example, to fear remote animals, like gorillas and lions, than familiar ones). What appears as unpredictability on a superficial level is, May argues, quite consistent on a deeper one: a child's fears are "objectivated forms of underlying anxiety." May discloses, "Jersild remarked to me in personal conversation that these (children's) fears really expressed anxiety. He was surprised that he had never seen this earlier. I think his not seeing it shows how hard it is to get out of our traditional ways of thinking."[65]

Behavioral research has delineated many situations that arouse fear in human children. The same question may be asked of this experimental data. Why does the child fear strangers, or a "visual cliff" (a glass table with what appears to be a chasm underneath it), or an approaching object (looming), or darkness? Obviously each of these situations—as well as animals, ghosts, and separation—represents a threat to survival. Yet with the exception of Melanie Klein and D. W. Winnicott, who emphasize that primal anxiety is anxiety about annihilation, ego dissolution, or being devoured,[66] the question, Why is the child fearful of these life-threatening situations? is rarely asked. Child developmentalists or child analysts frequently draw highly inferential conclusions about the inner life of the child when it involves object relations or infantile sexuality; but, in considering the child's conception of death, their intuition and imagination remain checked.

The evidence for the existence of separation anxiety is based on solid behavioral observations. Throughout the mammalian species a child separated from its mother evinces signs of distress—both external motoric signs and internal physiological ones. There is also no doubt, as Bowlby ably demonstrates, that separation anxiety is evident early in the life of the human infant, and that concerns about separation remain a major motif in the inner world of adults.

But what behavioral research cannot reveal is the nature of the young child's inner experience or, as Anna Freud puts it, the "mental representation" of the behavioral reaction.[67] It is possible to know what evokes the apprehensiveness but not what the apprehensiveness is. Empirical research demonstrates that the child is fearful when separated, but in no way demonstrates that separation anxiety is the primal anxiety from which death anxiety is derived. At a level prior to thought and language the child may experience the inchoate anxiety of nonbeing; and that anxiety, in the child as in the adult, seeks to become fear: it is, in the only "language" available to the older child, bound and transformed into separation anxiety. Developmentalists eschew the idea that a young child—say, before the age of thirty months—could experience death anxiety, because the child has little concept of a self that is separate from surrounding objects. But the same may be said about separation anxiety. What is it that the child experiences? Certainly not separation, because without a conception of self, the child cannot conceive of separation. What is it, after all, that is being separated from what?

There are limits to our knowing about an inner experience that cannot be described, and in this discussion I run the peril of "adultomorphizing" the child's thought. It must be kept in mind that the term "separation anxiety" is a convention, an agreed-upon term founded upon empirical research, and refers to some ineffable inner state of apprehensiveness. But for the adult it makes no sense whatever to translate death anxiety into separation anxiety (or "fear of loss of object") or to argue that death anxiety derives from a more "fundamental" separation anxiety. As I discussed in the previous chapter, one must distinguish between two meanings of "fundamental": "basic" and "chronologically first." Even were we to accept the argument that separation anxiety is chronologically the first anxiety, it would not follow that death anxiety "really" is fear of object loss. The most fundamental (basic) anxiety issues from the threat of loss of self; and if one fears object loss, one does so because loss of that object is a threat (or symbolizes a threat) to one's survival.

Why? The omission of death fear from dynamic theory is obviously not oversight. Nor, as we have seen, is there substantial reason to justify translating this fear into other concepts. There is, I believe, an active repressive process at work—a process that stems from the universal tendency of mankind (including behavioral researchers and theoreticians) to deny death—to deny it both personally and in life work. Others who have studied the fear of death have arrived at a similar conclusion. Anthony remarks:

> The illogicity and the patent insensibility (of child developmental researchers) to the phenomenon of man's fear of death, which anthropology and history have demonstrated to be one of the most common and powerful of human motivations, can be attributed only to conventional (i.e. culturally induced) repression of this fear by the writers themselves and those whose researches they report.[68]

Charles Wahl, in the same vein, comments:

> It is a surprising and significant fact that the phenomenon of the fear of death, or anxiety about it (thanato-phobia as it is called), while certainly no clinical rarity, has almost no description in the psychiatric or psychoanalytic literature. It is conspicuous by its absence. Could this suggest that psychiatrists, no less than other mortal men, have a reluctance to consider or study a problem which is so closely and personally indicative of the contingency of the human estate? Perhaps they, no less than their patients, would seem to confirm de La Rochefoucauld's observation that "One cannot look directly at either the sun or death."[69]

Death Anxiety and the Development of Psychopathology

If death anxiety is a major factor in the development of psychopathology, and if coming to terms with the concept of death is a major developmental task of every child, then why do some individuals develop crippling neurotic disorders and others reach adulthood in relatively well-integrated fashion? There is no empirical research to help answer this question, and for the present I can do no more than suggest possibilities. Undoubtedly a number of factors interact in a complex fashion. There must be some "ideal" timing or sequence of developmental events: the child must deal with the issues at a pace compatible with his or her inner resources. "Too much, too soon" obviously creates an imbalance. A child who is harshly confronted with death before having developed appropriate defenses, may be severely stressed. Severe stress, unpleasant at all times of life, has for the young child implications that transcend transient dysphora. Freud, for example, spoke of the disproportionately severe and enduring damage to the ego caused by massive trauma early in life, and cited, by way of illustration, an experiment in biology which demonstrated the catastrophic effects on an adult organism caused by the tiny prick of a needle into the embryo at the very beginning of its development.[70]

What type of trauma may be involved? Several obvious possibilities present themselves. Exposure to death in the child's environment is an important event; some types of contact with death may—in proper dosage and in the presence of already existing ego resources, salubrious constitutional factors, and supportive adults who are themselves able to deal adaptively with death anxiety—result in innoculation, whereas some types may exceed the child's capacity to shield himself or herself. Every child is exposed to death in encounters with insects, flowers, pets, and other small animals, and these deaths may be sources of puzzlement or anxiety and stimulate the child to discuss with his or her parents questions and fears about death. But for a child faced with the death of a human, the possibility of trauma is much greater.

The death of another child is, as I have discussed, especially frightening because it undermines the consoling belief that only very old people die. The death of a sibling, who is both young and important to the child, is a major trauma. The child's reaction may be very complex, for several issues are involved: guilt emanating from sibling rivalry (and from the pleasure of commanding more parental attention), loss, and the evocation of fear of one's personal death. The literature deals primarily with the first issue, guilt, and occasionally with the second, loss, but almost never with the third. For example, Rosenzweig and Bray presents data that indicates that among schizophrenic patients, when compared with a normal population, with a manic-depressive sample, and with a general paretic sample, there is a significantly greater incidence of a sibling dying before a patient's sixth year.[71]

Rosenzweig offers the standard analytic interpretation of this result—namely, that overwhelming guilt ensuing from inter-sibling hostility and incestuous feelings is a significant factor in the production of schizophrenic behavior patterns. To support this conclusion, he presents three brief (one paragraph) case reports. Despite the brevity of the reports and the selection from a huge sample of clinical material to support his thesis, there is evidence of fear of personal death in two of the three vignettes. One patient who had lost his mother and two sibs early in life responded strongly to the death of a cousin: "He was so deeply disturbed that he became ill and had to go to bed: he feared persistently that he was going to die. The doctor gave the diagnosis of a nervous breakdown. The patient soon began to display bizarre behavior of a schizophrenic kind."[72] Another patient lost three brothers, the first when he was six years old. He developed a psychosis at seventeen, shortly after the death of the third brother. The only statement quoted from the patient suggests that more than guilt was involved in his reaction to the death. "I've heard his voice occasionally. I almost seem to be him at times. I don't know, there's some void that seems to be in the way.... Well, how can I get over a void like his death? My brother's dead and I'm—well I'm alive, but I don't know...."[73] This highly selective form of case report proves nothing. I belabor the point to illustrate the problems of interpreting the research literature. Researchers and clinicians become "grooved" and have difficulty changing set even when, as in this research, another explanation seems entirely plausible and consistent with the data.

If one considers loss of a parent as well as loss of a sibling, then one finds in Rosenzweig's research that *over 60 percent* of schizophrenic patients suffered an early loss. Perhaps, then, schizophrenic patients have had "too much, too soon." Not only did these patients have too much exposure to death but, because of the degree of pathology in the family environment, the families and the patients were particularly unable to cope with death anxiety. (Harold Searles, as I will discuss in chapter 4, reached the same conclusions based on his psychotherapeutic work with adult schizophrenic patients.[74])

The death of a parent is a catastrophic event for the child. The latter's reactions depend upon a number of factors: the quality of his relationship to the parent, the circumstances of the parent's death (was, for example, the child witness to a natural or a violent death?), the parent's attitude during his or her final illness, and the existence of a strong surviving parent and a network of community and family resources.[75] The child suffers a deep loss and, furthermore, is extraordinarily beset with concern that his or her aggressive behavior or fantasies concerning the parent may have been instrumental in the latter's death. The role of loss and guilt is well known and has been competently discussed by others.[76] Omitted from traditional bereavement literature, however, is a consideration of the impact of a parent's death upon the child's awareness of his or her own death. As I have emphasized previously, annihilation is the individual's primary dread and supplies much of the anguish in his or her reaction to the loss of another. Maurer puts it well: "At some level below true cognition, the child with naive narcissism 'knows' that the loss of his parents is the loss of his tie to life. . . . Total terror for his life rather than jealous possessiveness of a lost love object is the etiology of the distress of separation anxiety."[77]

It is not difficult to demonstrate that psychiatric patients, neurotic and psychotic, have lost a parent more frequently than have individuals in the general population.[78] But the implications of a parent's death for the child are so extensive that it is not possible for research to disentangle and to assign weight to all the separate components of the experience. It is known, for example, from animal experimentation that the young, if separated from their mothers, will develop an experimental neurosis and respond far more adversely to stress than do those who remain with their mothers. In humans the immediate presence of a maternal figure lessens anxiety caused by unfamiliar events. It follows then that a child who has lost a mother is far more vulnerable to *all* the stresses he or she must face. The child is not only exposed to anxiety emanating from death awareness but suffers inordinately with anxiety from many other stresses (interpersonal, sexual, school-related) with which he or she is poorly able to cope. Thus the child is likely to develop symptomatology and neurotic mechanisms of defense which will be layered, one upon the other, as he or she proceeds in life. The fear of personal death may rest at the deepest layers, breaking through in undisguised form only rarely in nightmares or other expressions of the unconscious.

Josephine Hilgard and Martha Newman studied psychiatric patients who had lost a parent early in life, and reported an intriguing finding (which they termed the "anniversary reaction"): a significant correlation between a patient's age at psychiatric hospitalization and his or her parent's age at death.[79] In other words, when a patient is hospitalized there is a greater-than-chance possibility that he or she will be the same age as his or her parent was when the latter died. For example, if a patient's mother died at the age of thirty, the patient is "at risk" at the age of thirty. Furthermore, the patient's oldest child is likely to be the same age as the patient was when the parent died. For example, a patient who was six years old when her mother died, is "at risk" psychiatrically when her oldest daughter is six years old. Though the researchers did not raise the issue of death anxiety, it would seem possible that the death of the original mother hurled the child—the later patient—into a confrontation with contingency: the mother's death signaled to the child that she, too, must die. The child repressed this conclusion, and its associated anxiety, which remained unconscious until triggered by the anniversary—by the patient's attaining the age when her parent died.

The degree of trauma is to a large extent a function of a family's degree of anxiety about death. Children in many cultures participate in rituals surrounding the dead. They may have assigned roles in funerals or other death rituals. In the Foré culture of New Guinea, for example, children participate in the ritual devouring of a dead relative. Most likely this experience is not catastrophic for the child because the adults participate in the activities without severe anxiety; it is part of a natural, un-selfconscious stream of life. However, if, as is often true in Western culture today, a parent experiences severe anxiety about the issue of death, then the child is given the message that there is much to fear. This parental communication may be especially important for those children who have severe physical illness. As Marian Breckenridge and E. Lee Vincent put it, "The children feel the anxiety of their parents that they may die, and hence tend to carry a vague uneasiness which healthy children do not experience."[80]

The Death Education of Children

Many parents, perhaps most, in our culture attempt gradually to escalate reality in regard to death education. Young children are shielded from death; they are explicitly misinformed; denial is implanted early in life with tales of heaven, or of return of the dead, or with assurances that children do not die. Later, when the child is "ready to take it," a parent gradually increases the dose of reality. Occasionally, enlightened parents take a determined stand against self-deception and refuse to teach their children to negate reality. They find it difficult, however, when a child is frightened or anguished, to refrain from offering solace through some reality-negating reassurance—either a flat denial of mortality or a "long journey" afterlife myth.

Elisabeth Kübler-Ross disapproves strongly of traditional religion's practice of indoctrinating children with "fairy tales" of heaven, God, and angels. Yet when she describes her work with children who are concerned about death—their own or their parents—it is obvious that she, too, offers denial-based consolation. She informs children that at the moment of death one is transformed or liberated "like a butterfly" to a comforting, beckoning future.[81] Although Kübler-Ross insists that this is not denial but instead is reality based on objective research on life-after-death-experiences, the empirical evidence remains unpublished. The current position of this remarkable therapist who once confronted death unflinchingly indicates how difficult it is to face death without self deception. Insofar as I can judge, Kübler-Ross's "objective data" differ in no significant manner from traditional religion's "knowing" through faith.

There exist clear educational guidelines in our Western culture for such areas as physical development, information acquisition, social skills, and psychological development; but when it comes to death education, parents are very much on their own. Many other cultures offer some culturally sanctioned myths about death which, with no ambivalence or anxiety, are transmitted to the children. Our culture offers no identifiable guidelines for parents to follow; despite the universality of the issue and its crucial importance in the development of the child, each family must determine, willy-nilly, what to teach their children. Often the child is given information that is obscure, commingled with parental anxiety, and likely to be contradicted by other sources of information in the environment.

There is sharp disgreement about death education within the ranks of professional educators. Anthony recommends that parents negate reality to the child. She quotes Sandor Ferenczi who said that "negation of reality is a transition phase between ignoring and accepting reality," and suggests that parents' failure to assist the child's denial may result "in a neurosis in which death-associations played a part."[82] Anthony continues:

> The arguments in favour of supporting reality-acceptance are strong. Nevertheless in this context there is a danger in doing so. The knowledge that the denial is itself an easing of acceptance may make the parent's task easier. He may anticipate a charge of unreliability, of lying, when the child's own need for denial is past. If openly accused, he may answer, "You could not take it, *then*."[83]

On the other hand, many professional educators accept Jerome Bruner's view that "any subject can be taught effectively in some intellectually honest form to any child at any stage of development,"[84] and attempt to assist the child's gradual realistic understanding of the concept of death. Euphemisms ("gone to sleep," "went to heaven," "is with the angels") are "wafer-thin barricades against death fears and only bewilder the child."[85] Ignoring the issue results in a fool's paradise for parents: children do not ignore the issue and, as is true for sex, find other sources of information that are often unreliable or are even more frightening or bizarre than reality.

In summary, there is convincing evidence that children discover death at an early age, that they apprehend that life will ultimately be extinguished, that they apply this knowledge to themselves, and that as a result of this discovery they suffer great anxiety. A major developmental task is to deal with this anxiety, and the child does so in two major ways: by altering the intolerable objective reality of death and by altering inner subjective experience. The child denies the inevitability and the permanence of death. He or she creates immortality myths—or gratefully embraces myths offered by elders. The child also denies his or her own helplessness before the presence of death by altering inner reality: the child believes both in his or her personal specialness, omnipotence, and invulnerability and in the existence of some external personal force or being that will deliver him or her from the fate that awaits all others.

"What is remarkable is," as Rochlin states, "not that children arrive at adult views of the cessation of life, but rather how tenaciously throughout life adults hold to the child's beliefs and how readily they revert to them."[86] Thus, the dead are not dead; they rest, they slumber on in memorial parks to the sound of eternal music, they enjoy an afterlife in which they will ultimately be reunited with their loved ones. And, regardless of what happens to others, one as an adult denies death for oneself. The mechanisms of denial are incorporated into one's life style and character structure. The individual's burden, as an adult no less than as a child, is to deal with personal finiteness; and the study of psychopathology, to which I now turn, is the study of failed death transcendence.

CHAPTER 4

Death and Psychopathology

THE RANGE of psychopathology, the types of clinical picture with which patients present, is so broad that clinicians require some organizing principle that will permit them to cluster symptoms, behaviors, and characterological styles into meaningful categories. To the extent that clinicians can apply some structuring paradigm of psychopathology, they are relieved of the anxiety of facing an inchoate situation. They develop a sense of recognition or of familiarity and a sense of mastery which, in turn, engender in patients a sense of confidence and trust—prerequisites for a truly therapeutic relationship.

The paradigm that I shall describe in this chapter rests, as do most paradigms of psychopathology, on the assumption that psychopathology is a graceless, inefficient mode of coping with anxiety. An existential paradigm assumes that anxiety emanates from the individual's confrontation with the ultimate concerns in existence. I shall present in this chapter a model of psychopathology based upon the individual's struggle with death anxiety, and in later chapters models applicable to patients whose anxiety is more closely related to other ultimate concerns—freedom, isolation and meaninglessness. Though for didactic purposes I must discuss these concerns separately, all four represent strands in the cable of existence, and all must eventually be recombined into a unified existential model of psychopathology.

All individuals are confronted with death anxiety; most develop adaptive coping modes—modes that consist of denial-based strategies such as suppression, repression, displacement, belief in personal omnipotence, acceptance of socially sanctioned religious beliefs that "detoxify" death, or personal efforts to overcome death through a wide variety of strategies that aim at achieving symbolic immortality.

Either because of extraordinary stress or because of an inadequacy of available defensive strategies, the individual who enters the realm called "patienthood" has found insufficient the universal modes of dealing with death fear and has been driven to extreme modes of defense. These defensive maneuvers, often clumsy modes of dealing with terror, constitute the presenting clinical picture.

Psychopathology (in every system) is, by definition, an *ineffective* defensive mode. Even defensive maneuvers that successfully ward off severe anxiety, prevent growth and result in a constricted and unsatisfying life. Many existential theorists have commented upon the high price exacted in the struggle to cope with death anxiety. Kierkegaard knew that man limited and diminished himself in order to avoid perception of the "terror, perdition and annihilation that dwell next door to any man."[1] Otto Rank described the neurotic as one "who refused the loan (life) in order to avoid the payment of the debt (death)."[2] Paul Tillich stated that "neurosis is the way of avoiding non-being by avoiding being."[3] Ernest Becker made a similar point when he wrote: "The irony of man's condition is that the deepest need is to be free of the anxiety of death and annihilation; but it is life itself which awakens it and so we must shrink from being fully alive."[4] Robert Jay Lifton used the term "psychic numbing" to describe how the neurotic individual shields himself from death anxiety.[5]

Naked death anxiety will not be easily apparent in the paradigm of psychopathology I shall describe. But that should not surprise us: primary anxiety in pristine form is rarely visible in any theoretical system. The defensive structures exist for the very purpose of internal camouflage: the nature of the core dynamic conflict is concealed by repression and other dysphoria-reducing maneuvers. Eventually the core conflict is deeply buried and can be inferred—though never wholly known—only after laborious analysis of these maneuvers.

To take one example: an individual may guard himself from the death anxiety inherent in individuation by maintaining a symbiotic tie with mother. This defensive strategy may succeed temporarily, but as time passes, it will itself become a source of secondary anxiety; for example, the reluctance to separate from mother may interfere with attendance at school or the development of social skills; and these deficiencies are likely to beget social anxiety and self-contempt which, in turn, may give birth to new defenses which temper dysphoria but retard growth and accordingly generate additional layers of anxiety and defense. Soon the core conflict is heavily encrusted with these epiphenomena, and the excavation of the primary anxiety becomes exceedingly difficult. Death anxiety is not immediately apparent to the clinician: it is discovered through a study of dreams, fantasies, or psychotic utterances or through painstaking analysis of the onset of neurotic symptoms. For example, Lewis Loesser and Thea Bry[6] report that first phobic attacks that are analyzed carefully are invariably characterized by a breakthrough of death anxiety. The understanding of later attacks is confounded by the presence of elaborations, substitutions, and displacements.

The derivative, secondary forms of anxiety are nonetheless "real" anxiety. An individual may be brought down by social anxiety or by pervasive self-contempt; and, as we shall see in the next chapter, treatment efforts generally are directed toward derivative rather than toward primary anxiety. The psychotherapist, regardless of his or her belief system concerning the primary source of anxiety and the genesis of psychopathology, begins therapy at the level of the patient's concerns: for example, the therapist may assist the patient by offering support, by propping up adaptive defenses, or by helping to correct destructive interpersonal modes of interaction. Thus in the treatment of many patients the existential paradigm of psychopathology does not call for a radical departure from traditional therapeutic strategies or techniques.

Death Anxiety: A Paradigm of Psychopathology

A clinical paradigm that I believe to be of considerable practical and heuristic value was adumbrated in the previous chapter. The child's mode of coping with the awareness of death is denial-based, and the two major bulwarks of that denial system are the archaic beliefs that one is either personally inviolable and/or protected eternally by an ultimate rescuer. These two beliefs are particularly powerful because they receive reinforcement from two sources: from the circumstances of early life, and from widespread culturally sanctioned myths involving immortality systems and the existence of a personal, observing deity.

The clinical expression of these two fundamental defenses became particularly clear to me one day when I saw two patients, whom I shall call Mike and Sam, in two successive hours. They provide a powerful study in the two modes of death denial; the contrast between the two is striking; and each, by illustrating the opposite possibility, sheds light on the dynamics of the other.

Mike, who was twenty-five years old and had been referred to me by an oncologist, had a highly malignant lymphoma and, though a new form of chemotherapy offered his only chance for survival, he refused to cooperate in treatment. I saw Mike only once (and he was fifteen minutes late for that meeting), but it was readily apparent that the guiding motif of his life was individuation. Early in life he had struggled against any form of control and developed remarkable skills at self-sufficiency. Since the age of twelve he had supported himself, and at fifteen he moved out of his parental home. After high school he went into contracting and soon mastered all aspects of the trade—carpentry, electrical work, plumbing, masonry. He built several houses, sold them at substantial profits, bought a boat, married, and sailed with his wife around the world. He was attracted to the self-sufficient individualistic culture that he had found in an underdeveloped country, and was preparing to emigrate when, four months before I saw him, his cancer was discovered.

The most striking feature of the interview was Mike's irrational attitude toward the chemotherapy treatment. True, the treatment was markedly unpleasant, causing severe nausea and vomiting, but Mike's fear exceeded all reasonable bounds: he could not sleep the night before treatment; he developed a severe anxiety state and obsessed about methods of avoiding treatment. What was it precisely that Mike feared about the treatment? He could not specify, but he did know that it had something to do with immobility and helplessness. He could not bear to wait while the oncologist prepared his medication for injection. (It could not be done in advance, since the dosage depended upon his blood count, which had to be examined before each administration.) Most terrible of all, however, was the intravenous: he hated the penetration of the needle, the taping, the sight of the drops entering his body. He hated to be helpless and restrained, to lie quietly on the cot, to keep his arm immobile. Though Mike did not consciously fear death, his fear of therapy was an obvious displacement of death anxiety. What was truly dreadful for Mike was to be dependent and static: these conditions ignited terror, they were death equivalents; and most of his life he had overcome them by a consummate self-reliance. He believed deeply in his specialness and his invulnerability and had, until the cancer, created a life that reinforced this belief.

I could do little for Mike except to suggest to his oncologist that Mike be taught to prepare his own medications and be permitted to monitor and adjust his own intravenous. These suggestions helped, and Mike finished his course of treatment. He did not keep his next appointment with me but called to ask for a self-help muscle-relaxation cassette. He chose not to remain in the area for the oncological follow-up and decided to pursue his plans to emigrate. His wife so disapproved of his plan that she refused to go, and Mike set sail alone.

Sam was approximately the same age as Mike but resembled him in no other way. He came to see me in extremis following his wife's decision to leave him. Though he was not, like Mike, confronted with death in a literal sense, Sam's situation was similar on a symbolic level. His behavior suggested that he faced an extraordinarily severe threat to his survival: he was anxious to the point of panic, he wailed for hours on end, he could not sleep or eat, he longed for surcease at any cost and seriously contemplated suicide. As the weeks passed, Sam's catastrophic reaction subsided, but his discomfort lingered. He thought about his wife continuously. He did not, as he stated, "live in life" but slunk about outside life. "Passing time" became a conscious and serious proposition: crossword puzzles, television, newspapers, magazines were seen in their true nature—as vehicles for filling the void, for getting time over with as painlessly as possible.

Sam's character structure can be understood around the motif of "fusion"—a motif dramatically opposed to Mike's of "individuation." During the Second World War, Sam's family had, when he was very young, moved many times to escape danger. He had suffered many losses, including the death of his father when Sam was a preadolescent and the death of his mother a few years later. He dealt with his situation by forming close, intense ties: first with his mother and then with a series of relatives or adopted relatives. He was everyone's handyman and perpetual babysitter. He was an inveterate gift giver, bestowing generous amounts of time and money on a large number of adults. Nothing seemed more important to Sam than to be loved and cared for. In fact, after his wife left him, he realized that he felt he existed only if he were loved: in a state of isolation he froze, much like a terrified animal, into a state of suspended animation—not living but not dying either. Once when we talked about his pain following his wife's departure, he said, "When I'm sitting home alone, the most difficult thing is

114

to think that no one really knows I'm alive." When alone, he scarcely ate or sought to satisfy any but the most primitive needs. He did not clean his house, he did not wash, he did not read; though he was a talented artist, he did not paint. There was, as Sam put it, no point in "expending energy unless I am certain it will be returned to me by another." He did not exist unless someone was there to validate his existence. When alone, Sam transformed himself into a spore, dormant until another person supplied life-restoring energy.

In his time of need Sam sought help from the elders in his life: he flew across the country for the solace of a few hours in the home of adopted relatives; he received support by simply standing outside the house he and his mother had once lived in for four years; he ran up astronomical phone bills soliciting advice and comfort; he received much support from his in-laws who, because of Sam's devotion to them, threw their lot (and love) in with Sam rather than with their daughter. Sam's efforts to help himself in his crisis were considerable but monothematic: he sought in a number of ways to reinforce his beliefs that some protective figure watched over and cared for him.

Despite his extreme loneliness, Sam was willing to take no steps to alleviate it. I made a number of practical suggestions about how he might meet friends: singles' events, church social activities, Sierra Club events, adult education courses, and so forth. My advice, much to my puzzlement, went completely unheeded. Gradually I understood: what was important for Sam was not, despite his loneliness, to be with others but to confirm his faith in an ultimate rescuer. He was explicit in his unwillingness to spend time away from his home on singles or dating activities. The reason? He was afraid of missing a phone call! One phone call from "out there" was infinitely more precious than joining dozens of social activities. Above all, Sam wanted to be "found," to be protected, to be saved *without* having to ask for help and without having to engineer his own rescue. In fact, at a deep level, Sam was made *more* uncomfortable by successful efforts to assume responsibility for helping himself out of his life predicament. I saw Sam over a four-month period. As he became more comfortable (through my support and through "fusion" with another woman), he obviously lost motivation for continued psychotherapeutic work, and we both agreed that termination was in order.

TWO FUNDAMENTAL DEFENSES AGAINST DEATH

What do we learn from Mike and Sam? We see clearly two radically different modes of coping with fundamental anxiety. Mike believed deeply in his specialness and personal inviolability; Sam put faith in

115

the existence of an ultimate rescuer. Mike's sense of self-sufficiency was hypertrophied, while Sam did not exist alone but strove to fuse with another. These two modes are diametrically opposed; and, though by no means mutually exclusive, they constitute a useful dialectic which permits the clinician to understand a wide variety of clinical situations.

We meet Mike and Sam in a time of urgent experience. In neither man does the crisis elicit new defenses; in the starkest possible manner, it highlights the nature and the limitations of their modes of being. Extreme adherence to either an individuation or a fusion mode results in a characterological rigidity that is obviously maladaptive. Mike and Sam exhibit extreme styles that increase stress, prevent coping, and retard growth. Mike refused to participate in a life-saving therapy and later refused follow-up evaluation. Sam's intense desire for all of his wife's attention was responsible for her decision to leave; his passion for fusion resulted in an augmentation of the pain of loneliness and in an inability to cope resourcefully with his new situation in life. Neither Mike nor Sam was able to grow in any way as a result of their crises. Maladaptive and rigid behavior that precludes personal growth is, by definition, neurotic behavior.

In a crude, sweeping way, the two defenses constitute a dialectic—two diametrically opposed modes of facing the human situation. The human being either fuses or separates, embeds or emerges. He affirms his autonomy by "standing out from nature" (as Rank put it[7]), or seeks safety by merging with another force. Either he becomes his own father or he remains the eternal son. Surely this is what Fromm meant when he described man as either "longing for submission or lusting for power."[8]

This existential dialectic offers one paradigm that permits the clinician to "grasp" the situation. There are many alternate paradigms, each with explanatory power: Mike and Sam have character disorders—schizoid and passive-dependency, respectively. Mike can be viewed from the vantage points of a continued rebellious conflict with his parents, of counterdependency, of neurotic perpetuation of the oedipal struggle, or of homosexual panic. Sam can be "grasped" from the vantage points of identification with Mother and unresolved grief, or of castration anxiety, or from a family dynamic one in which the clinician focuses attention on Sam's interaction with his wife.

The existential approach is, therefore, one paradigm among many, and its *raison d'être* is its clinical usefulness. This dialectic permits the therapist to comprehend data often overlooked in clinical work. The therapist may, for example, understand why Mike and Sam responded so powerfully and manneristically to their painful situations, or why Sam balked at the prospect of "improving" his situation by the assumption of responsibility for himself. This dialectic permits the therapist to engage the patient on the deepest of levels. It is based on an understanding of primary anxiety that exists in the immediate present: the therapist views the patient's symptoms as a response to death anxiety that currently threatens, not as a response to the evocation of past trauma and stress. Hence, the approach emphasizes awareness, immediacy, and choice—an emphasis that enhances the therapist's leverage.

I shall, in the remainder of this chapter, describe these two basic forms of death denial and the types of psychopathology that spring from them. (Though many of the familiar clinical syndromes can be viewed and understood in terms of these basic denials of death, I make no pretense of an exhaustive classifying system—that would suggest greater precision and comprehensiveness than is the case.) Both beliefs, in specialness and in an ultimate rescuer, can be highly adaptive. Each, however, may be overloaded and stretched thin, to a point where adaptation breaks down, anxiety leaks through, the individual resorts to extreme measures to protect himself or herself, and psychopathology appears in the form of either defense breakdown or defense runaway.

For the sake of clarity I shall first discuss each defense separately. I shall then need to integrate them again because they are intricately interdependent: the great majority of individuals have traces of both defenses woven into their character structures.

Specialness

No one has ever described the deep irrational belief in our own specialness more powerfully or poignantly than Tolstoy who, through the lips of Ivan Ilyich, says:

> In the depth of his heart he knew he was dying, but not only was he not accustomed to the thought, he simply did not and could not grasp it.
> The syllogism he had learnt from Kiezewetter's Logic: "Caius is a man, men are mortal, therefore Caius is mortal," had always seemed to him correct as applied to Caius, but certainly not as applied to himself. That Caius—man in the abstract—was mortal, was perfectly correct, but

> he was not Caius, not an abstract man, but a creature quite, quite separate from all others. He had been little Vanya, with a mamma and a papa, with Mitya and Volodya, with the toys, a coachman and a nurse, afterwards with Katenka and with all the joys, griefs, and delights of childhood, boyhood, and youth. What did Caius know of the smell of that striped leather ball Vanya had been so fond of? Had Caius kissed his mother's hand like that, and did the silk of her dress rustle so for Caius? Had he rioted like that at school when the pastry was bad? Had Caius been in love like that? Could Caius preside at a session as he did? "Caius really was mortal, and it was right for him to die; but for me, little Vanya, Ivan Ilyich, with all my thoughts and emotions, it's altogether a different matter. It cannot be that I ought to die. That would be too terrible."[9]

We all know that in the basic boundaries of existence we are no different from others. No one at a conscious level denies that. Yet deep, deep down each of us believes, as does Ivan Ilyich, that the rule of mortality applies to others but certainly not to ourselves. Occasionally one is caught off guard when this belief pops into consciousness, and is surprised by one's own irrationality. Recently, for example, I visited my optometrist to complain that my eyeglasses no longer functioned as of yore. He examined me and asked my age. "Forty-eight," I said, and he replied, "Yep, right on schedule." From somewhere deep inside the thought welled up and hissed: *"What* schedule? *Who's* on schedule? You or others may be on a schedule, but certainly not I."

When an individual learns he or she has some serious illness—for example, cancer—the first reaction is generally some form of denial. The denial is an effort to cope with anxiety associated with the threat to life, but also it is a function of a deep belief in one's inviolability. Much psychological work must be done to restructure one's lifelong assumptive world. Once the defense is truly undermined, once the individual really grasps, "My God, I'm really going to die," and realizes that life will deal with him or her in the same harsh way as it deals with others, he or she feels lost and, in some odd way, betrayed.

In my work with terminally ill cancer patients I have observed that individuals vary enormously in their willingness to know about their deaths. Many patients for some time do not hear their physician tell them their prognosis. Much internal restructuring must be done to allow the knowledge to take hold. Some patients become aware of their deaths and face death anxiety in staccato fashion—a brief moment of awareness, brief terror, denial, internal processing, and then preparedness for more information. For others the awareness of death and the associated anxiety flood in with a terrible rush.

118

One of my patients, Pam, a twenty-eight-year-old woman with cervical cancer, had her myth of specialness destroyed in a striking fashion. After an exploratory laparotomy, her surgeon visited her and informed her that her condition was grave indeed, and that her life expectancy was in the neighborhood of six months. An hour later Pam was visited by a team of radiotherapists who had obviously not communicated with the surgeon, and who informed her that they planned to radiate her and that they were "going for a cure." She chose to believe her second visitors, but unfortunately her surgeon, unbeknownst to her, spoke with her parents in the waiting room and gave them the original message—namely, that she had six months to live.

Pam spent the next few months convalescing at her parents' home in the most unreal of environments. Her parents treated her as though she were going to be dead in six months. They insulated themselves and the world from her; they monitored her phone calls to screen out unsettling communications; in short, they made her "comfortable." Finally Pam confronted her parents and demanded to know what in God's name was going on. Her parents told her about their conversation with the surgeon; Pam referred them to the radiotherapist, and the misunderstanding was quickly cleared up.

Pam, however, was deeply shaken by the experience. The confrontation with her parents made her realize, in a way that a death sentence from the surgeon had not, that she was indeed veering toward death. Her comments at this time are revealing:

> "I did seem to be getting better and it was a happier situation but they began to treat me like I was not going to live and I was stung into this terrible feeling of realization *that they had already accepted my death.* Because of an error and a miscommunication I was already dead to my family, and I started being dead and it was a very hard way back to get myself to be alive. It was worse later on as I was getting better than it was when I was very sick because when the family suddenly realized that I was getting better then they left and went back to their daily chores and I was still left with being dead and I couldn't handle it very well. I'm still frightened and trying to cross the boundary line that seems to be in front of me—the boundary line of, am I dead or am I alive?"

The point is that Pam truly understood what it meant to die not from anything her doctors told her but from the crushing realization that her parents would continue to live without her and that the world would go on as before—that, as she put it, the good times would go on without her.

Another patient with widespread metastatic cancer had arrived at the same point when she wrote a letter to her children instructing them how to divide some personal belongings of sentimental value. She had rather mechanically performed the other dreary administrative chores of dying—the writing of a will, the purchase of a burial plot, the appointment of an executor—but it was the personal letter to her children that made death real to her. It was the simple but dreadful realization that when her children read her letter she would no longer exist: neither to respond to them, to observe their reactions, to guide them; they would be there but she would be nothing at all.

Another patient, after months of procrastination, arrived at the painful decision to discuss with her teen-age sons the fact that she had advanced cancer and not long to live. Her sons responded with sadness but with courage and self-sufficiency. A bit too much courage and self-sufficiency for her: in some far-off place in her mind she could feel some pride—she had done what a good parent must do, and they would pattern their lives along the lines she had laid out for them—but they took her death too well; and, though she hated her irrationality, she was troubled because they would persist and thrive without her.

Another patient, Jan, had breast cancer that had spread to her brain. Her doctors had forewarned her of paralysis. She heard their words but at a deep level felt smugly immune to this possibility. When the inexorable weakness and paralysis ensued, Jan realized in a sudden rush that her "specialness" was a myth. There was, she learned, no "escape clause." She said all this during a group therapy meeting and then added that she had discovered a powerful truth in the last week—a truth that made the ground shake under her. She had been musing to herself about her preferred life span—seventy would be about right, eighty might be too old—and then suddenly she realized, "When it comes to aging and when it comes to dying, *what I wish has absolutely nothing to do with it.*"

Perhaps these clinical illustrations begin to transmit something of the difference between knowing and truly knowing, between the everyday awareness of death we all possess and the full facing of "my death." Accepting one's personal death means facing a number of other unpalatable truths, each of which has its own force-field of anxiety: that one is finite; that one's life really comes to an end; that the world will persist nonetheless; that one is one of many—no more, no less; that the universe does not acknowledge one's specialness; that all our lives we have carried counterfeit vouchers; and, finally, certain stark immutable dimensions of existence are beyond one's influence. In fact, what one wishes "has absolutely nothing to do with it."

120

When an individual arrives at the discovery that personal specialness is mythic, he or she feels angry and betrayed by life. Surely this sense of betrayal is what Robert Frost had in mind when he wrote: "Forgive, O Lord, my little jokes on Thee/And I'll forgive Thy great big one on me."[10]

Many people feel that if they had only known, really known, earlier they would have lived their lives differently. They feel angry; yet the rage is impotent, for it has no reasonable object. (The physician is, incidentally, often a target for displaced anger, and especially for that of so many dying patients.)

The belief in personal specialness is extraordinarily adaptive and permits us to emerge from nature and to tolerate the accompanying dysphoria: the isolation; the awareness of our smallness and the awesomeness of the external world, of our parents' inadequacies, of our creatureliness, of the bodily functions that tie us to nature; and, most of all, the knowledge of the death which rumbles unceasingly at the edge of consciousness. Our belief in exemption from natural law underlies many aspects of our behavior. It enhances courage in that it permits us to encounter danger without being overwhelmed by the threat of personal extinction. Witness the psalmist who wrote, "A thousand shall fall at thy right hand, ten thousand at thy left, but death shall not come nigh thee." The courage thus generated begets what many have called the human being's "natural" striving for competence, effectance, power, and control. To the extent that one attains power, one's death fear is further assuaged and belief in one's specialness further reinforced. Getting ahead, achieving, accumulating material wealth, leaving works behind as imperishable monuments becomes a way of life which effectively conceals the mortal questions churning below.

COMPULSIVE HEROISM

For many of us, heroic individuation represents the best that man can do in light of his existential situation. The Greek writer, Nikos Kazantzakis was such a spirit, and his Zorba was the quintessential, self-sufficient man. (In his autobiography Kazantzakis cites the last words of the man who was his model for Zorba the Greek: " . . . if any priest comes to confess me and give me communion, tell him to make himself scarce, and may he give me his curse! . . . Men like me should live a thousand years."[11]) Elsewhere, through the lips of his Ulysses, Kazantzakis advises us to live life so completely that we leave death nothing but a "burned-out castle."[12] His own tombstone on the ramparts of Herakleion bears the simple heroic epitaph: "I want nothing, I fear nothing, I am free."

Push it a bit farther though, and the defense becomes overextended: the heroic pose caves in on itself, and the hero becomes a compulsive hero who, like Mike, the young man with cancer, is driven to face danger in order to escape a greater danger within. Ernest Hemingway, the prototype of the compulsive hero, was compelled throughout his life to seek out and conquer danger as a grotesque way of proving there was no danger. Hemingway's mother reports that one of his first sentences was, " 'fraid of nothin'."[13] In an ironic way he was afraid of nothing precisely because he, like all of us, was afraid of nothingness. The Hemingway hero thus represents a runaway of the emergent, individualistic solution to the human situation. This hero is not choosing; his actions are driven and fixed; he does not learn from new experiences. Even the approach of death does not turn his gaze within or increase his wisdom. The Hemingway code contains no place for aging and diminishment, for they have the odor of ordinariness. In *The Old Man and the Sea*, Santiago meets his approaching death in a stereotyped way—the same way he faced every one of life's basic threats—by going out alone to search for the great fish.[14]

Hemingway himself could not survive the dissolution of the myth of his personal invulnerability. As his health and physical prowess declined, as his "ordinariness" (in the sense that he like everyone must face the human situation) became painfully evident, he grew bereft and finally deeply depressed. His final illness, a paranoid psychosis with persecutory delusions and ideas of reference, temporarily bolstered his myth of specialness. (All persecutory trends and ideas of reference flow from a core of personal grandiosity; after all, only a very special person would warrant that much attention, albeit malevolent attention, from his environment.) Eventually the paranoid solution failed; and, left with no defense against the fear of death, Hemingway committed suicide. Though it seems paradoxical that one would commit suicide because of a fear of death, it is not uncommon. Many individuals have said in effect that "I so fear death I am driven to suicide." The idea of suicide offers some surcease from terror. It is an active act; it permits one to control that which controls one. Furthermore, as Charles Wahl has noted, many suicides have a magical view of death and regard it as temporary and reversible.[15] The individual who commits suicide to express hostility or to generate guilt in others may believe in the continued existence of consciousness, so that it will be possible to savor the harvest of his or her death.

THE WORKAHOLIC

The compulsive heroic individualist represents a clear, but not clinically common, example of the defense of specialness which is stretched too thin and fails to protect the individual from anxiety or degenerates into a runaway pattern. A commonplace example is the "workaholic"—the individual consumed by work. One of the most striking features of a workaholic is the implicit belief that he or she is "getting ahead," "progressing," moving up. Time is an enemy not only because it is cousin to finitude but because it threatens one of the supports of the delusion of specialness: the belief that one is eternally advancing. The workaholic must deafen himself or herself to time's message: that the past grows fatter at the expense of a shrinking future.

The workaholic life mode is compulsive and dysfunctional: the workaholic works or applies himself not because he wishes to but because he *has* to. The workaholic may push himself without mercy and without regard for human limits. Leisure time is a time of anxiety and is often frantically filled with some activity that conveys an illusion of accomplishment. Living, thus, becomes equated with "becoming" or "doing"; time not spent in "becoming" is not "living" but waiting for life to commence.

Culture, of course, plays an important role in the shaping of the individual's values. Regarding "activity," Florence Kluckholm suggests an anthropological classification of value orientations that postulates three categories: "being," "being-in-becoming," and "doing."[16] The "being" orientation emphasizes the activity rather than the goal. It focuses on the spontaneous natural expression of the "is-ness" of the personality. "Being-in-becoming" shares with the "being" orientation an emphasis on what a person is rather than on what the person can accomplish, but emphasizes the concept of "development." Thus, it encourages activity of a certain type—activity directed toward the goal of the development of all aspects of the self. The "doing" orientation emphasizes accomplishments measurable by standards outside of the acting individual. Obviously contemporary conservative American culture, with its emphasis on "what does the individual do?" and "getting things done," is an extreme "doing" culture.

Still, in every culture there are wide ranges of individual variation. Something within the workaholic individual interacts with the cultural standard in a manner that breeds a hypertrophied and rigid internalization of the value system. It becomes difficult for individuals to assume a bird's-eye view of their culture and to view their value system as one among many possible stances. I had one workaholic patient who treated himself to a rare noonday walk (as a reward for some particularly important accomplishment) and was staggered by the sight of hundreds of people standing around simply sunning themselves. "What do they *do* all day? How can people live that way?" he wondered. A frantic fight with time may be indicative of a powerful death fear. Workaholic individuals relate to time precisely as if they were under the seal of imminent death and were scurrying to get as much completed as possible.

Embedded in our culture, we accept unquestioningly the goodness and rightness of getting ahead. Not too long ago I was taking a brief vacation alone at a Caribbean beach resort. One evening I was reading, and from time to time I glanced up to watch the bar boy who was doing nothing save languidly staring out to sea—much like a lizard sunning itself on a warm rock, I thought. The comparison I made between him and me made me feel very smug, very cozy. He was simply doing nothing—wasting time; I was, on the other hand, doing something useful, reading, learning. I was, in short, getting ahead. All was well, until some internal imp asked the terrible question: Getting ahead of what? How? And (even worse) why? Those questions were, and are still, deeply disquieting. What was brought home to me with unusual force was how I lull myself into a death-defeating delusion by continually projecting myself forward into the future. I do not exist as a lizard exists; I prepare, I become, I am in transit. John Maynard Keynes puts it this way: "What the 'purposeful' man is always trying to secure is a spurious and illusive immortality, immortality for his acts by pushing his interest in them forward in time. He does not love his cat, but his cat's kittens; nor, in truth the kittens, but only the kittens' kittens, and so on forward forever to the end of catdom."[17]

Tolstoy, in *Anna Karenina*, describes the collapse of the "upward spiral" belief system in the person of Alexey Alexandrovitch, Anna's husband, a man for whom everything has always ascended, a splendid career, a brilliant marriage. Anna's leaving him signifies far more than the loss of her: it is the collapse of a personal *Weltanschauung*.

> He felt that he was standing face to face with something illogical and irrational, and did not know what was to be done. Alexey Alexandrovitch was standing face to face with life, with the possibility of his wife's loving some one other than himself, and this seemed to him very irrational and incomprehensible because it was life itself. All his life Alexey Alexandrovitch had lived and worked in official spheres, having to do with the reflection of life. And every time he had stumbled against life itself he had shrunk away from it. Now he experienced a feeling akin to that of a man who, while calmly crossing a precipice by a bridge, should sud-

denly discover that the bridge is broken, and that there is a chasm below. That chasm was life itself, the bridge that artificial life in which
Alexey Alexandrovitch had lived.[18]

"The chasm was life itself, the bridge that artificial life . . . " No one
has said it more clearly. The defense, if successful, shields the individual from the knowledge of the chasm. The broken bridge, the failed defense, exposes one to a truth and a dread that an individual in midlife
following decades of self-deception is ill equipped to confront.

NARCISSISM

The person who copes with basic anxiety with a prepotent belief in
his or her specialness will often encounter major difficulties in interpersonal relationships. If a belief in personal inviolability is coupled,
as it often is, with a corresponding diminished recognition of the
rights and the specialness of the other, then one has a fully developed
narcissistic personality. Fromm is supposed to have described the narcissistic personality by reporting a conversation between such an individual and a physician. The patient requested an appointment that day.
The physician said that it would not be possible since his schedule was
filled. The patient exclaimed, "But, doctor, I just live a few minutes
from your office."

The narcissistic personality pattern is more blatantly apparent in the
group therapy format than in individual therapy. In individual therapy
the patient's every word is listened to; each dream, fantasy, and feeling
is examined. Everything is given to the patient; little reciprocation is
asked; and months may go by before narcissistic features are evident.
In the therapy group, however, the patient is required to share time, to
understand and empathize with others, to form relationships and be
concerned about the feelings of others.

The narcissistic pattern manifests itself in many ways: some patients
feel they may offend others but are entitled to be exempt from personal
criticism; they naturally feel that anyone with whom they fall in love
will reciprocate in kind; they feel they should not have to wait for others; they expect gifts, surprises, and concern though they give none;
they expect to be loved and admired for simply being there. In the
therapy group they feel they should receive maximum group attention,
and that it should be forthcoming without any effort expended on
their part; they expect the group to reach out to them though they
themselves reach out to no one. The therapist must point out to such
patients over and over again that there is only one time in life when

125

this expectation is appropriate—when one is an infant and can demand unconditional love from mother without any question of reciprocation.

Hal, a patient in a therapy group, illustrates many of these points. He was a bright, exceedingly articulate physicist who entertained the group for months with spellbinding Faulknerian tales of his childhood in the South (consuming in the process about 40 percent of the time of an eight-person group). He was also sharp-tongued, but his sarcasm was so clever and colorful that the group members took no offense and allowed themselves to be entertained by him. Only gradually did the other members grow to resent his attention-seeking greed, and hostility. They began to grow impatient with his tales, then to shift the focus off of Hal and onto other members, and, finally, to label him explicitly as a time and attention hog. Hal's anger intensified; it outgrew its casing of well-tempered sarcasm and erupted in a chronic continuous stream of bitterness. His personal and professional life began to deteriorate: his wife threatened to leave him, and his department chairman admonished him for relating poorly to his students. The group urged him to examine his anger. Repeatedly the group members asked him, "What are you angry about?" When he discussed some concrete event, they asked him to go down to a deeper level and to answer once again, "What are you angry about?" At the deepest level Hal said, "I'm angry because I'm better than everyone here, and nobody recognizes me for it. I'm smarter, I'm quicker, I'm better and, goddammit, nobody appreciates me. I should be rich—Arabian rich—I should be recognized as a Renaissance man, but I'm treated just like everybody else."

The group was useful to Hal in a number of ways. Simply helping him to excavate and air these feelings and to consider them rationally was an essential and enormously beneficial first step. Slowly the other members helped Hal to recognize that they, too, were sentient beings; that they, too, felt special; that they, too, wanted succor, attention, and center stage. Others, Hal learned, were not simply wellsprings of appreciation and astonishment from which he could endlessly draw support for his own solipsism. "Empathy" was a key concept for Hal, and the group helped him experience his empathy by, on occasion, asking him to go around the group and guess what each of the other members were feeling. At first Hal characteristically answered by guessing what each was feeling about him; but gradually he was able to sense what they were experiencing—for example, that they, too, wanted time or were angry, disillusioned, or pained.

Narcissism is so integral that often a patient has difficulty finding a "ledge" outside his "specialness" on which to stand and observe him-

126

self. Another patient who resembled Hal in many ways had his ego-centricity brought home to him in a curious fashion. He had been in a therapy group for two years and made striking improvement especially in his ability to love and to commit himself to another. I saw him in a debriefing session six months after termination and asked him if he could recall some particularly critical incident in his therapy. He singled out a session in which the group viewed a videotape of the previous meeting; he had been stunned at the discovery that he remembered only those parts of the meeting that focused on him; there were vast stretches of the session that he saw as though for the first time. Others had criticized him frequently for his self-centeredness, but it was only brought home to him (as are all important truths) when he discovered it for himself.

AGGRESSION AND CONTROL

Specialness as a primary mode of death transcendence takes a number of other maladaptive forms. The drive for power is not uncommonly motivated by this dynamic. One's own fear and sense of limitation is avoided by enlarging oneself and one's sphere of control. There is some evidence, for example, that those who enter the death-related professions (soldiers, doctors, priests, and morticians) may in part be motivated by a need to obtain control over death anxiety. For example, Herman Feifel has shown that, though physicians have less conscious death concern than contrast groups of patients or of the general population, they have, at deeper levels, a greater fear of death.[19] In other words, conscious death fears are allayed by the assumption of power, but deeper fears, which in part dictated the choice of profession, operate still. When the dread is particularly strong, the aggressive drive is not contained by peaceful sublimation, and it accelerates. Arrogance and aggression are not uncommonly derived from this source. Rank writes that "the death fear of the ego is lessened by the killing, the sacrifice, of the other; through the death of the other, one buys oneself free from the penalty of dying."[20] Obviously Rank refers to more than literal killing: more subtle forms of aggression—including domination, exploitation, or "soul murder," as Ibsen put it[21]—serve the same purpose. But this mode of adaptation often decompensates into a runaway defense. Absolute power, as we have always known, corrupts absolutely; it corrupts because it does not do the trick for the individual. Reality always creeps in—the reality of our helplessness and our mortality; the reality that, despite our reach for the stars, a creaturely fate awaits us.

THE DEFENSE OF SPECIALNESS: FALTERING AND ANXIETY

In discussing the specialness mode of coping with death fear, I have focused on maladaptive forms of the individualistic or agentic solution: a runaway heroic individualism (with its attendant dread of any sign of human frailty), a compulsive workaholic solution, a depression ensuing from an interruption of the eternal spiral upward, a severe narcissistic character disorder with its accompanying problematic interpersonal ramifications and maladaptive aggressive and controlling life styles. But there is another even more serious and intrinsic limitation to the defense of specialness. Many keen observers have noted that though great exhilaration may for some time accompany individualist expression and achievement, there comes a point where anxiety sets in. The person who "emerges from embeddedness" or "stands out from nature" must pay a price for his success. There is something frightening about individuation, about separating oneself from the whole, about going forward and living life as a separate isolated being, about surpassing one's peers and one's parents.

Many clinicians have written on the "success neurosis"— a curious condition where individuals on the point of the crowning success for which they have long striven, develop not euphoria but a crippling dysphoria which often ensures that they do not succeed. Freud refers to the phenomenon as the "wrecked by success" syndrome.[22] Rank describes it as "life anxiety"[23]—the fear of facing life as a separate being. Maslow notes that we shrink away from our highest possibilities (as well as from our lowest), and terms the phenomenon the "Jonah complex," since Jonah like all of us could not bear his personal greatness and sought to avoid his destiny.[24]

How is one to explain this curious, self-negating human tendency? Perhaps it is a result of an entanglement of achievement and aggression. Some people use achievement as a method of vindictively surpassing others; they fear that others will become aware of their motives and retaliate when success becomes too great. Freud thought it had much to do with the fear of surpassing one's father and thereby exposing oneself to the threat of castration. Becker advances our understanding when he suggests that the terrible thing in surpassing one's father is not castration but the frightening prospect of becoming one's own father.[25] To becomes one's own father means to relinquish the comforting but magical parental buttress against the pain inherent in one's awareness of personal finiteness.

Thus the individual who plunges into life is doomed to anxiety. Standing out from nature, being one's own father or, as Spinoza put it, "one's own god," means utter isolation; it means standing alone without the myth of rescuer or deliverer and without the comfort of the human huddle. Such unshielded exposure to the isolation of individuation is too terrible for most of us to bear. When our belief in personal specialness and inviolability fails to provide the surcease from pain we require, we seek relief from the other major alternative denial system: the belief in a personal ultimate rescuer.

The Ultimate Rescuer

Ontogeny recapitulates phylogeny. In both the physical and the social development of the individual, the development of the species is mirrored. In no social attribute is this fact more clearly evident than in the human belief in the existence of a personal omnipotent intercessor: a force or being that eternally observes, loves, and protects us. Though it may allow us to venture close to the edge of the abyss, it will ultimately rescue us. Fromm characterizes this mythic figure as the "magic helper,"[26] and Masserman as the "omnipotent servant."[27] In chapter three I traced the development of this belief system in early childhood: like the belief in personal specialness, it is rooted in events of early life when parents seemed eternally concerned and satisfied one's every need. Certainly humankind from the beginnings of written history has clung to the belief in a personal god—a figure that might be eternally loving, frightening, fickle, harsh, propitiated, or angered, but a figure that was always *there*. No early culture has ever believed that humans were alone in an indifferent world.

Some individuals discover their rescuer not in a supernatural being but in their earthly surroundings, either in a leader or in some higher cause. Human beings, for milleniums, have conquered their fear of death in this manner and have chosen to lay down their freedom, indeed their lives, for the embrace of some higher figure or personified cause. Tolstoy was keenly aware of our need to manufacture a godlike figure and then to bask in the illusion of safety emanating from our creation. Consider in *War and Peace*, Rostov's battlefield ecstasy at the thought of the Tsar's proximity:

> He was entirely absorbed in the feeling of happiness at the Tsar's being near. His nearness alone made up to him by itself, he felt, for the loss of

129

the whole day. He was happy, as a lover is happy when the moment of the longed-for meeting has come. Not daring to look around from the front line, by an ecstatic instinct without looking around, he felt his approach. And he felt it not only from the sound of the tramping hoofs of the approaching cavalcade, he felt it because as the Tsar came nearer everything grew brighter, more joyful and significant, and more festive. Nearer and nearer moved this sun, as he seemed to Rostov, shedding around him rays of mild and majestic light, and now he felt himself enfolded in that radiance, he heard his voice—that voice caressing, calm, majestic, and yet so simple. . . . And Rostov got up and went out to wander about among the campfires, dreaming of what happiness it would be to die—not saving the Emperor's life—(of that he did not dare to dream), but simply to die before the Emperor's eyes. He really was in love with the Tsar and the glory of the Russian arms and the hope of coming victory. And he was not the only man who felt thus in those memorable days that preceded the battle of Austerlitz: nine-tenths of the men in the Russian army were at that moment in love, though less ecstatically, with their Tsar and the glory of the Russian arms.[28]

"As the Tsar came nearer everything grew brighter, more joyful and significant, and more festive. Nearer and nearer moved this sun . . . " How beautifully clear is Tolstoy's depiction of the internal defensive ecstasy—not only, of course, of the Russian soldier but of the legions of Everyman and Everywoman whom therapists see in everyday clinical work.

THE RESCUER DEFENSE AND PERSONALITY RESTRICTION

Overall the ultimate rescuer defense is *less* effective than the belief in personal specialness. Not only is it more likely to break down but it is intrinsically restrictive to the person. Later I shall report on empirical research that demonstrates this ineffectiveness, but it is an insight that Kierkegaard arrived at intuitively over one hundred years ago. He has a curious statement contrasting the perils of "venturing" (emergence, individuation, specialness) and not venturing (fusion, embeddedness, belief in ultimate rescuer):

> . . . it is dangerous to venture. And why? Because one may lose. Not to venture is shrewd. And yet, by not venturing, it is so dreadfully easy to lose that which it would be difficult to lose in even the most venturesome venture, . . . one's self. For if I have ventured amiss—very well, then life helps me by its punishment. But if I have not ventured at all— who then helps me? And, moreover, if by not venturing at all in the highest sense (*and to venture in the highest sense is precisely to become conscious of oneself*) I have gained all earthly advantages . . . and lose myself. What of that?[29]

To remain embedded in another, "not to venture," subjects one then to the greatest peril of all—the loss of oneself, the failure to have explored or developed the manifold potentials within oneself.

When too much is asked of the rescuer defense, a highly restricted life mode results, as in the case of Lena, a thirty-year-old member of a therapy group. Lena was deeply depressed, flooded with suicidal ideation, and often lapsed into depressive stupors during which she stayed in bed for days on end. She lived an isolated existence, spending most of her time alone in her sparsely furnished room. Her personal appearance was striking: in every aspect—from her long careless blonde hair to her decorated jeans and combat fatigue jacket, to her youthful posturing and gullibility—she resembled a girl in midadolescence. She had lost her mother at age five and her father at twelve and had grown exceedingly attached to her grandparents and other parent surrogates. As her grandparents grew old and infirm, she developed a horror of the telephone—the phone had been the messenger of her father's death—and she refused to answer it lest it bring news of her grandparents' death.

Lena was overtly terrified of death and avoided any contact with death motifs, and she attempted to deal with her terror in a most ineffective and magical mode—a mode that I have seen many patients use: she attempted to elude death by refusing to live. Like Oskar in Günter Grass's *The Tin Drum*, she attempted to conquer time, to fix it permanently by remaining a child forever. She devoted herself to avoiding individuation and sought safety by attempting to submerge herself in a protector. An axiom of group therapy is that the members display, in the here and now of the group, their internal defenses as they interact with one another. Lena's defensive posture became exceedingly transparent as the group proceeded. Once she began a session by announcing that she had, the previous weekend, been involved in a serious automobile accident. She had gone to visit a friend in a city 150 miles away and through gross negligence had run off the road, overturned her car, and narrowly escaped death. Lena commented that it would have been so easy and desirable not to have regained consciousness.

The group members responded accordingly. They felt concerned and frightened for Lena. They outdid one another in offering her nurturance. The group therapist responded in the same fashion until he began to analyze, silently, the process of the meeting. Lena was always dying, always frightening the group, always mobilizing massive concern from the other members. In fact, during her first months in the group the members assumed the task of keeping Lena alive, keeping her eating, keeping her from suicide. The therapist wondered, "Does anything good ever happen to Lena?"

Lena's accident had occurred on the way to visit a friend. Suddenly the therapist asked himself the question, "What friend?" Lena had relentlessly presented herself to the group as an isolated individual sans friends, relatives, even acquaintances. And yet she described driving 150 miles to see a friend. When the therapist asked the question, he learned that, yes, Lena had a boyfriend; that, yes, she had spent every weekend with him for months; and that, yes, he wished to marry her. Yet she had chosen not to share this information with the group. Her reasons were obvious: what was important to Lena was not growth but survival, and survival seemed possible only by soliciting care and protection from the group and the therapist. Her major dilemma was how to retain protection in perpetuity: she must give no evidence of growth or change lest the group members and the therapist conclude she was well enough to terminate therapy.

During the course of the group therapy Lena was highly threatened by incidents that challenged her major defensive system: that is, the belief that help was "out there," and that only the continued presence of the deliverer ensured her safety. Lena's passion for fusion with the therapist resulted in many transference distortions that required continuous attention throughout therapy. She was exquisitely sensitive to any sign of rejection by him and reacted strongly to evidences of his mortality, fallibility, or unavailability. She, more than the other members, was alarmed (and angry) when he took vacations, or became ill, or was obviously mistaken or confused in the group. Much of the therapeutic work with patients who have a hypertrophied craving for an ultimate rescuer will, as I demonstrate in the next chapter, center about the analysis of transference.

THE COLLAPSE OF THE RESCUER

Through much of life the belief in an ultimate rescuer provides considerable solace and functions smoothly and invisibly. Most individuals remain unaware of the structure of their belief system until it fails to serve its purpose; or until, as Heidegger put it, there is a "breakdown in the machinery."[30] There are many possibilities for breakdown and many forms of pathology associated with the collapse of the defense.

Fatal Illnesses. Perhaps the severest test for the effectiveness of the ultimate rescuer delusion is presented by fatal illness. Many individuals, so stricken, channel a great deal of energy into bolstering their belief in the presence and power of a protector. As the obvious candidate for the role of rescuer is the physician, the patient-doctor relationship becomes charged and complex. In part, the robe of rescuer is thrust upon the physician by the patient's wish to believe; in part, however, the physician dons the robe gladly because playing God is the physician's method of augmenting his belief in his personal specialness. Either way, the result is the same: the doctor becomes larger than life, and the patient's attitude to him or her is often irrationally obeisant. Commonly, patients with a fatal illness dread angering or disappointing their physicians; these patients apologize for taking a physician's time and are so flustered in a physician's presence that they forget to ask the pressing questions they have prepared. (Some patients attempt to cope with this problem by preparing a written checklist of questions to ask the physician.)

To patients it is so important that doctors retain their power that a patient will neither challenge nor doubt one. Many patients, in fact, in a highly magical way, permit physicians to maintain the role of the successful healer by concealing important information from them about their (the patients') psychological and even physical distress. Often, thus, the physician is the last to know about the depth of a patient's despair. A patient who is perfectly able to talk openly to nurses or social workers about his anguish, maintains a cheery, plucky face toward the physician, who concludes that the patient is handling the situation as well as could be expected. (Consequently physicians are notoriously reluctant to refer terminally ill patients for psychological treatment.)

Individuals differ in the tenacity with which they cling to denial, but eventually all denial crumbles in the face of overwhelming reality. Kübler-Ross, for example, reports that in her long experience she has seen only a handful of individuals maintain denial to the moment of death. A patient's reaction to learning that no medical or surgical cure exists is catastrophic. He or she feels angry, deceived, and betrayed. At whom, however, can one be angry? At the cosmos? At fate? Many patients are angry at the doctor for failing them—not for failing medically but for failing to incarnate the patient's personal myth of an ultimate deliverer.

Depression. In his study of psychotically depressed individuals, Silvano Arieti describes a central motif, a life ideology that precedes and "prepares the ground" for depression.[31] His patients lived a type of mediated existence; they lived not for themselves but for either the "dominant other" or the "dominant goal." Though the terminology differs, Arieti's description of these two ideologies coincides closely

133

with the two defenses against the fear of death I have described. The individual who lives for the "dominant goal" is the individual who fashions his or her life around a belief in personal specialness and inviolability. As I discussed earlier, depression often ensues when the belief in an ever-ascending spiral ("dominant goal") collapses.

To live for the "dominant other" is to attempt to merge with another whom one perceives as the dispenser of protection and meaning in life. The dominant other may be one's spouse, mother, father, lover, therapist, or an anthropomorphization of a business or a social institution. The ideology may collapse for many reasons: the dominant other may die, leave, withdraw love and attention, or prove too fallible for the task.

When patients recognize the failure of their ideology, they are often overwhelmed; they may feel that they have sacrificed their lives for a currency that has proven counterfeit. Yet they have available no alternative strategy for coping. Discussing a patient, Arieti puts it:

> The patient has reached a critical point at which a realignment of psychodymanic forces and a new pattern of interpersonal relationships are due, but she is not able to muster them. This is her predicament. She is helpless. She either cannot visualize alternative cognitive structures that lead to recuperative steps or, if she is able to visualize them, they appear unsurmountable. At other times these alternatives do not seem unrealizable, but worthless, since she has learned to invest all her interest and desires only in the relationship that failed.[32]

The patient may attempt to re-establish the relationship or to search for another. If these attempts fail, the patient is without resources and feels both depleted and self-condemnatory. Restructuring a life ideology is beyond comprehension; and many patients, rather than question their basic belief system, conclude that they are too worthless or too bad to warrant the love and protection of the ultimate rescuer. Their depression is abetted, furthermore, by the fact that, unconsciously, suffering and self-immolation function as a last desperate plea for love. Thus, they are bereft because they have lost love, and they remain bereft in order to regain it.

Masochism. I have described a cluster of behaviors associated with the hypertrophied belief in the ultimate rescuer: self-effacement, fear of withdrawal of love, passivity, dependency, self-immolation, refusal to accept adulthood, and depression at collapse of the belief system. When accented, each of these may produce a characteristic clinical syndrome. When self-immolation dominates, the patient is referred to as "masochistic."

Karen, a forty-year-old patient I treated for two years, taught me a great deal about the dynamics behind the urge to inflict pain on oneself. Karen entered therapy for a number of reasons: masochistic sexual propensities, an inability to achieve sexual pleasure with her "straight" boyfriend, depression, a pervasive inertia, and terrifying nightmares and hypnagogic experiences. In therapy she rapidly developed a powerful positive transference. She devoted herself to the project of eliciting care and concern from me. Her masturbatory fantasies consisted of her becoming very ill (either with a physical disease like tuberculosis, or a psychotic breakdown) and my feeding and cradling her. She delayed leaving my office so as to spend a few extra minutes with me; so as to have my signature, she saved her canceled checks with which she had paid my bills; she attempted to visit my lectures so as to catch sight of me. Nothing seemed to please her more than for me to be stern with her; in fact, if I expressed any irritation, she experienced sexual excitation in my office. In every way she made me bigger than life and selectively ignored all of my obvious flaws. She read a book I had written with a patient in which I had been highly self-revelatory about my own anxieties and limitations.[33] But rather than to appreciate my limitations, her response was to admire me even more for the great courage I had shown in publishing such a book.

She responded similarly to signs of weakness or limitation in other important and powerful figures in her life. If her boyfriend became ill or evinced any sign of weakness, confusion, or indecision, she experienced much anxiety. She could not bear to see him falter. Once when he was severely injured in an auto accident, she became phobic about visiting his hospital room. She responded similarly to her parents and was sorely threatened by their increasing age and frailty. As a child, she had related to them through illness. "Being sick was the lie of my life," said Karen. She sought pain to get succor. On more than one occasion during her childhood, she spent weeks in bed with a fictitious disease. During adolescence she became anorexic, only too glad to exchange physical starvation for the attention and solicitude it incited.

Her sexuality joined in the pursuit for safety and deliverance: force, restraint, strength, and pain aroused her, while weakness, passivity, even tenderness repulsed her. To be punished was to be protected; to be bound, confined, or restricted was wonderful: it meant that limits were being set, and that some powerful figure was setting them. Her masochism was overdetermined: she sought survival not only through subjugation but also through the symbolic and magical value of suffering. A small death, after all, is better than the real thing.

Treatment was successful in alleviating the acute depression, the nightmares, the suicidal preoccupation; but there came a time when treatment with me seemed to impede further growth, since, to avoid losing me, Karen continued to immolate herself. I, therefore, set a termination date six months in the future and told her that after that time I would not see her again in treatment. Over the next few weeks we weathered the storm of a severe recrudescence of all symptomatology. Not only did her severe anxiety and nightmares return, but she had terrifying hallucinatory experiences consisting of gigantic swooping bats attacking her whenever she was alone.

This was a period of great fear and despair for Karen. Her delusion of the ultimate rescuer had always protected her against the terror of death and its removal left her overly exposed to dread. Wonderful poems she wrote in her journal (mailed to me after termination of therapy) describe her terror graphically.

> With death in my mouth I speak to you
> And maggots eating at my heart.
> In the cacophony of bells
> My protests go unheard.
> Death is disappointment,
> A bitter bread.
> You cram it down my throat
> To stifle my screams.

Karen's deeply entrenched and powerful belief that, by merging with me, she could escape death was overtly expressed in this poem:

> I would take Death as my master,
> Call his whip a gentle hand,
> And ride with him to those fell caves
> Wherein he dwells;
> Willingly forsake the ripe smell of summer
> Seed pods bursting with ebullient life,
> To sit with him on thrones of ice,
> And know his love.

As the termination date approached, Karen pulled out all stops. She threatened suicide if I would not continue treating her. Another poem expressed her mood and her threat:

> Death is no pretense.
> It is as stark a reality,
> as complete a presence as life itself,
> the other ultimate choice.

I feel myself running into shadows,
clothing myself in cobwebs,
hiding from the reality you thrust at me.
I want to hold up my dark cloak, death,
and threaten you with it.

Do you understand?
I will wrap myself in this if you persist.

Though I felt frightened by Karen's threats and provided her as much support as possible, I decided not to budge from my stand and maintained that at the end of the six months I would not continue to see her regardless of how ill she was. Our termination was to be final and irrevocable; no degree of distress on her part could influence it. Gradually her efforts to merge with me subsided, and she turned toward the task at hand: how to use our final sessions as constructively as possible. It was only then, when she had relinquished all hope of my continued, eternal presence, that she could work truly effectively in therapy. She allowed herself to know and to make known her strengths and her growth. She rapidly obtained a full-time position commensurate with her talents and skills (she had procrastinated finding this work for four years!). She changed her demeanor and grooming radically from woebegone waif to mature attractive woman.

Two years after termination she asked to see me again because of the death of a friend. I agreed to meet with her for a single session and learned that not only had she maintained her changes but had undergone considerably more growth. It seems that one important thing for patients to learn is that, though therapists can be helpful, there is a point beyond which they can offer nothing more. In therapy, as in life, there is an inescapable substrate of lonely work and lonely existence.

The Rescuer Defense and Interpersonal Difficulties. The fact that some individuals avoid the fear of death through a belief in the existence of an ultimate rescuer offers the clinician a useful frame of reference for some baffling, interpersonal minuets. Consider the following examples of a common clinical problem: the patient who is enmeshed in a patently ungratifying, even destructive relationship and yet is unable to wrench free.

Bonnie was forty-eight years old, had a severe circulatory disorder (Buerger's disease), and, after a twenty-year childless marriage, had been separated for ten years. Her husband, a fervent outdoorsman, appeared to be a highly insensitive, self-centered autocrat who finally left Bonnie when her poor health made it impossible for her to accompany him on hunting and fishing expeditions. He provided her no financial support during the ten years of separation, had affairs with numerous women (descriptions of which he did not fail to share with her), and visited Bonnie's home once every week or two to use the washing machine, to pick up recorded phone messages for the business phone he maintained there, and, once or twice a year, to have sexual relations with her. Bonnie, because of strong moral standards, refused to date other men while she was still married. She continued to be obsessed with her husband—at times enraged at the sight of him, at times enamored of him. Her life diminished, as she became ill, lonely, and tormented by his weekly washing machine visits. Yet she could neither divorce him, disconnect his phone, or terminate his laundry privileges.

Delores had a long series of unsatisfying relationships with men and finally, at the age of thirty-five, married an extraordinarily compulsive, unpsychologically minded individual. Before her marriage she had been in therapy because of chronic anxiety and duodenal ulcer. After marriage her husband's controlling punctiliousness soon made her prenuptial anxiety state blissful in comparison. He kept time sheets for Delores's weekend schedule (9:00–10:15 gardening, 10:30–noon, grocery shopping, etc.) and a careful chart of her expenditures; he monitored all phone calls and rebuked her for spending time with anyone but him. Soon Delores was raw with anxiety and suppressed rage; yet she was terror-stricken at the very thought of separation or divorce.

Martha was thirty-one years old and desperate to marry and raise a family. For several years she had been involved with a man who belonged to a mystical religious sect that taught him that the fewer commitments an individual makes, the greater is his freedom. Consequently, though he enjoyed Martha, he refused to live with her or make any long-term commitment to her. He was alarmed by her need for him; and, the tighter she clutched, the less was he willing to promise. Martha was obsessed with binding him and was pained beyond description at his lack of commitment. Yet she felt addicted and was unable to wrench herself free; each time she broke with him, she suffered a painful state of withdrawal and finally in depression or panic reached for the telephone to call him. He, during times of separation, was maddeningly tranquil; he cared for her but could manage well without her. Martha was too consumed with him to search effectively for other relationships: her major project in life was to extract a commitment from him—a commitment that reason and experience strongly suggested was not to be forthcoming.

138

Each of these three patients was involved in a relationship that was responsible for considerable anguish; each realized that continuing in the relationship was self-destructive. Each tried, in vain, to wrench herself free; in fact these futile attempts constituted the major theme of the therapy of each woman. What made disengagement so difficult? What welded each of them so tightly to another person? An obvious and a common thread runs through the concerns of the three patients, and it quickly became apparent when I asked each one to tell me what came to mind when she thought of separating from her mate.

Bonnie had a twenty-year marriage to a husband who had made every decision for her. He was a man who could do everything and "took care" of her. Of course, as she was to learn when she separated, "being taken care of" restricted her growth and self-sufficiency. But it was so comforting to know that someone was always there to protect and rescue her. Bonnie had a serious illness and doggedly continued to believe, even after ten years' separation, that her husband was "out there" taking care of her. Every time I urged her to reflect on life without his presence (and I speak here of symbolic presence; aside from the shared washing machine and a few mechanical coital acts, there had been no meaningful physical presence for years), she became very anxious. What would she do in an emergency? Whom would she call? Life would be unbearably lonely without him. Obviously he was a symbol that shielded her from confronting the harsh reality that there is no one "out there," that the "emergency" is inevitable and no person, symbolic or real, can obviate it.

Delores, like Bonnie, was terrified of being alone. Though her husband was unspeakably restrictive, she preferred the prison of her marriage to, as she put it, the freedom of the streets. She would be nothing, she said, but an outcast, a soldier in the army of misfit women searching for the occasional stray single man. Merely asking her, in the therapy hour, to reflect on a separation was sufficient to bring on a severe bout of anxious hyperventilation.

Martha permitted her life to be governed by the future. Whenever I asked her to meditate on what it would be like to give up her relationship with her uncommitted boyfriend, she always responded that all she could think of was "eating alone at sixty-three." When I asked her for her definition of commitment, she replied, "It's the assurance I'll never have to live alone or die alone." The thought of dining alone or going to the movies alone filled her with shame and dread. What was it

139

that she really wanted from a relationship? "Being able to get help without having to ask for it," she replied.

Martha was tyrannized by the always present, desperate fear that she would be alone in the future. Like many neurotic patients, she did not really live in the present, but instead attempted to find the past (that is, the comforting bond with mother) in the future. Martha's fear and her need were so great that they ensured that she would not establish a gratifying relationship with a man. She was too frightened of loneliness to give up her current unsatisfying relationship, and her need was so obviously frenzied that she frightened away prospective partners.

For each of these women, then, the bonding force was not the relationship per se but the terror of being alone; and what was especially fearful about being alone was the absence of that magical, powerful other who hovers about each of us, observing, anticipating our needs, providing each of us with a shield against the destiny of death.

That the belief in the ultimate rescuer may result in restrictive interpersonal relationships is illustrated exceptionally clearly in the relationship between some adults and aging parents. Irene was forty years old and had long had an intensely ambivalent relationship with her mother. The mother was hostile, demanding, and chronically depressed, and toward her Irene felt, for the most part, loathing and great rage. Yet when her mother complained about her living conditions, Irene invited her to move across the country in order to live with her. Though Irene was in therapy at the time, she did not discuss with the therapist her invitation to her mother until after she had sent the invitation. It would seem as though she was well aware of the self-destructive nature of her behavior but was compelled to barrel ahead and did not wish anyone to dissuade her. Not long after her mother's arrival, Irene decompensated: she had severe bouts of anxiety, intractable insomnia, and an acute flare-up of asthma. So long as we focused in therapy on her mother's guilt-producing maneuvers, intrusiveness, and venomous disposition, we made no progress. That was not to come until we turned to another question—the question crucial to the understanding of many tortured relationships between adults and their parents: *Why was mother so important to Irene?* Why was it her responsibility and task to ensure mother's happiness? Why could she not separate herself from her mother?

When I asked Irene to reflect on the texture of her life without her mother, her first association was interesting: "Without mother no one would care about what I eat!" Mother was out there hovering somewhere over her right shoulder watching, taking note of Irene's eating.

At a conscious level her mother's presence had always infuriated Irene, but now as she looked deeper into it, it was reassuring. If mother monitored what she ate, then it followed that mother would in other ways ensure her daughter's well-being. Irene needed mother not only alive but vigorous; signs of infirmity, apathy, or depression in her mother were, at a deep level, distressing for Irene.

Toward an Integrated View of Psychopathology

I have, for didactic purposes, focused separately on two major modes of coping with death anxiety and presented vignettes of patients who show extreme forms of one of these two basic defenses, but now it is time to integrate them. Most patients do not, of course, present with clear and monothematic clinical pictures. Generally one does not construct a single ponderous defense but instead uses multiple, interlaced defenses in an attempt to wall off anxiety. Most individuals defend against death anxiety through both a delusional belief in their own inviolability *and* a belief in the existence of an ultimate rescuer. Although I have thus far presented these two defenses as a dialectic, they are closely interdependent. *Because* we have an observing, omnipotent being or force continuously concerned with our welfare, we are unique and immortal and have the courage to emerge from embeddedness. *Because* we are unique and special beings, special forces in the universe are concerned with us. Though our ultimate rescuer is omnipotent, he is at the same time, our eternal servant.

Otto Rank in a thoughtful essay entitled "Life Fear and Death Fear" posited a basic dynamic that illuminates the relationship between the two defenses.[34] Rank felt that there is in the individual a primal fear that manifests itself sometimes as a fear of life, sometimes as a fear of death. By "fear of life" Rank meant anxiety in the face of a "loss of connection with a greater whole." The fear of life is the fear of having to face life as an isolated being, it is the fear of individuation, of "going forward," of "standing out from nature." Rank believed that the prototypical life fear was "birth," the original trauma and the original separation. By "fear of death" Rank referred to the fear of extinction, of loss of individuality, of being dissolved again into the whole.

Rank stated that, "Between these two fear possibilities, these poles of

141

fear, the individual is thrown back and forth all his life . . ." The individual attempts to separate himself, to individuate, to affirm his autonomy, to go forward, to fulfill his potential. Yet there comes a time when he develops fear in the face of life. Individuation, emergence, or, as I put it in this chapter, affirmation of specialness, are not duty-free: they entail a fearful, lonely sense of unprotectedness—a sense that the individual assuages by reversing direction: one goes "backward," relinquishes individuation, finds comfort in fusing, in dissolving oneself, in giving oneself up to another. Yet the comfort is unstable because this alternative evokes fear also—the fear of death: relinquishment, stagnation, and, finally, inorganicity. Between these two poles of fear, *life fear* and *death fear*, the individual shuttles throughout life.

Though the paradigm I offer here of the dual defenses of specialness and the ultimate rescuer is not identical with Rank's life-fear, death-fear dialectic, they obviously overlap. Rank's poles of fear correspond closely to the inherent limits of the defenses I have described. "Life anxiety" emerges from the defense of specialness: it is the price one pays for standing out, unshielded, from nature. "Death anxiety" is the toll of fusion: when one gives up autonomy, one loses oneself and suffers a type of death. Thus one oscillates, one goes in one direction until the anxiety outweighs the relief of the defense, and then one moves in the other direction.

This oscillation may be demonstrated in some of the clinical material I have already presented. Consider Lena, who avoided anxiety by choosing to be frozen in adolescence. She continuously sought to merge herself with some rescuer. Yet she was often terrified by her situation: she clung to others but stubbornly rebelled against them. She craved closeness; yet when it was offered, she fled. Much of her energy seemed to be directed toward avoiding "life anxiety" with its change and growth. She sought peace, comfort, and safety; yet when she got them, she was engulfed in death anxiety: she abhorred sleep or any stillness and, to avoid either, engaged in frenzied activity—often, for example, driving aimlessly all night.

Then there was Karen who was masochistic and chose to immolate herself, if necessary, to obtain my embrace. But she, too, was frightened of her objective. Merging with another meant comfort and safety, but it also meant the loss of herself. One of her poems clearly illustrates her dilemma:

> I want to shake, like a dog out of water,
> to free myself from your influence.
> I was too free with you,

let you too near my heart
and got stuck like flesh to icy metal.
Warm to me, and let me go.
To free myself, I must tear flesh,
make wounds that will not heal.

Is that what you want from me?

Emergence-fusion oscillation is often displayed particularly clearly in family therapy sessions where the major problem centers around a teen-ager's preparing to leave home. In one such family I treated, Don, the nineteen-year-old identified patient, was ostensibly fed up with his parents' controlling his life. Among his spasmodic efforts to be his own man was his insistence that his parents not participate in his choice of college or in the college admission procedure. However, he procrastinated too long to gain admission to the colleges of his choice and decided to live at home and attend a local junior college.

Don's continued presence at home resulted in a chaotic family environment. He was wildly ambivalent about freedom. Though painfully sensitive to any of his parents' actions that suggested limitation of his freedom, he covertly but unmistakably asked for curtailment: he persisted in playing the stereo at a deafening pitch till late in the night; he demanded the use of the family car but gunned it, tires screeching out of the driveway, and often returned it with a gas tank so empty that it offered his father, at best, a slim chance of making it to a service station the next morning. He demanded money for dating but "inadvertently" left condoms on his dresser for his strict Mormon parents to find.

Don insisted on freedom but would not take it. On numerous occasions he angrily left home to seek harbor with a friend for a few days, but he never seriously explored getting his own apartment. His parents were wealthy, but he would not allow them to pay his apartment rent, nor would he pay it himself. (He had sufficient funds from summer work but refused to spend these, since he wished to save for a time when he might "really" need the money!) Though Don yearned and fought for freedom, he simultaneously said to his parents, "I'm immature, irresponsible, take care of me, but pretend I didn't ask you."

Don's parents were by no means disinterested bystanders in this drama. Don was the oldest child; his leaving home signified a milestone in his parents' life cycle. Don's father, a fiercely competitive workaholic, was especially threatened by this milestone: it uncovered the illusory nature of his specialness project; it signified personal diminishment, the beginning of a new, less vital, less useful stage of life; it signified displacement and decline and, lurking beyond both, death. Don's mother, whose major identity was that of mother and housekeeper, was similarly threatened by Don's departure. She feared loneliness and the loss of meaning in her life. Consequently, Don's parents, in the subtlest of ways, impeded his growth; they prepared him for life as an autonomous adult (is that not the goal of the successful parent?), yet pleaded *sotto voce*, "do not grow up, do not leave us, stay young forever, and so shall we."*

Another individual oscillating between emergence and fusion was Rob, a thirty-year-old successful business executive, who consulted me because of his transvestism. He had cross-dressed, always in private, since adolescence; and the pattern had, until the present, always been ego-syntonic: that is, the urge seemed to come from the very center of himself—cross-dressing provided much pleasure, and he wished to do it. Recently, however, the behavior seemed to be taking over. He was often anxious and was aware of *having* to cross-dress to relieve anxiety. The symptom demanded more: it wanted him to appear in public as a woman; it wanted him to shave all his body hair (which he did) and, finally, to cut off his penis and become a woman. Thus he was anxious either way: anxious if he did not cross-dress, and anxious if he did.

Ordinarily, psychotherapists understand the transvestite patient by assuming that the sexual perversion is an attempt to ward off castration anxiety. The symptom of cross-dressing serves two functions: it is a symbolic castration (that is, if one is already castrated, one is safe from attack) and at the same time permits the individual to have some form of genital satisfaction. This paradigm had, for Rob, some explanatory power. It clarified, for example, why he could masturbate only while dressed in women's clothes and fantasizing himself as a woman. Yet it left much unexplained, and an existential paradigm provided a broader view of Rob's behavior.

Rob's fantasies were rarely explicitly sexual. Generally he imagined himself as a woman being greeted and admired by a group of women who accepted him into their circle; they would accept him for his looks or simply for his person but would require of him no specific act. He wished to blend in with them, to be one of them, to be a practical nurse, a housekeeper, or a typist. He commented that what was particularly important was not having to perform: he was so weary of the

---

*Similar dynamics are generally found in the families of children with school phobia. W. Tietz presents several cases of a patient's fear of death resulting in a school phobia: a child attempts to defend himself or herself from death anxiety by refusing to separate from the family; the family, because of ambivalence about the child's growing autonomy, colludes in the sympton.[35]

stress inherent in being a man—of competing, standing out, struggling, showing his skill.

The cross-dressing hid much preoccupation with and fear of death. Rob's mother had died slowly and painfully from cancer when he was a teen-ager; and for over fourteen years he had continued to dream of her. Cross-dressing was a symbol of merging with mother and with all women; the transvestite act for most of his life had bound the anxiety inherent in individuation. Always a high achiever, Rob had long ago surpassed his father but, in so doing, had to face what Rank calls "life fear." Rob had always responded to this anxiety of individuation by a fantasy life in which fusion through the mechanism of cross-dressing was the dominant theme. However, the defense of cross-dressing was no longer effective; it evoked too much "death fear," and Rob was terrified that his fantasies would take over, that he would lose himself in that fusion.

The attempt to assuage individuation anxiety through sexual merger is common. The successful man who devotes himself utterly to power, to getting ahead, standing out, and making a name for himself must at some point come face to face with the lonely unprotectedness inherent in individuation. Often this point is reached on business trips. When a hard-striving man can no longer channel his energies and attention into his work, when he must slow down in an unfamiliar setting, he often experiences terrible loneliness and deep frenzy. He searches for sex, not a loving embrace, from a woman (which would stir up fears of losing himself): he searches for manipulative sex, a sexual union that permits him to continue to control life and limit awareness but that provides a poultice for isolation and the underlying death anxiety. The relationship is, of course, a charade; and at some deep level the individual recognizes his inauthentic mode of encountering another. The ensuing guilt joins the anxiety and results in greater isolation and frenzy, and in the need for still another woman, sometimes within minutes of leaving the first.

Sexual activity as a mode of assuaging death anxiety is often clinically observed. Patricia McElveen-Hoehn has reported a series of such incidents: the sexually conservative woman who returns home for the funeral of a parent or some close relative and takes with her a diaphragm and uncharacteristically engages in a sexual relationship with a stranger or a casual friend; or the man who has had a severe coronary and on the way to the hospital fondles his wife's breasts and presses for some sexual exchange; or the man who, with a child dying of leukemia, becomes highly promiscuous.[36]

Another clinical example is provided by Tim, a thirty-year-old patient whose wife was dying of leukemia. Tim began therapy not because of overt grief but because of an alarming degree of sexual preoccupation and compulsivity. He had led a monogamous life prior to his wife's illness; but as she approached death, he began compulsively to visit pornography films and singles' bars (running great risks of public exposure) and masturbated several times a day, often while in bed with his dying wife. On the night of his wife's funeral he sought out a prostitute. Tim's grief and his fear of his own death were easily discernible beneath the sexual compulsivity. His dreams, which I shall describe in the next chapter, give clear evidence of such concerns.

A striking example of the relationship between sex and death occurred when a patient of mine developed widespread, inoperable cancer of the cervix. Despite her obvious pain and cachexia, she had no end of suitors—more, she said, than she had ever had during her bloom. Her mates were dealing with death fears counterphobically. They reported an exhilaration at being so close to the hub of life or, as one put it, to the "bowels of the earth." They were, I believe, elated to come so close to death, to spew in its face, and to emerge each time intact and unscathed. The patient had a different motivation: despite intense pelvic pain, she had a powerful craving for sex. She was so close to death and so terrified of the loneliness of dying that she was engulfed by the need to merge with another person. Ellen Greenberger studied women with terminal cancer and on the basis of TAT scores reports a significantly high incidence of illicit sexuality themes. [37]

The task of satisfying both needs—for separateness and autonomy and for protection and merger—and of facing the fear inherent in each, is a lifelong dialectic that govern one's inner world. It is a task that begins in the first months of life, when the child, who first is symbiotically merged with the mother (and thereafter has an ever-diminishing emotional dependence on her) must, in order to develop a sense of identity, of wholeness and separateness, disengage and differentiate from the mother—a task referred to by Margaret Mahler as "separation-individuation." [38]

THE COST OF NEUROTIC ADAPTATION

The attempt to escape from death anxiety is at the core of the neurotic conflict. Behavior becomes "neurotic" when it is extreme and rigid; and hypertrophy of either of the major defenses against death results, as we have seen, in some form of neurotic adaptation. The neurotic life style is generated by a fear of death; but insofar as it limits one's ability to live spontaneously and creatively, the defense against death is itself a partial death. That is what Rank meant when he said that the neurotic refuses the loan of life to escape the debt of death: he buys himself free from the fear of death by daily partial self-destruction.[39]

But self-restriction is not the end of the cost of neurotic adaptation. Because of guilt, the neurotic individual cannot escape scot-free even with the remnants of a life. Traditionally guilt is defined as the feeling that ensues from a real or fantasied transgression against another. It was Kierkegaard,[40] and later Rank and Tillich,[41] who called attention to another source of guilt—the transgression against oneself, the failure to live the life allotted to one. As Rank put it: "When we protect ourselves . . . from a too intensive or too quick living out or living up, we feel ourselves guilty on account of the unused life, the unlived life in us."[42] Repression is thus a double-edged sword; it provides safety and relief from anxiety, while at the same time it generates life restriction and a form of guilt, henceforth referred to as "existential guilt." In chapter 6 I shall explore existential guilt in depth.

Thus far I have discussed well-delineated neurotic adaptations to death anxiety. Let me now turn briefly to the consideration of the more primitive, fragmentary defenses against death anxiety that are found in schizophrenia.

Schizophrenia and the Fear of Death

Though evidence is mounting that many forms of schizophrenia have an important biochemical component, there can be no evasion of the fact that schizophrenia is also a tragic human experience—one that can be apprehended from both a longitudinal (historical) and a cross-sectional (phenomenological) perspective. Crushing developmental stresses have contributed to the development of the schizophrenic patient's world view, and he or she inhabits a terrifying and chaotic experiental world.

Perhaps no contemporary therapist has made a more concerted and heroic effort to comprehend and explicate the world of the schizophrenic patient than has Harold Searles who treated deeply psychotic patients for many years at Chestnut Lodge in Rockville, Maryland. In 1958 he wrote a deeply insightful but neglected article entitled "Schizophrenia and the Inevitability of Death" expressing his views on the psychodynamics of the schizophrenic patient. Searles's thesis is summarized in this passage:

> The ostensibly prosaic fact of the inevitability of death is, in actuality, one of the supremely potent sources of man's anxiety, and the feeling-responses to this aspect of reality are among the most intense and complex which it is possible for us to experience. The defense-mechanisms of psychiatric illness, including the oftentimes exotic-appearing defenses found in schizophrenia, are designed to keep out of the individual's awareness—among other anxiety-provoking aspects of inner and outer reality—this simple fact of life's finitude.[43]

Searles submits that the dynamics of the schizophrenic patient, like those of the neurotic patient, may be fully understood only from the perspective of the patient's response to the inevitability of his or her death. Obviously the schizophrenic patient's defenses are more exotic, more extreme, and more disabling than those of the neurotic patient. Furthermore, the schizophrenic patient has an early life experience far more devastating than that of the neurotic patient. But the existential nature of human reality makes brothers and sisters of us all. Though the magnitude of the threat or the characteristics of the response differ, it is human finitude that bedevils the schizophrenic no less than the neurotic. Searles states this brilliantly:

> To be sure, schizophrenia can be considered a *result* of exotic, warping experiences in the past—predominantly in infancy and early childhood; but it can equally accurately, and with greater clinical usefulness, the writer thinks, be seen as consisting in the use of certain defense-mechanisms, learned very early, to cope with *present-day* sources of anxiety. And of these latter, none is more potent than the existential circumstance of life's finitude. In essence, then, the hypothesis here is that schizophrenia can be seen, from one among various other possible vantage-points as an intense effort to ward off or deny this aspect of the human situation.
>
> The author wishes to make quite clear that, in his experience, the fact of death's inevitability has a more than merely tangential relation to schizophrenia. That is, it is not a matter of the patient's becoming able, as he grows free here from his schizophrenia, to turn his attention yonder to that great life-circumstance of the inevitability of death—a circumstance which had previously lain inertly at the periphery of, or even quite totally beyond, his ken. On the contrary, the author's clinical work has indicated that the relationship is a much more central one than that: It is a matter, rather, of the patient's having become, and having long remained, schizophrenic (and reference here, of course, is to largely or wholly *unconscious* purposiveness) *in order to avoid facing,* among other aspects of internal and external reality, the fact that life is finite.[44]

Traditional case histories of schizophrenic patients have always stressed their bleak, conflicted early childhoods and the severe pathology of their early family environments. But how would it be if a patient's *real* case history, an existential case history, were written? Part of a psychiatric examination includes a mental status inquiry where the interviewer attempts to discover whether the patient is oriented for time, place, and person. Searles hypothesizes what one patient would respond were he or she to be truly "oriented":

> I am Charles Brennan, a man who is now, this being April 15, 1953, 51 years of age; who is living here in Chestnut Lodge, a psychiatric hospital in Rockville, Maryland; who has been living in a series of psychiatric hospitals constantly for eight years now; who has been seriously ill for over 25 years, with a mental illness which has robbed me of any realistic prospect, considering my present age, of ever being able to marry and have children, and which, quite possibly, will require my being hospitalized for the remainder of my life. I am a man who was once a member of a family which included two parents and seven children, but who has seen, over the years, a crushing series of tragedies strike this family: Years ago my mother died, in a state of long-standing mental illness; one of my brothers developed a mental illness as a young man, requiring extended hospitalization; another brother committed suicide; still another brother was killed in action in the Second World War; and a third was murdered only recently, at the height of his legal career, by a mentally ill client. My remaining parent, my father, is now elderly, a man pathetically far removed from the strong man he used to be, and death cannot be far off for him.[45]

There is something stark and shocking about this particular case history, but perhaps more shocking yet is the knowledge that a similarly tragic case history, one that focuses not on early development, education, military service, object relations, sexual practices, but on the existential facts of life, can be written for every patient (and, indeed, for every therapist).

Searles described the course of therapy of a floridly psychotic patient whom he treated for several years. At first the patient showed "abundant evidence of a richly detailed, fascinatingly exotic and complex, extremely rigorously defended delusional system, replete with all manner of horrendous concepts, ranging from brutal savagery to witchcraft and to the intricate machinations of science fiction." Though the patient's world experience was terrifying, Searles noted that she expressed little concern about those givens that are terrifying to all humans—such as illness, aging, and inescapable death. She dealt with

149

these issues with explicit and massive death denial: "There's no reason for anybody in the world to be unhappy or miserable today; they have antidotes for everything . . . people don't die but in actuality are simply 'changed,' moved about from place to place or are made the unwitting subjects of motion pictures."

After three-and-one-half years of psychotherapy, the patient began to develop a reality-based view of life and to accept that life—including human life—is finite. During the months before this realization, she had shown evidence of a last-ditch intensification of her delusional defenses against the recognition of death's inevitability.

> . . . She came to spend most of her time picking up dead leaves and the occasional dead birds and small animals which hours of searching revealed, and buying all sorts of articles from the stores in the nearby community, then by various alchemy-like processes, attempting to bring these to one or another form of life. It became very clear (and she herself substantiated this) that she felt herself to be God, selecting various dead leaves and other things to be brought to life. Many times the psychotherapeutic sessions were held out on the hospital grounds; the therapist sat on a bench, while she went on with her daylong scrutinizing of the lawn nearby.
>
> But as these months wore on, toward the end of this period of denial of death, she came to express more and more openly a feeling of despair about this activity. Then there came an autumn day when, during the session, patient and therapist sat on benches not far apart and gazed together at the leaf-strewn lawn. She let it be known, mainly in nonverbal ways, that she was filled with mellowness, tenderness, and grief. She said, with tears in her eyes, in a tone as of resignation to a fact that simply has to be accepted, "I can't turn those leaves into sheep, for instance." The therapist replied, "I gather that you're realizing, perhaps, that it's this way with human life, too—that, as with the leaves, human life ends in death." She nodded, "Yes."

This realization marked the beginning of solid therapeutic progress. The patient gradually relinquished her major defense against death: her belief in her own omnipotence and invulnerability. She realized:

> . . . that she was not God . . . and that we human beings are mortal. This showed that the very foundation of her paranoid schizophrenic illness was now crumbling, an illness which had involved her years-long conviction, for example, that both her deceased parents were still living.[46]

Though the defenses of this woman, and of other schizophrenic patients whom Searles describes, are extreme and exceedingly primitive, they are nonetheless homologous to the defensive patterns found in neurotic patients. The paranoid patient, for example, evinces, in delusions of grandeur and omnipotence, one of the primary modes of evading death—a belief in one's own specialness and immortality.

Many if not all schizophrenic patients are unable to experience themselves as fully alive. No doubt this deadness is a function of the global repression of all affect in the schizophrenic patient, but it may also serve, Searles suggests, an additional defensive purpose: being "dead" may protect the patient from death. A limited death is better than the real death. One need not fear death if one is dead anyway.

But all of us must face death. If the fear of death is a core dynamic in the schizophrenic patient, we must answer the riddle why it is that the schizophrenic patient is brought down by this ubiquitous fear. Searles suggests several reasons.

First, the anxiety of facing death is infinitely greater in those who do not have the strengthening knowledge of personal wholeness and of whole participation in living. "A person," Searles writes, "cannot bear to face the prospect of inevitable death until he has had the experience of fully living, and the schizophrenic has not yet fully lived."[47] Norman Brown in his extraordinary book, *Life Against Death*, makes a similar statement: "Only he who can affirm birth can affirm death. . . . The horror of death is the horror of dying with unlived lives in our bodies."[48] (This thesis—that death anxiety is greatly heightened by life failure—has considerable implications for therapy and is discussed in the following chapter.)

A second reason that the schizophrenic is overwhelmed by death anxiety is that the patient has suffered enormous losses so early in development that he or she has not been able to integrate them. Owing to having an immature ego, the patient reacts to the losses pathologically, generally by a reinforcement of subjective infantile omnipotence, which serves to negate the loss (one cannot suffer loss if one is the whole world). Thus, not having been able to integrate losses in the past, the patient is unable in the present to integrate the prospect of the greatest of all losses—the loss of oneself and of everyone one knows. The patient's primary shield against death, then, is a sense of omnipotence, a key feature in any schizophrenic illness.

A third source of intense death anxiety emanates from the nature of the schizophrenic patient's early relationship to mother—a symbiotic union from which the patient has never emerged but in which he or she continues to oscillate between a position of psychological merger and a state of total unrelatedness. The patient's experience of relating to mother is not unlike negotiating a magnetic field: veer too close and be suddenly sucked in, move away too far and drift away into nothingness. The symbiotic relationship requires, for its maintenance, that neither party experience himself or herself as independently whole: each needs the other to complete his or her wholeness. Thus the patient never develops the sense of wholeness necessary to experience life fully.

Furthermore, the schizophrenic patient perceives that the symbiotic relationship is absolutely necessary to survival: the patient needs protection against any threats to the relationship; and among those threats none is as dangerous as his or her (and his or her mother's) intense ambivalence. The child has a sense of profound helplessness in feeling the deepest hate toward the person whom he or she most deeply loves. The child is helpless, too, in the face of the knowledge that this same person loves and hates him or her with great intensity. This helplessness requires continued maintenance of the fantasy, normal only in infancy, of personal omnipotence. Nothing would so completely destroy the sense of personal omnipotence than the acceptance of the inevitability of death, and the schizophrenic patient clings to his or her denial of death with a fierce desperation.

An Existential Paradigm of Psychopathology: Research Evidence

In this chapter I postulate that, though denial of death is ubiquitous, and though the specific modes of death denial are highly varied, there are two major bulwarks of denial: belief in personal specialness and belief in an ultimate rescuer. These defenses originate early in life and greatly influence the individual's character structure. An individual believing strongly in an ultimate rescuer (and striving toward fusion, merger, or embeddedness) will look for strength outside of himself or herself; will take a dependent, supplicant pose toward others; will repress aggression; may show masochistic trends; and may become deeply depressed at the loss of the dominant other. The individual oriented toward specialness and inviolability (and striving toward emergence, individuation, autonomy, or separateness) may be narcissistic; is often a compulsive achiever; is likely to direct aggression outward; may be self-reliant to the point of rejecting necessary, appropriate help from others; may be harshly unaccepting of his or her own personal frailties and limits; and is likely to show expansive, sometimes grandiose trends.

There is no direct empirical evidence for the existence of this emergence-embeddedness dialectic—but neither is there any for other clinical psychopathology paradigms posited by Freud, Sullivan, Horney, Fromm, or Jung: clinical paradigms always emerge intuitively and are justified and validated by their clinical usefulness. However, analogous personality constructs have been posited and closely studied along two robust avenues of inquiry: laboratory research on cognitive styles and personality research on locus of control.

COGNITIVE STYLE

Herman Witkin in 1949 identified two basic perceptual modes—field dependence and field independence—which seem analogous to ultimate rescuer and specialness personality organization.[49] In the "field-dependent" mode (analogous to the ultimate rescuer style) the individual's perception is strongly dominated by the global organization of the field. In the "field-independent" mode (analogous to the specialness style) parts of the field are experienced as discrete from the background. A great deal of research has demonstrated that a tendency toward one or the other modes of perception is a consistent and pervasive characteristic of an individual's functioning. Across a wide variety of perceptual tasks* the field-dependent individual is unable to keep foreground apart from environmental context, whereas the field-independent individual has no difficulty with these tasks. Thus the tests demonstrate a stylistic tendency of the individual which, as it turns out, is not limited to perception but is a pervasive cognitive style, evi-

---

*There are many perceptual tests that can be used to demonstrate this phenomenon. For example, in the body-adjustment test, an individual is placed in a chair that can be tilted right or left, and the chair is placed in a small room that can also be tilted right or left. The subject is asked to make his or her body upright with respect to gravity while the room about him or her is tilted. The field-dependent individuals are not able to separate themselves from the position of the surrounding room. In other words, if the room is tilted, they will tilt themselves accordingly and report that they are upright even though their bodies may be objectively tilted as much as forty-five degrees. The field-independent subjects are, regardless of the position of the surrounding room, able to bring their bodies close to the true upright. Thus, the field-dependent individuals seem to have a fusion of body and field, whereas the field-independent individuals seem to have an immediate sense of the separateness of their bodies from the background.

In an analogous test the individual is presented with a luminous rod and frame (the only objects visible in a darkened room) and asked to place the rod to the true upright position regardless of the tilt of the frame. The embedded-figures test asks an individual to study some complex designs in which are imbedded some particular simple figures. The field-dependent individuals cannot perceive the simple figure, while for the field-independent individual the simple figure is obvious and "pops out" of the design.

dent in the individual's intellectual activities, body concept, and sense of separate identity.

Intellectual Activities.   The field-dependent individual does less well than the field-independent one at solving problems that require the isolation of a central element from its context. Such tendencies are called "cognitive styles." There is a consistent tendency at one extreme for experience to be global and diffuse, and at the other for it to be delineated and structured. Witkin refers to these poles of cognitive style as "global" and "articulated," respectively. It is important, however, to underscore the fact that the world is not peopled by two kinds of being: scores on cognitive style show continuous distribution rather than bipolar distribution.

Body Image.   Not only do the styles of an individual influence what is perceived "out there," but they also influence experience "within." Tests of body image (for example draw-a-person tests) strongly suggest that the way an individual perceives his or her body is significantly related to his or her performance on perceptual and cognitive tests. Individuals with a field-dependent (*"global"*) style demonstrate little detail, unrealistic representation of proportion and body parts, and little attempt at sex role representation; field-independent (*"articulated"*) individuals show clear representation of proportion and sex differences.

Identity.   Persons with a field-independent cognitive style give evidence of a developed sense of separate identity: that is to say, they have an awareness of needs, feelings, attributes that they recognize as their own and that they identify as distinct from those of others. On the other hand, individuals with a field-dependent cognitive style rely heavily on external sources for definition of their attitudes, judgments, sentiments, and of their views of themselves.* For example, studies have demonstrated that field-dependent persons look at the face of the adult examiner much more frequently than do field-independent ones. Furthermore, field-dependent persons are better at recognizing faces of those whom they have seen earlier, and more often have dreams concerned with their own relation to the experimenter.

Cognitive Style and Death Denial.   The "field-dependent" individual, defined experimentally, closely resembles the clinical characterization

---

* A field-dependent individual who is placed in an autokinetic situation changes his or her judgment about the movement of a point of light in conformance with the suggestion of a planted confederate. (The autokinetic situation asks an individual to look at a stationary point of light in a dark room and to estimate how much this point of light has moved. The light itself does not move but the individual may be more or less influenced by estimates of experimental subjects, or confederates, who precede him or her in the experiment.)

of the individual oriented toward the existence of an ultimate rescuer; the "field-independent" person resembles one oriented toward a belief in personal specialness. The field-dependence and field-independence dialectic is derived entirely from empirical studies of perceptual and cognitive function but is devoid of subjective content. I would submit that the existential dialectic described herein is related to this empirical dialectic in the same way that "dread" is related to galvanic skin response: the existential dialectic provides the personal meaning, the phenomenological experience, of the individual who is categorized according to one of these cognitive styles. Let me carry the analogy farther and compare the empirical linkage between cognitive style and psychopathology with the observations made earlier in this chapter about the psychopathology associated with each of the major defenses against death anxiety.

Psychopathology and Cognitive Styles. The individual's cognitive style is closely related to "choice" of psychological defense and to the form of psychopathology. Field dependence-independence is a continuum, at both extremes of which psychopathology occurs; furthermore, pathology takes quite different forms at the two extremes.

A field-dependent individual with personality disturbances is likely to have severe identity problems, with symptoms often considered suggestive of deep-seated problems of dependence, passivity, and helplessness. Several studies indicate that such a patient develops symptoms related to lack of development of a "sense of separate identity," such as alcoholism, obesity, inadequate personality, depression, and psychophysiological reactions (for example, asthma). A psychotic patient is likely to hallucinate—as compared with a field-independent one who is likely to be delusional.[50]

A field-independent individual who develops pathology is likely to show outward aggression, delusions, expansive and euphoric ideas of grandeur, paranoid syndromes, and depressive compulsive character structures.

Interesting observations have also been made about differences between field-dependent and field-independent persons who enter psychotherapy. The major difference centers around the transference. As one could predict, a field-dependent patient tends to develop a quick and highly positive transference to the therapist and to feel better earlier than a field-independent patient. A field-dependent patient tends to "fuse" with the therapist, whereas a field-independent one is likely to be much more cautious in the development of a relationship with the therapist. A field-independent patient comes to the first session with an articulated account of and ideas about his or her problems, whereas a field-dependent patient is nonspecific. A field-dependent individual readily accepts the therapist's suggestions and solicits support from him or her, and attempts to prolong the sessions owing to feelings of anxiety at the end of the hour.

The cognitive style of the psychotherapist is an important determinant of the psychotherapeutic context. Psychotherapists who are themselves field-independent tend to favor either a directive or passive, observational approach to a patient, whereas field-dependent therapists favor personal and mutual relationships with their patients.

The similarities are obvious: extremity, either in field dependency or in orientation toward an ultimate rescuer results in pathology characterized by passivity, dependency, orality, lack of autonomous function, inadequacy; an extreme field independence or specialness may result in pathological expansiveness, paranoid syndromes, aggression, or compulsivity. These observations receive additional support from another line of inquiry—locus of control, an empirically derived personality paradigm that also closely resembles the specialness-ultimate rescuer clinical paradigm.

LOCUS OF CONTROL

Beginning with the work of Joseph Rotter[51] and E. Jerry Phares,[52] many researchers have been interested in a paradigm of personality that investigates whether the individual has either an internal or an external locus of control. Does one feel that one controls the events of one's life, or does one feel that these events occur independently of one's actions? Most of the research in internal-external control is based on an instrument—the I.E. scale * developed by Rotter in 1966 and used in several hundred research studies[55] since that time.

---

* The I.E. (Internal-External) scale is a twenty-three-item forced-choice self-assessment questionnaire. Some sample paired items:
   a. People are lonely because they don't try to be friendly.
   b. There's not much use in trying too hard to please people, if they like you they like you.

   a. What happens to me is my own doing.
   b. Sometimes I feel that I don't have enough control over the direction my life is taking.[53]

There is also a form for preschool children with such items as:

   a. When you get a hole in your pants, is that
      a) because you tore them, or
      b) because they wore out.
   b. If you had a shiny new penny and lost it, would that be
      a) because you dropped it, or
      b) because there was a hole in your pocket.[54]

"Internals" have an internal locus of control and feel they control their personal destiny; "externals" place control external to themselves and look outside themselves for answers, support and guidance.

Internals differ from externals in a vast number of ways. Internals tend to be more independent, more achieving, more politically active, and have a greater sense of personal power. They are more power seeking, they direct their efforts toward gaining mastery over their environment. "Internal" patients hospitalized for tuberculosis know more about their condition, are more inquisitive about the disease and their situation, and indicate that they are not satisfied with the amount of information they are getting from physicians and nurses.[56] When given TAT cards and subtly prompted by the tester, internals are far less open to suggestion and influence than are externals.[57]

In general, then, internals acquire more information and are better at retaining and utilizing it to control their own world. Internals are less suggestible and are more independent and more reliant upon their own judgment. They, in contrast to externals, evaluate information on the basis of its merit rather than responding on the basis of the prestige or expertise of the source of the information. Internals are more likely to be high achievers and more likely to delay gratification so as to attain larger rewards at a later date. Externals are far more suggestible, tend more often to be smokers or to take high risks at gambling, and are lower in achievement, dominance, and endurance and higher in desiring succor from others and self-abasement.[58]

These characterizations and the previous ones about field-independents (or believers in specialness) and field-dependents (or believers in the rescuer) are clearly similar. We may integrate these findings by imagining a continuum with field dependency, external locus of control, and orientation toward an ultimate rescuer on one pole and field independence, internal locus of control, and orientation toward personal specialness on the other. A position on either extreme end of the continuum is highly correlated with clinically evident psychopathology. Much research, however, indicates that one pole of the continuum constitutes a personality organization that is less effective and more likely to result in psychopathology. Individuals at the field-*dependent*, the *external* locus of control pole are more likely to have demonstrable psychopathology than individuals at the field-independent, or internal locus of control, pole.[59] Individuals with high external locus of control scores are more likely to feel inadequate;[60] to be more anxious, hostile, fatigued, confused, and depressed,[61] to have less vigor and resiliency.[62] Severely impaired psychiatric patients are more likely to be externals.[63] Schizophrenics are far more likely to be externals.[64] A great deal of research demonstrates a strong relationship between external locus of control and depression.[65]

These research findings accord with clinical experience. More individuals seek therapy because of the failure of the rescuer defense (dependency cravings, low self-esteem, self-contempt, helplessness, masochistic trends, depression because of the loss, or threat of loss, of their dominant other) than because of specialness breakdown. One team of investigators reported a positive correlation between the external locus of control mode and death anxiety.[66] In other words, the external mode seemed a less effective shield against death anxiety than did the internal mode. (However, another experiment, using different death anxiety instruments, failed to replicate these findings.)[67]

The defense of belief in an outside deliverer seems inherently limited. Not only does it not entirely contain primal anxiety but by its very nature it spawns additional pathology: the belief that one's life is controlled by external forces is associated with a sense of powerlessness, ineffectualness, and low self-regard. One who does not rely on or believe in oneself limits accordingly one's acquisition of information and skills, and may relate to others in an ingratiating manner. It is readily apparent that low self-esteem, a tendency toward self-abasement, few skills on which to build a sense of self-worth, and unsatisfying interpersonal relationships, all prepare the soil for psychopathology.

CHAPTER 5

Death and Psychotherapy

T HE LEAP from theory to practice is not easy. In this chapter I shall transport us from metaphysical concerns about death to the office of the practicing psychotherapist and attempt to extract from those concerns what is relevant to everyday therapy.

The reality of death is important to psychotherapy in two distinct ways: death awareness may act as a "boundary situation" and instigate a radical shift in life perspective; and death is a primary source of anxiety. I shall discuss the application of each way, in turn, to the technique of therapy.

Death as a Boundary Situation

A "boundary situation" is an event, an urgent experience, that propels one into a confrontation with one's existential "situation" in the world. A confrontation with one's personal death ("my death") is the nonpareil boundary situation and has the power to provide a massive shift in the way one lives in the world. "Though the physicality of death destroys an individual, the *idea* of death can save him." Death acts as a

159

catalyst that can move one from one state of being to a higher one: from a state of wondering about *how* things are to a state of wonderment *that* they are. An awareness of death shifts one away from trivial preoccupations and provides life with depth and poignancy and an entirely different perspective.

Earlier I considered illustrative examples from literature and clinical records of individuals who, after a confrontation with death, have undergone a radical personal transformation. Tolstoy's Pierre in *War and Peace* and Ivan Ilyich in "The Death of Ivan Ilyich" are obvious instances of "personality change" or "personal growth." Another striking illustration is everyone's favorite miraculously transformed hero: Ebenezer Scrooge. Many of us forget that Scrooge's transformation was not simply the natural result of yule warmth melting his icy countenance. What changed Scrooge was a confrontation with his own death. Dickens's Ghost of the Future (Ghost of the Christmas Yet to Come) used a powerful form of existential shock therapy: Scrooge was permitted to observe his own death, to overhear members of the community discuss his death and then dismiss it lightly, and to watch strangers quarreling over his material possessions, including even his bedsheets and nightshirt. Scrooge then witnessed his own funeral and, finally, in the last scene before his transformation, Scrooge knelt in the churchyard and examined the letters of his name inscribed on his tombstone.

DEATH CONFRONTATION AND PERSONAL CHANGE: MECHANISM OF ACTION

How does death awareness instigate personal change? What is the inner experience of the individual thus transformed? Chapter 2 presents some data that indicates the type and the degree of positive change that some terminal cancer patients have undergone. Interviews with these patients provide insights into some of the mechanisms of change.

Cancer Cures Psychoneurosis. One patient had disabling interpersonal phobias that almost miraculously dissolved after she developed cancer. When asked about this cure, she responded, "Cancer cures psychoneurosis." Although she tossed this statement off almost flippantly, there is an arresting truth in it: not the dismal truth that death eliminates life with all its attendant sorrows, but the optimistic truth that the anticipation of death provides a rich perspective for life concerns. When asked to describe her transformation, she stated that it was a simple process: having faced and, she felt, conquered her fear of death—a fear that had dwarfed all her other fears—she experienced a strong sense of personal mastery.

Existence Cannot Be Postponed. Eva, forty-five years old and deeply depressed, had advanced ovarian cancer and was highly conflicted about whether she should take one last trip. In the midst of our therapeutic work she reported this dream:

> There was a large crowd of people. It looked something like a Cecil B. DeMille scene. I can recognize my mother in there. They were all chanting, "You can't go, you have cancer, you are ill." The chanting went on and on. Then I heard my dead father, a quiet reassuring voice, saying, "I know you have lung cancer like me, but don't stay home and eat chicken soup, waiting to die like me. Go to Africa—live."

Eva's father had died many years ago of a lingering cancer. She last saw him several months before his death and had sorrowed not only at her loss but at the way he died. No one in the family had dared tell him about his cancer, and the symbol of staying home and eating chicken soup was apt: his remaining life and his death were unenlightened and unheroic. The dream bore powerful counsel; Eva heeded it well and altered her life dramatically. She confronted her physician and demanded all available information about her cancer and insisted that she share in the decisions made about her treatment. She re-established old friendships; she shared her fears with others and helped them share their grief with her. She did take that last journey to Africa which, though it was cut short by illness, did leave her with the satisfaction of having drunk deeply from life until the last draught.

The matter can be summed up simply: "Existence cannot be postponed." Many patients with cancer report that they live more fully in the present. They no longer postpone living until some time in the future. They realize that one can really live *only* in the present; in fact, one cannot outlive the present—it always keeps up with you. Even in the moment of looking back over one's life—even in the last moment—one is still there, experiencing, living. The present, not the future, is the eternal tense.

I remember a thirty-year-old patient who was obsessed by the vision of herself as an old woman spending Christmas alone. Haunted by this vision, she spent much of her adult life in frantic pursuit of a mate—so frantic a pursuit that she frightened away any prospective suitors. She rejected the present and devoted her life to rediscovering the security of early childhood. The neurotic obliterates the present by trying to find the past in the future. It is, of course, paradoxical; and I shall have more to say of this later, that it is the person who will not "live" who is most terrified of dying. "Why not," Kazantzakis asked, "like a well-filled guest, leave the feast of life?"[1]

Another individual, a university professor, as a result of a serious bout with cancer, decided to enjoy the future in the immediate present. He discovered, with astonishment, that he could choose not to do those things he did not wish to do. When he recovered from his surgery and returned to work, his behavior changed strikingly: he divested himself of onerous administrative duties, immersed himself in the most exciting aspects of his research (eventually attaining national prominence), and—let this be a lesson to us all—never attended another faculty meeting.

Fran was chronically depressed and fearful and had for fifteen years been locked into a highly unsatisfying marriage which she could not bring herself to end. The final obstacle to separation was her husband's extensive home aquarium! She wished to remain in the house so that her children could keep their friends and remain in the same school; yet she could not undertake the two hours of time needed for the daily feeding of the fish. Nor could the huge aquarium be moved except at enormous expense. The problem seemed insoluble. (On such trifling issues is a life sacrificed.)

Fran then developed a malignant form of bone cancer which brought home to her the simple fact that this was her one and only life. She said that she suddenly realized that time's clock runs continuously, and that there are no "time-outs" when it stops. Though her illness was so severe that her need for her husband's physical and economic support were very great indeed, she was nonetheless able to make the courageous decision to separate, the decision she had postponed for a decade.

Death reminds us that existence cannot be postponed. And that there is still time for life. If one is fortunate enough to encounter his or her death and to experience life as the "possibility of possibility" (Kierkegaard)[2] and to know death as the "impossibility of further possibility" (Heidegger),[3] then one realizes that, as long as one lives, one has possibility—one can alter one's life until—but only *until*—the last moment. If, however, one dies tonight, then all of tomorrow's intentions and promises die stillborn. That is what Ebenezer Scrooge learned; in fact, the pattern of his transformation consisted of a systematic reversal of his misdeeds of the previous day: he tipped the caroler he had cursed, he donated money to the charity workers he had spurned, he embraced the nephew he had scorned, he gave coal, food, and money to Cratchit whom he had tyrannized.

Count Your Blessings. Another mechanism of change energized by a confrontation with death was well illustrated by a patient who had cancer that had invaded her esophagus. Swallowing became difficult; gradually she shifted to soft foods, then to puréed foods, then to liquids. One day in a cafeteria, after having been unable even to swallow some clear broth, she looked around at the other diners and wondered, "Do they realize how lucky they are to be able to swallow? Do they ever think of that?" She applied this simple principle to herself and became aware of what she *could* do and *could* experience: the elemental facts of life, the changing seasons, the beauty of her natural surroundings, seeing, listening, touching, and loving. Nietzsche expresses this principle in a beautiful passage:

> Out of such abysses, from such severe sickness one returns newborn, having shed one's skin, more ticklish and malicious, with a more delicate taste for joy, with a more tender tongue for all good things, with merrier senses, with a second dangerous innocence in joy, more childlike and yet a hundred times subtler than one has ever seen before.[4]

Count your blessings! How rarely do we benefit from that simple homily? Ordinarily what we *do* have and what we *can* do slips out of awareness, diverted by thoughts of what we lack or what we cannot do, or dwarfed by petty concerns and threats to our prestige or our pride systems. By keeping death in mind, one passes into a state of gratitude, of appreciation for the countless givens of existence. This is what the Stoics meant when they said, "Contemplate death if you would learn how to live."[5] The imperative is not, then, a call to a morbid death preoccupation but instead an urging to keep both figure and ground in focus so that being becomes conscious and life becomes richer. As Santayana put it: "The dark background which death supplies brings out the tender colors of life in all their purity."[6]

Disidentification. In everyday clinical work the psychotherapist encounters individuals who are severely anxious in the face of events that do not seem to warrant anxiety. Anxiety is a signal that one perceives some threat to one's continued existence. The problem is that the neurotic person's security is so tentative that he or she extends his or her defensive perimeter a long way into space. In other words, the neurotic not only protects his or her core but defends many other attributes (work, prestige, role, vanity, sexual prowess, or athletic ability) with the same intensity. Many individuals become inordinately stressed, therefore, at threats to their career or to any of a number of other attributes. They believe in effect, "I *am* my career," or "I *am* my sexual attractiveness." The therapist wishes to say, "No, you are not your career,

163

you are not your splendid body, you are not mother or father or wise man or eternal nurse. You are your *self*, your core essence. Draw a line around it: the other things, the things that fall outside, they are not you; they can vanish, and you will still exist."

Unfortunately such self-evident exhortations, like all self-evident exhortations, are rarely effective in catalyzing change. Psychotherapists look for methods to increase the power of the exhortation. One such method I have used, with groups of cancer patients as well as in the classroom, is a structured "disidentification" exercise.* The procedure is simple and takes approximately thirty to forty-five minutes. I choose a quiet peaceful setting and ask the participants to list, on separate cards, eight important answers to the question "Who am I?" I then ask them to review their eight answers and to arrange their cards in order of importance and centricity: the answers closest to their core at bottom, the more peripheral responses at the top. Then I ask them to study their top card and meditate on what it would be like to give up that attribute. After approximately two to three minutes I ask them (some quiet signal like a bell is less distracting) to go on to the next card and so on until they have divested themselves of all eight attributes. Following that, it is advisable to help the participants integrate by going through the procedure in reverse.

This simple exercise generates powerful emotions. I once led three hundred individuals in an adult education workshop through it; and, even years afterward, participants gratuitously informed me how momentously important the procedure had been to them. Disidentification is an important part of Roberto Assagioli's system of psychosynthesis. He tries to help an individual reach his "center of pure self-consciousness" by asking him to imagine shedding, in a systematic way, his body, emotions, desires, and finally intellect.[7]

The individual with a chronic illness who copes well with his or her situation often spontaneously goes through this process of disidentification. One patient whom I remember well had always closely identified herself with her physical energy and activities. Her cancer gradually weakened her to the point where she could no longer backpack, ski, or hike, and she mourned these losses for a long time. Her range of physical activities inexorably diminished, but eventually she was able to transcend her losses. After months of work in therapy she was able to accept the limitations, to say, "I cannot do it" without a sense of per-

---

*Suggested to me by James Bugental.

sonal worthlessness and futility. Then she transmuted her energy into other forms of expression that were within her limits. She set feasible final projects for herself: completing personal and professional unfinished business, expressing unvoiced sentiments to other patients, friends, doctors, and children. Much later she was able to take another, major step—to disidentify even with her energy and impact and to realize that she existed apart from these, indeed apart from all other qualities.

Disidentification is an obvious and ancient mechanism of change— the transcendence of material and social accouterments has long been embodied in ascetic traditions—but is not easily available for clinical use. It is the awareness of death that promotes a shift in perspective and makes it possible for an individual to distinguish between core and accessory: to reinvest one and to divest the other.

DEATH AWARENESS IN EVERYDAY PSYCHOTHERAPY

If we psychotherapists accept that awareness of personal death can catalyze a process of personal change, then it is our task to facilitate a patient's awareness of death. But how? Many of the examples I have cited are of individuals in an extraordinary situation. What about the psychotherapist treating the everyday patient—who does not have terminal cancer, or who is not facing a firing squad, or who has not had a near fatal accident?

Several of my cancer patients posed the same question. When speaking of their growth and what they had learned from their confrontation with death, they lamented, "What a tragedy that we had to wait till now, till our bodies were riddled with cancer, to learn these truths!"

There are many structured exercises that the therapist may employ to simulate an encounter with death. Some of these are interesting, and I shall describe them shortly. But the most important point I wish to make in this regard is that the therapist does not need to *provide* the experience; instead, the therapist needs merely to help the patient *recognize* that which is everywhere about him or her. Ordinarily we deny, or selectively inattend to, reminders of our existential situation; the task of the therapist is to reverse this process, to pursue these reminders, for they are not, as I have attempted to demonstrate, enemies but powerful allies in the pursuit of integration and maturity.

Consider this illustrative vignette. A forty-six-year-old mother takes the youngest of her four children to the airport where he departs for college. She has spent the last twenty-six years rearing her children and longing for this day. No more impositions, no more incessantly living for others, no more cooking dinners and picking up clothes, only to be reminded of her futile efforts by dirty dishes and a room in new disarray. Finally she is free.

Yet, as she says goodbye, she unexpectedly begins sobbing loudly, and on the way home from the airport a deep shudder passes through her body. "It is only natural," she thinks. It is only the sadness of saying goodbye to someone she loves very much. But it is more than that. The shudder persists and shortly turns into raw anxiety. What could it be? She consults a therapist. He soothes her. It is but a common problem: the "empty nest" syndrome. For so many years she has based her self-esteem on her performance as mother and housekeeper. Suddenly she finds no way to validate herself. Of course she is anxious: the routine, the structure of her life have been altered, and her life role and primary source of self-esteem have been removed. Gradually, with the help of Valium, supportive psychotherapy, an assertiveness training women's group, several adult education courses, a lover or two, and a part-time volunteer job, the shudder shrinks to a tremble and then vanishes altogether. She returns to her "premorbid" level of comfort and adaptation.

This patient, treated by a psychiatric resident, some years ago, was part of a psychotherapy outcome research project. Her treatment results could only be described as excellent: on each of the measures used—symptom check lists, target problem evaluation, self-esteem—she had made considerable improvement. Even now, in retrospect, it seems clear that the psychotherapist fulfilled his function. Yet I also look upon this course of treatment as a "misencounter," as an instance of missed therapeutic opportunities.

I compare it with another patient I saw recently in almost precisely the same life situation. In the treatment of this patient I attempted to nurse the shudder rather than to anesthetize it. The patient experienced what Kierkegaard called "creative anxiety," and her anxiety led us into important areas. It *was* true that she had problems of self-esteem, she *did* suffer from "empty nest" syndrome, and she also was deeply troubled by her great ambivalence toward her child: she loved him but also resented and envied him for the chances in life she had never had (and, of course, she felt guilty because of these "ignoble" sentiments).

We followed her shudder, and it led us into important realms and raised fundamental questions. It was true enough that she could find ways to fill her time, but what was the *meaning* of the fear of the empty nest? She had always desired freedom but now, having achieved it, was terrified of it. Why?

A dream helped to illuminate the meaning of the shudder. Her son who had just left home for college had been an acrobat and a juggler in high school. Her dream consisted simply of herself holding in her hand a 35-millimeter photographic slide of her son juggling. The slide was peculiar, however, in that it was a slide in movement: it showed her son juggling and tumbling in a multitude of movements all at the same time. Her associations to the dream revolved around time. The slide captured and framed time and movement. It kept everything alive but made everything stand still. It froze life. "Time moves on," she said, "and there's no way I can stop it. I didn't want John to grow up. I really treasured those years when he was with us. Yet whether I like it or not, time moves on. It moves on for John and it moves on for me as well. It is a terrible thing to understand, to really understand."

This dream brought her own finiteness into clear focus, and rather than rush to fill time with distractions, she learned to wonder at and to appreciate time and life in richer ways than she previously had. She moved into the realm that Heidegger describes as authentic being: she wondered not at the *way* that things are but *that* things are. In my judgment, therapy helped the second patient more than the first. It would not be possible to demonstrate this conclusion on standard outcome measures; in fact, the second patient probably continued to experience more anxiety than the first did. But anxiety is a part of existence, and no individual who continues to grow and to create will ever be free of it. Nevertheless, such a value judgment evokes many questions about the therapist's role. Is the therapist not assuming too much? Does the patient engage his or her services as a guide to existential awareness? Or do not most patients say in effect, "I feel bad, help me feel better"; and if this is the case, why not use the speediest, most efficient means at one's disposal—for example, pharmacological tranquilization or behavioral modification? Such questions, which pertain to all forms of treatment based on self-awareness, cannot be ignored, and they will emerge again and again in this text.

In the treatment of every patient, situations arise that, if sensitively emphasized by the therapist, would increase the patient's awareness of the existential dimensions of his or her problems. The most obvious situations are the stark reminders of finiteness and the irreversibility of time. The death of someone close will, if the therapist persists, always lead to an increased death awareness. There are many components to grief—the sheer loss, the ambivalence and guilt, the disruption of a life plan—and all need to be thoroughly dealt with in treatment. But, as I stressed earlier, the death of another also brings one closer to facing one's own death; and this part of the grief work is commonly omitted. Some psychotherapists may feel that the bereaved is already too overwhelmed to accept the added task of dealing with his or her own finiteness. I think, however, that assumption is often an error: some individuals can grow enormously as a result of personal tragedy.

The Death of Another and Existential Awareness. For many, the death of a close fellow creature offers the most intimate recognition one can have of one's own death. Paul Landsburg, discussing the death of a loved one, says:

> We have constituted an "us" with the dying person. And it is in this "us," it is through the specific power of this new and utterly personal being that we are led toward the living awareness of our own having to die. . . . My community with that person seems to be broken off; but this community in some degree was I myself, I feel death in the heart of my own existence.[8]

John Donne made the same point in his famous sermon: "And therefore never send to know for whom the bell tolls. It tolls for thee."[9]

The loss of a parent brings us in touch with our vulnerability; if our parents could not save themselves, who will save us? With parents gone nothing stands between ourselves and the grave. On the contrary, we become the barrier between our children and death. The experience of a colleague after the death of his father is illustrative. He had long been expecting his father's death and bore the news with equanimity. However, as he boarded an airplane to fly home for the funeral, he panicked. Though he was a highly experienced traveler, he suddenly lost faith in the plane's capacity to take off and land safely—as though his shield against precariousness had vanished.

The loss of a spouse often evokes the issue of basic isolaton; the loss of the significant other (sometimes the dominant other) increases one's awareness that, try as hard as we may to go through the world two by two, there is nonetheless a basic aloneness that we must bear. No one can die one's own death with one or for one.

A therapist who attends closely to a bereaved patient's associations and dreams, will discover considerable evidence of the latter's concern with his or her own death. For example, a patient reported this nightmare on the night after learning that his wife had inoperable cancer:

> I was living in my old house in _____. [A house that had been in the family for three generations.] A Frankenstein monster was chasing me

through the house. I was terrified. The house was deteriorating, decaying. The tiles were crumbling and the roof leaking. Water leaked all over my mother. [His mother had died six months ago.] I fought with him. I had a choice of weapons. One had a curved blade with a handle, like a scythe. I slashed him and tossed him off the roof. He lay stretched out on the pavement below. But he got up and once again started chasing me through the house.

The patient's first association to the dream was: "I know I've got a hundred thousand miles on me." The symbolism of the dream seemed clear. His wife's impending death reminded him that his life, like his house, was deteriorating; he was inexorably pursued by death, personified, as in his childhood, by a monster who could not be halted.

Another patient, Tim, whose wife had terminal cancer, had this dream the night after she, near death, had had to be hospitalized because of severe respiratory problems:

I had just returned from some type of trip and found that I was pushed into some back room area. Someone had done me in. It was all filled with old stuffed furniture, plywood, dusty and everything was covered with chicken wire. There was no exit. It reminded me of Sartre's play. I felt stifled. I couldn't breathe, something was bearing in on me. I picked up some plywood box or crate that was crudely built. It hit against the wall or floor and had a crushed corner. That crushed corner really stuck out in my mind. It sort of blazed. I decided to take it up with the boss at the very top. I'll go right up to the top and complain. I'll go to the vice president. I then went up an extremely elegant stairway that had mahogany rails and marble floors. I was angry. I had been shuffled aside. They put it to me. Then I became confused about who I should complain to.

Tim's associations to the dream indicated clearly that his wife's impending death hurled him into a confrontation with his own. The outstanding image in the dream, the "blazing" crushed corner of the plywood box, reminded him of the crushed body of his automobile after a serious accident in which he had almost been killed. The plywood box also reminded him of the plain coffin he would have to order for his wife (according to Jewish burial ritual). In the dream it is he who finds himself in his wife's situation. He, too, cannot breathe. He, too, is pushed aside, trapped, crushed by something bearing down upon him. The major affect of the dream was anger and bafflement. He felt angry at the things happening to him, yet to whom could he issue a complaint? He awoke deeply confused about who, upstairs, would be the proper person to consult.

In therapy this dream opened up important vistas. It enabled the patient, who had been previously in a panic state, to sort out his feelings and to work on each cluster in a more meaningful way. He had been overwhelmed with death anxiety, with which he had attempted to cope by physically avoiding his wife and by compulsive sexuality. For example, he masturbated several times a day in bed next to his wife (I described this patient briefly in chapter 4). As we worked overtly on his anxiety about his own death, he was finally able to remain near his wife, comforting her by holding her and, in so doing, avoiding a considerable measure of guilt that would have ensued after her death.

After the death of his wife therapy focused both on the loss of his wife and on his own existential situation which his wife's death helped him to see more clearly. For example, he had always been achievement-oriented but, after his wife's death, began to ask: "For whom am I working?" "Who will see it?" Slowly Tim began to glimpse what his wife's constant nurturing and his obsession with sex had obscured for him: his isolation and his own finiteness. He was highly promiscuous after his wife's death, but gradually he grew disenchanted with the sexual chase and began to grapple with the question of what he wanted to do in life for himself. An enormously fertile period in therapy began, and in the course of the succeeding months Tim made substantial personal change.

The loss of a son or daughter is often the bitterest loss of all to us and we simultaneously mourn our child and ourselves. Life seems to hit us, at such a time, on all fronts at once. Parents first rail at the injustice in the universe but soon begin to understand that what seemed injustice is, in reality, cosmic indifference. They also are reminded of the limit of their power: there is no time in life when they have greater motivation to act and yet are helpless; they cannot protect a defenseless child. As night follows day, the bitter lesson follows that we, in our turn, will not be protected.

The psychiatric grief literature does not emphasize this dynamic but instead often focuses on the guilt (thought to be associated with unconscious hostility) that parents experience at the death of a child. Richard Gardner[10] studied parental bereavement empirically by systematically interviewing and testing a large sample of parents whose children suffered from some type of fatal illness. Though he confirmed that many parents suffered considerable guilt, his data indicated that the guilt, rather than emanating from "unconscious hostility," was four times more commonly an attempt by the parent to assuage his or her own existential anxiety, to attempt to "control the uncontrollable." After all, if

170

one is guilty about not having done something one should have done, then it follows that *there is something that could have been done*—a far more comforting state of affairs than the hard existential facts of life.

The loss of a child has another portentous implication for the parents. It signals the failure of their major immortality project: they will not be remembered, their seed will not take root in the future.

Milestones. Anything that challenges the patient's permanent view of the world can serve as a fulcrum with which the therapist can wedge open the patient's defenses and permit him a view of life's existential innards. Heidegger emphasizes that only when machinery suddenly breaks down do we become aware of its functioning.[11] Only when defenses against death anxiety are removed do we become fully aware of what they shielded us from. Therefore the therapist who looks may find existential anxiety lurking when any major event, expecially an irreversible one, occurs in a patient's life. Marital separation and divorce are prime examples of such events. These experiences are so painful that therapists often make the error of focusing attention entirely on pain alleviation and miss the rich opportunity that reveals itself for deeper therapeutic work.

For some patients, the commitment to a relationship, rather than the termination of one, acts as a boundary situation. Commitment carries with it the connotation of finality, and many individuals cannot settle into a permanent relationship because that would mean "this is it," no more possibilities, no more glorious dreams of continued ascendancy. In chapter 7 I shall discuss how irreversible decisions evoke existential anxiety precisely because they exclude other possibilities and confront the individual with the "impossibility of further possibility."

The passage into adulthood is often particularly difficult. Individuals in their late teens and early twenties are often acutely anxious about death. In fact, a clinical syndrome in adolescents called the "terror of life" has been described: it consists of marked hypochondriasis and preoccupation with the aging of the body, with the rapid passage of time, and with the inevitability of death.[12]

Therapists who treat medical residents (to take one example) sometimes note considerable existential anxiety in the thirtyish individual who is finally completing training and must, for the first time, shed a student identity and face the world as a grown-up. I have long observed that psychiatric residents, upon nearing completion of training, go through a period of major inner turmoil—a turmoil that has roots reaching far below such immediate concerns as finances, selection of an office and establishment of referral networks for private practice.

171

Jaques, in his wonderful essay "Death and the Mid-Life Crisis," stresses that the individual in midlife is especially bedeviled by the thought of death.[13] This is the time of life when a person may become preoccupied with the thought, often unconscious, that he or she "has stopped growing up and has begun to grow old." Having spent the first half of life in the "achievement of independent adulthood," one may reach the prime of life (Jung called age forty the "noon of life")[14] only to become acutely aware that death lies beyond. As one thirty-six-year-old patient, who had become increasingly aware of death in his analysis, put it: "Up till now, life has seemed an endless upward slope with nothing but the distant horizon in view. Now suddenly I seemed to have reached the crest of the hill, and there stretching ahead is the downward slope with the end of the road in sight—far enough away, it's true—but there is death observably present at the end." Jaques remarked upon the difficulty of working through the layers of death denial and gave an example of how he helped one patient become aware of death by analyzing his inability to mourn the death of friends.

A threat to one's career or the fact of retirement (especially in individuals who had believed that life was an ever-ascending spiral) can be a particularly potent catalyst for increasing one's awareness of death. A recent study of individuals making a midlife radical career shift suggests that most of them had made the decision to "drop out" or to simplify their lives in the context of a confrontation with their existential situation.[15]

Simple milestones, such as birthdays and anniversaries, can be useful levers for the therapist. The pain elicited by these signs of the passage of time runs deep (and for that reason is generally dealt with by reaction formation, in the form of a joyous celebration). Sometimes mundane reminders of aging offer an opportunity for increased existential awareness. Even a penetrating look in the mirror can open the issue. One patient told me that she said to herself, "I'm just a little gnome. I'm the same little Isabelle inside, but outside I'm an old lady. I'm sixteen going on sixty. I know it's perfectly all right for others to age, but somehow I never thought it would happen to me." The appearance of old people's characteristics, such as the loss of stamina or senile plaques on the skin, stiff joints, wrinkles, balding, or even the recognition that one enjoys "old people's" pleasures—watching, walking, serene quiet times—may act as a spur to death awareness. The same may be said about looking at old photographs of oneself and noting how one resembles one's parents when they were considered old, or seeing friends after long intervals and noting how they have aged. The therapist who listens carefully will be able to use any of these everyday occurrences. Or the therapist may tactfully contrive such situations. Freud, as I described in chapter 1, had no qualms about requesting Fraulein Elisabeth to meditate at the site of her sister's grave.

A careful monitoring of dreams and fantasies will invariably provide material to increase death awareness. Every anxiety dream is a dream of death; frightening fantasies involving such themes as unknown aggressors breaking into one's home always, when explored, lead to the fear of death. Discussions of unsettling television shows, movies, or books may similarly lead to essential material.

Severe illness is such an obvious catalyst that no therapist should let this opportunity pass by unmined. Noyes studied two hundred patients who had had near-death experiences through sudden illness or accident and found that a substantial number (25 percent) had a new and powerful sense of death's omnipresence and nearness. One of his subjects commented, "I used to think death would never happen or, if it did, I would be eighty years old. But now I realize it can happen any time, any place, no matter how you live your life. A person has a very limited perception of death until he is confronted with it." Another described his death awareness in these terms: "I have seen death in life's pattern and affirmed it consciously. I am not afraid to live because I feel that death has a part in the process of my being." Though a few of Noyes's subjects reported an increased terror of death and a greater sense of vulnerability, the great majority reported that their increased death awareness had been a positive experience resulting in a greater sense of life's preciousness and a constructive reassessment of their life's priorities.[16]

Artificial Aids to Increase Death Awareness. Though the naturally occurring reminders of death's presence are numerous, they are not, therapists often find, sufficiently potent to combat a patient's ever-vigilant denial. Consequently many therapists have sought vivid techniques to bring patients to face the fact of death. In the past, intentional and unintentional reminders of death were far more common than they are today. It was precisely for the purpose of reminding one of life's transiency that a human skull was a common furnishing in a medieval monk's cell. John Donne, the seventeenth-century British poet and clergyman, wore a funeral shroud when he preached "Look to eternity" to his congregation; and earlier, Montaigne, in his splendid essay "That to Philosophize Is to Learn How to Die," had much to say on the subject of intentional reminders of our finiteness:

> . . . we plant our cemeteries next to churches, and in the most frequented parts of town, in order (says Lycurgus) to accustom the common people, women and children, not to grow panicky at the sight of a dead man,

and so that the constant sight of bones, tombs, and funeral processions should remind us of our condition. . . . To feasts, it once was thought, slaughter lent added charms/Mingling with foods the sight of combatants in arms,/And gladiators fell amid the cups, to pour/Onto the very tables their abundant gore. . . . And the Egyptians, after their feasts, had a large image of death shown to the guests by a man who called out to them: "Drink and be merry, for when you are dead you will be like this."

So I have formed the habit of having death continually present, not merely in my imagination, but in my mouth. And there is nothing that I investigate so eagerly as the death of men: what words, what look, what bearing they maintained at that time; nor is there a place in the histories that I note so attentively. This shows in the abundance of my illustrative examples; I have indeed a particular fondness for this subject. If I were a maker of books, I would make a register, with comments, of various deaths. He who would teach men to die would teach them to live.[17]

Some therapists who have used LSD as an aid to psychotherapy speculate that an important mechanism of action is that LSD brings the patient into a dramatic confrontation with death.[18] Other therapists have suggested that shock therapy (electrical, Metrazol, and insulin) has its effect through a death-rebirth experience.[19]

Some encounter-group leaders have used a form of "existential shock" therapy by asking each member to write his or her own epitaph or obituary. "Destination" labs held for harried business executives commonly began with this structured exercise:

On a blank sheet of paper draw a straight line. One end of that line represents your birth; the other end, your death. Draw a cross to represent where you are now. Meditate upon this for five minutes.

This short, simple exercise almost invariably evokes powerful and profound reactions.

"Calling out" is an exercise* used in large groups to increase awareness of finiteness. The members are divided into triads and assigned a conversational task. Each individual's name is written on a slip of paper, placed in a bowl, and then randomly chosen and called aloud. An individual whose name is called stops talking and turns his back to the others. Many participants report that, as a result of this exercise, they have an increased awareness of the arbitrariness and the fragility of existence.

Some therapists and encounter-group leaders have used a guided

---

* Suggested by James Bugental.

fantasy technique to increase death awareness. Individuals are asked to imagine their deaths—"Where will it occur?" "When?" "How?" "Describe a detailed fantasy." "Imagine your funeral." A philosophy professor describes a number of exercises that he employs in the classroom to increase death awareness. For example, students are requested to write their obituaries (their "real" obituary and their "ideal" one), to record their emotional responses to a tragic story of the death of a six-year-old orphan, and to write the script for their own deaths.[20]

A "life cycle" group experience offered by Elliot Aronson and Ann Dreyfus, at the National Training Laboratory summer program at Bethel, Maine, helped the participants to focus on the major issues in each stage of life. In the time devoted to old age and death, these participants spent days living like old people. They were instructed to walk old, to dress old, to powder their hair and attempt to play elderly people they have known well. They visited a local cemetery. They walked alone in a forest, imagined passing out, dying, being discovered by friends, and being buried.[21]

Several death-awareness workshops have been reported that employ structured exercises designed to provide the individual with an encounter with his or her death.[22] For example, W. M. Whelan describes a workshop consisting of a single eight-hour, eight-member group session with the following format: (1) Members complete a death anxiety questionnaire and discuss anxiety-provoking items. (2) Members, in a state of deep muscle relaxation, fantasize in great detail, with awareness of all five senses, their own (comfortable) death. (3) Members are asked to construct a list of their values and then asked to imagine a situation in which a life-saving nuclear fallout shelter is able to save only a limited number of people: each member has to make an argument, on the basis of his or her value hierarchy, why he or she should be saved (this exercise was, according to the authors, designed to re-create Kübler-Ross's stage of bargaining!). (4) Again in a state of muscle relaxation, the members are asked to fantasize their own terminal illnesses, their inability to communicate, and, finally, their own funerals.[23]

Interaction with the Dying. As intriguing as many of these exercises are, they nonetheless are make-believe. Though one can be drawn into such an exercise for a period of time, denial quickly sets in, and one reminds oneself that one still exists, that one is merely observing these experiences. It was precisely because of the persistence and ubiquity of denial to assuage dread that several years ago I started to treat individuals with a fatal illness, individuals who were continually in the midst of urgent experience and could not deny what was happening to them.

175

My hope was not only to be useful to these patients but to be able to apply what I learned to the treatment of the physically healthy patient. (It is difficult to phrase that sentence because the very essence of this approach is that, from the very beginning of life, dying is a part of living. Consequently I shall use the phrase "everyday psychotherapy"— or better perhaps "psychotherapy of those not imminently dying.")

Group therapy sessions with terminal patients are often powerful with the evocation of much affect and the sharing of much wisdom. Many patients feel that they have learned a great deal about life but are frustrated in their efforts to be helpful to others. One patient put it, "I feel I have so much to teach, but my students will not listen." I have searched for ways to expose everyday psychotherapy patients to the wisdom and power of the dying and shall describe some limited experience with two different approaches: (1) inviting everyday psychotherapy patients to observe meetings of a group of terminally ill patients, and (2) introducing an individual with terminal cancer into an everyday psychotherapy group.

Observation of a terminal cancer group by everyday psychotherapy patients. One patient who observed a meeting of the group of cancer patients was Karen, whom I discussed in chapter 4. Karen's major dynamic conflict was her pervasive search for a dominant other—an ultimate rescuer—which took the form of psychic and sexual masochism. Karen would limit herself or inflict pain on herself, if necessary, to gain the attention and protection from some "superior" figure. The meeting she observed was particularly powerful. One patient, Eva, announced to the group that she had just learned she had a recurrence of cancer. She said that she had done something that morning that she had long postponed: she had written a letter to her children giving instructions about the division of minor sentimental items. In placing the letter in her safe deposit box, she realized with a clarity she had never before attained that indeed she would cease to be. As I described in chapter 4, she realized that when her children read that letter, she would not be there to observe or to respond to them. She wished, she said, that she had done her work on death in her twenties rather than waiting until now. Once one of her teachers had died (Eva was a school principal); and, rather than concealing the death from the students, she realized how right she had been to hold a memorial service and openly discuss death—the death of plants, animals, pets, and humans—with the children. Other group members, too, shared their moments of full realizations about their deaths, and some discussed the ways they had grown as a result of that realization.

176

An interesting debate developed as one member told about a neighbor who had been perfectly healthy and had died suddenly during the night. "That's the perfect death," she said. Another member disagreed and in a few moments had presented compelling reasons that that type of death was unfortunate: the dead woman had had no time to put her affairs in order, to complete unfinished business, to prepare her husband and her children for her death, to treasure the end of life as some of the members in the group had learned to do. "Just the same," the first quipped, "that's still the way I'd like to die. I've always loved surprises!"

Karen reacted strongly to the meeting she had observed. It was immediately thereafter that she arrived at the many deep insights about herself I described in chapter 4. For example, she realized that because of her fear of death, she had sacrificed much of her life. She had so feared death that she had organized her life around the search for an ultimate rescuer; therefore she had feigned illness during her childhood and stayed sick in adulthood to remain near her therapist. While observing the group, she realized with horror that she would have been willing to have cancer in order to be in that group and sit next to me, perhaps even hold my hand (the group ended with a hand-holding period of meditation). When I pointed out the obvious—that is, that no relationship is eternal, that I, as well as she, would die—she said that she felt that she would never be alone if she could die in my arms. The evocation and the subsequent working through of this material helped move Karen into a new phase of therapy, especially into a consideration of termination—an issue that previously she had never been willing to broach.

Another everyday therapy patient who observed the group was Susan, the wife of an eminent scientist who, when she was fifty, had sued her for divorce. In her marriage she had lived a mediated existence, serving him and basking in his accomplishments. Such a life pattern, not uncommon among wives of successful husbands in these days, had certain inevitable tragic consequences. First, she did not live her life; in her effort to build up credit with the dominant other she submerged herself, she lost sight of *her* wishes, her rights, and her pleasure. Secondly, because of the sacrifice of her own strivings, interests, desires, and spontaneity, she became a less stimulating partner and was considerably more at risk for divorce.

In our work Susan passed through a deep depression and gradually began to explore her *pro-active* feelings, not the reactive ones to which she had always limited herself. She felt her anger—deep, rich, and vibrant; she felt her sorrow—not at loss of her husband but at the loss of herself all those years; she felt outraged at all the restrictions to which she had consented. (For example, to ensure that her husband had optimal working conditions at home, she was not permitted to watch television, to speak on the phone, to garden while he was home—his study looked out on the garden and her presence distracted him.) She ran the risk of being overcome with regret for so much wasted life, and the task of therapy was to enable her to revitalize the remainder of her life. After two months of therapy she watched a poignant meeting of the cancer group, was moved by the experience, and immediately plunged into productive work which finally permitted her to understand that the divorce might be salvation rather than requiem. After therapy she moved to another city and several months later wrote a debriefing letter which included:

> First of all, I've thought that those women with cancer need not be reminded of the inevitability of death; that the awareness of death helps them to see things and events in their proper proportions and corrects our ordinarily poor sense of time. The life ahead of me may be very short. Life is precious, don't waste it! Make the most of every day in the ways you value! Reappraise your values! Check your priorities! Don't procrastinate! Do!
>
> I, for one, have wasted time. Every once in a while in the past, I'd feel vividly that I was only a spectator or an understudy watching the drama of life from the wings, but always hoping and believing that one day I'd be on the stage myself. Sure enough there had been times of intense living, but more often that not life seemed just a rehearsal for the "real" life ahead. *But what if death comes before the "real" life has started?* It would be tragic to realize when it's too late, that one has hardly lived at all.

Introduction of a patient facing death into an everyday psychotherapy group. "Death's rather like a certain kind of lecturer," wrote the novelist John Fowles. "You don't really hear what is being said until you're in the front row."[24] Some time ago I attempted to seat the seven members (who were all everyday psychotherapy patients) of a therapy group in the very first row by introducing into the group Charles, a patient with an incurable cancer.

Much data exists on this experiment. I wrote a detailed summary after each meeting, including a review both of the narrative flow and of process, and mailed it to the group members (a technique I have used in groups for many years).[25] In addition to these summaries I have my own personal records of the group. Furthermore, since ten psychiatric residents observed each meeting through a one-way mirror and discussed the meeting after each session, this group was heavily studied. From all these observations and records, I shall select and discuss some of the most salient issues arising in the first twelve months after Charles entered the group.

The group was an outpatient psychotherapy one, meeting once weekly for an hour and a half. It was an open group: as members improved and graduated, new members were introduced. At the time when Charles entered, two members had been in the group for two years, and four others had been there for periods of time ranging from three to eighteen months. The age range was from twenty-seven to fifty. The types of psychopathology of the members would generally be considered neurotic or characterologic, though two members had borderline traits.

Charles was a thirty-eight-year-old divorced dentist who, three months before consulting me, had learned that he had a form of cancer for which there was no medical or surgical cure. In our initial interview he stressed that he did not feel that he needed any help in coping with his cancer. He had spent many days in medical libraries, familiarizing himself with the course, the treatment, and the prognosis of his cancer. He arrived with a graph that he had drawn of his projected clinical course, and had concluded that he had approximately one and one half to three years of good, useful life ahead of him and, following that, a rapid one-year decline. I remember having two strong impressions during that initial interview. First, I marveled at his lack of manifest feelings: he seemed detached—as though he were talking about some stranger who had had the misfortune to contract a rare disease. Secondly, though I was jarred by his isolation from feeling, I was also struck by the fact that his detachment was serving him extraordinarily well in this instance. He stressed that he needed no help in dealing with his fear of death but wished assistance in getting more out of the life remaining to him. His cancer had caused him to take stock of the pleasures he was getting in life, and he realized that, aside from his work, he received few important gratifications. He especially wanted help in improving the quality of his relationship with other people. He felt distant from others and missed the personal closeness that he perceived so many others to enjoy. His relationship to a woman with whom he had lived for three years was severely strained, and he urgently wanted to be able to express, and receive, the love that existed between them only in chrysalis.

I had been looking for some time for a person with cancer to introduce into a general psychotherapy group, and Charles looked to be the perfect candidate. He wanted help in the very areas where the therapy group can most provide it; furthermore, I suspected that he would be of enormous assistance to others in the group. It was evident that Charles was not in the habit of asking for help: his request was creaking and awkward, but at the same time it was urgent and sincere and could not be refused.

The therapy of seven individuals interlocked in the network of a therapy group is highly complex; and over the next twelve months a marvelously intricate series of interpersonal and intrapersonal issues arose, were worked upon, and occasionally were worked through. I cannot, of course, describe all these events and shall instead place the beacon of attention upon Charles and upon the impact he and the other members had on one another.

To leap ahead of myself, I wish to state that the presence of an individual facing death did not bring the therapy group down: the atmosphere of the group did not become morbid, the feeling tone did not become blackened silk or the perspective limited and fatalistic. Charles gained a great deal from his work in the group, and in a number of ways his situation deepened the level of discourse for each of the other members. The group did not become monolithic but discussed the same wide array of life issues. In fact, there were times when mass denial was in operation, and for weeks on end Charles's cancer seemed all but forgotten by the members.

Self-disclosure is essential in psychotherapy—in group no less than in individual therapy. At the same time it is important that the members not experience the group as a forced confessional. Consequently, in my orientation session with Charles before he entered the group, I was careful to inform him (as I inform all incoming members) that to gain help from the group he would need to be wholly honest about both his physical condition and his psychological concerns—but that he should be so at his own pace. Charles, accordingly, attended the group for ten weeks before informing the group about his cancer. In retrospect, his decision to withhold this information was wise. The group never experienced Charles as a "cancer patient" but instead as a person who had cancer.

One of the basic axioms of interactional group therapy is that the group develops into a social microcosm for each of the members. Each person, sooner or later, begins to relate to the other members in the group in the same manner that he relates to individuals outside the group; each person, thus, carves out his or her own characteristic interpersonal niche. That rapidly occurred with Charles. In his first few meetings the group members began to note that he seemed either dis-

180

interested or critical and judgmental of many of their statements. They gradually learned that he was isolated, that he had difficulty getting close to people, that he could not experience or express his feelings, and that he was self-critical.

He was especially impatient and condescending to the women in the group. He considered one a "gadfly," "childish," or on other occasions "a lightweight" whose opinion did not matter a great deal to him. He was impatient with another woman because of her lack of a logical train of thought, and he generally dismissed her intuitive comments as "interference" or as "white noise" in the system. On one occasion when the other three men in the group were absent, Charles was almost entirely silent—not considering it worth his while to participate in a totally female group. The recognition, the understanding, and the resolution of his attitudes toward the female members were important in helping him to understand some of the basic issues of conflict between him and the woman with whom he lived.

Although these issues were salient to Charles's interpersonal conflict and led him into the areas upon which he wanted to work, there remained a great deal of puzzlement in the group. Periodically, over Charles's first several meetings, members would remark that they did not really *know* Charles, and that he seemed hidden, unreal, and distant to them. (Another axiom of group therapy is that when someone is keeping an important secret, he or she tends to be globally inhibited. The individual with the secret not only withholds the core secret but become careful about traversing any avenue that might conceivably lead to it.) Eventually, in the tenth session, the members and the therapists encouraged Charles to share more of himself, and he then discussed his cancer in much the same way that he had presented it in his pre-group individual sessions: detached, matter-of-fact, and with considerable scientific detail.

The group members responded to Charles's disclosure in highly individual fashion. Several talked about his courage and about the type of model he provided for them. One man was especially impressed at the way Charles talked about his goal of wanting to get as much as he could from the life remaining to him. This patient, Dave, became aware of how much he himself postponed life and of how little he savored his present life.

Two members had severe and inappropriate reactions. One, Lena (whom I described briefly in chapter 4), had lost both parents at an early age and had remained thereafter terrified of death. She sought for the protection of an ultimate rescuer and remained passive, dependent, and childlike. Lena, predictably, became frightened and responded in an angry almost bizarre fashion by assuming that Charles had the same type of cancer that had caused her mother's death and then, in a highly inappropriate fashion, described to the group in lurid detail the debilitating physical changes that had occurred in her mother. The other patient, Sylvia, a forty-year-old woman with massive death anxiety, immediately flared up angrily at Charles's passivity in the face of his disease. She berated him for not having investigated other possible sources of help: faith healers, Laetrile, Philippine psychic surgeons, megavitamins, and so forth. When one of the other members of the group came to Charles's rescue, a heated argument ensued. Sylvia was so frightened by Charles's cancer that she attempted to pick a fight in the hope that it would provide her with reasons to drop out of the group. Throughout the year Sylvia's response to Charles continued to be tumultuous. Her continued contact with him evoked great anxiety, which resulted in brief decompensation and eventual salubrious resolution. As Sylvia's clinical course illustrates vividly some important principles in the management and working through of death anxiety, I shall describe her treatment thoroughly later in this chapter.

Over the next four weeks several important events occurred in the group. One of the members, a pediatric nurse, described for the first time her close relationship with one of her patients, a ten-year-old child, who had died a few months previously. She was painfully aware of the fact that even in the short space of ten years that child had lived more fully than she. The death of the child in concert with Charles's terminal illness propelled her into trying to break out of her self-imposed restrictions and to increase the depth of her own life.

Another patient, Don, had been locked in a transference struggle with me for many months. Although he felt strong yearnings for my guidance and counsel, he felt himself defying me in a number of destructive ways. For example, he systematically arranged on many occasions to meet each of the members of the group outside for some type of social interaction. Although we had discussed on several occasions the fact that this sabotaged the work of the group, Don nonetheless felt that it was important for him to develop allies in the group against me. After Charles revealed to the group that he had cancer, Don began to feel quite differently toward me, and the tension and antagonism between us seemed visibly less. Don mentioned how much I had changed over the weeks since Charles had entered the group. He stated that he couldn't easily put it into words but then suddenly blurted out, "Somehow I know now that you're not immortal." He was able to discuss in detail some of his ultimate rescuer fantasies—the belief that I was infallible, that I was able to plot out his future with great certainty. He was able to express his anger at my apparent unwillingness to give him what I was capable of giving. Charles's presence reminded Don that I, as well as he, had to face death, that we were all united and equal in that way, that as Emerson somewhere said, "Let us keep cool for it will all be one in a hundred years." Suddenly his battle with me seemed foolish and trivial, and he and I soon became allies rather than combatants.

Lena's relationship to Charles was extraordinarily complex. She first found herself full of anger at him because of her anticipation of his leaving her, as her mother and father had done. She began to recall, for the first time, the events of her mother's death (when Lena was five) and repeatedly relived the experience in her mind. Her mother had become very emaciated before death; and during Charles's first few months in the group after his disclosure, Lena became anorexic and lost an alarming amount of weight. Lena's dynamics became much clearer: she felt so overwhelmed by the death of people close to her that she chose a state of suspended animation. Her formula was: "No friendships, no losses." She had four aged grandparents and lived in daily expectation of news of their death. Her dread was so great that she deprived herself of the pleasures of knowing and being close to them. She said once in the group, "I wish they'd all hurry up and die and get it over with." Gradually she broke the pattern and in a poignant manner allowed herself to reach out to Charles. She gingerly began to touch him by, for example, helping him off with his coat at the beginning of a meeting. Throughout, Charles remained the most important person in the group for Lena; and by accepting the fact that the deep pleasure she had in being close to him was worth the pain of the eventual separation, she was gradually able to establish other important relationships in her life. Eventually she was to profit considerably from the group experience with Charles. During their time together in the group she regained her lost weight, her suicidal yearnings disappeared, her depression lifted, and after three years of unemployment she obtained a responsible and gratifying job.

Another member derived another type of benefit from "sitting in the front row." She was divorced, had two small children, and generally felt suffused with resentment and impatience toward them. Only occasionally, when one of them was injured or sick, was she able to reach her positive tender feelings. Her relationship with Charles brought home to her, in vivid fashion, the passage of time and the finiteness of life. Gradually she was able to dip into the well of loving feelings toward her children without provocation of illnesses, accidents, or other stark reminders of mortality.

Although deep emotion was experienced in the group, there was never more affect present that could be assimilated and worked through. In large part, no doubt, this was a function of Charles's style. He rarely showed or appeared to experience deep affect. This was highly functional for the group work to the extent that it allowed titration of affect: emotion emerged slowly and in manageable degrees. Eventually, however, the time came for Charles's emotion-stifling style to come under direct surveillance. One meeting, a couple of months after Charles's revelation to the group, is particularly illustrative. Charles seemed pressured and began the meeting in an unusual way by stating that he had some specific questions he wished to ask the therapist. The questions were general, and his expectations of precise, authoritative answers were unrealistic. He asked for some specific techniques in order to overcome his distance from others, and he asked for a specific recommendation about how to resolve a conflict with his girlfriend. Charles posed these questions after the fashion of an efficient engineer and obviously anticipated answers in kind.

The group attempted to respond to Charles's questions, but he insisted on hearing from the group leader and impatiently dismissed the other members. They refused to be silenced, however, and shared their feelings of hurt and annoyance at being shut out. One member gently asked if the frantic quality of Charles's questions related to his sense of time running out and to a need to increase the efficiency of the process in the group. Gently, gradually, the group helped Charles talk about what had been brewing deep inside him over the past few days. With tears in his eyes, he revealed that he had been terribly shaken up by a couple of events: he had watched a long television movie on the death of a child from cancer and had, in connection with his profession as dentist, attended a long and "gruesome" conference on oral cancer.

With this information the group turned again to Charles's unusual behavior in the meeting. His insistence on a precise answer to his questions from the therapist was an expression of his wish to be taken care of. He went about it indirectly, he said, because he feared expressing "effusive" feelings openly. If effusive, smothering sentiments were offered him, he felt he would be mortified.

Charles's initial questions were answered in the meeting, not through "content" (that is, through specific suggestions by the therapist) but through an analysis of "process" (that is, through an analysis of his relationships to others). He learned that problems of intimacy with others, including his ex-wife and his girlfriend, were related to his stifling of his affect, his fear of "effusive" sentiments by others, his judgmentalism and dismissal of peers in the hopes of getting a systems-oriented solution from authority.

A few weeks later a similar episode occurred that corroborated and reinforced this instruction for Charles. He started the meeting in an obviously belligerent way. He was often upset by the amount of alimony he had to pay, and he remarked on a newspaper article that day demonstrating how women and divorce lawyers were exploiting helpless men. He then extended these remarks to the women in the group and in general belittled their contributions. When the group, once again, explored what had been happening to him, Charles described some highly emotional events of the last two days. His only child had just left home for college, and their last day together had been disappointing to Charles. He had so much wanted to tell his son how much he loved him. Yet they passed their last meal together in silence, and Charles felt despair at having lost this precious opportunity. Since his son's departure Charles had been preoccupied with "what's next?," with "everything seems terminal," and he felt that he was entering into a new, and final, phase of life. He did not fear death or pain, Charles said; what he really feared was disability and helplessness.

Obviously everyone shared Charles's fear of disability and helplessness; yet it had a particular terror for Charles whose dread of helplessness was evident in his reluctance to reveal vulnerability or to ask for help. In this particular meeting, rather than come to the group with an open description of his pain and a request for help, Charles had begun with a belligerent, distancing manner. His cancer would one day render him physically dependent on others, and he lived in dread of that day. Gradually the group helped allay that dread by, on numerous occasions, affording him the opportunity to disclose his feelings of vulnerability and to request help from the others.

One of the members of the group, Ron, who had been in the group for over two years, was obviously well enough to graduate and had been deliberating termination for some time. Furthermore, he was romantically involved with Irene, one of the female members; and as long as he was present, she found it difficult to make good use of the group. Whenever members of a therapy group form a subgroup or dyad and develop an allegiance to that subgroup which surpasses in importance their dedication to the primary task of the large therapy group, then therapeutic work becomes seriously impaired. This point had been reached with Ron and Irene; and at one meeting I not only supported Ron's decision to terminate the group but urged him to do so in such a forthright manner that it hastened his decision to terminate. The meeting after Ron's departure was tumultuous. Another axiom of small therapy groups is that members of a group who are exposed to a common stimulus will have highly individual responses to that stimulus. There can only be one possible explanation for this phenomenon: each of the members has a different internal world. Thus the investigation of varying responses to the same stimulus often provides a high yield in therapy.

The responses of Sylvia and Lena were especially striking. Both were extraordinarily threatened. They believed that I had kicked Ron out of the group—a view that was not held by the other members. Furthermore, they saw my decision as extremely arbitrary and unfair. They were angry; yet they feared to express their anger lest they, too, be thrown out of the group.

The work done on these feelings led into an investigation of Sylvia's and Lena's major defensive structures—a belief in deliverance by an ultimate rescuer. Both were so terrified of being abandoned by me that they took great pains to appease and placate me. In order to stay near me, they both, at an unconscious level, resisted getting well and, at a conscious level, declined to report to the group any change that might be construed as positive. Charles's presence in the group brought much closer to the fore their fears of abandonment and, beneath that, of death. Both Lena and Sylvia gradually realized that they had overreacted to the situation—that Ron's departure was the proper decision for Ron and for the group, and that no one else felt fearful about being thrown out of the group. Eventually they understood that their reaction to this incident was reflective of their general behavior, of their dependency, their fear of abandonment, and their self-crippling tendencies.

Charles's reaction to Ron's leaving was also very stong, as was his later reaction to other members in the group preparing to terminate. He said that it actually provoked a physical pain right in the middle of his chest. It was as though something were being wrenched away from him, and he felt extremely threatened at the possible dissolution of the group. In one meeting Charles—the same Charles who a few months previously had said that he was sterile emotionally, and that no one meant anything to him—told the group how much they meant to him and, with tears streaming down his face, thanked them for, as he put it, saving his life.

On one occasion a young man in the group made the curious statement that he envied Charles for having a fatal illness; if he, too, had a fatal illness, he might be plunged into making something more of his life. The group was quick to remind the young man he did indeed have a fatal illness, and that the difference between Charles and the others was simply the difference between sitting in the front, rather than in the back, row. Frequently Charles attempted to bring that point home to the others in the group. On one memorable occasion one of the older members lamented that he had "wasted" his life: there had been so many missed opportunities, so many undeveloped potential friend-ships, so many untapped career possibilities. He was full of self-pity and avoided experiencing the present by a remorseful trudging about in the past. Charles was especially effective by pointing out forcefully to him that while he had not wasted his life, he was at that very mo-ment in the process of "wasting" it.

The group members would from time to time suddenly be reminded that Charles had cancer and was going to die in the not too distant fu-ture. Periodically each was thrown into a confrontation with Charles's death and his or her own as well. One member who had always denied death commented that Charles's hunger for life, his courage, and his mode of dealing with his death had given her strength and a model for both living and dying.

At the time of this writing Charles continues to be an active member of the group. He has long outlived his prognosis and is in good phys-ical condition. Moreover, he has achieved his original goals in therapy. He feels more human and is no longer isolated: he relates far more openly and intimately with others. He entered couples' therapy with his girlfriend; and his relationship to her vastly improved. His pres-ence in the group has touched almost all the members in profound ways; their experience with Charles shifted each of them from a preoc-cupation with a relatively narrow band of existence toward a desire to plunge into life in all its breadth and intensity.

Death as a Primary Source of Anxiety

The concept of death provides the psychotherapist with two major forms of leverage. I have discussed the first: that death is of such mo-mentous importance that it can, if properly confronted, alter one's life perspective and promote a truly authentic immersion in life. The second, to which I shall now turn my attention, is based on the premise that the fear of death constitutes a primary source of anxiety, that it is present early in life, is instrumental in shaping character structure, and continues throughout life to generate anxiety that results in manifest distress and in the erection of psychological defenses.

First, some general therapeutic principles. It is important to keep in mind that death anxiety, though it is ubiquitous and has pervasive ramifications, exists at the deepest levels of being, is heavily repressed, and is rarely experienced in its full sense. Death anxiety per se is not easily evident in the clinical picture of most patients; nor does it often become an explicit theme in the therapy, especially not in brief therapy, of most patients. Some patients are, however, suffused with overt death anxiety from the very onset of therapy. There are also life situations in which the patient has such a rush of death anxiety that the therapist, try as he or she might, cannot evade the issue. Furthermore, in long-term intensive therapy which explores deep levels of concern, explicit death anxiety is always to be found and must be considered in the therapeutic process.

Since death anxiety is so intimately tied to existence, it has a different connotation from "anxiety" in other frames of reference. Though the existential therapist hopes to alleviate crippling levels of anxiety, he or she does not hope to eliminate anxiety. Life cannot be lived nor can death be faced without anxiety. Anxiety is guide as well as enemy and can point the way to authentic existence. The task of the therapist is to reduce anxiety to comfortable levels and then to use this existing anxiety to increase a patient's awareness and vitality.

Another major point to keep in mind is that, even though death anxiety may not explicitly enter the therapeutic dialogue, a theory of anxiety based on death awareness provides the therapist with a frame of reference, an explanatory system, that may greatly enhance his or her effectiveness.

REPRESSION OF DEATH ANXIETY

In chapter 2 I described a head-on automobile collision where, had circumstances been less fortunate, I would have lost my life. My response to that accident serves as a transparent model for the workings of death anxiety in neurotic reactions. Recall that within a day or two I no longer experienced any explicit death anxiety but instead noted a specific phobia surrounding luncheon discussions. What happened was that I "handled" death anxiety by repression and displacement. I bound anxiety to a specific situation. Rather than being fearful of death or of nothingness, I became anxious about something. Anxiety is always ameliorated by becoming attached to a specific object or situation. Anxiety attempts to become fear. Fear is fear of some thing; it has a location in time and space; and, because it can be located, it can be tolerated and even "managed" (one may avoid the object or develop some systematic plan of conquering one's fear); fear is a current sweeping over one's surface—it does not threaten one's foundation.

I believe that this course of events is not uncommon. Death anxiety is deeply repressed and not part of our everyday experience. Gregory Zilboorg, in speaking of the fear of death, said: "If this fear were constantly conscious, we should be unable to function normally. It must be properly repressed to keep us living with any modicum of comfort."[26]

No doubt the repression, and subsequent invisibility, of death anxiety is the reason that many therapists neglect its role in their work. But surely the same state of affairs applies to other theoretical systems. The therapist always works with tracings of and defenses against primal anxiety. How often, for example, does an analytically oriented therapist encounter explicit castration anxiety? Another source of confusion is that the fear of death can be experienced at many different levels. One may, for example, consider death dispassionately and intellectually. Yet this adult perception is by no means the same as the dread of death that resides in the unconscious, a dread that is formed early in life at a time prior to the development of precise conceptual formulation, a dread that is terrible and, inchoate and exists outside of language and image. The original unconscious nucleus of death anxiety is made more terrifying yet by the accretion of a young child's horrible misconceptions of death.

As a result of repression and transformation, existential therapy deals with anxiety that seems to have no existential referent. Later in this chapter I shall discuss patients who have much overt death anxiety and also how layers of explicit death anxiety must always be reached through long and intensive therapy. But even in those courses of therapy where death anxiety never becomes explicit, the paradigm based on death anxiety may enhance the therapist's effectiveness.

The Therapist Is Provided with a Frame of Reference That Greatly Enhances His or Her Effectiveness.   As nature abhors a vacuum, we humans abhor uncertainty. One of the tasks of the therapist is to increase the patient's sense of certainty and mastery. It is a matter of no small importance that one be able to explain and order the events in our lives into some coherent and predictable pattern. To name something, to locate its place in a causal sequence, is to begin to experience it as under our control. No longer, then, is our internal experience or behavior frightening, alien or out of control; instead, we behave (or have a particular inner experience) because of something we can name or identify. The "because" offers one mastery (or a sense of mastery that phenomenologically is tantamount to mastery). I believe that the sense of potency that flows from understanding occurs even in the matter of our basic existential situation: each of us feels less futile, less helpless, and less alone, even when, ironically, what we come to understand is the fact that each of us is basically helpless and alone in the face of cosmic indifference.

In the previous chapter I presented an explanatory system of psychopathology based on death anxiety. The importance of such an explanatory system is as important for the therapist as it is for the patient. Every therapist uses an explanatory system—some ideological frame of reference—to organize the clinical material with which he or she is faced. Even if the therapist's explanatory system is so complex and abstract and so rooted in unconscious structures that it cannot be explicitly transmitted to the patient, it nonetheless enhances the therapist's effectiveness in numerous ways.

First, a belief system provides therapists with a sense of security for the same reasons that explanation is useful to patients. By allowing the therapist to control, and not be overwhelmed by, a patient's clinical material, a belief system enhances a therapist's self-confidence and sense of mastery and results in the patient's developing trust and confidence in the therapist—an essential condition for treatment. Furthermore, a therapist's belief system often serves to augment his or her interest in a patient—an interest that vastly facilitates the development of the necessary therapist-patient relationship. For example, I believe that the search for a genetic causal explanation (that is, "Why from the standpoint of a patient's past history is that patient the way he or she is?") is a wrong steer in the therapeutic process; nevertheless, the explanation of the past often serves an important function in therapy: it provides therapist and patient with a joint, purposeful project, an intellectual bone to gnaw upon, which brings them together and keeps them cemented to one another while the real agent of change, the therapeutic relationship, germinates and matures.

The therapist's belief system provides consistency to his or her remarks to patients: it permits the therapist to know what to explore and what *not* to push, so that he or she does not confuse a patient. Even if the therapist does not make full and explicit interpretations about the unconscious roots of a patient's problems, the therapist may still, with subtlety and good timing, make comments that, at a deep unspoken level, "click" with the patient's unconscious and allow the latter to feel completely understood. A belief system that is deeply rooted, grounded in fact in the deepest levels of being, has the particular advantage of conveying to the patient that there are *no* taboo areas, that any topic may be discussed, and, furthermore, that his deepest concerns are not idiosyncratic but are shared by all human beings.

The therapist's sense of certainty issuing from an explanatory system of psychopathology has a benefit for therapy which is curvilinear in nature. There is an optimal amount of therapist certainty: too little *and* too much are counterproductive. Too little certainty, for reasons already discussed, retards the formation of the necessary level of trust. Too *much* certainty, on the other hand, becomes rigidity. The therapist rejects or distorts data that will not fit into his system; furthermore, the therapist avoids facing, and helping the patient to face, one of the core concepts in existential therapy—that uncertainty exists, and that all of us must learn to coexist with it.

INTERPRETATIVE OPTIONS: AN ILLUSTRATIVE CASE STUDY

In chapter 4 I described some general existential dynamics underlying common clinical syndromes involving death anxiety, I shall present here specific interpretative options in a case of compulsive sexuality.

Bruce was a middle-aged male and had since adolescence been continually, as he put it, "on the prowl." He had had sexual intercourse with hundreds of women but had never cared deeply for any one of them. Bruce did not relate to a woman as to a whole person but as a "piece of ass." The women were more or less interchangeable. The important thing was bedding a woman—but, once orgasm was reached, he had no particular desire to remain with her. It was not unusual, therefore, once a woman had left, for him to go out searching for another, sometimes only minutes later. The compulsive quality of his behavior was so clear that it was evident even to him. He was aware often of "needing" or "having" to pursue a woman when he did not wish to.

Now Bruce could be understood from many perspectives, none of which had exclusive hegemony. The oedipal overtones were clearly evident: he desired but feared women who resembled his mother. He was usually impotent with his wife. The closer he came in his travels to the city his mother inhabited, the stronger was his sexual desire. Furthermore, his dreams groaned with incestuous and castration themes. There was also evidence that his compulsive heterosexuality was powered by the need to handle the eruption of unconscious homosexual impulses. Bruce's self-esteem was severely impaired, and the successful seduction of women could be understood as an attempt to bolster his self-worth. Still another perspective: Bruce had both a need and a fear of closeness. The sexual encounter, at once closeness and caricature of closeness, honored both the need and the fear.

During more than eight years of analysis and several courses of therapy with competent therapists, all of these explanations, and many others besides, were explored fully, but without effect on his compulsive sexual drive.

During my work with Bruce I was struck by the rich, unmined existential themes. Bruce's compulsivity could be understood as a shield against confrontation with his existential situation. For example, it was apparent that Bruce was fearful of being alone. Whenever he was away from his family, Bruce took great pains to avoid spending an evening alone.

Anxiety can be a useful guide, and there are times when the therapist and patient must openly court anxiety. Accordingly, when Bruce had increased his ability to tolerate anxiety, I suggested that he spend an evening entirely alone and record his thoughts and feelings. What transpired that night was exceedingly important in his therapy. Raw terror is the best term for the experience. He encountered, for the first time since childhood, his fear of the supernatural. By sheer chance there was a brief power failure and Bruce grew terrified of the dark. He imagined that he saw a dead woman lying on the bed (resembling the old woman in the film *The Exorcist*); he imagined he saw a death's head in the window; he feared that he might be touched by "something, perhaps a hand of a skeleton all dressed in rags." He gained enormous relief from the presence of a dog and for the first time realized the strong bond between some individuals and their pets: "What is needed," he said, "is not necessarily a human companion but something alive near you."

The terror of that evening was gradually, through the work of therapy, transformed into insight. Spending an evening alone made the function of sex abundantly clear. Without the protection of sex Bruce encountered massive death anxiety: the images were vivid—a dead woman, a skeleton's hand, a death's head. How did sex protect Bruce from death? Through a number of ways, each of which we analyzed in therapy. Sexual compulsivity, like every symptom, is overdetermined. For one thing sex was a form of death defiance. There was something frightening about sex for Bruce; no doubt sex was deeply entangled with buried incestuous yearnings and with fears of retaliatory castration—and by "castration" I mean not literal castration but annihilation. Thus the sexual act was counterphobic. Bruce stayed alive by jamming his penis into the vortex of life. Viewed in this way, Bruce's sexual compulsivity dovetailed with his other passions—parachuting, rock climbing, and motorcycling.

Sex also defeated death by reinforcing Bruce's belief in his personal specialness. Bruce stayed alive, in one sense, by being the center of his universe. Women revolved about him. All over the world women adored him. They existed for him alone. Bruce never thought of them as having independent lives. He imagined they remained in suspended animation for him; that, like Joseph K.'s flagellators in Kafka's *The Trial*, they were there for him every time he opened their doors, and that they froze into immobility when he did not call upon them. And of course sex served the function of preventing the conditions necessary for a true confrontation with death. Bruce never had to face the isolation that accompanies the awareness of one's personal death. Women were "something alive and near," much like the dog on the night of his terror. Bruce was never alone, he was always in the midst of coitus (a frenetic effort to fuse with a woman), searching for a woman, or just having left a woman. Thus, his search for a woman was not truly a search for sex, nor even a search powered by infantile forces, by "the stuff from which" as Freud liked to say "sex will come,"[27] but instead it was a search to enable Bruce to deny and to assuage his fear of death.

Later in therapy an opportunity arose for him to go to bed with a beautiful woman who was the wife of his immediate boss. He deliberated about this chance and discussed it with a friend who counseled him against taking it because it might have destructive ramifications. Bruce also knew that the toll he would have to pay in anxiety and guilt would be prohibitive. Finally with a mighty wrench he, for the first time in his life, decided to forgo the sexual conquest. In our next therapy hour I agreed with him that he was acting indeed in his best interests.

His reaction to his decision was enlightening. He accused me of taking his life's pleasures away from him. He felt "done for," "finished." The following day, at a time when he could have had a sexual assignation, he read a book and sunbathed. "This is what Yalom wanted," he thought, "for me to grow old, sit in the sun and bleach like an old dog turd." He felt lifeless and depressed. That night he had a dream that illuminates better than any dream I have known the use of dream symbolism:

I had a beautiful bow and arrow, I was proclaiming it as a great work of art that possessed magical qualities. You and X [a friend] differed and pointed out that it was just a very ordinary bow and arrow. I said, "No, it's magic, look at those features, and these!" [pointing at two protuberances]. You said, "No, it's very ordinary." And you proceeded to demonstrate to me how simply the bow was constructed, how simple twigs and bindings accounted for its shape.

What Bruce's dream illustrates so beautifully is another way that sex is death defeating. Death is connected with banality and ordinariness. The role of magic is to allow one to transcend the laws of nature, to transcend the ordinary, to deny one's creaturely identity—an identity that condemns one to biological death. His phallus was an enchanted bow and arrow, a magic wand lifting him above natural law. Each affair magically constituted a mini-life; although each of his affairs was a maze ending in a cul-de-sac, his affairs, all of them taken together, provided him with the illusion of a constantly lengthening life line.

As we worked through the material generated by his taking these two stands—spending time alone and *not* accepting a sexual invitation—a great deal of insight ensued to illuminate not only his sexual pathology but many other aspects of his life. For example, he had always related to others in a highly limited, sexual way. When his sexual compulsiveness waned, he began for the first time to confront the question, What are people for?—a question that launched a valuable exploration of Bruce's confrontation with existential isolation. I shall discuss this phase of Bruce's therapy in chapter 9. Indeed, Bruce's course of therapy illustrates the interdependence of all the ultimate concerns. Bruce's decision, and his subsequent reluctance to accept that decision, to pass up a sexual invitation was the tip of the iceberg of another extraordinarily important existential concern, freedom, and especially of the issue of assuming responsibility—the theme of chapter 6. Lastly, Bruce's eventual relinquishment of his sexual compulsion confronted him with another ultimate concern—meaninglessness. With the removal of his major *raison d'être*, Bruce began to confront the problem of purpose in life—the subject of chapter 9.

DEATH ANXIETY IN LONG-TERM THERAPY

Though brief courses of therapy often entirely circumvent any explicit consideration of death anxiety, any long-term intensive therapy will be incomplete without working through awareness and fear of death. As long as a patient continues to attempt to ward off death through an infantile belief that the therapist will deliver him or her from it, then the patient will not leave the therapist. "As long as I am with you, I will not die" is the unspoken refrain that so often emerges in late stages of therapy.

May Stern, in an important article, describes six patients mired in an interminable analysis.[28] In each instance the working through of death anxiety brought the analysis to a successful conclusion. One representative patient was a thirty-eight-year-old obsessive-compulsive male with symptoms of insomnia, nightmares, hypochondriasis, and the obsessive fantasy occurring in sexual relations that he was being sat upon and breathed into. Much analytic work had been done on oedipal and preoedipal levels. The meaning of his symptoms in terms of castration anxiety, incestuous feminine identification, pregenital regression, oral incorporation, and so forth had been explored, but without therapeutic effect. Only when the analyst moved to a deeper level—the meaning of his symptoms in the context of death fear—did the clinical picture alter.

> Finally, transference material referring to a wish to get from the analyst a magical formula elicited the interpretation that he conceived of analysis as protection against fear of death, and that no one was able to protect him against inevitable death. This interpretation effected a surprising, almost dramatic turn. It brought into analysis his permanent fears of dying manifested in his hypochondriacal complaints, his desperate struggle with the fear of nothingness in the beginning of his latency period, and his wish to stay forever in analysis.

Another patient who had many self-destructive symptoms—gambling, drinking, continual quarreling, and masochistic sexual trends—also had had little success in a lengthy analysis.

> In analysis, no technical device was able to make him give up acting out the fantasy that by his perverse activities he would arouse the anger of the analyst, which to him meant being beaten. Any interpretation by the analyst was used for gratification of his wish to be scolded and beaten; silence was interpreted as the sullen response of the angered father. His analysis seemed to have reached an impasse. . . . Finally, the therapist interpreted that through fusion with the analyst (father), he wanted to win protection against death. This interpretation brought out a wealth of material hitherto withheld. "Death is and always was around me." He remembered having thought a lot about death as a child. "I have solved my fear of death through submission. . . . Being raped anally is protection against death." He resented that this had not been pointed out to him earlier.

In this case, as in the first, the working through of transference was the *via regia* to the subterranean layers of death anxiety. The historical view of transference (that is, the transfer of affect from some prior cathexis to a current one) is of only limited value in the actual process of therapy. What is important is the immediate, here-and-now function of the patient's distortion. Stern's patient learned that he used the therapist as a shield against current death awareness and fear. Gradually he confronted his death and grew to understand that not only his transference but his symptoms, too, represented infantile magical ways of warding off death (for example, drinking represented "symbolic ecstatic fusion with mother as a defense against death").

Each of these patients underwent subsequent marked improvement, but the author was careful to note that "the dramatic turn in the treatment situation of these patients might be due to the fact that the interpretation of fear of death was introduced after years of tedious working through, after a possible termination of the analysis had appeared on the horizon." In every neurotic individual there is a substratum of death anxiety, which can be worked through in extensive therapy—a process that the therapist facilitates by interpreting both the patient's symptoms and the transference as an attempt to cope with death.

Death cannot be ignored in an extensive venture of self-exploration, because a major task of the mature adult is to come to terms with the reality of decline and diminishment. *The Divine Comedy*, which Dante wrote in his late thirties, may be understood on many allegorical levels, but certainly it reflects its author's concern about his personal death. The opening verses describe the fearful confrontation with one's own mortality that frequently occurs in midlife.

> In the middle of the course of our life, I came to myself within a dark wood, having lost the direct way. Ah, how difficult it is to describe what that wood was like, thick and savage and harsh, just the thought of which renews my fear.[29]

Individuals who have had significant emotional distress in their lives, and whose neurotic defenses have resulted in self-restriction, may encounter exceptionally severe difficulty in midlife, the time when aging and impending death must be recognized. The therapist who treats a patient in midlife must remind himself or herself that much psychopathology emanates from death anxiety. Jaques, in his essay on the midlife crisis, states this clearly:

> A person who reaches mid-life, either without having successfully established himself in marital and occupational life, or having established himself by means of manic activity and denial with consequent emotional impoverishment, is badly prepared for meeting the demands of middle age, and getting enjoyment out of his maturity. In such cases, the

mid-life crisis, and the adult encounter with the conception of life to be lived in the setting of an approaching personal death, will likely be experienced as a period of psychological disturbance and depressive breakdown. Or breakdown may be avoided by means of a strengthening of manic defenses, with a warding off of depression and persecution about aging and death, but with an accumulation of persecutory anxiety to be faced when the inevitability of aging and death eventually demands recognition.

The compulsive attempts, in many men and women reaching middle age, to remain young, the hypochondriacal concern over health and appearance, the emergence of sexual promiscuity in order to prove youth and potency, the hollowness and lack of genuine enjoyment of life, and the frequency of religious concern are familiar patterns. They are attempts at a race against time.[30]

DEATH ANXIETY AS A MAJOR SYMPTOM: A CASE STUDY

Often therapists encounter patients for whom death anxiety plays so central and explicit a role that no inferential leaps are needed. These patients are often trying, because their therapists, once they realize that there is no getting around the issue of death, become uncomfortably aware that they have no conceptual tools to guide them in their work.

Such a patient was Sylvia, who was mentioned earlier in this chapter as a member of the therapy group into which Charles, the patient with advanced cancer, was introduced. Sylvia was a divorced, thirty-six-year-old wealthy architect who had been in psychotherapy on and off over the previous ten years. She was alcoholic, chronically depressed, anxious, obese, lonely, and subject to a wide variety of psychophysiological complaints, including headaches, urticaria, back pain, hearing difficulties, and asthma. She was involved in a severe conflict with her thirteen-year-old daughter and with two older children who, because of her alcoholism and unpredictable behavior, had elected to live with their father. Her previous therapy (individual, group, and family formats) had effected little improvement. A year and a half of therapy in a specialized group for alcoholics had helped Sylvia gain some control over her drinking. In most other ways, though, she remained on a plateau of stress; and therapy was merely a "holding operation."

Charles's entrance into the therapy group (where she had been a member for several months) radically altered the course of her therapy. It forcibly confronted her with the idea of death; and some important themes hitherto overlooked emerged in her clinical picture.

Sylvia's first reaction when Charles informed the group that he had incurable cancer was irrational. Earlier I described her strong anger at him for passively giving in to cancer and not seeking other than conventional medical modes of help. A couple of weeks after Charles had informed the group about his cancer, Sylvia had a panic reaction. She had bought a new leather sofa for her home but was strangely distressed by its smell. Furthermore she had a house guest who was an artist, and she became convinced that the fumes from the oil paints were toxic. That evening she developed a slight rash on her face and in the middle of the night woke up in severe panic, convinced that she was going to die as a result of respiratory failure caused by an allergic reaction to the sofa and to the paint fumes. She grew more and more frightened and finally called an ambulance in the middle of the night. She began drinking again and, three weeks after Charles's entrance, was arrested for drunken driving. She stated that her driving was a form of suicide; she felt that suicide was a mode of achieving some mastery over death because it gives one an active control of one's fate rather than waiting for "something horrible to engulf you." Her anxiety level continued high for several weeks, and she was so uncomfortable that she raised the question of leaving the therapy group. At the same time she developed the conviction that "her number was up in the group," and that I was trying to get rid of her. When, because of her continued headaches, I referred her to an internist for a physical examination, she went into an acute depression and interpreted this referral as my saying to her that I refused to take care of her any more and was sending her to someone else. When new people were introduced into the group, she was convinced that they were being brought in to replace her.

After her initial anxiety subsided, Sylvia stopped avoiding Charles and began to make contact with him, at first in a tentative and then in a much more positive manner. There was meetings in which Charles was depressed or anxious, and it was Sylvia who, of all the members, found the courage to wonder aloud whether Charles was concerned about his cancer or about time running out. Gradually Sylvia began thinking and talking more about some of her central concerns: aging, her fear of getting cancer, her dread of loneliness. She became preoccupied with her mother's death and began thinking about the events around it with greater detail and more intensity than she had for the last fifteen years. These themes had always been present; yet they had never been formally worked on in her therapy.

Sylvia's case provides wonderful proof of how the therapist's frame of reference controls the content of the material provided by the patient. For example, Sylvia had had severe insomnia for fifteen years and had been treated by many clinicians with a variety of approaches and a vast number of sedatives. A few weeks after Charles entered the group, she again described her intractable insomnia but this time, because the therapist was tuned to a different channel, she added the information that for years she had awakened virtually every night between 2:00 and 4:00 A.M. in a sweat, saying to herself, "I don't want to die, I don't want to die." In her previous ten years of therapy (including two years with me) she had never told that to a therapist!

When I invoked death anxiety as a central organizing principle, many disparate symptoms and events fell into a coherent pattern. Sylvia's panic attacks, which often initiated eating and drinking binges, were almost invariably precipitated by some type of insult to her body, some suggestion of physical illness or deterioration. Sylvia's death anxiety was always greatest when she was alone. The implicit message she delivered to her thirteen-year-old daughter was "Don't grow up and leave me. I can't bear to be alone. I need you to stay as young as you are and to remain with me. If you don't grow up, I won't grow older." This message seriously affected her daughter, who displayed severe delinquent behavior.

Sylvia's chief mechanism of defense against her anxiety was her belief in the existence of an ultimate rescuer, a belief that lay at the root of her pervasive orality (manifested in part by her alcoholism and obesity) and was particularly evident in her relationship toward therapy and her therapists. She was perpetually obsequious and deferential to them. She feared nothing more than the possibility of being rejected or abandoned by them. To this end she exaggerated her needfulness, concealed any positive gains that she made, and often presented herself as exaggeratedly confused and helpless. Her task in therapy was, it seemed, to present herself, through a number of strategies, as so enfeebled that the therapist would be forced to take her in hand and give her succor.

The more Sylvia confronted these issues, the higher her anxiety mounted. Soon she was so uncomfortable that she needed to be seen more frequently than once a week in the group meeting. I saw her for a series of individual sessions in which we did a focal analysis of her death concerns.

The death of her mother had been the most painful event of Sylvia's life, and she could not think about it without horror. Her mother had developed cancer of the cervix, and at the age of twenty-five, Sylvia left her family, flew to her mother's bedside, and nursed her for the last month of her life. Her mother at this point was either unconscious or in a highly irrational state of consciousness, where she was hallucinatory and very paranoid. Without bladder or bowel control, her mother needed Sylvia's continual nursing. Finally, in the mist of excrement and overwhelming stench, with gurgling sounds in her throat and with blood and mucous running out of her mouth, her mother died. Sylvia remembers feeling at that time that her head was disconnected from her body, that it was swelling and would split apart (similar to the headaches she experienced after Charles entered the group).

Sylvia has many frightening childhood memories about death. Her grandfather had died when she was seven, and her grandmother six months later. She remembers seeing her grandmother in the casket and remembers her conviction that they had cut her grandmother's throat. (In retrospect, she thinks her grandmother had had thyroid surgery.) When she was twelve a schoolmate drowned, and she went to his funeral—also a very frightening experience for her.

Sylvia herself had been a sickly child and was told on many occasions by her mother (and recalls her mother telling friends and relatives) how close she had come to dying when young. She had several bouts with pneumonia in the first five years of her life. At the age of six she had a broken arm and chronic osteomyelitis. She required surgery at that time and remembers with great dread the suffocating ether cone. Ever since than she had had severe anxiety with anesthesia. During the birth of each of her children the anesthesia evoked so much death anxiety that she had brief psychotic episodes.

Her earliest memory is of "being dead" as a very young child, and of an aunt massaging her legs, perhaps trying to bring her back to life. She thinks she may have been in a coma and remembers that her aunt was crying. She also remembers that every time her body was touched, she felt intense pain but could not speak or communicate in any other way to ask her aunt to stop massaging her. A second early memory is a recollection of being dead and floating out of her body and trying desperately, but in vain, to rejoin it.

In addition to these early sensitizing experiences, which exposed her to death "too much and too soon," several other important factors in Sylvia's life prevented her from building traditional defenses against death terror. She had no sense of reliance on either her mother or her father. Her father deserted the family when she was a young child, and her recollection of her mother is that she was undependable and irresponsible. Her mother panicked at any sickness or physical injury and called in some other member of the family to do the necessary nursing if anyone was ill. Her mother had not been available to her emotionally or physically: even when Sylvia was a preadolescent, the mother left home, presumably with a man, for days on end, leaving the family entirely in Sylvia's care. Her mother faced her own death with unrelenting terror and provided Sylvia with a model that sensitized her even more to a fear of death. (Many patients report that their parents' mode of facing death is extremely important in shaping their own attitudes toward death. There are, in this observation, some obvious implications for the treatment of the dying patient: one way to maintain meaning in life until the very end is to consider the model one sets for others.)

Sylvia's death anxiety was obviously overdetermined. Not only had she had too much, too soon—early life-threatening experiences and frequent reminders of her close brush with death by her mother—but she also was not able to develop traditional denial-based defenses against death anxiety. She could not expect protection or rescue from her parents: her father had, in effect, died, and her mother was herself overwhelmed by life. She could neither exile death to a distant realm nor develop credence in her own inviolability. Death was an imminent presence, it had almost snared her on more than one occasion, and she viewed herself as very vulnerable and very fragile.

Sylvia remembers trying to take solace in religious doctrine and pleading with her grandmother to prove to her that there was a God, because if there were, He would prevent her from dying or take care of her when she died. She was raised a Southern Baptist with all that religion's hell and brimstone accouterments. On several occasions when she was ill as a child she had made a bargain with God: "Spare my life, and I will become a nun and devote my life to you." Now, decades later, Sylvia still brooded over her betrayal of that contract.

Our individual sessions devoted to death anamnesis were productive, and Sylvia became much more aware of the extent of her fear of death and of the role this fear played in her life. As she proceeded in the therapy group, she became aware of her terror of growing old and of her exceedingly maladaptive defense, which consisted of a "freeze and camouflage" maneuver. In other words, she suspended living and growing, in the magical hope that death might simply overlook her. She neglected her physical appearance and spent evenings and weekends vegetating. She had become increasingly obese because of some magical belief that, if she could avoid becoming thin and emaciated like her mother, then she could avoid death. (Hattie Rosenberg describes identical dynamics in one of her patients.[31]) Her suspension of living was brought home to her in the group when one of the men brought her flowers on her birthday. She caught her breath as she became aware of how much she wanted a lover, and of how much she had missed over the last several years by straddling the fence between living and not living.

Sylvia also became aware of the fact that she treated herself like a dy-

ing person and made certain demands on others to treat her accordingly. Once, when she was attacked for her hypochondriacal rumination
in the group, she blurted out, "How can you treat me like this when
I'm dying?" She realized the absurdity of the statement but also that it
was a phrase she had muttered *sotto voce* for many years.

Much of Sylvia's work in the group centered about her relationship
with Charles and with me. Her relationship with Charles became much
more real: she stopped denying his illness, stopped urging him to seek
a healer's help, and stopped competing with him for the title of the individual in the group most close to death. Week by week she slowly began to relinquish her belief in my omnipotence. While she tried to
hold on to her image of me as a figure larger than life, she also became
aware of her impatience with me for my fallibility. Accordingly, I was
careful not to assume a post of omniscience but was as open and transparent as possible. Sylvia's improvement became noticeable and solid.
She began facing death rather than being paralyzed by it. She realized
that to escape death anxiety she had attempted in the past to merge
with her therapist or friends. Even television served that purpose, and
when she was very much afraid of death, she would watch television
for long periods of time because "simply hearing a voice makes me realize I'm still alive." She stopped being afraid of loneliness and began
to feel that it would be possible for her to live a satisfying life even
without a comforting dependent relationship with a child or a man.
(There is an old saying: "He who carries his own light need not fear
the dark.")

She began to groom herself, to lose weight, and to build up a social
life outside the group. The group had, for two years, constituted her
entire social world, and we realized that she was approaching termination when in one meeting she announced that she had to leave thirty
minutes early because of a dinner date. The most striking occurrence,
however, was her announcement to the group that for several weeks
she had been meditating daily on her mother's death—not an obsessive
rumination as had often been the case in the past, but a conscious
meditation on all the horrible aspects of her mother's death, with the
deliberate plan for mastering it through total familiarity. This decision
was especially important since it was a plan she had conceived herself
rather than one suggested by the therapist. For years she had been obsessed with the idea that she would die at the same age as her mother.
The group observed that she no longer spoke of this obsession, and she
replied "I haven't thought about that for a long time. It simply isn't
part of my experience any more. I'm into living now."

She made a firm decision to terminate the group and, expectedly, suffered recrudescence of many of her symptoms. She experienced some nightmares, some death panics in the middle of the night, and fleeting desires to petition some superior figure for relief. This exacerbation of symptomatology, however, was brief, perhaps in part because the therapist had predicted that it would occur in the face of the pain of termination. At her last session she brought this dream:

> I was in a large cave and there was a guide there who promised, I thought, to show me some dazzling exhibition. However, there was nothing at all in the cave, no paintings or art work of any sort. He then took me into another room which was a rectangular room, perhaps the size of the group therapy room here and once again there was no paintings or any kind of exhibition. Finally the only thing I could see were a couple of windows overlooking some drab, gray skies and oak trees. Then on the way going out the guide suddenly changed, he had red hair and incredible magnetism so that I thought he was absolutely electric. There was something very very strong going on between the two of us. A very short time later I saw him again and he had seemed to have lost all of the magnetism and become a normal man in blue jeans again.

This dream is a splendid and poignant depiction of the relinquishment of magic; it portrays Sylvia's coming to terms with the illusory quality of her belief in the ultimate rescuer. In the dream I cannot show her a dazzling exhibition; instead of enchanting paintings, I offer only windows looking out at the drab reality of the world. Toward the end of the dream Sylvia makes one final attempt to encloak me in magic: I suddenly become a figure with extrahuman qualities. But the old self-deceptive spell has lost its staying power, and I soon revert back into what I really am—a guide, no more, no less.

In her previous therapies Sylvia had always made spasmodic terminations. She so dreaded the separation, the saying goodbye, and the realization that the therapist's powers were limited that she avoided the final sessions and broke off contact abruptly. Now she directly confronted the separation process (and the underlying reminders of death) in the same way she confronted death anxiety: rather than being overcome by it, she took it into herself and moved *through* the anxiety to experience a richer life than she had known before.

Problems of Psychotherapy

DENIAL BY PATIENT AND THERAPIST

Despite the omnipresence of death and the vast number of rich opportunities available for exploring it, most therapists will find extraordinarily difficult the tasks of increasing the patient's death awareness and working through death anxiety. Denial confounds the process every step of the way. Fear of death exists at every level of awareness—from the most conscious, superficial, intellectualized levels to the realm of deepest unconsciousness. Often a patient's receptivity, at superficial levels, of the therapist's interpretation acts in the service of denial at deeper layers. A patient may be responsive to the therapist's suggestion that the patient examine his or her feelings about his or her finiteness, but gradually the session becomes unproductive, the material runs dry, and the discourse moves into an intellectualized discussion. It is important at these times that the therapist not leap to the erroneous conclusion that he or she is drilling a dry well. The blocking, the lack of associations, the splitting off of affect are all manifestations of resistance and should be treated accordingly. One of Freud's first discoveries in the practice of dynamic therapy was that the therapist repeatedly comes up against a psychological force in the patient that opposes the therapeutic work. ("Through my psychic work I had to oppose a psychic force in the patient which opposed the pathogenic idea from becoming conscious.")[32]

The therapist must persevere. The therapist must continue to collect evidence, to work with dreams, to persist in his or her observations, to make the same points, albeit with different emphases, over and over again. Observations about the existence of death may seem so banal, so overly obvious that the therapist feels fatuous in persisting to make them. Yet simplicity and persistence are necessary to overcome denial. One patient, a depressed, masochistic, suicidal individual, in a debriefing session some months after termination of therapy, described the most important comment I had made to her during therapy. She had frequently described her yearning for death and, at other times, the various things she would like to do in life. I had made, more than once, the embarrassingly simple observation that there is only one possible sequence for these events: experience first and death last.

The patient is not the only source of denial, of course. Frequently the denial of the therapist silently colludes with that of the patient. The therapist no less than the patient must confront death and be anxious in the face of it. Much preparation is required of the therapist who must in everyday work be aware of death. My co-therapist and I became acutely aware of this necessity while leading a group of patients with metastatic cancer. During the first months of the group the discussion remained superficial: much talk about doctors, medicines, treatment regimes, pain, fatigue, physical limitations, and so forth. We considered this superficiality to be defensive in nature—a signal of the depth of the patients' fear and despair. Accordingly, we respected the defense and led the group in a highly cautious manner.

Only much later did we learn that we therapists had played an active role in keeping the group superficial. When we could tolerate our anxiety and follow the patients' leads, then there was no subject too frightening for the group to deal with explicitly and constructively. The discussion was often extraordinarily painful for the therapists. The group was observed through a one-way mirror by a number of student mental health professionals, and on several occasions some had to leave the observation room to compose themselves. The experience of working with dying patients has propelled many therapists back for another course of personal therapy—often highly profitable for them, since many had not dealt with concerns about death in their first, traditional therapy experiences.

If a therapist is to help patients confront and incorporate death into life, he or she must have personally worked through these issues. An interesting parallel is to be found in the initiation rites of healers in primitive cultures, many of which have a tradition requiring that a shaman pass through some ecstatic experience that entails suffering, death, and resurrection. Sometimes the initiation is a true sickness, and the individual who hovers long between life and death is selected for shamanism. Generally the experience is a mystical vision. To take one, not atypical example, a Tungus (a Siberian tribe) shaman described his initiation as consisting of a confrontation with shaman ancestors who surrounded him, pierced him with arrows, cut off his flesh, tore out his bones, drank his blood, and then reassembled him.[33] Several cultures require that the novice shaman sleep on a grave or remain bound for several nights in a cemetery.[34]

WHY STIR UP A HORNET'S NEST?

Many therapists avoid discussions of death with a patient not because of denial but because of a deliberate decision based on the belief that the thought of death would aggravate that patient's condition. Why stir up a hornet's nest? Why plunge the patient deeply into a theme that can only increase anxiety and about which one can do nothing? Everyone must face death. Does not the neurotic patient have quite enough troubles without being burdened with reminders of the bitter quaff awaiting all humans?

It is one thing, these therapists feel, to excavate and examine neurotic problems; there at least they can be of some help. But to explore the real reality, the bitter, immutable facts of life, seems not only folly but antitherapeutic. The patient dealing with unreconciled oedipal conflicts, for example, is hamstrung by phantasmal torments: some constellation of internal and external events that occurred long ago persists in the timeless unconscious and haunts the patient. The patient responds to current situations in distorted fashion: to the present as though it were the past. The therapist's mandate is clear: to illuminate the present, to expose and scatter the demons of the past, to help the patient detoxify events that are intrinsically benign but irrationally experienced as noxious.

But death? Death is not a ghost from the past. And it is not intrinsically benign. What can be done with it?

Increased Anxiety in Therapy. First, it is true that the thought of our finitude has a force field of anxiety about it. To enter the field is to heighten anxiety. The therapeutic approach I describe here is dynamic and uncovering; it is not supportive or repressive. Existential therapy does increase the patient's discomfort. It is not possible to plunge into the roots of one's anxiety without, *for a period of time,* experiencing heightened anxiousness and depression.

The case of Sylvia is clearly illustrative. After Charles told the group about his cancer, she experienced a violent eruption of anxiety and a recrudescence of many primitive defenses against this anxiety. Earlier I described two patients reported by Stern who were in long-term individual analysis and who successfully terminated therapy only after an explicit and exhaustive working through of the mortal terror emanating from the fear of death.[35] Once the therapy of each of these two patients entered the realm of death anxiety, each experienced a dramatic recrudescence of dysphoria. When one patient worked through his fantasy of the analyst's protecting him against death and realized that there was to be no deliverer, he was plunged into a deep depression. "His hyperactivity in his work and in his hobbies turned into feelings of being utterly helpless, of living in a haze, of dissolution of his identity. This induced a regression to ambivalent symbiotic wishes, wishes for oral incorporation of his wife, of the analyst, and tremendous rage against both." The other patient, too, realized that his neurotic defenses would not protect him against death, and his analysis took a similar course. "He became depressed, felt constantly in a haze, and experienced the recrudescence of many infantile patterns which attempted a last-ditch defense against death." Each of the four other cases that Stern reported also experienced a temporary dysphoria and depression as they confronted the future trauma of death.

Bugental, in his excellent discussion of the subject, refers to this phase of treatment as the "existential crisis"—an inevitable crisis which occurs when the defenses used to forestall existential anxiety are breached, allowing one to become truly aware of one's basic situation in life.[36]

Life Satisfaction and Death Anxiety: A Therapeutic Foothold

From a conceptual standpoint the therapist does well to keep in mind that the anxiety surrounding death is *both* neurotic and normal. All human beings experience death anxiety, but some experience such excessive amounts of it that it spills into many realms of their experience and results in heightened dysphoria and/or a series of defenses against anxiety which constrict growth and often themselves generate secondary anxiety. Why some individuals are brought down by the conditions that all must face is a question I have already addressed: the individual, because of a series of unusual life experiences, is both unduly traumatized by death anxiety and fails to erect the "normal" defenses against existential anxiety. What the therapist encounters is a failure of the homeostatic regulation of death anxiety.

One approach available to the therapist is to focus on the patient's current dynamics that alter that regulation. I believe that one particularly useful equation for the clinician is: *death anxiety is inversely proportional to life satisfaction.*

John Hinton reports some interesting and relevant research findings.[37] He studied sixty patients with terminal cancer and correlated their attitudes (including "sense of satisfaction or fulfillment in life") with their feelings and reactions during terminal illness. The sense of satisfaction in life was rated from interviews with the patient and the patient's spouse. The feelings and reactions during the terminal illness were measured by interviews with the patients and by rating scales completed by nurses and spouses. The data revealed that, to a highly significant degree, "When life had appeared satisfying, dying was less troublesome. . . . Lesser satisfaction with past life went with a more troubled view of the illness and its outcome." The lesser the life satisfaction, the greater was the depression, anxiety, anger, and overall concern about the illness and levels of satisfaction with the medical care.

These results seem counterintuitive because, on a superficial level, one might conclude that the unsatisfied and disillusioned might welcome the respite of death. But the opposite is true: a sense of fulfillment, a feeling that life has been well lived, mitigates against the terror of death. Nietzsche, in his characteristic hyperbole, stated: "What has become perfect, all that is ripe—wants to die. All that is unripe wants to live. All that suffers wants to live, that it may become ripe and joyous and longing—longing for what is further, higher, brighter."[38]

Surely this insight gives the therapist a foothold! If he can help the patient experience an increased satisfaction in life, he can allay excessive anxiety. Of course, there is a circularity about this equation since it is *because* of an excessive death anxiety that the individual lives a constricted life—a life dedicated more to safety, survival, and relief from pain than to growth and fulfillment. Searles poses the same dilemma: "The patient cannot face death unless he is a whole person, yet he can become a truly whole person only by facing death." The problem (and it is especially critical with schizophrenic patients, Searles believes) is that "the anxiety concerning life's finitude is too great to face unless one has the strengthening knowledge that one is a whole person. . . . A person cannot bear to face the prospect of inevitable death unless he has had the experience of fully living, and the schizophrenic has not yet fully lived."[39]

Yet still there is a foothold. The therapist must not be overawed by the past. It is not necessary that one experience forty years of whole, integrated living to compensate for the previous forty years of shadow life. Tolstoy's Ivan Ilyich, through his confrontation with death, arrived at an existential crisis and, with only a few days of life remaining, transformed himself and was able to flood, retrospectively, his entire life with meaning.

The less the life satisfaction, the greater the death anxiety. This principle is clearly illustrated by one of my patients, Philip, a fifty-three-year-old, highly successful business executive. Philip had always been a severe workaholic; he worked sixty to seventy hours a week, always lugged a briefcase brimming with work home every evening, and during one recent two-year period worked on the east coast and commuted weekends to his home on the west coast. He had little life satisfaction: his work afforded safety not pleasure; he worked not because he wanted to, but because he had to, to assuage anxiety. He hardly knew his wife and children. Years ago his wife had had a brief extramarital affair, and he had never forgiven her—not so much for the actual act, but because the affair and its attendant pain had been a major source of distraction from his work. His wife and children had suffered from the estrangement, and he had never dipped into this potential reservoir of love, life satisfaction, and meaning.

Then a disaster occurred that stripped Philip of all his defenses. Because of severe setbacks in the aerospace industry, his company failed and was absorbed by another corporation. Philip suddenly found himself unemployed and possibly, because of his age and high executive position, unemployable. He developed severe anxiety and at this point sought psychotherapy. At first his anxiety was entirely centered on his work. He ruminated endlessly about his job. Waking regularly at 4 A.M., he lay awake for hours thinking of work: how to break the news to his employees, how best to phase out his department, how to express his anger at the way he had been handled.

Philip could not find a new position and, as his last day of work approached, he became frantic. Gradually in therapy we pried loose his anxiety from the work concerns to which it adhered like barnacles to a pier. It became apparent that Philip had considerable death anxiety. Nightly he was tormented by a dream in which he circled the very edge of a "black pit." Another frightening recurrent dream consisted of his walking on the narrow crest of a steep dune on the beach and losing his balance. He repeatedly awoke from the dream mumbling "I'm not going to make it." (His father was a sailor who drowned before Philip was born.)

Philip had no pressing financial concerns: he had a generous severance settlement, and a recent large inheritance provided considerable security. But the time! How was he going to use the time. Nothing meant very much to Philip, and he sank into despair. Then one night an important incident occurred. He had been unable to go to sleep and at approximately 3:00 A.M. went downstairs to read and drink a cup of tea. He heard a noise at the window, went over to it, and found himself face to face with a huge stocking-masked man. After his startle and the alarm had subsided, after the police had left and the search was called off, Philip's real panic began. A thought occurred to him, a jarring thought, that sent a powerful shudder through his frame, "Something might have happened to Mary and the children." When, during our therapy hour, he described this incident, his reaction, and his thought, I, rather than comfort him, reminded him that something *will* happen to Mary, to the children, and to himself as well.

Philip passed through a period of feeling wobbly and dazed. All of his customary denial structures no longer functioned: his job, his specialness, his climb to glory, his sense of invulnerability. Just as he had faced the masked burglar, he now faced, at first flinchingly and then more steadily, some fundamental facts of life: groundlessness, the inexorable passage of time, and the inevitability of death. This confrontation provided Philip with a sense of urgency, and he worked hard in therapy to reclaim some satisfaction and meaning in his life. We focused especially on intimacy—an important source of life satisfaction that he had never enjoyed.

Philip had invested so much in his belief in specialness that he dreaded facing (and sharing with others) his feelings of helplessness. I urged him to tell all inquirers the truth—that he was out of a job and having trouble finding another—and to monitor his feelings. He shrank away from the task at first but gradually learned that the sharing of vulnerability opened the door to intimacy. At one session I offered to send his résumé to a friend of mine, the president of a company in a related field, who might have a position for him. Philip thanked me in a polite, formal manner; but when he went to his car, he "cried like a baby" for the first time in thirty-five years. We talked about that cry a great deal, what it meant, how it felt, and why he could not cry in front of me. As he learned to accept his vulnerability, his sense of communion, at first with me and then with his family, deepened; he achieved an intimacy with others he had never previously attained. His orientation to time changed dramatically: no longer did he see time as an enemy—to be concealed or killed. Now, with day after day of free time, he began to savor time and to luxuriate in it. He also became acquainted with other, long dormant parts of himself and for the first time in decades allowed some of his creative urges expression in both painting and writing. After eight months of unemployment, Philip obtained a new and challenging position in another city. In our last session he said, "I've gone through hell in the last few months. But, you know, as horrible as this had been, I'm glad I couldn't get a job immediately. I'm thankful I was forced to go through this." What Philip learned was that a life dedicated to the concealment of reality, to the denial of death, restricts experience and will ultimately cave in upon itself.

Death Desensitization

Another concept that offers a therapeutic foothold against death anxiety is "desensitization." "Desensitization to death"—a vulgar phrase, which is demeaning because it juxtaposes the deepest human concerns with mechanistic techniques. Yet it is difficult to avoid the phrase in a discussion of the therapist's techniques for dealing with death anxiety. It seems that, with repeated contact, one can get used to anything— even to dying. The therapist may help the patient deal with death terror in ways similar to the techniques that he uses to conquer any other form of dread. He exposes the patient over and over to the fear in attenuated doses. He helps the patient handle the dreaded object and to inspect it from all sides.

Montaigne was aware of this principle and wrote:

> It seems to me, however, that there is a certain way of familiarizing ourselves with death and trying it out to some extent. We can have an experience of it that is, if not entire and perfect, at least not useless, and that makes us more fortified and assured. If we cannot reach it, we can approach it, we can reconnoiter it; and if we do not penetrate as far as its fort, at least we shall see and become acquainted with the approaches to it.[40]

In several years of working with groups of cancer patients, I have seen desensitization many times. Over and over a patient approaches his or her dread until gradually it diminishes through sheer familiarity. The model set by other patients and by the therapist—whether it be resoluteness, uneasy stoic acceptance, or equanimity—helps to detoxify death for many patients.

A basic principle of a behavioral approach to anxiety reduction is that the individual be exposed to the feared stimulus (in carefully calibrated amounts) in a psychological state and setting designed to retard the development of anxiety. The group approach employed this strategy. The group often began (and ended) with some anxiety-reducing meditational or muscle-relaxing exercise; each patient was surrounded by others with the same illness; they trusted each other and felt completely understood. The exposure was graduated in that one of the operating norms of the group was that each member be allowed to proceed at his or her own speed and that no pressure be placed on anyone to confront more than he or she wished to.

Another useful principle in anxiety management is dissection and analysis. One's feeling of organismic catastrophic dread generally includes many fearful components that can yield to rational analysis. It may be helpful to encourage the patient (both the everyday psychotherapy patient and the dying one) to examine his or her death and sort out all the various component fears. Many individuals are over-whelmed by a sense of helplessness in the face of death; and, indeed, the groups of dying patients I have worked with devoted much time to counteracting this source of dread. The major strategy is to separate ancillary *feelings* of helplessness from the true helplessness that issues from facing one's unalterable existential situation. I have seen dying patients regain a sense of potency and control by electing to control those aspects of their lives that were amenable to control. For example, a patient may change his mode of interacting with his physician: he may insist on being informed fully about his illness or on being included in important treatment decisions. Or he may change to another physician if he is dissatisfied with the current one. Other patients involve themselves in social action. Others develop a sense of choicefulness; they discover with exhilaration that they can elect not to do the things they do not wish to do. Others who believe that developing new ways to manage psychological stress will influence the course of their cancer, engage actively in psychotherapy. And, when all else seems beyond one's control, one, even then, has the power to control one's attitude toward one's fate—to reconstrue what one cannot deny.

There are other component fears: the pain of dying, afterlife, the fear of the unknown, concern for one's family, fear for one's body, loneliness, regression. In achievement-oriented Western countries death is curiously equated with failure. Each of these component fears, examined separately and rationally, is less frightening than the entire gestalt. Each is an obviously disagreeable aspect of dying; yet, neither separately nor in concert, do these fears need to elicit a cataclysmic reaction. It is significant, however, that many patients, when asked to analyze their death terrors, find that they correspond to none of these but to something primitive and ineffable. In the adult unconscious dwells the young child's irrational terror: death is experienced as an evil, cruel, mutilating force. Recall the terrifying children's fantasies of death described in chapter 3, views of death far more horrible than those of the mature adult. These fantasies, no less than oedipal or castration fears, are atavistic unconscious tags that disrupt the adult's ability to recognize reality and to respond appropriately. The therapist works with such fears as with any other distortions of reality: he attempts to identify, to illuminate, and to scatter these ghosts of the past.

5 / Death and Psychotherapy

DEATH DESENSITIZATION: EMPIRICAL EVIDENCE

Several reports in the literature (all psychology doctoral dissertations) describe workshops on death awareness that employ many of these approaches to death desensitization and measure quantitative changes in death anxiety. One eight-hour marathon workshop—which consisted of discussions of death, the viewing of a movie about death, guided fantasies (in a state of deep muscle relaxation) of each member's own terminal illness, death, and funeral—reported that the eight experimental subjects (in contrast to a control no-group sample) "reorganized their ideas about death," used less denial in confronting their own deaths, and, after an eight-week follow-up, had lower death anxiety scores. In post-group interviews some of the subjects gratuitously averred that the workshop catalyzed significant other life changes. One alcoholic, for example, reported that the laboratory had had an enormous impact on him: he had decided that he did not wish to die the demeaning death of an alcoholic, and had become totally abstinent.[41]

Another similar death desensitization program, SYATD ("shaping your attitudes toward death") reduced death fears (as measured by two manifest death anxiety scales).[42] A "death and self-discovery workshop" laboratory resulted in increased death anxiety—but also in an *increase* in a sense of purpose in life.[43] Other programs have shown an immediate post-workshop reduction in anxiety, with a return to preworkshop levels in four weeks.[44] Finally, a six-week death education class for nurses did not affect death anxiety immediately but resulted in a significant reduction four weeks later.[45]

Death is only one component of the human being's existential situation, and a consideration of death awareness illuminates only one facet of existential therapy. To arrive at a fully balanced therapeutic approach, we must examine the therapeutic implications of each of the other ultimate concerns. Death helps us understand anxiety, offers a dynamic structure upon which to base interpretation, and serves as a boundary experience that is capable of instigating a massive shift in perspective. Each of the other ultimate concerns, to which I now turn, contributes another segment of a comprehensive psychotherapy system: *freedom* helps us understand responsibility assumption, commitment to change, decision and action; *isolation* illuminates the role of relationship; whereas *meaninglessness* turns our attention to the principle of engagement.

PART II

Freedom

I N THE SECTION on the concept of death in psychotherapy I suggested that the clinician would find the discussion strange, yet oddly familiar: "strange" because the existential approach cuts across traditional categories and clusters clinical observations differently; but "familiar" because in his or her bones the experienced clinician apprehends the importance and the omnipresence of the concept of death. "Strange yet familiar" will apply to this section as well. Though the term "freedom" is not found in the psychotherapist's lexicon, the concept of freedom plays an indispensable role in both theory and practice of all traditional and innovative therapies. To illustrate, consider these incidents in therapy that have come to my attention over the past several years.

- To a patient, who insists that her behavior is controlled by her unconscious, a therapist says, "Whose unconscious is it?"
- A group leader has a "can't" bell which he rings whenever a patient in his group says "I can't." The patient is asked to recant and then to restate the phrase as "I won't."
- A patient caught up in a highly self-destructive relationship stated: "I cannot decide what to do, I can't bring myself to end the relationship, but I pray that I could catch him in bed with another woman so that I would be able to leave him."
- My first supervisor, an orthodox Freudian analyst who firmly believed in Freud's deterministic view of behavior, said to me twenty years ago in our first meeting, "The goal of psychotherapy is to bring the patient to the point where he can make a free choice." Yet, though we had over fifty more supervisory sessions, I do not recall his ever having said another word about "choosing"—which he pronounced as *the* goal of therapy.
- Many therapists repeatedly ask patients to change their speech and "own" what happens to them. Not "he bugs me," but "I let him bug me." Not "I have a mind that skips," but "when I get hurt and feel like crying, I defend myself by being confused."
- A therapist asked a forty-five-year-old patient to have a dialogue with his dead mother and to repeat this sentence several times: "I will not change until you treat me differently when I was ten years old."
- Otto Will, a legendary therapist, is reported to have periodically interrupted the interminable ruminations of a highly restricted obsessive patient with such suggestions as: "Say, why don't you change your name and move to California?"
- At 5:00 P.M. a sexually compulsive man arrived by plane in a city where he had a professional commitment the following morning. While still at the airport he hurriedly began phoning a series of women acquaintances to arrange for a sexual liaison that evening. No luck! They all had previous engagements. (Of course, he could easily have phoned them days or, indeed, weeks earlier.) His response was relief: "Thank God, now I can read and get a good night's sleep, *which is what I really wanted to do all along.*"

These incidents may appear to be a potpourri of patients' thoughtless utterances and of smug, gimmicky therapists' ploys. Yet, as I shall demonstrate, they are all of a piece, bound together by the conceptual thread of freedom. Furthermore, though these incidents are frocked in insubstantial garb, they do not represent insubstantial concerns. Each, properly considered, will be seen to have implications that stretch down into the socket of existence. Each incident offers a perspective on the theme of freedom, and each will serve as a springboard for the discussion of some therapeutically relevant aspect of freedom.

To the philosopher, "freedom" has broad personal, social, moral, and political implications and consequently encompasses a wide terrain.

Moreover, the issue is intensely controversial: the philosophical debate concerning freedom and causality has not ceased for two thousand years. Throughout the centuries the concept of absolute freedom has always engendered bitter opposition because it has clashed with prevailing world views: first, with the belief in divine providence; later, with the laws of scientific causality; still later, with the Hegelian view of history as a meaningful progression, or with Marxist or Freudian deterministic theories. However in this section, as elsewhere in this book, I shall examine only those aspects of freedom that have important, everyday relevance to the clinician: specifically, in chapter 6, the individual's freedom to create his or her own life, and in chapter 7 the individual's freedom to desire, to choose, to act and—more important for the purposes of psychotherapy—to change.

CHAPTER 6

Responsibility

RESPONSIBILITY has many connotations. We label a trustworthy, dependable person "responsible." "Responsibility" also implies accountability—legal, financial, or moral. In the mental health field, "responsibility" refers to the patient's capability for rational conduct as well as to the therapist's moral commitment to the patient. Although none of these connotations is entirely irrelevant to this discussion, I use "responsibility" here in a specific sense—in the same sense as did Jean-Paul Sartre when he wrote that to be responsible is to be "the uncontested author of an event or a thing."[1] Responsibility means authorship. To be aware of responsibility is to be aware of creating one's own self, destiny, life predicament, feelings and, if such be the case, one's own suffering. For the patient who will not accept such responsibility, who persists in blaming others—either other individuals or other forces—for his or her dysphoria, no real therapy is possible.

Responsibility as an Existential Concern

But how is responsibility existential? That death is an existential issue is self-evident: Mortality and finiteness are obvious givens of existence.

6 / Responsibility

But when we speak of responsibility or, as in the following chapter, of willing, then the existential referent is not immediately evident.

At the deepest level, responsibility accounts for existence. This was brought home to me many years ago by a simple experience so potent that it has remained vividly with me. I was snorkling alone in the warm, sunny, clear waters of a tropical lagoon and experienced, as I often do while in the water, a deep sense of pleasure and coziness. I felt at home. The warmth of the water, the beauty of the coral bottom, the sparkling silver minnows, the neon-bright coral fish, the regal angel fish, the fleshy anemone fingers, the esthetic pleasure of gliding and carving through the water, all in concert created an underwater elysium. And, then, for reasons I have never understood, I had a sudden radical shift in perspective. I suddenly realized that none of my watery companions shared my cozy experience. The regal angel fish did not know that it was beautiful, the minnows that they sparkled, the coral fish that they were brilliant. Nor for that matter did the black needle urchins or the bottom débris (which I tried not to see) know of their ugliness. The at-homeness, the coziness, the smiling hour, the beauty, the beckoning, the comfort—none of these really existed. I had created the entire experience! I could by the same token glide through oil-slicked waters bobbing with empty plastic Clorox containers and choose to consider it either beautiful or disgusting. At the deepest level the choice and the creation were mine. In Husserl's terms my *noema* ("meaning") had exploded, and I had become aware of my constitutive function. It was as though I peered through a rent in the curtain of daily reality to a more fundamental and deeply unsettling reality.

In his novel *Nausea*, in one of the great passages of modern literature, Sartre describes this moment of illumination—the discovery of responsibility.

> The roots of the chestnut tree were sunk in the ground just under my bench. I couldn't remember it was a root any more. The words had vanished and with them the significance of things, their methods of use, and the feeble points of reference which men have traced on their surface. I was sitting, stooping forward, head bowed, alone in front of this black, knotty mass, entirely beastly, which frightened me. Then I had this vision.
>
> It left me breathless. Never, until these last few days, had I understood the meaning of "existence." I was like the others, like the ones walking along the seashore, all dressed in their spring finery. I said, like them, "The ocean *is* green; that white speck up there *is* a seagull," but I didn't feel that it existed or that the seagull was an "existing seagull."
>
> ... And then all of a sudden, there it was, clear as day: existence had suddenly unveiled itself. It had lost the harmless look of an abstract cate-

ry: it was the very paste of things, the root was kneaded into existence. Or rather the root, the park gates, the bench, the sparse grass, all that had vanished: the diversity of things, their individuality, were only an appearance, a veneer. This veneer had melted, leaving soft, monstrous masses, all in disorder—naked, in a frightful, obscene nakedness. . . . This root, on the other hand, existed in such a way that I could not explain it. Knotty, inert, nameless, it fascinated me, filled my eyes, brought me back unceasingly to its own existence. In vain to repeat: "This is a root"—it didn't work any more.[2]

Sartre's protagonist confronts the raw "monstrous masses," the "very paste of things"—stuff that has no form, no meaning until he supplies it. The knowledge of his true "situation" crashes in on him as he discovers his responsibility for the world. The world acquired significance only through the way it is constituted by the human being—in Sartre's terms the "for-itself." There is not meaning in the world outside of or independent of the for-itself.

Western and Eastern philosophers alike have pondered the problem of man's responsibility for the nature of reality. The heart of Kant's revolution in philosophy was his position that it is human consciousness, the nature of the human being's mental structures, that provides the external form of reality. Space itself, according to Kant, "is not something objective and real but something subjective and ideal; it is, as it were, a schema issuing by a constant law from the nature of the mind for the coordinating of all outer sensa whatever."[3]

What are the implications of this world view for the psychology of the individual? it was Heidegger, and then Sartre, who explored the meaning of responsibility for the individual being. Heidegger referred to the individual as *dasein* (not as "I" or "one" or "ego" or a "human being") for a specific reason: he wished always to emphasize the dual nature of human existence. The individual is "there" (*da*), but also he or she constitutes what is there. The ego is two-in-one: it is an *empirical* ego (an objective ego, something that is "there," an object in the world) and a *transcendental* (constituting) ego which constitutes (that is, is "responsible" for) itself and the world. Responsibility viewed in this manner is inextricably linked to freedom. Unless the individual is free to constitute the world in any of a number of ways, then the concept of responsibility has no meaning. The universe is contingent; everything that is could have been created differently. Sartre's view of freedom is far-reaching: the human being is not only free but is doomed to freedom. Furthermore, freedom extends beyond being responsible for the world (that is, for imbuing the world with significance): *one is also entirely responsible for one's life, not only for one's actions but for one's failures to act.*

6 / Responsibility

There is, as I write, mass starvation in another part of the world. Sartre would state that I bear responsibility for this starvation. I, of course, protest: I know little of what happens there, and I feel I can do little to alter the tragic state of affairs. But Sartre would point out that I choose to keep myself uninformed, and that I decide at this very instant to write these words instead of engaging myself in the tragic situation.[4] I could, after all, organize a rally to raise funds or publicize the situation through my contacts in publishing, but I choose to ignore it. I bear responsibility for what I do and for what I choose to ignore. Sartre's point in this regard is not moral: he does not say that I *should* be doing something different, but he says that what I *do* do is my responsibility. Both of these levels of responsibility—significance attribution and responsibility for life conduct—have, as we shall see, enormous implications for psychotherapy.

Both to constitute (to be responsible for) oneself and one's world and to be aware of one's responsibility is a deeply frightening insight. Consider its implication. Nothing in the world has significance except by virtue of one's own creation. There are no rules, no ethical systems, no values; there is no external referent whatsoever; there is no grand design in the universe. In Sartre's view, the individual alone is the creator (this is what he means by "man is the being whose project is to be god").[5]

To experience existence in this manner is a dizzying sensation. Nothing is as it seemed. The very ground beneath one seems to open up. Indeed, *groundlessness* is a commonly used term for a subjective experience of responsibility awareness. Many existential philosophers have described the anxiety of groundlessness as "ur-anxiety"—the most fundamental anxiety, an anxiety that cuts deeper even than the anxiety associated with death. In fact, many consider death anxiety as a symbol for the anxiety of groundlessness. Philosophers often make the distinction between "my death" and death, or the death of another. What is truly terrifying about "my death" is that it implies the dissolution of my world. With "my death," the meaning giver and spectator of the world dies, too, and is truly confronted with nothingness.[6]

The concerns of "nothingness" and of self-creation have another deep and unsettling implication: loneliness, an existential loneliness, which—as I shall discuss in chapter 8—extends far beyond ordinary social loneliness; it is the loneliness of being separated not only from people but from the world, as one ordinarily experiences it, as well. "The responsibility of the 'for-itself' [that is, the individual consciousness] is overwhelming, since it is thanks to the 'for-itself' that it happens there is a world."[7]

We respond to the anxiety of groundlessness as we do when confronted with anxiety: we seek relief. There are many ways to shield ourselves. First, unlike death anxiety, the anxiety of groundlessness is *not* evident in everyday experience. It is not easily intuited by the adult and probably not experienced at all by the child. Some individuals, like Sartre's Roquentin in *Nausea*, have flashes of their constitutive activity on several occasions in life, but generally it remains far from awareness. One avoids situations (for example, making decisions, isolation, autonomous action) that, if deeply considered, would make one aware of one's fundamental groundlessness. Thus one seeks structure, authority, grand designs, magic, something that is bigger than oneself. Even a tyrant, as Fromm reminds us in *Escape from Freedom*, is better than no leader at all.[8] Thus it is that children are upset by freedom and demand limit setting; panicky psychotic patients exhibit the same need for structure and limits. The same dynamic underlies the development of transference in the course of psychotherapy. Other defenses against the anxiety of groundlessness include the common ones used against full awareness of "my death," because death denial is an ally of groundlessness denial.

Perhaps the most potent defense of all, however, is simply reality as it is experienced—that is, the appearance of things. To view ourselves as primal constitutors is to fly in the face of reality as we ordinarily experience it. Our sense data tell us that the world is "there," and that we enter and leave it. Yet, as Heidegger and Sartre suggest, appearances enter the service of denial: *we constitute the world in such a way that it appears independent of our constitition.* To constitute the world as an empirical world means to constitute it as something independent of ourselves.

To be taken in by any of these devices that allow us to flee from our freedom is to live "inauthentically" (Heidegger) or in "bad faith" (Sartre). Sartre considered it his project to liberate individuals from bad faith and to help them assume responsibility. It is the psychotherapist's project as well; in much of the remainder of this chapter I shall explore the clinical ramifications of responsibility avoidance and the techniques available to the therapist to facilitate the process of assumption of responsibility.

Responsibility Avoidance: Clinical Manifestions

Even the most casual historical review of the field of psychotherapy reveals radical changes in the modes whereby therapists offer help to patients. The riotous proliferation of new, competing therapies appears to defy any coherent pattern and consequently has at times undermined the general public's confidence in the field. But a careful look at these new therapies—as well as at new developments in traditional therapies—reveals that they have one outstanding feature in common: an emphasis on the assumption of personal responsibility.

That this is so, that modern approaches focus heavily on responsibility, is no accident. Therapies reflect, and are shaped by, the pathology that they must treat. *Fin de siècle* Vienna, incubator and cradle of Freudian psychology, had all the characteristics of late Victorian culture: instinctual (especially sexual) repression, heavily structured and clearly defined rules of behavior and manners, separate spheres for men and women, an emphasis on will power and moral strength, and an intoxicating optimism springing from a scientific positivism that promised to explain all aspects of the natural order, not excluding human behavior. Freud realized, quite correctly, that such rigid suppression of natural inclinations was detrimental to the psyche; libidinal energy that could not be permitted to surface nakedly begat restrictive defenses and indirect means of expression. The defenses and the oblique mode of libidinal expression together comprised the clinical picture of the classical psychoneurosis.

But what would Freud emphasize were he to examine contemporary American culture—especially in California, which has been the birthplace of so many of the newer therapeutic approaches? Natural instinctual strivings are given considerable free expression; sexual permissiveness, beginning in early adolescence, is, as many surveys have demonstrated, a reality. A generation of young adults have been nursed and spoonfed according to a compulsively permissive regimen. Structure, ritual, boundaries of every type, are being relentlessly dismantled. In the religious orders, Catholic sisters defy the Pope, priets refuse to remain celibate, women and gay men divide the Episcopal church on their right to be ordained, and women rabbis lead services in many synagogues. Students address professors by their first names. Where are the forbidden dirty words, the professional titles, the manuals of manners, the dress codes? A friend of mine, an art critic, characterized the new California culture by describing an incident that occurred on his first visit to Southern California. He stopped at a fast-food drive-in and was given, with his hamburger, a small plastic container of ketchup. Elsewhere these containers have a dotted line and the notation to "tear here"; the California container had no dotted lines, only the simple inscription "tear anywhere."[9]

The picture of psychopathology has changed accordingly. The classical psychoneurotic syndromes have become a rarity. Even a decade ago an individual with a true psychoneurotic clinical picture was a treasure eagerly vied for by both young trainees and senior staff. Today's patient has to cope more with freedom than with suppressed drives. No longer pushed from within by what he or she "has" to do, or pulled from without by what he or she "must" or "ought" to do, the patient has to cope with the problem of choice—with what he or she *wants* to do. With increasing frequency patients seek therapy with vague, ill-defined complaints. Indeed, I often finish my first consultative session with no clear picture of a patient's problem; I consider the fact that the patient cannot define the problem *as* the problem. The patient complains of "something missing" from life, of being cut off from feelings, of emptiness, of zestlessness, or of a sense of being cast adrift. The course of therapy of such patients is similarly diffuse. The word "cure" has been banished from the vocabulary of therapy; instead, the therapist speaks of "growth" or "progress." Since the goals are indistinct, the end point of therapy is similarly blurred, and courses of therapy often continue aimlessly year after year.

The atrophy of structure-providing social (and psychological) institutions in our lives has served to confront us with our freedom. If there are no rules, no grand designs, nothing we *must* do, then we are free to do as we choose. Our basic nature has not changed; one might say that, with the stripping away of freedom-concealing diversions, with the deconstitution of externally imposed structure, we are today closer than ever to experiencing the existential facts of life. But we are unprepared; it is too much to bear, anxiety clamors for release, and, at both individual and social levels, we engage in a frenetic search to shield ourselves from freedom.

Let me turn now to an examination of the specific psychic defenses that protect the individual from responsibility awareness. No therapist goes through a day of clinical work without encountering several examples of responsibility-avoiding defenses. I shall discuss some of the more common ones: compulsivity, displacement of responsibility to another, denial of responsibility ("innocent victim," "losing control"), avoidance of autonomous behavior, and decisional pathology.

6 / *Responsibility*

One of the more common dynamic defenses against responsibility awareness is the creation of a psychic world in which one does not experience freedom but exists under the sway of some irresistible ego-alien ("not-me") force. We call this defense "compulsivity."

A clinical illustration of it is provided by Bernard, a twenty-five-year-old salesman whose major problems centered on guilt and "drivenness." He was driven in his sexual behavior, in his work, and even in his leisure. He was the man who (in the example in the introduction to Part II), upon failing to arrange a sexual liaison (he had deliberately phoned too late), breathed a sigh of relief: "Now I can read and get a good night's rest which is what I really wanted all along." In that remarkable phrase—"which is what I really wanted all along"—lies the crux of Bernard's problem. The obvious question is, "Why, Bernard, if this is what you *really* want, did you not simply do that directly?"

Bernard answered that query in several ways: "I didn't know that was what I really wanted until I felt the wave of relief that came over me when the last woman refused me." At another time he stated, in effect, that he was unaware there was a choice involved: "Making a woman is what it's all about." The drive was so compelling that it was unthinkable for him not to bed an available woman, even though it was perfectly clear that the brief sexual exhilaration was heavily outweighed by the associated dysphoria: anticipatory anxiety, feelings of self-dissatisfaction because his sexual ruminations reduced his effectiveness at work, guilt and fear that his sexual promiscuity would be discovered by his wife, self-contempt because of his awareness that he acted in bad faith by using women as one would use a machine.

Bernard, then, avoided the problem of responsibility and choice by a compulsivity that obliterated choice; his subjective experience was similar to hanging on for dear life to a frenzied, uncontrollable bronco. He sought therapy to find relief from his dysphoria but was blind to the fact that at some level he was responsible for having created his dysphoria, his compulsivity—in short, for having created every aspect of his life predicament.

DISPLACEMENT OF RESPONSIBILITY

Many individuals avoid personal responsibility by displacing it to another. This maneuver is exceptionally common in the psychotherapy situation. One of the major themes in my work with Bernard was his effort to shift the burden of responsibility from himself to me. He did not think about his problem from one session to the other; instead, he merely stored up the material and "dumped" it in my lap. (He countered this observation with the cunning rejoinder that if he "processed" the material beforehand, spontaneity would be stripped from the sessions.) He rarely produced dreams, because he could not will himself to write down the dreams during brief awakenings in the night, and by morning he had forgotten them. On the rare occasions when he did write down a dream, he never once looked at the dream between the time of writing it and his session; consequently, he often could no longer decipher his own script.

During a summer break when I was away on vacation he "marked time" waiting for my return and dreamed, the night before we resumed, that he was at a football game and watching himself *perched upon my shoulders* catching a touchdown pass. His behavior during that first session was a symbolic re-enactment of the dream: he deluged me with detailed accounts of his summer anxieties, guilt, sexual behavior, and self-depreciations. He had for four weeks given in to his compulsivity and anxiety, waiting for me to return to show him how to take a stand against them. Though he had often used brain-storming exercises in his work, he seemed dismayed when I suggested a simple exercise for him (reflecting on himself for twenty minutes and then writing down his observations). After a few (fruitful) attempts he "could not find the time" for the exercise. After a session in which I persisted in pointing out how he dumped his problems on me, he dreamed:

> A man X [an individual who resembled Bernard—obviously a double] called me for an appointment. He said I had known his mother and that he, himself, now wanted to see me. I felt I didn't want to see him. I then thought that since he was in public relations maybe I ought to think of what I can get from him. But then we couldn't work out a meeting time; our schedules were incompatible. I said to him, "Perhaps we ought to schedule a meeting to talk about your schedule!" I woke up laughing.

Bernard drove fifty miles to see me and never once felt burdened by the long commute. Yet, as the dream clearly illustrates, he could not and would not find the time for a session with himself. Obviously for Bernard, and for every patient who will not work in the absence of the therapist, it is not a matter of time or convenience. What is at stake is the facing of one's own personal responsibility for one's life and one's process of change. And always lurking beyond that awareness of responsibility is the dread of groundlessness.

The assumption of responsibility is a precondition of therapeutic change. As long as one believes that one's situation and dysphoria are produced by someone else or by some external force, then what sense is there in committing oneself to personal change? People show indefatigable ingenuity in finding ways to avoid awareness of responsibility. One patient, for example, complained of severe, long-standing sexual problems in his marriage. I believe that by facing his responsibility for his situation he would have had a frightening confrontation with freedom and discovered that he was locked up in a prison of his own creation. In fact he was free, if sex were important enough, to leave his wife or find another woman, or to *consider* leaving his wife (the mere thought of separation was sufficient to propel him into paroxysms of anxiety). He was free to change any aspect of his sexual life; and that fact, too, was momentous, because it meant that he would have to assume the responsibility of a life-long stifling of his sexual feelings and many other aspects of his affective life as well. Consequently he doggedly avoided facing responsibility and attributed the sexual problems to a number of factors outside of himself: that is, to his wife's sexual lack of interest and her disinclination to change; to squeaky bedsprings (so noisy that the children would overhear the sounds of coitus, and, for many absurd reasons, the bed could not be replaced); to his aging (he was forty-five) and innate libidinal deficit; to his unresolved problems with his mother (which, as is so often true for genetic explanations, served more as apologia for responsibility avoidance than as catalyst for change).

Other modes of displacing responsibility are commonly seen in clinical practice. Paranoid patients obviously displace responsibility to other individuals and forces. They disown and attribute to others their own feelings and desires and invariably explain their dysphoria and failures as the result of external influence. The major, and often impossible, therapeutic task with paranoid patients to help them accept authorship of their projected feelings.

The avoidance of responsibility is also the major obstacle in the psychotherapy of the patient with a psychophysiological illness. The assumption of responsibility in these patients is twice removed: they experience somatic rather than psychological distress; and even when they recognize the psychological substrate to their somatic distress, they still characteristically employ externalization defenses attributing their psychological dysphoria to "bad nerves" or to adverse work or environmental conditions.

DENIAL OF RESPONSIBILITY: INNOCENT VICTIM

A particular type of responsibility avoidance is often seen in individuals (generally thought of as hysterical personalities) who deny responsibility by experiencing themselves as innocent victims of events that they themselves have (unwittingly) set into motion.

For example, Clarissa, a forty-year-old practicing psychotherapist, entered a therapy group to work on her long difficulties in developing intimate relationships. She had particularly severe problems in relating to men who, beginning with a brutal, punitive father, characteristically rejected and punished her. During our initial intake session she told me that several months previously she had terminated a lengthy psychoanalysis, and that she now felt that her problems would be better dealt with in a group setting. After several months in the group she informed us that she had re-entered analysis shortly after beginning the group but had not considered it of sufficient import to report to the group. At this point, however, her analyst, who strongly disapproved of group therapy, interpreted her membership in a therapy group, as "acting-out."

It is obvious that a patient cannot work in a therapy group if his or her individual therapist opposes and undermines the work. I attempted, at Clarissa's suggestion, to communicate with her analyst, but he elected to maintain a psychoanalytic posture of total confidentiality and—somewhat haughtily, I thought—refused even to converse with me about the matter. I felt betrayed by Clarissa, irritated with her analyst, and dazed by the turn of events. Throughout, Clarissa remained ingenuous and slightly bewildered at the confusing events occurring to her. The group members viewed her as "playing dumb"; and, in an effort to help her see her role in these events, they became increasingly forceful, almost punitive, in their comments. Clarissa felt once again victimized, especially by men, and "due to circumstances beyond her control" was forced to leave the group.

This incident was a miniature version of Clarissa's core problem: an avoidance of responsibility, which she accomplished by playing the role of innocent victim. Though she was not yet prepared to see it, the incident held the key to her difficulties in establishing intimate relationships. Two important men in her life, her analyst and her group therapist, felt manipulated and, speaking for myself, annoyed with her. The other group members felt similarly used. She did not relate to them in good faith; but instead, they felt they were mere pawns in a drama she was enacting with her therapists.

Recall that Clarissa entered therapy because of her problems in developing intimate relationships. Her responsibility for these difficulties was crystal clear in the group. She was never *with* a person. While next to the group members, she was with me. While next to me, she was with her analyst; and, no doubt, when next to him, she was with her father. Clarissa's dynamics of innocent victimhood were especially obvious because she was herself an experienced psychotherapist, had led therapy groups, and well knew the importance of communication between individual and group therapists.

DENIAL OF RESPONSIBILITY: LOSING CONTROL

Another mode of shucking responsibility is to be temporarily "out of one's mind." Some patients enter a temporary irrational state in which they may act irresponsibly, for they are not accountable, even to themselves, for their behavior. It was this problem that, in one of the examples at the beginning of Part II, the therapist addressed when he asked a patient (who was lamenting that her behavior was not deliberate), "Whose unconscious is it?" It is important to note that careful examination of such patients will reveal to a therapist that the "losing control" behavior is by no means disorderly: it is purposeful and offers the patient both secondary gains ("payoffs") and a self-deceptive avoidance of responsibility.

A patient who was brutalized and then rejected by an insensitive, sadistic lover, "lost control," and by "going crazy" radically changed the balance of control in the relationship. She followed him around for weeks, repeatedly broke into and vandalized his apartment, created scenes by screaming and throwing dishes when he was dining in restaurants with friends. Her crazy, unpredictable behavior defeated him utterly: he panicked, sought protection from the police, and eventually required emergency psychiatric care. At this point, her goal accomplished, she—*mirabile dictu*—regained control and behaved thenceforth in an entirely rational manner. In muted form this dynamic is by no means uncommon. Many an individual is tyrannized by the potential irrationality of a partner.

Losing control offers another common payoff: nurturance. Some patients so deeply crave to be nursed, to be fed, to be cared for in the most intimate ways by their therapist that to gain those ends, they "lose control" even to the point of deep regression requiring hospitalization.

AVOIDANCE OF AUTONOMOUS BEHAVIOR

Therapists are often baffled by patients who know very well what they can do to help themselves feel better but inexplicably refuse to take that step. Paul, a patient who was depressed and in the process of changing jobs, went to New York for job interviews. He felt desperately lonely: the interviews themselves filled only six hours of a three-day period, and the rest of the time was spent in lonely, frenzied waiting. Having in the past lived many years in New York, Paul had many friends there, whose presence would have no doubt heartened him. He spent two lonely nights looking at the telephone, wishing they would call—an impossibility since they had no way of knowing he was in town. Yet he could not pick up the telephone to call them.

Why? We analyzed this at length beginning with such explanations as "no energy," "too humiliated to ask for company," "they'd feel I only call them when I need them." Only gradually did we understand that his behavior was a reflection of his unwillingness to recognize that his well-being and his comfort rested in his own hands, and that help would not come unless he acted to create that help. At one point I commented that it was frightening to be one's own father; that phrase reverberated powerfully for Paul, and during subsequent therapy he often referred back to it. The paradox for him (as for Sam, in chapter 4, who, after his wife left him, would not go out and search for friends lest he miss an incoming phone call) was that to alter his social loneliness, he had to encounter a deeper existential loneliness. In these examples we see the confluence of two frames of reference: the assumption of responsibility results also in the relinquishment of one's belief in the existence of the ultimate rescuer—an exceedingly difficult task for an individual who has constructed his *Weltanschauung* around that belief. These two frames of reference acting in concert constitute the basic dynamics of dependency and provide the therapist with a coherent and powerful explanatory system by which to understand the pathologically dependent character.

DISORDERS OF WISHING AND DECIDING

The next chapter will discuss in depth the relationship between responsibility assumption and willing (that is, wishing and deciding), and I need pause only briefly here to note that when one in full awareness wishes and decides, one is confronted with responsibility. The central thesis of this chapter is that one creates oneself; the central thesis of the next is that wishing and deciding are the building blocks of creation. As Sartre has often told us, an individual's life is constituted by his or her choices. An individual wills himself into being what he is. If one is terrified by self-constitution (and by the groundlessness inherent in such knowledge), then one may avoid willing by, for example, deadening oneself to wishing or feeling, by abdicating choice, or by transferring one's choice to other individuals, institutions, or external events. In chapter 7 I shall consider these mechanisms of responsibility avoidance through willing-denial.

Responsibility Assumption and Psychotherapy

To assist the patient in assuming responsibility, the therapist's first step is not a technique but the adoption of an attitude upon which subsequent technique will rest. The therapist must continually operate within the frame of reference that a patient has created his or her own distress. It is *not* chance, or bad luck or bad genes, that has caused a patient to be lonely, isolated, chronically abused, or insomniac. The therapist must determine what role a particular patient plays in his or her own dilemma, and find ways to communicate this insight to the patient. Until one realizes that one has created one's own dysphoria, there can be no motivation to change. If one continues to believe that distress is caused by others, by bad luck, by an unsatisfying job—in short, by something outside oneself—why invest energy in personal change? In the face of such a belief system, the obvious strategy is not therapeutic but activist: to change one's environment.

Readiness to accept responsibility varies considerably from patient to patient. For some patients it is extraordinarily difficult and constitutes the bulk of the therapeutic task; once they assume responsibility, therapeutic change almost automatically and effortlessly transpires. There are others who recognize responsibility more quickly but balk repeatedly at other stages of treatment. Generally responsibility awareness does not proceed evenly on a unified front, individuals may accept responsibility on some issues and deny it on others.

IDENTIFICATION AND LABELING

The first task of the therapist is to be attentive to the issue, to identify instances and methods of responsibility avoidance and to make these known to the patient. Therapists, depending on stylistic preference, use a vast variety of techniques to focus a patient's attention on responsibility. Take several of the examples at the beginning of Part II: A therapist who counters a patient's excuse for behavior ("It was not deliberate. I did it unconsciously.") with the question "Whose unconscious is it?" is encouraging responsibility awareness. As is the therapist who asks a patient to "own" what happens to him or her: (not "he bugs me," but "I let him bug me.") The "can't" bell, which summons individuals to change "cannot" into "will not," is a ploy designed to enhance the awakening of responsibility. As long as one believes in "can't," one remains unaware of one's active contribution to one's situation. The patient instructed to say, "I will not change, mother, until you treat me differently when I was ten years old" is in effect being asked to ponder her *refusal* (rather than her inability) to change. Furthermore, she is confronted with the absurdity of her situation and with her tragic and futile sacrifice of a life upon the altar of spitefulness.

Vera Gatch and Maurice Temerlin studied audiotapes of psychotherapy sessions and report a potpourri of confrontative (at times insensitively so) interventions designed to enhance responsibility awareness:

> When one man complained, bitterly and passively, that his wife would not have sexual intercourse with him, a therapist clarified the implicit choice with the remark, "You must like her that way; you've been married to her a long time." A housewife complained, "I cannot manage my child, all he does is sit and watch TV all day." The therapist explicated the implicit choice with: "And you're too little and helpless to turn off the TV." An impulse-ridden, obsessional man cried: "Stop me, I'm afraid I'm going to kill myself." The therapist said: "I should stop you? If you really want to kill yourself—to actually die—nobody can stop you—except you." Interacting with a passive, oral-dependent man who felt that life held nothing for him because he suffered from the unrequited love of an older woman, one therapist began singing, "Poor little lamb that has lost its way."[10]

The general principle is obvious: whenever the patient laments about his or her life situation, the therapist inquires how the patient has created this situation.

It is often helpful if the therapist keeps the patient's initial complaints in mind and, at appropriate points in therapy, juxtaposes these complaints with the latter's in-therapy attitudes and behavior. For example, consider a patient who sought therapy because of feelings of isolation and loneliness. During therapy he discussed his sense of superiority and his scorn and disdain of others. His resistance to changing these attitudes was significant: they were ego-syntonic and doggedly maintained. The therapist helped the patient understand his responsibility for his uncomfortable predicament by commenting, whenever the patient discussed his scorn of others, "And you are lonely."

A patient who resents the restriction in his or her life, must be helped to appreciate how he or she has contributed to that situation: for example, by choosing to stay married, to hold two jobs, to keep three dogs, to maintain a formal garden, and so forth. Generally one's life becomes so structured that one begins to consider it as a given, as a concrete structure that one must inhabit, rather than as a web, spun by oneself, which could be spun again in any number of ways. This is why, I am sure, that Otto Will said to his constricted, obsessive patient, "Why don't you change your name and move to California?" He confronted the patient forcefully with his freedom; with the fact that he really was free to change the structure of his life—to constitute it in an entirely different way.

Of course, there is a ready rejoinder: "There are many things that cannot be changed." One must earn a living, one must be father or mother to one's children, one must fulfill one's moral obligations. One must accept one's limitations: a paraplegic has no freedom to walk; a poor man no freedom to retire; an aging widow may have little possibility to marry; and so on. This objection—a fundamental objection to the concept of human freedom—may arise at any stage of therapy and is so important that I shall consider it at length in a separate section (pages 268–76).

Though there is a place for these techniques of labeling , and underscoring responsibility, there is a limit to their therapeutic effectiveness. "Can't" bells or slogans like "Take charge of your life" or "Own your feelings" are often arresting, but most patients require more than exhortation, and therapists must employ methods that have a deeper impact. The most potent methods available to therapists involve analyzing the patient's current (here-and-now) in-therapy behavior and demonstrating that the patient recreates microcosmically, in the therapy situation, the same situation that he or she faces in life. Indeed, as I shall discuss, psychotherapy may be structured specifically for the purpose of illuminating the patient's awareness of responsibility.

RESPONSIBILITY AND THE HERE-AND-NOW

The therapist who attempts to analyze a patient's narrative in an effort to demonstrate the latter's responsibility for a life situation often wanders into quicksand. The patient says *sotto voce*, "This is all very well. He can sit there in his comfortable office and tell me I got myself into this, but he doesn't *really* know what a sadistic bully my husband is" (or "what an impossible boss I have," or "how really overwhelming my compulsion is," or "what it's really like in the business world," or any other of an unlimited number of unsurmountable obstacles). There are no limits to this resistance because, as every experienced therapist knows, the patient is not an objective observer of his or her own life predicament. The patient may use externalizing mechanisms of defense or, in a number of other ways, distort the data to fit his or her assumptive world. Thus, it is only on rare occasions that the therapist can facilitate responsibility assumption by working solely with second-hand data.

Leverage is vastly increased if the therapist works with first-hand material that manifests itself in the here-and-now of treatment. By focusing on experiences that have transpired in the therapy situation, experiences in which he or she has participated, the therapist may help the patient examine the latter's own responsibility for nascent behavior—before it becomes encrusted and obscured by mechanisms of defense. The therapeutic impact is considerably increased if the therapist selects an incident or an aspect of behavior, with obvious similarities to the problem that brought the patient to therapy.

A patient, Doris, provides a clinical illustration. She sought therapy because of severe anxiety centering largely upon her relationship with males. Her major problem, as she described it, was to involve herself in relationships to abusive men from which she was unable to extricate herself. Her father had abused her as had her first husband, her current husband, and a long string of employers. Her account of her difficulty was persuasive, and my inclination was to empathize with Doris for having been so ill fated as to be thrown time and time again into the clutches of tyrannical bastards. She had been in a therapy group for several months when she had a severe anxiety storm. Unable to wait until the next group meeting, she called me one morning for an emergency individual appointment. With considerable difficulty I rearranged my schedule and agreed to see her at 3:00 P.M. that afternoon. At twenty minutes to three she called and left a message canceling the appointment. A few days later, in the group meeting, I inquired what had happened. She replied that she had felt slightly better that afternoon, and since my rule was that I would see a group member for an individual hour only once during the entire course of therapy, she had decided to save her hour for a time when she might need it even more.

Now I never made such a rule! I would never refuse to see a patient in an emergency. Nor had any of the group members heard me make any statement to that effect. But Doris was convinced I had told it to her. She chose to recall other incidents of our relationship in a highly selective fashion. For example, she remembered with astonishing clarity a single, impatient comment that I had once made to her months before (about her monopolistic tendencies), and she frequently repeated it in the group. However, she had forgotten many positive supportive statements I had made to her in subsequent months.

Doris's interaction with me in the microcosm of the here-and-now was representative of her relationship with men and illuminated her role (that is, her responsibility) in her life situation. She distorted her perception of me in the same way that she distorted her perception of other men—that is, by seeing us all as authoritarian and uncaring. But there was still more to be learned from the incident. I felt annoyed with Doris for canceling the appointment at the last moment, after I had made such an effort to clear the time for her. I felt irritated, too, at her insistence, even though seven other members disagreed with her, that I had voiced a "rule" about only one individual session. With some effort I tempered my irritation and maintained my therapeutic objectivity, but I could easily imagine how difficult it would be to relate to Doris in a nontherapeutic real-life situation.

In essence, then, what happened was that Doris had certain beliefs about men, certain expectancies about how they would behave toward her. These expectancies distorted her perception, and perceptual distortion resulted in her behaving in ways *that elicited the very behavior she dreaded*. This maneuver, the "self-fulfilling prophecy," is common: the individual first expects a certain event to occur, then behaves in such a way as to bring the prophecy to pass, and finally *relegates awareness of his or her behavior to the unconscious.*

This incident was crucial in Doris's therapy because it had such far-reaching implications for her basic problem. If she could understand and accept her responsibility for the way she related to me, then it was only a short step, requiring minimal generalization, for her to become aware of her responsibility for her mode of relating to other men in her life. The therapist should, I believe, seize such an incident and hang on to it with tenacity. I label it explicitly and underscore its importance: "Doris, I believe what just happened between you and me is exceedingly important because it gives us an important clue to some of the problems that exist between you and men in your life." If the patient is not yet prepared to accept the interpretation, repeat it in the future when there is additional corroborative evidence or when the therapist-patient relationship is more solid.

Awareness of one's own feelings constitute a therapist's most important instrument for identifying a patient's contribution to his or her life predicament. For example, a depressed forty-eight-year-old woman complained bitterly about the way her children treated her. They dismissed her opinions, dealt with her in cavalier fashion, and, when some serious issue was at stake, addressed their comments to their father. I tuned into my feelings about her and became aware of a whining quality in her voice which tempted me not to take her seriously and to treat her as a child. Sharing my feeling with the patient was enormously useful to her: it helped her become aware of her childlike behavior in many areas. The analysis of the here-and-now (her whining) was extremely important in helping her to solve the puzzle of her children's treatment of her. After all, they merely followed her instructions: they treated her precisely as she asked to be treated (that is, asked nonverbally through whining, through her excuses based on weakness, and through her helpless depression).

Not only is the patient's responsibility avoidance recapitulated in the patient therapist relationship, but it is also re-enacted in the patient's basic posture toward therapy. Patients, often with the silent collusion of the therapist, may settle comfortably, passively, and permanently into therapy, expecting little to happen or, if anything is to happen, that it will come from the therapist.

A therapist who has a sense of being heavily burdened by a patient, who is convinced that nothing useful will transpire in the hour unless he or she brings it to pass, has allowed that patient to shift the burden of responsibility from his or her own shoulders to those of the therapist. Therapists may deal with this process in a number of ways. Most therapists choose to reflect upon it. The therapist may comment that the patient seems to dump everything in his or her (the therapist's) lap, or that he or she (the therapist) does not experience the patient as actively collaborating in therapy. Or the therapist may comment upon his or her sense of having to carry the entire load of therapy. Or the therapist may find that there is no more potent mode of galvanizing a sluggish patient into action than by simply asking, "Why do you come?"

There are several typical resistances on the part of patients to these interventions, and they center on the theme of "I don't know what to do," or "If I knew what to do, I wouldn't need to be here," or "That's why I'm coming to see you," or "Tell me what I have to do." The patient feigns helplessness. Though insisting that he or she does not know what to do, the patient has in fact received many explicit and implicit guidelines from the therapist. But the patient does not disclose his or her feelings; the patient cannot remember dreams (or is too tired to write them down, or forgets to put paper and pencil by the bed); the patient prefers to discuss intellectual issues or to engage the therapist in a never-ending discussion of how therapy works. The problem, as every experienced therapist knows, is not that the patient does not know what to do. Each of these gambits reflects the same issue: the patient refuses to accept responsibility for change just as, outside the therapy hour, he or she refuses to accept responsibility for an uncomfortable life predicament.

6 / Responsibility

Ruth, a patient in a therapy group, illustrates this point. She avoided responsibility in every sphere of her life. She was desperately lonely, she had no close women friends, and all of her relationships with males had failed because her dependency needs were too great for her partners. More than three years of individual therapy had proved ineffective. Her individual therapist reported that Ruth seemed like a "lead weight" in therapy: she produced no material aside from circular rumination about her dilemmas with men, no fantasies, no transference material, and, over a three-year span, not a single dream. In desperation, her individual therapist had referred her to a therapy group. But in the group Ruth merely recapitulated her posture of helplessness and passivity. After six months she had done no work in the group and made no progress.

In one crucial meeting she bemoaned the fact that she had not been helped by the group, and announced that she was wondering whether this was the right group or the right therapy for her.

> Therapist: Ruth, you do here what you do outside the group. You wait for something to happen. How can the group possibly be useful to you if you don't use the group?
>
> Ruth: I don't know what to do. I come here every week and nothing happens. I get nothing out of therapy.
>
> Therapist: Of course you get nothing out of it. How can something happen until you make it happen?
>
> Ruth: I feel "blanked out" now. I can't think of what to say.
>
> Therapist: It seems important for you never to know what to say or do.
>
> Ruth: (*crying*) Tell me what you want me to do. I don't want to be like this all my life. I went camping this weekend—all the other campers were in seventh heaven, everything was in bloom and I spent the whole time in complete misery.
>
> Therapist: You want me to tell you what to do, even though you have a good idea of how you can work better in the group.
>
> Ruth: If I knew, I'd do it.
>
> Therapist: On the contrary! It seems very frightening for you to do what you can do for yourself.
>
> Ruth: (*sobbing*) Here I am again in the same shitty place. My mind is scrambled eggs. You're irritated with me. I feel worse, not better in this group. I don't know what to do.

At this point the rest of the group joined in. One of the members resonated with Ruth, saying he was in the same situation. Two others expressed their annoyance at her eternal helplessness. Another commented, accurately, that there had been endless discussions in the group about how members could participate more effectively. (In fact, a long segment of the previous meeting had been devoted to that very issue.)

She had innumerable options, another told her. She could talk about her tears, her sadness, or about how hurt she was. Or about what a stern bastard the therapist was. Or about her feelings toward any of the other members. She knew, and everyone knew that she knew, these options. "Why," the group wondered, "did she need to maintain her posture of helplessness and pseudo dementia?"

Thus galvanized, Ruth said that for the last three weeks during her commuting to the group she had made a resolution to discuss her feelings toward others in the group, but always reneged. Today she said she wanted to talk about why she never attended any of the post-group coffee klatches. She had wanted to participate but had not done so because she was reluctant to get any closer to Cynthia (another member of the group) lest Cynthia, whom she saw as exceptionally needy, would begin phoning her in the middle of the night for help. Following an intense interaction with Cynthia, Ruth openly showed her feelings about two other members of the group and by the end of the session had done more work than in the six previous months combined. What is worth underlining in this illustration is that Ruth's lament, "Tell me what to do," was a statement of responsibility avoidance. When sufficient leverage was placed upon her, she knew very well what to do in therapy. But she did not want to know what to do! She wanted help and change to come from outside. To help herself, to be her own mother, was frightening; it brought her too close to the frightening knowledge that she was free, responsible, and fundamentally alone.

RESPONSIBILITY ASSUMPTION IN GROUP THERAPY

The concept that therapy is a social microcosm—a setting in which the patient not only recites but displays his or her psychopathology in the here-and-now—pertains to all therapy settings (individual, couples, families, or groups). It is particularly relevant to the group situation. First, the large number of individuals, eight to ten (including the therapist or therapists) provides the opportunity for most of the patient's conflict areas to be ignited. In the individual setting the patient often encounters, in interaction with the therapist, his or her conflicted problems surrounding authority or problems relating to parents or to parental surrogates. But in the group setting the patient encounters so many others who activate so many different interpersonal issues (sibling rivalry, heterosexuality, homosexuality, competition with peers, intimacy, self-disclosure, generosity, giving and receiving, and so forth) that we are justified in considering the therapy group as a miniaturized social universe for each of its members.

The here-and-now of the small interactional therapy group provides especially optimal conditions for therapeutic work on responsibility awareness. One of the most fascinating aspects of group therapy is that the members are all born simultaneously: each starts out in the group on an equal footing. Each, in a way that is visible to the other members and—if the therapist does his job—apparent to himself, gradually scoops out and shapes a particular life space in the group. Thus, one is responsible for the interpersonal position one scoops out for oneself in the group (and, by analogy, in life as well) and for the sequence of events that will occur to one. The group has many eyes. Members do not need to accept another's description of how he or she is victimized by external persons or events. If the group functions at a here-and-now level (that is, the primary focus is upon experiencing and analyzing intermember relationships), then the members will observe how each creates his own self-victimization—and they will eventually feed these observations back to each member in turn.

Though we therapists do not often think of the group process in this manner, I believe that the major activities of the group, especially in the initial stages of therapy, are directed toward each member's becoming aware of personal responsibility. Why do we encourage members to be direct and honest in the group (that is, to be themselves)? Why do we encourage feedback? Why do we encourage members to share their impressions and feelings for the other members? I believe that the group therapist—often without necessarily being aware of doing so—attempts to escort each patient through the following sequence:

1. *Patients learn how their behavior is viewed by others.* Through feedback and, later, through self-observation, patients learn to see themselves through others' eyes.
2. *Patients learn how their behavior makes others feel.*
3. *Patients learn how their behavior creates the opinions others have of them.* Members learn that, as a result of their behavior, others value them, dislike them, find them unpleasant, respect them, avoid them, exploit them, fear them, and so on.
4. *Patients learn how their behavior influences their opinion of themselves.* Building on the information gathered in the first three steps, patients formulate self-evaluations; they make judgments about their self-worth and their lovability, and they learn how their behavior leads to these judgments.

Each step begins with the patient's own behavior and attempts to demonstrate the repercussions of that behavior. The end point of this sequence is that the group member apprehends that one is oneself responsible for how others see one, treat one, and regard one. Furthermore, one is also responsible for the manner in which one regards oneself. That one's group experience is a microcosm of one's life experience is an obvious and compelling fact; and in my experience patients have no difficulty generalizing assumption of individual responsibility from in-group situations to life situations. Once having reached this point, a patient has entered the vestibule of change; and the therapist then embarks on the venture of facilitating the process of willing, as I shall discuss in the next chapter.

The interactional therapy group enhances responsibility assumption not only by making members aware of their personal contribution to their unsatisfying life situations but also by accentuating each member's role in the conduct of the group. The underlying principle is that if members assume responsibility for the functioning of the group, then they become aware that they have the ability (and the obligation) to assume responsibility in all spheres of life.

The effective therapy group is one in which the members themselves are the primary agents of help. As patients look back over a successful therapy group experience, they rarely attribute their improvement directly to the therapist: either to specific comments by the therapist or to their overall relationship with the therapist. Instead, patients generally cite some aspect of their relationships with other members: either support, conflict and resolution, acceptance or, often, the experience of having been helpful to others. The leader-centered group fails to foster such events, and in it often all hope and all help are seen as emanating from the leader. (Such leader-centered approaches as Gestalt therapy groups and transactional analytic groups fail, in my opinion, to take full advantage of the therapeutic potential inherent in the group format.)

It is important, therefore, that the group leader be aware that his or her task is to create a social system—a system in which the group and the members themselves are the agents of change. The leader must be acutely sensitive to the location of responsibility in the group. If he or she looks forward with dismay to the therapy group meetings and ends each one feeling drained and fatigued, then it is clear that something has gone seriously wrong in the shaping of an optimal therapeutic culture. If the leader has the sense that everything depends on him or her, that if he or she doesn't work nothing will happen in the group, that the members are moviegoers coming to see what's playing that week, then the members of the therapy group have successfully transferred the burden of responsibility onto the shoulders of the therapist.

How does the group therapist help to shape a group that assumes responsibility for its own functioning? First, the leader must be aware of being generally the only person in the group who, on the basis of past experience, has a relatively clear definition in mind of what constitutes a good work meeting versus a nonwork meeting. The leader must help the members acquire such a definition and then encourage them to act accordingly. A number of techniques are available. The leader may use process checks—breaking into the meeting from time to time and asking the members to evaluate how the meeting has been going for them over the past thirty minutes or so. If the meeting has been painfully lumbering along, the leader may ask them to compare it with a previous, dynamic session, so that they gradually begin to differentiate work meetings from nonwork ones. If everyone is in accord that the meeting has been fruitful and compelling, the leader encourages the members to fix that session in their minds as a standard with which to compare subsequent meetings.

If in response to the leader's question about members' evaluation of the meeting, a member comments that he or she was involved only for the first fifteen minutes but then tuned out for the next thirty minutes after Joe or Mary started talking, the leader may, in a variety of ways, question why that particular member let the meeting go on in a manner that was personally unrewarding. How could that person have rechanneled the meeting? The leader may poll the group and, finding that there was a general consensus that the meeting was unrewarding, ask, "All of you seem to have known this. Why did you not stop the meeting and redirect it? Why is it left to me to do what everyone here is capable of doing?" Many variations in technique are possible, of course, depending upon the stylistic preferences of the therapist; what is important is the underlying strategy of encouraging patients to take responsibility for their lives through the process of taking responsibility for their therapy.

Large Group Therapy. The same principle operates in the larger therapeutic groups. Facilitation of the patient's assumption of personal responsibility has been a major impetus in the creation of the therapeutic community. Confinement in a psychiatric hospital has always been an autonomy-stripping experience: patients are deprived of power, of decision making, of freedom, of privacy, and of dignity. Maxwell Jones designed the therapeutic community so that the hospital experience would augment rather than diminish the patient's autonomy. The hospital ward was restructured so that patients had broad responsibility for their own treatment and their own environment. The patient government assumed the rights to decide upon ward rules, furloughs, ward personnel decisions, and even discharges and medication regimens.

A synonym for responsibility assumption is "life management." Many therapeutic approaches emphasize the teaching of life management skills. Inpatient units commonly conduct life management or "contract" groups in which each patient's "contract" (an agreement to take over the management of his or her life) is reviewed, and various contractual issues are discussed. The group may then systematically focus on what each person can do to take charge of such specific issues as personal finances, physical health, or social companionship.

RESPONSIBILITY ASSUMPTION AND THE THERAPIST'S STYLE

Activity and Passivity. The facilitation of responsibility assumption often poses a dilemma for the therapist. A too-active therapist takes over for the patient; a passive therapist conveys a sense of powerlessness to the patient. The problem is especially pronounced in psychoanalytic technique when the analyst's narrow range of behavior and relative inactivity may foster prolonged dependency. Milton Mazer, an analyst concerned with this problem, warns that excessive therapist passivity may discourage the patient's assumption of responsibility:

> ... the analyst's passivity in the presence of the patient's expression of helplessness confirms what he chooses to believe, namely, that he is not responsible for his actions and therefore may simply follow his impulses. Hearing no word of warning and no definition of the possible consequences, may he not with some justice conclude that he cannot help himself, particularly when the conclusion permits him to fulfill the aim of his drives?

Mazer warns also that the alternative—excessive activity, either in the form of guidance or limit setting—may also interfere with the assumption of responsibility: "It is not suggested that the analyst attempt to forbid the contemplated act, for this would also indicate that the patient is not to be held responsible and can be curbed only by an outside force, the authority of the analyst."

How to steer a middle course? What facilitative posture can the therapist assume? Mazer suggests that the therapist should attempt to help the patient recognize this process of choosing:

> ... it is the analyst's job to point out that the patient is in the process of deciding whether or not to engage in a particular act, for in so doing he clearly outlines the responsibility of the patient for his future. By this

means, the patient is given the opportunity to make a choice between neurotic necessity and responsible freedom. If he is able to choose responsible freedom, he makes his first cleavage in his neurotic structure.[11]

In other words, the therapist concentrates upon increasing the patient's awareness that (like it or not) he or she is faced with choice and cannot escape this freedom.

Other therapists have sought for more active ways of encouraging responsibility assumption. Transactional analysts, for example, place heavy emphasis upon the therapeutic "contract." They devote the initial sessions not toward establishing a diagnosis (which would merely accentuate the definition of the therapist-patient relationship as healer-supplicant) but toward developing a contract. The contract must emanate from the individual rather than from the wishes of others which have been internalized (in the "parent" ego state) as "shoulds" or "oughts." Furthermore, the contract must be action-oriented: not "to understand myself better" but "I want to lose thirty pounds" or "I want to be able to get an erection with my wife at least once a week." By setting concrete attainable goals—goals that the patient has defined—and by continuing to call the patient's attention to the relationship between work in therapy and these goals, transactional therapists hope to increase the patient's sense of responsibility for individual change.

Active suggestions on the part of the therapist may, properly employed, be used to increase awareness. I do not mean here that the therapist take over for the patient, making decisions and, in short, telling him or her how to live. However, there are times when the therapist may make a suggestion that seems an obvious behavioral option, but that the patient, because of a restricted perspective, has never considered. Thus, the question Why not? may be far more useful than the question Why? It is not even important that the patient follow the suggestion; the most important message of the procedure may be precisely that the patient's attention is called to the fact that he or she has never considered obvious options. Therapy may then proceed to consider the possibility of choice, the myth of choicelessness, and the feelings evoked by a confrontation with freedom. The following clinical vignette is illustrative.

George was a thirty-year-old successful dentist whose major problem centered about responsibility avoidance. He had been married once, but the marriage had failed in general because of his dependent posture toward his wife and specifically because he had "found himself" involved with another woman. Since then he had experienced considerable torment in regard to his efforts to decide upon remarriage. He was faced with a decision among several women, all of whom were interested in him, and went to great lengths to induce others—his friends, his therapist, and the women themselves—to make the decision for him.

An episode that illuminated for him his difficulties in assuming responsibility involved a visit to his parents whom he saw approximately once a year. His father had always been viewed as the family villain, and George's relationship to him had always been highly conflicted and dissatisfying for both. For over a decade their fighting had revolved about automobiles. Whenever George returned home, he wanted to use one of the family cars, and his father, an automobile mechanic, consistently objected, claiming that he needed the car or that the car was mechanically malfunctioning. George described his mother as a powerful woman who controlled every aspect of the family life aside from the automobiles, the one province where she allowed her husband dominion.

George anticipated his upcoming visit to his parents with considerable trepidation. He anticipated what would happen: he would want to use the car; his father would object, claiming that the brakes or the tires were bad, and would then insult him and ask him why couldn't he be a *mensch* and rent a car. "What kind of family is that?" George asked. "I come to see them once a year and they don't care enough even to pick me up at the airport."

"Why not rent a car?" I asked him. "Is the idea so outlandish? Why have you never considered it? After all, you make four times as much money as your father, are unmarried, and have no outstanding expenses. What would the extra few dollars a day mean to you?" George seemed startled at my suggestion. As obvious as it was, it was clear that he had never seriously considered it before. He thought about it and called his family the next day to tell them when he would be arriving. George suggested to his mother that he would rent a car, and his mother instantly assured him that the car was fixed now, that his father would pick him up at the airport, that they much looked forward to seeing him, and there would be no question about other forms of transportation.

The inevitable scene at the airport came to pass. His father greeted him with "Why didn't you rent a car? Look at that car rental counter. For eight ninety-five you could have rented a car." They had a loud embarrassing quarrel. George ran over to the car rental stall, rented a car, and angrily and self-righteously spurned his father's offer to pay for it. He and his father went home in separate cars. His father immediately went into the bedroom and left for work early in the morning. Since George was there for only a day, he did not see his father again.

We discussed this incident at great length in therapy. George considered it a prototypical example of his family interaction and as apologia for his current state. "As much as this disturbed me now, think of what it must have been like to grow up in a family like that." It was, George thought, especially illustrative of why he had such doubts about his masculinity: consider the model his father constituted, and consider also how impossible it was to talk to his father.

I provided an entirely different perspective. How much effort had he made to speak to his father? Consider his father's position: George's mother had offered his father's services without consulting him, as though he were the family butler. His father felt controlled and angry and attempted to exert himself in his only domain of power—the use of the car. But what efforts had George made to speak to his father? Could he not have spoken to his father as well as to his mother on the phone? What stopped him from simply phoning his father and saying, "Dad, I'll rent a car at the airport since I need one the next day. I won't be in till ten o'clock, but please wait up for me so we'll have a chance to talk." George seemed flabbergasted. "That's impossible!" he exclaimed. "Why?" "I can't talk to my father on the phone. You just don't know my family, that's all."

But George continued to feel a vague sense of guilt about his father—about that gray-headed, stubborn old man who had survived a concentration camp and who for thirty years had gone to work every day at 6:00 A.M. to put four children through college and graduate school. "Write him a letter and tell him just how you feel," I suggested. George once again seemed stunned at my suggestion, as well as annoyed with my naïveté. "That's impossible!" "Why?" I asked. "We don't write letters. I've never written my father a letter in my life." "And yet you complain about being alienated from him, about not being able to communicate with him. If you really want to communicate with him, then do so. Write him. No one prevents you from doing so. You can't pass this buck."

This simple interchange profoundly unsettled George, and that evening he tremulously and tearfully began to compose a letter to his father—a letter that would begin "Dear Dad" and *not* "Dear Mom and Dad" or "Dear Folks." As fate would have it, the spirit of freedom and responsibility stalked his father that same night; and before he had finished the letter, his father telephoned him to apologize—the first time that his father had ever phoned him. George told his father about the letter he was writing, and was so moved that he sobbed like a child. Suffice it to say that things were never the same again between George and his father, and that an analysis of George's immediate disclaimer that it was "impossible" to phone his father or to write a letter opened up rich vistas in therapy.

Fritz Perls, Gestalt Therapy, and Responsibility Assumption. Of the proponents of an active therapist style in the approach to responsibility, none have been more vigorous or inventive than Fritz Perls. Perls's approach rests on the basic concept that responsibility avoidance must be recognized and discouraged.

> As long as you fight a symptom, it will become worse. If you take responsibility for what you are doing to yourself, how you produce your symptoms, how you produce your illness, how you produce your existence—the very moment you get in touch with yourself—growth begins, integration begins.[12]

Perls was acutely sensitive to the patient's use (or avoidance) of the first-person pronoun and to any switch from active to passive voice:

> We hear the patient first depersonalize himself into "it" and then become the passive recipient of the vicissitudes of a capricious world. "I did this" becomes "It happened." I find that I must interrupt people repeatedly, asking that they own themselves. We cannot work with what occurs somewhere else and happens to one. And so I ask that they find their way from "It's a busy day" to "I keep myself busy," from "It gets to be a long conversation" to "I talk a lot." And so on.[13]

Once Perls had identified the modes of responsibility avoidance, he then urged the patient to translate helplessness back into unwillingness. The patient was urged to take responsibility for every gesture, every feeling, every thought. Perls sometimes used an "I take responsibility" structured exercise:

> With each statement, we ask patients to use the phrase, ". . . and I take responsibility for it." For example, "I am aware that I move my leg . . . and I take responsibility for it." "My voice is very quiet . . . and I take responsibility for it." "Now I don't know what to say . . . and I take responsibility for not knowing."[14]

Perls asked patients to take responsibility for all of their internal conflicting forces. If a patient was caught in an agonizing dilemma and, while discussing it, experienced a knot in his stomach, Perls asked the patient to have a conversation with the knot. "Place the knot in the other chair and talk to it. You lay the role of you and the role of the knot. Give it a voice. What does it say to you?" Thus he asked the patient to take responsibility for both sides of a conflict in order to be aware that nothing "happens" to one, that one is the author of everything—of every gesture, every movement, every thought.

> T: Are you aware of what your eyes are doing?
> P: Well, now I realize that my eyes keep looking away——
> T: Can you take responsibility for that?
> P: ——that I keep looking away from you.
> T: Can you be your eyes now? Write the dialogue for them.
> P: I am Mary's eyes. I find it hard to gaze steadily. I keep jumping and darting about.[15]

We choose each of our symptoms, Perls felt; "unfinished" or unexpressed feelings find their way to the surface in self-destructive, unsatisfying expressions. (This is the source of the term "Gestalt" therapy. Perls attempted to help patients to complete their gestalts—their unfinished business, their blocked-out awareness, their avoided responsibilities.)

A description of a therapeutic encounter illustrates Perls's approach to responsibility:

> Two weeks ago I had a wonderful experience—not that it was a cure, but at least it was an opening up. This man was a stammerer, and I asked him to increase his stammer. As he stammered, I asked him what he feels in his throat, and he said, "I feel like choking myself." So, I gave him my arm and said, "Now, choke me." "God damn, I could kill you!" he said. He got really in touch with his anger and spoke loudly, without any difficulties. So, I showed him he had an existential choice, to be an angry man or to be a stutterer. And you know how a stutterer can torture you, and keep you on tenterhooks. Any anger that is not coming out, flowing freely, will turn into sadism, power drive, and other means of torture.[16]

This approach to symptoms—asking the patient to produce or augment a symptom—is often an effective mode of facilitating responsibility awareness: by deliberately producing the symptom, in this instance a stammer, the individual becomes aware that the symptom is *his*, it is of his own creation. Though they have not conceptualized it in terms of responsibility assumption, several other therapists have simultaneously arrived at the same technique. Viktor Frankl, for example, describes a technique of "paradoxical intention"[17] in which a patient is asked deliberately to increase a symptom, be it an anxiety attack, compulsive gambling, fear of a heart attack, or binge eating. Don Jackson, Jay Haley, Milton Erickson, and Paul Watzlawick have all written on the same approach, which they label "symptom prescription."[18]

Perls developed a unique method of working with dreams—a method ingeniously designed to facilitate the individual's assumption of responsibility for all his or her mental processes. Throughout most of history, human beings have considered dreaming as a phenomenon beyond the realm of personal responsibility. This viewpoint is reflected in the common idiom: if a person wishes to disclaim an act or thought, he says, "I wouldn't even dream of it." Before the advent of Freudian dynamic psychology, dreams were generally considered to be divine visitations from without or chance occurrences. For example, one theory suggested that the cells of the cortex slept, and that as the toxic metabolites of the day were cleaned away, clusters of cells "awoke" in strictly random patterns. The dream, according to this theory, is comprised by the output of the cells as they awaken: the nonsensical quality of most dreams is, therefore, a function of the adventitious sequence in which cells are aroused; and an intelligible dream is formed serendipitously in much the same way that a horde of monkeys punching at typewriters by chance compose a comprehensible paragraph.

Freud argued persuasively that dreams were products of neither chance nor outside visitation but instead of the conflicting, interacting components of the personality: the id impulses, the manifest day's residue of the subconscious, the dream censor (an unconscious machinist of the ego), the conscious ego ("secondary revision"). Though Freud discovered that the individual—or at least the interplay of these parts of the individual—was the sole author of the dream, his compartmentalization of the psyche resulted, Perls insisted (and quite correctly, I believe) in personal responsibility's being lost in the component crevices.

Perls, who termed the dream "the existential messenger,"[19] aimed to maximize the individual's appreciation of his or her own authorship of the dream. First, Perls attempted to bring the dream to life by changing its tense: he asked the patient to repeat the dream in the present tense and then to re-enact the dream by turning it into a play in which the patient becomes the director, the props, and the actors. The patient is asked to play the parts of all the objects in the dream drama. For example, I observed Perls working with a patient who dreamed of driving his car, which began to sputter and finally died altogether. Under Perl's instruction the patient played multiple parts: the driver, the car, the empty gas tank, the sluggish spark plugs, and so on. By this strategy Perls hoped that the patient could begin to reassemble into a whole the scattered bits of his personality (that is, to complete the individual gestalt).

Responsibility assumption meant to Perls that the individual has to take responsibility for all his or her feelings, including unpleasant ones that are often projected upon others.

> We are not willing to take the responsibility that we are critical, so we project criticism onto others. We don't want to take the responsibility for being discriminating, so we project it outside and then we live in fear of being rejected. And one of the most important responsibilities is to take responsibility for our projections and become what we project.[20]

By reclaiming all previously disowned parts of oneself, the individual's experience becomes richer: one is at home within oneself and within one's world.

> Of course, taking responsibility for your life and being rich in experience and ability is identical. And what I hope to do is . . . to make you understand how much you gain by taking responsibility for every emotion, every movement you make, every thought you have—and shed responsibility for anybody else . . .[21]

Shedding "responsibility for anybody" else is vitally important for the psychotherapist. Perls was acutely aware of the patient's effort to manipulate others, especially the therapist, into taking care of him or her.

> The therapist has three immediate tasks: to recognize how the patient tries to get support from others rather than to provide his own, to avoid getting sucked in and taking care of the patient and to know what to do with the patient's manipulative behavior.[22]

Not "getting sucked in" is not easy, and the therapist must be accustomed to recognizing and resisting a patient's many and varied means of persuasion:

> "I can't cope, in this situation, and you can. I 'need' you to show me the way, so that I can go on with my life." This is sometimes not much of a life at all, but rather an existence which includes a succession of propositions submitted by the patient to people who like to take over the management of others. The therapist is merely the latest try. Hopefully, "the buck stops here."[23]

In order to resist being manipulated, Perls took an extreme position on stopping the buck. He began his workshops in this manner:

So if you want to go crazy, commit suicide, improve, get "turned on," or get an experience that will change your life, that's up to you. I do my thing and you do your thing. Anybody who does not want to take responsibility for this, please do not attend this seminar. You came here out of your own free will. I don't know how grown up you are, but the essence of a grown-up person is to be able to take responsibility for himself—his thoughts, feelings, and so on . . .[24]

Perls's position here is extraordinarily severe and may, especially with severely disturbed patients, require modification. Many patients require months of work to become able to assume responsibility, and it is often unrealistic to make full responsibility assumption a prerequisite for therapy. Occasional situations arise, however, where the therapist is well advised to require some degree of responsibility assumption at the onset of therapy. Many therapists insist that highly suicidal patients make a "no suicide" pact in which they agree not to attempt suicide for a specified period of time. Properly used, such an approach can significantly diminish suicide risk.[25]

Though Perls's words leave no doubt that he was highly sensitive to the issue of responsibility and cognizant of the fact that the therapist must not accept the burden of the patient's responsibility, he was never able to solve (or for that matter, I believe, to recognize fully) the paradox of his approach to therapy. "Assume responsibility" the patient is told. But what is the rest of the patient's experience? An encounter with an enormously powerful, charismatic, wise old man who pronounces nonverbally: "And I'll tell you precisely how, when and why to do it." Perls's active personal style, his aura of power and omniscience contradicted his words. To receive two simultaneous, conflicting messages, one explicit and the other implicit, is to be placed in a classical double bind. Let me describe another therapeutic approach that attempts to avoid that pitfall.

Helmuth Kaiser and Responsibility Assumption. Of the many therapists who have confronted the dilemma of how to increase responsibility assumption without at the same time "taking over" for the patient, Helmuth Kaiser's contributions stand out for thoughtfulness and consistency. Though both Kaiser and Perls built their approaches to therapy around the axis of responsibility, the style and the structure of their approaches were diametrically opposed. Kaiser, who died in 1961, was a highly inventive therapist who, because he wrote little, has never enjoyed wide recognition. A book of his collected works was issued in 1965 under the title *Effective Psychotherapy.*[26] Kaiser believed that patients have a universal conflict, a "condition of the mind, common to all neurotics,"[27] which issues from the fact that "mature adulthood entails a complete, a fundamental, an eternal and insurmountable isolation."[28]

Kaiser tells the story of a medical school chum, Walter, who in the midst of his studies accepted a role in an amateur dramatic production and became impassioned with the theater. He was clearly talented and deliberated abandoning his medical studies and throwing his whole life into the career of an actor. But *how* talented was he? Would he become a great actor? Walter agonized over his decision and sought the opinion of expert after expert. Kaiser observed the torments of his friend, and suddenly it dawned upon him that Walter was expecting the impossible. He did not merely want an opinion. He wanted much more: he wanted someone else to take the responsibility of his decision.

> In the time that followed, G. [that is, Kaiser] could observe how Walter slowly, step by step, discovered that no judgment, no advice from any other person could contribute anything to the decision he had to make. Feeling compassionate towards Walter's struggle, he was always willing to discuss with his friend all the innumerable pros and cons which could possibly have a bearing on the step considered. Yet, when they had gone through all the possible consequences, had estimated chances, weighed indications, sifted information and only the ultimate conclusion was missing, they regularly fell into a deep, painful silence. G. then sensed Walter's unspoken question, "Now, what do you think?"[29]

What Walter faced, and recoiled from, is a profound human paradox: we yearn for autonomy but recoil from autonomy's inevitable consequence—isolation. Kaiser called this paradox "mankind's congenital achilles heel" and said that we would suffer enormously from it if we did not cover it over with some "magician's trick," some device to deny isolation. That "magician's trick" is what Kaiser called the "universal symptom"—a mechanism of defense which denies isolation by softening one's ego boundaries and fusing with another. Earlier I discussed fusion or merger as a defense against death anxiety in the description of man's yearning for an ultimate rescuer. Kaiser reminds us that isolation, and (though he does not explicitly make this point) the groundlessness beneath isolation, is a powerful instigator of one's efforts to fuse with another.

What events hurl us into a confrontation with isolation? According to Kaiser, those events that most make one aware that one is entirely responsible for one's own life—especially the confrontation with a life-altering decision or the development of a conviction that is not supported by authority. At these times we strive, as did Kaiser's friend Walter, to find others who will assume responsibility for us.

Kaiser was exquisitely sensitive to the efforts of the patient to avoid the isolation of responsibility by transferring executive powers to the therapist. How can the therapist thwart these efforts of the patient? Kaiser pondered this question, and posited several approaches but finally decided that the issue was so important that it must be dealt with by a modification in the very structure of therapy. To discourage responsibility transfer, therapy should be *entirely* unstructured, the therapist *entirely* nondirective, the patient *entirely* responsible not only for the *content* but for the *procedure* of therapy. Kaiser declared that "there should be no rules for the therapist." His description of a therapist-patient interaction is illustrative:

> P: May I ask what the therapy will consist of? I mean, what is the procedure?
>
> T: The procedure . . . ? I am not sure that I understand you fully, but if I do, I would say: There is no procedure!
>
> P: (Smiling politely) Oh, of course, I meant only: What do you want me to do?
>
> T: That is exactly what I thought you meant by "procedure."
>
> P: I do not understand (20 seconds silence). I mean . . . of course, there must be something I am supposed to do. Isn't there?
>
> T: You seem certain that there is something you are supposed to do here.
>
> P: Well, isn't that so?
>
> T: As far as I am concerned, no.
>
> P: Well . . . I . . . I . . . I do not understand.
>
> T: (Smiling) I think you understand what I said but you cannot quite believe it.
>
> P: You are right. I really don't think that you mean it literally.
>
> T: (after 10 seconds pause) I meant it literally.
>
> P: (after an uneasy silence of 60 seconds with some effort) Is it all right if I say something about my anxiety attacks?
>
> T: It seems impossible for you to believe that I meant what I said.
>
> P: I am sorry . . . I did not mean to . . . but, indeed, I am not sure at all that I really . . . excuse me, what did you say?
>
> T: I said: It seems impossible for you to believe that I meant what I said.
>
> P: (shaking his head slightly as if irritated) No, I mean: is it all right for me . . . (he looks up and when his eyes meet those of the therapist he starts laughing.)[30]

Kaiser believed that "anything that increases the patient's feeling of responsibility for his own words must tend to cure him"; and as this illustration indicates, he refused even to accept the responsibility of instructing the patient how to operate in therapy.

There are obvious limitations to such extreme technique. I believe that Perls erred in the direction of supplying too much structure and energy to the patient, and that Kaiser erred in precisely the opposite direction. No therapist can help a patient who, because of bewilderment, lack of structure, or lack of confidence, prematurely drops out of therapy. Because the therapist ultimately hopes to assist the patient assume responsibility, it does not follow that the therapist must demand that the patient do so at each step, even in the onset of therapy. The therapeutic situation usually requires flexibility; often to keep patients in therapy, therapists must be active and supportive in initial sessions. Later, once the therapist alliance is welded fast, the therapist may accent those therapeutic conditions that enhance acceptance of responsibility.

Elsewhere Kaiser stresses the importance of the therapeutic relationship and of communicational directness;[31] and no doubt in actual therapy situations he made the necessary adjustments. He wrote an intriguing play, *Emergency*,[32] which, in fact, illustrates therapeutic flexibility par excellence. The protagonist of *Emergency*, a psychiatrist, Dr. Terwin, is consulted by Mrs. Porfiri, the wife of a psychiatrist, who states that her husband is deeply disturbed but refuses to seek help. Dr. Terwin pretends to be a patient and consults Dr. Porfiri. Gradually, almost imperceptibly, he then proceeds under the rubric of "Patient" to treat the therapist. Obviously Dr. Porfiri was not able to assume responsibility, not even the responsibility of requesting therapy; and the therapist did not demand it of him but instead did what all good therapists must do: he modified the therapy to fit the patient.

Responsibility Awareness American-Style—Or, How to Take Charge of Your Own Life, Pull Your Own Strings, Take Care of Number One, and Get It

Responsibility awareness has come of age in America. What once was the discourse—often obscure—of the professional philosopher and later the *bon mot* of the Left Bank avant-garde has become a major consumer item in the New World today. Many nationwide best sellers have as their central theme, responsibility assumption. *Your Erroneous Zones*, to take one example, has these chapter headings: "Taking Charge of Yourself," "Choice—Your Ultimate Freedom," "You Don't Need Their Approval," "Breaking Free from the Past," "Breaking the Barrier of Convention," "Declare Your Independence."[33] The central message of the book is clearly stated: "Begin to examine your life in the light of choices you have made or failed to make. This puts all responsibility for what you are and how you feel on you."[34] Similar books, for example, *Pulling Your Own Strings*,[35] and *Self-Creation*[36] have also zoomed quickly to the top of the best-seller lists.

Mass consumerism requires that a product be attractive, well packaged, and, most important of all, easily and quickly consumed. Unfortunately these requirements are generally incompatible with the effort and the thoughtfulness that are needed if one is truly to examine and alter one's life and world perspective. Thus a "leveling-down" occurs: we are subjected to exhortation, and best sellers, such as *Your Erroneous Zones*, tell us how to "put an end to procrastination":

> Sit down and get started on something you've been postponing. Begin a letter or a book. Simply beginning will help you to eliminate anxiety about the whole project.... Give yourself a designated time slot (say Wednesday from 10:00 to 10:15 P.M.) which you will devote exclusively to the task you've been putting off.... Quit smoking. Now! Begin your diet ... this moment! Give up booze ... this second. Put this book down and do one push-up as your beginning exercise project. That's how you tackle problems ... with action now. Do it! Decide not to be tired until the moment before you get into bed. Don't allow yourself to use fatigue or illness as an escape or to put off doing anything.[37]

Or "rid yourself of dependency":

> Give yourself five-minute goals for how you're going to deal with dominant people in your life. Try a one-shot "No, I don't want to," and test the reaction of your reaction in the other person.... Stop taking orders![38]

"Responsibility" has caught the public eye, and professional workshops with a responsibility theme have burgeoned across the country. For example, a large workshop, called "Taking Charge of Your Own Life" (and subtitled "The Psychology of Health Care, The Role of Individual Responsibility") was offered at several locations in 1977–78. It included on its program: Rollo May, in a keynote address, on the existential struggle toward personal and spiritual freedom; Albert Ellis, on his rational-emotive approach to the individual's responsibility for

254

growth and change in the area of sexuality and intimacy; and Arnold Lazarus, on multimodal therapy—an approach to self-healing described in his book *"I Can If I Want To."*[39] Other topics in the workshop included behavioral stress-management approach to helping the hard-driving ("Type-A") patient change behavioral patterns, stress and biofeedback, overcoming shyness, Eastern (meditational) approaches to self-control, and changing "no-change" habit patterns. Of particular interest is the great diversity of clinical approaches clustered on the same program. In the past one would not have perceived the common theme of these various approaches; currently they are grouped together under the rubric of "responsibility."

EST

The mass merchandising of responsibility assumption is nowhere more evident than in est—the most publicized and commercially successful of the growth workshops of the 1970s. Owing to this success and to its concern with the concept of responsibility, est warrants a particularly close examination.

A slickly packaged, mass-produced, enormously profitable, large-group approach to personal change founded by Werner Erhard, est has spiraled in a few short years from a one-man operation to a massive organization. By 1978 it had over 170,000 graduates, and in 1978 it grossed over nine million dollars, with a paid staff of 300 and a volunteer unpaid staff of 7,000; and it includes on its advisory boards prominent business executives, attorneys, university presidents, the former chancellor of the University of California Medical School, eminent psychiatrists, government officials, and popular entertainers.

The est format consists of a large group of individuals (approximately 250) who spend two weekends listening to a trainer who instructs them, interacts with them, insults them, shocks them, and guides them through a number of structured exercises. Though the est packet is a potpourri of techniques borrowed from such personal growth technologies as Scientology, Mind Dynamics, encounter groups, Gestalt therapy, and Zen meditation,[40] its primary thrust is *assumption of responsibility*. Participants and est leader statements make that crystal clear:

> The leader explained, "Each of us is different because each of us makes different choices. It is the inability to choose that keeps us stuck in our lives. When you make a choice your life moves forward. The choice usually boils down to a simple yes or no. "I don't know" is also a choice—the choice to evade responsibility."[41]

255

One participant describes her recollections of the workshop in this manner:

> "When you are responsible," Stuart [the trainer] thundered, "you find out you just didn't happen to be lying there on the tracks when the train passed through. You are the asshole who put yourself there."
>
> The theme of responsibility pervades every aspect of the training. In fact, if I were to sum up in a few words what I got from the training data it would be that we are each the cause of our own experience and responsible for everything that happens in our experience.[42]

The theme of responsibility assumption is an explicit part of the est catechism. In this interaction an est trainer argues, and argues effectively, that one is responsible for being mugged:

> "You are each the sole source of your own experience, and thus TOTALLY RESPONSIBLE FOR EVERYTHING YOU EXPERIENCE. When you *get* that, you're going to have to give up ninety percent of the bullshit that's running your lives. Yes, Hank?"
>
> "Look," says burly Hank, looking quite irritated, "I get that I'm responsible for everything I do. I see that. But when I get mugged, there's no way I'm gonna accept responsibility for getting mugged."
>
> "Who's the source of your experience, Hank?"
>
> "In this case, it would be the mugger."
>
> "The mugger would take over your mind?"
>
> "My mind and my wallet!"
>
> (Laughter)
>
> "Do you take responsibility for getting out of bed that morning?"
>
> "Sure"
>
> "For being on that street?"
>
> "Yes"
>
> "For seeing a man with a gun in his hand?"
>
> "For seeing him?"
>
> "Yes, seeing the mugger."
>
> "Take responsibility for seeing him?"
>
> "Yes"
>
> "Well," says Hank. "I would certainly see him."
>
> "If you had at that moment no eyes, no ears, nose, or sensations in the skin, you wouldn't experience this mugger, would you?"
>
> "Okay, I get that."
>
> "That you are responsible for being at that street at that hour with money that might be stolen?"
>
> "Okay, I get that."
>
> "That you chose not to risk your life by resisting this man and that you chose to give up your wallet?"
>
> "When a guy says give me your money with a gun in his hand, there's no choice."
>
> "Did you choose to be at that place at that time?"

"Yeah, but I didn't choose to have that guy show up."

"You saw him, didn't you?"

"Sure."

"You take responsibility for seeing him, don't you?"

"For seeing him, yeah."

"Then get it: EVERYTHING THAT YOU EXPERIENCE DOESN'T EXIST UNLESS YOU EXPERIENCE IT."

"EVERYTHING A LIVING CREATURE EXPERIENCES IS CREATED UNIQUELY BY THAT LIVING CREATURE WHO IS THE SOLE SOURCE OF THAT EXPERIENCE. WAKE UP, HANK!"[43]

Most est graduates, when discussing their gains, emphasize, above all, the assumption of responsibility. One est graduate stated that people

realized they created their own backaches, migraines, asthma, ulcers and other ailments. . . . Illness doesn't just *happen* to us. It was remarkable to watch person after person get up and admit that they and they alone were responsible for their physical ailments. Once these people faced the experiences of their life honestly, their ailments vanished.[44]

In the following interaction an est trainer goes even further and argues that a man is responsible for his wife's having cancer:

"How the hell am I responsible for my wife's getting cancer?"

"You're responsible for creating the experience of your wife's manifesting behavior which you choose to call, by agreement with others, a disease called cancer."

"But I didn't cause the cancer."

"Look, Fred, I get that what I'm saying is hard for you to fit into your belief system. You've worked hard for forty years to create your belief system and though I get that right now you're being as open-minded as you can be, for forty years you've believed that things happen out there and that you, passive, innocent bystander, keep getting RUN OVER—by cars, buses, stock-market crashes, neurotic friends, and cancer. I get that. Everyone in this room has lived with that same belief system. ME, INNOCENT; REALITY OUT THERE, GUILTY.

"BUT THAT BELIEF SYSTEM DOESN'T WORK! IT'S ONE REASON WHY YOUR LIFE DOESN'T WORK. The reality that counts is your experience, and you are the sole creator of your experience.[45]

"You are the sole creator of your experience." This statement is strikingly similar to many of Sartre's statements about freedom and responsibility. The core of est—the "it" of "getting it"—is responsibility assumption. It would appear, then, that est works with some important but obscure concepts and rephrases them into arresting language—an accessible, Californian, "Pop" Sartre. If this ingenious application of philosophical thought works, then professional therapists may have a great deal to learn from est methodology.

But does it work? Unfortunately we have no definitive answers to that question. No controlled outcome research on est has been done; and though est graduate testimonials are legion, they may not be relied upon as a measure of effectiveness. A similar enthusiastic chorus of testimonials has surrounded every new personal growth technology from T-groups, encounter groups, nude encounters, and marathons, to Esalen body awareness, psychodrama, rolfing, TA, Gestalt, Lifespring, Synanon. Yet the natural history of so many of these approaches (which will most likely be the history of est as well) includes a period of bright pulsation, then a gradual dimming, and ultimate replacement by the next technology. Indeed, many of the participants in each of these have had a history of prior attendance and allegiance to some other approach. What is behind this history? Does it raise doubts about whether the approach has a truly substantial, enduring effect?

Follow-up studies have shown that an extremely high percentage of est graduates rated their experiences as highly positive and constructive. Yet one must be cautious in evaluating research whose design does not include adequate controls; much empirical research suggests that there is no outcome assessment more susceptible to error than a simple follow-up, which is in essence a compilation of testimonials. To examine only one aspect of research design, consider the problem of self-selection. Who chooses to go to est? Is it possible that those who elect to attend, to part with a large sum of money, to put up with a grueling weekend, are going to change (or to say they change) *regardless* of the content of the program?

The answer is, most assuredly, yes! Research on placebo reactors, on subject expectational sets, and on the psychological attitudes of volunteers strongly indicates that the outcome to the individual is heavily influenced by factors that exist *before* the workshop. This tendency, of course, makes research very difficult: the common design of recruiting volunteers for a personal growth procedure (such as an encounter group) and contrasting their outcomes with those of a similar number of nonvolunteer control subjects, is highly flawed. In fact, a growth group or workshop composed of dedicated individuals who have committed themselves to the experience, who are desirous of personal growth, and who have high expectational sets (created in part by an effective pre-group "hype"), will *always* be deemed successful by the great majority of participants. To deny benefit would create significant cognitive dissonance. The post-group "high," the glowing testimonials, are ubiquitous. Only a particularly inept leader could fail under these circumstances.

If there is no reliable outcome evidence, on what can we rely? I suggest that if we examine the internal evidence available on est, we shall discover a serious and alarming inconsistency. While avowing the goal of responsibility assumption, est is at the same time *extraordinarily heavily structured.* In the est weekend there are numerous, heavily enforced ground rules: no alcohol, drugs, tranquillizers, or watches. No one is permitted to go to the bathroom except at the four-hour bathroom breaks. Name tags are to be worn at all times. Chairs are not to be moved. Punctuality is stressed; latecomers are punished by not being permitted entry or by public humiliation.[46] Members are not permitted to eat except at widely spaced meal breaks and are required to turn over snacks hidden in their pockets.

Many est graduates volunteer to be nonpaid assistants and, judging from their description of their experiences, are enormously exhilarated by the act of giving up their autonomy and basking in the powerful rays of authority. Consider these comments made by an est volunteer, a clinical psychologist:

> My next task was to arrange the name tags. They had to be ten in a vertical row, not touching, in perfect parallel columns. Now I was to become aware of est's meticulous attention to detail. The instructions for each chore were exact, deliberate with the precision one would expect from an excellent instruction manual. I was expected to carry out the task with the same precision.
>
> From name tags I went to table cloths ... Each table cloth was to be pinned with a square corner and should almost but not quite touch the floor ... I looked up to see the person supervising the assistants standing alongside me. "It touches the floor" ...
>
> I redid the table cloth with full attention. My square corners were perfect and the cloth hung to precisely the right length. I had completed the job, which in est terms meant that I had finished it with nothing left out of the experience.[47]

"Perfect parallel columns." "Meticulous attention to detail." "The precision one would expect from an instruction manual." Table cloths hung to "precisely the right length." Where amid this lust for conformity and structure is one to find freedom and responsibility? I became even more troubled when at a workshop I noted a cadre of est assistants, all of whom dressed like Werner Erhard (blue blazer, white open-collared shirt, gray slacks) and had their hair cut like Werner Erhard. And, like Werner Erhard, began their sentences with "and" and spoke about est in hushed, almost religious tones. Consider other reports of volunteers (which I have drawn without much selective effort from est books endorsed by Werner Erhard and sent to me by est to inform me about the organization):

> A young woman who had volunteered to clean the San Francisco town house where Werner has his office told me that she had been instructed in detail about how to do the job. "I had to clean under each object, such as those found on a coffee table, and then replace it precisely where I found it, not a half inch away."[48]

> The person assigned to clean toilets at headquarters reported that there was one, and only one, est way to do the job. He shared that he had been astonished to discover how much thought and effort could go into cleaning toilets the est way: i.e., completely.[49]

> We were instructed to smile in the role of "greeter," . . . [at other times] we were to remain poker faced. When I remarked on this to my supervisor, he said, simply, "The purpose of assisting is to assist. Do what you're doing now. Do your *humor* at humor time."[50]

A practicing psychologist describes her volunteer work:

> The high point of the weekend came when the man in charge of logistics said to me, after I had mapped the shortest and most efficient route to the bathrooms, "Thank you, Adelaide. You've done an excellent job in writing these instructions." Wow! I was high for hours.[51]

Doing things the "right" way. Cleaning toilets the est way. Replacing coffee table objects precisely—not a half-inch away. Doing humor at "humor time." "High for hours" after being complimented for mapping the most efficient route to the bathroom. These words reflect an obvious satisfaction in the losing of one's freedom, in the joy of surrendering autonomy and donning the blinders of a beast of burden.

Many est graduate statements reflect not a sense of personal power but a giving up oneself to a higher being. Judgment and decision making are ceded; nothing is more important than being smiled on by a divine providence. An est volunteer states ingeniously:

> Werner can become very loud when a job isn't completed. I quake, but I know he loves me. Does that sound really crazy? That's the way it is and so you go about your job the way Werner wants the job done.[52]

Erhard becomes a figure larger than life, his blemishes are "touched up," his shortcomings turned into virtues, his talents turned into superhuman qualities. A clinical psychologist gives her impressions of her first exposure to Werner Erhard:

At that time, I had not yet met Werner. A friend had told me that "he makes you feel as though you are the whole world, as though nothing else exists." The lights dimmed promptly at 8:00 and Werner emerged . . . looking much younger than his forty years, his skin and eyes incredibly clear, dressed in an impeccably tailored beige jacket, open-necked white shirt and dark slacks. The audience rose and applauded. Werner had come to be with them.[53]

The audience had settled in and was intensely focused on this magnetic and attractive (but not quite handsome) man with the body of a tennis player and the eyes of a prophet.[54]

"Incredibly clear eyes." "The eyes of a prophet." "Werner had come to be with them!" It was such pronouncements—pronouncements that signal the end of personal judgment and freedom— that prompted another est graduate, also a clinical psychologist, to write: "The more I envision the goose-stepping corps at the center of the est organization, the more virtue I see in anarchy."[55] Thus the major critique that may be levied against est is—not that it is simplistic (there may be virtue in that), not that it is mass production (every great system of thought demands a popularizer)—but that it is fundamentally inconsistent. Authoritarianism will not breed personal autonomy but, on the contrary, always stifles freedom. It is sophistry to claim, as est presumably does, that a product of personal responsibility may emerge from a procedure of authoritarianism. Which, after all, is the product and which the procedure? The wish to escape from freedom, as Fromm has taught us, is rooted deep. We will go to any length to avoid responsibility and to embrace authority *even, if necessary, if it requires us to pretend to accept responsibility.* Is it possible that the authoritarian procedure has become the product? Perhaps it was from the onset—we shall never know!

Responsibility and Psychotherapy: Research Evidence

The connection between responsibility and psychotherapy rests on two related propositions: responsibility avoidance is not conducive to mental health; and responsibility acceptance, in psychotherapy, leads to therapeutic success. Let me examine the available research to determine what empirical evidence exists to support these propositions.

First, it is important to recognize that these propositions oversimplify the matter. Consider, for example, the nature of defense mechanisms, some of which result in responsibility avoidance (such as innocent victim, externalization, or losing control) and are maladaptive, while others (such as those with considerable social reinforcement like belief in grace or divine providence) may stand one in good stead. Some individuals may, on the other hand, face responsibility too fully, too openly, and without the internal resources to face the ensuing anxiety. A certain amount of ego strength is necessary if one is to face one's existential situation and the anxiety inherent therein.

IS RESPONSIBILITY AVOIDANCE BAD FOR MENTAL HEALTH?

It is no easy matter to find evidence that responsibility avoidance is bad for mental health, since neither "responsibility" nor "freedom" nor "willing" has been explicitly studied by researchers. A computerized search yielded no empirical studies whatsoever. The term "responsibility" is not to be found in the formal nosological categories, nor is the concept of responsibility avoidance or acceptance to be found in studies of psychotherapy. Consequently I approached the literature obliquely and inquired whether there were studies that bore even a possible relevance to responsibility. The most relevant construct, discussed in chapter 4, was locus of control.* External locus of control may be considered as lack of responsibility acceptance. If responsibility avoidance is "bad" for one's health, then I expected external locus of control to be positively correlated with abnormal personal functioning. I found research that has demonstrated that externals, when contrasted with internals, have greater feelings of inadequacy;[56] have more mood disturbances,[57] are more tense, anxious, hostile, and confused;[58] are lower achievers, less politically active, and more suggestible;[59] are less imaginative, more frustrated, and more apprehensive.[60] Schizophrenic patients are far more likely to score in an external direction.[61] Severely impaired psychiatric patients are more likely to be externals than are mildly impaired patients.[62]

Depression is the disorder that has been most researched with the locus of control construct, since the clearly evident hopelessness and fa-

* Recall that locus of control measures, at a superficial level, whether an individual accepts personal responsibility for his or her behavior and life experiences, or whether the individual believes that what happens to him or her is unrelated to personal behavior and is therefore beyond personal control. Individuals who accept responsibility are considered to have an "internal" locus of control, and those who reject it have an "external" locus of control.

talism of the depressed patient suggest, even to the untrained observer, that such patients have lost the belief that they have the power to act in their own behalf and to influence their own experiential worlds. Many have demonstrated that depressed individuals have an external locus of control and, as a result of the breakdown of a perceived correction between behavior and outcome, develop a deep sense of helplessness and hopelessness.[63]

A major theory of depression is the "learned-helplessness" model formulated by Martin Seligman which postulates that the various components of depression (affective, cognitive, and behavioral) are consequences of one's learning early in life that outcomes (that is, rewards and punishments) are out of one's control.[64] A person who learns that there is no causal relationship between his or her behavior and outcome not only ceases to act in an effective manner but also begins to evince aspects of depression. Translated into existential terms, this model postulates simply that those who believe that they are not responsible for what happens to them in the world may pay a heavy penalty. Though they avoid paying the price of existential anxiety associated with awareness of responsibility, they may, as Seligman claims, develop a fatalism and depression.

The learned-helplessness model of depression is rooted in the experimental laboratory and is based on observations that experimental animals exposed to unavoidable stress become less adaptive at avoiding subsequent escapable stress. For example, dogs given inescapable shock were subsequently poorer at escaping from avoidable shocks than were dogs given prior escapable shock or no shock at all.[65] There have been many attempts to design comparable laboratory studies with humans. For example, subjects have been exposed to inescapable noise and on subsequent testing exhibit more failures to escape an escapable noise when placed in a human analogue of an animal shuttle box[66] or showed debilitated performance on certain problem-solving tests.[67]

These results demonstrate, then, that if individuals are "taught" in the laboratory that their behavior cannot extricate them from situations, then subsequent coping behavior is impaired. Furthermore, David Klein and Martin Seligman found that depressed individuals (who did not receive pretreatment of inescapable noise) performed in a comparable manner with those nondepressed subjects who did receive inescapable noise.[68] William Miller and Seligman found comparable findings with problem-solving experiments.[69] In other experiments it has been found that depressed subjects (unlike nondepressed subjects) have low expectancies for future successes on laboratory tasks, and that these expectancies are not influenced by reinforcement.*[70]

To summarize, the locus of control, a widely used psychological instrument, which can be conceptually compared to responsibility acceptance and avoidance, offers some evidence that responsibility avoidance (external locus of control) is associated with some forms of psychopathology, especially depression. The learned-helplessness laboratory paradigm of depression offers further corroborative evidence.

What does research tell us about the origins of the individual's posture toward control or responsibility? There is some evidence that the antecedents of internality and externality lie in early family environment: a consistent, warm, attentive, and responsive milieu is a precursor of the development of an internal locus of control, while an inconsistent, unpredictable, and relatively uncongenial milieu (much more frequently found in lower socioeconomic classes) begets a sense of personal helplessness and an external locus of control.[73] Ordinal position, too, makes a difference: first-borns are more likely to be internals (possibly because they are more often placed in positions of responsibility for household affairs and for their own conduct and are often put in charge of younger siblings as well).[74]

DOES PSYCHOTHERAPY INCREASE RESPONSIBILITY AWARENESS? IS THAT HELPFUL?

Several research projects have investigated the relationship between therapeutic outcome and shifts in the locus of control. John Gillis and Richard Jessor demonstrated that hospitalized patients who improved shifted from externality to internality on locus of control.[75] P. S. Dua reported that a behavioral therapy program with a population of delinquent adolescents resulted in increased internality of locus of control.[76] Stephen Nowick and Jarvis Bernes demonstrated a rise in internality by using effectance training in a summer camp of deprived inner-city adolescents.[77] Several studies of members of encounter experiential groups found that the group experience shifted members toward internality.[78] Unfortunately these studies are slender contributions, not rig-

---

* An interesting conceptual paradox exists between the learned-helplessness model of depression and the cognitive model of depression described by Aaron Beck[71] which posits that a depressive patient is characterized by negative expectations and a powerful tendency to assume personal responsibility for outcome. Thus depressed patients blame themselves for events clearly out of their control (for example, psychotically depressed patients may blame themselves for starting war or for a natural catastrophe). Lynn Abramson and Harold Sackeim discuss this still unreconciled paradox in an excellent review.[72]

orously designed, and use either no control groups at all or a "no-treatment" control which fails to control for Hawthorne effects. Furthermore, the results are correlational and do not tell whether a patient improves because of a shift in locus of control, or whether a patient shifts locus of control because of improvement.

Another research approach has been to study the subjective reports of patients who have completed therapy. If patients are asked about the aspects of therapy which they found particularly useful, they often cite the discovery and assumption of personal responsibility. In a study of twenty successful group therapy patients my colleagues and I administered a sixty-item Q-sort* reflecting "mechanisms of change" in therapy.[79] These sixty items were developed from twelve "curative factor" categories (each consisting of five items): (1) catharsis, (2) self-understanding, (3) identification—that is, with other members than the therapist, (4) family re-enactment, (5) instillation of hope (6) universality—that is, learning that others have similar problems, (7) group cohesiveness—acceptance by others, (8) altruism—being helpful to others, (9) suggestions and advice, (10) interpersonal learning "input"—learning about how others perceive one, (11) interpersonal learning "output"—improving skills in interpersonal relationships, (12) existential factors.

The "existential" category consisted of these five items:

1. Recognizing that life is at times unfair and unjust.
2. Recognizing that ultimately there is no escape from some of life's pain and from death.
3. Recognizing that no matter how close I get to other people, I must still face life alone.
4. Facing the basic issues of my life and death, and thus living my life more honestly and being less caught up in trivialities.
5. Learning that I must take ultimate responsibility for the way I live my life no matter how much guidance and support I get from others.

The therapists in this study were not existentially oriented but instead led traditional, interactionally based groups, and the "existential factor" category was inserted almost as an afterthought. Hence, when the results were tabulated, it was with much surprise that we learned that many patients attributed considerable importance to these "throw-in" items which are not part of a traditional therapeutic program. The

---

* Patients were presented with the sixty items (each on a separate card) and asked to force-sort them into seven categories (from "most helpful" to "least helpful").

entire category of existential factors was ranked sixth in importance of the twelve categories (arrived at by summing and averaging the rank order of the individual items). One item 5—*"Learning that I must take ultimate responsibility for the way I live my life no matter how much guidance and support I get from others"*—was especially highly valued. Of the sixty items, *it was ranked fifth most important by the patients.*

D. York and C. Eisman repeated this experiment with eighteen drug and alcohol addicts who received six months of intensive six days a week psychotherapy (with heavy emphasis on group methods) and fourteen parents of drug addicts, also in an intensive treatment program. These researchers found, too, that this "responsibility" item was often chosen (*it ranked first of the sixty items in one group and second in the other*).[80]

J. Dreyer administered a "curative factor" instrument to patients entering a psychiatric hospital and again eight days later. He demonstrated that the majority of patients entering an acute psychiatric hospital expected that the chief mode of help would be that others would give them concrete advice or suggestions to help them deal with their major life problems. By the eighth day of treatment the majority had altered that belief: rather than believe that help would come from a source outside of themselves they now stated that they knew they must assume greater personal responsibility.[81]

In an extensive study of the effects of women's consciousness-raising groups, Morton Lieberman et al. reports that "interviews with group members repeatedly revealed a thematic concern that 'I alone am responsible for my own happiness.' "[82]

Leonard Horowitz studied three videotaped interviews with forty patients. (The first tape was before therapy, the second after eight months of therapy, and the third after twelve months of therapy.) He did a systematic count of the number of statements made by a patient beginning with "I can't . . ." or "I have to . . ." or close synonyms thereof ("I am not able to," "I must," "I need to," and so on), and reported a significant decrease of such statements, less of a sense of powerlessness and gradual assumption of personal responsibility as therapy progressed.[83]

These data all suggest that the successful psychotherapy patient becomes more aware of personal responsibility for life. It seems that one of the results of effective therapy is that one not only learns about relatedness and intimacy—that is, about what one can obtain from relating to others; but also that one discovers the limits of relatedness—that is, what one *cannot* get from others, in therapy and in life as well.

Therapist Style: Research Evidence. Patients, especially those who seek to avoid responsibility, prefer therapists who are active and directive and who structure the therapy sessions (just as, after all, what good guides are supposed to do). Three projects using the locus of control instrument provide research evidence of this preference.

G. C. Helweg asked psychiatric patients and college students to view films of two therapists conducting an interview—Carl Rogers, a nondirective interviewer, and Albert Ellis, an extremely active directive interviewer—and then to select the therapist each would most prefer. The subjects who had an external locus of control (that is, avoided responsibility awareness) much preferred the active directive therapist.[84]

R. A. Jacobsen asked therapists of behavioristic and of analytic orientations to construct profiles of their therapeutic approaches. She then asked subjects to select the therapist they would prefer, and found that individuals with an external locus of control preferred directive, behavioral therapists, while those with an internal locus of control preferred nondirective, analytic therapists.[85] K. G. Wilson, using similar techniques, found that the critical variable was the therapist's position (as perceived by the patient) toward control and participation. Internals will select therapists who they (the patients) perceive will permit them full participation and control in the therapy process.[86]

The problem for patients with responsibility avoidance (that is, with external locus of control) is that the choice of an active-directive therapist may be self-defeating: the control requested is not the control required. *The more active and forceful the therapist (even if ostensibly in the service of helping the patient assume responsibility), the more is the patient infantilized.*

An outcome project my colleagues and I conducted demonstrates this point.[87] We studied eighteen encounter groups, which met for thirty hours over a ten-week period, led by leaders from a wide variety of ideological schools. Observers rated every aspect of a leader's behavior: total level of activity, content of comments, the degree of executive function (setting limits, rules, norms, goals; managing time; pacing, stopping interceding), and the number of structured exercises (that is, some specific task or exercise which the therapist asked the group to perform, such as feedback exercises, hot seat, or psychodrama). All leaders used structured exercises: some used many structured exercises each session; some, very few. When we analyzed the relationship between leader behavior and outcome (self-esteem, coping mechanisms, interpersonal style, peer evaluations, life values, and so forth), some interesting correlations emerged:

1. A curvilinear relationship existed between amount of executive function and outcome. In other words the rule of the golden mean prevailed: *too much or too little correlated with poor outcome*. *Too much* executive function resulted in a highly structured authoritarian group in which members failed to develop a sense of autonomy. Too little—a laissez-faire style—resulted in a bewildered floundering group.
2. The more structured exercises used by the leader, *the more competent did the members deem him to be* immediately at the end of the group but *the less successful* was the outcome of his group members (measured six months later).

The moral of this latter finding is obvious: if you want patients to think you know what you're doing, be an active, vigorous, structuring guide. However, be prepared to accept the fact that such a strategy gets in the way of the growth of the patient and probably impedes responsibility assumption.

Limits of Responsibility

The concept of responsibility is crucial to psychotherapy—and it is pragmatically true, it "works": acceptance of it enables the individual to achieve autonomy and his or her full potential.

But how far does this truth go? Many therapists are professional advocates of responsibility but secretly, in their own hearts and in their own belief systems, are environmental determinists. I have for many years treated psychotherapists, both in individual therapy and in a therapy group for psychotherapists, and have discovered how frequently psychotherapists (and I do not exclude myself) maintain a double standard: patients constitute and are responsible for their worlds, while therapists themselves live in a no-nonsense objective, structured world and do their best to adjust to what "really" is.

Both therapists and patients pay a penalty for their inconsistent belief systems. The therapists advocate responsibility assumption, but their secret doubt leaks out; they cannot convince patients of something they themselves do not believe. They are unconsciously sympathetic to and, consequently, are soon ensnared by a patient's resistance. For example, in the treatment of a divorced depressed woman who is desperate in her search for another mate, the therapist may begin to waver in his or her efforts to help the patient assume responsibility. Her resistance strikes a responsive chord in the therapist, who begins to think, "The patient seems like an engaging, attractive person, the culture *is* rough for a single forty-eight-year-old woman, the singles' scene *is* in many ways uninviting, there *are* very few attractive, single straight men in San Francisco. Her job, which she needs for survival, does not provide opportunities to meet other people. Perhaps she's right: if only Mr. Right would come along, ninety percent of her problems would vaporize. This patient is a casualty of destiny." And so the therapist enters into collusion with the patient's resistance and is soon reduced to suggesting strategies for meeting men—singles clubs, computer dating, parents without partners, and so on (as though the patient were incapable of such planning on her own).

The real education of the therapist occurs when "Mr. Right" does come along and somehow "happily ever after" never transpires. "Mr. Right" is not quite smart enough, or he is too dependent or too independent, or too poor or too rich, or too cold. Or she doesn't want to give up her freedom, or she clasps him with such desperation that he is frightened away, or she is so anxious that her spontaneity is stifled and he finds her empty and uninteresting. In fact the therapist will, in time, find that there is no end to the number of ways that an individual who is conflicted about intimacy can manage to unhinge a relationship.

Obviously double standards in the therapeutic as well as in any other relationship will not do; the therapist must examine his or her own beliefs about responsibility and arrive at a consistent position. The relationship between environment and personal freedom is extraordinarily complex. Do individuals carve their own destinies, or are they, as environmental determinists like B. F. Skinner claim, entirely determined by environmental contingencies. ("A person does not act upon the world, the world acts upon him.")[88]

Generally in a debate between a determinist and a libertarian (one who believes in freedom of the will) logic and reality seem to be on the side of the determinist; the libertarian is "softer" and appeals to unmeasurable, emotional argument. Psychotherapists are thus in a dilemma. To work effectively, they must be libertarian; yet many, with extensive backgrounds in science, in either experimental or social psychology, or in the biological or medical sciences, find themselves wishing they could manage a leap of faith into a free choice perspective but believe secretly that the determinist argument is unassailable.

Yet there are substantial arguments for the position of personal responsibility, some of which have the backing of empirical research and may offer therapists a way out of this dilemma. First one must recognize that an exceptionless environmental determinism is an extreme position which no longer can claim exclusive support of "hard" empirical research. Skinner contends that since we are determined by our environment, each of us may manipulate behavior by manipulating environment; but this contention is internally inconsistent. Who is it, after all, who is manipulating the environment? Not even the most fanatical determinist can contend that we are determined by our environment to alter our environment; such a position obviously leads to an infinite regress. If we manipulate our environment, then we are no longer environmentally determined; on the contrary, the environment is determined. Binswanger, in a 1936 essay commemorating Freud's eightieth birthday, makes this point by noting that Freud's personal stature and contributions were a marvelous example of the limitations of his deterministic theory:

> The fact that our lives are determined by the forces of life is only one side of the truth; the other is that we determine these forces as our fate. Only the two sides together can take in the full problem of sanity and insanity. Those who, like Freud, have forged their fates with the hammer—the work of art he has created in the medium of language is sufficient evidence of this—can dispute this fact least of all.[89]

In his presidential address to the American Psychological Association in 1974, Albert Bandura referred to this viewpoint as "reciprocal determinism" and distinguished between the potential and the actual environments: though all individuals may have the same *potential* environment, each *actually* regulates his or her environment.[90]

> A researcher once studied schizophrenic and normal children in a setting containing an extraordinary variety of attractive devices, including television sets, phonographs, pinball machines, electric trains, picture viewers, and electric organs. To activate these playthings, children had simply to deposit available coins, but only when a light on the device was turned on; coins deposited when the light was off increased the period that the device would remain inoperative. Normal children rapidly learned how to take advantage of what the environment had to offer and created unusually rewarding conditions for themselves. By contrast, schizophrenic children, who failed to master the simple controlling skill, experienced the same potentially rewarding environment as a depriving, unpleasant place.[90]

Thus there is a reciprocal relationship between behavior and environment: one's behavior can influence one's environment. Bandura pointed out: "We are all acquainted with problem-prone individuals who, through their obnoxious conduct, predictably breed negative social climates wherever they go. Others are equally skilled at bringing out the best in those with whom they interact." The environment that each individual creates, in turn, influences future behavior. Environment and behavior are interdependent; environments are not given but, like behavior, have causes. Bandura claimed that, "in the regress of prior causes, for every chicken discovered by a undirectional environmentalist, a social learning theorist can identify a prior egg."

A vast body of empirical research supports the position of reciprocal determinism. This material has been ably reviewed elsewhere,[91] and I shall not cite it except to note that it is substantial and rigorous and stems from such areas as human communicational interaction, expectational set, reciprocal relationships between personal preferences and mass media content, cognition and perception, self-regulatory functions of the self system (that is, a psychocybernetic model of self), and biofeedback.

Though many libertarians are pleased with the unexpected empirical support offered by the theory of reciprocal determinism, many will say it does not go far enough. They will argue that a fatal flaw exists in social psychological and behavioral experimental methods: the flaw is that the dependent variable is "behavior." In discussing the relationship between freedom and determinism, Bandura began with this self-evident (from the behaviorists' standpoint) argument:

> In deciding which movie to attend from many alternatives in a large city there are few constraints on the individual so that personal preferences emerge as the predominant determinants. In contrast, if people are immersed in a deep pool of water, their behavior will be remarkably similar however uniquely varied they might be in their cognitive and behavioral make-up.[92]

The phrase that creates vast problems for the libertarian is that the *behavior* of people immersed in water will be "remarkably similar." The issue, of course, is "behavior." How was it determined that behavior should be the criterion by which choice or freedom is measured? If one measures limb thrashing, bodily activity, or physiological indices, then certainly it is true that the human's physical range or behavioral options, like that of any other creature, will be drastically curtailed. But, even immersed to the neck, a human being has freedom: he or she chooses how to feel about the situation, what attitudes to adopt, whether to be courageous, stoic, fatalistic, cunning, or panicked. There is no limit to the range of psychological options available. Almost two thousand years ago Epictetus said:

> I must die. I must be imprisoned. I must suffer exile. But must I die groaning? Must I whine as well? Can anyone hinder me from going into exile with a smile? The master threatens to chain me: what say you? Chain me? My leg you will chain—yes, but not my will—no, not even Zeus can conquer that.[93]

This is no minor quibble. Even though the image of a drowning man's possessing freedom may appear ludicrous, the principle behind the image is of great significance. One's attitude toward one's situation is the very crux of being human, and conclusions about human nature based solely on measurable behavior are distortions of that nature. It cannot be denied that environment, genetics, or chance plays a role in one's life. The limiting circumstances are obvious: Sartre speaks of a "coefficient of adversity."[94] All of us face natural adversities that influence our lives. For example, contigencies may hinder any one of us from finding a job or a mate—physical handicaps, inadequate education, poor health, and so forth—but that does not mean that we have no responsibility (or choice) in the situation. We are responsible still for what we make out of our handicaps; for our attitudes toward them; for the bitterness, anger, or depression that act synergistically with the original "coefficient of adversity" to ensure that a handicap will defeat the individual. Despite, for example, the high market value on physical attractiveness, many people have a style and charm that transcend unattractive physical features. (It was Abraham Lincoln, I believe, who said that after forty everyone is responsible for his face.) When all else fails, when the coefficient of adversity is formidable, still one is responsible for the attitude one adopts toward the adversity—whether to live a life of bitter regret or to find a way to transcend the handicap and to fashion a meaningful life despite it.

A patient of mine, the likelihood of whose finding a desirable mate was severely jeopardized by a serious physical deformity, tormented herself by "choosing" to believe that life without a love-sexual relationship with a man was without value. She closed off many options for herself, including the deep pleasure of an intimate friendship with another woman or a nonsexual friendship with a man. The bulk of the therapeutic work with this patient consisted of challenging this basic assumption—that one was either coupled or one was nothing (a view that has always had strong social reinforcement, especially for women). Eventually she arrived at the realization that, though she bore no responsibility for her deformity, she bore complete responsibility for her attitude toward it and for her decision to adhere to a belief system that resulted in severe self-deprecation.

Recognition and acceptance of the external "given" (the coefficient of adversity) do not involve a passive stance toward one's external environment. Indeed neo-Marxists and proponents of radical psychiatry have often levied this very charge toward the mental health movement: that is, that it neglects the adverse material circumstances of the individual, whom it urges to accept unquestioningly his or her (capitalist-imposed) lot in life. But a full acceptance of responsibility implies not only that one imbues the world with significance but also that one has the freedom and the responsibility to change one's external environment whenever possible. The important task is to identify one's true coefficient of adversity. The ultimate task of therapy in this regard is to help patients reconstrue that which they cannot alter.

PHYSICAL DISEASE

Personal responsibility extends farther than responsibility for one's psychological state. Considerable medical evidence demonstrates that bodily ailments are influenced by an individual's psychological state. The field of body-mind interdependence in physical disease is so vast that space prevents more than a quick obeisance in the proper direction and a brief discussion of recent developments about responsibility for one particular illness—cancer.

Freud adumbrated the field of stress-disease linkage in 1901 in *The Psychopathology of Everyday Life,* where he suggested that accidental injuries are not accidental but instead are a manifestation of psychic conflict; he described the "accident prone" individual who suffers an unusual amount of accidental injury.[95] Following Freud, two generations of analysts developed the field of psychosomatic medicine in which a number of medical illnesses (for example, arthritis, ulcers, asthma, ulcerative colitis) were discovered to be powerfully influenced by a patient's psychological state. Modern biofeedback technology, meditation, a wide variety of autoregulatory mechanisms has heralded a surge of renewed interest in the individual's control, and responsibility, for aspects of bodily function that are controlled by the autonomic nervous system (a division of the nervous system long referred to as the "involuntary nervous system").

The concept of personal responsibility is now being applied in the treatment of such illnesses as cancer—long thought to be far beyond the purview of individual control. Cancer has always been viewed as the prototype of externally based disease: it strikes without warning, and the patient can do little to influence either its onset or its course. Recently there have been highly publicized attempts to reverse this attitude toward cancer: patients are being urged to examine their own roles in the disease. O. Carl Simonton, a radiation oncologist, has spearheaded this attempt by proposing a psychologically based therapy for cancer.[96] His rationale is based on current disease theory which suggests that the individual is constantly exposed to cancer cells, and that one's body resists these cells unless resistance has been lowered by some factor, thus making one susceptible to cancer. There is considerable evidence that stress diminishes resistance to disease by affecting both the immunological system and the hormonal balance. If this evidence is further borne out, Simonton reasons, then psychological forces may well be marshaled to influence the course of cancer.

Simonton's treatment method consists of daily visual meditation in which the patient first concentrates upon a visual metaphor of how he or she imagines the cancer to appear, and then meditates upon some visual metaphor of the body defenses defeating that cancer. For example, one patient visualized the cancer as a mound of raw hamburger and the body's defenses, the white blood cells, as a band of wild dogs devouring the hamburger. Simonton urges patients to examine their modes of dealing with stress. Of a patient whose disease spreads, the first question asked is "What did you do that brought this upon yourself?"

To the best of my knowledge, there has been no trustworthy evidence that this approach increases survival time; and one must be skeptical of a system that promises so much but neglects to do the relatively simple research that would substantiate (or disprove) its claims. Nonetheless, the Simonton approach teaches us something important about the role of responsibility in the management of severe illness, because even those patients using visual meditation who are not helped physically are often helped psychologically by assuming a more active, responsible stance toward their disease. This is of great importance, because helplessness and profound demoralization are often major problems in the treatment of patients with cancer. Cancer, perhaps more than any other disease, fosters a sense of helplessness—patients feel unable to exert any personal control over their condition. Patients with almost any other disease (such as heart disease or diabetes) have many ways in which they can participate in treatment: they can diet, follow medical regimens, rest, adhere to physical exercise schedules, and so on; but patients with cancer feel they can do nothing but wait— wait until the next cancer cell pops up somewhere in the body. This sense of helplessness is augmented often by attitudes of doctors who frequently do not include patients in decision making about the course of therapy. Many doctors are reluctant to share information with patients and often bypass them and consult with the family about important decisions that need to be made concerning future therapy.

But if the Simonton method is indeed unsubstantiated and does not increase survival time, then is it not based on a lie and destined to cave in on itself? And what therapeutic methods are available to help those patients who cannot accept his premise and method? I believe that the concept of responsibility assumption offers therapeutic leverage for any cancer patient, even those whose disease is far advanced.[97] First it must be noted that regardless of one's physical circumstances (that is, coefficient of adversity), one is always responsible for the attitude one assumes toward one's burden. In my work with patients with metastatic cancer (cancer that has spread to other parts of the body and is no longer amenable to surgical or medical cure) I have been singularly impressed with major differences between individuals in their attitude toward their illness. Some individuals give in to despair and die a premature psychological death and, as some research suggests,[98] a premature physical death as well. Others, as I described in chapter 5, transcend their illness and use their impending death as a catalyst to improve their quality of life. Responsibility for one's attitude does not necessarily mean responsibility for one's *feelings* (although Sartre would claim that to be the case) but for the *stand* that one takes toward one's feelings. A joke told by Viktor Frankl illustrates this point.

> During World War I a Jewish army doctor was sitting in a fox hole with his gentile friend, an aristocratic colonel, and heavy shooting began. Teasingly the colonel said, "You are afraid, aren't you? That's just another proof that the Aryan race is superior to the Semitic one." "Sure I'm afraid," was the doctor's answer. "But who is superior? If you, my dear colonel, were as afraid as I am, you would have run away long ago."[99]

The therapist working with the cancer patient may offer a great deal by concentrating on the latter's hopelessness and helplessness. In our work with cancer patients in support groups, my colleagues and I[100] developed several approaches geared to bolster a sense of power and control. For example, cancer patients often feel powerless and infantilized in relation to their physicians. My group focused sharply upon this issue and was effective in helping many patients assume responsibility for their relationship to their doctors. After patients described their relationships to their doctors, other members suggested other methods; role playing was done in which the patients practiced new methods of asserting themselves with physicians. Patients learned to request time from a physician, to demand information (if they wished it) about their illness; some learned to ask to see their medical charts or to view their X-rays; and some, when it seemed to make sense, assumed ultimate responsibility and refused further medication.

Many patients in the therapy group developed a sense of potency through social action. Many spoke out for the rights of cancer patients and campaigned for political issues affecting them (such as, for tax credit for breast prostheses). Finally, in ways already described, the group therapist helped patients regain a sense of potency by encouraging them to assume responsibility for the course of their own group. By increasing their awareness that they can shape the group to suit their needs—indeed, that it is their *responsibility* to shape the group—the therapist can increase each individual's assumption of responsibility in other spheres of life.

Responsibility and Existential Guilt

In attempting to facilitate a patient's awareness of responsibility, the therapist soon discovers an uninvited presence in the therapeutic arena. That presence is guilt, the dark shadow of responsibility, which often trespasses into the process of existential psychotherapy.

In existentially based therapy "guilt" assumes a somewhat different meaning from its meaning in traditional therapy, where it refers to a feeling state related to a sense of wrongdoing—a pervasive, highly uncomfortable state which has been described as anxiety plus a sense of badness. (Freud comments that, subjectively, "the sense of guilt and the sense of inferiority are difficult to distinguish.")[101] A distinction may be made between neurotic guilt and "real" guilt or, in Buber's terms, between "guilt" and "guilt feelings."[102]

Neurotic guilt emanates from *imagined* transgressions (or minor transgressions that are responded to in a disproportionately powerful manner) against another individual, against ancient and modern taboos, or against parental or social tribunals. "Real" guilt flows from an *actual* transgression against another. Though the subjective dysphoric experience is similar, the meaning and the therapeutic management of these forms of guilt are very different: neurotic guilt must be approached through a working through of the sense of badness, the unconscious aggressivity, and the wish for punishment; whereas "real" guilt must be met by actual, or symbolically appropriate, reparation.

An existential perspective in psychotherapy adds important dimensions to the concept of guilt. First, the full acceptance of responsibility for one's actions broadens the scope of guilt by diminishing escape hatches. No longer can the individual comfortably rely on such alibis as: "I didn't mean it," "It was an accident," "I couldn't help it," "I followed an irresistible impulse." Thus real guilt and its role in one's interpersonal dealings frequently enters into the existential therapeutic dialogue.

But the existential concept of guilt adds something even more important than the broadening of the scope of "accountability." Most simply put: one is guilty not only through transgressions against another or against some moral or social code, but *one may be guilty of transgression against oneself.* Of all the existential philosophers Kierkegaard and then Heidegger most fully developed this concept. It is important that Heidegger uses the same word (*schuldig*) to refer to both guilt and responsibility. After discussing traditional uses of the term "guilty," he states: "being guilty also has the signification of 'being responsible for'—that is, being the cause, or author or even the occasion for something."[103]

One is thus guilty to the same extent that one is responsible for oneself and one's world. Guilt is a fundamental part of *Dasein* (that is, human be-ing): "Being guilty does not first result from an indebtedness, but on the contrary indebtedness becomes possible only on the basis of a primordial being guilty."[104] Heidegger then proceeds to develop the theme that "in the idea of 'guilty' there lies the character of the 'not.'" *Dasein* is always constituting, and it "constantly lags behind its possibilities."[105] *Guilt is thus intimately related to possibility or potentiality.* When the "call of conscience" is heard (that is, the call that brings one back to facing one's "authentic" mode of being), one is always "guilty"—and *guilty to the extent that one has failed to fulfill authentic possibility.*

This extraordinarily important concept has been developed more fully (and far less obscurely) by many others. Paul Tillich's contributions are particularly relevant to psychotherapy. In *The Courage to Be*, he discusses man's anxiety at the idea of nonbeing and distinguishes three sources of anxiety—three major modes by which nonbeing threatens being. Two of these (the threat to objective existence—*death*, and the threat to spiritual existence—*meaninglessness*), I examine elsewhere. The third is germane to this discussion. Nonbeing threatens being by threatening our moral self-affirmation—and we experience guilt and the anxiety of self-condemnation. Tillich's words are exceedingly clear:

> Man's being is not only given to him but also demanded of him. He is responsible for it; literally, he is required to answer, if he is asked, *what he has made of himself*. He who asks him is his judge, namely he himself. The situation produces the anxiety which in relative terms is the anxiety of guilt, in absolute terms the anxiety of self-rejection or condemnation. Man is asked to make of himself what he is supposed to become, to fulfill his destiny. In every act of moral, self-affirmation man contributes to the fulfillment of his destiny, to the actualization of what he potentially is.[106]

Tillich's view that man is "asked to make of himself what he is supposed to become, to fulfill his destiny" derives from Kierkegaard who described a form of despair that emerged from not being willing to be oneself. Self-reflection (awareness of guilt) tempers the despair, whereas not to know that one is in despair is a deeper form of despair yet.[107] The same point is made by the Hasidic rabbi, Susya, who shortly before his death said, "When I get to heaven they will not ask me, 'Why were you not Moses?' Instead they will ask 'Why were you not Susya? Why did you not become what only you could become?'"[108] Otto Rank was acutely aware of these issues and wrote that when we restrict ourselves from a too intensive or too quick living out, or living up, *we feel ourselves guilty on account of the unused life, the unlived life in us.*[109]

Rollo May suggested that the concept of repression be understood from the perspective of one's relationship to one's own potential, and that the concept of the unconscious be enlarged to include the individual's unrealized repressed potential:

> We must ask the following questions, therefore, if we are to understand repression in a given person: *What is this person's relation to his own potentialities?* What goes on that he chooses or is forced to choose, to block off from his awareness something that he knows and on another level *knows that he knows?* ... The unconscious, then, is not to be thought of as a reservoir of impulses, thoughts, and wishes that are culturally unacceptable. I define it rather as those potentialities for knowing and experiencing that the individual cannot or will not actualize.[110]

Elsewhere May describes guilt (that is, existential guilt) as "a positive constructive emotion ... a perception of the difference between what a

278

thing is and what it ought to be."[111] Therefore existential guilt (as well as anxiety) is compatible with, even necessary for, mental health. "When the person denies his potentialities, fails to fulfill them, his condition is guilt."[112]

It is an ancient idea that each human being has a unique set of potentials that yearn to be realized. Aristotle's "entelechy" referred to the full realization of potentiality. The fourth cardinal sin, sloth, or accidie has been interpreted by many thinkers as "the sin of failing to do with one's life all that one knows one can do."[113] It is an extremely popular concept in modern psychology and appears in the writings of almost every modern humanistic or existential theorist or therapist.* Although it has been given many names (that is, "self-actualization," "self-realization," "self-development," "development of potential," "growth," "autonomy," and so on), the underlying concept is simple: each human being has an innate set of capacities and potentials and, furthermore, has a primordial knowledge of these potentials. One who fails to live as fully as one can, experiences a deep, powerful feeling which I refer to here as "existential guilt."

Karen Horney's mature work, for example, is based solidly on the concept that, under favorable conditions, the human being will naturally develop his or her intrinsic potential just as an acorn will develop into an oak tree.[123] Horney's major work, *Neurosis and Human Growth*, is subtitled *The Struggle toward Self-Realization*. Psychopathology, in her view, occurs when adverse circumstances inhibit a child from growing toward the realization of his or her own possibilities. The child then loses sight of its potential self and develops another self image: an "idealized self" toward which it directs its life energies. Though Horney does not use the term "guilt," it is clear that she is well aware of the price paid by the individual for not fulfilling his or her own destiny. She speaks of the sense of alienation, of being split from what one really is, which results in one's overriding one's genuine feelings, wishes, and thoughts. One senses the existence of one's potential self, however, and, at an unconscious level, continuously compares it with one's "actual" self (that is, the self that actually lives in the world). The discrepancy between what one is and what one could be generates a flood of self-contempt with which the individual must cope throughout life.

Abraham Maslow, much influenced by Horney, was the first, I be-

---

* Notably Buber,[114] Murphy,[115] Fromm,[116] Buhler,[117] Allport,[118] Rogers,[119] Jung,[120] Maslow,[121] and Horney.[122]

lieve, to use the term "self-actualization." He, too, believed that individuals naturally actualize themselves unless circumstances in their development are so adverse that they must strive for safety rather than for growth (that is, they must adopt a "deficiency motivation" rather than a "growth motivation").

> If the essential [intrinsically given] core of the person is denied or suppressed, he gets sick, sometimes in obvious ways sometimes in subtle ways. . . . This inner core is delicate and subtle and easily overcome by habit and cultural pressure. . . . Even though denied, it persists underground, forever pressing for actualization. . . . Every falling away [from our core], every crime against our nature records itself in our unconscious and makes us despise ourselves.[124]

But how is one to find one's potential? How does one recognize it when one meets it? How does one know when one has lost one's way? Heidegger, Tillich, Maslow, and May would all answer in unison: "Through Guilt! Through Anxiety! Through the call of conscience!" There is general consensus among them that existential guilt is a positive constructive force, a guide calling oneself back to oneself. When patients told her that they did not know what they wanted, Horney often replied simply, "Have you ever thought of asking yourself?" In the center of one's being one knows oneself. John Stuart Mill, in describing this multiplicity of selves, spoke of a fundamental, permanent self which he referred to as the "enduring I."[125] No one has said it better than Saint Augustine: "There is one within me who is more myself than my self."[126]

A clinical vignette illustrates the role of existential guilt as a guide. A patient consulted me because of severe depression and feelings of worthlessness. She was fifty years old and for thirty-two years had been married to a highly disturbed, spiteful man. On many occasions in her life she had considered entering therapy but had decided against it because she feared that self-examination would lead to the breakup of her marriage and she could not bring herself to face isolation, pain, disgrace, economic hardship, and acknowledgement of failure. Finally she became so incapacitated that she was forced to seek help. However, though she appeared physically in my office, she refused to commit herself to therapy, and we made little headway. There was a dramatic turning point one day as she was speaking of aging and her fear of death. I asked her to imagine herself close to death, to look back over her life and to describe her feelings. Without hesitation, she answered, "Regret." "Regret for what?" I asked. "Regret for wasting my life, for never knowing what I could have been." "Regret" (her term for existential guilt) was the key to therapy. We used it as a constant guide from that time forward. Though months of hard work lay ahead for her, there was never a doubt about the outcome. She *did* examine herself (and she did break up her marriage), and she was able, by the time therapy ended, to experience her life with a sense of possibility rather than of regret.

The relationship between guilt, self-contempt, and self-fulfillment is clearly illustrated in the treatment of Bruce, the middle-aged patient I discussed in chapter 5. Since adolescence Bruce had been preoccupied by sex, and especially by breasts. He had been, throughout his life, self-contemptuous. "Relief" was what Bruce wanted from therapy—relief from anxiety, self-hatred, and the persistent sense of guilt that gnawed away at his innards. It is an understatement to say that Bruce did not experience himself as the author of his life. The concept that he had personal responsibility for his life situation was like a foreign language to him; he felt so driven, so perpetually panicked that, like Kafka, he felt "fortunate to be able to sit in the corner and breathe."[127]

For many long months of therapy we examined his guilt and self-hatred. Why was he guilty? What transgressions had he committed? He confessed to banal, tired, petty crimes and obsessively paraded them back and forth hour after therapy hour: as a child he had stolen loose change from his father; he had padded figures on insurance claims, cheated on his income tax, stolen his neighbor's morning newspaper, and, above all, screwed women. We investigated each at length and each time determined anew that the self-punishment exceeded the crime. For example, when he discussed his promiscuity, he realized that he had injured no one; he treated his lady friends well, used no deceit and was considerate of their feelings. He worked through each of his "offenses" on a rational level and realized that he was "innocent" and unfairly harsh on himself. Yet the guilt and self-hatred persisted undiminished.

The first glimmer of responsibility awareness occurred as he was discussing his fear of assertiveness. Though his professional position called for him to do so he could not represent his company well in public discussions. It was especially difficult to disagree or to be publicly critical of another; nothing terrified him more than a public debate. "What could happen in that situation?" I asked. "What is the ultimate calamity?" Bruce had no doubt about the answer. "Exposure." He feared his adversary would insouciantly read aloud a list of all the shameful sexual episodes in his life. He identified with the nightmare of James Joyce's Leopold Bloom in *Ulysses* who, when placed on trial for his secret desires, is humiliated when evidence of his many pecca-

281

dillos is paraded before the court. I wondered which he feared most—exposure of past or of current sexual adventures? He answered, "The present. I could handle the past affairs. I could say to myself, perhaps even aloud, 'That was then, the way I used to be. Now I've changed. I'm a different person.' "

Gradually Bruce began to hear his own words, which were saying in effect, "My current behavior, what *I* am doing *right* now, is the source of my fear of assertiveness and is the source of my self-contempt and my guilt as well." Bruce eventually realized *that he was immediately and entirely the source of his own self-hatred.* If he wanted to feel better about himself, or even to love himself, he had to stop doing things of which he was ashamed.

But an even greater realization was to follow. After Bruce made a stand (which I described in chapter 5) and chose, for the first time, to forgo a sexual conquest, he gradually began to improve. In the following months he underwent many changes (including the expected period of impotency), but gradually his compulsivity gave way and his sense of choicefulness increased. As his behavior changed, his self-image dramatically changed also, and he grew immensely in self-confidence and self-love. Toward the end of therapy Bruce gradually discovered two roots for his guilt. One stemmed from the way he had demeaned his encounters with other beings (which I shall have more to say about in chapter 8). The second source of guilt was the crime he committed against himself. For much of his life, his attentions and energies had been focused, animalistically, on sex, on breasts, genitals, copulation, seduction, and various ingenious, extravagant modifications of the sexual act. Bruce had, until his change in therapy, rarely given his mind free rein, rarely engaged in other thoughts, rarely read (except to impress females), rarely listened to music (except as a prelude to sex), rarely truly encountered another person. Bruce, who had a way with words, said that he had "lived like an animal constantly in heat yanked to and fro by a tube of flesh dangling between his legs." "Suppose," he said one day, "that we had the means to study closely the life of an insect species. Imagine that we find that the male insects are transfixed by two bumps on the thorax of the female and devote all their days on earth to finding ways of touching these bumps. What would we think? Why, what a peculiar way to spend one's life! Surely there must be more to life than the touching of bumps. Yet I was like that insect." Small wonder Bruce felt guilty. His guilt, as Tillich knew, came from his life denial and restriction, from his self-immolation and his refusal to become what he could become.

No one has depicted existential guilt more vividly and arrestingly than has Franz Kafka. The refusal to acknowledge and to confront one's existential guilt is a recurrent theme in Kafka's work. *The Trial* begins, "Someone must have maligned Joseph K., for without having done anything wrong, he was arrested one fine morning." Joseph K. is asked to confess but declares, "I am completely guiltless." The entire novel is a depiction of Joseph K.'s efforts to free himself from the court. He seeks help from every conceivable source, but to no avail because he faces no ordinary official court of law. As the reader gradually realizes, Joseph K. is confronted with an internal court, one residing in his private depths.[128] Julius Heuscher calls attention to the court's physical contamination with primitive instinctual material: for example, the desks of the judges are littered with pornographic books; the court is located in a grimy attic of a slum dwelling.[129]

When Joseph K. enters a cathedral, he is addressed by a priest who attempts to help him by urging him to look within at his guilt. Joseph K. replies that everything is a misunderstanding, and then rationalizes, "And if it comes to that, how can any man be called guilty? We are all simply men here, one as much as the other." The priest appeals, "But that's how all guilty men talk" and once again counsels him to look within rather than to attempt to dissolve his guilt in collective guilt. When Joseph K. describes his next step ("I'm going to get more help"), the priest becomes angry: "You cast about too much for outside help." Finally, the priest shrieks from the pulpit: "Can't you see one pace before you?"

Joseph K. then hopes to obtain from the priest a method to circumvent the court, "a mode of living completely outside the jurisdiction of the court," by which he means a mode of living outside of the jurisdiction of his own conscience. Is there a way, Joseph K. asks in effect, that one may never have to face existential guilt? The priest replies that the hope of escape is a "delusion" and tells him a parable "in the writings that preface the law" which describes "that particular delusion." This parable is the searing tale of the man and the doorkeeper. A man from the country begs for admittance to the law. A doorkeeper in front of one of the innumerable doors greets him and announces that he may not be admitted at the moment. When the man attempts to peer through the entrance, the doorkeeper warns him: "Try to get in without my permission. But note that I am powerful. From hall to hall, keepers stand at every door, one more powerful than the other and the sight of the third man is already more than even I can stand."

The supplicant decides that he had better wait until he gets permission to enter. He waits for days, for weeks, for years. He waits outside that door for his entire life. He ages; his vision dims; and as he lies dying, he poses one last question to the doorkeeper, a question he had never asked before: "Everyone strives to attain the law. How does it come about then, that in all these years no one has come seeking admittance but me?" The doorkeeper bellows in the man's ear (for his hearing, too, is fading): "No one but you could gain admission through this door, since this door was intended for you. I am now going to shut it."

Joseph K. does not understand the parable; and, indeed, until the very end when he dies "like a dog," he continues to search for help from some external agency.[130] Kafka himself, as he records in his diaries did not at first understand the significance of the parable.[131] Later, as Buber points out,[132] Kafka fully expressed the parable's significance in his notebooks: "Confession of guilt, unconditional confession of guilt, door springing open. It appears in the interior of the house of the world whose turbid reflection lay behind walls." Kafka's man from the country was guilty—not only guilty of living an unlived life, of waiting for permission from another, of not seizing his life, of not going through the door intended for him alone, but he was guilty, too, of not accepting his guilt, of not using it as a guide to his interior, of not "unconditionally" confessing—an act that would have resulted in the door "springing open."

We are not told much about Joseph K.'s life anterior to the call of guilt and therefore cannot with precision delineate the reasons for his existential guilt. However, Heuscher, in a remarkably illuminating case report, provides a proxy Joseph K.—a patient, Mr. T, whose offenses against himself are readily apparent:

> Mr. T consulted me because he could no longer swallow. For weeks he had limited himself to frequent small sips of liquids and consequently had lost some forty pounds. Before he became ill, his time was spent either in the plant where his functions were interesting but well defined, or in his home where an intelligent but chronically neurotic, depressed, and alcoholic wife rendered impossible all social outings and all entertaining. Sexual intimacies had stopped years ago, allegedly by mutual consent, and the activities at home were restricted to reading, television viewing, impersonal conversation when the wife was not intoxicated, and an occasional visit by a distant relative. Though well liked and an excellent conversationalist, he had no close friend, much as he wished for one, nor did he ever venture to develop some social activities in which his wife would not be included. Stuck in this rigid and restricted world, he cleverly parried any of the therapist's suggestions to the effect that he further this or that potential, pursue this or that option.[133]

Though Mr. T's symptomatology ameliorated, two years of therapy did nothing to alter his general life style. Mr. T, like Joseph K., did not listen to himself and, in his therapy, studiously avoided a deep examination of his life. Yet he insisted on continuing therapy, and the therapist regarded his insistence as an indication of a dormant sense that a richer life might be available to him.

One day Mr. T brought in a dream, a dream that amazed him by its extreme clarity. Though he had not read Kafka, his dream has an uncanny resemblance to *The Trial*, which, like many of Kafka's works, had its origin in a dream. It is too long to repeat here in its entirety, but it begins:

> I was arrested by the police and taken to the police station. They would not tell me what I was arrested for, but muttered something about a "misdemeanor" and asked me to plead guilty. When I refused, they threatened to charge me with a felony. "Book me for anything you want!" I retorted, and so they did charge me with a felony. As a result of this I was convicted and ended up in a prison farm since this was, according to one of the policemen, the place for "nonviolent felonies." Initially I had felt panicky for being asked to plead guilty; then I felt angry and confused. I never found out what I was charged with, but the arresting officer had told me it was stupid to refuse to plead guilty, since a misdemeanor conviction would get me only six months, while a felony conviction carried at least five years. I got five to thirty years![134]

Mr. T and Joseph K. are both summoned by existential guilt, and both choose to avoid the summons by interpreting guilt in the traditional manner. They both proclaim their innocence. After all, neither has committed a crime. "There must have been some mistake," they reason, and each devotes himself to convincing the external authorities of the miscarriage of justice. But existential guilt is not the result of some criminal act that the individual has committed. Quite the contrary! Existential guilt (by any of its many names—"self-condemnation," "regret," "remorse," and so forth) issues from *omission*. Joseph K. and Mr. T are both guilty for what they have *not* done with their lives.

The experiences of Joseph K. and Mr. T have rich implications for the psychotherapist. "Guilt" is a dysphoric subjective state experienced as "anxious badness." Yet there are different meanings of subjective guilt. The therapist must help the patient distinguish between real guilt, neurotic guilt, and existential guilt. Existential guilt is more than a dysphoric affect state, a symptom to be worked through and eliminated; the therapist should regard it as a call from within which, if heeded, can function as a guide to personal fulfillment. One who, like Joseph K. or Mr. T, has existential guilt, has transgressed against one's own destiny. The victim is one's own potential self. Redemption is achieved by plunging oneself into the "true" vocation of the human being, which, as Kierkegaard said, "is to will to be oneself."[135]

CHAPTER 7

Willing

Responsibility, Willing, and Action

A JAPANESE proverb states: "To know and not to act is not to know at all." Awareness of responsibility in itself is not synonymous with change; it is only the first step in the process of change. That was what I meant when, in the last chapter, I said that the patient who becomes aware of responsibility enters the vestibule of change. This chapter will consider the rest of the journey—the passage from awareness to action.

In order to change, one must first assume responsibility: one must commit oneself to some action. The word "responsibility" itself denotes that capability: "response" + "ability"—that is the ability to respond. Change is the business of psychotherapy, and therapeutic change must be expressed in action—not in knowing, intending, or dreaming.

How obvious this seems; yet the field of psychotherapy has traditionally obfuscated this self-evident fact. Early analysts were so convinced that self-knowledge was tantamount to change that they tended to see knowledge as the end point of therapy. If change did not occur, then it was assumed that the patient had not achieved sufficient insight. In a well-known 1950 article in a leading psychiatric journal, Allen Wheelis thought it necessary to remind psychotherapists: "Therapy can bring about personality change only in so far as it leads a patient to adopt a new mode of behavior. A real change occurring in the absence of action is a practical and theoretical impossibility."[1]

From the standpoint of psychotherapy, what is action? Is thinking action? After all, thought can be demonstrated to consume energy. Wheelis argued that to extend the concept of action to include thought would rob action of its meaning. Thought, *in and of itself*, has no external consequences—although it may be an indispensable overture to action: one may, for example, plan, rehearse, or muster the resolve for action. Action extends one beyond oneself; it involves interaction with one's surrounding physical or interpersonal world. Action need not entail gross, or even observable, movement. A slight gesture or glance toward another may be action of momentous import. Action has two sides: its obverse, the *absence* of action—for example, *not* acting in habitual fashion, *not* overeating, *not* exploiting others, *not* being dishonest—may be a major action indeed.

The therapist must court action. He or she may pretend to pursue other goals—insight, self-actualization, comfort—but in the final analysis, change (that is, action) is every therapist's secret quarry. The problem is that nowhere in training does the therapist learn about the mechanics of action: instead, the therapist is schooled in history taking, interpretation, and relationship and takes the secular leap of faith that pursuance of these activities will ultimately generate change.

But what if this faith is mistaken? The therapist then becomes bewildered and pushes for more insight, more self-scrutiny; analysis and therapy stretch over three, four, and five years. Indeed, many courses of psychoanalysis consume seven and eight years, and a second analysis is so common it is no longer a mark of distinction. The therapist loses sight of how change is to come about, but hopes merely that, through a process of mutual fatigue—to use Wheelis's felicitous phrase[2]—the patient's neurotic structure will crumble.

But what if still no change occurs? The therapist lose patience and starts to gaze directly at volition and action instead of glancing surreptitiously at them—as he or she has been trained to do. In Wheelis's words:

> . . . the therapist may find himself wishing that the patient were capable of more "push," more "determination," a greater willingness to "make the best of it." Often this wish eventuates in remarks to the patient: "People must help themselves"; "Nothing worthwhile is achieved without effort"; "You have to try." Such interventions are seldom included

287

in case reports, for it is assumed that they possess neither the dignity nor effectiveness of interpretation. Often an analyst feels uncomfortable about such appeals to volition, as though he were using something he didn't believe in, and as though this would have been unnecessary had only he analyzed more skillfully.[3]

"You have to try." "People must help themselves!" Wheelis says that this type of intervention is seldom included in case reports. Indeed, they are not. They are entirely "off the record." Yet they are commonplace; every therapist thinks these thoughts and in a vast variety of ways conveys them to the patient.

But when therapists say *sotto voce*, "You have to try harder," or "One must make an effort," to whom are they speaking? The problem that most therapists face is that *there is no psychic agency in the analytic (or behavioristic) model of the mind to which such an appeal can be made*. Freud's model of the mind, as I described in chapter 2, was based on Helmholtzian principles—that is, it was an antivitalistic, deterministic model where the human being is activated and controlled by "chemical-physical forces reducible to the force of attraction and repulsion."[4] Freud was unrelenting on this issue. "Man" Freud said, "is lived by the unconscious. . . . The deeply rooted belief in psychic freedom and choice is quite unscientific and must give ground before the claims of a determinism which governs mental life."[5] Freud's man, as May said, is "not driving any more but driven."[6] Behavior is a vector, a resultant of the interplay of internal forces. But if that is true, if all a human being's mental and physical activity is determined, if there is no driver, then precisely *who* or *what* is it that can "try harder" or demonstrate "resoluteness" or "courage"?

The therapist who adopts a "scientific" deterministic position in clinical work soon encounters a serious problem: in a model of man subdivided into such interrelating but conflicting fractions as ego, superego, and id, where does the ultimate seat of responsibility lie? The issue was framed clearly by my supervisor whom I quoted at the beginning of Part II "*The* goal of psychotherapy is to bring the patient to the point where he can make a free choice." But where is the "choosing agency" located in a deterministic model? No wonder that in our fifty sessions together he never elaborated further upon "the goal of psychotherapy"!

Freud never reconciled the contradiction between his deterministic model and his therapeutic endeavors; and in *The Ego and the Id*, written when he was sixty-seven, he noted that the therapist's task is "to give the patient's ego freedom to choose one way or another."[7] This often-quoted statement is supreme proof of the unacceptability of his deterministic model of man. Even though traditional analytic thought views human behavior as completely determined, even though it splits the human psyche into conflicting fractions (ego, superego, and id; or preconscious, unconscious, and conscious), still it seems necessary to include a core that is not determined. The latter-day ego analysts who proffer the concept of the "autonomous ego" continue to beg the question. It is as if a freely choosing homunculus were placed within one of the parts. But of course this makes no sense at all because, as May has noted, "how can a part be free without the whole being free?"[8]

Some therapists have attempted to deal with this dilemma by stating that, even though humans experience a subjective sense of freedom and choice (and the therapist attempts to augment this state), nonetheless the state is an illusion—as determined as any other subjective state. This is precisely the argument made by such rationalists as Hobbes and Spinoza. Hobbes described man's sense of freedom as a phantasm of consciousness. "If a wooden top, lashed by the boys . . . sometimes spinning, sometimes hitting men on the shins were sensible of its own motion [it] would think it proceeded from its own will."[9] Similarly, Spinoza said that a self-conscious and sentient stone that was set into motion by some external (unknown) force "would believe itself to be completely free and would think that it continued in motion solely because of its own wish."[10] However, psychotherapists who believe that freedom is an illusionary subjective state paint themselves into a corner: since they state that successful psychotherapy results in the patient's *feeling* a greater sense of choice, they are in effect proclaiming that the purpose of therapy is to create (or to restore) an illusion. This view of the therapeutic process is, as May points out, entirely incompatible with one of psychotherapy's overarching values: the quest for truth and self-knowledge.[11]

The analytic model of the psyche omits something vital, something that constitutes a major psychological construct and plays a central role in every course of psychotherapy. Before I christen this construct, let me review its characteristics and functions. It is the mental agency that transforms awareness and knowledge into action, it is the bridge between desire and act. It is the mental state that precedes action (Aristotle).[12] It is the mental "organ of the future"—just as memory is the mental organ of the past (Arendt).[13] It is the power of *spontaneously* beginning a series of successive things (Kant).[14] It is the seat of volition, the "responsible mover" within (Farber).[15] It is the "decisive factor in translating equilibrium into a process of change . . . an act occurring between insight and action which is experienced as effort or determination" (Wheelis).[16] It is responsibility assumption—as opposed to responsibility awareness. It is that part of the psychic structure that has "the capacity to make and implement choices" (Arieti).[17] It is a force composed of both power and desire, the "trigger of effort,"[18] the "mainspring of action."[19]

To this psychological construct we assign the label "will," and to its function, "willing." Frankly, I should much prefer some happier term—one simpler, less controversial, one not so encrusted with two thousand years of theological and philosophical polemic. "Will" has the disadvantage of multiple, often conflicting definitions. For example, Schopenhauer, in his major work *The World as Will and Representation*, regards will as the life force—"a nonrational force, a blind striving power whose operations are without purpose or design";[20] whereas Nietzsche, in the *Will to Power*, equates "willing" with power and command: "to will is to command; inherent in will is the commanding thought."[21]

One of the major sources of controversy stems from the fact that will is inextricably bound with freedom; for it makes little sense to speak of an unfree will, unless we, like Hobbes and Spinoza, change the meaning of will so that it becomes an illusionary subjective state rather than an actual seat of volition. Throughout history free will has always managed to offend the prevailing world view. Though the controversy regarding free will has continued without cessation, the opponents of the concept have changed over the centuries. The Greek philosophers had no term for "free will"; the very concept was incompatible with the prevailing belief in eternal recurrence, with the belief that, as Aristotle held, that "coming-into-being necessarily implies the pre-existence of something which is potentially but not actually."[22] The Stoic fatalists, who believed that whatever is or will be "was to be," rejected the idea of a freely willing agency in man. Christian theology could not reconcile the belief in divine providence, in an omniscient, omnipotent god, with the claims of free will. Later, free will clashed with scientific positivism, with Isaac Newton's and Pierre Laplace's belief in an explicable and predictable universe. Still later, the Hegelian idea of history as a necessary progress of the world spirit clashed with a free-will ideology that, by its very nature, rejects necessity and holds that all that *was* or *is* done could, as well, *not* have been done. Lastly, free will is opposed by all deterministic systems whether they be based on economic, behavioristic, or psychoanalytic principles.

The term "will" presents a problem to the psychotherapist. It was banished so long ago from the lexicon of therapy that when "will" is invoked now, the clinician has difficulty recognizing it—much as though it were an old weathered acquaintance returning from exile. Perhaps, too, the clinician is not certain that he or she wishes to recognize it. Many years ago "will" was replaced by "motive," and therapists have learned to explain one's actions on the basis of one's motives. Thus, behavior such as paranoia is "explained" (that is, "caused") by the unconscious motivation of homosexual impulses; genital exhibitionism is "explained" by unconscious castration anxiety. Yet to explain behavior on the basis of motivation is to absolve one of ultimate responsibility for one's actions. Motivation can influence but cannot replace will; despite various motives, the individual still has the option of behaving or not behaving in a certain fashion.

Despite these many problems, no term other than "will" serves our purpose. The definitions of will that I cited earlier ("trigger of effort," "responsible mover," "mainspring of action," "seat of volition") are marvelously descriptive of the psychological construct appealed to by the psychotherapist. Many have noted the rich connotations of the word "will."[23] It conveys determination and commitment—"*I will do it.*" As a verb "will" connotes volition. As an auxiliary verb it designates the future tense. A last will and testament is one's final effort to lunge into the future. Hannah Arendt's felicitous phrase "the organ of the future" has particularly important implications for the therapist, because the future tense is the proper tense of psychotherapeutic change. Memory ("the organ of the past") is concerned with *objects*; the will is concerned with *projects*; and, as I hope to demonstrate, effective psychotherapy must focus on patients' *project relationships* as well as on their *object relationships*.

THE CLINICIAN AND THE WILL

If will is the "responsible mover" (and that is, I believe, a particularly useful definition of "will"), and if therapy requires movement and change, then it follows that the therapist, regardless of his or her frame of reference, must attempt to influence the will.

To return for a moment to the previous chapter on responsibility—what happens once the clinician has succeeded in helping a patient become aware that each person bears primary responsibility for his or her unhappy life predicament? The most simple therapeutic approach available to the therapist is exhortative: "You are responsible for what happens to you in your life. Your behavior is, as you yourself know, doing you in. It is not in your best interests. This is not what you want for yourself. Damn it, change!"

The guileless expectation that an individual will change as a result of this approach stems directly from the moral philosophical belief that if one truly knows the good (that is, what is, in the deepest sense, in one's best interest), one will act accordingly. ("Man, insofar as he acts willfully, acts according to some imagined good." [Aquinas]) Occasionally—very occasionally—this exhortative approach is effective. Individuals who undergo change as a result of short-term individual therapy, or especially of a short-term experiential group experience (which generally focuses on awareness of responsibility), often change as a result of this petition to conscious will.

However, as I shall discuss, "will power" constitutes only the first layer, and a thin layer at that, of "willing." Few changes are made as a result of "a deliberate, slow, dead heave of the will," as William James put it.[24] Well-entrenched psychopathology simply will not yield to exhortation; more therapeutic power is needed. Some therapists may attempt to increase therapeutic leverage by accenting the individual's *sole* responsibility. The therapist helps the patient realize that not only is the individual responsible for his situation but that *only* he is responsible. The corollary of this realization is that the individual is also *solely* responsible for the transmutation of his or her world. In other words, no other can change one's world for one. One must (actively) change if one is to change.

This appeal to the will may generate some twitching or stirring in a patient but generally is insufficient for sustained movement, and the therapist then embarks on the long, hard middle work of therapy. Though the particular tactics, strategy, formulated mechanisms, and goals depend upon the therapist's ideological school and upon personal style, I submit that the therapy is effective insofar as it influences the patient's will. The therapist may explicitly focus on interpretation and insight, interpersonal confrontation, development of a trusting and caring relationship, or analysis of maladaptive interpersonal behavior, but each of these may be viewed as a will-influencing venture. (I deliberately use the term "influence" rather than "create" or "generate." The therapist can neither create will nor inspirit or infuse the patient with will; what the therapist can do is to liberate will—to remove encumbrances from the bound, stifled will of the patient.)

But still I am vague. In my clinical work I sometimes think of the will, that responsible mover within the patient, as a turbine encased and concealed by ponderous layers of metal. I know that the vital, moving part is lodged deep in the innards of the machine. Puzzled, I circle it. I try to affect it from a distance by exhortation, by poking, tapping, or incantation, by performing those rites that I have been led to believe will influence it. These rites require much patience and much blind faith—more, in fact, than many contemporary free-thinking therapists are able to muster. What is required is a more expedient, rational approach to the will. In the remainder of this chapter I shall attempt to dismantle the turbine and systematically to examine will in its naked form and separate the mutative steps in psychotherapy from the ritualistic, decorative ones.

Because of will's long banishment from the psychological-psychotherapeutic literature, I shall first sketch the contours of a psychology of will. I shall examine relevant clinical observations on will made by three outstanding psychotherapist-theorists—Otto Rank, Leslie Farber, and Rollo May—and then, with their insights as a guide, discuss the clinical strategies and tactics of a will-influencing psychotherapy.

Toward a Clinical Understanding of Will: Rank, Farber, May

OTTO RANK—WILL THERAPY

A discussion of the will in clinical work must include the contributions of Otto Rank, for it was he who introduced the concept of the will into modern psychotherapy. Rank joined Freud in 1905 as one of his first students and was one of his close associates until 1929 when ideological differences created an unbridgeable chasm between the two men. A lay analyst and humanist with a deep and broad array of interests and knowledge, Rank's intellectual intensity in conjunction with his protruding fiery eyes transfixed both students and patients. His position as editor of the leading psychoanalytic journal and as founder and director of the powerful Viennese Psychoanalytic Institute made him a highly influential figure in the early development of psychoanalysis. But in the United States, destiny, abetted by wretched translations of his major works on psychotherapy which now (almost mercifully) are out of print, has not dealt well with Rank. Although he has been an influential intellectual force at the Pennsylvania School of Social Work, he has had—until the recent voice of Ernest Becker[25]—no one else to speak for him. Becker considers Rank as the brooding genius waiting in the wings; and indeed, I gasped at his prescience, when reading his works, especially his books, *Will Therapy* and *Truth and Reality.*[26]

Rank's system of behavior and therapy was built around the concept of will and is far too rich and complex to allow, in a short space, more than a brief summary of clinically relevant issues. His departure from Freud resulted from his disagreement with the latter's psychic determinism. Despite Freud's belief that behavior is a vector of opposing drives and counterforces, a freely choosing homunculus has been, as I noted earlier, smuggled into the ego. Rank chose as his starting place that homunculus with executive function and labeled it "will." He retained the concept of instinctual drives but placed them under the jurisdiction of the will: "I understand by will a positive, guiding organization which utilizes creatively as well as inhibits and controls the instinctual drives.[27] Rank was concerned more with therapeutic outcome than with the construction of a model of the mind and was convinced that strict psychic determinism was incompatible with effective psychotherapy. A therapeutic procedure dedicated to uncovering influences upon the patient (both historical and unconscious) could only, Rank insisted, result in the patient's *avoiding* responsibility and becoming less able to act: "It is astonishing how much the patient knows and how relatively little is unconscious if one does not give the patient this convenient excuse for refusing responsibility."[28] Rank suggested that Freud's theory elevated the unconscious to a responsibility-dissolving function, the precise function played by a deity in previous systems:

> The unconscious, just as the original meaning of the word shows, is a purely negative concept, which designates something momentarily not conscious, while Freud's theory has lifted it to the most powerful factor in psychic life. The basis for this, however, is not given in any psychological experience but in a moral necessity, that is, to find an acceptable substitute for the concept of God, who frees the individual from responsibility.[29]

The Development of the Will. In the development of the individual, the will, Rank believed, arises in relation to instinctual impulses. The shaping of the will is influenced by the manner in which parents deal with impulse education. At first the child's community is concerned primarily with restricting the child's impulse life in order to make the child fit for the community. The child responds to these parental restrictions with a counterforce: the *anlage* of the will or, as Rank put it, "negative will."[30] Gradually the child begins to exert personal control over his or her impulses and decides, for example, on the basis of love for his or her parents to curb those aggressive impulses. Thus, the will's function at first is inextricably tied up with impulse: either it controls impulse, or it resists outside efforts to control impulse. The child's emotional life, too, Rank stated, develops in relation to the impulses. Emotions are different from impulses: we seek to discharge impulses, but we seek to prolong or dam up emotions. (Rank referred here to pleasurable emotions but does not discuss dysphoric emotions.) Hence "the emotional life corresponds, so to say, to an inhibited or dammed up impulse life."[31]

Thus Rank suggested that the emotional life is a mirror image of the impulse life, whereas the will is a separate executive entity equal in power to the impulse system. "The will is an impulse, positively, actively placed in the service of the ego, and not a blocked impulse, as is the emotion."[32] Later Rank referred to the will as an "ego impulse."[33] Rank was striving to wrench himself away from Freud but could not divest himself of Freudian drive theory. By continuing to use psychic compartmentalization, Rank created difficulties for himself: the will, a freely choosing agency, is described as an "ego impulse"—a term that creates as much confusion as clarity.

Rank viewed the parent-child relationship and, indeed, the entire assimilative process—and, as we shall see, the therapeutic relation as well—as a struggle of wills and urged that parents pay exquisite sensitivity to this issue. Negative will should not be squelched but should be accepted in such a way that it is transformed into positive or "creative" will.

Rank subordinated other major issues of early life to the basic will struggle. "The Oedipus complex has no other significance than that of a great—if not the first—will conflict between the growing individual and the counter-will of a thousand-year-old moral code, represented in the parents." He continued (ironically): "The child must subject himself to it, not in order that he should let his father live and not marry his mother but that he should not believe in general that he can do what he wishes, that he should not trust himself to will."[34]

Rank described three developmental stages of the will: (1) counter will—opposition to another's will, (2) positive will—willing what one must, (3) creative will—willing what one wants. The goal of child rearing (and of therapy) is to transform the first two stages into creative will. The major "error" of child rearing, Rank suggested, is the squelching of impulse life and of early will ("counter" or "negative" will). If parents teach the child that all free impulse expression is undesirable and all counter will is bad, the child suffers two consequences: suppression of his or her entire emotional life, and stunted, guilt-laden will. The child then grows into an adult who suppresses his or her emotions and regards the very act of willing as evil and forbidden.

These consequences are of the utmost importance for the therapist who frequently sees patients who are unable to feel and unable, because of guilt, to will.

Rank's nosological system was based on the developmental vagaries of the will. He described three basic character types: creative, neurotic, and antisocial. The creative character has access to emotions and wills what he or she wants. The neurotic character has a will ensnarled with guilt and an inhibited emotional life. The antisocial character has a suppressed will and is dominated by impulse.

The Will and Psychotherapy. Rank felt that both Freud and Alfred Adler annihilated the will. Freud interpreted the will as sublimated sexual striving, and Adler viewed the will as a compensatory tendency to adjust for the child's sense of smallness and inferiority. Both men thus "explained away" the will by considering it as a derivative function. In contrast, Rank posited an "a priori will" and emphasized the central role of will not only in child development but also in therapy (which, he felt, was always carried out against the backdrop of the will).

Rank viewed therapist-patient interaction in much the same way as he did the parent-child experience. In therapy "two wills clash, either the one overthrows the other or both struggle with and against one another for supremacy."[35] The goal of therapy should be for the neurotic to learn to will and, above all, to learn to will without guilt.[36] Will enters the therapeutic situation in the very first sessions, Rank observed. The beginning of therapy is "therefore nothing other than the opening of a great duel of wills, in which the first easy victory over the apparently weak-willed patient is bitterly avenged many times."[37] The patient engages in a will conflict with the therapist and wishes both to resist and to submit. Freud, Rank felt, made a serious error in ignoring this will conflict: "The battle for supremacy [between analyst and patient] is so clear that only the wish not to see it can explain its neglect by Freud."[38] Rather than strengthening will, Rank felt that Freudian technique undermined it in two ways: through its basic procedure and through its management of "resistance."

First, Rank felt that the basic procedure in psychoanalysis—a procedure that requires a state of "will-lessness" by both patient and therapist—acts to weaken will. "The basic analytic rule of free association specifically states, eliminate entirely the little bit of will which your neurotic weakness has perhaps not yet undermined and resign yourself to the guidance of the unconscious. . . ."[39] (This comment is prescient of criticisms levied at psychoanalysis decades later: for example, Sylvan

Tomkins referred to psychoanalysis as a "systematic training in indecision,"[40] and Allen Wheelis stated "knowledgeable moderns put their back to the couch and in so doing may occasionally fail to put their shoulders to the wheel."[41])

During the course of therapy the patient opposes what he perceives to be the will of the therapist. Freud labeled this opposition "resistance," considered it an obstacle, and suggested various techniques (patience, guidance, interpretation) to overcome it. To Rank, this view of resistance was a serious error: he believed that the patient's protest was a valid and important manifestation of counter will and, as such, must not be eliminated but instead supported and transformed into creative will. "The task of the therapist is to function in such a way that the will of the patient shall not be broken but strengthened."[42] If the therapist tries to force the patient to do what is "right," the patient will resist, and therapy will fail. (Certainly within this statement lies the germ of the modern-day tactic of "paradox" in psychotherapy.) Rank, therefore, systematically reinforced all manifestations of the patient's will: if the patient resisted or the patient suggested termination, Rank was careful to point out that he considered these stands as progress. He stated: "The neurotic cannot will without guilt. That situation can be changed not by himself but only in relation to a therapist who accepts the patient's will, who justifies it, submits to it, and makes it good."[43]

One situation where the patient's and the therapist's wills are certain to clash is the termination of therapy. Some patients choose to terminate precipitately; while others refuse to terminate and, if necessary, cling to their symptoms to resist the therapist's efforts to bring therapy to a conclusion. Rank felt that this clash of wills contained so much therapeutic potential that it was unfortunate that it had to be carried out at the end of therapy—and, indeed, often outside of therapy altogether. Would it not be more sensible to transfer this will conflict to the center of the therapeutic arena—indeed, even to the beginning of therapy? Rank attempted to do just that by the special device of setting, at the beginning of therapy, a precise "time limit." His "end-setting" thus projected the final phase of therapy forward to the onset of treatment.

These therapeutic strategies pertaining to will represent only one aspect of Rank's therapeutic approach. Later I shall discuss his views on "experiencing," on the importance of the present and the future tenses, and on the nature of the therapeutic relationship.

In his effort to counter what he perceived in Freud and Adler as an undermining of will and responsibility, Rank may have overstated the role of will power and willfulness. By and large, patients do not change in therapy as a result of an act of conscious will. In fact, what is so often perplexing to the therapist (and maddening to the researcher) is that change occurs at a subterranean level, far out of the ken of either the therapist or the patient.

Is subterranean, "nonvolitional" change an act of will? It is precisely this question, this connection between willful acts and unconsciously based change, that has created so much difficulty for psychologists who have tried to fashion a succinct, workable definition of will. Leslie Farber's contribution to a psychology of will offers a vital corrective to an exaggerated emphasis on conscious will.[44] Farber suggests that efforts to define will have failed because there are two different realms of will, each so distinct from the other that only the most vapid definition can straddle them.

Farber's first realm of the will—and it is here that he makes his most important contribution—is *not* experienced consciously during an act and must be inferred after an *event*; this realm may be said to be unconscious. Farber cites W. H. Auden:

> When I look back at the three or four choices in my life which have been decisive, I find that, at the time I made them, I had very little sense of the seriousness of what I was doing and only later did I discover what had seemed an unimportant brook was, in fact, a Rubicon.[45]

Thus Farber suggests that the important choices that one makes in life (and, I am certain he would say, in therapy) are not consciously experienced as choices. In fact, only *after the fact* is one able to deduce that one has actually made a choice. This realm of will may be thought of as a subterranean life current that has direction but not discrete objects or goals. It provides propulsion to the individual but eludes immediate and direct scrutiny.

The second realm of will is the conscious component: it is experienced during the event. One can describe, without much difficulty, its presence, shape, and magnitude. This second realm of will presses toward some specific object (unlike the first which is pure propulsion) and is utilitarian in character: "I do this to get that." The goal of this realm of the will is known from the beginning (for example, weight loss, a change in interpersonal style, or graduation from college).

These two realms of will must be approached differently in therapy.

The second (conscious) realm of will is approached through exhortations and appeals to will power, effort, and determination. The first realm is impervious to these enjoinders and must be approached obliquely. A serious problem occurs when one applies exhortative second-realm techniques to first-realm activities. Farber offers some examples:

> I can will knowledge, but not wisdom; going to bed, but not sleeping; eating, but not hunger; meekness, but not humility; scrupulosity, but not virtue; self-assertion or bravado, but not courage; lust, but not love; commiseration, but not sympathy; congratulations, but not admiration; religiosity, but not faith; reading, but not understanding.[46]

Here Farber provides an extraordinarily important insight to the therapist, an insight to which I shall return many times in this chapter. However, it is clear from some of the goings-on in the psychotherapy field—the "can't" bells ringing and the "winning through intimidation" genre of self-help books cascading off the presses—that Farber's warning has not been heeded, and that many psychotherapists make the mistake of trying to make the will of the second (conscious) realm do the work of the will of the first.

ROLLO MAY—THE WISH AND THE WILL

Rollo May's excellent book *Love and Will* brims with rich clinical insights, among which is the incorporation of "wish" into the psychology of the will.[47] May reminds us that wish is anterior to will, that there can be no meaningful action without a prior wish.[48] Willing is not only power and resolve but potentiality that is intimately bound up with the future.[49] Through the will we project ourselves into the future, and the wish is the beginning of that process. The wish is "an admission that we want the future to be such and such; it is a capacity to reach down deep into ourselves and preoccupy ourselves with a longing to change the future."[50]

It is important to distinguish May's "wish" from the wish, defined differently, that plays an important role in the analytic model of mental functioning. Freud referred to wish throughout his metapsychology as the "mental representation of a drive." "Only a wish can set the mental apparatus into motion"; "Wish is the desire to relieve tension"—as Freud stated repeatedly.[51]

The most complete statement of this position is to be found in the often-cited chapter 7 of *The Interpretation of Dreams*,[52] where Freud stated clearly his view that man operates on the constancy principle: that is, man attempts to maintain the level of cortical excitation at a constant level. When a disequilibrium occurs (for example, when the infant experiences hunger), the organism experiences a "wish" to be fed and acts in such a way (for example, cries or signals discomfort in some manner) to restore equilibrium. Gradually, as hunger is repetitively followed by feeding, the infant acquires a visual representation (an image or a "hallucination") of being fed. Later, under the pressure of the reality principle, the child learns to delay gratification by evoking the visual representation of the feeding experience. This process of wishing and internal, temporary gratification of the wish, Freud argued, is the *anlage* of all thinking. A wish can exist on various levels of consciousness. An unconscious wish is the mental representation of an id impulse. Conscious wishes are generally compromise formations—that is, unconscious wishes tempered and molded by the superego and by unconscious parts of the ego. To Freud, then, wish is an unfree force akin to a tropism.

Sartre criticized Freud's theory of repression on the ground that it omitted the self. "How can there be a lie without a liar?" Sartre asked. Or deception without a deceiver? Or denial without a denier? Freud's concept of the wish is open to the same criticism: How can there be a wish without a wisher?

May emphasizes that wishes differ from needs, forces, or tropisms in one important aspect: wishes are imbued with meaning. An individual does not wish blindly. A man does not merely wish, for example, for sex with a woman: he finds one woman attractive, another repugnant. Wishing is selective and highly individualized. If a man indiscriminately desires sexual relationships with all women, then something is seriously wrong. This state occurs either as a result of unusual environmental press, as in the case of soldiers stationed for long periods in an isolated Arctic station,[53] or else as a result of psychopathology: one gives up one's freedom and is then no longer the driver but the driven. It is precisely the state of "wishing" without a wisher that we term "neurosis." That is what May meant when he said: "It is the symbolic meanings that have gone awry in neurosis, and not the id impulses."[54]

Wish, which May defines as "the imaginative playing with the possibility of some act or state occurring,"[55] is the first step of the process of willing. Only after wishing occurs can the individual pull the "trigger of effort" and initiate the remainder of the act of willing, commitment and choice, which culminates in action.

> "Wish" gives the warmth, the content, the imagination, the child's play, the freshness, and the richness to "will." "Will" gives the self-direction, the maturity, to "wish." Without "wish," "will" loses its life-blood, its

viability, and tends to expire in self-contradiction. If you have only "will" and no "wish," you have the dried-up, Victorian, neopuritan man. If you have only "wish" and no "will," you have the driven, unfree, infantile person who, as an adult-remaining-an-infant, may become the robot man.[56]

The Will and Clinical Practice

The will is not an esoteric concept of interest only to the unusual patient and therapist, but it enters, in a number of ways, into the course of therapy of every patient. Some patients seek therapy for problems of disordered will. Of course, since there is no place for will in the standard nosology, the problem is not referred to by that name. Instead, one may be considered obsessive-compulsive and forced by internal pressures to act against one's will. Or one may be indecisive, unable to wish, to want something for oneself, or to act. Or one may be caught in the throes of some particularly agonizing decision. Or one may be timid, shy, unassertive, or flooded with guilt when one attempts to will. As Rank suggested, an individual may have learned early in life that impulse expression is bad, and generalized that verdict of badness to the entire realm of volition.

Even if there is no apparent willing disorder in the presenting clinical picture, it is inevitable that the issue of will will arise during psychotherapy. Will is inherent in the very act of change. At some point the patient must come to terms with what he or she truly wishes, must become committed to a certain course, must take a stand, must choose, must say yea to something and nay to something else. Will is also present in every therapist-patient relationship. Although Rank overstated the issue by characterizing therapy as a "duel of two wills,"[57] he made a valuable contribution by calling attention to this important aspect in the therapeutic process. Some patients and therapists do indeed lock horns over issues of dominance, and in these instances Rank's observations are germane. Resistance or obstinacy on the part of the patient is not always an impediment to therapy, nor is it necessarily to be analyzed away. Instead, as Rank suggests, it is a stand that the patient is taking; and, by accepting and reinforcing that stand, the therapist may facilitate the patient's ability to will guiltlessly.

One of the major obstacles to the therapist's acceptance of a theory of will is the erroneous belief that "will" is synonymous with "will power." But, as Farber's "two realm" concept tells us, much more than conscious, teeth-gritting resolution is involved in willing. In fact, as I shall discuss shortly, a full consideration of the meaning and roots of "willing" leads us into the area of the deepest unconscious concerns. But even unconscious willing does not occur without determination and commitment. Effortless change is not possible; the patient must transport himself or herself to therapy, must pay money, must bear the burden of responsibility, must experience the conflict and the anxiety that inevitably accompany the work of therapy. In short, the therapy vehicle has no slick, noiseless automatic transmission; effort is required, and will is the "trigger of effort."

The concept of will is so broad and so unwieldy that only generalized, trivial comments may be made about it as an entity. To discuss will in a clinically useful way, I must consider its component parts separately. Hannah Arendt's philosophical treatise on the will provides a natural cleavage:

> [There are] two altogether different ways of understanding the faculty of the will: as a faculty of choice between objects or goals, the liberum arbitrium, which acts as arbiter between given ends and deliberates freely about means to reach them; and, on the other hand, as our "faculty for beginning spontaneously a series in time (Kant) or Augustine's "initium ut esset homo creatus est," man's capacity for beginning because he himself is a beginning.[58]

These two ways of understanding will—"spontaneously beginning a series in time," and deciding between given ends and choosing the means to reach them—have obvious and valuable clinical referents. One initiates through *wishing* and then enacts through *choice*.

The clinician's goal is change (action); responsible action begins with the *wish*. One can only act for oneself if one has access to one's desires. If one lacks that access and cannot wish, one cannot project into the future, and responsible volition dies stillborn. Once wish materializes, the process of willing is launched and is transformed finally into action. What shall we call this process of transformation? The process between wish and action entails commitment; it entails "putting myself on record (to myself) to endeavor to do it."[59] The happiest term seems to me to be "decision"—or, "choice,"* which is used by both clinicians

---

*I shall use "decision" and "choice" interchangeably. They are synonymous but each emanates from a different tradition: "choice" is the preferred philosophical term; "decision" the preferred social-psychological one. Used interchangeably, they reflect my effort to span these disciplines in this discussion.

and social scientists. To decide means that action will follow. If no action occurs, then no true decision has been made. If wishing occurs without action, then there has been no genuine willing. (If action occurs without wishing, then, too, there is no "willing"; there is only impulsive activity.)

Either of these phases of willing—wishing and deciding—can break down in a number of ways, each with a different clinical picture, each requiring a different therapeutic approach.

Wish

> "What shall I do? What shall I do?"
> "What stops you from doing what you want to do?"
> "But I don't *know* what I want! If I knew I wouldn't be here!"

How often does the therapist participate in some such sequence as this? How often do therapists work with patients who know what they should do, ought to do, or must do but have no experience of what they *want* to do. To work with individuals with a profound incapacity to wish is a particularly frustrating experience, and few therapists have not shared May's inclination to shout, "Don't you ever *want* anything?"[60] The wish-blocked individual has enormous social difficulties. Others, too, wish to shout at such persons. They have no opinions, no inclinations, no desires of their own. They become parasitic on the wishes of others, and finally others become bored, drained, or fatigued at having to supply wish and imagination for them.

"Incapacity" to wish is too strong a phrase. More often the individual distrusts or suppresses his or her wishes. Many people, in an effort to appear strong, decide that it is better not to want; wanting makes one vulnerable or leaves one exposed: "If I never wish, I'll never be weak." Others, demoralized, deaden themselves to internal experience: "If I never wish, I will never again be disappointed or rejected." Others submerge their wishes in the infantile hope that eternal caretakers will be able to read their wishes for them. There is something infinitely reassuring about having someone else meet one's unexpressed wishes. Still others so fear abandonment by caretakers that they repress all direct expression of personal desire. They do not permit themselves the right to wish, as though their wishing would irritate, threaten, or drive away others.

THE INABILITY TO FEEL

The inability to wish, or to experience one's wishes, has not been widely and explicitly discussed in clinical literature; it is generally embedded in a global disorder—the inability to feel. The psychotherapist frequently encounters patients who seem unable to feel or to express their feelings in words. They are unable to differentiate between various affects and seem to experience joy, anger, sorrow, nervousness, and so on, all in the same manner. They cannot localize feelings within their body and have a particularly striking lack of fantasies referable to inner drives and affects. In 1967, Peter Sifenos suggested a term, "alexithymia" (from the Greek, meaning "no words for feelings") to describe this clinical picture; and a large body of literature has since accumulated about the alexithymic patient.[61] The psychosomatic patient is particularly likely to be alexithymic, although many alexithymic individuals present with other clinical pictures.

The expression of affect has always been considered an important part of psychotherapy. Freud, in 1895 in *Studies in Hysteria*, first postulated that hysteria was caused by the presence of some strong affect (resulting, for example, from a traumatic incident) in the individual.[62] Unlike most strong emotional reactions which are eliminated through "the normal wearing away process of abreaction," this particular affect persists and is repressed into the unconscious. Once that occurs, the "constancy principle"* is violated: the level of intracerebral excitation" is increased, and the individual, to restore equilibrium, develops a symptom that symbolically provides an outlet for the tension. Thus, psychiatric symptomatology is caused by "strangulated affect"; and psychiatric treatment should consist of releasing this imprisoned affect and, allowing it to enter consciousness and to be discharged through catharsis.

Though this was Freud's first formulation of the therapeutic mechanism, and though he rapidly realized that catharsis *per se* was an insufficient means of therapy, this formulation is so beautiful in its simplicity that it has persisted throughout the decades. Certainly it is the popular view incarnated in innumerable Hollywood films. The contemporary view is that, though catharsis does not in and of itself produce change, it plays a necessary role in the therapeutic process. Certainly there is considerable research to support this view. For example,

---

*That is, the need of the organism to maintain an optimal level of tension.

my colleagues and I studied a series of patients who had had highly successful psychotherapy outcomes.[63] In an effort to delineate the effective therapeutic mechanisms, we developed a list of sixty items (see chapter 6) and asked the patients to rank them in the order of the importance of each item to their personal change. Of the sixty items, the patients selected "catharsis" items as the second and the fourth most important mechanisms.

Recently there has been an explosion of new therapies (for example, Gestalt therapy, intense feeling therapy,[64] implosive therapy,[65] bioenergetics,[66] emotional flooding,[67] psychodrama, primal scream therapy,[68]) which closely resemble one another in the importance placed on awareness and expression of feelings. Though each of these therapies advances its own rationale for this emphasis, they have, I believe, important views in common. They all hold that awareness and expression of feelings is helpful to the individual in two primary ways: by facilitating interpersonal relationships, and by facilitating one's capacity to wish.

FEELING AND INTERPERSONAL RELATIONSHIPS

The role of affect expression in interpersonal relationships is self-evident. Significant problems arise in relationships for the alexithymic individual. Others never know how that person feels; he or she seems unspontaneous, wooden, heavy, lifeless, and boring. The other person feels burdened by having to generate all the affect in the relationship, and begins to question whether he or she is really cared for by the blocked person. The movements of the blocked individual are so deliberate and unspontaneous that they seem forced and ungenuine. There is no play, no fun, only an awkward, ponderous self-consciousness. One who does not feel is not sought out by others, but exists in a state of loneliness, cut off not only from one's feelings but from those of others.

FEELING AND WISHING

One's capacity to wish is automatically facilitated if one is helped to feel. Wishing requires feeling. If one's wishes are based on something other than feelings—for example, on rational deliberation or moral imperatives—then they are no longer wishes but "shoulds" or "oughts," and one is blocked from communicating with one's real self.

One patient in a therapy group found himself unable to understand another patient who was upset because her therapist was leaving for a month's vacation. "Why get yourself in a turmoil if there's nothing you

305

can do about it?" In other words, he placed feelings and wishes secondary to a utilitarian goal and said, in effect, "If nothing useful will come of it, why wish and why feel?" This type of individual acts and has an internal sense of guidance, but does not wish. His or her wishes emanate from without, not from within. The exigencies of the environment and the dictates of rationality determine his or her internal state of wishing and feeling; to the observer, this individual may seem mechanical, predictable, and lifeless.

Another individual—and this one is especially obvious in a therapy group—tries to find out what he or she should feel and wish by attempting to find out what the *other* wants and then appeasing that other. These individuals are nonspontaneous; their behavior is highly predictable; and, consequently, they are invariably boring to others.

Wish is more than thought or aimless imagination. Wish contains an affect and a component of force. If affect is blocked, one cannot experience one's wishes, and the entire process of willing is stunted. No one has written a more arresting description of a man who could neither act nor wish because he could not reach his feelings, than has Sartre in *The Age of Reason*:

> He closed the paper and began to read the special correspondent's dispatch on the front page. Fifty dead and three hundred wounded had already been counted, but that was not the total, there were certainly corpses under the debris. . . . There were thousands of men in France who had not been able to read their paper that morning without feeling a clot of anger rise in their throat, thousands of men who had clenched their fists and muttered: "Swine!" Mathieu clenched his fists and muttered: "Swine!" and felt himself still more guilty. If at least he had been able to discover in himself a trifling emotion that was veritably if modestly alive, conscious of its limits. But no: he was empty, he was confronted by a vast anger, a desperate anger, he saw it and could almost have touched it. But it was inert—if it were to live and find expression and suffer, he must lend it his own body. It was other people's anger. "Swine!" He clenched his fists, he strode along, but nothing came, the anger remained external to himself. . . . Something was on the threshold of existence, a timorous dawn of anger. At last! But it dwindled and collapsed, he was left in solitude, walking with the measured and decorous gait of a man in a funeral procession in Paris. . . . He wiped his forehead with his handkerchief and he thought: "One can't force one's deeper feelings." Yonder was a terrible and tragic state of affairs that ought to arouse one's deepest emotions. . . . "It's no use, the moment will not come. . . ."[69]

Feeling is prerequisite to wish but not identical with it. One can feel without wishing and, consequently, without willing. Some of the best known "wishless" figures in modern literature—for example, Meursault in Albert Camus's *The Stranger* and Michel in André Gide's *The Immoralist*—were keen sensualists but were isolated from their own wishes and especially from wishes in the sphere of interpersonal relationships. Their actions were impulsively explosive and ultimately profoundly destructive to others and to themselves.

AFFECT-BLOCK AND PSYCHOTHERAPY

Psychotherapy with the affect-blocked (that is, feeling-blocked) patient is slow and grinding. Above all, the therapist must persevere. Time after time he will have to inquire, "What do you feel?" "What do you want?" Time after time he will need to explore the source and the nature of the block and of the stifled feelings behind it. The blockade is so apparent, even to the untrained eye, that it would be easy to conclude that if only it could be broken, if only the dam holding back the patient's affect could be dynamited away, then health and wholeness would come cascading through the breach. Consequently many therapists in search of a breakthrough have used some of the new sophisticated Gestalt, psychodrama, bioenergetic, and encounter affect-generating techniques in working with the affect-blocked patient.

Does the breakthrough strategy work? Can the therapist blast a way through the affect-blocked patient's perimeter of defenses and allow the dammed-up emotion to escape? My colleagues and I attempted to test this in a research project where we studied thirty-five patients in the midst of long-term psychotherapy (many of whom were affect-blocked and stuck in therapy) and attempted to determine whether, as a result of an affect-arousing experience, the subsequent course of individual therapy would be significantly altered.[70] We sent these patients to one of three different groups for a weekend experience. Two of these groups used powerful encounter and Gestalt affect-arousing techniques; the third, a meditation, body-awareness group, served as an experimental control in that it provided a weekend with neither affect arousal nor interpersonal interaction. The results indicated that, though during the group weekend many patients had intense emotional breakthroughs, these were not sustained: there were no discernible effects on the subsequent course of individual therapy.

Thus, while it is important to generate affect in therapy, there is no evidence that rapid intensive affect arousal *per se* is therapeutic. Much as we would like it otherwise, psychotherapy is "cyclotherapy"[71]—a long, lumbering process in which the same issues are repeatedly worked through in the therapy environment and are tested and retested in the patient's life environment. If affect breakthrough is not an effective therapy model, neither is the opposite approach—the sterile, overly intellectualized, highly rational approach to therapy. Affective engagement—Franz Alexander termed it "the corrective emotional experience"[72]—is a necessary component of successful therapy. Though many early therapists (such as Sandor Ferenczi, Otto Rank, Wilhelm Reich, and Julius Moreno) recognized the need for affective engagement and introduced techniques to make the therapeutic encounter more real and affect-laden, Fritz Perls more than any other must be credited with the development of an approach designed to increase the individual's awareness of affect.

Fritz Perls: "Lose Your Head and Come to Your Senses." Perls focused doggedly on awareness. His therapy is an "experiential therapy rather than a verbal or interpretative therapy,"[73] and he worked only in the present tense, because he felt that neurotics live too much in the past:

> Gestalt therapy is a "here and now" therapy in which we ask the patient during the session to turn all his attention to what he is doing in the present, during the course of the session—right here and now . . . to become aware of his gestures, of his breathing, of his emotions and of his facial gestures as much as his pressing thoughts.[74]

Perls would often begin with awareness of sensory impressions and kinesthetic impressions. For example, if a patient complained of a headache, Perls might ask the patient to focus on the headache until he or she found that it was associated with contractions of facial muscles. Perls might ask the patient then to exaggerate the contractions and at each step to talk about what he or she was aware of. Gradually the patient would be led from kinesthetic sensation to affect. For example, a woman patient might then describe her face: "It's as if I were screwing up my face to cry." At this point the therapist might encourage the affect by asking, "Would you like to cry?"[75]

Perls began with awareness and gradually worked toward "wish."

> I am convinced that the awareness technique alone can produce valuable therapeutic results. If the therapist were limited in his work only to asking three questions, he would eventually achieve success with all but the most seriously disturbed of his patients. These three questions are "What are you doing?" "What do you feel?" "What do you want?"[76]

Perls attempted to help patients feel things, to "own" these feelings, and then to become aware of wishes and desires. For example, if a patient intellectualized or addressed repeated questions to the therapist,

Perls might urge him or her to verbalize the statement and the wish behind the question.

> Patient: What do you mean by support?
> Therapist: Could you turn that into a statement?
> Patient: I would like to know what you mean by support?
> Therapist: That's still a question. Could you turn it into a statement?
> Patient: I would like to tear hell out of you on this question if I had the opportunity.[77]

At this point the patient has greater access to his affect and also access to his wishes.

The purpose of affect arousal is not sheer catharsis but to help patients rediscover their wishes. One major problem of Gestalt therapy is that many therapists become so preoccupied with affect-arousing techniques that they lose sight of the deeper purpose of the technique. To some degree this is a result of therapists modeling themselves after Perls, who was a great showman and enjoyed short, dramatic encounters with patients conducted before large audiences. But Perls, in his reflective moments, expressed dismay at the tendency of therapists to focus excessively on technique:

> It took us a long time to debunk the whole Freudian crap, and now we are entering a new and more dangerous phase. We are entering the phase of the turner-onners: turn on to instant cure, instant joy, instant sensory-awareness. We are entering the phase of the quacks and the conmen, who think if you get some break-through, you are cured. . . . I must say I am *very* concerned with what's going on right now.
> . . . A technique is a gimmick. A gimmick should be used only in the extreme case. We've got enough people running around collecting gimmicks, more gimmicks and abusing them. These techniques, these tools, are quite useful in some seminar on sensory awareness or joy. . . . But the sad fact is that this jazzing-up more often becomes a dangerous substitute activity, another phony therapy that *prevents* growth.[78]

Other Therapeutic Approaches. Perls is not the only worker who grappled with the problem of affect block. Psychodrama, encounter groups, hypnotic therapy, and bioenergetics have all developed techniques designed to arouse affect and to increase the individual's awareness of wishes. In fact, there has been such a vast proliferation of approaches that it is no longer possible to trace their genealogy. All the techniques, however, rest on the assumptions that at some deep level one knows one's wishes and feelings, and that the therapist, through proper focusing, can increase the patient's conscious experience of such internal states.

Postural, gestural, or other subtle nonverbal cues may provide important information about underlying but dissociated feelings and wishes. Therapists must attend closely to such clues as clenched fists, the pounding of one fist into one's palm, or the assumption of a closed (crossed arms and legs) position. Each of these is a manifestation of an underlying feeling or wish. (In such instances Perls attempted to facilitate the emergence of the repressed feeling by calling attention to the behavior and then requesting the patient to exaggerate it—for example, to hit the fist into the palm harder and faster.) Indeed, some patients are so affect-isolated that physical or physiological data are their only contacts with their inner world—for example, "I must be sad if my eyes are teary," or "I must be embarrassed if I'm blushing."

The question, "What do you want?" often takes patients by surprise since they rarely ask it of themselves. Erving and Miriam Pohlster provide an illustration:

> A college professor was feeling overburdened by having to cram each day with what seemed to be overwhelming requirements to write, read, teach—until his time felt like it was ready to burst at the seams. After a long recital of all the demands he experienced on his already overcommitted life, I asked him, "What do you want?" A pause . . . and a gesture with his hands showing one hand fitting—but *very loosely* and with space left over—into another . . . and then, "I want some *slop* in my life!" These recognitions are simple enough, but to many people they are not readily accessible. Until these wants can be at least recognized, though, focused action is unlikely.[79]

If patients are severely schizoid and deeply isolated from their wishes, a focused inquiry on the immediate here-and-now interaction may be productive. For example, in a group session a deeply troubled young man lamented, in response to my question, that he had no feelings and wishes, and indicated that he could feel if only he knew what he *should* feel. Other members pursued the issue, asking him about how he felt about a number of topics (such as loneliness, strong tranquilizers, some problems on the ward), all of which left the patient feeling more confused and discouraged. We finally became more helpful to him when we focused the inquiry onto immediate process: "How do you feel about being questioned about your feelings?" At this level he was able to experience a number of genuine feelings and wishes. Though he was frightened by all of the attention, he also felt pleased and grateful and wanted the group to continue to press him. He also felt like a hog for talking so much and feared that others would resent his taking away their time. Gradually, starting from this base of immediate affect, the patient gained confidence with his ability to *have* feelings and to identify them.

Another patient had for years distrusted and devalued the importance of her feelings. She considered feelings phony and contrived because whenever she was aware of a particular feeling, she could also generate an opposing feeling equal in magnitude. Endless hours of therapy had been wasted in block-busting efforts to break down this defense. Progress only occurred by helping her to identify some feeling (and wish) of incontestable valence in the immediate here and now. She was in a therapy group on a hospital ward which was observed by the ward staff, and then had the opportunity to observe the observers' open rehash of the meeting. When asked to describe her reaction to the rehash, she said that she had been annoyed by the fact that she was rarely discussed. When we investigated her annoyance (since it appeared without question to be deeply felt), it turned to pain—her hurt at being ignored—and then to fear—fear that the therapist had, in his mind, filed her, as she put it, in the "C" (chronic) file. She was then urged to express what she wished the therapist had said or done. In this manner she was gradually led to experience such non-phony wishes as her desire that he cradle and shelter her.

Freud pointed out long ago that fantasies are wishes; and the investigation of fantasy—either spontaneous or guided fantasy—is often a productive technique in the uncovering and the assimilation of wishes. For example, one patient could not decide whether to continue seeing his girlfriend or to break off the relationship. His response to such questions as "What do you want to do?" or "Do you care for her?" was invariably a bewildered and frustrated "I don't know." The therapist asked him to fantasize receiving a phone call from her in which she suggested that they end their relationship. The patient visualized this clearly, sighed with relief, and became aware of feeling liberated after the phone call. From this fantasy it was only a short step to realize his true wish about the relationship and to begin working on those factors that inhibited the recognition and the enactment of his wish.

IMPULSIVITY

A disorder of wishing does not necessarily lead to inhibition and paralysis. Some individuals avoid wishing by not discriminating among wishes, but act promptly and impulsively on all wishes. One who acts immediately on each impulse or whim avoids wishing as neatly as does one who stifles or represses wishes. Thus, one avoids having to choose among various wishes which, if experienced simultaneously, may be contradictory. Peer Gynt, as Rollo May points out, is an excellent example of a person who cannot discriminate among his wishes, attempts to fulfill all of them, and in so doing loses his true self—the self that wants one thing more deeply than another thing.[80] A wish always involves direction and time. To wish is to lunge into the future, and the indivudal must consider the future implications and the consequences of acting upon a wish. Nowhere is this necessity more evident than in the wish involving another person. Impulsive Peer Gyntish enactment of all interpersonal wishes results in violation or rape of the other rather than a true encounter. What is required is internal discrimination among wishes and assigning priorities to each. If two wishes are mutually exclusive, then one must be relinquished. If, for example, a meaningful, loving relationship is a wish, then a host of conflicting interpersonal wishes—such as conquest, power, seduction, or subjugation—must be denied. If a writer's primary wish is to communicate, he must relinquish other, interfering wishes (such as the wish to appear clever). Impulsive and indiscriminate enactment of all wishes is a symptom of disordered will: it suggests an inability or a reluctance to project oneself into the future.

Another way to describe the basic disorder of wishing which underlies behavioral impulsivity is to consider two forms of ambivalence: sequential and simultaneous ambivalence.[81] In "sequential ambivalence" the individual experiences first one and then the other wish. When one is dominant, it is acted upon, and the individual does not have full access to the other. In "simultaneous ambivalence" one is confronted by both wishes fully and directly. James Bugental describes a patient who was tossed about in an agonized state of sequential ambivalence:

> At 42 Mabel had been married for 17 years to a man whom she loved deeply and with whom she had much that was meaningful and satisfying. Then, through a series of circumstances not important here, she found herself also very much in love with another man, a widower, and he returned her feeling. She had not lost her love for her husband, Greg, nor did she want only a simple "fling" with the other man, Hal.
>
> Thus, Mabel, when she was at home with Greg would be very aware of how rich her life was with him and would wonder that she could be tempted to overturn it with all the pain, guilt, and disruption of her own and his futures that would be involved. Then when she was with Hal or perhaps just away from Greg, she would be swept by anguish as she knew how vital was her feeling for Hal and her yearning for the different life she would have were she to go to him.[82]

The therapist's task is to help the impulsive patient transform sequential ambivalence into simultaneous ambivalence. The experiencing of conflicting wishes sequentially is a method of defending oneself from anxiety. When one fully experiences conflicting wishes *simultaneously*, one must face the responsibility of choosing one and relinquishing the other. Simultaneous ambivalence results in a state of extreme discomfort; and, as Bugental notes, it is extremely important that the therapist avoid diluting the pain or the autonomy of the patient. The therapist is strongly tempted to advise, to succor, to (as Heidegger puts it) "leap in ahead of the other";[83] yet if one is able to confront deeply and with full intensity all one's relevant wishes, then one will eventually fashion a creative, innovative solution—a solution that another could not have foreseen.

In the preceding case Mabel used her conflict to arrive at a truly creative insight: "She realized how, all along, she had subtly used her husband to define her own being and how she had come near to doing the same thing with Hal." She began to realize her own identity as separate from either Hal or Greg. This did not mean that she would cease to love her husband, with whom she chose to remain, but it meant loving him in a different fashion: it meant loving *him*, not loving herself and him as a fused entity; it meant being able to face life alone without a loss of selfhood and without a devastating sense of loneliness.

COMPULSIVITY

Compulsivity, a defense against responsibility awareness, also constitutes a disorder of wishing—one that appears more organized and less capricious than impulsivity. The compulsive individual acts in accordance with inner demands that are *not* experienced as wishes. Something "ego-alien" directs such an individual. He is propelled to act, often against his wishes, and, if he does not act, feels acutely uncomfortable. Though he wishes not to act in a particular way, he finds it extraordinarily difficult not to follow the dictates of the compulsion. Camus caught it perfectly when, through the protagonist of *The Fall*, he said, "Not taking what one doesn't desire is the hardest thing in the world."[84] The compulsive individual is generally not aware of an inability to wish: he or she does not feel empty or rudderless. On the contrary, such an individual is active, often forceful, and at all times possessed with a sense of purpose. But there are often waves of doubt—times when the individual realizes that though he or she has a purpose, it is not his or her own purpose; that though he or she has desires and

313

goals, they are not his or her own desires and goals. The individual is so busy, so driven that he feels he has neither the time nor the right to ask himself what he wishes to do. It is only when the defense cracks (for example, the "externally imposed" goals may become irrelevant because of some environmental alteration such as loss of job or breakup of family, or they have been attained—money, prestige, power) that the individual becomes aware of the suffocation of his or her real self.

Decision—Choice

Once an individual fully experiences wish, he or she is faced with decision or choice. Decision is the bridge between wishing and action.* To decide means to commit oneself to a course of action. If no action ensues, I believe that there has been no true decision but instead a flirting with decision, a type of failed resolve. Samuel Beckett's *Waiting for Godot* is a monument to aborted decision. The characters think, plan, procrastinate, and resolve, but they do not decide. The play ends with this sequence.

> Vladimir: Shall we go?
> Estragon: Let's go.
> [Stage directions:] No one moves.[85]

DECISION AND THE THERAPEUTIC CONTRACT

Therapy and a Specific Decision.   The concept of decision enters into psychotherapy in many ways. Some patients seek therapy specifically because they are caught in the throes of a specific decision—often one related to relationship or career. Consequently, therapy will center about this decision. If the therapy is brief, focused, and task-oriented, the therapist will enable the patient to make the decision. The therapist will consider, with the latter, the pros and cons of the decision and will try to help the patient sort out both conscious and subconscious implications of each choice. If, on the other hand, therapy is more intensive

---

* I use "action" not in an energic but in a therapeutic sense. The slightest movement or the obliteration of some previous habitual action may constitute momentous therapeutic action.

and the goals are more extensive, the therapist uses the specific decision as a central trunk from which, as therapy proceeds, a diversity of
themes will radiate. The therapist helps the patient understand the unconscious meaning of the decisional anxiety, reviews other past decisional crises and, though the treatment goal is not specifically to help
the patient make a particular decision, hopes nonetheless to resolve the
conflicted areas so that the patient may make that decision and related
ones in an adaptive fashion.

Therapy and Unconscious Decision. Many therapists focus closely on
decision even if the patient does not enter therapy for some particular
crisis of decision. In an effort to augment the patient's sense of personal responsibility, these therapists emphasize that every act (including
personal change) is preceded by a decision. Therapists who focus on
decision in this manner often assume that decisions are involved in behavior not ordinarily associated with decision. Thus, the therapist focuses on the decision that the patient makes to fail, to procrastinate, to
withdraw from others, to avoid closeness, or even to be passive, depressed, or anxious. Obviously these decisions were never consciously
made; the therapist assumes that, since individuals are responsible for
their behavior, each must have "chosen" to be as he or she is. What
kind of choosing is this? It is the choosing that Farber referred to as the
"first realm" of will. Few major decisions are made with a full sense of
deliberate, conscious effort. William James, who thought deeply about
how decisions are made, described five types of decision, only two of
which, the first and the second, involve "willful" effort:

1. *Reasonable decision.* We consider the arguments for and against a given
   course and settle on one alternative. A rational balancing of the books;
   we make this decision with a perfect sense of being free.
2. *Willful decision.* A willful and strenuous decision involving a sense of
   "inward effort." A "slow, dead heave of the will." This is a rare decision;
   the great majority of human decisions are made without effort.
3. *Drifting decision.* In this type there seems to be no paramount reason for
   either course of action. Either seems good, and we grow weary or frustrated at the decision. We make the decision by letting ourselves drift in
   a direction seemingly accidentally determined *from without.*
4. *Impulsive decision.* We feel unable to decide and the determination seems
   as accidental as the third type. But it comes from *within* and not from
   without. We find ourselves acting automatically and often impulsively.
5. *Decision based on change of perspective.* This decision often occurs suddenly
   and as a consequence of some important outer experience or inward
   change (for example, grief or fear) which results in an important change
   in perspective or a "change in heart." [Such were the decisions made by
   many of the cancer patients I described in chapter 5].[86]

315

As James suggests, then, "decision" refers to a wide array of activities that have different subjective experiences—differing degrees of effort, rationality, consciousness, impulsivity, and sense of responsibility.

Therapy, Decision, and Character Structure.   Some therapists—for example, those of the transactional analysis (T.A.) school—use "decision" in an even more radically unconscious sense. They suggest that individuals make early "archaic" decisions that shape their lives in critical ways. A typical formulation of psychopathological development by a T.A. therapist asserts: "The individual gets an Injunction from his parent, which is implanted by strokes (i.e. reinforcements), makes a Decision around that Injunction, and then develops a script to support the Injunction."[87] Thus, according to Eric Berne, the individual "decides" on a "Life script"—an unconscious blueprint for one's life course which encompasses personality variables and repetitive interpersonal interactions. Berne's "Life script" is not very different from Adler's "guiding fiction" or Horney's idealized image system. Though it is more interpersonally based, it is loosely equivalent to the Freudian concept of character structure.

According to the T.A. approach, the child makes a decision that determines his or her character structure and is thus responsible for it. Yet problems arise when "decision" is used only in a conscious willful sense. The definition of "decision" offered by T.A. reflects the confusion about the term: "The decision is the point in time when the youngster, applying all the adaptive resources of his ego, modifies his expectations and tries to align them with the realities of the home situation."[88] Note that the definition begins "The decision is the point in time . . ." as though there were a specific moment of decision, as though between the original state and the changed state there must have been some conscious decision.

The therapist who takes seriously the notion that the child made some concrete momentous archaic decision, runs the danger of developing a concrete, simplistic approach to therapeutic change. Indeed, that is precisely what has happened: T.A. texts, for example, suggest that the therapist's task is to help the patient go back to the "original decision," the "first act experience,"[89] (not unlike the original trauma of early Freudian theory), relive it, and make a "redecision." The problem with this formulation is that the patient may be asked to make a current, rational decision in order to neutralize an early decision of an entirely different type. This is what Farber warned against when he said it is important that one not try to force the will of the second (conscious) realm to do the work of the will of the first (unconscious) realm.

What is lost in this radical view of decision making is the subtlety of the developmental process. An individual's character structure is not the result of a single momentous decision that can be traced and erased, but instead is constituted by a lifetime of innumerable choices made and alternatives relinquished. Although the child has, of course, no awareness of adult characterological options, nonetheless the child always has a modicum of ability to affirm or reject what is presented to him or to her, to submit or rebel, to identify positively or, as Erik Erikson has taught us, to form a negative identification with certain role models.[90] As I discussed in the last chapter, it is necessary to the treatment process that the patient accept responsibility for what he or she is—as well as for what he or she will become. Only then can the individual experience the power (and the hope) necessary for the process of change. But psychotherapeutic change will not consist of a single momentous willful decision; instead, it will be a gradual process of multiple decisions, each paving the way for the next.

WHY ARE DECISIONS DIFFICULT?

"Shall we go? Let's go. No one moves." What happens between the resolve and the committed decision to act? Why do so many patients find it so extraordinarily difficult to decide? Indeed, as I think of my current patients, almost every one is wrestling with some decision. Some patients are concerned with a specific life decision: what to do about an important relationship, whether to stay married or to separate, whether to return to school, whether to attempt to have a child. Other patients say they know what they have to do—say, stop drinking or smoking, lose weight, try to meet people, or try to establish an intimate relationship—but cannot decide—that is, commit themselves—to do it. Still others say they know what is wrong—for example, they are too arrogant, too workaholic, or too uncaring—but do not know how to decide to change and, consequently, do not commit themselves to work in therapy.

There is something highly painful about these unmade decisions. As I review my patients and attempt to analyze the meaning (and the threat) that decision has for them, I am struck first of all by the diversity of response. Decisions are difficult for many reasons: some obvious, some unconscious, and some, as we shall see, that reach down to the deepest roots of being.

Alternatives Exclude. The protagonist of John Gardner's novel *Grendel* made a pilgrimage to a old priest to learn about life's mysteries. The wise man said, "The ultimate evil is that Time is perpetual perishing and being actual involves elimination." He summed up his meditations on life in two simple but terrible propositions, four devastating words: "Things fade: alternatives exclude."[91] I regard that priest's message as deeply inspired. "Things fade" is the underlying theme of the first section of this book, and "alternatives exclude" is one of the fundamental reasons that decisions are difficult.

For every yes there must be a no. To decide one thing always means to relinquish something else. As one therapist commented to an indecisive patient, "Decisions are very expensive, they cost you everything else."[92] Renunciation invariably accompanies decision. One must relinquish options, often options that will never come again. Decisions are painful because they signify the limitation of possibilities; and the more one's possibilities are limited, the closer one is brought to death. Indeed, Heidegger defined death as "the impossibility of farther possibility."[93] The reality of limitation is a threat to one of our chief modes of coping with existential anxiety: the delusion of specialness—that, though others may be subject to limitations, one is exempt, special, and beyond natural law.

One may, of course, avoid awareness of renunciation by avoiding awareness of one's decisions. Wheelis, in a metaphor where decision is a crossroads on a journey and renunciation is the road not taken, states the issue beautifully:

> Some persons can proceed untroubled by proceeding blindly, believing they have traveled the main highway and that all intersections have been with byways. But to proceed with awareness and imagination is to be affected by the memory of crossroads which one will never encounter again. Some persons sit at the crossroads, taking neither path because they cannot take both, cherishing the illusion that if they sit there long enough the two ways will resolve themselves into one and hence both be possible. A large part of maturity and courage is the ability to make such renunciations, and a large part of wisdom is the ability to find ways which will enable one to renounce as little as possible.[94]

Sitting "at the crossroads, taking neither path because they cannot take both" is a wonderfully apt image of one who is unable to relinquish possibility. Ancient philosophical metaphors depict the same dilemma: Aristotle's example of the hungry dog unable to choose between two equally attractive portions of food, or the celebrated problem of Buridan's ass, a poor beast starving between two equally sweet smelling bundles of hay.[95] In each instance the creature would have died if it had refused to relinquish options; the salvation of each lay in trusting desire and grasping what lay within reach.

The metaphor has clinical relevance to those patients who suffer paralysis of willing not only because they cannot say yes but because they cannot say no. At an unconscious level they refuse to accept the existential implications of renunciation.

Decisions as a Boundary Experience. To be fully aware of one's existential situation means that one becomes aware of self-creation. To be aware of the fact that one constitutes oneself, that there are no absolute external referents, that one assigns an arbitrary meaning to the world, means to become aware of one's fundamental groundlessness.

Decision plunges one, if one permits it, into such awareness. Decision, especially an irreversible decision, is a boundary situation in the same way that awareness of "my death" is a boundary situation. Both act as a catalyst to shift one from the everyday attitude to the "ontological" attitude—that is, to a mode of being in which one is mindful of being. Although, as we learn from Heidegger, such a catalyst and such a shift are ultimately for the good and prerequisites for authentic existence, they also call forth anxiety. If one is not prepared, one develops modes of repressing decision just as one represses death.

A major decision not only exposes one to the anxiety of groundlessness but also threatens one's defenses against death anxiety. By facing one with the limitation of possibilities, decision challenges one's myth of personal specialness. And decision, insofar as it forces one to accept personal responsibility and existential isolation, threatens one's belief in the existence of an ultimate rescuer.

A fundamental decision also confronts each of us with existential isolation. A decision is a lonely act, and it is *our* own act; no one can decide for us. Many people, therefore, are highly distressed by decision and, as I shall discuss shortly, attempt to avoid it by coercing or persuading others to make the decision for them.

Decision and Guilt. Some individuals find decisions difficult because of guilt which, as Rank emphasized, is entirely capable of paralyzing the willing process. Will is born in a caul of guilt; it arises, said Rank, first as counter will. The child's impulses are opposed by the adult world, and the child's will first arises to oppose that opposition. If the child is unfortunate enough to have parents who attempt to squelch all impulsive expression, then the child's will becomes heavily laden with guilt and experiences all decisions as evil and forbidden. Such an individual cannot decide because one feels one does not have the *right* to decide.

Masochistic characters who are encased in a symbiotic relationship with a parent have particular trouble with guilt and decision. Ester Menaker suggests that each of these patients has a parent who in effect

319

said, "You dare not be yourself, you have not the ability to be yourself; you need my presence to exist."[96] During development such individuals experience any free expression of choice as forbidden since it represents a violation to the parental mandate. In adulthood major decisions elicit dysphoria stemming both from the fear of separateness and from the guilt at transgressing against the dominant other.

Existential guilt goes beyond the traditional guilt whereby the individual regrets a real or fantasized transgression against another. In chapter 6 I defined existential guilt as arising from one's transgressions against oneself; it emanates from regret, from an awareness of the unlived life, of the untapped possibilities within one. Existential guilt, too, may be a powerful decision-blocking factor, in that a major decision to change causes the individual to reflect upon wastage, upon how he has sacrificed so much of his one and only life. Responsibility is a two-edged sword: if one accepts responsibility for one's life situation and makes the decision to change, the implication is that one alone is responsible for the past wreckage of one's life and *could* have changed long ago.

Bonnie, a forty-eight-year-old woman, whom I discussed briefly in chapter 4, illustrates some of these issues. For many years Bonnie had suffered from Buerger's disease, a disorder resulting in the occlusion of small blood vessels in the extremities. There is well-established medical evidence that nicotine is extremely toxic in Buerger's disease: patients who smoke accelerate the course of the disease and generally must face early amputation of one or more limbs. Bonnie had always smoked and could not—would not—stop. Various hypnotic and behavioral approaches had all failed, and she seemed unable—unwilling—to make the decision to stop smoking. She felt that in many ways her life had been ruined by her smoking habit. She had been married to a rather ruthless, authoritarian man who, ten years previously, had left her because of her poor physical health. He was an avid outdoorsman and decided that he would be far better off with a mate with whom he could share outdoor activities. That Bonnie had brought about her own disability through her "filthy habit" (as he put it) and her weakness of will sharply compounded the problem. Eventually he gave Bonnie an ultimatum: "Choose smoking or marriage." When she continued to smoke, he left her.

When Bonnie and I considered the reasons that made it difficult for her to decide to stop smoking, one of the important themes that arose was her realization that, if she stopped smoking now, then that would mean that *she could have stopped smoking before.* The implications of that insight were far-reaching indeed. Bonnie always considered herself as a victim: a victim of Buerger's disease, of her habit, of a cruel, insensitive husband. But if, in fact, her fate had always been under her control, then she would have to face the fact that she must bear the entire responsibility for her disease, for the failure of her marriage, and for the wreckage (as she put it) of her adult life. To decide to change would entail accepting existential guilt—the guilt for the atrocity she had committed against herself. In therapy Bonnie had to be helped to understand the implication of deciding something for herself—that is, of not basing her decision upon the wishes of anyone else, her husband, her parents, or her therapist. She had to accept the guilt (and the ensuing depression) for having thwarted her own growth. She had to accept the crushing responsibility for her actions in the past by grasping her responsibility for the future. The best way—perhaps the only way—of dealing with guilt—guilt from violation either of another or of oneself—is through atonement. One cannot will backward. One can atone for the past only by altering the future.

METHODS OF AVOIDING DECISION: CLINICAL MANIFESTATIONS

Since decisions are extraordinarily difficult and painful for many individuals, it is not unexpected that one should develop methods of decision avoidance. The most obvious method of avoiding a decision is procrastination, and every therapist sees patients who pace tormentedly before the door of decision. But there are many, more subtle methods of dealing with the intrinsic pain of decision—methods that permit one to decide while concealing from oneself that one is deciding. After all, it is the *process*, not the content, of decision that is painful; and if one can decide without knowing one is doing so, then *tant mieux*. I answered the question Why are decisions difficult? by stressing the renunciation, the anxiety, and the guilt that accompany decision. To soften the awareness and pain of decision, one must erect defenses against these threats: one can avoid the sense of renunciation by distorting the alternatives and/or can avoid existential anxiety and guilt by arranging for someone or some thing else to make the decision.

AVOIDANCE OF RENUNCIATION

Trading down. If decision is difficult because one must relinquish one possibility at the same time as one chooses another, then the decision becomes happier if one arranges the situation so that one renounces less. For example, my patient Alice sought therapy because she could not decide to divorce her husband. He had made the decision to leave her, had moved out one year ago, but occasionally returned for sexual relations. Alice mourned him continually, and her fantasies brimmed with visions of winning him back. She schemed to find ways to meet him, and she humiliated herself by pleading with him to give their marriage another trial. Reason told her that the marriage never had or never would work and that she was far better off alone. But she continued to give him all the power in the relationship and refused to consider that she, too, had a decision to make in the matter. Her decision, as she viewed it, consisted of a choice between a comfortable, dependent relationship with her husband and a fearful isolation.

With the help of a few supportive counseling sessions Alice finally handled her dilemma by becoming involved with another man. By using him as a support, she was able to let her husband go completely. (And, in fact, soon took the ultimate step of hauling him into court for refusing to pay child support.) Alice was able to make the decision by stripping the deeper implications from it. She avoided the awareness of renunciation by altering the formula of the decision: no longer did she have to choose between a husband (who was unavailable and toward whom she had good reason to feel much enmity) and a state of loneliness; instead, she could choose between this husband and a loving boyfriend—not a difficult decision at all.

In one sense, the brief supportive therapy was helpful, since it freed Alice from the agonizing throes of indecision. On the other hand, though, she missed an opportunity for growth, by avoiding the deeper implications of her decision. For example, she might, had she been willing to plunge into these implications, have dealt with the fear of loneliness, her inability to face life in an autonomous fashion, and her ensuing proclivity to surrender herself to a dominant male. As it turned out, Alice learned little from the experience and, a few months later, was in the same situation. The relationship with the boyfriend turned sour, she could not terminate it, and she again sought therapy in the throes of a decisional crisis.

Devaluation of the Unchosen Alternative. It is freedom we fear; and common sense, clinical experience, and psychological research all indicate that the sense (and the discomfort) of freedom increases when alternatives in a decision are perceived to be nearly equivalent. Comfortable decision-making strategy demands therefore that the chosen alternatives be regarded as attractive, and the unchosen alternative as unattractive. One proceeds by magnifying, at an unconscious level, slight differences between two fairly equal options so that the decision between them is both obvious and painless. Thus, decisions may be made effortlessly, and the painful confrontation with freedom entirely avoided.

For example, a schizoid affect-stifled patient had for many years "decided" not to make an effort to change. Change, for reasons not germane to this discussion, was a terrifying prospect for him, and consequently he refused to commit himself to therapy and carved out a muted, isolated life for himself. Viewed objectively, his choice lay between a pervasive intra- and interpersonal isolation and a more spontaneous and expressive affective life. To continue in the decision not to change, the patient distorted the options available to him and devalued the unchosen alternative and overvalued the chosen one. He viewed affect suppression as "dignity" or "decorum" and spontaneity as an "animalistic loss of control" where he would run the risk of being overcome by rage and tears. Another patient of mine decided to stay in a highly unsatisfying marriage because the alternative (as she distorted and devalued it) was to join the singles horde—the "vast, pathetic army of freaks, cast-offs, and misfits."

Social psychological research confirms that the devaluation of the unchosen alternative is a common psychological phenomenon.[97] After a subject makes a decision in which the chosen alternative does not have a clear edge over the unchosen one, he or she experiences postdecisional regret. To the degree that the alternative is attractive, the individual has an uncomfortable "What have I done?" feeling which is in the literature often referred to as "cognitive dissonance": that is, an individual's choice appears inconsistent—"dissonant"—with his or her values. Cognitive dissonance theory holds that the tension of dissonance is highly unpleasant, and that the individual engages (though not at a conscious level) in some activity to reduce that tension.[98] Laboratory research indicates a number of ways that one uses to decrease the pain of renunciation. A common method that has obvious clinical relevance is information distortion: one is open to information that either upgrades the chosen alternative or downgrades the nonchosen alternative; and, conversely, one is closed to information that increases the attractiveness of the nonchosen alternative or decreases the attractiveness of the chosen one.[99]

Delegating the Decision to Someone. Decision, as I have discussed, is also painful because it, if deeply considered, confronts each of us not only with freedom but with fundamental isolation—with the fact that each of us alone is responsible for our individual situations in life. One can have one's decision and avoid the pain of isolation if one can locate and persuade another to make that decision for one. Erich Fromm has repeatedly emphasized that human beings have always had a highly ambivalent attitude toward freedom. Though they fight fiercely for freedom, they leap at the opportunity to surrender it to a totalitarian regime that promises to remove the burden of freedom and decision from them. The charismatic leader—one who makes every decision crisply and confidently—has no difficulty recruiting subjects.

In therapy the patient strives mightily to coax or persuade the therapist to make decisions for him or her; and one of the therapist's chief tasks is to resist being manipulated into taking care of, or taking over, the patient. To manipulate the therapist, a patient may exaggerate helplessness or withhold evidence of strengths from him or her. Many patients caught in a decisional crisis scan the therapist's every syllable, gesture, or shift of posture as though each were the expression of an oracle; they rummage about in their post-session recollections of the therapist's words in search of clues to the latter's view of the proper decision. Regardless of their level of sophistication, patients secretly yearn for the therapist who will provide structure and guidance. The anger and the frustration that at some level occurs in every course of therapy stems from the patient's dawning recognition that the therapist will not relieve him or her of the burden of decision.

There are innumerable strategies by which one may find another to make the decision for one. Two acquaintances of mine recently divorced in such a manner that each believed the other had made the decision. The wife did not request a divorce but did inform her husband that she was in love with another man. The husband, predictably, automatically concluded in accordance with certain standards of his that they must divorce, and so they did. Husband and wife each avoided decisional pain (and post-decisional regret) by concluding that the other had made the decision. The wife had only stated her affection for another man and had not asked for a divorce. The husband felt that his wife had, by her declaration, *de facto* made the decision.

One may avoid a decision by procrastinating until it is made for one by an outside agent or circumstance. Though such an individual may not apprehend that he or she is making a decision—for example, to fail a course—in fact, procrastination obscures the decision to fail by placing it in the hands of the instructor. Similarly, it might appear that an employer had made a decision to discharge an employee when in fact it was the employee who, by performing inadequately, covertly made the decision to leave the job. Another may not be able to decide to terminate a relationship and by acting cold, indifferent, or withdrawn forces the other into making the decision.

324

In a vignette at the beginning of this section a woman expressed the wish to catch her husband in bed with another woman and thus be able to leave him. Obviously she wished to leave her husband but could not transform the wish into action: the pain of decision (or the anticipation of post-decisional regret) was too great. Therefore she hoped that he, by breaking some definite rule of the relationship, would make the decision for her. She was, however, by no means limited to sheer waiting and hoping. She discovered many other ways of hastening the decision while still concealing from herself that it was she who was making it: for example she subtly distanced herself from him, and withheld sex while covertly implying that he could find it elsewhere.

Another patient, George, presented a similar problem. He would not take responsibility for an overt decision. He was particularly conflicted about a relationship to a woman; he enjoyed her sexually yet disliked her in many other ways. He refused to make a decision about the relationship—either to say no and terminate it or to say yes and commit himself to work on it. Consequently he was forced to "find" a decision without "making" one. Unconsciously he attempted to force her to make the decision. He stayed out of his apartment as much as possible so she could not phone him, or he "accidentally" neglected to clean his car so that another woman's objects (cigarette butts, hairpins, etc.) were clearly in evidence. If, during this time, however, anyone had suggested to him that he was deciding to end the relationship, George would have vigorously denied it.

His woman friend would not make the decision to end the relationship; instead, she put pressure on him to move in with her. At that point George searched for other individuals to make the decision for him. He canvassed all his friends for advice and repeatedly attempted to solicit his therapist's guidance in the matter. When the therapist finally succeeded in helping him sit still long enough to examine his behavior, George made an interesting comment: "If someone else makes the decision, then I will not be committed to making the decision work." [A substantial body of social psychological research indicates that an individual who participates in a decision—that is, the democratic process—takes responsibility for making that decision work, in contrast to the relatively apathetic or resisting posture one takes toward the decision another has forced upon one.]

George knew that it was in his best interests to end the relationship. (It was better for his woman friend, too, that he end it, although for a long time he clung to the rationalization that he did not want to hurt

325

her—as though long, agonizing, covert rejection were painless. Yet he could not bring himself to make the decision, and he slowly twisted in the wind because he could not find another to make his decision for him.

Many patients "act out" in therapy in order to persuade the therapist to make their decisions for them. Another patient, Ted, who was himself a psychotherapist, had for months struggled with strong dependency yearnings. Ted's therapist had in one session reflected on the difficulty of being one's own father and mother. (This concept, stated in one form or another, must emerge in every existential therapeutic investigation of freedom.) At the next session Ted was extraordinarily distressed and announced that during the week he had "lost control" and became sexually involved with one of his patients, and that he needed someone to "blow the whistle" on him. This situation seemed powerfully designed to force the therapist to take over decisions for Ted. After all, how could a responsible therapist sit passively and allow a patient to injure another patient and, in the process, to ruin his own professional career?

The therapist, however, chose to examine all aspects of the "acting out," and it was soon apparent that Ted was not wholly out of control but had made several decisions that indicated he had assumed some degree of responsibility. Rather than becoming involved with a psychotic or borderline patient, he had "chosen" a mature, well-integrated patient ready to terminate after three years of therapy. Furthermore, though he had violated the professional ethical code, he had, in fact, stopped far short of intercourse and had immediately brought the situation up for scrutiny in his personal therapy. Ted's interest's were best served in the long run by the therapist's refusal to be manipulated into making Ted's decision ("whistle blowing") and by the therapist's persistence in demonstrating to Ted that, though it was frightening to make his own decisions, he was entirely capable of doing so.

Delegating the Decision to Some Thing. An ancient mode of decision making was to consult fate. Whether fate's answer was to be found in sheep entrails, tea leaves, the *I Ching*, meteorological changes, or any of a vast array of portents was of no matter. What was important was that, by transferring decision to an outside agency, the individual was spared the existential pain inherent in decision.

A modern version of total reliance on chance is to be found in Luke Rhinehart's novel *The Dice Man*, in which the protagonist makes one fundamental decision: to leave all other decisions up to chance—the toss of the dice.[100] Thereafter he makes every major life decision by drawing up a list of options and allowing the dice to decide. True, some decisions have to be made in respect to which options are placed on the list, but these are minor and relatively uncommitting, since each option has so many odds against it. The dice man's rationale for his behavior is that many aspects of his personality are permanently squelched by the "majority rule" of his other traits. By leaving the decision to the dice, he is permitting each part some opportunity to exist. Although the dice man is presented as an existential hero—an individual who embraces total freedom (that is, randomness) and contingency, he may be also viewed as the opposite—one who has surrendered freedom and responsibility. Indeed, whenever the dice man is called upon to answer for some particularly outrageous act, he has one response, "The dice told me to do it."

"Rules" are another handy decision-making agency, and individuals have always sought the comfort of a comprehensive set of rules to relieve them from the pain of decision. The Orthodox Jews who follow the 513 Judaic laws are spared many decisions, since so much of their behavior is prescribed for them, ranging from the daily rituals accompanying each of the day's events to the proper course of action when faced with major life crises. The rules of traditional societies often stifle initiation and limit ambition and choice, but they do offer blessed relief from such decisions as, Whom should I marry? Should I divorce? What career shall I pursue? How shall I spend my free time? Whom shall I befriend?—and so forth.

Bugental, in describing the treatment of a patient, an undergraduate dean of students, beautifully illustrates how "rules" allow one to avoid decision:

> Dean Stoddert smiled understandingly but with a trace of sadness at the girl as she said, "I certainly understand now why you did as you did, but you see I really have no choice in the matter. If I made an exception for you now, then I'd have to make an exception for everyone else who had good reasons for breaking the rules. Pretty soon the rules would be meaningless, wouldn't they? So, although I really am sorry about it, the situation is clear, and it calls for you to be restricted to campus for the next month."
>
> The student looked appreciatively at the Dean through her tears. "It helps to know that you understand, but somehow it just doesn't seem fair under the circumstances. This will mean I'll lose my job, and I don't know whether Dad will be able to keep me in school or not." The Dean was sympathetic but made it evident that she had no choice.
>
> When the student was gone, Dean Stoddert sat back in her chair for a minute, herself swept by contradictory feelings. On the one hand, she felt a certain satisfaction that she had finally trained her feelings and her

judgment to the point where she could stand firm when the regulations required it. For so many years she had found herself carried away by her sympathies so that she almost never was able to combine understanding with consistent application of the rules. . . .

Ruefully, Margaret Stoddert reflected that it had been a real struggle to be able to handle a situation as she had just handled this one. Yet, and here the irony came in, somehow she wasn't content. Somehow, she felt vaguely uneasy even as she reassured herself that she had done the job well. Later in the day, on the couch in my office, she found herself ruminating: "I don't know what it is that keeps bothering me about that interview, but I feel restless whenever I think about it. And I keep thinking about it. It's like there's something I've overlooked, but I can't think what it might be. . . ."[101]

Margaret, as Bugental points out, had, instead of administering the rules, become administered *by* the rules. She concluded that "rules have meanings in themselves," that rules and consistency transcend consideration of human understanding and human needs. Margaret sensed that there was danger if choice was exercised. Her rationale of the danger was that "if I make an exception for you now, then I'd have to make an exception for everyone else who has good reasons for breaking the rules."

But why should this be so? Why should consistency be elevated above all else? No, there were other more urgent reasons for Margaret's following the rules, though these reasons are not explicit in the clinical report: it is apparent that by avoiding decision Margaret avoided the role of "decision maker." She embraced and cherished the comforting illusion that there is some absolute external referent, that there is a prescribed right and wrong. And, in so believing, Margaret avoided the existential isolation inherent in her "real" situation—that is, that she herself has fashioned her world and imbued it with structure and meaning.

DECISION: CLINICAL STRATEGY AND TECHNIQUES

Decision plays a central role in every successful course of therapy. Even though a therapist may not explicitly focus on decision or even acknowledge it, even though a therapist may believe that change is brought about by exhortation or interpretation, or by virtue of the therapeutic relationship, nonetheless it is a decision that slips the machinery of change into gear. No change is possible without effort, and decision is the trigger of effort.

Here I shall consider some therapeutic approaches to decision—both conscious and unconscious decision. Some patients come to therapy in the throes of some active decision making; some have periodic decision crises during the course of therapy; others have long-term problems in being unable to make decisions. Even though the therapist does not formulate the patient's dynamics in terms of problems in decision making, still the therapist's goal is, as I mentioned in the vignette at the beginning of Part II, "to bring the patient to the point where he or she can make a free choice."

Therapeutic Approaches to Decision: Conscious Levels.   Beatrice, a patient in a therapy group, called me for an emergency session because of an acute decisional crisis. Three months previously she had invited her Italian boyfriend to live with her. At that time it appeared to be a short-term arrangement, since he was slated to return to his own country in a month. However, his departure date had been postponed, and their relationship had rapidly deteriorated. He was drinking heavily, was verbally abusive to her, and had borrowed large sums of money, her car, and her apartment. Beatrice was overwhelmed with anxiety and in great despair about her inability to act. Finally, after weeks of struggling with the decision, she had asked him that morning to leave, but he refused to go, stating he had no money and no place to stay. Furthermore, since she had no lease on the apartment, he now had as much right to it as she. She considered calling the police but doubted that they could be effective because of the lack of a lease. Besides, she dreaded angering her boyfriend because he had a bad temper and was entirely capable of engaging in a prolonged vendetta against her.

What should she do? He would leave in another four or five weeks; she had hoped to stick it out till then, but the situation had so deteriorated that she no longer felt she could do so. If she asked him to leave, he might harm her physically or destroy her furniture or car. Furthermore, it was vitally important to her that she end the relationship in a way that would result in his continuing to care for her. What should she do?

Beatrice felt paralyzed, with apparently no possible course of effective action. During the emergency consulation she appeared so distraught that I entertained the idea of hospitalizing her. I attempted directly to confront the decision panic and paralysis by asking repeatedly, "What are your alternatives?" Beatrice felt that there were none; but when I persisted, she listed a number of options. She could confront him much more openly, honestly, and forcibly than she had before. She could let him know precisely how devastating an experience this had been for her, and how determined she was not to spend another day with him in the apartment. She could insist that he leave, and then she could seek legal advice and police protection. She could enlist the help of some of her friends to help her confront him. She could move out of the apartment (she had neither lease nor particular attachment committing her to it). If she feared he would destroy her furniture, then she could call a moving company and have her furniture put into storage. (Expensive? Yes, but not as costly as the large sums she was giving him.) She could easily stay with her sister, and so on, and so on. By the end of this option-listing exercise, Beatrice no longer felt trapped, her sense of paralysis had diminished, and she was able to plan a course of action.

The follow-up of this session leads into areas that are not entirely germane to this discussion but that nonetheless illuminate the clinical problems surrounding decision making sufficiently to warrant a digression. Beatrice felt better after the session. She reviewed all her options and chose to confront her tormentor. She braced herself and timorously told him that she could bear the situation no longer, and asked him to leave. Although she had reported to me that she had spoken so to him previously, the message had apparently not gotten through since his response to this statement was immediate acquiescence. He packed up his belongings, found another place to stay, and agreed to leave the next day!

That evening she agreed to have a last dinner with him, and in the course of conversation he remarked soulfully that it was a pity that two rational individuals who liked one another could not find some way to live together as good friends. And what did Beatrice reply? "I'd like that, too," she said. And so they unpacked his bags, and he settled in again.

In the therapy group four days later, Beatrice began the meeting with a brief report of the incident. She described a brief argument, a crisis session with me, a resolve to ask her boyfriend to leave, a rapprochement, and an ensuing couple of days of a dramatically improved relationship. She did not mention extraordinary distress, the abuse she had suffered, the drinking, the financial exploitation, the threats. I was stunned by her account; and after Beatrice had finished, I told the group that I, too, had had an experience in the past week which I wished to share with them. "A young woman in extraordinary anguish called me," I began, and in that vein proceeded to describe my version of our session. Indeed, the accounts were so different that it was several minutes before the group realized that Beatrice and I had been describing the same incident!

Why did Beatrice distort the information she relayed to the group?

Unconsciously she must have realized that, if she provided the group—and, for that matter, herself—with an accurate portrayal of the relationship, the members would conclude that she should end the relationship. (And, indeed, every one of her friends had responded in that fashion. Among the more dispassionate responses were, "Kick the son of a bitch out!" "Are you crazy?" "Get rid of the jerk!" "Why do you put up with that shit?") At a deep level, Beatrice appreciated that she had made an irrational decision—one clearly not in her best interests. But she *had* decided, and she wished to avoid the anxiety of cognitive dissonance. As she valued the opinions of the group members, it was clearly in the interest of her personal comfort that she withhold the facts that would allow them to conclude that she had decided incorrectly.

In my emergency session with her I had alleviated Beatrice's panic by helping her consider the available options. That technique is generally effective in the face of decision panic; but it is important for the therapist to keep in mind that it is the *patient—not the therapist*—who must generate and choose among those options. In helping patients to communicate effectively, one of the first principles psychotherapists teach is that one "owns" one's feelings. *It is equally important that one owns one's decisions.* A decision made by another is no decision at all: one is not likely to commit oneself to it; and even if one does, no change in the process of decision making has been effected—one will not generalize to the next decision. The therapist must resist the patient's entreaties to make a decision. Neophyte therapists often succumb and fall into the trap of deciding for patients. Such a therapist later feels not only disappointed but curiously betrayed or angry when a patient fails to commit himself or herself to that decision. If the therapist takes over the patient's decision-making function, then the entire focus of therapy may be displaced from the crucial area of responsibility and decision to the area of obedience or defiance of authority.

It is important to remember that deciding does not end either with a decision or with a failure to make one. The individual must re-decide over and over. Failing to carry out a decision does not "blow it" for ever and need not carry implications for the next decision; and much can be learned from such failure. There are times also when a patient is not ready or able to make a decision: the alternatives are too equal; and the patient's anxiety and anticipation of regret are too high, and his or her awareness of the "meaning" of a decision (which I shall discuss shortly) is too limited. The therapist may afford the patient much relief by supporting the latter's decision not to decide at such a time.

Many patients' decision-making abilities are paralyzed by "what ifs." What if I quit this job and can't find another one? What if I leave my children alone, and they get hurt? What if I consult another doctor, and my pediatrician finds out about it? A logical, systematic analysis of the possibilities is sometimes useful. The therapist may, for example, ask the patient to consider the whole scenario of each "what if" in turn: to fantasize its happening, with possible ramifications, and then to experience and analyze his or her emergent feelings.

Though these conscious approaches have some usefulness, they have severe limitations because so much of a decision dilemma exists at a subterranean level and is impervious to a rational approach. Two thousand years ago Aristotle said, I believe, that the whole is greater than the sum of the parts, and folk wisdom has always reflected this insight, as in the Yiddish joke about the kreplach aversion. A boy's mother is trying to rid the child of his extraordinarily powerful repugnance to kreplach (a meat-filled pastry). Painstakingly she prepares the kreplach while he is in the kitchen. Patiently she presents and discusses each of the ingredients. "See, you like flour, and eggs, and meat," and so on. He agrees readily. "Well, then, that settles it, because that's all there is in kreplach." But at the word "kreplach" the child once again promptly retches.

Therapeutic Approaches to Decision: Unconscious Levels. How can the therapist approach the unconscious aspects of decision making—what Farber refers to as the "first realm of will." The answer: "Indirectly." Much as they might wish to, therapists cannot create will or commitment, cannot flick the decision switch or inspirit a patient with resoluteness. But they can influence the factors that influence willing. No one has a congenital absence of will. Part of one's constitutional heritage, as Robert White[102] and Karen Horney[103] have ably argued, is a drive toward effectance, toward mastering one's environment, toward becoming what one is capable of becoming. Will is blocked by obstacles in the path of the child's development; later these obstacles are internalized, and the individual is unable to act even though no objective factors are blocking him or her. The therapist's task is to help remove those obstacles. Once that is done, the individual will naturally develop—just, as Horney put it, as an acorn develops into an oak.[104] *Thus, the therapist's task is not to create will but to disencumber it.*

I shall describe several approaches to this task. The therapist must first help the patient become aware of the inevitability and the omnipresence of decision. The therapist helps the patient "frame" or gain perspective upon a particular decision, and then assists in laying bare the deeper implications (the "meaning") of that decision. Finally, through the leverage of insight the therapist attempts to awaken the dormant will.

The inevitability and the omnipresence of decision. One cannot not decide. Much as each of us would like it otherwise, decisions are unavoidable. If it is true that one constitutes oneself, then it follows that decisions are the atoms of the being that one creates. Acceptance of one's decisions is a step first taken in therapy during the work of assumption of responsibility. In later stages the therapeutic work consists of sharpening and deepening that insight. The patient is helped not only to assume responsibility but to discover, one by one, each of his or her avoidance tactics.

If one fully accepts the ubiquity of one's decisions, then one confronts one's existential situation in authentic fashion. Procrastination is a decision—as are failure, and drinking, and being seduced, exploited, or trapped. One decides even to stay alive. Nietszche said that only after one has fully considered suicide does one take one's life seriously. Many cancer patients with whom I have worked have had adrenalectomies (part of the treatment program of metastatic breast carcinoma) and must take cortisone replacement therapy every day. Many take their daily tablets as automatically as they brush their teeth, but others are very much aware of making a decision every day to remain alive. My impression is that awareness of this decision enriches life and encourages one to commit oneself to the task of living as fully as possible.

Some therapists reinforce a patient's awareness of the omnipresence of decisions by reminding him or her of the decisions that must be made about therapy. Thus, Kaiser, as we have seen, recommends a therapeutic format with "no conditions" whatsoever, and Greenwald persistently asks the patient to make decisions about the format of therapy—that is, whether he or she wants to work on dreams, how many sessions to meet, and so on.[105]

Therapists should help patients become fully aware of meta-decisions—that is, decisions about decisions—for some individuals attempt to deny the importance of decisions by persuading themselves that they have decided not to decide. Such a decision is in actuality a decision not to decide *actively*. One cannot evade decision altogether, but one may decide to decide *passively*—by, for example, letting another decide for one. I believe that the *way* one makes a decision is of the utmost importance. An active approach to decision is consonant with an active acceptance of one's own power and resources.

Many of the patients I described earlier illustrate this principle. For example, Beatrice, whose boyfriend would not leave her apartment had little question about which decision was in her best interests. When I asked her to imagine how she would feel a month hence when he finally left the country, her response was a full-bodied "blissful." The patient who prayed that she could catch her husband in bed with another woman also had little question about what she wanted. However, each woman balked at making an active decision to throw out the man in her life; and, by arranging for another to make that decision, each had made another decision to decide passively. Each, however, paid a price for the decision about how to decide. Both patients had severely impaired self-esteem, and the way by which they avoided decisions contributed to that self-contempt. If one is to love oneself, one must behave in ways that one can admire.

My patient Bill agonized for a year about ending a relationship with a woman, Jean. I had persistently taken the approach that the *way* he made the decision was extremely important, but he persistently denied that he was deciding. He said he could not decide about the relationship because his work was overwhelming, and Jean was being very helpful to him in it. I reminded him that he chose to invite her to come to his office in the evenings to help him. Jean was wonderfully supportive when he was in a crisis, he said. I suggested that not only did he have some choice about entering a crisis (for example, by needlessly missing a deadline at work and, as a result, having a humiliating confrontation with his boss), but that he freely had chosen to tell Jean about his crisis and to solicit her help.

Finally Bill made a decision to terminate the relationship, but it was a decision he concealed from himself. The decision was to decide passively: to persuade Jean to terminate the relationship. He chose a plan of subtle, gradual disengagement; he gave Jean so little affection that eventually she left him for another man. He had gone through this cycle on many previous occasions, and each time he was left feeling rejected and worthless. Bill's primary problem was that he was flooded with self-contempt; an important function of therapy was to help him understand that the ignoble way he made decisions contributed to his self-contempt.

Framing a decision. In describing the difference between the two realms of will (conscious and unconscious), Farber says, you can will "going to bed but not going to sleep."[106] The therapist may occasionally be able to influence the deeper levels of will by changing the frame of a decision, by providing the patient with a different perspective on a decision. A personal incident is illustrative.

Once many years ago I had a severe siege of insomnia. The insomnia was linked to tension and was greatly exacerbated whenever I traveled to deliver a lecture. I was particularly apprehensive about an upcoming lecture trip to Cleveland, which I considered a "bad sleeping city" because I had once spent an extraordinarily uncomfortable, sleepless night there. This apprehension, of course, initiates a vicious circle: anxiety about not sleeping begets insomnia.

I have always taken advantage of episodes of personal distress to familiarize myself with various approaches to therapy, and on this occasion I consulted a behavior therapist. In the four to five sessions I met with him, we worked with a systematic desensitization approach and with muscular relaxation tapes, neither of which was particularly helpful. However, as I was leaving his office after a session, the therapist made a casual remark that proved of enormous benefit. He said, "When you're packing your bag to go to Cleveland, don't forget to put in a revolver." "Why"? I asked him. "Well," he replied, "if you can't sleep you can always shoot yourself." That comment "clicked" deep inside; and even now, years later, I regard it as an inspired therapeutic maneuver.

How did it work? It is difficult to explain precisely, but it reframed the situation and put it into a meaningful existential perspective. This is precisely the experience that I have observed in patients who have had some massive encounter with death. In chapter 2, I described a patient with advanced cancer who reported that her confrontation with death allowed her to "trivialize the trivia in life" or to stop doing those things she did not wish to do. Such patients, as a result of an encounter with death, have been able to remove the frame surrounding their everyday life and to experience the relative unimportance of everyday decisions from the perspective of their one and only life cycle.

If all but a small segment of a large tapestry is covered from view, then the details of that small segment emerge and appropriate a new vividness—a vividness that pales when the rest of the tapestry is again uncovered. Similarly, the "shift of perspective" technique is a process of deframing and uncovering. But *how* does the therapist deframe and unveil the tapestry of existence? Some therapists make an explicit appeal to reason. For example, I have observed how Viktor Frankl, an existential therapist, attempted to treat a patient who was being smothered by a series of tormenting decisions: Frankl asked him to meditate upon his core being and then suggested that he simply draw a line around this core and become aware of the fact that these decisions involved concerns in outlying and, in the long run, petty areas of life.

Such appeals to reason, however, are generally ineffective in gener-

ating a major shift of perspective. What is often required is some immediate confrontation with a boundary situation that propels the individual into an awareness of his or her existential situation. Accordingly,
many of the techniques I have described in chapter 5 to help one to
confront one's own mortality will often influence the decision process.

The meaning of decision.   Every decision has a visible conscious component and a massive, submerged unconscious component. A decision
has its own dynamics and is a choice among several factors, some of
which are beyond awareness. To help a patient caught in the throes of
a particularly tormenting decision, the therapist must inquire about its
many subterranean, unconscious meanings. A decision with which
Emma, a sixty-six-year-old widow, struggled is illustrative.

Emma asked to be seen because of her anguish about whether to decide to sell her summer home, a luxurious estate about one hundred
and fifty miles away from her permanent residence. The house required frequent visits, constant attention to gardening, maintenance,
police protection, and servants, as well as a substantial expense for up-
keep. It seemed an unnecessary burden to a frail old woman in poor
health. There were, of course, financial factors to consider. Was the
market at its peak, or would the estate continue to increase in value?
Could she invest the money more profitably elsewhere? Emma ruminated continuously about these issues. But though they were important
and complex, they seemed insufficient to account for her profound distress. Accordingly, I proceeded to explore the deeper meaning of her
decision.

Her husband had died a year ago, and she mourned him yet. They
had spent many a good summer together at the house, and every room
was rich still with his presence. Emma had changed the house very little: every nook and corner contained her husband's personal effects;
drawers and closets brimmed with his clothes. She clung to the house
just as she clung to his memory. Thus, a decision to sell the house required a deeper decision for Emma—a decision to come to terms with
her loss and with the fact that her husband would never return.

The house was so often visited by large numbers of friends that she
referred to it as her "hotel." Though she hated the long three-hour
drive and resented the expenses of entertaining, she also was extremely lonely and felt grateful for the companionship. Emma had always
felt that she had few internal provisions to offer friends, and since her
husband's death she had felt particularly depleted and superfluous.
"Who would," she thought, "visit me to see *me*?" The house was her
drawing card. Thus, a decison to sell the house meant testing the loyal-
ty of her friends and risking loneliness and isolation.

Her father had designed and built the house, and the land on which it stood had been in her family for generations. The great tragedy of Emma's life had been that she had no children. She had always envisaged the estate passing on through time to her children and to her children's children. But she was the last leaf; the line ended with her. A decision to sell the house thus was a decision to acknowledge the failure of one of her major symbolic immortality projects.

Emma's decision, then, was no ordinary one. When the *meaning* of her decision was explored, it became clear that the implications were indeed staggering: she was deciding whether to punctuate the loss of her husband, to confront isolation and possible loneliness, and to accept her own finiteness. If I had been content to help her decide on the basis of convenience, poor health, or financial factors, I would have missed both the whole point of Emma's turmoil and the opportunity to help her in a fundamental way. I used the house-selling decision as a springboard to these deeper issues and helped Emma mourn both her husband, herself, and her unborn children. Once the deeper meanings of a decision are worked through, the decision itself generally glides easily into place; and after a dozen sessions Emma effortlessly made the decision to sell the house.

Many therapists today inquire about the "meaning" of a decision when they explore the "payoff" of a decision. Greenwald, who bases an entire approach ("decision therapy") to psychotherapy around decision making, emphasizes the importance of investigating payoffs.[107] In every decision there are payoffs—some conscious, some unconscious. If the patient is unable to stick with a decision, the therapist must assume that the patient has made another decision, which has its own corpus of payoffs. If the patient wishes to change but cannot decide to change, the therapist may focus, not on the refusal to decide, but on the decision that *was* in fact made—the patient's decision to stay the way he or she is. Staying sick is a decison and invariably has tangible or symbolic payoffs—for example, the patient may obtain a pension, the solicitude of friends, or the therapist's continued ministrations.

A decison will not stick unless one "owns" it and recognizes and discards the payoffs of opposing decisions. Thus, of a patient who expresses the wish to kick a narcotic habit, Greenwald asks, "Why?" and explores with him or her all the payoffs of drug taking—such as anxiety relief, euphoria, or absolution from responsibility.[108] One is more likely to "own" a decision if one discovers the limits to each of the opposing payoffs. Two patients in a therapy group that I conducted wanted to have a sexual relationship but decided not to because of my "rules." I pointed out that I had made no rules and then asked the patients about the "payoffs" of their decision. When they had fully discussed their awareness both that the group meant a great deal to them, and that a sexual relationship would sabotage the group, the decision became *their* decision, and much more firmly rooted than if I, the therapist, had made it for them.

"Payoff" is a new term but an old concept. Whether we speak of exploring "meaning" or "payoff" or "secondary gratification," we are referring to the fact that every decision that one makes has benefits for that individual. If the decision seems to be self-destructive, we will invariably find that it makes sense in the patient's experiential world, and that in some highly personalized or symbolic mode, it is self-preservative. However, there will be many decisions whose full meaning the therapist will find difficult to comprehend, because of their deep roots in the unconscious.

INSIGHT AND DECISION

The precise relationship between insight and the decision to change has always remained elusive. Although psychoanalytic texts generally equate insight and change, they employ a circular type of logic that guarantees the truth of the proposition that the reason the patient does not change is that he or she has not acquired enough insight. The issue is made even more problematic by the lack of a precise definition of "insight." In its broadest clinical sense, "insight" refers to self-discovery—a "sighting inwards." But clinicians differ widely in their conception of the *type* of self-discovery that instigates change. Is it insight into the way one behaves with other individuals? or insight into the current motivation behind one's behavior? or insight into childhood sources, often erroneously referred to as the genetic "causes," of behavior? Freud always held that mutative insight was insight into the early sources of behavior, and believed that successful therapy hinged on the excavation of the earliest layers of life's memories. Other therapists believe that effective insight is the discovery of currently active dynamics. For example, Emma, the widow faced with the decision to sell her summer home, improved by discovering the currently active dynamics without considering the genetic issue, or "How did you get to be that way?"

Is insight always necessary? Most assuredly not. Every clinician has worked with patients who have undergone substantial change in the absence of insight. Earlier I discussed those who changed as a result of some radical shift in perspective—a shift that often one can explain only with a pallid "I learned to count my blessings," or "I decided to live my life rather than postpone it"—comments that hardly qualify as insight. Individuals go through therapy in a variety of ways: some profit from insight; some from other mechanisms of change; some may even obtain insight as a *result* of change, rather than the other way around. May states, "I cannot perceive something until I can conceive it."[109] One is often unable to perceive truths about oneself only after taking some stand toward change. Once having made a decision, once having put oneself on record to oneself, then one has constituted one's world differently and is able to seize truths that one had previously hidden from oneself.

Though there is considerable discussion and controversy about the *type* of insight most likely to produce change, the literature is relatively silent about *how* insight effects change. Many of the traditional explanations—for example, making the unconscious conscious, undermining resistance, the working through of the past, the reintegration of dissociated material, a corrective emotional experience—all elaborate upon the problem but still beg the question and fall short of providing a precise mechanism of the influence of insight.

The psychological construct of willing and particularly the concept of decision—that process that stretches from wish into action—provides the clinician with a model to explain how insight catalyzes change. The therapist's task is to disencumber will; insight is one of the important tools that the therapist can use to accomplish that task.

In the following section I shall argue that insight effects change through (1) facilitating the development of the therapist-patient relationship, and (2) a series of maneuvers that help the therapist liberate the patient's stifled will: these maneuvers are designed to enable patients to realize that *only* they can change the world they have created; that there is no danger in change; that to get what they *really* want, they must change; and that each individual has the power to change.

FACILITATION OF THE PATIENT-THERAPIST RELATIONSHIP

An accepting, trusting patient-therapist relationship is crucial to the process of change. As a result of the therapist's concern and unconditional regard, the patient's self-love and self-regard gradually increase. Self-regard begets a belief that one has the right to wish and to act. The patient's will is first exercised in the therapeutic area where it is accepted and reinforced by the therapist. Once the patient's belief in the destructiveness of his or her will is disconfirmed in the therapeutic situation, he or she is gradually able to will effectively in other domains.

How does insight catalyze the therapeutic relationship? Indirectly!

Insight is an epiphenomenon—a means to a means to an end. It is a fertilizer of the relationship! The search for understanding provides a context for the formation of the therapist-patient relationship; it is the glue that binds patient and therapist together; it keeps them occupied in a mutually satisfying task (The patient is gratified by having his or her inner world scrutinized with such thoroughness; the therapist is charmed by the intellectual challenge); and all the while the *real* agent of change, the therapeutic relationship, is silently germinating.

LEVERAGE-PRODUCING INSIGHTS

In addition to its function in the development of the therapist-patient relationship, insight may catalyze willing more directly. The therapist assists the patient in obtaining self-knowledge that applies leverage to the will. The following "insights" are four of the most common leverage-producing statements made by the therapist to the will-stifled patient.

"Only I can change the world I have created." In the previous chapter I described many techniques to help patients become aware of their responsibility for their life predicaments. Once a patient truly grasps the full implications of his or her responsibility, then the therapist must help that patient to understand that responsibility is continuous: one does not create one's situation in life once and for all; rather, one is continuously creating oneself. Thus, responsibility for past creation implies responsibility for future change. Next, the therapist helps the patient take the short step toward realizing that, just as one is *solely* responsible for being what one is, one is *solely* responsible for changing what one is. A patient who is to change must arrive at the insight: "If I, and only I, have created my world, then *only* I can change it." Change is an active process: it will not occur unless we actively change. No one else can change us or change for us.

This insight is at once simplistic and profound. Though the insight is easily stated, and its mechanism fundamentally exhortative, nonetheless its implications run very deep.

"There is no danger in change." Many patients cannot make the crucial decision to change because of a powerful, often unconscious belief that some calamity would befall them if they were to change. The nature of the fantasied calamity varies from person to person: one fears being engulfed if he or she were to engage another; another fears rejection or humiliation if he or she were to be more spontaneous or self-disclosing, or catastrophic retribution as a result of self-assertion, or abandonment and isolation as a result of autonomous behavior.

These fantasied calamities are encumbrances to the will, and the

340

therapist must search for methods to eliminate these encumbrances. The process of identifying and naming the fantasied calamity may in itself enable a patient to understand how far his or her fears are removed from reality. Another approach is to encourage the patient to perform by degrees in the therapy session various aspects of the behavior whose consequences the patient dreads. The fantasied calamity does not, of course, ensue, and the dread is gradually extinguished. For example, a patient may avoid aggressive behavior out of a deep-seated fear of having a dammed-up reservoir of homicidal fury that requires constant vigilance lest it be unleashed and bring down on the patient retribution from others. The therapist helps such a patient express aggression in carefully calibrated doses in therapy: pique at being interrupted, irritation at the therapist's fallibility, anger at the therapist for charging him money, and so on. Gradually the patient learns to demythologize himself as an alien and homicidal being.

"To get what I really want, I must change." What prevents individuals from making decisions that are clearly in their best interests? An obvious answer is that the patient who seems to be sabotaging his or her own mature needs and goals, is satisfying *another* set of needs that are often unconscious and that are incompatible with the first. In other words, the patient has conflicting motivations that cannot be simultaneously satisfied. For example, the patient may consciously wish to establish mature heterosexual relationships, but unconsciously wish to be nurtured, to be cradled endlessly, to be sheltered from the terrifying freedom of adulthood, or—to use another vocabulary in the case of a man—to assuage castration anxiety by a maternal identification. Obviously the patient cannot satisfy both sets of wishes: he cannot establish an adult heterosexual relationship with a woman if he is saying *sotto voce*, "Take care of me, protect me, nurse me, let me be a part of you."

The therapist uses insight to attack this obstacle to the functioning of the will and helps the patient to become aware that he or she has conflicting needs and goals, and that each decision, including a decision not to decide, satisfies some needs—that is, has some "payoff." When the patient is fully aware of the nature of his or her conflicting needs, the therapist helps the former to realize that since all needs cannot be satisfied, the patient must choose among them and relinquish those that cannot be fulfilled except at enormous cost to his or her integrity and autonomy. Once the patient realizes what he or she "really" wants (as an adult), and that his or her behavior has been designed to fulfill opposing growth-retarding needs, he or she gradually concludes that "to get what I really want, I must change."

"I have the power to change." Many individuals are aware that they

do not, will not, make decisions that are in their best interests. Their internal experience is one of confusion-spawned impotence; they experience themselves as victims rather than masters of their conduct. As long as this subjective state prevails, there is little possibility of willful, constructive action on the part of a patient.

The therapist attempts to counter the patient's confusion and impotence with explanation, and says in effect, "You behave in certain fashions because. . . ." The "because" clause generally involves motivational factors that lie outside the patient's awareness. How does this strategy help the patient change?

Explanation is a potent enemy of the powerlessness that emanates from ignorance. Explanation, identifying, and labeling are all part of the natural sequence of the development of mastery—or of a *sense* of mastery which, in turn, begets effective behavior. Human beings have always abhorred uncertainty and have sought through the ages to order the universe by providing explanations, primarily religious or scientific. The explanation of a phenomenon is the first step toward control of that phenomenon. If, for example, natives live in terror of the unpredictable eruptions of a nearby volcano, their first step toward mastery of their situation is explanation. They may, for example, explain the volcano's eruption as the behavior of a displeased volcano god. Although their external circumstances may be entirely the same, their phenomenological world is altered by explanation. Furthermore—and this is very important—a course of action is available that augments their sense of mastery: if the volcano explodes because the god is displeased, then there must be methods of placating and eventually controlling the god.

Jerome Frank, in a study of Americans' reactions to an unfamiliar South Pacific disease (schistosomiasis) demonstrated that secondary anxiety stemming from uncertainty often creates more havoc than does the primary disease.[110] Similarly with psychiatric patients: fear and anxiety that stem from uncertainty of the source, the meaning, and the seriousness of psychiatric symptoms may so compound the total dysphoria that effective exploration becomes vastly more difficult. The therapist may effectively intervene by providing a patient with an explanation that allows that patient to view his or her dysphoria in some coherent and predictable schema. Through explanation the therapist helps a patient to order previously unfamiliar phenomena and to experience them as being under his or her control. Thus, insight permits a patient to feel, *"I am potent, I have the power to change."*

The implication of this sequence is that it is primarily the *process* (that is, the provision of insight), rather than the precise *content* of the insight, that is important. The function of the interpretation is to provide the patient with a sense of mastery; accordingly, the value of an interpretation should be measured by this criterion. To the extent that it offers a sense of potency, insight is valid, correct, or "true." Such a definition of truth is completely relativistic and pragmatic. It argues that no explanatory system has hegemony or exclusive rights, that no system is the correct, the fundamental, or the "deeper"—and therefore better—one.

In a study of encounter groups my colleagues and I learned that positive outcome was highly correlated with insight.[111] Those subjects who obtained insight and were able to organize their experience in some coherent pattern had a positive outcome. Furthermore, the successful group leaders were those who provided some type of cognitive framework for their members. The type of insight that the successful members had, and the specific content of the ideological school from which the successful leaders sprang, had little to do with the positive outcome. The important feature was not *what* they had learned but *that* they had learned.

Therapists may offer the patient any of a number of explanations to clarify the same issue; each may be made from a different frame of reference (for example, Freudian, Jungian, Horneyan, Sullivanian, Adlerian, and transactional analytic) and each may be "true" in that each provides an explanation that begets a sense of potency. None, despite vehement claims to the contrary, has sole rights to the truth. After all, they are all based on imaginary "as if" structures. They all say, "You are behaving (or feeling) as if such and such a thing were true."

The superego, the id, the ego; the archetypes, the idealized and the actual selves, the pride system; the self system and the dissociated system, the masculine protest; parent, child, and adult ego states—none of these really exists. They are all fictions, all psychological constructs created for semantic convenience, and they justify their existence only by virtue of their explanatory power. The concept of the will provides a central organizing principle for these diverse explanatory systems. They all act by the same mechanism: they are effective to the degree that they afford a sense of personal mastery and thus inspirit the dormant will.

Does this mean that psychotherapists abandon their attempts to make precise, thoughtful interpretations? Not at all. Only that they recognize the purpose and function of an interpretation. Some interpretations may be superior to others, not because they are "deeper" but because they have more explanatory power, are more credible, provide more mastery, and therefore better catalyze the will. Interpretations, to be truly effective, must be tailored for the recipient; in general, they are more effective if they make sense, if they are logically consistent with sound supporting arguments, if they are bolstered by empirical observation, if they are consonant with the patient's frame of reference, if they "feel" right, if they "click" with the internal experience of the patient, and if they can be applied to many analogous situations in the life of the patient. Global interpretations generally offer a novel explanation to the patient for some large pattern of behavior (as opposed to a single trait or act). The novelty of the therapist's explanation stems from his unusual frame of reference, which permits him to unify data about the patient in an original fashion; indeed, often this data is material that has been overlooked by, or is out of the awareness of, the patient.

When I present this relativistic thesis to students, they respond with such questions as "Do you mean that an astrological explanation is also valid in psychotherapy?" In spite of my own intellectual reservations, I have to respond affirmatively. If an astrological or a shamanistic or a magical explanation enhances one's sense of mastery, and leads to inner, personal change, then it is valid (keeping in mind the proviso that it must be consonant with one's frame of reference). There is much evidence from cross-cultural psychiatric research to support my position; in most primitive cultures *only* the magical or the religious explanation is acceptable, and hence valid and effective.

An interpretation, even the most elegant one, has no benefit if a patient does not hear it. The therapist should take pains to review some of the evidence with the patient and to present the explanation clearly. (A therapist who cannot do so does not understand the explanation; it is not, as some claim, because the therapist is speaking directly to the patient's unconscious.) A patient may not be able to accept an interpretation the first time a therapist makes it, but may hear the same interpretation many times until one day it seems to click. Why does it click that one day? The important thing for the therapist to recognize is that, even though it appears that a decision to change may be made in an astonishingly short period of time, nevertheless the groundwork for that change often takes many, many long months or even years. Many therapists are impressed and puzzled by reports of individuals who report a dramatic, sudden life transformation as a result of some brief therapeutic encounter or short participation in a personal growth workshop. It is extremely difficult to evaluate these reports. Richard

Nisbett and Tim Wilson have demonstrated that individuals who make decisions are often inaccurate in their descriptions of the antecedants of that decision.[112] From my interviews with those who have undergone dramatic breakthroughs I have found that these life transformations are by no means sudden: the groundwork for change has been laid over preceding weeks, months, and years. By the time they have reached the point of seeking therapy or some other type of personal growth experience, many individuals have already, at a deep level, done the work and are on the brink of dramatic change. In these instances therapy—that is, the decision to seek therapy—is the *manifestation*, not the *cause*, of change.

Decisions to change generally require considerable time, and the therapist must exercise patience. Interpretations must be properly timed. The experienced therapist knows that an interpretation prematurely given will have little therapeutic impact. An illustrative clinical example is provided by a patient in a therapy group who had been involved for several years in an exceedingly unsatisfying marriage. All attempts to improve the marriage had failed; and though she realized that it was destroying her, she clung to it because she was terrified of facing life alone. She perceived her husband not as a real person but as a figure who protected her from loneliness. Though the relationship was obviously unsatisfactory, she was so terrified of losing it that she refused to commit herself to a plan for change. Without any real relatedness and without any commitment for change, there was little possibility of the marriage working. It seemed clear to me that only if she could face separateness and autonomy could she have a chance at a genuine, undistorted human encounter. Consequently, I ventured the opinion: *"Only if you are willing to give up the marriage can you save it."* That interpretation was deeply meaningful to her: she said that it struck her like a thunderbolt; and subsequently it catalyzed considerable change.

The fascinating aspect of this situation was that she had been in a therapy group after each meeting of which I had for many years written a summary to mail to the group members before the following session (see my book on group therapy[113] for the rationale of this procedure). Thus, there was a written history of the therapy group—a chronicle that the patients had read after each meeting. This particular patient was an assiduous reader of the summaries and filed them, so that she had an ongoing log of the group to which she referred from time to time. Shortly after I made this effective interpretation to her, I reviewed the summaries of the group over the past couple of years in conjunction with some writing I was doing, and discovered, to my astonishment, that I had made the precise interpretation to her one year previously! Though the wording was identical and the interpretation had been underscored and heavily emphasized, she had not heard it previously because she was not ready to hear it.

The Past versus the Future in Psychotherapy

It is a matter of no small significance that the word "will" has a double meaning: it suggests resolution and determination, and it also denotes the future tense—"I will do it—not at this moment, but in the future." As every therapist recognizes, psychotherapy is successful to the extent that it allows the patient to alter his or her future. Yet it is not the future but the past tense that dominates psychotherapy literature. To a large extent this domination by the past is a result of a confusion between explanation and "originology." Psychotherapists, especially those of a Freudian persuasion, often believe that in order to explain something—that is, to provide insight—one must lay bare its origins or, at the very least, relate the present event to some past situation. In this frame of reference, the causes of individual behavior are to be found in antecedent circumstances of a person's life.

Yet, as I suggested in the previous section, there are many modes of explanation or systems of causality that do not rely on the past. For example, the future (our present idea about the future) is, no less than the past, a powerful determinant of behavior, and the concept of future determinism is fully defensible. The "not yet" influences our behavior in many, formidable ways. Within one, at both conscious and unconscious levels, there is a sense of purpose, an idealized self, a series of goals for which one strives, an awareness of destiny and of ultimate death. These constructs all stretch into the future, yet they powerfully influence inner experience and behavior.

Another mode of explanation applies a Galilean concept of causality which stresses the current field forces operating upon the individual. As we hurtle through space, our behavioral trajectories are influenced not only by the nature and the direction of the original push and the nature of the goal that beckons, but also by all the current field forces operating upon them. Thus, the therapist may "explain" a patient's behavior by examining the concentric rings of conscious and unconscious

346

current motivations which envelop that individual. Consider, for example, one who has a strong inclination to attack others. Exploration of this behavior may reveal that the patient's aggression is a reaction formation concealing a layer of strong dependency wishes that are not expressed because of anticipation of rejection. This explanation need not include the question "How did the patient get that way?"

Still, the therapist's natural tendency is to focus on the past in psychotherapy. Most long-term intensive treatment devotes much energy to looking backward. Long developmental histories are gathered, recollections about one's early relations with parents and siblings are explored at length, early memories and infantile roots of dreams are painstakingly examined. Freud laid the foundations of this approach. He was a committed psycho-archeologist who, to the end of his life, believed that the excavation of the past was essential, even tantamount, to successful therapy. In fact, in one of his last papers he makes an extended comparison between the work of the analyst and that of the professional archeologist. He describes the therapist's task as "construction of the past":

> We all know that the person who is being analyzed has to be induced to remember something that has been experienced by him and repressed. The analyst has neither experienced nor repressed any of the material under consideration; his task cannot be to remember anything. What then *is* his task? His task is to make out what has been forgotten from the traces which it has left behind or, more correctly, to *construct*.... His work of construction, or, if it is preferred, of reconstruction, resembles to a great extent an archeologist's excavation of some dwelling place that has been destroyed and buried. The two practices are in fact identical, except that the analyst works under better conditions and has more material at his command to assist him.[114]

Freud goes on to argue that the therapist, like the archaeologist, must often reconstruct the available fragments (as supplied by the patient) and then offer this construction to the patient. In fact, Freud suggests that the word "construction" is a more appropriate label than "interpretation" for the therapist's activity. An analyst who is not successful in helping the patient to recollect the past should, Freud suggests, nonetheless give the patient a construction of the past as the analyst sees it. Freud believed that this construction would offer the same therapeutic benefit as would actual recollection of past material:

> Quite often we do not succeed in bringing the patient to recollect what has been repressed. Instead of that, if the analysis is carried out correctly, *we produce in him an assured conviction of the truth of the construction which achieves the same therapeutic results as a recaptured memory.*[115]

347

This latter remarkable statement is in agreement with the point I made earlier—namely, that it is not the content but the process of interpretation or explanation that is important.

Freud's emphasis on reconstruction of the past as an explanatory system is intimately related to his deterministic doctrine: all behavior and mental experience are the result of antecedent events—events either environmental or instinctual in nature. The problem with such an explanatory system is that it contains within it the seeds of therapeutic despair. If we are determined by the past, whence comes the ability to change? It is evident from Freud's later works, especially *Analysis Terminable and Interminable*, that his uncompromising deterministic view of man led him to a position of therapeutic nihilism.

Any system that explains behavior and mental experience on the basis of phenomena (for example, past or present environmental events, instinctual drives) outside the domain of individual responsibility leads to a treacherous position for the therapist. As Rank puts it: "The causality principle means the denial of the will principle since it makes the feeling, thinking and acting of the individual dependent on forces outside of himself and thus frees him from responsibility and guilt."[116]

Of course, it is often useful to free oneself from guilt about past events and actions. The therapist who adheres to a deterministic doctrine is able to examine the past in such a way as to demonstrate to the patient that he or she was a victim of environmental events—that, given the circumstances, he or she could not have acted differently. Thus, exploration of the past serves to absolve guilt but leaves the therapist with the problem of how to deal with the past from one frame of reference (to offer absolution) and the future with another (to invoke responsibility).

Gatch and Temerlin studied transcripts of twenty therapists—ten Freudian and ten existential analysts—to determine how they dealt with this paradox.[117] They found that, as expected, the existential therapists made significantly more comments that underscored the patients' choices, freedom, and responsibility. However, none of the twenty therapists ever spoke as if patients were currently victims of circumstances beyond their control. For a patient contemplating change, all therapists attempted to acknowledge and to underscore the alternatives available to that patient. Furthermore, when a patient spoke of his or her infancy or childhood, all therapists appeared to take a deterministic position: that circumstances had been beyond the control of the patient as a child.

It is apparent, then, that therapists learn to live with this inconsistent position. They may reduce the inconsistency by ameliorating the deterministic doctrine to one of reciprocal determinism: they assume that in the past the coefficient of adversity was too great; that, given the patient's youth and experience and the power of adult forces acting upon him, he or she could not have acted otherwise.

Most existential therapists tend to focus less on the past than do therapists of other persuasions, and more on the future tense, on the decisions beckoning one, the goals stretching out before one. When existential therapists deal with guilt, it is not for the bad choices made but for the refusal to make new ones. It is extraordinarily difficult to absolve guilt for the past in the presence of ongoing guilt-provoking behavior. One must learn first to forgive oneself for the present and the future. So long as one continues to operate toward the self in the present in the same way that one has acted in the past, then one cannot forgive oneself for the past. But even when working with the past, it is important that the individual does not assume disproportionate responsibility. One important concept is the categorical imperative for responsibility: what is true for one regarding responsibility is true for all. Many individuals assume excessive responsibility and guilt for others' actions and feelings. Though the patient may truly have transgressed against another, there's also a realm of responsibility of the other who allowed him- or herself to be hurt, scorned, or otherwise mistreated by the patient. Thus, the therapist must help the patient locate the boundaries of responsibility.

Not only is there serious question about the therapeutic efficacy of a causal explanatory system based on the past, but there is a serious methodological problem—namely, that psychological reality is not identical with historical reality. As Rank notes, Freud's natural science ideology led him to attempt to reconstruct the historical past from the patient's recollection of it. But "the reconstruction of the past depends not on the facts but on the attitude or reaction of the individual to them. . . . The problem of the past is a problem of memory and therefore a problem of consciousness."[118] In other words, the past is reconstituted by the present. Even in a lengthy anamnesis, one recalls only a minute fraction of one's past experience and may selectively recall and synthesize the past so as to achieve consistency with one's present view of oneself. (Goffman, for this reason, suggests the term "apologia" for this reconstruction of the past.)[119] As one through therapy changes one's present image of oneself, one may reconstitute or reintegrate one's past; for example, one may recall long-forgotten positive experiences with parents. One may humanize them and, rather than experiencing them solipsistically (as figures who existed by virtue of their service to one), one may begin to understand them as harried, well-intentioned individuals struggling with the same overwhelming facts of the human condition that anyone faces. This process is epitomized in a remark attributed to Mark Twain: "When I was seventeen I was convinced my father was a damn fool. When I was twenty-one I was astounded by how much the old man had learned in four years."

The hermeneutic approach to interpretation considers the relationship between understanding and background: it posits that grasping an understanding requires a certain background, but that this new understanding alters the perception of the background. Consequently, interpretation is an organic process in which background and understanding sequentially reconstitute one another. The same principle applies to the relationship between past and present: a human being's past, unlike the ruins of some ancient temple, is neither fixed nor finite; it is constituted by the present and, in its ever-changing symbolic immanence, influences the present.

If the past as a system of explanation is of limited value, what role does the past play in the process of psychotherapy? Earlier I alluded to the role of the search for genetic insight in the development of the therapeutic relationship. The intellectual venture, which Freud likens to an archeological dig, provides a shared, apparently meaningful activity in which patient and therapist engage, while the *real* agent of change, the therapeutic relationship, unfolds. But the past facilitates relationship in another important manner: the explicit understanding of the early development of a particular interpersonal stance enhances the possibility of engagement. For example, a woman with a regal air conveying hauteur and condescension may suddenly seem understandable, even winsome, when the therapist learns of her immigrant parents and her desperate struggle to transcend the degradation of her slum childhood. Knowing another's process of becoming is often an indispensable adjunct to knowing the person. What is important in this regard is the accent. The past is explored in order to facilitate and deepen the present relationship. This is precisely the reverse of Freud's formula, where the present relationship serves as a means to deepen understanding of the past. Charles Rycroft states this exceptionally clearly:

> It makes better sense to say that the analyst makes excursions into historical research in order to understand something which is interfering with his present communication with the patient (in the same way that a translator might turn to history to elucidate an obscure text) than to say that he makes contact with the patient in order to gain access to biographical data."[120]

PART III

Isolation

CHAPTER 8

Existential Isolation

T HE PROCESS of deepest inquiry—a process that Heidegger refers to as "unconcealment,"[1]—leads us to recognize that we are finite, that we must die, that we are free, and that we cannot escape our freedom. We also learn that the individual is inexorably alone.

As freedom and death are concepts that traditionally lie outside of the psychotherapist's domain, in early chapters I felt it necessary to elaborate on their specific relevance to psychotherapy. The situation is different with isolation since it is a familiar concept and arises frequently in everyday therapy. In fact, isolation is so familiar and used in so many different fashions that my first task must be to define it in an existential context. The clinician, it seems to me, encounters three different types of isolation: interpersonal, intrapersonal and existential.

Interpersonal isolation, generally experienced as loneliness, refers to isolation from other individuals. It is a function of many factors: geographic isolation, the lack of appropriate social skills, heavily conflicted feelings about intimacy, or a personality style (such as schizoid, narcissistic, exploitative, or judgmental) that precludes gratifying social interaction. Cultural factors play an important role in interpersonal isolation. The decline of intimacy-sponsoring institutions—the extended family, the stable residential neighborhood, the church, local merchants, the family doctor—has, in the United States at least, inexorably led to increased interpersonal estrangement.

Intrapersonal isolation is a process whereby one partitions off parts of oneself. Freud used the term "isolation" to describe a defense mechanism, especially apparent in obsessional neurosis, in which an unpleasant experience is stripped of its affect, and its associative connections are interrupted, so that it is isolated from ordinary processes of thought.[2] Harry Stack Sullivan was particularly interested in the phenomenon by which one excludes experience from conscious awareness and/or makes parts of the psyche inaccessible to the self. He referred to this process as "dissociation" (abandoning the term "repression") and elevated it to a central position in his schema of psychopathology.[3] In the contemporary psychotherapy scene "isolation" is used not only to refer to formal defense mechanisms but in a more casual way to connote any form of fragmentation of the self. Thus, intrapersonal isolation results whenever one stifles one's own feelings or desires, accepts "oughts" or "shoulds" as one's own wishes, distrusts one's own judgement, or buries one's own potential.

Intrapersonal isolation is a widely used and current paradigm of psychopathology. Modern theorists such as Horney, Fromm, Sullivan, Maslow, Rogers, and May all posit that pathology is the result of obstructions that, occuring early in life, act to derail the individual's natural development. Carl Rogers in a discussion of Ludwig Binswanger's famous case of Ellen West clearly describes intrapersonal isolation: "Though as a child she was wholly independent of opinion of others, she now is completely dependent on what others think. She no longer has any way of knowing what she feels or what her opinion is. This is the loneliest state of all, an almost complete separation from one's autonomous organism."[4]

Contemporary therapists focus closely on the goal of helping patients reintegrate previously split-off parts of themselves. In a research project that I described in chapter 6, successful patients were asked to rank-order sixty factors in therapy according to degree of helpfulness.[5] The single most frequently chosen item by far was "discovering and accepting previously unknown or unacceptable parts of myself." To make oneself whole again is the goal of most psychotherapies (excluding symptom-oriented ones). Perls, for example, christened his approach "Gestalt" therapy to emphasize his dedication to the aim of "wholeness." (Note in this regard the common etymological root of "whole," "heal," "healthy," "hale.")

In the remainder of this chapter I shall focus on a third form of isolation—existential isolation. This is not to say that *inter*personal and *intra*personal isolation are not crucial issues in clinical work; but if I am to keep this treatise within manageable length, I must be content to recommend to the reader the relevant literature.[6] There will be many occasions, however, when I shall refer to interpersonal and intrapersonal isolation, for they are closely related to existential isolation (interpersonal and existential isolation especially share a common boundary). The types of isolation are similar subjectively; that is, they may feel the same as and masquerade for one another. Frequently therapists mistake them and treat a patient for the wrong type of isolation. Furthermore, their boundaries are semipermeable: existential isolation, for example, is often kept within manageable bounds through interpersonal affiliation. All these issues will be discussed in due time, but first existential isolation must be defined.

What Is Existential Isolation?

Individuals are often isolated from others and from parts of themselves, but underlying these splits is an even more basic isolation that belongs to existence—an isolation that persists despite the most gratifying engagement with other individuals and despite consummate self-knowledge and integration. Existential isolation refers to an unbridgeable gulf between oneself and any other being. It refers, too, to an isolation even more fundamental—a separation between the individual and the world. "Separation from the world"—that seems to be the right phrase, yet still it is vague. One of my patients provided an embodied definition. She experienced periodic panic attacks that occurred whenever her relationship with a dominant other was endangered. When describing her experience, she said to me: "Remember the movie *West Side Story*, when the two lovers meet, and suddenly everything else in the world mystically fades away, and they are absolutely alone with one another? Well, that's what happens to me at these times. Except there's no one else there but me."

Another patient had a recurrent nightmare that dated back to early childhood and now, in adulthood, resulted in severe insomnia—in fact, in a sleep phobia, since he was terrified of going to sleep. The nightmare is unusual in that the dreamer himself suffered no harm. Instead, his world melted away, exposing him to nothingness. The dream:

I am awake in my room. Suddenly I begin to notice that everything is changing. The window frame seems stretched and then wavy, the bookcases squashed, the doorknob disappears, and a hole appears in the door which gets larger and larger. Everything loses its shape and begins to melt. There's nothing there any more and I begin to scream.

Thomas Wolfe was forever haunted by his unusually acute awareness of existential isolation. In the autobiographical *Look Homeward, Angel* the protagonist muses on isolation even while an infant in the crib:

> Unfathomable loneliness and sadness crept through him: he saw his life down the solemn vista of a forest aisle, and he knew he would always be the sad one: caged in that little round of skull, imprisoned in that beating and most secret heart, his life must always walk down lonely passages. Lost. He understood that men were forever strangers to one another, that no one ever comes really to know anyone, that imprisoned in the dark womb of our mother, we come to life without having seen her face, that we are given to her arms a stranger, and that, caught in that insoluble prison of being, we escape it never, no matter what arms may clasp us, what mouth may kiss us, what heart may warm us. Never, never, never, never, never.[7]

Existential isolation is a vale of loneliness which has many approaches. A confrontation with death and with freedom will inevitably lead the individual into that vale.

DEATH AND EXISTENTIAL ISOLATION

It is the knowledge of "my death" that makes one fully realize that no one can die with one or for one. Heidegger states that "though one can go to his death for another, such 'dying-for' can never signify that the other has had his death taken away in even the slightest degree. *No one can take the other's death away from him.*"[8] Though we may be surrounded with friends, though others may die for the same cause, even though others may die at the same time (as in the ancient Egyptian practice of killing and burying servants with the pharoah, or in suicide pacts), still at the most fundamental level dying is the most lonely human experience.

Everyman, the best-known medieval morality play, portrays in a powerful and simple manner the loneliness of the human encounter with death.[9] Everyman is visited by Death who informs him that he must take his final pilgrimage to God. Everyman pleads for mercy, but to no avail. Death informs him that he must make himself ready for the day that "no man living may escape away." In despair Everyman hurriedly casts about for help. Frightened and, above all, isolated, he pleads to others to accompany him on his journey. The character Kindred refuses to go with him:

> Ye be a merry man:
> Take good heart to you and make no moan
> But one thing I warn you, by Saint Anne,
> As for me, ye shall go alone.

As does Everyman's cousin, who pleads that she is indisposed:

> No, by our Lady! I have the cramp in my toe
> Trust not to me. For so God me speed,
> I will deceive you in your most need.

He is forsaken in the same way by each of the other allegorical characters in the play: Fellowship, Worldly Goods, and Knowledge. Even his attributes desert him:

> Beauty, strength and discretion.
> When death bloweth his blast
> They all run from me full fast.

Everyman is finally saved from the full terror of existential isolation because one figure, Good Deeds, is willing to go with him even unto death. And, indeed, that is the Christian moral of the play: good works within the context of religion provide a buttress against ultimate isolation. Today's secular Everyman who cannot or does not embrace religious faith must indeed take the journey alone.

FREEDOM AND EXISTENTIAL ISOLATION

The Loneliness of Being One's Own Parent.   To the extent that one is responsible for one's life, one is alone. Responsibility implies authorship; to be aware of one's authorship means to foresake the belief that there is another who creates and guards one. Deep loneliness is inherent in the act of self-creation. One becomes aware of the universe's cosmic indifference. Perhaps animals have some sense of shepherd and shelter, but humankind, cursed by self-awareness, must remain exposed to existence.

Erich Fromm believed that isolation is the primary source of anxiety. He especially emphasized the sense of helplessness inherent in the human being's basic separateness.

> The awareness of his aloneness and separateness, of his helplessness before the forces of nature and of society, all this makes his separate dis-

united existence an unbearable prison. The experience of separateness arouses anxiety; it is indeed the source of all anxiety. Being separate means being cut off, without any capacity to use my human powers. Hence to be separate means to be helpless, unable to grasp the world—things and people—actively; it means that the world can invade me without my ability to react.[10]

This fused affect of loneliness-helplessness is an understandable emotional response to our finding ourselves inserted, without our consent, into an existence not of our choosing. Heidegger uses the term "thrownness" to refer to this state. Though one creates oneself, one's project—what one ultimately fashions for oneself— is limited by one's having been thrown alone onto the easel of existence.

Defamiliarization. Not only do we constitute ourselves but we constitute a world fashioned in such a way as to conceal that we have constituted it. Existential isolation impregnates the "paste of things," the bedrock of the world. But it is so hidden by layer upon layer of worldly artifacts, each imbued with personal and collective meaning, that we experience only a world of everydayness, of routine activities, of the "they." We are surrounded, "at home in," a stable world of familiar objects and institutions, a world in which all objects and beings are connected and interconnected many times over. We are lulled into a sense of cozy, familiar belongingness; the primordial world of vast emptiness and isolation is buried and silenced, only to speak in brief bursts during nightmares and mythic visions.

Yet there are moments when the curtain of reality momentarily flutters open, and we catch a glimpse of the machinery backstage. In these moments, which I believe every self-reflective individual experiences, an instantaneous defamiliarization occurs when meanings are wrenched from objects, symbols disintegrate, and one is torn from one's moorings of "at-homeness." Albert Camus, in an early works, described such a moment when he was in a hotel room in an alien country.

> Here I am defenseless in a city where I cannot read the signs . . . without friends to speak to, in short, without diversion. In this room penetrated by the sounds of a strange city, I know that nothing will draw me toward the more delicate light of a home or another cherished place. Am I going to call out? cry out? Strange faces would appear. . . . And now the curtain of habit, the comfortable tissue of gestures and words, wherein the heart grows sluggish, rises slowly and finally unveils the pale face of anxiety. Man is face to face with himself: I defy him to be happy. . . .[11]

In these moments of deep existential anguish one's relationship to the world is profoundly shaken. One of my patients, a highly successful, hard-driving executive, described such an incident: it lasted only a few minutes, yet was so powerful that it retained its vividness forty years later. At the age of twelve he was sleeping outside, looking at the sky, and suddenly felt himself separated from mother earth and drifting between the stars. Where was he? Where did he come from? Where did God come from? Where did something (rather than nothing) come from? He felt overcome with aloneness, with helplessness, and with groundlessness. Though I find it hard to believe that lifelong decisions are made in an instant, he insists that then and there he decided he would make himself so renowned and mighty that he would never again have this feeling.

Of course, this empty, lost, disenfranchising experience is not "out there": it is within us, and no external stimulus is necessary to find it. All that is required is an earnest, inward search. Robert Frost phrases it beautifully:

> They cannot scare me with their empty spaces
> Between stars—on stars where no human race is.
> I have it in me so much nearer home
> To scare myself with my own desert places.[12]

When one falls into one's own "desert places," the world is suddenly unfamiliar. At these times Kurt Reinhardt says:

> Something utterly mysterious intervenes between him and the familiar objects of his world, between him and his fellowmen, between him and all his "values." Everything which he had called his own pales and sinks away, so that there is nothing left to which he might cling. What threatens is "nothing" (no thing), and he finds himself alone and lost in the void. But when this dark and terrible night of anguish has passed, man breathes a sigh of relief and tells himself: it was "nothing," after all. He has experienced "nothingness."[13]

Heidegger uses the term "uncanny" ("not at home") to refer to the state in which one loses one's sense of familiarity in the world. When one (*dasein*) is totally involved in the familiar world of appearance and has lost contact with one's existential situation, Heidegger considers one to be in the "everyday," "fallen" mode. Anxiety serves as a guide to lead one back, by way of uncanniness to awareness of isolation and nothingness:

> As dasein falls, anxiety brings it back from its absorption in the "world." Everyday familiarity collapses. . . . "Being-in" enters into the existential "mode" of the "not-at-home." Nothing else is meant by our talk of "uncanniness."[14]

In another passage Heidegger states that when one is brought back from "absorption in the world" and objects are divested of their meaning, one experiences anxiety at confronting the world's loneliness, mercilessness, and nothingness.* Thus, to escape uncanniness we use the world like a tool and absorb ourselves in the diversions provided by Maya—the world of appearances. The ultimate dread occurs when we confront nothing. In the face of nothing, no thing and no being can help us; it is at that moment when we experience existential isolation in its fullness. Both Kierkegaard and Heidegger were fond of word play involving "nothing." "Of what is man afraid?" "Of nothing!"

The Italian film maker, Antonioni was a master at portraying defamiliarization. In many of his films (for example, *The Eclipse*) objects are seen in stark clarity, with a kind of cold mysteriousness. They are detatched from their meaning, and the main character simply drifts past them unable to act, while everyone around her goes on busily using them.[16]

Defamiliarization involves more than objects in the world; other entities invented to provide structure and stability—such as roles, values, guidelines, rules, ethics—can similarly be stripped of meaning. In chapter 5 I described a simple "disidentification" exercise in which individuals list answers to the question "Who am I?" on cards and then meditate upon the experience of giving up, one by one, each of these roles (for example, a man, a father, a son, a dentist, a walker, a reader of books, a husband, a Catholic, or Bob). By the time the exercise is completed, the individual has divested himself or herself of all roles and becomes aware that being is independent of accouterments, that one persists, as Nietzsche said, even after the "last cloudy streak of evaporating reality."[17] Some of the fantasies reported by subjects at the end of the exercise (such as "a disembodied spirit gliding in a void") suggest clearly that role divestment propels one into an experience of existential isolation.

---

* Heidegger refers to objects in the world as "ready-to-hand" or "present-at-hand," depending upon whether the object is considered "equipment" or is grasped in pure essence:

> The threatening does not come from what is ready-to-hand or present-at-hand, but rather from the fact that *neither of these "says" anything any longer.* The world in which I exist has sunk into insignificance. Anxiety is anxious in the face of the "nothing" of the world; but this does not mean that in anxiety we experience something like the absence of what is present-at-hand within-the-world. The present-at-hand must be encountered in just such a way that it does not have *any involvement whatsoever,* but can show itself in an empty mercilessness. This implies, however, that our concernful awaiting finds nothing in terms of which it might be able to understand itself; it clutches at the "nothing" of the world.[15]

Experiences where one is alone, and everyday guidelines are suddenly stripped away, have the power to evoke a sense of the uncanny—of not being at home in the world. The hiker who loses his or her way, the skier who suddenly finds himself or herself off the trail, the driver who in a dense fog can no longer see the road—the individual in these situations often experiences a rush of dread, a dread independent of the physical threat involved, a lonely dread that is a wind blowing from one's own desert place—the nothing that is at the core of being.

Uncanny are the social explosions that suddenly uproot the values, ethics, and morals that we have come to believe exist independently ourselves. The Holocaust, mob violence, the Jonestown mass suicide, the chaos of war, all of these strike horror in us because they are evil, but they also stun us because they inform us that nothing is as we have always thought it to be, that contingency reigns, that everything could be otherwise than it is; that everything we consider fixed, precious, good can suddenly vanish; that there is no solid ground; that we are "not-at-home" here or there or anywhere in the world.

GROWTH AND EXISTENTIAL ISOLATION

The word "exist" implies differentiation ("ex-ist" = "to stand out"). The process of growth, as Rank knew, is a process of separation, of becoming a separate being. The words of growth imply separateness: autonomy (self-governing), self-reliance, standing on one's own feet, individuation, being one's own person, independence. Human life begins with a fusion of ova and sperm, passes through an embryonic stage of complete physical dependence on the mother, into a phase of physical and emotional dependency on surrounding adults. Gradually the individual establishes boundaries demarking where he or she ends and others begin, and becomes self-reliant, independent, and separate. Not to separate means not to grow up, but the toll of separating and growing up is isolation.

The tension inherent in this dilemma is, in Kaiser's term, the human being's "universal conflict." "Becoming an individual, entails a complete, a fundamental, an eternal and insurmountable isolation."[18] Fromm makes the same point in *Escape from Freedom*:

> To the extent to which the child emerges from that world it becomes aware of being alone, of being an entity separate from all others. This separation from a world, which in comparison with one's own individual existence is overwhelmingly strong and powerful, and often threatening and dangerous, creates a feeling of powerlessness and anxiety. As long as one was an integral part of that world, unaware of the possibili-

ties and responsibilities of individual action, one did not need to be afraid of it. When one has become an individual, one stands alone and faces the world in all its perilous and overpowering aspects.[19]

To relinquish a state of interpersonal fusion means to encounter existential isolation with all its dread and powerlessness. The dilemma of fusion-isolation—or, as it is commonly referred to, attachment-separation—is the major existential developmental task. This is what Otto Rank meant when he emphasized the importance of birth trauma. To Rank, birth was symbolic of all emergence from embeddedness. What the child fears is life itself.[20]

It becomes clear now that existential isolation and interpersonal isolation are intricately interwoven. Emergence from interpersonal fusion thrusts the individual into existential isolation. A dissatisfying state of fusion-existence or too early or too tentative emergence leaves the individual unprepared to face the isolation inherent in autonomous existence. The fear of existential isolation is the driving force behind many interpersonal relationships and is, as we shall see, a major dynamic behind the phenomenon of transference.

The problem of relationship is a problem of fusion-isolation. On the one hand, one must learn to relate to another without giving way to the desire to slip out of isolation by becoming part of that other. But one must also learn to relate to another without reducing the other to a tool, a defense against isolation. Bugental (in his discussion of the problems of relatedness) plays on the word "apart."[21] The human being's basic interpersonal task is to be at once "a-part-*of*" and "a-part-*from*." Interpersonal and existential isolation are way stations for each other. One must first separate oneself from the other in order to encounter isolation; one must be alone to experience aloneness. But, as I shall now discuss, it is the facing of aloneness that ultimately allows one to engage another deeply and meaningfully.

Isolation and Relationship

The experience of existential isolation produces a highly uncomfortable subjective state and, as is the case with any form of dysphoria, is not tolerated by the individual for long. Unconscious defenses "work" on it and quickly bury it—out of the purview of conscious experience. The defenses must work without respite because the isolation is within one, always waiting to be recognized. "The waves of the ether," as Martin Buber says, "roar on always, but for most of the time we have turned off our receivers."[22]

How does one shield oneself from the dread of ultimate isolation? One may take a portion of the isolation into oneself and bear it courageously or, to use Heidegger's term, "resolutely." As for the rest, one attempts to give up singleness and to enter into relationship with another, with either a being like oneself or a divine being. The major buttress against the terror of existential isolation is thus relational in nature, and my discussion of the clinical manifestations of existential isolation must perforce center on interpersonal relationships. In accent, however, I shall differ from traditional discussions of interpersonal psychology: I shall focus not on such needs as security, attachment, self-validation, satisfaction of lust, or power, but instead shall view relationships according to how they assuage fundamental and universal isolation.

No relationship can eliminate isolation. Each of us is alone in existence. Yet aloneness can be shared in such a way that love compensates for the pain of isolation. "A great relationship," says Buber, "breaches the barriers of a lofty solitude, subdues its strict law, and throws a bridge from self-being to self-being across the abyss of dread of the universe."[23]

I believe that if we are able to acknowledge our isolated situations in existence and to confront them with resoluteness, we will be able to turn lovingly toward others. If, on the other hand, we are overcome with dread before the abyss of loneliness, we will not reach out toward others but instead will flail at them in order not to drown in the sea of existence. In this instance our relationships will not be true relationships at all but out of joint, miscarriages, distortions of what might have been. We will not relate to others with a full sense of them as like ourselves, as sentient beings, also alone, also frightened, also carving out a world of at-homeness from the paste of things. We behave toward other beings as toward tools or equipment. The other, now no longer an "other" but an "it," is placed there, within one's circle of world, for a *function*. The fundamental function, of course, is *isolation denial*, but awareness of this function is too close to the lurking terror. Greater concealment is needed; metafunctions emerge; and we constitute relationships that provide a product (for example, power, fusion, protection, greatness, or adoration) that in turn serves to deny isolation.

There is nothing novel in this psychic defensive organization: every explanatory system of behavior posits some core conflict that is encrusted with layers of protective and concealing dynamisms. These miscarried "relationships," with their products, their functions, and their metafunctions, constitute what clinicians refer to as "interpersonal psychopathology." I shall describe the clinical picture of many forms of pathological relationship and discuss the existential dynamics of each. But in order to understand fully what relationship is not, it is necessary first to apprehend what, in the best of ways, a relationship can be.

NEED-FREE LOVE

A relationship, at its best, involves individuals who relate to one another in a need-free fashion. Yet how is it possible to love another for the other and not for what that other provides for the lover? How can we love without using, without a *quid pro quo*, without a mainsail of infatuation, lust, admiration, or self-service? Many wise thinkers have addressed this question, and I shall begin by reviewing their contributions.

Martin Buber. "In the beginning is the relation."[24] Thus proclaimed Martin Buber, a philosopher and theologian, whose patriarchal appearance, complete to piercing gaze and full white beard, augmented the power of his philosophical pronouncements. Buber has had an extraordinary impact on both religious philosophy and modern psychiatric theory. His posture is an unusual one, straddling Jewish mystical thought and hasidism on the one hand and modern relational theory on the other. His proclamation "In the beginning is the relation" is rooted in these traditions. Buber was part of a mystical tradition that believes that every individual is part of the Covenant; each contains a divine spark that in concert reveal the holy presence. Thus every individual is united in that each has a cosmic, spiritual association to the universe.

Buber believed that longing for relationship was "innate" and given, "and that in his mother's womb everyman knows [that is, is related to] the universe and forgets it at birth." The child has a "drive" for contact—originally tactile, and then "optimal," contact with another being.[25] The child knows of no "I"; he knows of no other state of being than relation.

"Man," Buber stated, does not exist as a separate entity: "Man is a creature of the between."[26] There are two basic types of relationships—thus, two types of in-betweenness—which Buber characterized "I-Thou" (sometimes translated as "I-You") and "I-It." The "I-It" relationship is the relationship between a person and equipment, a "functional" relationship, a relationship between subject and object wholly lacking mutuality.

The I-Thou relationship is a wholly mutual relationship involving a full experiencing of the other. It differs from empathy (imaginatively viewing a situation from the other's perspective) because it is more than an "I" attempting to relate to an "other." "There is no 'I' as such, but only the basic word I-Thou."[27]

"Relation is reciprocity."[28] Not only is the "Thou" of the I-Thou relationship different from the "It" in the I-It relationship, and not only are the *natures* of the I-Thou and the I-It relationships vastly different, but there is even a more fundamental difference. *The very "I" is different in the two situations.* It is not the "I" that has pre-eminent reality—an "I" that can decide to relate to "Its" or "Thous" that are objects floating into one's field of vision. No, the "I" is "betweenness"; the "I" *appears and is shaped* in the context of some relationship. Thus the "I" is profoundly influenced by the relationship with the "Thou." With each "Thou," and with each moment of relationship, the "I" is created anew. When relating to "It" (whether to a thing or to a person made into a thing) one holds back something of oneself: one inspects it from many possible perspectives; one categorizes it, analyzes it, judges it, and decides upon its position in the grand scheme of things. But when one relates to a "Thou," one's whole being is involved; nothing can be withheld.

> The basic word I-You can be spoken only with one's whole being. The concentration and fusion into a whole being can never be accomplished by me, can never be accomplished without me. I require a You to become; becoming I, I say You. . . .[29]

If one relates to another with less than one's whole being, if one holds something back by, for example, relating through greed or anticipation of some return, or if one remains in the objective attitude, a spectator, and wonders about the impression one's actions will make on the other, then one has transferred an I-Thou encounter into an I-It one.

If one is to relate truly to another, one must truly listen to the other: relinquish stereotypes and anticipations of the other, and allow oneself to be shaped by the other's response. Buber's distinction between "genuine" and "pseudo" listening obviously has important implications for the therapeutic relationship.

To relate to another in a need-less fashion, one must lose or transcend oneself. My favorite illustration of an I-Thou relationship is Buber's description of himself and his horse when he was a youth:

> When I was eleven years of age, spending the summer on my grandparents' estate, I used, as often as I could do it unobserved, to steal into

the stable and gently stroke the neck of my darling, a broad dapple-gray horse. It was not a casual delight but a great, certainly friendly, but also deeply stirring happening. If I am to explain it now, beginning from the still very fresh memory of my hand, I must say that what I experienced in touch with the animal was the Other, the immense otherness of the Other, which, however, did not remain strange like the otherness of the ox and the ram, but rather let me draw near and touch it. When I stroked the mighty mane, sometimes marvellously smooth-combed, at other times just as astonishingly wild, and felt the life beneath my hand, it was as though the element of vitality itself bordered on my skin, something that was not I, was certainly not akin to me, palpably the other, not just another, really the Other itself; and yet it let me approach, confided itself to me, placed itself elementally in the relation of Thou and Thou with me. The horse, even when I had not begun by pouring oats for him into the manger, very gently raised his massive head, ears flicking, then snorted quietly, as a conspirator gives a signal meant to be recognizable only by his fellow-conspirator; and I was approved. But one time—I do not know what came over the child, at any rate it was childlike enough—it struck me about the stroking, what fun it gave me, and suddenly I became conscious of my hand. The game went on as before, but something had changed, it was no longer the same thing. And the next day, after giving him a rich feed, when I stroked my friend's head he did not raise his head.[30]

The basic experiential mode of the I-Thou is "dialogue," in which, either silently or spoken, "each of the participants has in mind the other or others in their particular being and turns to them with the intention of establishing a living mutual relation between himself and them."[31] Dialogue is simply the turning toward another with one's whole being. When the young Buber turned away from the horse, became aware of his hand, and of how much pleasure the stroking afforded him, then dialogue vanished, and "monologue" and the I-It reigned. Buber termed this turning away from the other "reflexion." In reflexion not only is one "concerned with himself,"[32] but, even more important, one forgets about the particular being of the other.

Viktor Frankl makes a similar point when he deplores the present-day "vulgarization" of the concept of encounter.[33] Frankl argues, and quite correctly I believe, that "encounter" as it often occurs in the basic encounter group is no encounter at all but instead a self-expression, an adoration of affect-discharge whose rationale is rooted in a psychological "monadology" which pictures the human being as a windowless cell, a creature who cannot transcend oneself, who cannot "turn toward the other." Consequently there is, too often, an emphasis on getting one's aggression out, on beating a pillow or a punching bag, on self-esteem, on using others to solve ancient problems, on self-actualization. Instead of turning toward the other, there is, as Buber would say, sequential "monologues disguised as dialogue."[34]

Buber asked for a great deal in an I-Thou relationship. Once, for example, he was visited by a unknown young man who ostensibly had come for a chat. Buber found out much later that the stranger had a hidden agenda, that he was "borne by destiny" and was on the verge of a momentous personal decision. Though Buber treated him in a friendly, considerate fashion, he berated himself for "not being there in spirit" and for "omitting to guess the questions the man did not put."[35] But is it possible always to turn toward the other with such intensity? Obviously not, and Buber stressed that, though the I-Thou, constituted an ideal toward which one should strive, nonetheless it existed in only rare moments. One has to live primarily in the I-It world; to live solely in the "Thou" world would result in one's burning oneself up in the white flame of the "Thou."

> [The It-world is] the world in which one has to live and also can live comfortably. . . . The Thou-moments appear as queer lyric-dramatic episodes. Their spell may be seductive, but they pull us dangerously to extremes. . . . One cannot live in the pure present [that is, in the I-Thou] it would consume us . . . and in all the seriousness of truth, *listen*: [that is, be in the I-Thou] without it a human being cannot live. But whoever lives only with that is not human.[36]

This plea for balance is reminiscent of Rabbi Hillel's well-known aphorism: "If I am not for myself, who will be? And if I am only for myself, what am I?"[37]

I have cited Buber extensively because his formulation of a need-less love relationship is vivid and gripping. I cannot leave him without commenting upon an obvious tension between the fundamental position I have accorded to existential isolation and Buber's assertion that the human being does not exist as an "I" but is instead a "creature of the in-between." Since Buber held that the human being's basic mode of existence is relational, he would accord no place in his system for existential isolation. He would protest at my positing that isolation is a fundamental aspect of our existential situation; and even more vigorously would he protest at my citing his work as part of my discussion.

Yet let me look at an important dream with which Buber began *Between Man and Man*—a recurrent dream which visited him, sometimes after an interval of several years, all his life.[38] The dream, which Buber called "the dream of the double cry," begins with his finding himself alone "in a vast cave, or a mud building, or on the fringes of a gigantic forest whose like I cannot remember having seen." Then something extraordinary occurs, like, for example, an animal tearing the flesh from his arm, and then:

> I cry out. . . . Each time it is the same cry, inarticulate but in strict rhythm, rising and falling, swelling to a fullness which my throat could not endure were I awake, long and slow quite slow and very long, a cry that is a song. When it ends my heart stops beating. But then, somewhere, far away, another cry mourns toward me, another which is the same, the same cry uttered or sung by another voice.

The responding cry is the critical event for Buber:

> As the reply ends, a certitude, true dream certitude comes to me that *now it has happened.* Nothing more. Just this, and in this way—now it has happened. If I should try to explain it, it means that that happening which gave rise to my cry has only now, with the rejoinder, really and undoubtably happened.

Buber held that our basic mode of existence is relational; and in this dream, which he cited as a truth-giving vision, existence begins with the appearance of the relationship—the responding cry. Yet the dream text can, with grace, be interpreted differently. One begins, not in relationship, but alone and in an uncanny place. One is attacked and frightened. One cries out and, in anticipation of a reply, one's heart stops beating. The dream speaks to me of fundamental isolation and suggests that our existence begins with a solitary, lonely cry, anxiously awaiting a response.

Abraham Maslow. Abraham Maslow, who died in 1970, has had immense influence on modern psychological theory. More than any other person, he must be regarded as the progenitor of humanistic psychology—a field that, as I discussed in the initial chapter, overlaps existential psychology at many points. Maslow is destined, in my view, to be rediscovered many times before the richness of his thought is fully assimilated.

One of Maslow's fundamental propositions was that an individual's basic motivation is oriented toward either "deficit" or "growth." Psychoneurosis, he thought, is a deficiency disease resulting from a lack of fulfillment, beginning early in life, of certain basic psychological "needs"—that is, safety, belongingness, identification, love, respect, prestige.[39] Individuals who have these needs satisfied are growth-oriented: they are able to realize their own innate potential for maturity and self-actualization. Growth-oriented individuals, in contrast to those with a deficiency orientation, are far more self-sufficient and far less dependent upon their environment for reinforcement or gratification. In other words, the determinants that govern them are not social or environmental but inner:

> The laws of their own inner nature, their potentialities and capacities, their talents, their latent resources, their creative impulses, their needs to know themselves and to become more and more integrated and unified, more and more aware of what they really are, of what they really want, of what their call or vocation or fate is to be."[40]

Growth-motivated and deficiency-motivated individuals have different types of interpersonal relations. The growth-motivated person is less dependent, less beholden to others, less needful of others' praise and affection, less anxious for honors, prestige, and rewards. He or she does not require continual interpersonal need gratification and, in fact, may at times feel hampered by others and prefer periods of privacy. Consequently the growth-motivated individual does not relate to others as sources of supply but is able to view them as complex, unique, whole beings. The deficiency-motivated individual, on the other hand, relates to others from the point of view of usefulness. Those aspects of the other that are not related to the perceiver's needs are either overlooked altogether or regarded as an irritant or a threat. Thus, as Maslow said, love is transformed into something else and resembles our relationships "with cows, horses, and sheep, as well as with waiters, taxicab drivers, porters, policemen, or others whom we *use*."[41]

Accordingly, Maslow described two types of love that are consonant with these two types of motivation: "deficiency" and "growth." "D-love" (deficiency love) is "selfish love" or "love-need," whereas "B-love" (love for the *being* of another person) is "unneeding love" or "unselfish love." B-love, he felt, is not possessive and is admiring rather than needing; it is a richer, "higher," more valuable subjective experience than D-love. D-love can be gratified, whereas the concept of "gratification" hardly applies at all to B-love. B-love has within it a minimum of anxiety-hostility (but there can, of course, be anxiety-for-the-other). B-lovers are more independent of each other, more autonomous, less jealous or threatened, less needful, more disinterested, but also simultaneously more eager to help the other toward self-actualization, more proud of the other's triumphs, more altruistic, generous, and fostering. B-love, in a profound sense, creates the partner, provides self-acceptance and a feeling of love-worthiness, which enhances continued growth.[42]

Erich Fromm. In his jewel of a book, *The Art of Loving*,[43] Erich Fromm

369

addressed the question with which Buber and Maslow struggled: What is the nature of need-free love? Indeed it is striking, and reassuring, that these three seminal thinkers, each deriving from different backgrounds (theology-philosophy, experimental and social psychology, and psychoanalysis) arrived at similar conclusions.

Fromm's starting point is that the human being's most fundamental concern is existential isolation, that the awareness of separateness is "the source of all anxiety,"[44] and that our major psychological task, throughout the ages, has been the overcoming of separateness. Fromm discusses several historical attempts at solution: creative activity (the union of artist with material and product), orgiastic states (religious, sexual, drug-induced), and conformity with customs and beliefs of the group. All of these attempts fall short:

> The unity in productive (creative) work is not interpersonal; the unity achieved in orgiastic fusion is transitory; the unity achieved by conformity is only pseudo-unity. Hence they are only partial answers to the problem of existence. *The full answer lies in the achievement of interpersonal union, of fusion with another person, in love.*[45]

What Fromm meant by "the full answer" is not clear, but I assume it to be "the most satisfactory" answer. Love does not take away our separateness—that is a given of existence and can be faced but never erased. Love is our best mode of coping with the pain of separateness. Buber, Maslow, and, as we shall see, Fromm arrived at similar formulations of need-less love, but they started from different positions about the schema of love in the individual's life. Buber assumed that a state of love was the human being's natural state in existence, and that isolation was a fallen state. Maslow regarded love both as one of the innate human needs and potentials. Fromm considered love as a mode of coping, "an answer to the problem of existence"—a view close to my position in this book.

Not all forms of love answer equally well the anguish of separateness. Fromm differentiated "symbiotic union"—a form of fallen love—from "mature" love. Symbiotic love, consisting of an active (sadism) and a passive (masochism) form, is a state of fusion where neither party is whole or free (I shall discuss this among the forms of maladaptive love in the following section). Mature love is "union under the condition of preserving one's integrity, one's individuality. . . . In love the paradox occurs that two beings become one and yet remain two."[46]

Fromm traces the individual development of love from early childhood when one experiences being loved for what one is or, perhaps more accurately, because one is. Later, between eight and ten, a new factor enters the child's life: awareness that one produces love by one's own activity. As the individual overcomes egocentricity, the needs of the other become as important as his or her own; and gradually the individual transforms the concept of love from "being loved" into "loving." Fromm equates "being loved" with a state of dependency in which by remaining small, helpless, or "good," one is rewarded by being loved; whereas "loving" is an effective potent state. "Infantile love follows the principle 'I love because I am loved.' Mature love follows the principle: 'I am loved because I love.' Immature love says, 'I love you because I need you.' Mature love says, 'I need you because I love you.'"[47]

Fromm's point that love is an active, not a passive, process has extraordinary importance for the clinician. Patients complain of loneliness, of being unloved and unlovable, but the productive work is always to be done in the opposite realm: their inability to love. Love is a positive act, not a passive affect; it is giving, not receiving—a "standing in," not a "falling for."[48] A distinction must be made between "giving" and "depleting." An individual with a hoarding, a receptive, or an exploitative orientation* will feel depleted or impoverished by giving; one with a marketing orientation will feel cheated by giving and not receiving. But for the mature "productive" person, giving is an expression of strength and abundance. In the act of giving, one expresses and enhances one's aliveness. "When one gives, he brings something to life in the other person, and this which is brought to life reflects back to him; in truly giving, he cannot help receiving that which is given back to him. Giving makes the other person a giver also, and they both share in the joy of what they have brought to life."[50] Note how close this is to Buber: "Relation is reciprocity. My Thou acts on me as I act on it. Our students teach us, our works form us. . . . Inscrutably involved, we live in the currents of universal reciprocity."[51]

In addition to giving, mature love implies other basic elements: concern, responsivity, respect, and knowledge.[52] To love means to be actively concerned for the life and the growth of another. One must be responsive to the needs (physical and psychic) of the other. One must

---

* Fromm describes five basic types of interpersonally based character structure: receptive, exploitative, hoarding, marketing, and productive. The first four (the "nonproductive" types) believe that the "source of all good" is outside them, and that they must endeavor to get it by accepting, taking, preserving, or exchanging, respectively. The productive type is motivated from within and is a growth-motivated, actualized individual.[49]

respect the uniqueness of the other, to see him as he is, and to help him to grow and unfold in his own ways, for his own sake and not for the purpose of serving oneself. But one cannot fully respect the other without knowing that other deeply. True knowledge of the other, Fromm believes, is possible only when one transcends one's self-concern and sees the other person in the other's own terms. One needs to listen and to experience empathically (though Fromm does not use that word): that is, one needs to enter and become familiar with the private world of the other, to live in the other's life and sense the other's meanings and experiences. Note again how Fromm and Buber converge: compare Fromm's loving and Buber's "dialogue" and "genuine, presupposition-less, listening."

It is important to the clinician to think of love as "attitude" (something characteristic of the lover's orientation to the world) rather than in terms of the lover's relationship to his or her love "object." Too often we make the mistake of considering exclusive attachment to one person as proof of the intensity and purity of the love. But such a love is, in Fromm's terms, "symbiotic love" or "overinflated egotism"[53] and, in the absence of caring of others, is invariably destined to cave in on itself. *Need-less love is instead an individual's mode of relating to the world.*

A forty-year-old highly successful executive once consulted me because he had fallen in love with a woman and was in the throes of deciding whether to leave his wife and children. In therapy, after only a few sessions, he became impatient and highly critical of me for general inefficiency and for my failure to offer him a systematic well-planned course of action. Soon this criticism led us into his highly judgmental attitude toward people in general. In therapy we proceeded to investigate, not the immediate decision he faced, but his lack of love toward his world at large. Therapy proved of benefit to him by focusing, as effective therapy generally does, on the unexpected.

The most fundamental type of love, Fromm believes, is brotherly love—an experience of union with all individuals which is characterized by its very lack of exclusivity. The Bible stresses that the object of love should be the frail, the poor, the widow, the orphan, the stranger. These do not serve a purpose, and to love them is to love in need-less, "brotherly" fashion.

I began this section with the question, How is it possible to relate to another in a need-free fashion? Now, in the light of Buber, Maslow, and Fromm's similar conclusions, I shall describe the characteristics of a mature, need-free relationship and then use this prototype to illuminate by contrast the nature of various miscarried relationships.

1. To care for another means to relate in a selfless way: one lets go of self-consciousness and self-awareness; one relates without the overarching thought, What does he think of me? or, What's in it for me? One does not look for praise, adoration, sexual release, power, money. One relates in the moment solely to the other person: there must be no third party, actual or imagined, observing the encounter. In other words, one must relate with one's whole being: if part of oneself is elsewhere—for example, studying the effect that the relationship will have upon some third person—then to that extent one has failed to relate.

2. To care for another individual means to know and to experience the other as fully as possible. If one relates selflessly, one is free to experience all parts of the other rather than the part that serves some utilitarian purpose. One extends oneself into the other, recognizing the other as a sentient being who has also constituted a world about himself or herself.

3. To care for another means to care about the being and the growth of the other. With one's full knowledge, gleaned from genuine listening, one endeavors to help the other become fully alive in the moment of encounter.

4. Caring is active. Mature love is loving, not being loved. One gives lovingly to the other; one does not "fall for" the other.

5. Caring is one's way of being in the world; it is not an exclusive, elusive magical connection with one particular person.

6. Mature caring flows out of one's richness, not out of one's poverty—out of growth, not out of need. One does not love because one needs the other to exist, to be whole, to escape overwhelming loneliness. One who loves maturely has met these needs at other times, in other ways, not the least of which was the maternal love which flowed toward one in the early phases of life. Past loving, then, is the source of strength; current loving is the result of strength.

7. Caring is reciprocal. To the extent one truly "turns toward the other," one is altered. To the extent one brings the other to life, one also becomes more fully alive.

8. Mature caring is not without its rewards. One is altered, one is enriched, one is fulfilled, one's existential loneliness is attenuated. Through caring one is cared for. Yet these rewards flow from genuine caring; they do not instigate it. To borrow Frankl's felicitous word play—the rewards *ensue* but cannot be pursued.

Existential Isolation and Interpersonal Psychopathology

If we fail to develop the inner strength, the sense of personal worth and firm identity that enables us to face existential isolation, to say "so be it," and to take anxiety into ourselves, then we will struggle in oblique ways to find safety. In this section I shall examine these safety-seeking methods and their clinical manifestations. For the most part they are relational—that is, they involve interpersonal relationships—but, as we shall see, in each instance the individual does not relate to (that is, does not "care for") the other but instead *uses* the other for a function. The terror, the direct awareness of existential isolation, and the psychic defensive structure that we elaborate to assuage anxiety are all unconscious. One knows only that one cannot be alone, that one desperately wants from others something that one is never able to obtain and that, try as one might, something always goes wrong with one's relationships.

Yet another solution lies in the direction of sacrificing selfhood: one gains relief from isolation anxiety through immersion in some other individual, cause, or pursuit. Thus, individuals are, as Kierkegaard said, twice in despair:[54] to begin with, in a fundamental existential despair, and then further in despair because, having sacrificed self-awareness, they do not even know they are in despair.

EXISTING IN THE EYES OF OTHERS

"The worst thing about being alone, the thought that drives me bananas, is that, at that moment, no one in the world may be thinking about me." So declared a patient in a group session who had been hospitalized because of panic attacks when alone. There was, among the other patients in this inpatient therapy group, instantaneous agreement with this experience. One nineteen-year-old, who had been hospitalized for slashing her wrists following the break-up of a romantic relationship, said simply, "I'd rather be dead than alone!" Another said, "When I'm alone, that's when I hear voices. Maybe my voices are a way not to be alone!" (an arresting phenomenological explanation of hallucination). Another patient who, on several occasions, had mutilated herself stated that she had done so because of her despair about a highly unsatisfying relationship with a man. Yet she could not leave him because of her terror of being alone. When I asked her what terrified her about loneliness, she said with stark, direct, psychotic insight, "I don't exist when I'm alone."

The same dynamic speaks in the child's incessant plea, "Watch me," "Look at me"—the presence of the other is required to make reality real. (Here, as elsewhere, I cite the child's experience as anterior manifestation, not as cause, of an underlying conflict.) Lewis Carroll, in *Through the Looking Glass* wonderfully expressed the stark belief, held by many patients, that "I exist only so long as I am thought about." Alice, Tweedledee, and Tweedledum come upon the Red King sleeping:

374

"He's dreaming now," said Tweedledee, "and what do you think he's dreaming about?"

Alice said, "Nobody can guess that."

"Why, about *you*!" Tweedledee exclaimed, clapping his hands triumphantly. "And if he left off dreaming about you, where do you suppose you'd be?"

"Where I am now, of course," said Alice.

"Not you!" Tweedledee retorted contemptuously. "You'd be nowhere. Why you're only a sort of thing in this dream!"

"If that there King was to wake," added Tweedledum, "you'd go out—bang!— just like a candle!"

"I shouldn't!" Alice exclaimed indignantly. "Besides, if I'm only a sort of thing in his dream, what are *you*, I should like to know?"

"Ditto," said Tweedledum.

"Ditto, ditto!" cried Tweedledee.

He shouted this so loud that Alice couldn't help saying, "Hush! You'll be waking him, I'm afraid, if you make so much noise."

"Well, it's no use *your* talking about waking him," said Tweedledum, "when you're only one of the things in his dream. You know very well you're not real."

"I *am* real!" said Alice, and began to cry.

"You won't make yourself a bit realer by crying," Tweedledee remarked. "There's nothing to cry about."

"If I wasn't real," Alice said—half laughing through her tears, it all seemed so ridiculous—"I shouldn't be able to cry."

"I hope you don't suppose those are real tears?" Tweedledum interrupted in a tone of great contempt.[55]

One patient in a therapy group commented that once she had been in therapy for several months, and years later chanced to meet her therapist. She was "devastated" because the therapist took forty-five seconds to remember who she was. She then turned toward the group therapist and asked, "Will you always remember me? I can't go on if you won't." She was a high school teacher and was able gradually to accept the cruel fact that just as she would forget her students long before they forgot her, so it was with therapists. The therapist and the teacher are more important to the patient and the student than the other way around. (Still, this does not preclude the fact that, as I shall discuss later, when the therapist *is* with the patient, it is a full, deep presence.) Later in the same session the patient commented that she was beginning to understand why suicide had always appeared to be a compelling option for her. She believed that if she committed suicide, others would remember her for a very, very long time. This is an excellent example of "suicide as a magical act," which I described in chapter 2. There is in her view of suicide no idea of death; on the contrary, she clasped suicide as a way to defeat death—as one may do provided one believes that one can continue to live if one exists in the consciousness of another.

By searching for love, the neurotic individual flees from the dimly recognized sense of isolation and hollowness at the center of being. By being chosen and valued one feels affirmed in one's being. The pure sense of being, of "I AM," of being the source of things, is too frightening in its isolation; therefore, one denies self-creation and chooses to believe that one exists insofar as one is the object of others' consciousness. This solution is doomed to fail on several counts. The relationship generally fails because the other in time wearies of affirming the existence of the individual. Furthermore, the other senses that he or she is being not loved but needed. The other never feels wholly known and wholly embraced because the individual relates only to a part—the part that serves the function of affirming his or her existence. The solution fails because it is only stopgap: if one cannot affirm oneself, then one continually needs affirmation by the other. One is distracted permanently from facing one's fundamental isolation. The solution fails also because one misidentifies the problem: one considers it to be that one is unloved, whereas in actuality it is that one is unable to love. As we have seen, loving is more difficult that being loved and requires greater awareness and acceptance of one's existential situation.

The individual who needs the affirmation of others to feel alive must avoid being alone. True solitude comes too close to the anxiety of existential isolation, and the neurotic individual avoids it at all costs; isolated space is peopled with others; isolated time is extinguished ("killed") with busyness. (Solitary confinement has always been a particularly grim punishment.) Others combat isolation by escaping from the present, solitary moment: they comfort themselves with blissful memories of the past (even though at the time their experiences may have been far from blissful), or they project themselves into the future by enjoying the imagined spoils of as yet unrealized projects.

The recent swell of interest in meditation stems in part from its novelty and from a sense of mastery. It is rare indeed for the individual in the Western world simply to be with himself or herself and to experience, rather than dispatch, time. We have been taught to do several things at once—smoking, chewing, listening, driving, watching television, reading. We value time-saving machines, and we apply these machine values to ourselves. What can we do, however, with the time that we save except to find other ways to kill it?

When one's primary motive in engaging others is to ward off loneliness, then one has transformed the other into equipment. Not infrequently two individuals will each serve each other's primary function and, like socket and prong, fit snugly together. Their relationship may be so mutually functional that it remains stable; yet such an arrangement cannot help but be growth-stunting, since each partner is known, and knows the other, in only a partial manner. These relationships resemble "A-frame" dwellings where the component walls support each other; remove one partner (or strengthen one in psychotherapy), and the other falls.

Ordinarily, however, there is no such mutual fulfillment of needs. At some level one realizes one is being used rather than engaged and searches elsewhere for a more fulfilling partner. A thirty-five-year-old patient of mine, obsessed with the fear of loneliness, was plagued by the vision of "eating alone at sixty-three. She was consumed by the search for a permanent bond. Though she was an attractive, vivacious woman, one man after the other met her and after a short encounter broke off the relationship. They were driven away, I believe, both by the intensity and desperation of her love-need and by an awareness that she had little love to give. An important clue to an understanding of her dynamics was to be found in her other interpersonal relationships. Highly judgmental, she rapidly, and contemptuously, dismissed all those who were not potential mates. When treating a patient who has difficulty establishing an enduring relationship, it is always rewarding for the therapist to inquire deeply about the texture of the patient's other, less intense relationships. Love problems are not situation-specific. Love is not a specific encounter but an attitude. A problem of not-being-loved is more often than not a problem of not loving.

A particularly clear example of relating to others to avoid confronting isolation occurred in the treatment of Charles, the patient with cancer who was introduced into an outpatient psychotherapy group (see chapter 5). Charles began therapy because he wanted to improve his relationships with people. He had always been withdrawn and aloof and had settled comfortably into this distant mode of relating to others. The advent of his cancer and the prognosis of a two-year life expectancy resulted in his feeling of great isolation and catalyzed his efforts to get closer to others. The illustrative incident I shall describe began when one member, Dave, informed the group that because of his job in-service training requirements, he would have to leave town—and the group—for several months. Dave was highly upset by this move, as were all the other members—aside from Charles. The group members shared with Dave their feelings of sorrow, anger, and disappointment. I quote from the group summary (the summaries were mailed to the members after each meeting).[56]

> The floor gradually shifted to Charles by my pointing out that he was responding to Dave only in a problem solving fashion and I wondered what his feelings were. This opened up a truly remarkable episode in the group. For quite some period of time Charles denied having any feelings whatsoever about Dave's leaving the group. We tried to milk feelings out of him without success and wondered whether or not he would want people to miss him if he were leaving. That too didn't get anywhere. I pointed out to him that once he had stated he had a pain in his chest when people left the group and he underplayed that by saying that was only once. I kept pressing and said that once was enough but he smiled and laughed and pushed us all away. After a while then Charles told the group, almost as though it were in passing, that he had learned from his medical check-up that his cancer was doing much better than could possibly have been expected. We then learned that, in fact, his medical check-up had been on that very day. Dave asked him, Why didn't you tell us before? Charles's excuse was that he wanted to wait until Lena came (Lena arrived a few minutes late). I told him that I didn't see why he couldn't have told us and then told Lena again when she came. Then Charles said a really remarkable thing. *Now that he thinks his cancer is getting better, he suddenly finds he doesn't want to meet people any longer and he finds himself withdrawing.*

FUSION

The human being's "universal conflict" is that one strives to be an individual, and yet being an individual requires that one endure a frightening isolation. The most common mode of dealing with this conflict is through denial: one elaborates a delusion of fusion and proclaims in effect, "I am not alone, I am part of others." And so one softens one's ego boundaries and becomes part of another individual or of a group that transcends the individual.

Individuals whose major orientation is toward fusion are generally labeled "dependent." They live, as Arieti puts it, for the "dominant other"[57] (and are likely to suffer extraordinary distress in the event of separation from the dominant other). They submerge their own needs; they seek to find out what the others wish and make those wishes their own. Above all, they wish to avoid offense. They choose safety and merger over individuation. Kaiser's description of such individuals is particularly clear:

> Their behavior seems to suggest: "Do not take me seriously. I do not belong to the category of adults and cannot be counted as such." They

are playful but not like someone who likes to play, but like someone who does not want (or does not dare?) to appear serious and matter of fact. Distressing, and even tragic, events are mentioned laughingly, or in a hurried, nonchalant way, as if it were not worthwhile to waste time on them. There is also a readiness to talk of their own shortcomings with an inclination to exaggerate. Achievements and successes are put in a ridiculous light, or the report of them is followed by a compensatory enumeration of failures. Their talk frequently might appear chopped up by quick transitionless shifts in topic. By taking unusual liberties like blurting out naive questions, or using baby talk they indicate that they want to be put into the category "non-adult" and should not be counted among the grown-up people.[58]

Kaiser describes the clinical behavior of a patient particularly bent on merger with a more powerful figure:

> For eight months G—— had been seeing a man in his late thirties who appeared ready to do whatever he understood was being requested of him. Whenever G—— had wanted to switch the appointment to another day or another hour the patient's answer had invariably been, "Certainly, Doctor, certainly!" He was always on time, but never seemed to mind if G—— were delayed. When, during the hour, the sun came out and shone into the patient's eyes, he never would have dared to draw the drapes and lower the blinds. He sat in silence, painfully blinking and twisting his neck until G—— remarked on it. The patient then would respond as if G—— had asked him to let the blinds down, "Certainly, doctor, certainly!" he would say, jumping up from his chair and unhooking the cord. "This way, Doctor? Is this too much?"[59]

Fusion as an answer to existential isolation provides a construct by which many clinical syndromes may be understood. Consider, for example, transvestism. Ordinarily men with transvestism are understood to be motivated by castration anxiety. There is such threat in being a man, in competing for women with other men, that the man opts out of competition by dressing as a woman—at which point, his castration anxiety, assuaged by self-inflicted castration, is able to achieve genital sexual release. However, Rob, whom I discussed in Chapter 4, illustrates how "fusion" may be a central organizing dynamic. Rob had cross-dressed since he was thirteen first using the clothes of his sister and then those of his mother. Too frightened of males to develop relationships with them and too fearful of rejection to approach females, Rob had always been extraordinarily isolated. His fantasies while cross-dressing were always nonsexual and always variations on a fusion theme: he simply imagined going up to a group of women who would welcome him into their company and consider him one of them. His interpersonal style in a therapy group reflected his desire for merger—docile, obsequious, pleading for attention from the members but especially from the therapists whom he exalted. During the course of the therapy group Rob received an eye-opening education on the possibilities of relationship. He became fully aware—I believe for the first time—of the extent of his isolation. "I'm neither here nor there, neither man nor woman, isolated from everybody," he said one session. For a while his anxiety (and the incidence of cross-dressing) increased markedly. Gradually as he developed social skills and related in meaningful ways at first to the group members, and then to individuals in his life environment, all transvestite desires left him.

There is, of course, a heavy overlap between the concept of escaping existential isolation through fusion and the concept of escaping the terror of death through belief and immersion of oneself in an ultimate rescuer. Not only Rob, but many of the clinical examples of the defense of the ultimate rescuer in chapter 4, are descriptive, too, of fusion. Both concepts describe a mode of escaping anxiety by escaping individuation; in both one looks for solace outside the self. What differentiates the two is the impetus (isolation anxiety or death anxiety) and the ultimate goal (the search for ego boundary dissolution and merger or the search for a powerful intercessor). The distinction is, of course, academic: generally motivations and defensive strategies coexist in the same individual.

Fusion eliminates isolation in a radical fashion—by eliminating self-awareness. Blissful moments of merger are unreflective: the sense of self is lost. The individual cannot even say, "I have lost my sense of self," because there is in fusion no separate "I" to say that. The wonderful thing about romantic love is that the questioning lonely "I" disappears into the "we." "Love," as Kent Bach comments, "is the answer when there is no question."[60] To lose self-consciousness is often comforting. Kierkegaard said: "With every increase in the degree of consciousness, and in proportion to that increase, the intensity of despair increases: the more consciousness, the more intense the despair."[61]

One may also shed one's isolating sense of self by fusing, not with another individual, but with a "thing"—a group, a cause, a country, a project. There is something enormously compelling in merging with a larger group. Kaiser first became aware of this during an ice-skating show when two performers, dressed identically, skated a complicated number in perfect unison. After the applause they nonchalantly and indifferently adjusted their ties and simultaneously looked at their watches. Their post-applause synchronization excited the audience even more, and Kaiser along with them, and he reflected upon the joys of ego boundary softening:

> Uniformity of movement and synchronization of movement, if both come close enough to perfection, attract, thrill and fascinate an audience no matter whether or not the movements performed by a single individual would in themselves be pleasing.
>
> A single well-trained soldier going through the steps and paces, the turns and halts of his drill may please the eyes of the training officer; in the eyes of any outsider he looks ridiculous. If a whole battalion moves over the parade ground, all in step, breaking up the large column into smaller groups, all making the turn at exactly the same moment, turning again and forming one long straight line and maintaining this unbroken front, marching and pivoting around and then, on one short signal, freezes on the spot so that all the arms and legs, the helmets, canteens and rifles are suddenly at rest, all in exactly the same position with not even a single bayonet deviating in direction from all the others, then even an ardent antimilitarist cannot help being gripped by this spectacle. And what grips him is certainly not the beauty of right angles and straight lines, but the image . . . or rather the idea of the many acting as though animated by *one* mind.[62]

To be like everyone else—to conform in dress, speech, customs; to have no thoughts or feelings that are different—saves one from the isolation of selfhood. Of course the "I" is lost but so is the fear of aloneness. The enemies of conformity are, of course, freedom and self-awareness. The conforming-fusion solution to isolation is undermined by the questions: What do *I* want? What do *I* feel? What is *my* goal in life? What do I have in *me* to express and fulfill?

In the age-old struggle between self-expression and safety-in-fusion, it is usually the self that is compromised for the sake of isolation avoidance. The lure of the group is powerful indeed. The Jonestown tragedy demonstrates—to take one of countless examples—the power of the group. Identification with the group offered the members a haven from the fear of isolated existence—a product so valuable that they were willing to sacrifice everything for it: their worldly goods, their family, friends, country, and eventually their lives.

Mysticism, which involves heightened, marvelous moments of oneness with the universe, is also an instance of ego loss. Fusion with another individual, with group or cause, with nature or with the universe always involves a loss of self: it is a pact with Satan and eventuates in existential guilt—that guilt grief which laments the unlived life in each of us.

Sadism. The fusion-seeking individual who is dependent, obsequious, self-sacrificing, who will bear pain, who in fact enjoys pain because it dispells solitude, who, in short, is anything the other wishes in return for the safety of merger, has a curious counterpart. One who seeks to dominate the other, to humiliate the other, to inflict pain, to make oneself the absolute master over the other, seems very different from the dependent fusion seeker. Yet, as Fromm points out, "both tendencies are the outcomes of one basic need, springing from the inability to bear the isolation and weakness of one's own self. . . . The sadistic person needs his object just as much as the masochistic needs his."[63] The difference between the masochist and the sadist is between fuser and fusee. One seeks security by being swallowed by another; the other, by swallowing someone else. In both cases existential isolation is assuaged—either through losing one's separateness and isolation or through enlarging oneself by the incorporation of others. That is why masochism and sadism often oscillate within an individual: they are different solutions to the same problem.

SEX AND ISOLATION

Freud introduced the concept of the "symbol" in psychic organization. In chapter 5 of *The Interpretation of Dreams* he describes various symbols that represent a sexual theme—either the sexual organs or some sexual act.[64] The idea of one thing "standing in" for another could be carried too far, Freud warns: a cigar is not always a symbol for a penis; "Sometimes a cigar is just a cigar." But Freud does not go far enough in his warning. It is possible that sex may be a symbol of something else. If the deepest ultimate concerns of the human being are existential in nature and relate to death, freedom, isolation, and meaninglessness, then it is entirely possible that these fears may be displaced and symbolized by such derivative concerns as sexuality.

Sex may be used in the service of repression of death anxiety. On several occasions I have worked with patients with metastatic cancer who seemed obsessed with sexual concerns. I have met with married couples, one of whom had terminal cancer, who spoke of little else except their sexual maladjustment. At times, in the heat of the discussion, during the recriminations and countercharges, I forgot entirely that one of these individuals was facing imminent death. Such is the success of the defensive maneuver. In chapter 5 I described a young woman with advanced cervical cancer who found that her disease not only did not discourage male suitors but, on the contrary, seemed to increase their numbers and their sexual appetites. Ellen Greenspan described research demonstrating that women with severe breast cancer, in comparison with an age-matched healthy cohort, had a higher incidence of illicit sexual fantasies.[65]

There is something gloriously magic about the lure of sex. It is a powerful bulwark against the awareness and the anxiety of freedom, since, we, when under the spell of sex, have no sense whatsoever that we constitute our world. On the contrary, we are "captured" by a powerful external force. We are driven, enchanted; we "fall for." We can resist the lure, delay it, or give in to it, but we have no sense of "choosing" or "creating" our sexuality: it feels outside of us; it has a force of its own and seems "bigger than life." Sexually compulsive individuals in therapy report, as they get better, a sense of bleakness about their lives. The world is mundanized, and they ask, "Is this all there is?"

Compulsive sexuality is also a common response to a sense of isolation. Promiscuous sexual "coupling" offers a powerful but temporary respite to the lonely individual. It is temporary because it is not relatedness but only a caricature of relationship. Compulsive sex breaks all the rules of true caring. The individual uses the other as equipment. He or she uses, and relates to, only a part of the other. To relate in this mode means that one forms a relationship, and the quicker the better, to have sex—rather than the converse situation of sex both as a manifestation and a facilitation of a deeper relationship. The sexually compulsive individual is the example, *par excellence*, of one who does not relate to the whole being of the other. On the contrary, he relates only to that part which serves to meet his need. Our language well reflects this attitude, as when we speak of "a piece of ass," a "jock," a "stud." The stark language of sex ("laying," "making," "fucking," "screwing," "turning a trick," "scoring") denotes deceit, aggression, manipulation, almost anything in fact but caring and relatedness.

Above all, sexually compulsive individuals do not know their partners. In fact, it is often to their advantage not to know the other and to keep most of themselves hidden; therefore they show and see only those parts that facilitate seduction and the sexual act. One of the hallmarks of sexual deviation is that one individual relates not to another whole person but to some part of another. A fetishist, for example, has a relationship not with a woman (all published cases of fetishists are males) but with some part or some accouterment of a woman—for example, a shoe, a handkerchief, a piece of underclothing. One observer of human relationships went so far as to say, "If we make love to a woman without relating to her spirit we are fetishists, even if in the physical act we use the proper body orifice."[66]

Should, therefore, the thoughtful therapist deplore any sexual encounter that falls short of a true and caring interpersonal encounter? Is there, then, no place for sex as an act of uncommitted adult play? These questions are to a large extent ethical and moral, and the therapist does well to avoid making pronouncements on issues that lie outside of his or her field of expertise. But the therapist does have something of value to say in the case of those who relate sexually to others *only* in a partial, function-oriented manner. An essential part of the definition of sexual deviancy is that behavior is fixed and exclusive—that is, the deviant can relate sexually *only* in a prescribed deviant manner. Not only is rigid, exclusive sexual behavior indicative of deeper pathology, but such behavior cannot help but result in a sense of self-contempt and existential guilt. Kierkegaard drew an arresting sketch of such a situation in "The Diary of a Seducer," wherein the protagonist devotes his entire self to the seduction and abuse of a young girl.[67] Though he is successful in his aims, he pays a heavy price for his spoils: his life becomes empty, his spirit impoverished.

Thus, the sexually compulsive individual neither knows or engages the other. He never concerns himself with the other's growth. Not only does he never have the other fully in sight but he never loses sight of himself in the relationship. He does not exist "between" but always observes himself. Buber termed such an orientation "reflexion" and bemoaned a sexual relation where the partners do not engage in a full authentic dialogue but live in a world of monologue, a world of mirrors and mirroring. Buber's description of "erotic man" is particularly picturesque:

> Many years I have wandered through the land of men, and have not yet reached an end of studying the varieties of the "erotic man." There a lover stamps around and is in love only with his passion. There one is wearing his differentiated feelings like medal-ribbons. There one is enjoying the adventures of his own fascinating effect. There one is gazing enraptured at the spectacle of his own supposed surrender. There one is collecting excitement. There one is displaying his "power." There one is preening himself with borrowed vitality. There one is delighting to exist simultaneously as himself and as an idol very unlike himself. There one is warming himself at the blaze of what has fallen to his lot. There one is experimenting. And so on and on—all the manifold monologists with their mirrors, in the apartment of the most intimate dialogue![68]

Thus, one is in love with passion, one collects excitement and trophies, one warms oneself "at the blaze at what has fallen to his lot"—but what one does not do is to relate authentically to oneself or to another.

Many of these themes are illustrated in the dreams of Bruce, a sexually compulsive patient I described in chapters 5 and 6. Toward the end of therapy, as he was emerging from a sexually driven mode of relating, Bruce began to turn his attention to the problems, "If I do not attempt to screw women, what *do* I do with them?" "And what do I do with men?" "What are people for anyway?" That last question, "What are people for anyway?" emerges, in one form or another, in the treatment of all patients who begin to change their modes of relating from I-It to I-Thou. Three dreams heralded this stage in Bruce's therapy.

The first:

> I was lying in bed with my fourteen year old son. We were fully dressed but I was trying to have sex with him but I could not find his vagina. I woke up sad and frustrated.

This dream graphically depicts Bruce's dilemma about relationships. "Is there any other way than genitally" the dream seems to say, "that you can relate to someone, even to someone you care for very much?"

The second:

> I was playing tennis with a woman but every ball I hit came back to me rather than to her. It was as though there were an invisible glass backboard instead of a net separating the two of us.

The imagery is clear: Bruce was presumably engaging someone else in tennis but in fact was relating only to himself. The other person was extraneous in the game; and, furthermore, even though he tried to reach her, he could not.

The third:

> I wanted to be close to Paul [an acquaintance] but I kept bragging about how much money I had and he got angry. Then I tried to put my cheek next to his but our beards were so rough that we hurt one another.

Bruce had companions in activity—basketball, tennis, and bowling chums—but had never had a close male friend. He was dimly aware of his yearning for closeness but, as the dream illustrates, could find no way to relate to men except in a competitive fashion.

OTHER FORMS OF MISCARRIED RELATIONSHIP

We try to escape the pain of existential isolation in a variety of ways: we soften ego boundaries and attempt to fuse with another; we attempt to incorporate another; we take something from the other that makes us feel larger, more powerful, or cherished. The common interpersonal

385

theme in these attempts and in a number of others, which I shall now discuss, is that the individual is not with the other person. Instead, the individual uses the other person as equipment to serve a function, and a mutually enriching relationship never occurs; instead, there is some form of misalliance, a relational miscarriage which can only stifle growth and evoke existential guilt. As the sheer variety of unauthentic modes of relationship defies any exhaustive classificatory scheme, I shall describe a few common modes observed in clinical work.

The Other as Elevator. Barry was a thirty-five-year-old engineer with the "engineer syndrome": he was stiff, cold, and isolated. He displayed no emotion whatsoever and was generally aware of emotion only after he took note of a physiological cue (knot in stomach, tears, clenched fist, and so forth). His major goal in therapy was to "get in touch with" his feelings and to be able to establish a love relationship with another. A physically attractive man, he had little problem attracting the attention of women but was not able to develop a relationship further. Either he found a woman undesirable and dismissed her, or he found her desirable but was too anxious to pursue her.

Finally, after many hard months of therapy, Barry began dating and then living with Jamelia, a young woman whom he found very attractive. It immediately became apparent, however, that he invested little of himself in the relationship. He discussed in therapy his new problem of going to bed very early. Did it mean, he wondered (and this type of isolation from his feelings was highly characteristic), that he was already bored with Jamelia, or did it mean that he felt so comfortable with her that he allowed himself to relax with her? "How can you find out?" I asked. "What happens when you ask yourself whether you love Jamelia?" Barry responded, with unusual conviction for him, that he cared for Jamelia very much.

Still, he decided it was best to hold himself back so as not to arouse her hopes unduly. He explained that the relationship would never evolve into a long-term one because Jamelia did not quite match up to what he had been looking for in a woman. The main reason was that her social skills were not highly enough developed: she was not sufficiently articulate; she was too inhibited and too socially introverted. He knew that he did not speak well and wanted very much to marry a woman with greater verbal dexterity: since he learned well by imitating, he had hoped to improve as a result of contact with such a woman. He also expected a woman to provide him with a less restricted social life. Furthermore, he worried that if the two of them spent too much time alone and became very loving, then he would give all his caring to her and would never have any to give to others.

Barry's statements illustrate many of the most common problems that preclude the development of an authentic, loving relationship. The most basic one is that the *raison d'être* of Barry's mode of relating was to serve a function. Barry began from a position of extreme need and searched for someone to minister to this need. His need was for "elevation," and he searched for a "partner" who would be elevator: teacher, therapist, and purveyor of social life.

Barry often talked despairingly of his long fruitless search for a relationship. I felt that his use of the word "search" provided a key to understanding his problem. One, after all, does not *find* a relationship; one *forms* a relationship. Barry approached Jamelia in an inorganic rather than organic fashion. Not only did he view her as an "it," an object, as equipment to provide a particular product, but he viewed the relationship as static and inorganic—an entity that was "there" almost fully formed from the beginning—rather than as a developing process.

Another patient voiced the same theme when he said that the closer he got to another person, the more unattractive that person became—both physically and emotionally. As he physically approached a woman, he could see her faint skin blemishes, her varicosities, and the bags under her eyes. As he got to know her well, he became increasingly bored by her diminishing stock of anecdotes and facts. In such an inorganic approach to relationship, one views the other as an object with certain fixed properties and depletable resources. What one does not consider is that, as Buber reminds us, in a genuine organic relationship there is reciprocity: there is no unchanging I observing (and measuring) the other; the I in the encounter is altered, and the other, the Thou, is altered as well. Barry viewed love as an exhaustible commodity: the more he offered to one person, the less he would have for others. But, as Fromm has taught us, this marketing approach to love makes no sense: engaging others always leaves one richer not poorer.

Barry had always experienced intense anxiety at the prospect of approaching women whom he felt matched his standards. Often he ruminated for hours on the proper approach. He would start to call a woman; hand on the phone, number half-dialed, he would flush with anxiety and hang up the reciever. Other therapists had unsuccessfully attempted to afford Barry anxiety relief through behavioral approaches. In psychotherapy no progress occurred when we approached the problem from the obvious vantage point—that is, that Barry feared competition from other men and rejection from obviously attractive women; there was, however, considerable progress when we explored the ways that Barry used, or wished to use, the other. At a deep level Barry knew that he was not encountering but violating the other: he did not want her but wanted something from her. His anxiety was guilt because of the anticipated transgression against another and fear that the other would discover his motives.

How Many People Are in the Room?   In a mature, caring relationship one relates with one's whole being to the other. If one holds back part of oneself in order to observe the relationship or the impact one has upon the other, then, to that extent, one has failed to relate. Buber describes the situation that develops when two individuals who retain full self-consciousness try to relate.

> Let us now imagine two men, whose life is dominated by appearance, sitting and talking together. Call them Peter and Paul. Let us list the different configurations which are involved. First, there is Peter as he wishes to appear to Paul, and Paul as he wishes to appear to Peter. Then there is Peter as he really appears to Paul—that is, Paul's image of Peter, which in general does not in the least coincide with what Peter wishes Paul to see; and similarly there is the reverse situation. Further, there is Peter as he appears to himself, and Paul as he appears to himself. Lastly, there are the bodily Peter and the bodily Paul. Two living beings and six ghostly appearances, which mingle in many ways in the conversation between the two. Where is there room for any genuine interhuman life?[69]

One may fail to relate by relating only partly to the other and partly to some fantasized other person(s). In assessing the nature of my relationship with a patient, I find it helpful to inquire of myself, "How many people are in the room?" Am I, for example, thinking not only of the patient but also of how clever I will sound when I present this patient at a conference, or of the interesting "clinical material" which I can use to communicate more effectively with my readers? I pose the same questions to my patient. Is the patient really relating to me or to some ghostly figures from the past?

As the patient describes to me his important relationships, I wonder, "How many people are in each relationship? Are there only two people involved? Or three? Or a whole auditorium filled with people?"

Camus was a master of portraying, in his novels, characters who could not love but who feigned love for some ulterior purpose. In his first novel, *A Happy Death* (unpublished during his lifetime), Camus's protagonist says:

> He saw that what had attached him to Marthe was vanity not love. . . . What he had loved in Marthe were those evenings when they would walk into the movie theater and men's eyes turned towards her, that moment when he offered her to the world. What he had loved in her was his power and his ambition to live.[70]

"That moment when he offered her to the world." That captures it precisely. There were never two people in the relationship. He related not
to Marthe but to others through Marthe.

Similarly, Ken, a patient of mine who had deep-seated problems in
relating authentically to women, dreamed profusely but never had a
dream with only two people in it. An illustrative "tag-along" dream in
the middle of our work:

> I was with a woman in my old bedroom in San Francisco at 2:30 in the
> morning. My brother and father were watching through the window. I
> wasn't too interested in the woman or the lovemaking. I kept my father
> and brother waiting for an hour and let them in at 3:30.

Important associations to the dream included his attempts to identify
the woman. He realized that he was quite uninterested in her. She resembled a young cheerleader he had seen that day at a football game—
the kind of girl he never had the nerve to approach when he was in
college. She also resembled a girl, Christine, he had dated in high
school. He and a friend had both dated the same girl for several
months—a situation that he found both uncomfortable and exhilarat-
ing. Finally, he and his friend joined forces and pressured Christine
into choosing one of them as her steady boyfriend. Christine chose
Ken, much to his delight. However, within only a few weeks the
bloom had faded, Ken lost interest in Christine (he was never interested in *her* in the first place; he was interested only in her function in his
competition with his friend) and ended their relationship.

Ken had always viewed his father and brother as competitors—first
for his mother and then for other women. In the dream, his being with
a woman and keeping his father and brother waiting outside enviously
for an hour (until 3:30 which, incidentally, was the time of our regular
therapy hour) was a way of besting them through a woman. Ken could
not be "with" men either. He related to me, to his brother and father,
to all male friends, in a highly competitive fashion; when he was with
me, for example, he was so convinced that I wanted to subjugate him
that for months he withheld any important material he felt would give
me an "edge" over him. His only male friends were talented but did
not evoke competition since their talent lay in some entirely different
field (music, art, or athletics).

On the night following the analysis of this dream Ken had a series of
short dreams, all illuminating some aspect of the work to be done in relationships. In the first dream he went to a ski lodge and met several of

his male friends who greeted him warmly; then he found himself sitting next to them in a room where he was waiting to take his final real estate examinations (Ken was a realtor.) After a long wait the exams were passed out, but immediately the instructor (his therapist) announced the exam was canceled: they had come to the wrong place on the wrong day. This dream underscored Ken's fusion of friendship and competition; the work ahead, in therapy, would entail disentangling the two.

The second dream fragment was that Ken saw himself on a jumbo jetliner (he often, as do many dreamers, symbolized therapy as a journey on some vehicle). He strolled along in the aisle on the plane and was astounded to discover several hidden compartments, all of which were full of people. Although he saw them for the first time, he somehow knew that these people had been there all along. Obviously this dream represented another crucial task in therapy: the discovery of the others in the world.

His last dream that night was but a fragment: simply an image of a large toucan bird. Ken had no associations whatsoever to this bird, but my association to toucan was "two can"—a representation of the work in pairing that lay before Ken.

This "bad faith" mode of relating to others is so common that examples abound in everyday life and everyday therapy. For example, the woman who purposefully takes a new boyfriend to a gathering where she knows her old boyfriend will be is obviously not "with" her new friend. Karl, another patient, was with a new girlfriend when he received an angry, demanding phone call from his previous one. In a derisive manner he held the phone away from his ear pointing it to his new friend so that she, too, could hear. Each of an individual's relationships reflects the others: it is rare, I believe, for one to be able to relate in bad faith to some individuals and in an authentic, caring way to a select few. Karl's new friend was deeply troubled at his treatment of a previous friend. She suspected (and rightly so) that the telephone episode was an ominous portent of her future relationship with him.

Being with the other for the sake of another is particularly transparent in group therapy—a mode of therapy ideally suited to uncover and work through bad faith in interpersonal relationships. A graphic example unfolded over several weeks in one of my therapy groups. Ron, a forty-year-old married patient, systematically made extra-group contacts with every one of the members even though he and the rest of the members realized that such socializing often impeded therapy. Ron invited some members to go sailing, others to go skiing, and others to dinner and became intensely romantically involved with one, Irene. Extra-group socializing is usually destructive in group therapy only when it is surrounded by a conspiracy of silence. In this group, therapy ground to a halt because Ron refused to discuss his extra-group contacts, especially those with Irene; he saw nothing "wrong" with them and steadfastly refused to examine the meaning of his behavior.

In one session the group discussed his inviting my female co-therapist for a skiing weekend. Enormous pressure was placed on him to examine his behavior, and he left the session confused and shaken. On his way home Ron suddenly remembered that in his childhood his favorite story had been *Robin Hood*. Following an impulse, he drove to the children's section of the nearest public library and reread the story. Only then did the meaning of his behavior make sense. What he loved about the Robin Hood legend was the rescuing of individuals, especially women, from tyrants. That motif had played a powerful role in his life, beginning with oedipal struggles in his family. He had started a successful business by first working for someone else and then setting up a competitive firm and enticing his ex-boss's employees to work for him. So, too, with his wife whom he had married not so much because of love for her but to rescue her from a tyrannical father.

Similarly, the pattern unfolded in the group. He was strongly motivated to wrench the other members, even the co-therapist, from my grasp. The other members gradually expressed their deep dismay at having been mere pawns in Ron's struggle with me. When his predominant, inauthentic mode of relationship was laid bare and fully understood, Ron began to confront the question of "What else are people for?" He spent several months working on his relationship with each of the members, save Irene. He clung tightly to her; and even when it was clear that he had made all the progress possible for him in that group he resisted termination because, at an unconscious level, he wanted to be present so as to protect her from me. He eventually terminated, and a few months later Irene did as well. At that point, without the tyrant in the picture, Ron's love waned quickly, and he ended the relationship.

A full caring relationship is a relationship to another, not to any extraneous figure from the past or the present. Transference, parataxic distortions, ulterior motives and goals— all must be swept away before an authentic relation with another can prevail.

CHAPTER 9

Existential Isolation
and Psychotherapy

E XISTENTIAL ISOLATION has several major implications for psychotherapists. It provides them with a frame of reference that explains many complex, puzzling phenomena—explanations that therapists, through clarifying and interpretive comments, attempt to convey to their patients. The concept of existential isolation also provides the rationale for an important therapeutic maneuver—isolation confrontation. Finally, a consideration of existential isolation sheds considerable light upon that enormously important and complex phenomenon—the therapist-patient relationship.

A Guide to Understanding Interpersonal Relationships

Individuals who are terrified of isolation generally attempt to assuage that terror through an interpersonal mode: they need the presence of others to affirm their existence; they long to be swallowed by others greater than they, or they seek to alleviate their sense of lonely help-lessness by swallowing others; they attempt to elevate themselves through others; they search for multiple sexual bondings—a caricature of authentic relating. In short, the individual who is flooded with isolation anxiety reaches out desperately for help through a relationship. The individual reaches out, not because he or she wants to but because he or she has to; and the ensuing relationship is based on survival not on growth. The tragic irony is that those who so desperately need the comfort and pleasure of an authentic relationship are the very ones least able to form such a relationship.

One of the therapist's first tasks is to help the patient identify and apprehend what he or she does with others. The characteristics of a need-free relationship provide the therapist with an ideal or a horizon against which the patient's interpersonal pathology is starkly silhou-etted. Does, for example, the patient relate exclusively to those who can provide something for him? Is his love focused on receiving rather than giving? Does he attempt to know, in the fullest sense, the other person? How much of himself is held back? Does he genuinely listen to the other person? Does he use the other to relate to yet another—that is, how many people are in the room? Does he care about the growth of the other?

The group therapy situation offers a particularly rich arena for these patterns of distorted relationship to manifest themselves, as in the fol-lowing clinical cameo:

Eve had been attending a therapy group for six months and had gradually created (as patients always do) the same type of interpersonal pattern *in* the group that she inhabited ouside it. She was a marginal figure, passive, easily forgettable. No one took her seriously; she did not apparently take herself seriously and seemed content with being the group mascot. Over the Christmas holiday when the group was un-usually small since some members had gone out of town, Eve began the session by describing her discomfort at such a small group. She was not sure, she said, she was up to an "intense session." She continued to dis-cuss in a characteristically detached manner her feelings about a small group. Finally another woman member said she could not bear to listen to Eve any more. No one in the group felt that Eve was talking to them; Eve always spoke to an empty space in the group as though there was no one else present in the room. The members then commented that Eve engaged no one in the group, that no one really knew her, that she remained hidden from view; and that consequently none of the others allowed her to matter to them.

I asked Eve if she could try to engage any of the members. She compliantly went around the group and discussed, in a platitudinous manner, her feelings toward each person. "How would you rank," I asked, "your comments to each member on a one-to-ten risk-taking scale?" "Very low," she ventured, "about two to three." "What would happen," I said, "if you were to move up a rung or two?" She replied that she would tell the group that she was an alcoholic! This was, indeed, a relevation—she had told no one before. I then tried to help her open herself even more by asking her to talk about how she felt coming to the group for so many months and not being able to tell us that.* Eve responded by talking about how lonely she felt in the group, how cut off she was from every person in the room. But she was flushed with shame about her drinking. She could not, she insisted, be "with" others or make herself known to others because of her drinking.

I turned Eve's formula around (here the real therapeutic work began): *she did not hide herself because she drank, but she drank because she hid herself!* She drank because she was so unengaged with the world. Eve then talked about coming home, feeling lost and alone, and at that point doing one of two things: either slumping into a reverie where she imagined herself very young and being cared for by the big people, or assuaging the pain of her lostness and loneliness with alcohol. Gradually Eve began to understand that she was relating to others for a specific function—to be protected and taken care of—and that, in the service of this function, she was relating only partially. She saw only part of another individual and chose to disclose only those parts of herself that she felt would not drive away a protector.

After obtaining a clear view of how others viewed her behavior, Eve also was able to learn how her behavior made others feel. (This feature is one of the real strengths of the group therapy approach: though it is possible for the individual therapist to supply this information to a patient, the great diversity of feedback from a larger group is far more informative and powerful.) She discovered that her neediness did not elicit the caring she sought; quite the contrary, her reluctance to engage others with her whole self resulted in her not mattering to them. Eve failed to get what she wanted because she needed it too much.

There is, as this vignette illustrates, considerable therapeutic poten-

---

*As a general principle of therapy technique, it is always preferable to approach disclosure of a big secret by helping the patient to reveal more about the disclosure ("horizontal" or "meta"-disclosure) rather than asking for more of the specific details ("vertical" disclosure) of the secret. Thus, the patient may be enabled to make himself fully known to the others in the immediate moment.

tial in the understanding of current relationships—of which the therapist-patient relationship is the most accessible for study and is, in ways I shall discuss shortly, enormously effective in therapy. The patient's relationships with others should, however, always be investigated. Relationships among patients in treatment (therapy group, inpatient halfway house, day hospital, and so on) rarely develop into long-lasting, rewarding friendships outside of therapy. Nonetheless, through such relationships patients will display interpersonal pathology. In ways I have already described, therapists may use this first-hand data as a guide to understanding the specific form of their patients' misaligned relationships and to help patients to recognize the nature of their interpersonal behavior, its impact upon others, and their responsibility for their own isolation. In-treatment relationships also provide a "dress rehearsal" for a patient's future relationships in the "real world"—a low-risk venture in which he or she can test out new modes of relating.

Thus far I have described the *uses* of in-therapy relationships. But they are more than a forum for pathology display or a dress rehearsal: they are also real relationships with real people, which contain something in and for themselves that is meaningful and healing. Some patients enter a psychiatric ward and initiate little contact with others. They speak when spoken to; they stay in their rooms whenever possible; they occupy themselves with thinking, "sorting things out" in their minds, rug crocheting, reading, and so on.

Patients proffer many reasons for such withdrawal (such as depression, fear of rejection, or "nothing in common" with others), but one common reason is the feeling that there is no point in investing energy into something that will perforce be evanescent. A patient says that a relationship with another patient cannot last, that they travel in different "circles" (forgetting the "circles" they share—the terrestrial orbit, the life cycle)—why, then, get involved? Others point out that they cannot bear losses, and they prefer to cultivate only those relationships that have the potential to become long-term friendships.

These arguments have persuasive features. After all, one of the problems of modern life is its impermanence, its lack of stable institutions and social networks. Indeed, what point is there in cultivating yet another impermanent, "vacation cruise" relationship?

A clinical case provides us some insight into this issue. Anna, a borderline patient who had been hospitalized following a suicide gesture, was an exceptionally isolated, embittered young woman. One fundamental question she pondered continuously was "What are people for?" She avoided engagement with others in group meetings because she said that she refused to indulge in the phoniness surrounding superficial relationships. Whenever she reached out to another, or expressed any kind of sentiment, her inner voice soon reminded her of the fact that she was being a phony and that, verily, nothing she said was a true feeling. Anna felt lonely and frightened. She was always the outsider walking down the cold, dark street observing and coveting the warm lights and cozy gatherings in other people's homes. In her small group sessions I consistently urged her to attempt to engage others. "Stop analyzing, stop reflecting upon yourself," she was advised. "Just try to extend yourself to others in the group. Try to enter their experiential world. Try to open yourself up as much as possible and don't ask why." During a particularly intense group meeting Anna became deeply involved with several members, indeed weeping with and for one of them. Toward the end of this meeting Anna was asked to describe what her experience had been like over the past hour. (Effective use of the here-and-now in therapy always entails two processes: sheer experiencing and the subsequent examination of that experience.) Anna noted that she had been alive for an hour, swept along in life, involved with others and unaware of herself and of her sense of desolation. For an hour she had been inside life rather than outside staring at it through a chilly windowpane.

Anna's experience during the group supplied an answer to her question "What are people for?" She could, for a short time, appreciate that relationships enrich one's inner world. Though she would shortly, I was certain, try to take away the experience by labeling it phony, she had nonetheless experienced how a relationship can bridge the gulf of isolation. One is altered through an encounter with another, even a brief encounter. One internalizes the encounter; it becomes an internal reference point, an omnipresent reminder of both the possibility and the reward of a true encounter.

A striking example of the lasting impact of a brief encounter is provided by Bertrand Russell who in 1913 met Joseph Conrad:

> At our very first meeting, we talked with continually increasing intimacy. We seemed to sink through layer after layer of what was superficial, till gradually both reached the central fire. It was an experience unlike any other that I have known. We looked into each other's eyes, half appalled and half intoxicated to find ourselves together in such a region. The emotion was as intense as passionate love, and at the same time all-embracing, I came away bewildered, and hardly able to find my way among ordinary affairs.[1]

Though Russell spent but a few hours with Conrad, he reports that he was never the same again, that something of the moment of their touching remained always with him and played an instrumental role in shaping his attitudes toward war, minor misfortunes, and his subsequent human relations.[2]

It is possible to err in the opposite direction—to avoid enduring intimate relationships by involving oneself only in brief encounters; and the therapist must be attuned to this possibility. But one must also bear in mind that no relationship offers a guarantee of permanency. Because a relationship may have no future reality, why strip it of its current reality? Indeed, individuals who elect to relate only to a select few are most likely those who have the most difficulty engaging others. Their dread of isolation will be so great that, as I have described, they sabotage the possibility of relationship. Those, on the other hand, who are likely to extend themselves continuously and in authentic fashion to others will, through the peopling of their inner world, experience a tempering of their existential anxiety and be able to reach out to others in love rather than to grasp at them in need.

Confronting the Patient with Isolation

Another important step in treatment consists of helping the patient to address existential isolation directly, to explore it, to plunge into his or her feelings of lostness and loneliness. One of the fundamental facts that patients must discover in therapy is that, though interpersonal encounter may temper existential isolation, it cannot eliminate it. Patients who grow in psychotherapy learn not only the rewards of intimacy but also its limits: they learn what they *cannot* get from others. Some years ago in a project I described in chapter 6, my colleagues and I studied a number of successful psychotherapy patients and attempted to determine which aspects of their therapy experience had been most helpful to them. Of sixty items administered for a rank ordering (Q-sort) procedure, the one bearing on the limitations of intimacy ("Recognizing that no matter how close I get to other people, *I must still face life alone*") was highly ranked by many patients and over all ranked twenty-third of the sixty items.[3]

There is, of course, no "solution" to isolation. It is part of existence, and we must face it and find a way to take it into ourselves. Communion with others is our major available resource to temper the dread of isolation. We are all lonely ships on a dark sea. We see the lights of other ships—ships that we cannot reach but whose presence and similar situation affords us much solace. We are aware of our utter loneliness and helplessness. But if we can break out of our windowless monad, we become aware of the others who face the same lonely dread. Our sense of isolation gives way to a compassion for the others, and we are no longer quite so frightened. An invisible bond unites individuals who participate in the same experience—whether it be a life experience shared in time or place (for example, attending the same school) or simply as a member of an audience at some event.

But compassion and its twin, empathy, require a certain degree of equilibrium; they cannot be constructed on panic. One must begin to confront and tolerate isolation to be able to use the available resources to cope more fully with one's existential situation. God offers relief from isolation for many; but, as Alfred North Whitehead asserted, isolation is a condition of true spiritual belief: "Religion is what the individual does with his own solitariness . . . and if you are never solitary, you are never religious."[4] Part of the therapist's task consists of helping the patient confront isolation—an enterprise that first generates anxiety but ultimately catalyzes personal growth. In *The Art of Loving*, Fromm wrote that "the ability to be alone is the condition for the ability to love," and, in those days in the United States, before the 1960s and transcendental meditation, suggested modes of solitary concentration upon consciousness.[5]

Clark Moustakas, in his essay on loneliness, made the same point:

> The individual in being lonely, if let be, will realize himself in loneliness and create a bond or sense of fundamental relatedness with others. Loneliness rather than separating the individual or causing a break or division of self, expands the individual's wholeness, perceptiveness, sensitivity and humanity.[6]

Many others corroborate that isolation must be experienced before it can be transcended. Camus, for example: "When a man has learned—and not on paper—how to remain alone with his suffering, how to overcome his longing to flee, then he has little left to learn."[7] Similarly, Robert Hobson: "To be a human being means to be lonely. To go on becoming a person means exploring new modes of resting in our loneliness."[8]

I like the phrase "exploring new modes of resting in our loneliness." It is an arresting description of the task of the therapist. Yet the phrase contains the germ of the clinical problem: rather than "rest," the psychotherapy patient writhes in loneliness. The problem seems to be that the rich get richer and the poor get poorer. Those who can confront and explore their isolation can learn to relate in a mature loving fashion to others; yet only those who can already relate to others and have attained some modicum of mature growth are able to tolerate isolation. Robert Bollendorf, for example, demonstrated that the higher an individual's level of self-actualization (measured by the Personal Orientation Inventory) the less isolation anxiety (measured by the Anxiety Scale of the IGPE inventory) that individual experienced when placed in sixteen-hour solitary confinement.[9]

Otto Will, from the perspective of his long experience treating disturbed adolescents and young adults, observed that individuals from loving, reciprocally respectful families, are able, with relative ease, to grow away from their families and to tolerate the separation and the loneliness of young adulthood. What happens to those who grow up in tormented, highly conflicted families? One might expect that they would kick up their heels with joy at the prospect of dancing away from such a family. But the opposite occurs: the more disturbed the family, the harder it is for progeny to leave: they are ill equipped to separate, and cling to the family for shelter against isolation anxiety.[10]

The therapist must find a way to help a patient confront isolation in a dosage and with a support system suited to that patient. Some therapists, at an advanced stage of therapy (once other sources of anxiety are worked through and the therapeutic relationship has become positve and robust), advise or prescribe periods of self-enforced isolation during the course of therapy. There are two possible benefits of such isolation. First, important material may be generated. Recall Bruce, the patient in chapter 5, who, as a result of a few hours isolation, became aware of his terror of loneliness and death which he had all his life avoided through workaholism and compulsive sexuality. Secondly, the patient discovers hidden resources and courage. Linda Sherby describes a patient whose symptoms were frenzied activity and an unsatisfying, dependent posture toward would-be relationships.[11] In an effort to break through an impasse, the therapist suggested to the patient that she spend twenty-four hours alone in a motel cut off from all distractions (people, television, books, and so on), except for writing a diary of her thoughts and feelings. The major outcome, and it was of considerable import for this patient, was that she learned she could tolerate isolation without panic. The patient's notes are explicit in this regard: "I'm still amazed at how together my head must be—perhaps it's too soon for me to decompensate, but it's been nine hours so far, and I don't think I'm going to crash." Toward the end of the twenty-four hours she wrote to her therapist: "It is obvious I am not going to go berserk, and I expect you knew that all along. The sadness is becoming a part of me, and I doubt that it will be so easy to run from it again!"

Several years ago my colleagues and I performed an experiment that adventitiously demonstrated the degree to which personal growth is catalyzed by isolation.[12] In an effort to test the impact of affect arousal (in a weekend encounter group) upon long-term individual therapy, we sponsored weekend group experiences at a country inn for three groups of patients: two experimental affect-arousing gestalt groups and one control Zen meditation group. We attempted to measure the impact of the gestalt group experience on the subjects and assumed that the non-affect arousal meditation group would serve as a relatively stable control condition. The results indicated otherwise. There were unplanned "nonspecific" variables that vastly influenced the outcome. One of the important nonspecific variables was the experience of isolation. Many individuals in both the experimental and the control groups reported that a significant facet of their experience was that they were removed from their familiar surroundings and encountered isolation. Indeed, several of the women subjects said that the weekend was the first time in years (in one instance, twenty years) that they had been separated from their families and had spent a night alone without their husbands in bed beside them and their children sleeping nearby. The impact of the confrontation with isolation was so strong that for some it dwarfed the significance of the affect arousal, the variable under scrutiny.

The practice of meditation offers another avenue to isolation awareness. Though meditation therapists and teachers do not often conceptualize the benefit of meditation precisely in this manner, I believe that one of the primary growth-inducing factors in meditation is that it permits individuals in an anxiety-reduced state (that is, anxiety-relieving muscular relaxation, posture, breathing, mind cleansing) to face and to transcend the anxiety they associated with isolation.

Individuals learn to face what they fear the most. They are asked to plunge into isolation—and, even more important, to plunge nakedly, without customary shields of denial. They are asked to "let go" (rather than to achieve and acquire), to empty their minds (rather than to categorize and analyze experience), and to respond to and harmonize with the world (rather than to control and subdue it). Certainly one of the explicit goals of the meditational state, one of the states one must achieve on the path to enlightenment (satori), is awareness that physical reality is in fact a veil obscuring reality, and that only by reaching deep into one's isolation is one able to remove that veil. But recognition of the illusionary nature of reality or, as I described in chapter 6, awareness of one's constitutive function, invariably plunges one into a confrontation with existential isolation, into an awareness that not only is one isolated from others but, at the most fundamental level, isolated from world as well.

Isolation and the Patient-Therapist Encounter

IT IS THE RELATIONSHIP THAT HEALS

I remember two maxims of psychotherapy that I learned in the very beginning of my training. I discussed the first—"the goal of psychotherapy is to bring the patient to the point where he can make a free choice"—in the section on freedom. The second—"it is the relationship that heals"—is the single most important lesson the psychotherapist must learn. There is no more self-evident truth in psychotherapy; every therapist observes over and over in clinical work that the encounter itself is healing for the patient in a way that transcends the therapist's theoretical orientation.

If any single fact has been established by psychotherapy research, it is that a positive relationship between patient and therapist is positively related to therapy outcome. Effective therapists respond to their patients in a genuine manner; they establish a relationship that a patient perceives as safe and accepting; they display a nonpossessive warmth and a high degree of accurate empathy and are able to "be with" or "grasp the meaning" of a patient. Several reviews that summarize hundreds of research studies concur in this conclusion.[*][13]

In the first chapter I likened psychotherapy to an experience I had in

---

* Elsewhere in this book I have cited empirical research, but generally in a highly selective manner and with much caution. Either the research was scanty, poorly conceived or executed, or of doubtful relevance to the existential concern under discussion. In respect to the therapist-patient relationship, I shall also not fully cite the research literature—but for an entirely different reason: the overwhelming amount of high-quality research documenting the crucial importance of this relationship.

a cooking class: what seems to make the vital difference in both Armenian eggplant dishes and in psychotherapy are the "throw-ins," the "off the record" contributions. It is in the realm of the therapist-patient relationship that these "throw-ins" most frequently occur. During the course of effective psychotherapy the therapist frequently reaches out to the patient in a human and deeply personal manner. Though this reaching out is often a critical event in therapy, it resides outside official ideological doctrine; it is generally not reported in psychiatric literature (usually because of shame or fear of censure) nor is it taught to students (both because it lies outside of formal theory and because it might encourage "excesses").

An excellent illustration of the importance of the patient-therapist encounter is to be found in a book called *Critical Incidents in Psychotherapy* (1959), which described a number of incidents that therapists regarded as constituting turning points in therapy.[14] A substantial majority of these critical incidents consist of a therapist's stepping outside of his or her professional role and engaging a patient in a deeply human fashion. A few examples:

1. At this point Tom [the patient] looked me in the eye and very clearly and slowly said, "If you give me up, then there is no hope for me." At this moment I was overwhelmed with a complex and powerful set of emotions composed of sorrow, hatred, pity, and inadequacy. This sentence of Tom's became a "critical incident" for me. I was at that moment closer to him than I had ever been to any person on earth.[15]

2. A therapist saw an acutely ill patient for an emergency session Saturday afternoon and though the therapist was hungry and tired continued the session for several hours.[16]

3. A therapist met with a patient who during the course of therapy developed signs suggesting cancer. While she was awaiting the results of medical laboratory tests (which subsequently proved negative) he held her in his arms like a child while she sobbed and in her terror experienced a brief psychotic state.[17]

4. A male therapist working with a young female patient who had such a powerful positive eroticized transference to him that therapeutic work was not possible disclosed to her some aspects of his personal life which permitted the patient to sort out real from distorted perceptions of him.[18]

5. For several sessions a patient had been abusing a therapist by attacking him personally and by questioning his professional skills. Finally the therapist exploded: "I began pounding the desk with my fist and shouted, Dammit—look, why don't you just quit the verbal diarrhea and let's get down to the business of trying to understand yourself, and stop beating on me? Whatever faults I have, and I do have a lot of them, have nothing to do with your problems. I'm a human being too, and today has been a bad day. . . . "[19]

6. A patient had been abandoned in a desolate house perched on a cliff accessible only by a rickety wooden bridge. In extremis, she called her therapist who came to the house, crossed the bridge, consoled her and drove her to her home.[20]

The other critical incidents are similar: in each the thrust is clearly toward a human encounter and away from artificial or ideologically prescribed "handling" of the patient.

Corroborating illustrations of this phenomenon abound in the literature. In chapter 2 I discussed how, in 1895 in *Studies in Hysteria*, Freud and Breuer overlooked considerable material relating to death.[21] It is striking, too, that in his assessment of therapeutic mechanisms Freud may have overlooked the importance of the patient-therapist encounter. He attributed therapeutic change entirely to hypnotic suggestion and to interpretive work which makes possible "abreaction" and release of "strangulated affect." Yet note the nature of Freud's therapeutic involvement which he described in his case histories. He regularly gave some of his patients a massage and in one passage expressed his annoyance that the patient's menstrual period might make the massage impossible that day. On other occasions he "swings boldly" (to use Buber's term)[22] into the life of the patient by speaking to family members and by clarifying the patient's financial and marital prospects. At other times Freud was authoritarian and harsh. In one memorable encounter he adamantly told a patient that he would give her twenty-four hours to change her beliefs (about the nonpsychological causes of a symptom) or she would have to leave the hospital.[23]

Several years ago I established a contract (for reasons not germane to this discussion) with a patient which stipulated that we both would write impressionistic summaries after each individual therapy hour, deliver them sealed to my secretary, and every few months read each other's notes. (Later we published these notes in the book *Every Day Gets a Little Closer: A Twice-Told Therapy*[24]) What impressed me very much was the discrepancy between my perceptions of an hour and those of the patient. The patient and I attended to, and valued, very different aspects of the therapy experience. What of my precious and elegant interpretations? Alas, she never even heard them! What she cherished were the small personal touches—a warm look, a compliment about the way she looked, my unswerving interest in her, my asking her opinion about a movie she had seen.

What are we to make of these observations? It seems clear that in some as yet undefined fashion the therapist-patient personal relationship is crucial to the process of change, and also that the therapist often underestimates the importance of this factor and overestimates that of his cognitive contributions.

How Does the Therapeutic Relationship Heal? In the previous section I suggested that the patient's "in-therapy" relationships (those in his or her current life or with other members of a therapy group or psychiatric hospital ward) have two types of therapeutic effect: (1) they are "mediating," in that they improve the quality of other, future relationships by instructing patients about their maladaptive interpersonal behavior and by serving as "dress rehearsals" for new modes of relating; (2) they have value in and for themselves—as "real" relationships, they effect intrapersonal shifts.

The same paradigm holds for the therapist-patient relationship. It heals by illuminating other relationships and also by virtue of affording a real relationship to the patient. Let us consider each mode in turn.

Patient-therapist relationship: Illumination and facilitation of other relationships. The therapist, by helping a patient examine the patient-therapist relationship, illuminates and facilitates the patient's past or current relationships with those who, in some symbolic way, resemble the therapist.

The use of the relationship to illuminate the past is the traditional transference approach to the patient-therapist relationship, where the patient "transfers" feelings and attitudes from important figures, especially parental ones, onto the person of the therapist. The patient dresses the therapist, who serves as a mannikin, with feelings that have been stripped from others. The relationship with the therapist is a shadow play, reflecting the vicissitudes of a drama that transpired long ago. The analytic therapeutic goal of recapturing and illuminating events in early life is well served in this approach.

There are two basic objections to working with relationships in this manner. First, as I discussed in chapter 7, there is no evidence that uncovering and understanding the past is mutative in therapy. The second is that viewing the therapist-patient relationship primarily in terms of transference negates the truly human, and truly mutative, nature of the relationship. There is much evidence for the argument that it is the real relationship that heals; and to view the therapist-patient relationship as a crate to transport the merchandise of healing (insight, uncovering the events of early life, and so on) is to mistake the container for the contents. The relationship *is* the merchandise of healing; and, as I have stressed earlier, the search for insight, the task of excavating the past, are all interesting, seemingly profitable ventures that engage the attention of patient and therapist while the real agent of change, their relationship, is germinating.

Another use of the patient-therapist relationship is to help the patient understand current or future relationships. The patient almost invariably will distort some aspects of his or her relationship to the therapist. The experienced therapist, drawing from his or her own self-knowledge and wide experience of how others view him or her is able to help the patient distinguish distortion from reality. The therapist may represent different things to different patients, but to most patients he or she embodies images of authority—teacher, boss, parent, judge, supervisor, and so forth. By helping the patient improve his or her relationships to such individuals, the therapist performs a real service.

The "real" relationship between therapist and patient. There is enormous potential benefit in the patient's developing a real (as opposed to a tranferential) relationship to the therapist. Rather than the relationships being an "as if" phenomenon—one that, analyzed properly, will facilitate *other* relationships—the therapist helps to heal by developing a genuine relationship with the patient.

Kaiser, as I discussed earlier, believed that the individual, bedeviled by isolation (the "universal conflict"), attempts to deal with it by effecting a "fusion" with another. To pave the way for fusion, the "universal symptom," as Kaiser put it, arises. The "universal symptom" is "duplicity" or "ingenuineness" or "transference" and consists of both distorted perception of and behavior toward the therapist. Thus, the patient does not relate with his true self but engages the therapist in such a way as to escape isolation and to effect fusion.

And the antidote to this universal conflict and symptom? Kaiser's answer was "communication."[25] He posited that "it was the ability to communicate freely that prevented the universal conflict from forcing a person into the restrictive delusionary pattern of neurosis." The therapist healed, Kaiser believed, *simply by being with the patient.* Successful therapy requires "that the patient spends sufficient time with a person of certain personality characteristics."

What personality characteristics? Kaiser cited four: (1) an interest in people; (2) theoretical views on psychotherapy that do not interfere with his or her interest in helping the patient to communicate freely; (3) the absence of neurotic patterns that would interfere with the establishment of communication with the patient; (4) the mental disposition of "receptiveness"—being sensitive to duplicity or to the noncommunicative elements in the patient's behavior.

Kaiser offers only one rule for the therapist: "communicate." All other requirements pertain not to what the therapist must do but to what the therapist must *be*. Though Kaiser may overstate the matter, he nonetheless calls our attention to the essential cog in the process of therapeutic change. Psychotherapy for most patients is a cyclical process from isolation into relationship. Once a patient is able to relate deeply to a therapist (and to relate to him or her as a real person, *not* as a hologram manufactured by "technique"), then he or she has already changed. The patient learns that the potential for love exists within oneself and experiences feelings that have lain dormant in dissociated realms for years or decades. Recall Buber's comments about the I-Thou relationship: when the "I" truly relates to another, it is changed, it is different from the pre-Thou "I." It experiences new aspects of itself, it opens up not only to the other *but to itself as well*. No matter that the patient's relationship to the therapist is "temporary," the *experience* of intimacy is permanent. It can never be taken away. It exists in one's inner world as a permanent reference point: a reminder of one's potential for intimacy. The discovery of self that ensues as a result of intimacy is also permanent.

It scarcely needs to be said that the experience of an intimate encounter with a therapist has implications for the individual that extend beyond relationships with most other people. For one thing, the therapist is generally someone whom the patient particularly respects. But even more important, the therapist is someone, often the only one, who *really* knows the patient. To tell an individual all one's darkest secrets, all one's illicit thoughts, one's vanities, one's sorrows, one's passions and still be fully accepted by that person is enormously affirmative.

Earlier I said, "Psychotherapy is a cyclical process from isolation into relationship." It is cyclical because the patient, in terror of existential isolation, relates deeply and meaningfully to the therapist and then, strengthened by this encounter, is led back again to a confrontation with existential isolation. The therapist, out of the depth of relationship, helps the patient to face isolation and to apprehend his solitary responsibility for his own life—that it is the patient who has created his life predicament and that, alas, it is the patient, and no one else, who can alter it.

The therapist leads the patient back to isolation in yet another way. Earlier I stressed that one priceless thing the patient learns in therapy is the limits of relationship. One learns what one can get from others but, perhaps even more important, one learns what one *cannot* get from others. As patient and therapist encounter one another on a human level, the former's illusions inevitably suffer. The ultimate rescuer is seen in the full light of day as only another person after all. It is an isolating moment but also, as Kenneth Fisher states, an illuminating one "when the pilgrim chances to think: maybe no one knows—perhaps we are all pilgrims."[26] At the very least the patient is liberated from searching in the wrong place. Optimally he or she learns from the fullness of the encounter that patient and therapist and everyone else are brethren in their humanness and their irrevocable isolation.

THE IDEAL THERAPIST-PATIENT RELATIONSHIP

If it is the therapist's primary task to relate deeply and fully to the patient, does then the therapist form an I-Thou relationship with each patient? Does the therapist "love" (in Maslow or Fromm's sense) the patient? Is there a difference between a therapist and a true friend?

It is hard for a therapist to read (or to write) these questions without a certain uneasiness. "Squirm" is the word that springs to mind. There is an inescapable dissonance in the world of the therapist: no amount of polishing and lubricating make concepts like "friendship," "love," and "I-Thou" fit comfortably with other concepts like "fifty-minute sessions," "sixty-five dollars an hour," "case conferences," and "third-party payments." This incongruity is built into the therapist's, and the patient's, "situation" and cannot be denied or ignored.

There is one major aspect of a loving friendship or an I-Thou relationship which is perforce different in the therapist-patient relationship—reciprocity. The patient comes to the therapist for help. The therapist does not come to the patient. The therapist should have motivation, inclination, and ability to experience the patient as a person as fully as possible. The patient, by definition, has impaired ability to experience the other person fully and, furthermore, has another motive entirely—relief of suffering. Thus, the therapist has what Buber calls a "detached presence": the therapist is able to be in two places at once—at his or her own side and at the patient's side. "The therapist is able to be where he himself is and where the patient is; the patient cannot be but where he is."[27]

The therapist is interested in the "you" of the patient, not only the "you" that is present but the potential dormant "you." The therapist uses his or her intuitive sense of openness and closeness to the patient as a guide, seeking always to deepen the relationship. The patient at the onset of therapy has no ken of a reciprocal attitude toward the therapist. The patient may ask or think questions about the therapist, but these inquiries are generally not in the service of reaching out to "know" or to bring out the full potential of the therapist, but rather to establish the latter's credentials or to ascertain whether he is going to fill the patient's needs. Occasionally the patient's questions are part of a struggle for control in the relationship: the patient may feel less vulnerable in revealing himself or herself if the therapist is willing to self-disclose also.

Carlos Sequin in *Love and Psychotherapy*[28] describes the therapist-patient relationship as a special form of love: "psychotherapeutic eros." This form of love has several distinctive features. It is, as I have already indicated, nonreciprocal. The lack of reciprocity, I should note, is not fixed; as therapy proceeds, the improving patient becomes increasingly aware and increasingly caring (that is, need-free caring) about the person of the therapist. Psychotherapeutic eros is indestructible or, as Carl Rogers put it, "non-conditional." Other kinds of love can be eroded. A lover will ultimately cease to love when his or her love is not returned. Friends will part when they no longer have a great deal in common. Many circumstances exist that may result in estrangement between parent and child, teacher and student, worshiper and deity. But the mature therapist will care despite rebelliousness, narcissism, depression, hostility, and mendacity. In fact, one might say that the therapist cares *because of* these traits, since they reflect how much the individual needs to be cared for.

Another aspect of psychotherapeutic eros is that it implies a genuine caring for the person of the patient. In Sequin's[29] words, "it is not a 'humanitarian' love that the doctor should feel for the sick man, qua sick man. Rather, he should have an authentic feeling of love for the particular individual who is before him, who is *this* man and not another, who is not a 'sick man,' but rather a man." Fromm, Maslow, and Buber all stressed that true caring for another means to care about the other's growth and to bring something to life in the other. The therapist must have this attitude toward the patient. The therapist's *raison d'être* is to be midwife to the birth of the patient's yet unlived life.

The idea of "bringing to life" something in the other provides an important procedural strategy for the therapist. Buber distinguishes two basic modes of affecting another's attitude toward life.[30] Either one tries to impose one's attitude and opinions upon another (and in such a way that the other deems them to be his or her own views), or one attempts to help another discover his or her own dispositions and experience his or her own "actualizing forces." The first approach Buber terms "imposition" and is the way of the propagandist. The second approach is "unfolding" and is the way of the educator and the therapist. Unfolding implies that one uncovers what was there all along. The very term "unfolding" has rich connotations and stands in sharp contrast to other terms depicting the therapeutic process—for example, "reconstruction," "decondition," "behavioral shaping," "reparenting."

One helps the other unfold not by instruction but by "meeting," by "existential communication."[31] The therapist is not a director, not a shaper, but is instead a "possibilitator."[32] Heidegger, in analogous fashion, speaks two different modes of caring or "solicitude."* One can "leap in" for another—a mode of relating similar to "imposition"—and thus relieve another of the anxiety of facing existence (and, in so doing, limit the other to inauthentic existence). Or one can "leap ahead" (a not wholly satisfying term) and "liberate" the other by confronting the other with his or her existential situation.

In summary, the therapist relates to the patient in a genuine caring fasion and strives to achieve moments of authentic encounter. The therapist should be selfless in this endeavor—that is, concerned with the patient's growth and not with his or her personal needs. The therapist's caring should be indestructible and not dependent upon reciprocal caring by the patient. The therapist should be able to be both with himself or herself and with the patient and should thus be able, in caring, to enter the patient's world and to experience it as the patient experiences it. This requires the therapist to approach the patient without presuppositions, to focus on the project of sharing the patient's experience without rushing in to judge or stereotype the patient.

Many of these aspects of the therapeutic relationship have been described by Rogers and his co-workers in their triad of therapist characteristics—empathy, genuineness, and positive, unconditional regard; and considerable research evidence indicates that these characteristics facilitate positive therapy outcome. My chief concern about this characterization of therapist behavior is that others—despite Rogers's emphasis that the relationship must be genuine and deeply personal†—often present it as a technique, as something the therapist *does* in therapy. Accordingly, there are technical manuals that teach student therapists methods of conveying empathy, genuineness, and positive regard. To

---

* Heidegger distinguishes caring for things ("concern") and caring for other *daseins*.—that is, constituting beings ("solicitude").[33]

† Rogers was explicit about this point in a remarkable conversation with Buber, which indicates that these two seminal thinkers were in close agreement about the preferred nature of the therapist-patient relationship.[34]

an existential therapist, when "technique" is made paramount, every-thing is lost because the very essence of the authentic relationship is that one does not manipulate but turns toward another with one's whole being.

Diagnosis. Many therapists have difficulty relating authentically to patients because of presuppositions and stereotypes. The training of therapists emphasizes diagnosis and classification; they are taught to objectify patients, to arrive at a APA (American Psychiatric Association) code number that pins a patient like a specimen to an admission work-up or an insurance form. And, indeed, no responsible therapist can deny there is a place for diagnostic evaluation. For example, one needs to ascertain whether the patient has some organic illness or toxic condition that is affecting his or her psychological state. Or one needs to as-certain whether the patient is suffering from severe affective disorder of biochemical etiology (for example, endogenous depression or mani-depressive diathesis) which requires pharmacological treatment.

Even if a condition is primarily functional, the therapist needs to make other crude determinations. Is the patient's condition of such se-verity (for example, severe sociopathic character disturbance or well-systematized paranoid schizophrenia) that there is little likelihood of his or her benefiting from psychotherapy? For obvious reasons, the pa-tient's destructive tendencies (to self and others) must be ascertained. Even beyond that, the therapist can make determinations about a pa-tient's fragility and ability to tolerate closeness which will provide im-portant guidelines for the pace of therapy.

Beyond these relatively crude determinations which serve the func-tion of initial triage, further and "finer" diagnostic discriminations not only offer little help to the therapist but often interfere with the forma-tion of relationship. Intricate psychoanalytic diagnostic formulations about specific psychosexual dynamic organization are of little help to therapy and, to the extent to which they impede genuine listening, constitute a hindrance. Although some or most "hysterical personal-ities," to take one example, exhibit certain specific behavioral patterns and are plagued by certain common dynamic conflicts, not all do so. The standard diagnostic formulation tells the therapist nothing about the unique person he or she is encountering; and there is substantial evidence that diagnostic labels impede or distort listening.[35] Too often diagnostic categorization is a stimulating intellectual exercise whose sole function is to provide the therapist with a sense of order and mas-tery. The major task of the maturing therapist is to learn to tolerate un-certainty. What is required is a major shift in perspective: rather than strive to order the interview "material" into an intellectually coherent framework, the therapist must strive toward authentic engagement.

Therapist Self-disclosure. A therapist who is to know a patient must do more than observe and listen; he or she must fully experience the patient. But full experience of the other requires that one open oneself up to the other; if one engages the other in an open and honest fashion, one experiences the other as the other is responding to that engagement.

There is no way around the conclusion that the therapist who is to relate to the patient must disclose himself or herself as a person. The effective therapist cannot remain detached, passive, and hidden. Therapist self-disclosure is integral to the therapeutic process. But how much of self does the therapist disclose? Personal life problems? *All* feelings toward the patient? Boredom? Fatigue? Flatulence? Clever therapeutic strategies? Is there, in this regard, no difference between a therapist and a close friend?

Vexing problems indeed! Problems that in the first several decades of psychotherapeutic practice were never confronted, since it had been settled early in the analytic movement that therapists should maintain emotional distance and objectivity much as a surgeon dispassionately studies an ailing organ. Patients will develop strong feelings for therapists, warned Freud, but therapists must be on guard and suppress tender feelings. Therapists must realize that a patient's powerful feelings are "an unavoidable consequence of a medical situation, like the exposure of a patient's body or the imparting of a vital secret."[36]

Why should a dispassionate role for the therapist be so strictly prescribed? First, Freud suggested that a therapist who has ceased to be "objective" will lose control of the situation and be swept along by what a patient wishes rather than by what a patient requires:

> The patient would achieve *her* aim but the doctor would never achieve *his*. What would happen to the doctor and the patient would only be what happened, according to the amusing anecdote, to the pastor and the insurance agent. The insurance agent, a free-thinker, lay at the point of death and his relatives insisted on bringing in a man of God to convert him before he died. The interview lasted so long that those who were waiting outside began to have hopes. At last the door of the sick-chamber opened. The free-thinker had not been converted; but the pastor went away insured.[37]

So, in Freud's view, if therapists open themselves up to patients and involve themselves in normal human intercourse, they will sacrifice objectivity and, hence, effectiveness. A second, more pervasive argument for therapist opacity is grounded in the view that transference is the linchpin of psychotherapy. Freud believed, and the great majority of present-day psychoanalysts still believe, that analysis of transference is the paramount task of the therapist. As I discussed earlier, to Freud that transference was a living representation of what a patient had experienced early in life—in ages too ancient to be fully accessible to memory. Thus, by observing, understanding, and helping the patient to "work through" transference (that is, to experience it, to recognize its inappropriateness to the current situation, and to discover the infantile sources of the transferential feeling) the therapist uncovers the deepest strata of the individual's life experience.

Given the key role of transference, it follows that the therapist should facilitate its development. The less the therapist's real self appears, the more readily does the patient transfer onto him feelings that belong elsewhere. This is, of course, the rationale for the traditional "blank screen" role of the therapist and for the peculiar seating arrangement of the psychoanalytic session where the analyst remains behind the couch out of the patient's range of vision. This prescription against therapist self-disclosure paved the way for two generations of psychotherapy technique that argued against an authentic encounter between therapist and patient and insisted that the therapist's primary function—indeed, sole function—was interpretation.

Even some early theorists, however, dissented with this view of the therapist's role. Sandor Ferenczi, one of Freud's first and most loyal disciples, argued that the detached, omniscient posture of the therapist interfered with therapeutic effectiveness. Ferenczi, especially during his later years, openly acknowledged to patients his fallibility. For example, in response to a justified criticism, he felt comfortable in saying, "I think you may have touched upon an area in which I am not entirely free myself. Perhaps you can help me see what's wrong with me."[38]

For the most part, however, it was not until the 1950s when the issue of the real—that is, the "nontransference"—relationship was discussed in psychiatric literature. (Ralph Greenson and Milton Wexler's extensive review[39] cites only two studies before 1950.) In 1954, in an informal discussion of transference, Anna Freud commented:

> With due respect for the necessary strictest handling and interpretation of the transference, I feel still that we should leave room somewhere for the realization that analyst and patient are also two real people of equal adult status, in a real personal relationship to each other. I wonder whether our—at times complete—neglect of this side of the matter is not responsible for some of the hostile reactions which we get from our pa-

tients and which we are apt to ascribe to "true transference" only. But these are technically subversive thoughts and ought to be handled with care.[40]

Greenson and Wexler in 1969 gave some indication of the persistence of the traditional analytic view on this issue:

Although one no longer hears elaborate debates in analytic circles as to whether it is a mortal technical sin to offer a Kleenex to a patient weeping over the recent death of a parent, it is still highly suspect to do anything which resembles being kind to the patient.[41]

Although Greenson and Wexler argued for a more human therapist-patient relationship, I believe that they used the wrong reasons. In their discussion of the drawbacks to excessive therapist detachment, they said:

Perhaps we should be more aware of the fact that persistent anonymity and prolonged affective atherosclerosis can also be seductive, but generally in the direction of inviting an irreversible and uninterpretable hostile transference and alienation.[42]

Thus, these analysts argued for greater therapist involvement out of technical considerations: to keep the transference from becoming unworkable and to facilitate its analysis.*

To summarize, a singular focus on transference impedes therapy because it precludes an authentic therapist-patient relationship. First, it negates the reality of the relationship by considering the relationship solely as a key to understanding other more important relationships. Secondly, it provides therapists with a rationale for personal concealment—a concealment that interferes with the ability to relate in a genuine fashion with patients. Does this mean that therapists who faithfully maintain a detached, objectifying, "interpretation-only" posture toward patients are ineffective or even destructive? I believe that, fortunately, such therapists and such courses of therapy are exceeding-

---

* Incidentally the previous quotation contains the curious phrase that "prolonged affective atherosclerosis can also be seductive." I assume what is meant is that it is easier and requires less investment of energy for therapists to remain emotionally uninvolved. Possibly so, but therapists pay a terrible price as they themselves ultimately become deadened. Another professional hazard for therapists consists of using encounters with patients to avoid confronting and integrating their own isolation. Without such an integration some therapists never develop the autonomy to engage in gratifying and enduring love relationships instead, their personal lives become a staccato of intense but transient fifty-minute encounters.

ly rare. Here lies the importance of the "throw-ins" in therapy: therapists despite themselves and often unbeknownst to themselves reach out in a human manner in off-the-record moments.

What are other objections to therapist self-disclosure? Some therapists fear that if they open the door a little, patients will force it wider and demand more self-revelation. My personal experience is that this fear is unwarranted. I feel it is often important to reveal my immediate here-and-now feelings to the patient. I rarely find it necessary or particularly helpful to reveal many details of my personal past and current life. I have almost never found a patient whose demands escalate. The desire of the patient is not that the therapist be stripped but that the therapist relate to him or her as a person and be entirely present in the immediate encounter.

How much to reveal? What guidelines to use? It is important to keep in mind the overriding goal—authentic relationship. One of the outstanding characteristics of "psychotherapeutic eros" is the care for the other's becoming. Rollo May suggests the Greek term *agape* or the Latin *caritas*—a love that is devoted to the welfare of the other. What is important, then, is that therapist self-disclosure be in the service of the growth of the patient. Self-expression on the part of the therapist, or total honesty, or spontaneity, may each be a virtue in itself, but each is secondary to the overriding presence of agape. Therefore, it follows that therapists must keep some things to themselves, that they say nothing that may be destructive to a patient, that they respect the principle of timing and attend to the pace of therapy, to what a patient is or is not ready to hear.

The principle of self-restraint applies, incidentally, when we consider another objection to the therapist's involving himself or herself as a real person with the patient: loss of therapist objectivity, with resulting excesses and irresponsible behavior. Perhaps the most flagrant excess is the therapist who, as a "real person," becomes sexually involved with a patient. I have seen many patients who have had some prior sexual involvement with a therapist. My impression is that the experience is always destructive for the patient, and that invariably the therapist has violated the principle of agape—love for the being (and the becoming) of the other. Such therapists heeded not their patients' needs but their own and offered wretchedly transparent rationalizations—such as a patient's need for sexual affirmation. I have yet to hear of a therapist becoming sexually involved with one who might really need sexual affirmation—that is, with one who is remarkably unattractive, physically deformed, or surgically mutilated.

414

Another reason for the therapist to remain hidden is the fear that self-disclosure would lay bare some of those incongruities in the therapy situation I spoke of earlier: fee for service, the fifty-minute hour, the therapist's packed schedule. Will the patient ask, "Do you love me?" "If you really care for me, would you see me if I had no money?" "Is therapy really a purchased relationship?" It is true that these questions veer perilously close to that ultimate secret of the psychotherapist which is that the encounter with the patient plays a relatively small role in the therapist's overall life. As in Tom Stoppard's play *Rosencrantz and Guildenstern Are Dead*, a key figure in one drama becomes a shadow in the wings as the therapist moves immediately onto the stage of another drama. Indeed, this denial of specialness is one of the cruel truths and poorly kept secrets of therapy: the patient has one therapist; the therapist, many patients. The therapist is far more important to the patient than the patient to the therapist. To my mind there is only one response that therapists can make to such questions from patients: that when the therapist is with the patient, he or she is fully with the patient; the therapist strives to give his or her entire presence to the other. That is why earlier I stressed the importance of the immediate moment in an encounter. At the same time the therapist must know that, though the aim must be full encounter, he or she cannot continually relate at that level (recall Buber: "One cannot live in the pure present [that is, in the I-Thou], it would consume us"[43]) but must repeatedly during the hour bring himself or herself back to full engagement in the present moment.

I listen to a woman patient. She rambles on and on. She seems unattractive in every sense of the word—physically, intellectually, emotionally. She is irritating. She has many off-putting gestures. She is not talking to me; she is talking in front of me. Yet how can she talk to me if I am not here? My thoughts wander. My head groans. What time is it? How much longer to go? I suddenly rebuke myself. I give my mind a shake. Whenever I think of how much time remains in the hour, I know I am failing my patient. I try then to touch her with my thoughts. I try to understand why I avoid her. What is her world like at this moment? How is she experiencing the hour? How is she experiencing me? I ask her these very questions. I tell her that I have felt distant from her for the last several minutes. Has she felt the same way? We talk about that together and try to figure out why we lost contact with one another. Suddenly we are very close. She is no longer unattractive. I have much compassion for her person, for what she is, for what she might yet be. The clock races; the hour ends too soon.

PART IV

Meaninglessness

CHAPTER 10

Meaninglessness

Imagine a happy group of morons who are engaged in work. They are carrying bricks in an open field. As soon as they have stacked all the bricks at one end of the field, they proceed to transport them to the opposite end. This continues without stop and everyday of every year they are busy doing the same thing. One day one of the morons stops long enough to ask himself what he is doing. He wonders what purpose there is in carrying the bricks. And from that instant on he is not quite as content with his occupation as he had been before.

I am the moron who wonders why he is carrying the bricks.[1]

THIS SUICIDE NOTE, these last words written by a despairing soul who killed himself because he saw no meaning in life, serve as a stark introduction to a question that is, indeed, a matter of life and death.

The question takes many forms: What is the meaning of life? What is the meaning of *my* life? *Why* do we live? *Why* were we put here? What do we live *for*? What shall we live *by*? If we must die, if nothing endures, then what sense does anything make?

Few individuals were ever as tormented by such questions as was Leo Tolstoy, who for much of a long life grappled with meaninglessness. His experience (from *My Confession*, an autobiographical fragment) will launch us on our way:

Five years ago a strange state of mind began to grow upon me: I had moments of perplexity, of a stoppage, as it were, of life, as if I did not know

419

how I was to live, what I was to do. . . . These stoppages of life always
presented themselves to me with the same question: "why?" and "what
for?" . . . These questions demanded an answer with greater and greater
persistence and, like dots, grouped themselves into one black spot.[2]

During this crisis of meaning or, as he termed it, "life arrest," Tolstoy
questioned the meaning of everything he did. What was the point, he
asked, of managing his estate, of educating his son? "What for? I now
have six thousand desyatins in the province of Samara, and three hundred horses—what then?"[3] Indeed, he wondered why he should write:
"Well, what if I should be more famous than Gogol, Pushkin, Shake-
speare, Molière,—than all the writers in the world—well, and what
then? I could find no reply. Such questions demand an immediate answer; without one it is impossible to live. Yet answer there was none."[4]

With the dissolution of meaning, Tolstoy experienced a dissolution
of the foundations on which his life rested: "I felt that the ground on
which I stood was crumbling, that there was nothing for me to stand
on, that what I had been living for was nothing, that I had no reason
for living. . . . The truth was, that life was meaningless. Every day of
life, every step in it, brought me nearer the precipice and I saw clearly
that there was nothing but ruin.[5]

At age fifty Tolstoy veered close to suicide:

> The question, which in my fiftieth year had brought me to the notion of
> suicide, was the simplest of all questions, lying in the soul of every man
> from the undeveloped child to wisest sage: "What will come from what I
> am doing now, and may do tomorrow. What will come from my whole
> life?" otherwise expressed—"Why should I live? Why should I wish for
> anything? Why should I do anything?" Again, in other words: "Is there
> any meaning in my life which will not be destroyed by the inevitable
> death awaiting me?"[6]

Tolstoy is joined by a legion of others who have experienced a crisis
of meaning, a tormented "arrest of life." Albert Camus, to cite another
example, held that the only serious philosophical question is whether
to go on living once the meaninglessness of human life is fully
grasped. He stated, "I have seen many people die because life for them
was not worth living. From this I conclude that the question of life's
meaning is the most urgent question of all."[7]

How often do patients with Tolstoy's malady seek therapy? Though
no rigorous and comprehensive statistical studies exist, many experienced clinicians who are "tuned in" to the problem of meaninglessness
state that the clinical syndrome is very common. C. G. Jung, for exam-

ple, felt that meaninglessness inhibited fullness of life and was "therefore equivalent to illness."[8] He wrote: "Absence of meaning in life plays a crucial role in the etiology of neurosis. A neurosis must be understood, ultimately, as a suffering of a soul which has not discovered its meaning. . . . *About a third of my cases* are not suffering from any clinically definable neurosis but from the senselessness and aimlessness of their lives."[9]

Viktor Frankl states that 20 percent of the neuroses he encounters in clinical practice are "noogenic" in origin—that is, they derive from a lack of meaning in life. Frankl's conclusions are based on his own clinical impressions and upon statistical studies which unfortunately remain unpublished.[10] A meaninglessness crisis which has not yet crystallized into a discrete neurotic symptomatic picture (an "existential crisis") is even more common, occurring, according to Frankl, in over 50 percent of his patients in a Viennese hospital. Furthermore, Frankl, who has devoted his career to a study of an existential approach to therapy, has apparently concluded that the lack of meaning is *the* paramount existential stress. To him, existential neurosis is synonymous with a crisis of meaninglessness.

Other psychotherapists share that view. Salvatore Maddi, for example, in his splendid essay on the search for meaning, states that "existential sickness" stems from "a comprehensive failure in the search for meaning in life."[11] Maddi describes an "existential neurosis" in which the cognitive component is "meaninglessness, or a chronic inability to believe in the truth, importance, usefulness or interest value of any of the things one is engaged in or can imagine doing."[12] Benjamin Wolman defines existential neurosis in the same manner: "Failure to find meaning in life, the feeling that one has nothing to live for, nothing to struggle for, nothing to hope for . . . unable to find any goal or direction in life, the feeling that though individuals *perspire* in their work, they have nothing to *aspire* to."[13] Nicholas Hobbs agrees: "Contemporary culture often produces a kind of neuroses different from that described by Freud. Contemporary neuroses are characterized not so much by repression and conversion . . . not by lack of insight but lack of a sense of purpose, of meaning in life."[14]

Although such clinical impressions do not constitute firm evidence, certainly they suggest that the problem of meaning in life is a significant one that the therapist must confront frequently in everyday clinical work. Psychotherapy is a child of the Enlightenment. At bottom it always embraces the goal of unflinching self-exploration. The therapist must forthrightly accept and examine fundamental questions; and the question of meaning, that most perplexing and insoluble question of all, must not be denied in therapy. It will not do to inattend selectively to it, to shrink away from it, or to transform it into some lesser but more manageable question. But where in professional training curriculums does the therapist learn about the development of a sense of life meaning, about the psychopathology of meaninglessness, or about psychotherapeutic strategies available to assist patients in a crisis of meaning?

A small cohort of therapists have addressed these questions in informal works or in literature peripheral to mainstream therapeutic theory and practice. This chapter will place these neglected theorists on center stage and supplement their ranks with those philosophers and artists whose speculations on meaning in life have clinical relevance. A satisfying response to the riddle of life's meaning has throughout written history eluded the grasp of every great thinker. It will come as no surprise to anyone that these pages contain neither a solution nor a wholly satisfactory synthesis of the many attempted solutions. What I shall attempt to do is raise the therapist's consciousness to the issue of life meaning, and to survey the major approaches taken by others. It is my hope that the therapist who is fortified with knowledge about tested and serviceable trails through the morass of meaninglessness will act as an informed and creative guide to the patient suffering a crisis of meaning.

The Problem of Meaning

The dilemma facing us is that two propositions, both true, seem unalterably opposed:

1. The human being seems to require meaning. To live without meaning, goals, values, or ideals seems to provoke, as we have seen, considerable distress. In severe form it may lead to the decision to end one's life. Frankl noted that in the concentration camp the individual with no sense of meaning was unlikely to survive. As I shall discuss shortly, individuals facing death are able to live "better" lives, live with fullness and zest, if they are possessed of a sense of purpose. We apparently need absolutes—firm ideals to which we can aspire and guidelines by which to steer our lives.

2. Yet the existential concept of freedom described in chapters 6 and 7 posits that the only true absolute is that there are no absolutes. An existential position holds that the world is contingent—that is, everything that is could as well have been otherwise; that human beings constitute themselves, their world, and their situation within that world; that there exists no "meaning," no grand design in the universe, no guidelines for living other than those the individual creates.

The problem, then, in most rudimentary form is, How does a being who needs meaning find meaning in a universe that has no meaning?

Meanings of Life

DEFINITIONS

"Meaning" and "purpose" have different connotations. "Meaning" refers to sense, or coherence. It is a general term for what is intended to be expressed by something. A search for meaning implies a search for coherence. "Purpose" refers to intention, aim, function. When we inquire about the purpose of something, we are asking about its role or function: What does it do? To what end?

In conventional usage, however, "purpose" of life and "meaning" of life are used interchangeably, and I shall treat them accordingly as synonyms. "Significance" is another closely related term. Used in one sense, "significance" has the same implication as "meaning"; another sense confuses since it also refers to "importance" or "consequence."

What is the meaning of life? is an inquiry about *cosmic meaning*, about whether life in general or at least human life fits into some overall coherent pattern. What is the meaning of *my* life? is a different inquiry and refers to what some philosophers term "terrestrial meaning."[15] Terrestrial meaning ("the meaning of my life") embraces purpose: one who possesses a sense of meaning experiences life as having some purpose or function to be fulfilled, some overriding goal or goals to which to apply oneself.

Cosmic meaning implies some design existing outside of and superior to the person and invariably refers to some magical or spiritual ordering of the universe. *Terrestrial meaning* may, as we shall see, have foundations that are entirely secular—that is, one may have a personal sense of meaning without a cosmic meaning system.

One who possesses a sense of cosmic meaning generally experiences a corresponding sense of terrestrial meaning: that is, one's terrestrial meaning consists of fulfilling or harmonizing with that cosmic meaning. For example, one might think of "life" as a symphony in which each life is assigned some instrumental part to play. (Of course, one may believe in cosmic meaning but be unable to comprehend one's own place in that grand design or may even feel that one has behaved in such a way as to forfeit one's position in the cosmic plan; but such individuals suffer less from a sense of meaninglessness than from one of personal guilt or fallenness.)

COSMIC MEANING

Within the Western world, the Judeo-Christian religious tradition has offered a comprehensive meaning-schema based upon the principle that the world and human life are part of a divinely ordained plan. Divine justice is one corollary of that postulate: life, lived properly, will be rewarded. The individual being's meaning-in-life is divinely ordained: it is each human being's task to ascertain and to fulfill God's will. How is one to know that will? A fundamentalist approach holds that God's meaning is contained in the holy word, and that a good life may be based on a close, literal exegesis of the Scriptures. Others are certain only that one has to have faith, that one can never know with certainty and has to be satisfied with hints, with guesses, about God's ordained meaning or with the thought that a mere human cannot hope to know God's mind. "The branch," said Pascal in the seventeenth century, "cannot hope to know the tree's meaning."[16] Viktor Frankl explicates this point of view by the analogy of an ape that was used in medical research to find an effective poliomyelitis serum.[17] The ape suffered much pain and could never, because of its cognitive limitations, discover the meaning of the situation. So, too, Frankl argues, it must be with the human being who cannot hope to know with fullness a meaning that exists in a dimension beyond comprehension.

Another view of cosmic meaning stresses that human life be dedicated to the purpose of emulating God. God represents perfection, and thus the purpose of life is to strive for perfection. Of the various types of perfection to be sought, Aristotle (and the whole rational intellectual tradition he launched) considered intellectual perfection as the ultimate. God, in Aristotelian terms, is "thought thinking itself"; and one approaches the deity through perfection of one's rational faculties. In the twelfth century Moses Maimonides in *The Guide of the Perplexed* described the four major common modes of striving toward perfection.[18]

He dismissed the first, perfection of physical possession as imaginary and impermanent; and the second, perfection of the body, as failing to differentiate human from animal. The third, moral perfection, he found praiseworthy but limited in that it served others rather than oneself. The fourth, rational perfection, he considered to be "true human perfection," through which "man becomes man." This perfection is the ultimate goal and permits the human being to apprehend God.

The cosmic meaning afforded by a religious world view permits a vast number of interpretations of individual life purpose—some doctrinaire, some highly imaginative. In this century Jung, for example, had a deeply committed religious outlook and believed no one can be healed or find meaning unless one regains one's religious outlook.[19] Jung's view of his personal life purpose was to complete God's work of creation:

> Man is indispensable for the completion of creation; that is, in fact, he himself is the second creator of the world who alone has given to the world its objective existence—without which, unheard, unseen, silently eating, giving birth, dying, heads nodding through hundreds of millions of years, it would have gone on in the profoundest night of non-being down to its unknown end.[20]

Jung's idea that the human being completes the work of creation and "puts the stamp of perfection upon it," is a conclusion arrived at by others. Earlier Hegel wrote "without the world God is not god. . . . God is God only insofar as he knows himself and his self-knowledge is his consciousness of himself in man and man's knowledge of god."[21] Or the poet Rilke in this century:

> What will you do, God, if I die?
> I am your jug, what if I shatter?
> I am your drink, what if I spoil?
> I am your robe and your profession
> Losing me, you lose your meaning.[22]

A provocative comment by Thomas Mann echoes this thought: "With the generation of life from the inorganic, it was man who was ultimately intended. With him a great experiment is initiated, the failure of which would be the failure of creation itself. . . . Whether that be so or not, it would be well for man to behave as if it were so."[23]

Mann's thought that "it was man who was ultimately intended" forms the heart of the creative system of meaning posited by Pierre Teilhard de Chardin, the twentieth-century theologian who formulated an evolutionary synthesis in his remarkable book *The Phenomenon of Man*.[24] Teilhard de Chardin suggested a cosmic coherence in his law of "controlled complication": that life is a single unity, that the entire living world is a "single and gigantic organism* which, with predestined direction, enters into the evolutionary process. All of evolution is thus an orthogenetic process and, just as factors inside a single developing organism determine its ultimate outcome, so too do predetermined factors influence the ultimate outcome of the cosmic evolutionary process—a process destined to end with the human being in an absolute state of love and spiritual union.

In Teilhard de Chardin's system each individual, by playing a role in the shared enterprise, is provided with a personal sense of meaning: "Although only a small fraction of those who try to scale the heights of human achievement arrive anywhere close to the summit, it is imperative that there be a multitude of climbers. Otherwise the summit may not be reached by anybody. The individually lost and forgotten multitudes have not lived in vain, provided that they, too, made the efforts to climb."[27] Thus, there is shared, common entrance into a superhuman realm. "The gates of the future will admit only an advance of all together, in a direction in which all together could join and achieve fulfillment in a spiritual renovation of the earth."[28]

SECULAR PERSONAL MEANING

Personal Meaning in the Absence of Cosmic Meaning. Human beings are extraordinarily comforted by the belief that there is some supraordinate, coherent pattern to life and that each individual has some particular role to play in that design. One is not only provided a goal and a role but also a set of guidelines about how one should live life. Cosmic religious views constituted a major part of the belief system in the Western world until approximately three hundred years ago. Beginning at that time these views began to suffer an onslaught both from the burgeoning scientific attitude as well as from the Kantian questioning of the existence of a fixed objective reality. The more that the existence of something beyond man—either supernatural or some other

---

* The idea of the world as a single organism was a world view held by many primitive cultures and was prevalent in Western Europe until the sixteenth century. This scheme of cosmic meaning provided a firm, serviceable sense of terrestrial meaning, since each human being learned from birth that he or she was part of a larger unit and must conduct his or her life for the good of the mega-organism.[25] Thus, in the eighteenth century Alexander Pope could proclaim in his *Essay on Man* that "partial evil is for the universal good."[26]

abstract absolute—was called into doubt, the more difficult it was for the human being to embrace a cosmic meaning system.

But meaning systems cannot be relinquished without some substitute. Perhaps we can forgo the answer to the question, Why do we live? but it is not easy to postpone the question, How shall we live? Modern secular humans face the task of finding some direction to life without an external beacon. How does one proceed to construct one's own meaning—a meaning sturdy enough to support one's life?

Meaning in an Absurd World: Camus and Sartre.   Let me begin by examining the thinking of Albert Camus and Jean-Paul Sartre, two of the important thinkers who helped paint us into the corner of meaninglessness in the twentieth century. How did they deal with the question of life meaning?

Camus used the word "absurd" to refer to the human being's basic position in the world—the plight of a transcendent, meaning-seeking being who must live in a world that has no meaning. Camus stated that we are moral creatures who demand that the world supply a basis for moral judgment—that is, a meaning system in which is implicit a blueprint of values. But the world does not supply one: it is entirely indifferent to us. The tension between human aspiration and the world's indifference is what Camus referred to as the "absurd" human condition.[29]

What then are we to do? Are there no guidelines? No values? Nothing right or wrong? good or evil? If there are no absolutes, then nothing is more important than anything else, and everything is a matter of indifference. In his novels *A Happy Death*[30] and *The Stranger*,[31] Camus portrayed individuals who live in a state of value-nihilism. Meursault, in *The Stranger*, exists outside the moral world. "It's all the same to me," he says repeatedly. He attends his mother's funeral, copulates, works, and kills an Arab on the beach, all in the same state of profound indifference.

Earlier, in his essay *The Myth of Sisyphus*, Camus explored the tension between his nihilism and his ethical demands and gradually began to forge a new, secular, humanistically based vision of personal life meaning and a set of guidelines for life conduct that flow from that vision. His new vision posits that we can construct a new life meaning by cherishing our "nights of despair," by facing the very vortex of meaninglessness and arriving at a posture of heroic nihilism. A human being, Camus believed, can attain full stature only by living with dignity in the face of absurdity. The world's indifference can be transcended by rebellion, a prideful rebellion against one's condition. "There is

427

nothing equal to the spectacle of human pride." "There is no fate that cannot be surmounted by scorn."[32]

Camus's ideas were further shaped by the Second World War, during which he worked in the French Underground, and he conceived of an authentic revolt against the absurd as a fraternal revolt—a revolt in the name of the solidarity of humankind. In his novel *The Plague*, Camus described many human reactions to plague (in the book, a literal plague, but metaphorically the Nazi occupation of France or, beyond that, all forms of injustice and inhumanity).[33] The character who probably best represents the author's idealized self-image is Dr. Rieux, the tireless fighter of the plague who never fails to react with courage, vitality, love, and a sense of deep empathy with the plague's many victims.

In summary, then, Camus started from a position of nihilism—a position in which he despaired at the lack of meaning (and, thus, lack of purpose and values) in the world—and soon generated, gratuitously, a system of personal meaning—a system that encompasses several clear values and guidelines for conduct: courage, prideful rebellion, fraternal solidarity, love, secular saintliness.

Sartre, more than any other philosopher in this century, has been uncompromising in his view of a meaningless world. His position on the meaning of life is terse and merciless: "All existing things are born for no reason, continue through weakness and die by accident . . . It is meaningless that we are born; it is meaningless that we die."[34] Sartre's view of freedom (a view that I discussed in chapter 6) leaves one without a sense of personal meaning and with no guidelines for conduct; indeed, many philosophers have been highly critical of the Sartreian philosphical system precisely because it lacks an ethical component. Sartre's death in 1980 ended a prodigiously productive career, and his long-promised treatise on ethics will never be written.

However, in his fiction Sartre often portrayed individuals who discover something to live *for* and something to live *by*. Sartre's depiction of Orestes, the hero of his play *The Flies* (*Les Mouches*), is particularly illustrative.[35] Orestes, reared away from Argos, journeys home to find his sister Electra, and together they avenge the murder of their father (Agamemnon) by killing the murderers—their mother Clytemnestra and her husband Aegistheus. Despite Sartre's explicit statements about life's meaninglessness, his play may be read as a pilgrimage to meaning. Let me follow Orestes as he searches for values on which to base his life. Orestes first looks for meaning and purpose in a return to home, roots, and comradeship:

Try to understand I want to be a man who belongs to someplace, a man among comrades. Only consider. Even the slave bent beneath his load dropping with fatigue and staring dully at the ground and foot in front of him—why even that poor slave can say that he's in *his* town as a tree is in a forest or a leaf upon a tree. Argos is all around him, warm, compact, and comforting. Yes, Electra, I'd gladly be that slave and enjoy that feeling of drawing the city round me like a blanket and curling myself up in it.[36]

Later he questions his own life conduct and realizes that he has always done as they (the gods) wished in order to find peace within the status quo.

So that is the right thing. To live at peace—always at perfect peace. I see. Always to say "excuse me," and "thank you." That's what's wanted, eh? The right thing. Their Right Thing.[37]

At this moment in the play Orestes wrenches himself away from his previous meaning system and enters his crisis of meaninglessness:

What a change has come on everything ... until now I felt something warm and living round me, like a friendly presence. That something has just died. What emptiness. What endless emptiness.[38]

Orestes, at that moment, makes the leap that Sartre made in his personal life—not a leap into faith (although it rests on no sounder argument than a leap of faith) but a leap into "engagement," into action, into a project. He says goodby to the ideals of comfort and security and pursues, with crusader ferocity, his newfound purpose:

I say there is another path—my path. Can't you see it. It starts here and leads down to the city. I must go down into the depths among you. For you are living all of you at the bottom of a pit ... Wait. Give me time to say farewell to all the lightness, the aery lightness that was mine ... Come, Electra look at our city. ... It fends me off with its high walls, red roofs, locked doors. And yet it's mine for the taking. I'll turn into an ax and hew those walls asunder. ... [39]

Orestes's new purpose evolves quickly, and he assumes a Christlike burden:

Listen, all those people quaking with fear in their dark rooms—supposing I take over all their crimes. Supposing I set out to win the name of "guilt-stealer" and heap on myself all their remorse.[40]

Later Orestes, in defiance of Zeus, decides to kill Aegistheus. His declaration at that time indicates a clear sense of purpose: he chooses justice, freedom, and dignity and indicates that he knows what is "right" in life.

> What do I care for Zeus. Justice is a matter between men and I have no God to teach me it. It's right to stamp you out like the foul brute you are, and to free the people from your evil influence. It is right to restore to them their sense of human dignity.[41]

And glad he is to have found his freedom, his mission, and his path. Though Orestes must carry the burden of being his mother's murderer, it is better thus than to have *no* mission, no meaning, to wander pointlessly through life.

> The heavier it is to carry, the better pleased I shall be; for that burden is my freedom. Only yesterday I walked the earth haphazard; thousands of roads I tramped that brought me nowhere, for they were other men's roads . . . Today I have one path only, and heaven knows where it leads. But it is *my* path.[42]

Then Orestes finds another and, for Sartre, an important meaning—that there is no absolute meaning, that he is alone and must create his own meaning. To Zeus he says:

> Suddenly, out of the blue, freedom crashed down on me and swept me off my feet. My youth went with the wind, and I know myself alone . . . and there was nothing left in heaven, no right or wrong, nor anyone to give me orders . . . I am doomed to have no law but mine . . . Every man must find his own way.[43]

When he proposes to open the eyes of the townspeople, Zeus protests that, if Orestes tears the veils from their eyes, "they will see their lives as they are: foul and futile." But Orestes maintains that they are free, that it is right they face their despair, and utters the famous existential manifesto: "Human life begins on the far side of despair."[44].

One final purpose, self-realization, emerges when Orestes takes his sister's hand to begin their journey. Electra asks,"Whither?" and Orestes responds:

> Toward ourselves. Beyond the river and mountains are an Orestes and an Electra waiting for us, and we must make our patient way towards them.[45]

And so Sartre—the same Sartre who says that "man is a futile passion," and that "it is meaningless that we are born; it is meaningless that we die"— arrived at a position in his fiction that clearly values the search for meaning and even suggests paths to take in that search. These include finding a "home" and comradeship in the world, action, freedom, rebellion against oppression, service to others, enlightenment, self-realization, and engagement—always and above all, engagement.

And *why* are there meanings to be fulfilled? On that question Sartre is mute. Certainly the meanings are not divinely ordained; they do not exist "out there," for there is no God, and nothing exists "out there" outside of man. Orestes simply says, "I *want* to belong," or *"It is right"* to serve others, to restore dignity to man, or to embrace freedom; or every man *"must"* find his own way, must journey to the fully realized Orestes who awaits him. The terms "want to" or "it is right" or "must" are purely arbitrary and do not constitute a firm basis for human conduct; yet they seem to be the best arguments Sartre could muster. He seems to agree with Thomas Mann's pragmatic position in the passage cited earlier: "Whether that be so or not, it would be well for man to behave as if it were so."

What is important for both Camus and Sartre is that human beings recognize that one must invent one's own meaning (rather than discover God's or nature's meaning) and then commit oneself fully to fulfilling that meaning. This requires that one be, as Gordon Allport put it, "half-sure and whole-hearted"[46]—not an easy feat. Sartre's ethic requires a leap into engagement. On this one point most Western theological and atheistic existential systems agree: *it is good and right to immerse oneself in the stream of life.*

Let me survey the secular activities that provide human beings with a sense of life purpose. These activities are supported by the same arguments that Sartre advanced for Orestes: they seem right; they seem good; they are intrinsically satisfying and need not be justified on the basis of any other motivation.

Altruism.   Leaving the world a better place to live in, serving others, participation in charity (the greatest virtue of all)—these activities are right and good and have provided life meaning for many humans. Both Camus's Dr. Rieux and Sartre's Orestes fulfilled themselves through service—one by nursing plague victims, and the other by being a guilt-stealing Pied Piper who opens the eyes of others to dignity, freedom, and blessed despair.

In my clinical work with patients dying of cancer I have been in a particularly privileged position to observe the importance of meaning systems to human existence. Repeatedly I have noted that those patients who experience a deep sense of meaning in their lives appear to live more fully and to face death with less despair than those whose lives are devoid of meaning. (Jung commented, "Meaning makes a great many things endurable—perhaps everything."[47]) Though at this juncture patients experienced several types of meaning, both religious and secular, none seemed more important than altruism. Some clinical cases are illustrative.

Sal was a thirty-year-old patient who had always been vigorous and athletic until he developed multiple myeloma, a painful disabling form of bone cancer from which he died two years later. In some ways Sal's last two years were the richest of his life. Though he lived in considerable pain and though he was encased in a full body cast (because of multiple bone fractures), Sal found great meaning in life by being of service to many young people. Sal toured high schools in the area counseling teen-agers on the hazards of drug abuse and used his cancer and his visibly deteriorating body as powerful leverage in his mission. He was extraordinarily effective: the whole auditorium trembled when Sal, in a wheelchair, frozen in his cast, exhorted: "You want to destroy your body with nicotine or alcohol or heroin? You want to smash it up in autos? You're depressed and want to throw it off the Golden Gate bridge? Then give me your body! Let me have it! I want it! I'll take it! I want to live!"

Eva, a patient who died of ovarian cancer in her early fifties, had lived an extraordinarily zestful life in which altruistic activities had always provided her with a powerful sense of life purpose. She faced her death in the same way; and, though I feel uneasy using the phrase, her death can only be characterized as a "good death." Almost everyone who came into contact with Eva during the last two years of her life was enriched by her. When she first learned of her cancer and again when she learned of its spread and its fatal prognosis, she was plunged into despair but quickly extricated herself by plunging into altruistic projects. She did volunteer work on a hospital ward for terminally ill children. She closely examined a number of charitable organizations in order to make a reasoned decision about how to distribute her estate. Many old friends had avoided close contact with her after she developed cancer. Eva systematically approached each one to tell them that she understood their reason for withdrawal, that she bore no grudge, but that still it might be helpful to them when they faced their own death, to talk about their feelings toward her.

Eva's last oncologist, Dr. L., was a cold, steel-spectacled man who sat behind a desk the size of a football field and typed on Eva's medical record while he talked to her. Though Dr. L. was exceptionally skilled technically, Eva considered changing doctors in order to find someone warmer and more caring. She decided instead to stay with him and to make her final goal in life "the humanization of Dr. L." She demanded more time from him, requested that he not type and that he listen to her. She empathized with his position with patients: how hard it must be to see so many of his patients die—in fact, because of his specialty, almost *all* of his patients. Shortly before she died she had two dreams which she reported both to me and to Dr. L. The first was that he was in Israel but could not muster the resolution to visit the Holocaust museum. In the second dream she was in a hospital corridor and a group of doctors (including Dr. L.) were walking away from her very quickly. She ran after them and told them: "O.K. I understand that you can't deal with my cancer. I forgive you, it's all right. It's perfectly normal you should feel this way." Eva's perseverance won out, and eventually she had the gratification of breaking down Dr. L's barriers and touching him in a deeply human manner.

She was in a support group for patients with metastatic cancer and found meaning until the end of her life in the fact that her attitude toward her death could be of value to many other patients who might be able to use Eva's zest for life and courageous stance toward death as a model for their own living and dying. One of these patients, Madeline Salmon, a marvelous poet, wrote this poem to be read at Eve's memorial:

> Dear Eva,
> Whenever the wind is from the sea
> Salty and strong
> You are here.
>
> Remembering your zest for hilltops
> And the sturdy surf of your laughter
> Gentles my grief at your going
> And tempers the thought of my own.

"Tempers the thought of my own" expresses beautifully an important source of meaning for so many persons facing death. The idea of being a model for others, especially for one's children, of helping them to diminish or remove the terror of death can fill life with meaning until the moment of death. One extends oneself into one's children and into one's children's children and so on in the great chain of being. Eva, of course, influenced me profoundly and, in so doing, shares in the process by which I find my meaning by passing on her gift to my readers.

Altruism constitutes an important source of meaning for psychotherapists—and, of course, for all helping professionals—who not only invest themselves in helping patients grow but also realize that one person's growth can have a ripple effect whereby many others who touch on that patient's life are benefited. This effect is most obvious when the patient is someone who has a wide sphere of influence (teacher, physician, writer, employer, executive, personnel manager, another therapist), but in truth it obtains for every patient in that one cannot in one's everyday life avoid innumerable encounters with others. In my own clinical work I try with every patient to make this an explicit area of inquiry; I examine their interpersonal contacts, both intimate and casual; I explore with them what they want from others and what they contribute to the lives of others.

The belief that it is good to give, to be useful to others, to make the world better for others, is a powerful source of meaning. It has deep roots in the Judeo-Christian religious tradition and has been accepted as an *a priori* truth even by those who reject the theistic component.

Dedication to a Cause. "What man is, he has become through that cause he has made his own."[48] Karl Jasper's words indicate another important secular source of life meaning—devotion to a cause. Will Durant, the philosopher and historian, wrote a book entitled *On the Meaning of Life*, which consists of statements by eminent men on their notions of meaning in life. Working for some "cause" is a pervasive theme.

In his conclusions Durant states his personal position:

> Join a whole, work for it with all your body and mind. The meaning of life lies in the chance it gives us to produce, or to contribute to something greater than ourselves. It need not be a family (although that is the direct and broadest road which nature in her blind wisdom has provided for even the simplest soul); it can be any group that can call out all the latent nobility of the individual, and give him a cause to work for that shall not be shattered by his death."[49]

Many kinds of cause may suffice: the family, the state, a political or religious cause, secular religions like communism and fascism, a scientific venture. But the important thing, as Durant states, is that "it must, if it is to give life meaning, lift the individual out of himself, and make him a cooperating part of a vaster scheme."[50]

"Dedication to a cause" as a source of personal meaning is complex. Durant's statement contains several aspects. First, there is the altruistic component: one finds meaning by contributing to others. Many causes have altruistic underpinnings—either they are dedicated toward direct service, or they may be more complex movements whose direction is

434

ultimately utilitarian ("the greatest good for the greatest number"). It seems important, if an activity is to supply meaning, that it "lift the individual out of himself," even though it is not explicitly altruistic. This concept of "self-transcendence" is central to life-meaning schemas and will be discussed shortly. When, however, Durant speaks of a cause "that shall not be shattered by death" or of "becoming a part of something" greater than oneself," he is referring to other issues (for example, death transcendence, the anxiety of isolation and helplessness) rather than to meaninglessness *per se*.

Creativity.   Just as most of us would agree that service to others and dedication to a cause provide a sense of meaning, so too would we agree that a creative life is meaningful. To create something new, something that rings with novelty or beauty and harmony is a powerful antidote to a sense of meaninglessness. The creation justifies itself, it defies the question What for?, it is "its own excuse for being." It is right that it be created, and it is right that one devotes oneself to its creation.

Irving Taylor suggests that creative artists who have worked with the greatest personal handicaps and the greatest social constraints (only think of Galileo, Nietzsche, Dostoevsky, Freud, Keats, the Brontë sisters, Van Gogh, Kafka, Virginia Woolf) may have had faculties of self-reflection so highly developed that they had a keener vision than most of us of the human existential situation and the universe's cosmic indifference.[51] Consequently, they suffered more keenly from a crisis of meaninglessness and, with a ferocity born of desperation, plunged into creative efforts. Beethoven said explicitly that his art kept him from suicide. At the age of thirty-two, in despair because of his deafness, he wrote, "Little kept me back from putting an end to my life. Art alone held me back. Alas, it seems to be impossible for me to leave the world before I have done all that I feel inclined to do, and thus I drag on this miserable life."[52]

The creative path to meaning is by no means limited to the creative artist. The act of scientific discovery is a creative act of the highest order. Even bureaucracy may be approached creatively. A research scientist who changed fields described the importance and the feasibility of being creative in an administrative position.

> If you go into administration, you must believe that this is a creative activity in itself and that your purpose is something more than keeping your desk clean. You are a moderator and arbiter, and you try to deal equitably with a lot of different people, but you've also got to have ideas, and you've got to persuade people that your ideas are important and to see them into reality. . . . This is part of the excitement of it. In

both research and administration, the excitement and the elation is in the creative power. It's bringing things to pass. Now, I think administration is more exciting than research.[53]

A creative approach to teaching, to cooking, to play, to study, to bookkeeping, to gardening adds something valuable to life. Work situations that stifle creativity and turn one into an automaton will, no matter how high the salary scales, always generate dissatisfaction.

A friend of mine, a woman sculptor, when asked whether she found joy in her work pointed to another facet of creativity: self-discovery. Her work was dictated, in part, by unconscious forces within. Each new piece was doubly creative: the work of art in itself and the new inner vistas illuminated by it.[54]

This expanded view of creativity was exceptionally useful to a composer who sought therapy because the approach of his fifty-fifth birthday had impelled him to examine his life—a process that led him to conclude that he had contributed little to his field. He had a profound sense of purposelessness and was convinced that none of his efforts would have any lasting value. He sought therapy to increase his professional creativity, knowing at the same time that his talent as a composer was limited. Therapy was unproductive until I expanded the concept of creativity to include his entire life. He became aware of how stifled his life was in many areas. For one thing, he had been locked into an unsatisfying marriage for over thirty years and yet could bring himself neither to change it nor to end it. Therapy forged ahead when we reformulated his initial complaint into a new one: "How could he be creative in fashioning a new type of life for himself?"

Creativity overlaps with altruism in that many search to be creative in order to improve the condition of the world, to discover beauty, not only for its own sake but for the pleasure of others. Creativity may also play a role in a love relationship: bringing something to life in the other is part of mature loving and of the creative process as well.

The Hedonistic Solution. A philosophy professor asked members of an undergraduate class to write their own obituaries. One segment of the responses was characterized by such statements as:

Here I lie, found no meaning, but life was continuously astonishing.

or:

Shed your tears for those who have lived dying—
Spare your tears for me for I've died living.[55]

The purpose of life is, in this view, simply to live fully, to retain one's sense of astonishment at the miracle of life, to plunge oneself into the natural rhythm of life, to search for pleasure in the deepest possible sense. A recent textbook on humanistic psychology summed it up: "Life is a gift. Take it, unwrap it, appreciate it, use it, and enjoy it."[56]

This view has a long heritage. In the *Philebus*, Plato presented a debate about the proper goal of every human being. One view argues that one should aim toward intelligence, knowledge, and wisdom. The opposing position is that pleasure is the only true goal in life. This view, hedonism, has had many champions from the time of Eudoxus and Epicurus, in the third and fourth centuries B.C., through Locke and Mill, in the seventeenth and eighteenth centuries, until the present. The hedonists can muster powerful arguments that pleasure as an end in itself is a satisfactory and sufficient explanation for human behavior. One makes future plans and chooses one course over another if, and only if, says the hedonist, one thinks it will be more pleasant (or less unpleasant) for oneself. The hedonistic frame of reference is formidable because it is elastic and can include each of the other meaning schemes within its generous boundaries. Such activities as creativity, love, altruism, dedication to a cause, can all be viewed as important because of their ultimate pleasure-producing value. Even behavior that seems to aim at pain, displeasure, or self-sacrifice may be hedonistic since one may consider it as an investment in pleasure. This is an instance of the pleasure principle yielding to the reality principle—to temporary discomfort that will yield future dividends of pleasure.

Self-Actualization. Another source of personal meaning is the belief that human beings should strive to actualize themselves, that they should dedicate themselves to realizing their inbuilt potential. (See chapter 6 where I discuss the concept of self-actualization in the context of responsibility).

The term "self-actualization" is a modern reformulation of an ancient concept explicitly expressed as early as Aristotle in the fourth century B.C. in his system of teleological causation—a doctrine of internal finality which postulates that the proper end or aim of each object and each being is to come to fruition and to realize its own being. Thus, the acorn is realized in the oak, and the infant in a fully actualized adult.

Later the Christian tradition emphasized self-perfection and offered the figure of Christ, the man-God, as a model to be imitated by those seeking to perfect their God-given being. *The Imitation of Christ*—the fifteenth-century devotional work by Thomas à Kempis and second only to the Bible in its influence on the faithful—and numerous books on the lives of the saints provided guides for generations of practicing Christians, especially the literate ones, into our own time.

In today's secular world "self-actualization" is enmeshed in a humanistic, individualistic framework. Sartre's Orestes sets off on a journey, not toward God but toward the potential, the fully actualized Orestes awaiting within him.

Self-actualization has particular significance for Abraham Maslow who holds that one has within oneself proclivity toward growth and unity of personality and a type of inherent blueprint or pattern consisting of a unique set of characteristics and an automatic thrust toward expressing them. One has, according to Maslow, a hierarchy of inbuilt motives. The most fundamental of these—from the standpoint of survival—are physiological. When these are satisfied, the individual turns toward satisfaction of higher needs—safety and security, love and belongingness, identity and self-esteem. As these needs are met, then the individual turns toward satisfying self-actualizing needs which consist of cognitive needs—knowledge, insight, wisdom—and esthetic needs—symmetry, congruence, integration, beauty, meditation, creativity, harmony.

Self-actualization theorists propose an evolutionary morality. Maslow, for example, states "the human being is so constructed that he presses toward fuller and fuller being and this means pressing toward what most people would call good values, toward serenity, kindness, courage, honesty, love, unselfishness, and goodness."[57] Maslow thus answers the question What do we live *for*? by stating that we live in order to fulfill our potential. He answers the trailer question What do we live *by*? by claiming that the good values are, in essence, built into the human organism and that, if one only trusts one's organismic wisdom, one will discover them intuitively.

Thus, Maslow takes the position that actualization is a natural process, *the* basic organismic process in the human being, and will take place without the aid of any social structure. In fact, Maslow views society as an obstruction to self-actualization because it so often forces individuals to abandon their unique personal development and to accept ill-fitting social roles and stifling conventionality. I am reminded of an old psychology text where I once saw two pictures, juxtaposed. One showed children playing with one another in all the freshness and spontaneity of childhood exuberance and innocence; the other, a crowd of New York subway travelers with vacant stares and mottled gray faces dangling lifelessly from the subway straps and poles. Under the two pictures was the simple caption: "What happened?"

Self-Transcendence. The last two types of meaning (hedonism and self-actualization) differ from the previous ones (altruism, dedication to a cause, and creativity) in one important aspect. Hedonism and self-actualization are concerned with self, whereas the others reflect some basic craving to transcend one's self-interest and to strive toward something or someone outside or "above" oneself.

A long tradition in Western thought counsels us not to settle for a nonself-transcendent purpose in life. To take one example, Buber, in his discussion of hasidic thought, notes that, though human beings should begin with themselves (by searching their own hearts, integrating themselves, and finding their particular meaning), they should not end with themselves.[58] It is only necessary, Buber states, to ask the question "What for? What am I to find my particular way for? What am I to unify my being for?" The answer is: "Not for my own sake." One begins with oneself in order to forget oneself and to immerse oneself into the world; one comprehends oneself in order not to be preoccupied with oneself.

"Turning" is a crucial concept in Jewish mystical tradition. If one sins and then turns *away* from sin, toward the world and *toward* fulfillment of some God-given task, one is considered uniquely enlightened, standing above even the most pious holy man. If, on the other hand, one continues absorbed with guilt and repentance, then one is considered to be mired in selfishness and baseness. Buber writes: "Depart from evil and do good. You have done wrong? Then counteract it by doing good."[59]

Buber's essential point is that human beings have a more far-reaching meaning than the salvation of individual souls. In fact, through excessive preoccupation with gaining an advantageous personal place in eternity, a person may lose that place.

Viktor Frankl arrives at a similar position and expresses strong reservations about the current emphasis on self-actualization. It is his view that excessive concern with self-expression and self-actualization thwarts genuine meaning. He often illustrates this point with the metaphor of a boomerang that returns to the hunter who threw it only if it misses its target; in the same way human beings return to self-preoccupation only if they have missed the meaning that life has for them. He illustrates the same point with the metaphor of the human eye which sees itself or something in itself (that is, it sees some object in the lens or in the aqueous or vitreous humor) only when it is unable to see outside of itself.

The dangers of a nontranscendent posture are particularly evident in interpersonal relationships. The more one focuses on oneself, for example, in sexual relationships, the less is one's ultimate satisfaction. If one watches oneself, is concerned primarily with one's own arousal and release, and is likely to suffer sexual dysfunction. Frankl—quite correctly, I believe—feels that the contemporary idealization of "self-expression" often, if made an end in itself, makes meaningful relationships impossible. The basic stuff of a loving relationship is not free self-expression (although that may be an important ingredient) but reaching outside of oneself and caring for the being of the other.

Maslow uses different language to convey the same concept. In his view, the fully actualized person (a small percentage of the population) is not preoccupied with "self-expression." Such a person has a firm sense of self and "cares" for others rather than uses others as a means of self-expression or to fill a personal void. Self-actualized individuals, according to Maslow, dedicate themselves to self-transcendent goals. They may work on large-scale global issues—such as poverty, bigotry, or ecology—or, on a smaller scale, on the growth of others with whom they live.

Self-transcendence and the life cycle. These life activities that provide meaning are by no means mutually exclusive; most individuals derive meaning from several of them. Furthermore, as Erik Erikson long ago theorized[60] (a theory that has been thoroughly corroborated by the adult life cycle research in the 1970s[61]), there is gradual evolution of meanings throughout an individual's life cycle. Whereas in adolescence and early and middle adulthood one's concerns are centered on self as one struggles to establish a stable identity, to develop intimate relationships, and to achieve a sense of mastery in professional endeavors, in one's forties and fifties one passes (unless one fails to negotiate an earlier developmental task) into a stage where one finds meaning in self-transcendent ventures. Erikson defined this stage ("generativity") as "the concern in establishing and guiding the next generation,"[62] and it may take the form of specific concerns for one's progeny or, more broadly, in care and charity for the species.

George Vaillant, in his splendid longitudinal study of Harvard undergraduates, reported that during their forties and fifties successful men "worried less about themselves and more about the children."[63] One representative subject stated at fifty-five: "Passing on the torch and exposure of civilized values to children has always been of importance to me, but it has increased with each ensuing year." Another:

> The concerns I have now are much less self-centered. From 30–40 they had to do with too many demands or too little money, whether I could make it in my profession, etc. Past age 45 concerns are more philosophi-

cal, more long term, less personal . . . I am concerned about the state of human relations, and especially of our society. I am concerned to teach others as much as I can of what I have learned.

Another: "I don't plan on leaving any big footsteps behind, but I am becoming more insistent in my attempts to move the town to build a new hospital, support schools, and teach kids to sing."[64]

The emergence of self-transcendent concerns is reflected in the professional careers of several of Vaillant's subjects.[65] One scientist had pioneered, in his twenties, a new method of making poison gas; at fifty he chose to research methods of reducing air pollution. Another had, during his youth, worked for the military industrial establishment and helped calculate the blast radius of atomic warheads; at fifty he pioneered a college course in humanism.

A major longitudinal study at Berkeley, California, conducted by Norma Haan and Jack Block compared thirty-year-old and forty-five-year-old individuals to themselves as adolescents and arrived at similar findings. Altruism and other self-transcendent behavior increased over time. Individuals at forty-five were "more sympathetic, giving, productive and dependable" than they were at thirty.[66]

Much developmental research has dealt primarily with the male life cycle and has not taken special circumstances in the lives of women sufficiently into consideration. Recent feminist scholarship has offered an important corrective. Middle-aged women, for example, who earlier in their lives devoted themselves to marriage and motherhood, seek different meanings to fulfill than their middle-aged male counterparts. Traditionally women have been expected to meet the needs of others before their own, to live vicariously through husbands and children, and to play a nurturing role in society as nurses, volunteers, and purveyors of charity. Altruism has been imposed upon them rather than freely chosen. Thus, at a time when their male counterparts have achieved worldly success and are ready to turn to altruistic considerations, many middle-aged women are, for the first time in their lives, concerned primarily with themselves rather than with others.

THE CONTRIBUTIONS OF VIKTOR FRANKL

Self-transcendence is the cardinal feature of Viktor Frankl's approach to the question of meaning, and this is an appropriate place to consider some of Frankl's views on meaning and psychotherapy.

Few clinicians have made any substantial contributions to the role of meaning in psychotherapy, and virtually none have in their published work maintained a continued interest in this area. Viktor Frankl is the single exception; and from the beginning of his career, his professional interest has focused exclusively on the role of meaning in psychopathology and therapy. Frankl, a Viennese and an existentially oriented psychiatrist, first used the world "logotherapy" (*logos*="word" or "meaning") in the 1920s. Later he used the term "existential analysis" as a synonym; but to avoid confusion with other existential approaches (notably that of Ludwig Binswanger), Frankl has in recent years referred to his approach, in either a theoretical or a therapeutic context, as "logotherapy." Although Frankl is aware of the many clinical issues stemming from the other existential ultimate concerns, he maintains in all his work a singular accent on meaning in life. When he speaks of existential despair, he refers to a state of meaninglessness; and when he speaks of therapy, he refers to the process of helping the patient find meaning.

Before I discuss Frankl's contributions, a few words about his methods and style of presentation are in order. Despite his prolific output and the fact that he has, in my opinion, made an important contribution to psychotherapy theory, he has not gained the recognition he deserves from the academic community.

In part this neglect may be a function of the content of Frankl's thought which, like most contributions to existential therapy, can find no home in the "better" academic neighborhoods. Logotherapy belongs neither to psychoanalytically oriented schools, nor to formal psychiatry, nor to religious studies, nor to behaviorally oriented academic psychology, nor even to the "pop" personal growth movement. (Nonetheless his books have a wide general audience: his first book, *Man's Search for Meaning*, sold over two million copies.)

Furthermore, many scholars find Frankl's method offensive. His arguments are often appeals to emotion; he persuades, makes *ex cathedra* proclamations, and is often repetitive and strident. Furthermore, though he claims to present a secular approach to meaning (he states that as a physician who has taken the oath of Hippocrates, he is obliged to develop treatment methods that apply to all patients, atheists and devout alike), it is clear that Frankl's approach to meaning is fundamentally religious.

Serious readers are often troubled by many distractions in reading Frankl. In virtually every work there are numerous self-aggrandizing comments: self-citations, reminders about the many universities at which he has lectured, his many titles, the many eminent people who endorse his approach, the number of professionals who assist him, the occasions when medical students have broken out into unrestrained applause during one of his interviews, the foolish questions posed to him and his pithy rejoinders. Works by Frankl's disciples are particularly unenlightening and consist of a restatement of his remarks and an idealization of his person.

Still, I would urge the reader to persevere. Frankl has made a significant contribution in placing the issue of meaning before the therapist and in his many penetrating insights into the clinical implications of the search for meaning.

Frankl first presented his views on the role of meaning in psychotherapy in *From Death Camp to Existentialism* (later retitled *Man's Search for Meaning: An Introduction to Logotherapy*).[67] In the first part of this book Frankl describes his grim existence in Auschwitz from 1943–45, and in the remainder, a system of therapy that sprang from his insight that a continued sense of life meaning was crucial for survival in the concentration camp. His book was written on scraps of paper he sequestered in the camp and provided him with meaning and, thereby, with a reason to survive. Frankl's own meaning in life has been since that time "to help others find their meaning."[68]

Basic Assumptions. Frankl begins by taking issue with Freud's basic laws of motivation, the homeostasis principle, which posited that the human organism attempts unceasingly to maintain an inner equilibrium. The pleasure principle acts to maintain homeostasis and has as its fundamental goal the removal of tension. The pleasure principle operates in naked, unashamed form early in life; later, as the individual matures, the workings of the pleasure principle become more obscure when the reality principle requires delay or sublimation of gratification.

The problem with a theory that posits some inbuilt drive (that is, the "drive to pleasure" or "tension reduction") is that it is ultimately and devastatingly reductionistic. In this view man is "nothing but . . ." (and here may follow any of an infinite array of formulas). Frankl's favorite is: "Man is nothing but a complex biochemical mechanism powered by a combustion system which energizes computers with prodigious storage facilities for retaining encoded information."[69] Correspondingly, love, or altruism, or the search for truth, or beauty, is "nothing but" the expression of one or the other of the basic drives in duality theory. From this reductionistic point of view, as Frankl points out, "all cultural creations of humanity become actually by-products of the drive for personal satisfaction."[70]

The press toward reductionism in psychology has important implications for therapy. Human behavior is often motivated by unconscious forces, and it is the task of the therapist to lay bare the patient's under-lying psychodynamics. But Frankl argues (and quite correctly, I believe) that there comes a time when the unmasking has to stop. Materialism (that is, explaining the higher by the lower) is often undermining. Peace Corps volunteers do not always, to choose one example, elect to serve for self-serving reasons. Their desire to serve needs no "lower" or "deeper" justification; it reflects a will toward meaning, a reaching outside of self toward finding and fulfilling a purpose in life.

Frankl—along with many others (for example, Charlotte Buhler[71] and Gordon Allport[72])—believes that homeostatic theory fails to explain many central aspects of human life. What the human being needs, Frankl says, "is not a tensionless state but rather a striving and struggling for some goal worthy of him."[73] "It is a constitutive characteristic of being human that it always points, and is directed, to something other than itself."*[74]

Another major objection Frankl offers to a nontranscendent pleasure-principle view of human motivation is that it is always self-defeating. The more one seeks happiness, the more it will elude one. This observation (termed the "hedonistic paradox" by many professional philosophers[75]) led Frankl to say, "Happiness ensues; it cannot be pursued." (Alan Watts put it: "It's only when you seek it that you lose it."[76]) Pleasure is thus not the final goal but is a by-product of one's search for meaning.

Frankl calls his orientation the "third" Viennese school of psychotherapy:

> According to logotherapy, the striving to find a meaning in one's life is the primary motivational force in man. That is why I speak of a "will to meaning" in contrast to the pleasure principle (or as we could also term it the "will to pleasure") on which Freudian psychoanalysis is centered, as well as in contrast to the "will to power" stressed by Adlerian psychology.[77]

Elsewhere he states (following a suggestion of Aaron Ungersma[78]) that the primary motivating force in the human being undergoes a developmental sequence, and that the three Viennese schools reflect this evo-

---

* Frankl's position is supported by a long line of phenomenologists, beginning with Franz Brentano and later Edmund Husserl, who discovered that consciousness is always "intentional": it is always directed to something outside of itself. One is always conscious of something outside of oneself.

lution: "The Freudian pleasure principle is the guiding principle of the small child, the Adlerian power principle is that of the adolescent, and the will to meaning is the guiding principle of the mature adult."[79] Frankl is careful to distinguish between drives (for example, sexual or aggressive) that *push* a person from within (or, as we generally experience it, from below) and meaning (and the values implicit in the meaning system) that *pulls* a person from without. The difference is between drive and strive. In our most essential being, in those characteristics that make us human rather than animal, we are not driven but instead actively strive for some goal. Striving, as opposed to being driven, implies not only that we are oriented toward something outside of self (that is, we are self-transcendent) but also that we are free—free to accept or to deny the goal that beckons us. "Striving" conveys a future orientation: we are pulled by what is to be, rather than pushed by relentless forces of past and present.

Meaning is essential for life, Frankl claims. It was essential for survival and at Auschwitz, and it is essential for all people at all times. He cites a public opinion poll in France that showed that 89 percent of the general population believed that humans need "something" for the sake of which to live, and that 61 percent felt that there was something for which they would be willing to die.[80] Frankl is fond of commenting that, "though some psychiatrists state that life-meaning is nothing but defense mechanism and reaction formations, speaking for myself I would not be willing to live merely for my defense mechanisms and would be even less inclined to die for my reaction formations."[81]

Three Categories of Life Meaning. Though Frankl stresses that each individual has a meaning that no one else can fulfill, these unique meanings fall into three general categories: (1) what one accomplishes or gives to the world in terms of one's creations; (2) what one takes from the world in terms of encounters and experiences; (3) one's stand toward suffering, toward a fate that one cannot change.[82]

These three meaning systems—creative, experiential, and attitudinal—have all been touched upon in the previous discussion of various systems of personal meaning. Frankl defines creativity in conventional terms—that is, as a creative work or art or a scholarly endeavor that beckons one, and that each of us alone is uniquely equipped to fulfill. Frankl's sense that he, and only he, could write the book that illuminated the role of meaning in psychotherapy was, by his account, the major factor (aside from pure chance) that permitted him to endure and to survive Auschwitz. A wide array of life's activities, if approached creatively, may imbue one with meaning. "What matters," Frankl says, "is not how large is the radius of your activities but how well you fill its circle."[83]

Frankl is less clear about the meaning derived from experience, but in general he refers to what one derives from beauty, from truth, and especially from love. Engagement in deep experience constitutes meaning: "If someone tapped your shoulder while listening to your favorite music, and asked you if life were meaningful, would you not," asks Frankl, "answer Yes? The same answer would be given by the nature lover on a mountain top, the religious person at a memorable service, the intellectual at an inspiring lecture, the artist in front of a masterpiece."[84]

Frankl's personal life experiences in Auschwitz demanded that he think deeply about the relationships between meaning and suffering, between pain and death. Survival in extreme circumstances depends upon one's being able to find a meaning in one's suffering. In the depth of despair in the concentration camp Frankl searched for ways to give meaning to his suffering and to the suffering of others. He concluded that only by surviving could he give meaning to his anguish. For him, survival meant that he could complete his work, that he could forge a valuable psychotherapeutic approach out of the horrors of his Auschwitz experience. Some inmates wished to survive for the sake of others, for children or a spouse who awaited them; some for the sake of completing some unique life project; some wished to survive to tell the world about the camps; some wished to survive for revenge. (One thinks of the Lithuanian ghetto at Kovno whose citizens wished to stay alive for the sake of recording all the atrocities that were perpetrated upon them: written narrative accounts, artists' drawings of faces, uniform serial numbers of SS officers and men were carefully noted and stored in an underground vault where, after the war, they were retrieved and used to bring the guilty to trial). At other times Frankl found meaning in suffering by remembering another aphorism of Nietzsche's: "That which does not kill me makes me stronger."[85] Suffering can have a meaning if it changes one for the better. And finally, even when there is no hope of escape from suffering and death, Frankl states that there is meaning in demonstrating to others, to God, and to oneself that one can suffer and die with dignity.

Frankl's categories of meaning supply him with psychotherapeutic strategies to aid the patient who is in a crisis of meaning. I shall consider these contributions shortly in the discussion on therapy, but shall now turn to the clinical implications of the loss of life meaning.

Loss of Meaning: Clinical Implications

OUR CHANGING CULTURE: WHERE HAVE ALL THE MEANINGS GONE?

Many clinicians have noted that, with accelerating frequency, patients come in for therapy because of complaints associated with lack of a sense of meaning in life. Why? What are the factors in contemporary culture that contribute to a decreasing sense of life meaning?

Citizens of the pre-industrial agricultural world were beset by many life problems, but today's malady of meaninglessness does not seem to have been one of them. Meaning was supplied then in many ways. For one thing the religious world view supplied an answer so comprehensive that the question of meaning was obscured. Furthermore, people of earlier ages were often so preoccupied with the task of meeting other more basic survival needs, such as food and shelter, that they were not afforded the luxury of examining their need for meaning. Indeed, as I shall discuss later, meaninglessness is intricately interwoven with leisure and with disengagement: the more one is engaged with the everyday process of living and surviving, the less does the issue arise. Tolstoy, whose crisis of meaninglessness I described at the beginning of this chapter, observed that the simple peasant on his estate seemed relatively untroubled by fundamental doubts. Tolstoy concluded that the peasant knew something that he did not, and, accordingly, he sought for relief from his torment by attempting to emulate the peasant in order to discover the latter's secret knowledge.

Citizens of the pre-industrialized world had other meaning-providing activities in their everyday life. They lived close to the earth, felt a part of nature, fulfilled nature's purpose in plowing the ground, sowing, reaping, cooking, and naturally and unself-consciously thrusting themselves into the future by begetting and raising children. Their everyday work was creative as they shared in the creation of life amongst their livestock and seed and grain. They had a strong sense of belonging to a larger unit; they were an integral part of a family and community and, in that context, were provided scripts and roles. Moreover, their work was intrinsically worthwhile. Who, after all, can challenge the task of growing food with the question What for? Growing food is an endeavor that is simply right beyond questioning.

But all those meanings have vanished. A citizen of today's urbanized, industrialized secular world must face life *sans* a religiously based cosmic meaning-system and wrenched from articulation with the natural world and the elemental chain of life. We have time, too much time,

447

to ask disturbing questions. As the four- and three-day work week loom ahead, we must brace ourselves for increasingly frequent crises of meaning. "Free" time is problematic because it thrusts freedom upon us.

Work, what there is of it, no longer supplies meaning. Not even an extraordinarily fertile imagination could imbue many common forms of modern work with creative potential. The assembly line worker, for example, not only has no creative outlet on the job but systematically begins to consider himself or herself as a mindless cog in the factory machinery. Furthermore, much work lacks intrinsic value. How can the members of clerical armies performing "busy" work in vast, wasteful bureaucratic systems believe that their activities are worthwhile? With the population explosion, and its exposure on the mass media, how can the individual help but doubt that the begetting and rearing of children is doing a favor to anyone, least of all to the planet or the human species?

CLINICAL MANIFESTATIONS

How does the clinician encounter the phenomenon of meaninglessness in everyday clinical work? Few clinicians doubt that the complaint is common: earlier in this chapter I cited comments by Jung, Frankl, Maddi, Wolman, and Hobbs attesting to the frequency of meaninglessness as a clinical complaint. Unfortunately few systematic clinical inquiries have been made.

My colleagues and I conducted a project several years ago that, though it studied only a small clinical sample, lends some support to the claims that meaninglessness is a frequent clinical complaint.[86] The chief problems of forty consecutive patients applying for therapy at a psychiatric outpatient clinic were investigated in three different ways: patient's written self-report, therapist's report, conclusions of three clinicians observing a videotape of a clinical interview with each patient. Of the forty patients, nine listed some problem (most patients compiled a total list of three to six problems) centering around lack of meaning (such as "lack of purpose," "need for meaningfulness in my life," "don't know why I'm doing what I'm doing," "drifting without a goal," "lack of direction in my life"). The therapist and independent raters rated five of these nine patients as having a major problem surrounding meaning, but also included three additional patients (who listed the problems of "lacks meaning in life," "purposelessness," and "vague life goals"). Thus of forty patients, twelve (30 percent) had some major problem involving meaning (as adjudged from self-ratings, therapists, or independent judges).

Jill Gardner studied eighty-nine patients applying for therapy at an outpatient clinic.[87] The patients were asked to indicate the importance of sixteen different reasons for entering therapy. Of the patients 68 percent rated "to seek increased meaning in life" as "moderately" or "very" important. This item ranked ninth of the sixteen reasons and well ahead of such items as "to change how I relate to people" and "loneliness."

Meaninglessness is rarely mentioned as a clinical entity because it is generally considered to be a manifestation of some other, primary, and more familiar clinical syndrome. Indeed, Freud once stated, "The moment a man questions the meaning of life, he is sick. . . . By asking this question one is merely admitting to a store of unsatisfied libido to which something else must have happened, a kind of fermentation leading to sadness and depression."[88] Accordingly, meaninglessness is considered a symptom of some more significant underlying condition, such as chronic alcoholism, other forms of substance abuse, low self-esteem, depression, and identity crisis.

But let us examine what observations have been made of the clinical manifestations of meaninglessness. First, there is its ubiquity. I find that virtually every patient I have worked with has either gratuitously expressed concern about the lack of meaning in his or her life or has readily responded to inquiries I have made about the issue.

Existential Vacuum and Existential Neurosis. Frankl distinguishes two stages of a meaninglessness syndrome: the existential vacuum and the existential neurosis. The existential vacuum—or, as he sometimes terms it, "existential frustration"—is a common phenomenon and is characterized by the subjective state of boredom, apathy, and emptiness. One feels cynical, lacks direction and questions the point of most of life's activities. Some complain of a void and a vague discontent when the busy week is over (the "Sunday neurosis"). Free time makes one aware of the fact that there is nothing one *wants* to do. Frankl claims that existential frustration is increasing in frequency and spreading into all parts of the world. In one study he reports an incidence of "existential vacuum" of 40 percent for college students in Vienna and of 81 percent for American college students.[89] In another study he reports a rapid spread into such areas as Czechoslovakia, other Iron Curtain countries, and Africa.[90] Alois Habinger reports a rise in the incidence of existential frustration among youngsters over a two-year period in Vienna (1970–72)—30 to 80 percent![91] As the method of inquiry is not reported in any of these accounts (aside from the comment "improvised statistical survey"), we cannot take these hyperbolic data literally; but if they

449

even remotely reflect the incidence of existential vacuum, they are noteworthy.

If the patient develops, in addition to explicit feelings of meaninglessness, overt clinical neurotic symptomatology, then Frankl refers to the condition as an existential or "noogenic" neurosis. He posits a psychological *horror vacui: when there is a distinct (existential) vacuum, symptoms will rush in to fill it.* The noogenic neurosis may, according to Frankl, take any clinical neurotic form; he mentions various symptomatic pictures—alcoholism, depression, obsessionalism, delinquency, hyperinflation of sex, daredevilry. What differentiates noogenic neurosis from conventional psychoneurosis is that the symptoms are a manifestation of a thwarted will to meaning. Behavioral patterns also reflect a crisis of meaninglessness. Modern man's dilemma, Frankl states, is that one is not told by instinct what one *must* do, or any longer by tradition what one *should* do. Nor does one know what one *wants* to do. Two common behavioral reactions to this crisis of values are *conformity* (doing what others do) and *submission to totalitarianism* (doing what others wish).

Crusadism, Nihilism, and Vegetativeness.   Salvador Maddi suggests that a significant amount of current psychopathology emanates from a sense of meaninglessness.[92] (Note, however, that Maddi's clinical material is limited,[93] and his basic orientation is that of a macrotheoretician and academic psychologist.) He describes three clinical forms of "existential sickness" (as he terms pervasive meaninglessness): crusadism, nihilism, and vegetativeness.

Crusadism (also termed "adventurousness"[94]) is characterized by a powerful inclination to seek out and to dedicate oneself to dramatic and important causes. These individuals are demonstrators looking for an issue; they embrace a cause almost regardless of its content. As soon as one cause is finished, these hard-core activists must rapidly find another in order to stay one step ahead of the meaninglessness that pursues them.

The fact that the crusader searches out causes almost indiscriminately does not, of course, imply that most or even many supporters of any given social movement are motivated by similar factors. Nor is zeal for social change to be regarded as a defense mechanism. But involvement in a social movement is generally time-consuming, exhausting, and, if it involves civil disobedience, often dangerous. When a movement's purpose is accomplished, the participants, unlike the crusader, generally return to the business of their everyday lives. Crusadism, as Maddi describes it, is thus a reaction formation; the individual engages compulsively in activities in response to a deep sense of purposelessness.

Nihilism is characterized by an active, pervasive proclivity to discredit activities purported by others to have meaning. The nihilist's energy and behavior flow from despair; he or she seeks the angry pleasure involved in destruction to quote Maddi:

> He will be quick to point out that love is not altruistic but selfish, how philanthropy is a way of expiating guilt, that children are vicious rather than innocent, how leaders are vain and power-mad rather than inspired by a grand vision, and how work is not productive but rather a thin veneer of civilization hiding the monster in us all.[95]

Nihilism is so common, Maddi suggests, that it is not even recognized as a problem; in fact, it often masquerades as a highly enlightened, sophisticated approach to life. He cites the novelist and film maker Alain Robbe-Grillet, whose film, *Last Year at Marienbad*, contains seemingly meaningful threads but each defies the attempts of the moviegoer to discover its meaning. The film, Maddi suggests, was intended to frustrate any search for meaning in order to demonstrate the futility of believing in the meaningfulness of anything.

The *vegetative* form of existential sickness is the most extreme degree of purposelessness. One does not compulsively search for meaning in causes; nor does one angrily lash out at meaning embraced by others. Instead, one sinks into a severe state of aimlessness and apathy—a state that has widespread cognitive, affective, and behavioral expressions. The *cognitive* component is the chronic inability to believe in the usefulness or the value of any of life's endeavors. The *affective* tone is one of pervasive blandness and boredom, which are punctuated by episodic depressions. As the condition progresses, the individual settles into indifference, and periods of depression become less frequent. Overall *behavioral* levels are low to moderate, but even more important is the lack of selectivity of behavior: it becomes immaterial to the person which activities, if any, he or she pursues.

The vegetative trend is widespread in contemporary culture. Maddi suggests that it is clearly reflected in such artistic creations as the films of Antonioni, T. S. Eliot's *The Wasteland*, Edward Albee's *The Zoo Story*, Jean Genet's *The Balcony*. The contemporary film *Easy Rider* is a particularly vivid example of apathy and meaninglessness.

Individuals with a developing vegetative syndrome may seek therapeutic help for the associated depression and painful doubting. The therapist may note that such a patient is not troubled with guilt or esteem-identity problems or with manifestations of sexual or aggressive concerns. Instead, the patient voices such concerns as: Why bother working all your life if everything ends in death? Why spend half your life going to school? Why marry? Why raise a family? Why endure any deprivation? Aren't all values arbitrary, all goals illusionary?

If the condition progresses unchecked, the patient sinks deeper into indifference. He or she may withdraw from any engagement with life by becoming a recluse, a chronic alcoholic, or a hobo or by adopting some other analogous life pattern. Maddi suggests that many institutionalized patients are in a vegetative form of meaninglessness but, because they must be labeled with some official nosological diagnosis, are generally referred to as simple schizophrenics—a term now recognized to be a misnomer. Some vegetative patients are diagnosed as psychotically depressed. Even though they may not show the signs and symptoms of depression, the assumption is made that if they are vegetative they must be depressed. Maddi argues that at least some proportion of institutionalized patients with these diagnoses or other makeshift labels might, more appropriately, be considered existentially ill.

Compulsive Activity. The preceding clinical forms of meaninglessness are not, of course, observed commonly as full-blown entities but represent a clinical paradigm. Features and varying degrees of severity may be seen in many patients, often mingled with other clinical complaints. In my experience one of the more common clinical forms of meaninglessness is a pattern of frenetic activity that so consumes the individual's energy that the issue of meaning is drained of its toxin. This pattern is related to crusaderism but is broader in scope. Not only some dramatic social cause but any compelling human activity can be so cathected that it serves as a caricature of meaning. When the activity has no intrinsic "goodness" or "rightness," then it sooner or later will fail the individual. This phenomenon, which James Pike referred to as a "false centering" of life,[96] generally comes to the clinician's attention when the vehicle of meaning has collapsed or is in obvious danger of collapsing. Examples abound in which individuals in pursuit of meaning through social position, prestige, material acquisitions, or power suddenly are forced to question the value of these goals as life pursuits.

Harvey, a forty-two-year-old patient provides a clinical illustration. Harvey's original request for therapy was unusual: a quarrel with his wife over whether to buy first-class or tourist airline tickets propelled him into therapy. The circumstances were as follows. Harvey's father was a middle class, compulsively busy merchant. The whole family, including Harvey, worked long hours six to seven days a week in the family grocery store. Gradually the business expanded into a second and a third store. The business constituted the universe of the family and of Harvey as well. He subscribed to the family's work ethic and considered business prosperity as his *raison d'être*. His long working hours even as a child precluded his developing important chumships or heterosexual relationships, and at the time of graduation from high school he had never spent a night away from home. His identity was that of a "good boy," who never questioned, never rebelled, never thought deeply about himself or about life.

Following graduation from college (a business curriculum), he took over the family business (his father had died in harness) and had a highly successful business career. Through a variety of circumstances— an economically brilliant marriage, an excellent and experienced partner, and his own circumspect intelligence—he built up a nationwide chain of stores which he then sold for a dazzling sum to a large corporation. At thirty he had amassed a fortune of several million 1965 dollars. At this point he might have let up for a brief while, relaxed, perhaps even thought deeply about What next? Whither? or What for? Instead, he plunged immediately into another business enterprise, soon was working over seventy hours a week, and was so consumed with business concerns that his marriage was in peril. When he came for therapy, he had plans for a third empire, since he wanted to see if he could start a business from scratch, with little capital, no business partners, and no outside counsel (the business equivalent of wilderness survival).

Harvey became aware of certain troublesome incongruities. The economical practices of his family of origin stayed with him; and, despite the fact that his income from interest alone was enormous, he searched the newspaper for sales when he shopped and was perfectly willing to drive several miles to save a few dollars on a television set.

But it was the airline ticket caper that spurred him into taking a serious look at his goals in life. He, his wife, and another couple were planning a vacation to the Orient. The difference between first class and coach for the twelve-hour flight was several hundred dollars a ticket. Harvey's wife, his friend (who incidentally worked for Harvey), and the friend's wife all wished to fly first class. Harvey refused to spend the extra money for a wider seat and free champagne (as he put it); and he booked a coach ticket, while the other three, including his wife, traveled first class! Harvey had a good sense of humor and recognized the comedy of the situation; still, he was deeply troubled by the situation and developed anxiety, insomnia, and some hypochondriacal complaints. At this juncture he sought psychotherapy.

In therapy the airline ticket episode became the fulcrum for a far-ranging discussion of values. If money was to be spent lavishly for trivial comforts, why was Harvey killing himself to make more money? Why devote his entire life to money? He had already more than he could spend and had proved he could earn it. He began to question his basic life-long meaning system. One of the first insights Harvey acquired in therapy was that he had falsely centered his life, since material good constituted at best a fragile sense of life meaning—one that would not withstand examination.

The event that propelled Harvey into a crisis of meaning was that he had successfully and precociously achieved his life goal (always a danger in a nontranscendent life-meaning schema). Other events that may precipitate such a crisis include a confrontation with death or some urgent (boundary) experience that confronts the individual with his or her existential situation and illuminates the insubstantial nature of many systems of meaning. Some major upheaval that suddenly uproots the ritual and tradition of the social order may also throw certain values (for example, the social customs of "society") into sharp relief: one not only stops being rewarded extrinsically for adherence to ritual but, even more important, one becomes aware of the absolute relativity of the values one once considered as absolutes.

Some patients undergo a crisis of meaning as a result of psychotherapy. As patients explore themselves deeply and open new vistas within, old compulsive patterns are undermined and eventually decathected. Patients who for much of their life have lived narrowly within the confines of fixed repetitive patterns are faced with the freedom that their compulsivity has guarded them from. For example, the sexually compulsive patient Bruce, whom I described in chapter 5, had always filled "free" or reflective time with sexual fantasy or pursuit. When, in the course of successful therapy, Bruce's compulsivity weakened and then entirely loosened its hold on him, he passed through a crisis of meaning. (It was not that he had a prior, satisfying sense of meaning, but his compulsive activity had always provided a potent antidote to meaninglessness—namely *engagement*. The problem was that *content* of Bruce's compulsive engagement was so limited and restrictive that he failed to realize many of his deeply human potentials. Consequently he had no conscious crisis of meaning in his life, but in its place he experienced massive existential guilt—guilt at not becoming what he had it in him to be.)

When Bruce first faced life *sans* compulsive activity, life seemed to him flat, colorless, zestless, and, above all, pointless. Much time in therapy was then devoted to an exploration of goals, to examining what Bruce's internal wisdom told him about what should be the basis for his life.

454

Clinical Research

The Purpose in Life Test.   In 1964, James Crumbaugh and Leonard Ma-holick, two psychologists greatly influenced by the work of Viktor Frankl, published a psychometric instrument designed to measure purpose in life.[97] This questionnaire, *the Purpose in Life Test* (PIL), consists of twenty items to be rated on a seven-point scale.* On each item, position 4 is designated as "neutral," and different descriptive terms are given for positions 1 and 7. For example the first item reads: "I am usually . . ."; and position 1 is defined as "completely bored," while position 7 is "exuberant, enthusiastic." The other nineteen items, with their two defined anchor points, are:

2. Life to me seems: | (1) completely routine; | (7) always exciting.

3. In life I have: | (1) no goals or aims at all; | (7) very clear goals and aims.

4. My personal existence is: | (1) utterly meaningless, without purpose; | (7) very purposeful and meaningful.

5. Every day is: | (1) exactly the same; | (7) constantly new and different.

6. If I could choose, I would: | (1) prefer never to have been born; | (7) like nine more lives just like this one.

7. After retiring, I would: | (1) loaf completely the rest of my life; | (7) do some of the exciting things I've always wanted to.

8. In achieving life goals I have: | (1) made no progress whatever; | (7) progressed to complete fulfillment.

9. My life is: | (1) empty, filled only with despair; | (7) running over with exciting good things.

10. If I should die today, I would feel that my life has been: | (1) completely worthless; | (7) very worthwhile.

11. In thinking of my life I: | (1) often wonder why I exist; | (7) always see a reason for my being here.

12. As I view the world in relation to my life, the world: | (1) completely confuses me; | (7) fits meaningfully with my life.

13. I am a: | (1) very irresponsible person; | (7) very responsible person.

14. Concerning man's freedom to make his own choices, I believe man is: | (1) completely bound by limitations of heredity and environment; | (7) absolutely free to make all life choices.

---

*The instrument originally consisted of two additional sections: a thirteen-item completion part and an open-ended paragraph to be written on personal ambitions and goals; however, only the first section has been used in subsequent research.[98]

15. With regard to death, I am: (1) unprepared and frightened; (7) prepared and unafraid.

16. With regard to suicide, I have: (1) thought of it seriously as a way out; (7) never given it a second thought.

17. I regard my ability to find a meaning, a purpose, or mission in life as: (1) practically none; (7) very great.

18. My life is: (1) out of my hands and controlled by external factors; (7) in my hands and I am in control of it.

19. Facing my daily tasks is: (1) a painful and boring experience; (7) a source of pleasure and satisfaction.

20. I have discovered: (1) no mission or purpose in life; (7) clear-cut goals and a satisfying life purpose.

The PIL test has enjoyed wide usage; over fifty Ph.D. dissertations on purpose in life have been written which employ it as a major measuring tool; but before discussing some of the results of this research, I shall closely examine the validity of the instrument.

First, the face content of the items deals with several different concepts. Eight items (3,4,7,8,12,17,20) deal explicitly with life meaning (purpose, mission); six items (1,2,5,6,9,19) deal with life satisfaction (life is boring, routine, exciting, or painful); three items (13,14,18) deal with freedom, one item (15), with fear of death; one (16), with contemplation of suicide; and one (10) with worthwhileness of one's life. To my mind this conceptual confusion raises serious questions about the validity of the instrument. Although, for example, life satisfaction or consideration of suicide may be related to meaning in life, they are even more obviously related to other psychological states—most notably depression. Little information has been provided by the test authors about methods of item selection or of individual item behavior. In the light of these methodological shortcomings, one reviewer suggested that a single item "How meaningful is your life?" might be as valid as the entire scale.[99]

Furthermore, the PIL is obviously loaded in social desirability (a correlation coefficient of .57 is reported with the Marloew-Crowne Social Desirability scale).[100] The PIL, as critics have pointed out,[101] reflects certain values: for example, it assumes that responsibility acceptance is equivalent to a positive sense of life meaning. Although this is an interesting hypothesis, it is not clear that responsibility and meaning are so related.

Charles Garfield administered the PIL to subjects from several subcultures (ghetto residents, engineers, graduate students in psychology and religious studies, commune inhabitants) and then interviewed subjects with high, low, and intermediate scores to determine what each item meant to them.[102] Depending in part upon their culture, subjects interpreted the items in highly idiosyncratic ways. For example, on item 9 ("My life is: empty . . . [or] running over with exciting good things") ghetto residents thought of empty stomachs, commune residents viewed "empty" as associated with losing one's ego in meditation and bliss, engineers equated "empty" with dullness, and psychology students viewed "exciting" as not a good thing but associated it with agitation or nervous activity. Similar divergent responses on other items underscored the facts that not only is the wording ambiguous but also that the test is highly value-laden and based on assumptions inherent in a Protestant work ethic, with emphasis on goal-directed behavior, future orientation, activity over passivity, and the positivity of high levels of stimulation.

These criticisms are substantial, indeed devastating, and have never been satisfactorily answered by researchers using the PIL; they all make it difficult for one to have a high level of confidence in the instrument. Still, it is the only game in town, the only psychological instrument that has been used widely to study meaninglessness in a systematic manner. Keeping these reservations in mind, let me consider some of the research findings.

First, several validity studies have indicated that the test results correlate satisfactorily with therapists' ratings of life purpose in patients (correlation of .38) and with ministers' ratings of parishioners (.47).[103] By and large, patient populations have a lower PIL than have nonpatients (although some studies are equivocal; for example, one showed a surprisingly small difference in the scores of indigent psychiatric patients and undergraduate students—108 versus 106).*[104] Furthermore, the PIL seems to measure an independent personality variable: it does not correlate highly with other scales (aside from the MMPI Depression Scale,[105] some moderate overlap with the Srole Anomie Scale, and , as I already noted, the Social Desirability Scale).

The PIL has been employed in many clinical settings with diverse populations. Delinquent adolescents[106] and high school students[107] who abuse drugs have been shown to have low PIL scores. Patients hospitalized for chronic alcoholism and psychotic disorders have lower PIL

---

* Note that there are twenty items, each with a seven point scale: the highest score is, thus, 140; the lowest, 20.

scores than have neurotic outpatients.[108] The mean of both hospitalized patients and outpatients is significantly lower than in a nonpatient sample.[109] Alcoholics have been reported as having particularly low PIL scores.[110] Another study showed only low-normal scores for hospitalized alcoholics but did note that, with a month-long treatment program, the PIL score rose significantly.[111] A study of outpatients in a British clinic demonstrated that the more highly neurotic and socially introverted patients (as measured by the Eysenck Personality Inventory) have lower PIL scores.[112] Sexual adjustment was studied in a group of normal undergraduates, and it was found that the more sexually frustrated and maladjusted students have lower PIL scores.[113] One study compared PIL scores of physically ill patients and reported an interesting finding: patients who were critically ill had higher PIL scores than had patients with a minor ailment or nonpatients.[114] The authors speculated that these results indicate the approach of death catalyzed the critically ill patients to come to terms with their lives, to "work through" their doubts, and to come to some inner peace.

The relationship between social and religious attitudes and values (Rokeach Value Survey) has been much studied. A low PIL score has been shown to correlate with high valuing of hedonism, excitation, and comfort.[115] A high PIL has been shown to correlate with strong religious beliefs that play a central role in the individual's life.[116] (However, another study fails to replicate this finding.[117]) Another study demonstrates a correlation between a high PIL and conservatism, antihedonism, religious-puritanical values, and idealism.[118] Successfully matriculating Dominican nuns have higher PIL scores than have their less successful cohorts.[119] Two studies demonstrate that a high purpose in life is associated with low death anxiety.[120]

Earlier I discussed how involvement in a meaningful group or cause increases one's sense of meaning. Several studies have tested this concept and demonstrate that a high PIL score is correlated with involvement in organized groups (either religious, ethnic, political, or community service)[121] and involvement in sports and hobbies.[122] (One study, however, reveals no correlation between social activism [civil rights demonstrations] and PIL.[123] Could this be a result of the presence of some of Maddi's "crusaders"?) An Australian study reports a correlation between high PIL and a positive world view, goal orientation, and self-transcendent goals (that is, interests that extend beyond the individual's material and mental well-being).[124] Another study indicates that high PIL undergraduates are significantly more likely to have made vocational choices than are those with low PIL scores.[125] However, a study of business executives and nurses indicates no relation-ship between PIL scores and work attitudes or work motivation.[126]

Finally, it has been shown that ghetto residents, blacks[127] or Mexican-Americans[128] have lower PIL scores. There are contradictory findings on the general relationship between PIL and social-economic class[129] and also between males and females—with males generally found to have higher PIL scores.[130]

The Life Regard Index. Before considering the implications of these findings, let me briefly examine one other instrument designed to study life meaning. The Life Regard Index (John Battista and Richard Almond) is more conceptually sophisticated than the PIL but has unfortunately had no subsequent use.[131] The instrument differentiates "framework" items (such as "I have a clear idea of what I'd like to do with my life") from fulfillment items (such as "I feel that I am living fully"). The authors suggest that both a framework and a belief that one is fulfilling that framework is necessary to a sense of life meaning. The instrument was successfully validated via interviews of subjects, correlates highly with the PIL, and is probably free of the confounding effects of social desirability. The relation between self-esteem and a life-regard (meaning in life) was explored. The authors concluded that a satisfactory level of self-esteem is necessary but not sufficient for a well-developed sense of meaning: that is, it is possible for an in-dividual with high self-esteem to have low meaning in life but not for one with low esteem to have high meaning. One must, as Erik Erik-son suggested, solve the task of establishing self-worth and per-sonal identity before being able to develop a satisfying sense of life meaning.

The research suggests that positive life meaning is dependent upon some fit between one's goals and values and the roles and needs of the social structure in which one is enmeshed. Finally, the authors demon-strated that one has a greater sense of meaning if one perceives oneself as approaching one's goals at a satisfactory rate.

Summary of Research Results. The empirical research on meaning in life corroborates the following:

1. A lack of sense of meaning in life is associated with psychopathology in a roughly linear sense: that is, the less the sense of meaning, the greater the severity of psychopathology.
2. A positive sense of meaning in life is associated with deeply held reli-gious beliefs.
3. A positive sense of life meaning is associated with self-transcendent values.

4. A positive sense of meaning in life is associated with membership in groups, dedication to some cause, and adoption of clear life goals.

5. Life meaning must be viewed in a developmental perspective: the types of life meaning change over an individual's life; other developmental tasks must precede development of meaning.

A caveat: it is important to note the wording of these conclusions. The phrase "is associated with" recurs: for example, a low sense of meaning in life "is associated with" psychopathology. That does not mean, however, that there is any evidence that the absence of meaning *causes* psychopathology. All the research studies are correlative: they merely demonstrate that diminished life meaning and pathology co-occur. One might equally well argue from this research that diminished life meaning is a function—that is, a symptom—of pathology. Indeed, one study demonstrates that in depressed patients, the sense of life meaning is dramatically increased by electroshock therapy![132]

CHAPTER 11

Meaninglessness and Psychotherapy

I N the previous chapter I approached the question of life meaning as it is conventionally framed. Meaning-in-life is an important psychological construct which *prima facie* relates deeply to all of us. I accepted this construct at face value and, accordingly, discussed the array of meaning-offering life activities, and described the pathological clinical manifestations of the phenomenological state of meaninglessness.

Now I shall turn to the immediate everyday problem of therapists who are confronted with patients who state that they have no meaning in life. A therapist who accepts a patient's formulation of the problem is likely to share that patient's sense of entrapment. Such a therapist is reminded of his or her personal incomplete quest for meaning in life. How is it possible, the therapist wonders, for one to solve something for someone else one cannot solve for oneself? The therapist may well conclude that the problem is insoluble, and find ways to circumvent it in therapy.

To avoid this untherapeutic sequence of events, the therapist's first step must be *not* to accept at face value the patient's formulation of the problem. Instead, the therapist must rigorously examine the legitimacy

461

of the complaint that "life has no meaning." If one analyzes the ground on which the complaint rests—that is, the meaning of the question, "What meaning is there in life?"—one learns that, often to a great extent, the question is primitive and contaminated.

For one thing, the question, as conventionally posed, assumes that there is a meaning to life that a particular patient is unable to locate. The question is in conflict with the existential view of the human being as a meaning-giving subject. There is no pre-existing design, no purpose "out there." How could there be one when each of us constitutes our own "out there"?

Another major problem inherent in questions about life meaning is that they are so often confounded with a host of other issues. When these other concerns are dissected and discarded, the patient's primary meaning crisis is less lethal and far more manageable. I shall attempt to refine the clinical question of meaning in life by first considering why we need meaning and then examining the various concerns that often obscure the question.

Why Do We Need Meaning?

Decades of empirical research have established that our perceptual neuropsychological organization is such that we instantaneously pattern incoming random stimuli. The gestalt movement in psychology founded by Wolfgang Kohler, Max Wertheimer, and Kurt Koffka has spawned an enormous amount of research both in perception and in motivation which demonstrates that we organize molecular stimuli as well as molar behavioral and psychological data into *gestalten*, into configurations or patterns. Thus, when presented with random dots on wallpaper, one organizes them into figure and ground; when confronted with a broken circle, one automatically perceives it as complete; when presented with diverse behavioral data—for example, a strange noise at night, an unusual facial expression, a senseless international incident—one makes "sense" out of it by fitting it into a familiar explanatory framework. When any of these stimuli or situations do not lend themselves to patterning, one feels tense, annoyed, and dissatisfied. This dysphoria persists until a more complete understanding permits one to fit the situation into some larger, recognizable pattern.

The implications of such meaning-attribution tendencies are obvious. In the same way we face and organize random stimuli and events in our daily world, so too we approach our existential situation. We experience dysphoria in the face of an indifferent, unpatterned world and search for patterns, explanations, and the meaning of existence.

When one is unable to find a coherent pattern, on feels not only annoyed and dissatisfied but also helpless. The belief that one has deciphered meaning always brings with it a sense of mastery. Even if the meaning-schema that one has discovered involves the idea that one is puny, helpless, or dispensable, it is nonetheless more comforting than a state of ignorance.

It is evident that we crave meaning and are uncomfortable in its absence. One finds a purpose and clings to it for dear life. Yet the purpose one creates does not relieve discomfort effectively if one continues to remember that one forged it. (Frankl compares the belief in personally constructed, or "invented," life meanings to climbing a fakir's rope that one has oneself thrown into the air.) It is far more comforting to believe that the meaning is "out there," and that one has discovered it. Viktor Frankl insists that "meaning is what is meant by a situation which implies a question and calls for an answer. . . . There is one solution only to each problem, the right one; and there is one meaning only to each solution, and that is its true meaning."[1] He takes issue with Sartre's position that one of the burdens of being free is that one must invent meaning. Throughout his writing Frankl asserts: "Meaning is something to be found rather than given. Man cannot invent it but must discover it."[2] Frankl's position is basically religious and rests on the assumption that there is a God who has ordained a meaning for each of us to discover and fulfill. Even though we cannot comprehend the meaning in its entirety, Frankl insists we must accept on faith that there is a coherent pattern to life and a purpose to man's suffering. Just as the experimental animal cannot comprehend the reason for its pain, so too is it with human beings who cannot discover their meaning because it lies in a dimension beyond their comprehension. Yet are the basic premises of this argument tenable? After all, if there were a God, why should it follow that He had a purpose for life and, above all, a purpose for each of us. Let us not forget that it is man, not God, who is obsessed with purpose.

MEANING IN LIFE AND VALUES

Thus, one meaning of meaning is that it is an anxiety emollient: it comes into being to relieve the anxiety that comes from facing a life and a world without an ordained, comforting structure. There is yet another vital reason why we need meaning. Once a sense of meaning is developed, it gives birth to *values*—which, in turn, act synergistically to augment one's sense of meaning.

What are values and why do we need them? Tolstoy in his crisis of meaning not only asked Why questions ("Why do I live?") but also How questions, ("How shall I live? By what shall I live?")—all of which expressed a need for values—some set of guidelines or principles to tell him how to live.

A standard anthropological definition of a value is: *"A conception, explicit or implicit, distinctive of an individual or characteristic of a group, of the 'desirable' which influences the selection from available modes, means, and ends of action"*(my italics).[3] In other words, values constitute a code according to which a system of action may be formulated. Values allow us to place possible ways of behaving into some approval-disapproval hierarchy. For example, if one's meaning schema stresses service to others, then one is easily able to develop guidelines, or values, that permit one to say "this behavior is right or this behavior is wrong." I have stressed in earlier chapters that one creates oneself by a series of ongoing decisions. But one cannot make each and every decision *de novo* throughout one's life; certain superordinate decisions must be made that provide an organizing principle for subsequent decisions. If that were not the case, much of life would be consumed by the turmoil of decision making.

Values not only provide the individual with a blueprint for personal action but also make it possible for individuals to exist in groups: "Social life," Clyde Kluckholm tells us, "would be impossible without them. . . . Values add an element of predictability to social life."[4] Those belonging to a particular culture have some shared conception about "what is" and, from this conception, develop a shared belief system about "what must be done." Social norms emanate from a meaning schema that has the consensus of the group, and provide the predictability necessary for social trust and cohesion. A shared belief system not only tells individuals what they ought to do but what others probably will do as well.

MEANING OF LIFE AND OTHER ULTIMATE CONCERNS

Our human needs for overall perceptual frameworks and for a system of values on which to base our actions together constitute the "pure" reasons that we search for meaning in life. Generally, however, the question of meaning is contaminated: issues other than meaning *per se* are attached to and confound it.

Return for a moment to Tolstoy, who often asked: "Is there meaning in my life which will not be destroyed by the inevitable death awaiting me?"[5] "All my acts, whatever I do, will sooner or later be forgotten and I myself be nowhere. Why, then, busy one's self with anything?"[6] These questions are not about meaning but about meta-meaning concerns, and revolve about the issue of transience: will we leave anything enduring behind us? Do we vanish without a trace and, if so, how can our life matter? Is everything pointless if, as Bertrand Russell lamented, "All the labors of the ages, all the devotion, all the inspiration, all the noonday brightness of human genius, are destined to extinction in the vast death of the solar system, and the whole temple of man's achievement must inevitably be buried beneath the debris of a universe in ruins?"[7]

Ernest Becker argues persuasively that our "universal ambition" is "prosperity" (that is, "continued experience"), and that death is the chief enemy with which we must contend. Human beings try to transcend death not only in the many ways discussed in the first section of this book but also through "counting" or mattering or leaving something of themselves behind:

> Man transcends death not only by continuing to feed his appetites [that is, in simple-minded blissful visions of heaven] *but especially by finding a meaning for his life*, some kind of larger scheme into which he fits. . . . It is an expression of the will to live, the burning desire of the creature to count, to make a difference on the planet because he has lived, has emerged on it, and has worked, suffered, and died.[8] (my italics)

Thus, the wish to leave something behind of one's self to matter, to make a difference, Becker would argue, is an expression of an effort to transcend death. Meaning, used in the sense of one's life having made a difference, of one's having mattered, of one's having left part of oneself for posterity, seems derivative of the wish not to perish. When Tolstoy lamented that there was no meaning in his life that would not be destroyed by the inevitable death awaiting him, he was stating not that death destroyed meaning but that he failed to find a meaning that would destroy death.

We too easily assume that death and meaning are entirely interdependent. If all is to perish, then what meaning can life have? If our solar system is to be ultimately incinerated, why strive for anything? Yet though death adds a dimension to meaning, meaning and death are not fused. If we were able to live forever, we would still be concerned about meaning. What if experiences do pass into memory and then ultimately fade? What relevance does that have for meaning? That happens to be the nature of experiences. How could it be otherwise? Experiences are temporal, and one cannot exist outside of time. When they are over, they are over, and nothing can be done about it. Does the past vanish? Is it true, as Schopenhauer said, that "what has been exists as little as what has never been"? Is memory not "real"? Frankl argues that the past is not only real but permanent. He is sorry for the pessimist who despairs when he watches his wall calender grow thinner each day as a sheet is removed, and admires the man who saves each successive leaf and reflects with joy on the richness experienced in the days represented by the leaves. Such a person will think: "Instead of possibilities, I have realities."[9]

We are dealing with value judgments not with statements of fact. It is by no means an objective truth that nothing is important unless it goes on forever or eventually leads to something else that persists forever. *Certainly there are ends that are complete unto themselves* without requiring an endless series of justifications outside ourselves. As David Hume said in the eighteenth century, "It is impossible that there can be a progress ad infinitum, and that one thing can always be a reason why another is desired. *Something must be desirable on its own account* and because of its immediate accord or agreement with human sentiment or affection." (my italics)[10] If no ends were complete unto themselves, if everything had to be justified by something else outside of itself which must in its turn also be justified, then there is infinite regress: the chain of justification can never end.

Not only does death anxiety often masquerade as meaninglessness, but the anxiety stemming from awareness of freedom and isolation is also frequently confused with the anxiety of meaninglessness. Envisioning existence as part of some grand design that exists "out there" and in which one is assigned some role is a way of denying one's freedom and one's responsibility for the design and structure of one's own life and a way of avoiding the anxiety of groundlessness. Fear of absolute loneliness also propels one into a search for identification with something or someone. To be part of a larger group or to dedicate oneself to some movement or cause are effective ways of denying isolation.

MEANING OF LIFE—A CULTURAL ARTIFACT?

The question of meaning in life is not only confounded by issues belonging to the ultimate concerns of death, freedom, and isolation, but it is also extraordinarily difficult to comprehend it free of the biases inherent in a particular culture. A cartoon I once saw illustrates the problem aptly. It depicts a bevy of eager American travelers listening to the

466

words of a bearded Tibetan holy man on a precipitous mountain peak. The caption read: "The purpose of life? If I knew that I'd be rich!"

The cultural bias illustrated by the cartoon influences the views of a prominent psychiatrist who, when writing on meaning in life, asserts with full conviction:

> No human can always achieve, always create. No human being can be continuously successful in his endeavors. But to go in the right direction, not to have achieved, but achieving, not arriving at the inn but walking toward the inn, not resting on the laurels, but moving towards the laurels, putting one's talents to the most constructive, productive and creative use—this is perhaps the main sense of life and the only possible answer to the existential neurosis which cripples human efforts and maims human minds.[11]

With the same sense of conviction Frankl describes "achievement" or "accomplishment" as an "obvious and self-evident" category of life meaning.[12]

But is it obvious? Is striving, creating, achieving, or progressing part of existence, part of the deepest layers of human motivation. The answer is, most assuredly, no. There were other eras in our own culture where goal-directed striving was by no means accepted as a commonly sanctioned mode of finding meaning in life. An inscription on a sundial of great antiquity states: *Horas non numero nisi serena* ("The hours don't count unless they're serene"). Fromm notes that man's burning ambition for fame and lasting achievement has been common from the Renaissance up until the present day whereas it was little seen in medieval man. Furthermore, in northern European countries it was not until the sixteenth century that man's obsessional craving to work first appeared.[13] The belief in "progress," that civilization was inexorably heading in a desirable direction, is, similarly, a notion of relatively recent origin which did not take recognizable shape until the end of the seventeenth century.

Other contemporary cultures take issue not only with an achievement-oriented sense of life purpose but with the very concept of "purpose in life." One of the most articulate spokesmen for an alternate view is D. T. Suzuki, the Zen master. In an extraordinarily luminous essay,[14] Suzuki illustrates two opposing postures to life by comparing two poems. The first, a seventeenth-century haiku by Basho, reads:

> When I look carefully
> I see the Nazuma blooming
> By the hedge!

467

The second, a verse by Tennyson reads:

> Flower in the crannied wall,
> I pluck you out of the crannies;—
> Hold you here, root and all, in my hand.
> Little Flower—but if I could understand
> What you are, root and all, and all in all
> I should know what God and man is.

In the haiku Basho simply observes carefully a Nazuma (an inconspicuous, unpretentious, almost negligible plant) blooming by the hedge. The haiku conveys (though, Suzuki tells us, its subtlety is lost in translation) a tender, humble, close, and harmonious relationship to nature. Basho is quiet; he feels much but gently allows his last two syllables (called a "Kana" in Japanese and appropriately rendered in English by an exclamation point) to convey what he feels.

Tennyson is eloquent and active. He plucks the flower, he tears it away from nature "root and all" (which means that the plant must die) and inspects it closely (as though to dissect it). Tennyson attempts to analyze and to understand the flower; he stands away from it in a scientifically objective fashion. He uses the flower to know something else. He transforms his meeting with the flower into knowlege and, ultimately, into power.

Suzuki suggests that this contrast illustrates Western and Eastern attitudes toward nature and, by implication, toward life. The Westerner is analytical and objective and attempts to understand nature by dissecting and then subjugating and exploiting it. The Oriental is subjective, integrative, totalizing, and he attempts not to analyze and harness nature but to experience and harmonize with it. The contrast, then, is between a searching-action mode and a harmonizing-union one, and often is phrased in terms of "doing" versus "being."

If we step outside of our contemporary skins and look backward, we readily see that our posture toward "purpose" has undergone a gradual evolution. The early Christians valued contemplation above all else. Recall Christ's words: "They sow not, neither do they reap nor gather in the fields; yet your heavenly father feedeth them";[15] or "Consider the lilies of the field, how they grow; they toil not, neither do they spin."[16] The early Christians viewed work and wealth not as goals to be pursued but as obstructions, which clogged the mind with care and consumed the time that should be spent in the service of God. In the early monasteries the lay brothers did the manual labor; artistic expression (manuscript illustration) was more highly valued, whereas con-

468

templation was considered the most holy endeavor. That hierarchy is apparent in the stone carvings on Romanesque cathedral façades.

In the late Middle Ages human beings began to yearn to know the laws of nature and to work toward active subjugation of the physical world. A central motif in thirteenth-century astrological tracts was "The wise man will dominate the stars." Renaissance man explicitly assumed an active stance toward the world. Men like Leonardo da Vinci, Giordano Bruno, and Benvenuto Cellini believed the world existed to be transformed, and they rescued the concept of work (and of craftsmanship) from the neglect into which it had fallen.

In the sixteenth century John Calvin proposed a theological system that has, ever since, greatly influenced the West's attitudes toward life purpose. Calvin believed that humans were predestined by God's grace to be either elected or damned. The elected intuitively knew of their foreordained salvation and, by God's wish, were to participate actively in the affairs of this world. In fact, Calvin said that a sign that one was of the elect of God was one's worldly success. The damned, on the other hand, were the failures in worldly life.

The Puritan tradition, influenced by Calvin, and from which we are not yet entirely unshackled, valued sacrifice, hard work, ambition, and social position. Work was considered godly; the devil found work for idle hands. One's nation was viewed as a rowboat; each person was part of the crew and had to pull his or her own oar.[17] One could either row or be excess baggage—a parasite on the others. This ethic worked wonderfully well for the economic vitality of the young and developing United States; but for generations of individuals who in one way or another did not feel that they measured up, it set the stage for feelings of guilt and worthlessness.

The Western world has, thus, insidiously adopted a world view that there is a "point," an outcome of all one's endeavors. One strives for a goal. One's efforts must have some end point, just as a sermon has a moral and a story, a satisfying conclusion. Everything is preparation for something else. William Butler Yeats complained: "When I think of all the books I have read, wise words heard, anxieties given to parents . . . of hopes I have had, all life weighed in the balance of my own life seems to me *a preparation for something that never happens.*"[18]

A useful language for discussing this Western world view may be borrowed from aesthetics, where a distinction may be made, in a musical composition, between passages that have "introduction" (or "preparation") quality and those that have "exhibition" (or "fulfillment") quality.[19] In the West we view our life's activities in the same way: past

469

and present are preparation for what is to follow. But what is to follow? If we have no belief in an immortality system, then we come to feel that life is all preparation without "exhibition" quality. The sentiments "pointless" or "senseless" follow naturally from this belief.

It must be remembered, however, that art is not life. The distinction of art is that it can provide a balance of "preparation" and "exhibition" in a way that life cannot. The belief that life is incomplete without goal fulfillment is not so much a tragic existential fact of life as it is a Western myth, a cultural artifact. The Eastern world never assumes that there is a "point" to life, or that it is a problem to be solved; instead, life is a mystery to be lived. The Indian sage Bhaqway Shree Rajneesh says, "Existence has no goal. It is pure journey. The journey in life is so beautiful, who bothers for the destination?"[20] Life just happens to be, and we just happen to be thrown into it. Life requires no reason.

Psychotherapeutic Strategies

I began this chapter by stating that an important first step for the therapist is to reformulate the patient's complaint of meaninglessness in order to discover the presence of "contaminating" issues. The experience of meaningless may be a "stand-in" for anxiety associated with death, groundlessness, and isolation; and the therapist is well advised to analyze and approach these concerns along the lines discussed in previous chapters of this book. Often the therapist may be useful to the patient by maintaining a relatively culture-free perspective toward meaning and by helping the patient appreciate that "meaning" is highly relative. The formula that since life has no clear purpose, it follows that life is not worth living is based on culture-bound, arbitrary assumptions.

What other technical options are available to the therapist? I shall review the literature dealing with clinical approaches to meaninglessness but will first note that it is an impoverished literature. Aside from a few scattered clinical notes describing exhortative techniques and some superficial techniques offered by Frankl, the literature is mute.

Why should this be so? Perhaps it is because meaninglessness is so frequently a compound or derivative (rather than an elemental) concern, and appropriate therapist techniques have been developed and described elsewhere in appropriate contexts. Perhaps meaninglessness is such an inherently baffling issue that it defies the development of successful technology. Accordingly, therapists may have learned to in-attend selectively to the issue and to identify only those questions for which they have an answer. This is a discouraging state of affairs; but to those clinicians who are searching for a purpose in their clinical in-vestigative careers, it could be a beckoning opportunity. This chapter gathers together a wide range of reflections on the problem of mean-inglessness with the intention of providing a horizon against which therapists may fashion new and creative responses to an old problem.

THE THERAPIST'S "SET"

When the therapist approaches conflicts involving the ultimate con-cerns of death, freedom, and isolation, one of his or her first acts is "mind-setting." The same act is required of the therapist dealing with meaninglessness. Therapists must increase their sensitivity to the issue, listen differently, become aware of the importance of meaning in the lives of individuals. For many patients, the issue is not crucial: their lives seem filled with meaning. But for others the sense of meaning-lessness is profound and pervasive. Therefore, therapists must be at-tuned to meaning, they must think about the overall focus and direc-tion of the patient's life. Is the patient in any way reaching beyond himself or herself, beyond the humdrum daily routine of staying alive? I have treated many young adults who were immersed in a California singles' life style which is characterized to a large degree by sensuality, sexual clamor, and pursuit of prestige and materialistic goals. In my work I have become aware that therapy is rarely successful unless I help the patient focus on something beyond these pursuits.

But how? How does the therapist effect such a refocusing? If the therapist has a heightened, sensitivity to the importance of meaning in life, then the patient will, through picking up subtle cues from the therapist, become similarly sensitive to the issue. The therapist will, implicitly and explicitly, wonder about the patient's belief systems, in-quire deeply into the loving of another, ask about long-range hopes and goals, explore creative interests and pursuits. I have for example, found it singularly rewarding to take an in-depth history of the pa-tient's efforts to express himself or herself creatively.

All of these activities are an integral part of the patient's life. If one is to know and to value oneself, one must learn to identify and to value these parts. The therapist in order to "care" for the patient must know the patient as deeply as possible. That includes knowing these mean-ing-seeking, meaning-providing activities. I remember one young engineer, an extraordinarily isolated individual who worked at a solitary job during the day and spent evenings and weekends tinkering with his private computer that occupied almost his entire living space. I found it difficult to relate to him. He seemed restricted, lifeless, inexorably dull, and I often visualized him as a little laboratory mouse sniffing at me in my office. My therapeutic fantasy consisted of blowing up that damned computer and bringing some people into his life. We seemed at an impasse: I could develop no sense of caring for him and, accordingly, could not budge him from his isolated ways. Finally I began to inquire what he did every evening with his computer. He was reluctant to answer because he felt much shame about his solitary, reclusive, endless tinkering which, for most of his life, had constituted a symbol of his failure to relate to other people. Eventually, however, he opened up and spent two hours describing his tinkering in fascinating detail. Those sessions changed everything in therapy. He and I both finally understood that the "senseless" tinkering was in truth an important form of creative expression and not merely some sublimating or substitute activity. As a result of this sharing, our relationship became much closer, and he was willing to share other important secrets with me. I gradually helped him to bring other people into his life *along with*, rather than as a replacement for, his creative work and, finally, to share that work with others.

DEREFLECTION

Earlier I described Frankl's dictum that "happiness cannot be pursued, it can only ensue." The more we deliberately search for self-satisfaction, the more will it elude us. The more we fulfill some self-transcendent meaning, the more happiness will ensue. For patients in therapy it is necessary that therapists help them take their gaze off themselves. Frankl describes a specific technique—dereflection—which in principle involves diverting patients' gaze away from themselves, from their dysphoria, from the source of their neuroses and toward the intact parts of their personalities and the meanings that are available for them in the world.

The technique of dereflection, as described by Frankl, is simplistic and consists of little more than telling the patient to stop focusing on himself or herself and to search for meaning outside of self. This transcription of Frankl interviewing a nineteen-year-old schizophrenic girl is representative:

> Frankl: Now you are in a state where reconstruction of your life is the task awaiting you! But one cannot reconstruct one's life without a life goal, without anything challenging him.

Patient: I understand what you mean, Doctor; but what intrigues me is the question: What is going on within me?

Frankl: Don't brood over yourself. Don't inquire into the source of your trouble. Leave this to us doctors. We will pilot you through the crisis. Well, isn't there a goal beckoning you—say, an artistic accomplishment? Are there not many things fermenting in you—unformed artistic works, undrawn drawings which wait for their creation, as it were, waiting to be produced by you? Think about these things.

Patient: But this inner turmoil . . .

Frankl: Don't watch your inner turmoil, but turn your gaze to what is waiting for you. What counts is not what lurks in the depths, but what waits in the future, waits to be actualized by you. I know, there is some nervous crisis which troubles you; but let us pour oil on the troubled waters. That is our job as doctors. Leave the problem to the psychiatrists. Anyway, don't watch yourself; don't ask what is going on within yourself, but rather ask what is waiting to be achieved by you.

Patient: But what is the origin of my trouble?

Frankl: Don't focus on questions like this. Whatever the pathological process underlying your psychological affliction may be, we will cure you. Therefore, don't be concerned with the strange feelings haunting you. Ignore them until we make you get rid of them. Don't watch them. Don't fight them.[21]

For any patient who is excessively self-absorbed, Frankl feels that a long search within for causes of the anxiety generally compounds the problem and is ultimately counterproductive by making the patient even *more* self-absorbed. For such a patient he recommends that a therapist take the position (and convey this position to the patient) that, because of irreversible factors (the patient's family history, genetically transmitted anxiety, genetic imbalance of the autonomic system, and so forth), the patient is destined to experience a high baseline amount of anxiety, for which there is relatively little one can do except take medication or engage in exercise or some similar ameliorative activity. The therapist must then direct attention toward work on the patient's attitude toward his or her situation and toward the detection of meanings available for the patient.[22]

The specific technique depicted in the preceding vignette seems so authoritarian that it would be distasteful, and most likely ineffective, for many contemporary American therapists and patients. No doubt that is to some extent a cultural artifact: the average Viennese citizen is traditionally more likely to revere professional titles and knowledge. But it is problematic on another count: the appeal to authority ("we doctors will pilot you through the crisis") is ultimately undermining to personal growth, since it blocks the path to one's awareness and assumption of responsibility.

Frankl's point stands nonetheless: it is often vitally important to shift the patient's gaze from himself or herself onto others. The therapist must find a way to help the patient develop curiosity and concern for others. The therapy group is especially well suited for this endeavor. Self-absorbed, narcissistic proclivities are readily apparent, and inevitably the pattern of "taking without giving" becomes a key issue in the group. Therapists may ask patients to reflect on how others feel at the moment; therapists may in a flowing, unstructured manner provide training in empathy for others. In groups of acutely disturbed patients I have often assigned morbidly self-absorbed patients the task of introducing new patients to the group and of helping these patients express their pain and their problems to the others.

DISCERNMENT OF MEANING

Frankl suggests that it is the therapist's task to comprehend some coherent pattern, some meaning gestalt, in what would appear to be the random and tragic events of life. Often much ingenuity is required of the therapist, as one of Frankl's cases illustrates. He was consulted by an elderly, depressed general practitioner who could not overcome the loss of his wife two years previously. I quote Frankl:

> Now how could I help him? What should I tell him? Well, I refrained from telling him anything, but instead confronted him with the question, "What would have happened, Doctor, if you had died first, and your wife would have had to survive you?" "Oh," he said, "for her this would have been terrible; how she would have suffered!" Whereupon I replied, "You see, Doctor, such a suffering has been spared her, and it is you who have spared her this suffering; but now, you have to pay for it by surviving and mourning her." He said no word but shook my hand and calmly left my office.[23]

Frankl cites another example of how he has helped patients to detect their life meaning. The following transcript is from an interview with an eighty-year-old woman near death from cancer who was deeply depressed and ridden by anxiety and the feeling that she was useless:

> Frankl: What do you think of when you look back on your life? Has life been worth living?
> Patient: Well, Doctor, I must say that I had a good life. Life was nice indeed. And I must thank the Lord for what it held to me: I went to theaters, I attended concerts, and so forth.
> Frankl: You are speaking of some wonderful experiences; but all this will have an end now, won't it?
> Patient: (thoughtfully) In fact, now everything ends . . .
> Frankl: Well, do you think now that all of the wonderful things of

your life might be annihilated and invalidated when your end approaches? (And she knew that it did!)

Patient: (*still more thoughtfully*) All those wonderful things . . .

Frankl: But tell me: do you think that anyone can make undone the happiness, for example, that you have experienced—can anyone blot it out?

Patient: (*now facing me*) You are right, Doctor: Nobody can blot it out!

Frankl: Or can anyone blot out the goodness you have met in your life?

Patient: (*becoming increasingly emotionally involved*) Nobody can blot it out!

Frankl: What you have achieved and accomplished—

Patient: Nobody can blot it out!

Frankl: Or what you have bravely and honestly suffered: Can anyone remove it from the past wherein you have stored it, as it were?

Patient: (*now moved to tears*) No one can remove it! (*After a while*): It is true, I had so much to suffer; but I also tried to be courageous and steadfast in taking life's blows. You see, Doctor, I regarded my suffering as a punishment. I believe in God.

Frankl: But cannot suffering sometimes also be a challenge? Is it not conceivable that God wanted to see how Anastasia will bear it? And perhaps He had to admit, "Yes, she did so very bravely." And now tell me: Can anyone remove such an achievement and accomplishment from the world, Frau Anastasia?

Patient: Certainly no one can do it!

Frankl: What counts and matters in life is rather to achieve and accomplish something. And this is precisely what you have done. You have made the best of your suffering. You have become an example for our patients by the way and manner in which you take your suffering upon yourself. I congratulate you on behalf of this achievement and accomplishment, and I also congratulate your roommates who have the opportunity to watch and witness such an example.[24]

Frankl reports that the interview enhanced the patient's sense of meaningfulness, and that in her remaining week of life the patient's depression lifted and she died filled with pride and faith.

Terry Zuehlke and John Watkins report a study in which they treated twelve dying patients with a similar clinical approach which heavily emphasized the development of meaning.[25] The authors administered the Purpose in Life test (PIL) both before and after therapy and report a significant increase in purpose in life.

What type of meaning does the therapist help the patient find? Frankl stresses the uniqueness of each patient's meaning but does not, as we see from the clinical transcriptions, shrink from hinting broadly or providing some explicit formed meaning to the patient. The meanings he provides consist of the triad of meaning categories I described

earlier in this chapter: creative accomplishment, experience, and attitude toward suffering. When stressing either creative accomplishment
or experience, Frankl emphasizes the permanence of the past: accomplishments and experiences are stored away and endure forever. When
all other meaning seems obscured by present tragedy and suffering,
Frankl stresses that one may still find meaning in assuming a heroic
stance toward one's fate. One's attitude may serve as an inspiring model for others—children, relatives, friends, students, or even other patients on the ward. One's acceptance of inevitable suffering may be
seen as an embracement of God from whom the suffering emanated.
Or, finally, one's heroic attitude toward one's fate is meaningful in itself in much the same way that Camus regarded "prideful rebellion" as
the human being's final response to absurdity.

Frankl's therapeutic technique as illustrated by these two case examples, which are highly representative of his technical approach, is
problematic for the same reasons that his approach to dereflection is
problematic. In an authoritarian fashion he offers the patient a meaning. But, in so doing, does he not move the patient even farther from
the assumption of full personal autonomy? The same issue emerges
when we examine other therapists who focus on meaning.

Jung, for example, reports a case in which he also explicitly suggested a meaning schema to his patient.[26] The patient was a young, analyzed, secularized, enlightened Jewess with a severe anxiety neurosis.
Jung inquired about her background and learned that her grandfather
was a rabbi who had been widely regarded as a zaddick, a saint who
possessed second sight. She and her father had always scoffed at this
nonsense. Jung felt that he had an insight into the neurosis and told
her: "Now I am going to tell you something you may not be able to accept. Your grandfather was a Zaddick. . . . Your father betrayed the secret and turned his back on God. And you have your neurosis because
the fear of God has got into you." The interpretation, Jung reports,
"struck her like a bolt of lightning."

That night Jung had this dream: "A reception was taking place in my
house and, behold, this girl [the patient] was there. She came up to me
and asked, 'Haven't you got an umbrella? It is raining so hard?' I found
an umbrella and was on the verge of giving it to her. But what happened instead? I handed it to her on my knees as if she were a
goddess."

Jung's dream told him that the patient was not just a superficial little
girl, but that she had the makings of a saint. However her life was directed toward flirtation, sex, and materialism. She had no way to ex-

press the most essential feature of her nature—namely, that "in reality she was a child of God whose destiny was to fulfill His secret will." Jung told the patient his dream (as was his wont) and his interpretation of it. In a week, he reports, "The neurosis had vanished." (It is rare, incidentally, for Jung to report a successful brief therapy case.)

Peter Koestenbaum provides another example of the therapist who explicitly directs the patient toward some purpose.[27] The patient, a man in his early thirties, had a profound lack of self-worth and personal identity stemming in large part from parental neglect during his formative years. He had considerable amnesia for his life before age eight and in therapy persistently bemoaned his lost childhood. The therapist felt that one important way the patient could re-create his lost childhood and redefine himself as a person with a childhood was to commit himself to a child. The patient and his wife had made a firm contract not to have children; therefore, therapist and patient worked out a plan by which the latter would dedicate himself to working with a Big Brother organization. Koestenbaum reports that this worked out splendidly; contact with a child helped the patient view himself and his past differently. A year later the patient and his wife decided to have a child, at which point therapy successfully concluded.

PROGRAMED MEANING

James Crumbaugh reports on a systematic two-week "crash course" logotherapy* program with alcoholics, in which he attempted in a less authoritarian way to improve a patient's ability to seek and find mean-

---

*As I discussed in chapter 10, "logotherapy" is Frankl's term for his psychotherapeutic approach based on helping the patient regain meaning in life. There is a *Logotherapy Journal*, a logotherapy newsletter (with the banner "health through meaning"), a Logotherapy Institute, and several tests[28] on logotherapy. Yet, as I have implied earlier, there is, in my opinion, no coherent logotherapeutic system. Logotherapy consists of improvised attempts to help the patient detect meaning. Logotherapy manuals describe two basic techniques: the first, deflection, I have already discussed; the second is called "paradoxical intention"[29] and is basically a "symptom-prescription" technique where the patient is asked to experience and to exaggerage his or her symptoms. Thus, the stutterer is asked to stutter intentionally, the phobic patient to exaggerate that phobia, the obsessive patient to obsess even more, the compulsive gambler to lose money intentionally. Paradoxical intention is an interesting technique, which Frankl first described in 1938, and it anticipated the similar technique of symptom prescription and paradox employed by the school of Milton Erickson, Jay Haley, Don Jackson, and Paul Watzlawick.[30] There is some evidence that it is effective for brief therapy. Yet I cannot persuade myself that it is specifically related to life meaning. Paradoxical intention helps patients detach themselves from their symptoms; it allows them to view themselves dispassionately, even humorously; above all, it allows them to appreciate that they can influence—in fact, even create—their symptoms. To the extent that paradoxical intention allows one to assume responsibility for one's symptoms, it may be considered within the domain of existential therapy; but its function as a technique to provide meaning is, at best, obscure.

ing.[31] Crumbaugh makes the assumption that if one is to find some coherent pattern in complex life situations, one must be able to perceive
details and events in a comprehensive manner and then to recombine
this data into some new gestalt. Accordingly, the crash program attempts to expand perceptual awareness and stimulate creative
imagination.

The program for the expansion of perceptual awareness included exercises in recording visual stimuli (for example, a subject was exposed
to Rorschach cards and to seascape scenes and assisted in the recall of
details). The program for creative imagination consisted of such exercises as viewing a picture on a screen, projecting oneself into the picture, and relating the picture to some wish based on past experiences.

The pre-post (two weeks later) PIL tests showed an increase in Purpose in Life scores. However the follow-up time was inadequate, and
one has no way of ascertaining outcome specificity: that is, which features of the intensive course were responsible for what results? The inferential leap from visual perception and creative imagination to the
perception of a life meaning schema is broad and strains credulity; but
if positive outcome results are replicated, then a more detailed analysis
of this procedure is warranted.

ENGAGEMENT: THE MAJOR THERAPEUTIC ANSWER TO
MEANINGLESSNESS

Let me return for a moment to the suicide note with which chapter
10 began. Little is known about the man who wrote this note, but this
much stands out: he was not *in* life, but had removed himself from life,
removed himself so far that life and the activity and the experience of
human beings seemed puny and absurd. Even within his brief fable
one character (one of the brick-carrying morons) distances himself still
more by asking why he carries bricks; and from that moment he and
the writer as well are lost.

There is something inherently noxious in the process of stepping
back too far from life. When we take ourselves out of life and become
distant spectators, things cease to matter. From this vantage point,
which philosophers refer to as the "galactic"[32] or the "nebula's-eye"
view[33] (or the "cosmic" or "global" perspective[34]), we and our fellow
creatures seem trivial and foolish. We become only one of countless life
forms. Life's activities seem absurd. The rich, experienced moments are
lost in the great expanse of time. We sense that we are microscopic
specks, and that all of life consumes but a flick of cosmic time.

The galactic view presents a formidable problem for therapists. On the one hand, it seems unassailably logical. After all, the ability to be self-aware, to step outside of oneself, to view oneself from a distance is one of the human being's most valued attributes. It is what makes one human. In most situations a broader, more comprehensive perspective generally provides the observer with more objectivity: yet this particular perspective drains the vitality from life. For one to assume it for prolonged periods results in profound dispiritedness, and continual immersion in it may be lethal.

The tradition of philosophical pessimism, to take one example, is a natural derivative of the nebula's-eye view; and in the nineteenth century its leading spokesman, Schopenhauer, viewed temporality from such a distance that he concluded that it makes no sense to struggle for some goal that (from the galactic perspective) vanishes in an instant. Thus, happiness and goals are unattainable, because they are phantoms of the future or part of the vanished past. Predictably, he concluded: "Nothing is worth our striving, our efforts and struggles. . . . All good things are vanity, the world in all its ends, bankrupt, and like a business which does not cover its expenses."[35]

What Can Be Done?   What can the therapist offer to offset the noxious effects of the galactic view? First, there are logical inconsistencies in the argument that the nebula's-eye view must lead to Schopenhauer's position that "nothing matters, and since nothing matters, life is not worth living." For one thing, if nothing matters, it should not matter that nothing matters. In a penetrating essay on the absurd, Thomas Nagel suggests, in supremely unruffled fashion, that the absurdity that is made evident by the nebula's-eye view is not a *prima facie* disaster and simply does not warrant that much distress.[36] The ability to assume the nebula's-eye view is, Nagel states, one of our most advanced, precious, and interesting traits and is not agonizing unless we make it so. To allow it to matter so heavily betrays a failure to appreciate the cosmic unimportance of the situation. Nagel suggests that a true appreciation of the nebula's-eye view, coupled with the knowledge that it is our strength to be able to assume that view, should permit us to return to our absurd life "laced with irony" instead of with despair.

Another fact for therapists to note is that an actual mattering underlies the despair associated with the "not mattering" of the galactic view. For example, though Schopenhaurer concluded that nothing matters, "nothing is worth our striving," many things mattered to him. It mattered to him to convince others that things did not matter; it mattered to him to oppose a Hegelian system of thought, to continue writing actively until the end of his life, to philosophize rather than to commit suicide. Even to the man who wrote the suicide note about the brick-carrying morons, things mattered: it mattered that he try to comprehend the human condition and to communicate his conclusions to others. If he had sought my help before his suicide, I should have tried to communicate to this "mattering" life-searching part of him.

Kent Bach suggests another antidote to counteract the toxicity of the galactic view; keep in mind that, though that view undermines meaningfulness, it does not do so in any absolute sense; rather, it renders things meaningless *only when one is in that cosmic perspective*.[37] Such times are part of one's life—but only part. Meaninglessness is an experiential state; and though it is so consuming that it appears to render meaningless everything in the past and the future as well as in the present, it can do that *only when we view our lives from the galactic perspective*. "Meaning" is what something needs to matter only when in that perspective. At other times things matter because they matter. Things matter to us all the time. It matters to me that I communicate these ideas as clearly as possible. At other times other things matter—relationships, tennis, reading, chess, talking. Must the fact that these activities don't matter from the nebula's-eye view, that they don't hang together as some unified whole, take away their mattering? When things matter, they don't need meaning to matter!

This concept has immediate therapeutic implications: the therapist must help the patient to understand that current doubting (or the adoption of a new meaning schema) does not vitiate the reality of past mattering. Three patients come to mind. The first had been a nun for twenty-five years and then, after losing her faith, had left the order. Her current depression and sense of anomie was deepened by her belief that she had "lived a lie" for all of her adult life. Another patient had, at the age of fifty-five, begun writing poetry and soon discovered that she had enormous talent. I treated her at the age of sixty, when she was dying of cancer. She was deeply embittered at the fact she had "wasted" most of her life as a farmer's wife, raising children, washing dishes, digging potatoes—activities that did not accord to her current meaning schema. Another patient, in the midst of an acrimonious divorce battle, had been deeply wounded by her husband of twenty years who attempted to strip meaning from her by exclaiming that he had never loved her.

All three patients were helped by the realization that a new meaning schema or a deep state of doubt (that is, current viewing of life from a galactic perspective) does not vitiate the mattering that existed at other times. The former nun gradually understood that her current lack of faith did not erase the faith she had once had, nor did it erase the good she had done then as a teacher under the aegis of a different meaning system. The poet, too, learned in therapy that her earlier life had much meaning to her at the time. She had raised her children, grown food, mingled with the cycle of nature; and in the midst of all this her poetry had been conceived and silently germinated. Her poetry today was a product of her entire life; its particular character was shaped by her unique life experiences—even the ancient scraping of dirt from potatoes found its place in the vital texture of her verse. The third patient learned, too, that past mattering was not only imperishable but very precious. She grew bold in her defense of it and was able to say to her husband: "If you lived with me for twenty years without loving me, that's your tragedy! As for me, though I do not love you now, I once loved you very much and spent many of the best years of my life with you."

Engagement in Life. Though some of these philosophic rebuttals to the state of meaninglessness have some interesting implications for psychotherapy, they lack potency and remain for the most part psychotherapeutic curiosities. Reason, in this instance as in all other matters of therapeutic change, is not in itself sufficient. The therapist requires a more potent approach. David Hume, in a famous passage in the *Treatise*, points the way. As a result of musing while in the galactic perspective, he was beset by clouds of doubt ("philosophical melancholy"):

> Most fortunately it happens, that since reason is incapable of dispelling these clouds, nature herself suffices to that purpose, and cures me of this philosophical melancholy by some avocation, and lively impression of my senses, which obliterate all these chimeras. I dine, I play a game of backgammon, I converse, and am merry with my friends; and when after three or four hours' amusement, I would return to these speculations, they appear so cold, and strain'd, and ridiculous, that I cannot find in my heart to enter into them any farther.[38]

Hume's antidote to the meaninglessness inherent in the cosmic perspective is engagement; and engagement is Sartre's and Camus's solution as well; a leap into commitment and action. Tolstoy chose that solution, too, when he said, "It is possible to live only as long as life intoxicates us."* And engagement is the therapist's most effective approach to meaninglessness.

---

*But, alas, the tug of the galactic perspective was too great for him, and he concluded the sentence, "as soon as we are sober again we see that it is all a delusion, and a stupid delusion."[39]

Earlier I discussed the hedonistic paradox that the more we explicitly search for pleasure, the more it eludes us. Frankl argues that pleasure is a by-product of meaning, and that one's search should be directed toward the discovery of meaning. I believe that the search for meaning is similarly paradoxical: the more we rationally seek it, the less we find it; the questions that one can pose about meaning will always outlast the answers.

Meaning, like pleasure, must be pursued obliquely. A sense of meaningfulness is a by-product of engagement. Engagement does not logically refute the lethal questions raised by the galactic perspective, but it causes these questions not to matter. That is the meaning of Wittgenstein's dictum: "The solution to the problem of life is seen in the vanishing of the problem."[40]

Engagement is the therapeutic answer to meaninglessness regardless of the latter's source. Wholehearted engagement in any of the infinite array of life's activities not only disarms the galactic view but enhances the possibility of one's completing the patterning of the events of one's life in some coherent fashion. To find a home, to care about other individuals, about ideas or projects, to search, to create, to build—these, and all other forms of engagement, are twice rewarding: they are intrinsically enriching, and they alleviate the dysphoria that stems from being bombarded with the unassembled brute data of existence,

The therapist's goal, then, is engagement. The task is not to create engagement nor to inspirit the patient with engagement—these the therapist cannot do. But it is not necessary: the desire to engage life is always there within the patient, and the therapist's clinical activities should be directed toward removal of obstacles in the patient's way. What, for example, prevents the patient from loving another individual? Why is there so little satisfaction from relationships with others? What are the parataxic distortions that systematically poison his or her relationships? Why is there so little work satisfaction? What blocks the patient from finding work that is commensurate with his or her talents or finding pleasurable aspects of current work? Why has the patient neglected his or her creative or religious or self-transcendent strivings?

The therapist's most important tool in this context is his or her own person, through which the therapist engages with the patient. In the ways I have discussed earlier, the therapist guides the patient toward engagement with others by first personally relating deeply and authentically to the patient. Therapists also, as models of personal commitment to engagement, may offer themselves as objects with whom patients may identify: therapists care about their professional mission;

the growth of other human beings matters to them; they help others, often in creative ways, to search for meaning.

In summary, the therapist's first step in dealing with the question of meaninglessness is to analyze and refine the question. Much that is subsumed under the aegis of "meaninglessness" belongs elsewhere (either as a cultural artifact or as part of other ultimate concerns—death, freedom, and isolation) and must be treated accordingly. "Pure" meaninglessness, especially when it emanates from assuming a detached, galactic perspective, is best approached obliquely through engagement which vitiates the galactic perspective.

This therapeutic approach differs greatly from the therapeutic strategies I have described for dealing with other ultimate concerns. Death, freedom, and isolation must be grappled with directly. Yet when it comes to meaninglessness, the effective therapist must help patients to look *away* from the question: to embrace the solution of engagement rather than to plunge in and through the problem of meaninglessness. The question of meaning in life is as the Buddha taught, not edifying. One must immerse oneself in the river of life and let the question drift away.

Epilogue

THE DISCUSSION of meaninglessness brings me back full circle to the definition with which I began: existential therapy is a dynamic approach that focuses on concerns rooted in human existence. Each of us craves perdurance, groundedness, community, and pattern; and yet we must all face inevitable death, groundlessness, isolation, and meaninglessness. Existential therapy is based on a model of psychopathology which posits that anxiety and its maladaptive consequences are responses to these four ultimate concerns.

Though it was necessary to discuss each of the ultimate concerns separately, *in vivo* they are intricately interwoven and constitute the subtext of therapy. In the dialogue between patient and therapist they provide both content and process. The patient's confrontation with death, freedom, isolation, and meaninglessness offers the therapist explicit interpretive content. Even when these themes do not overtly arise in therapy, they still provide a *modus operandi*. Such psychic phenomena as willing, assuming responsibility, relating to the therapist, and engaging in life are the key processes of therapeutic change. It is precisely these crucial activities that are all too often considered unimportant "throw-ins" in many therapeutic systems.

Existential therapy compels attention in that it is firmly planted in ontological bedrock, the deepest structures of human existence. It is compelling, too, because it is humanistically based and, alone among

485

therapeutic paradigms, is entirely concordant with the intensely personal nature of the therapeutic enterprise. Moreover, the existential paradigm has a broad sweep: it gathers and harvests the insights of many philosophers, artists, and therapists about the painful and redemptive consequences of confrontation with ultimate concerns.

Yet it is a paradigm, a psychological construct that can be justified only by its clinical usefulness. As is the case with all constructs, it will eventually be followed by another construct with greater explanatory power. Every clinical paradigm is organic (unless it has been prematurely engraved in stone by some official institute): or by offering a novel perspective, it permits previously obscure data to emerge. These new data modify, in turn, the parent paradigm. I regard this existential paradigm as an early formulation based on clinical observations that are necessarily limited in source, scope, and number. It is my hope that this paradigm will be organic—that it not only will prove useful to clinicians in its present form, but will stimulate the discourse necessary to modify and enrich it.

NOTES

Chapter 1

1. J. Breuer and S. Freud, *Studies on Hysteria*, vol. II in *The Standard Edition of the Complete Works of Sigmund Freud*,* 24 vols., ed. James Strachey (London: Hogarth Press, 1955; originally published 1895), pp. 135–83.

2. Ibid., p. 158.

3. B. Spinoza, cited by M. de Unamuno, *The Tragic Sense of Life*, trans. J. E. Flitch (New York: Dover, 1954), p. 6.

4. A. Freud, *The Ego and the Mechanisms of Defense* (New York: International Universities Press, 1946).

5. H. Sullivan, *The Interpersonal Theory of Psychiatry* (New York: W. W. Norton, 1953).

6. O. Rank, *Will Therapy and Truth and Reality* (New York: Alfred A. Knopf, 1954), p. 121.

7. A. Malraux, cited in P. Lomas, *True and False Experience* (New York: Taplinger, 1973), p. 8.

8. T. Hardy, "In Tenebris," *Collected Poems of Thomas Hardy* (New York: Macmillan, 1926), p. 154.

9. *Encyclopedia of Philosophy*, vol. III (New York: Macmillan and Free Press, 1967), p. 147.

10. S. Kierkegaard, "How Johannes Climacus Became an Author," in *A Kierkegaard Anthology*, ed. R. Bretall (Princeton, N.J.: Princeton University Press, 1946), p. 193.

11. Ibid.

12. W. Barrett, *What Is Existentialism?* (New York: Grove Press, 1954), p. 21.

13. L. Binswanger, "Existential Analysis and Psychotherapy," in *Progress in Psychotherapy*, eds. F. Fromm-Reichman and J. Moreno (New York: Grune & Stratton, 1956), p. 196.

14. R. May, E. Angel, and H. Ellenberger, *Existence* (New York: Basic Books, 1958), pp. 3–35.

15. A. Sutich, American Association of Humanistic Psychology: Progress Report 1962, cited in J. Bugental, "The Third Force in Psychology," *Journal of Humanistic Psychology* (1964) 4:19–26.

16. J. Bugental, "The Third Force."

17. F. Perls, *Gestalt Therapy Verbatim* (New York: Bantam, 1971), p. 1.

18. S. Freud, *The Interpretation of Dreams*, vol. IV in *Standard Edition* (London: Hogarth Press, 1953; originally published 1900), p. 263.

19. T. Wilder, cited in *Reader's Digest* (January 1978), p. 133.

20. V. Frankl, oral communication, 1974.

21. May, Angel, and Ellenberger, *Existence*, p. 11.

22. C. Rogers, cited in D. Malan, "The Outcome Problem in Psychotherapy Research," *Archives of General Psychiatry* (1973) 29:719–29.

23. M. Lieberman, I. Yalom, and M. Miles, *Encounter Groups: First Facts* (New York: Basic Books, 1973).

24. Ibid., p. 99.

25. Personal communication, 1978.

Chapter 2

1. A. Meyer, cited by J. Frank, oral communication, 1979.

2. Cicero, cited in M. Montaigne, *The Complete Essays of Montaigne*, trans. Donald Frame (Stanford: Stanford University Press, 1965), p. 56.

---

*Hereafter referred to as *Standard Edition*.

3. Seneca, cited in Montaigne, *Complete Essays,* p. 61.

4. St. Augustine, cited in Montaigne, *Complete Essays,* p. 63.

5. Manilius, cited in Montaigne, *Complete Essays,* p. 65.

6. Montaigne, *Complete Essays,* p. 67.

7. M. Heidegger, *Being and Time* (New York: Harper & Row, 1962), pp. 210–24.

8. Ibid., passim.

9. K. Jaspers, cited in J. Choron, *Death and Western Thought* (New York: Collier Books, 1963), p. 226.

10. S. Freud, "Thoughts for the Times on War and Death," vol. XIV in *Standard Edition* (London: Hogarth Press, 1957; originally published 1915), p. 291.

11. Ibid., p. 290.

12. J. Giraudoux, cited in *The Meaning of Death,* ed. H. Feifel (New York: McGraw-Hill, 1965), p. 124.

13. Montaigne, *Complete Essays,* p. 67.

14. L. Tolstoy, *War and Peace* (New York: Modern Library, 1931), p. 57.

15. L. Tolstoy, *The Death of Ivan Ilych and Other Stories* (New York: Signet Classics, 1960).

16. D. Rosen, "Suicide Survivors," *Western Journal of Medicine* (April 1975) 122:289–94.

17. A. Schmitt, *Dialogue with Death* (Harrisonburg, Va.: Choice Books, 1976), pp. 55–58.

18. R. Noyes, "Attitude Changes Following Near-Death Experiences," *Psychiatry,* in press.

19. A. Hussain and S. Tozman, "Psychiatry and Death Row," *Journal of Clinical Psychiatry* (1978) 39 (3): 183–88.

20. R. Neuberger, cited in J. Frank in "Nuclear Death—The Challenge of Ethical Religion," *The Ethical Platform* (29 April 1962).

21. D. Spiegel, J. Blum, and I. Yalom, *Peer Support for Metastatic Cancer Patients: A Randomized Prospective Outcome Study,* in preparation.

22. K. Chandler, "Three Processes of Dying and the Behavioral Effects," *Journal of Consulting Psychology* (1965) 29:296–301; D. Cappon, "The Dying," *Psychiatric Quarterly* (1959) 33:466–89; A. Weisman and T. Hackett, "Predilection to Death," *Psychosomatic Medicine* (1961) 23:232–56; and E. Kübler-Ross, *On Death and Dying* (New York: Macmillan, 1969).

23. K. Weers, manuscript in preparation.

24. Schmitt, *Dialogue with Death,* p. 54.

25. R. Lifton, "The Sense of Immortality: On Death and the Continuity of Life," *Explorations in Psychohistory,* eds. R. Lifton and E. Olson (New York: Simon & Schuster, 1974), pp. 271–88.

26. J. Diggory and D. Rothman, "Values Destroyed by Death," *Journal of Abnormal and Social Psychology* (1961) 63(1): 205–10.

27. J. Choron, *Modern Man and Mortality* (New York: Macmillan, 1964), p. 44.

28. R. Kastenbaum and R. Aisenberg, *Psychology of Death* (New York: Springer, 1972), p. 44.

29. S. Kierkegaard, *The Concept of Dread* (Princeton, N.J.: Princeton University Press, 1957), p. 55.

30. R. May, *The Meaning of Anxiety,* rev. ed. (New York: W. W. Norton, 1977), p. 207.

31. S. Freud, "Inhibitions, Symptoms and Anxiety," vol. XX in *Standard Edition* (London: Hogarth Press, 1959; originally published 1926), p. 166.

32. Kierkegaard, *Concept of Dread,* p. 55.

33. May, *Meaning of Anxiety,* p. 207.

34. Heidegger, *Being and Time,* p. 223.

35. A. Sharp, *A Green Tree in Geddes* (New York: Walker, 1968).

36. R. Skoog, cited in J. Meyer, *Death and Neurosis* (New York: International Universities Press, 1975), p. 47.

37. E. Strauss, cited in E. Weigert, "Loneliness and Trust—Basic Factors of Human Existence," *Psychiatry* (1960) 23:121–30.

38. W. Schwidder, cited in J. Meyer, *Death and Neurosis* (New York: International Universities Press, 1975), p. 54.

39. H. Lazarus and J. Kostan, "Psychogenic Hyperventilation and Death Anxiety," *Psychosomatics* (1969) 10:14–22.

40. D. Friedman, "Death Anxiety and the Primal Scene," *Psychoanalytic Review* (1961) 48:108–18.

41. V. Kral, "Psychiatric Observations under Severe Chronic Stress," *American Journal of Psychiatry* (1951) 108:185–92.

42. Ibid., J. Meyer, *Death and Neurosis*, p. 58; and A. Heveroch, cited in J. Meyer, *Death and Neurosis*, p. 58.

43. M. Roth, "The Phobic Anxiety-Depersonalization Syndrome and Some General Aetiological Problems in Psychiatry," *Journal of Neuropsychiatry* (1959) 1:293–306.

44. R. Kastenbaum and R. Aisenberg, *Psychology of Death*.

45. D. Lester, "Experimental and Correlational Studies of Fear of Death," *Psychological Bulletin* (1967) 64(1); 27–36; and D. Templer and C. Ruff, "Death Anxiety Scale Means, Standard Deviations, and Embedding," *Psychological Reports* (1971) 29:173–74.

46. P. Livingston and C. Zimet, "Death Anxiety, Authoritarianism and Choice of Speciality in Medical Students," *Journal of Neurological and Mental Disorders* (1965) 140:222–30.

47. W. Swenson, "Attitudes toward Death in an Aged Population," *Journal of Gerontology* (1961) 16(1):49–52; D. Martin and L. Wrightsman, "The Relationship between Religious Behavior and Concern about Death," *Journal of Social Psychology* (1865) 65:317–23; and D. Templer, "Death Anxiety in Religiously Very Involved Persons," *Psychological Reports* (1972) 31:361–67.

48. N. Iammarino, "Relationship between Death Anxiety and Demographic Variables," *Psychological Reports* (1975) 37:262.

49. Iammarino, "Death Anxiety and Demographic Variables"; Swenson, "Attitudes toward Death"; A. Christ, "Attitudes toward Death among a Group of Acute Geriatric Psychiatric Patients," *Journal of Gerontology* (1961) 16(1):56–59; and P. Rhudick and A. Dibner, "Age, Personality, and Health Correlates of Death Concerns in Normal Aged Individuals," *Journal of Gerontology* (1961) 16(1):44–49.

50. M. Lieberman and A. Coplan, "Distance from Death as a Variable in the Study of Aging," *Developmental Psychology* (1970) 2:71–84.

51. M. Means, "Fears of One Thousand College Women," *Journal of Abnormal and Social Psychology* (1936) 31:291–311.

52. W. Middleton, "Some Reactions toward Death among College Students," *Journal of Abnormal and Social Psychology* (1936) 3:165–73.

53. Templer and Ruff, "Death Anxiety Scale Means"; Iammarino, "Death Anxiety and Demographic Variables"; and D. Templer, C. Ruff, and C. Franks, "Death Anxiety; Age, Sex, and Parental Resemblance in Disease Populations," *Developmental Psychology* (1971) 4:108.

54. P. Thauberger, "The Avoidance of Ontological Confrontation," unpublished Ph.D. dissertation, University of Saskatchewan, 1974.

55. C. Stacey and K. Markin, "The Attitudes of College Students and Penitentiary Inmates toward Death and a Future Life," *Psychiatric Quarterly*, supplement (1952) 26:27–32.

56. D. Templer, "Death Anxiety as Related to Depression and Health of Retired Persons," *Journal of Gerontology*, (1971) 26:521–23.

57. Swenson, "Attitudes toward Death"; J. Munnichs, *Old Age and Finitude* (Basel and New York: Karger, 1966); and S. Shrut, "Attitude toward Old Age to Death," *Mental Hygiene* (1958) 42:259–63.

58. Munnichs, *Old Age and Finitude*; A. Christ, "Attitude toward Death among a Group of Acute Geriatric Psychiatric Patients," *Journal of Gerontology* (1961) 16:56–59; and Kastenbaum and Aisenberg, *Psychology of Death*, p. 83.

59. Kastenbaum and Aisenberg, *Psychology of Death*, p. 107.

60. C. Stacy and M. Reichers, "Attitudes toward Death and Future Life among Normal and Subnormal Adolescent Girls," *Exceptional Children* (1959) 20:259–62.

61. A. Maurer, "Adolescent Attitudes toward Death," *Journal of Genetic Psychology* (1964) 105:79–80.

62. H. Feifel and A. Branscomb, "Who's Afraid of Death?" *Journal of Abnormal Psychology* (1973) 81(3):282–88; and H. Feifel and L. Herman, "Fear of Death in the Mentally Ill," *Psychological Reports* (1973) 33:931–38.

63. Feifel and Branscomb, "Who's Afraid of Death?"

64. W. Meissner, "Affective Response to Psychoanalytic Death Symbols," *Journal of Abnormal and Social Psychology* (1958) 56:295–99.

65. K. G. Magni, "Reactions to Death Stimuli among Theology Students," *Journal for the Scientific Study of Religion* (Fall 1970) 9(3):247–48.

66. Kastenberg and Aisenberg, *Psychology of Death*, p. 95.

67. Rhudick and Dibner, "Age, Personality, and Health Correlates."

68. Shrut, "Attitude toward Old Age."

69. Swenson, "Attitudes toward Death."

70. Templer, "Death Anxiety."

71. N. Kogan and R. Shelton, "Beliefs about 'Old People,'" *Journal of Genetic Psychology* (1962) 100:93–111.

72. M. Kramer, C. Winget, and R. Whitman, "A City Dreams: A Survey Approach to Normative Dream Content," *American Journal of Psychiatry* (1971) 127:86–92.

73. H. Cason, "The Nightmare Dream," *Psychology Monographs* (1935) 209:46.

74. M. Feldman and M. Hersen, "Attitudes toward Death in Nightmare Subjects," *Journal of Abnormal Psychology* (1967) 72:421–425; and D. Lester, "The Fear of Death of Those Who Have Nightmares," *Journal of Psychology* (1968) 69:245–47.

75. P. Handal and J. Rychlak, "Curvilinearity between Dream Content and Death Anxiety and the Relationship of Death Anxiety to Repression-Sensitivity," *Journal of Abnormal Psychology* (1971) 77:11–16.

76. W. Bromberg and P. Schilder, "The Attitudes of Psychoneurotics toward Death," *Psychoanalytic Review* (1936) 23:1–28.

77. C. Parks, "The First Year of Bereavement," *Psychiatry* (1970) 33:444–67.

78. *The Gilgamesh Epic and Old Testament Parallels,* trans. A. Heidel (Chicago: University of Chicago Press, 1946), pp. 63, 64.

79. A. Witt, personal communication, September 1978.

80. Personal communication from a friend.

81. Freud, "Thoughts for the Times," vol. XIV, *Standard Edition*, p. 298.

82. J. Breuer and S. Freud, *Studies on Hysteria*, vol. II in *Standard Edition* (London: Hogarth Press, 1955; originally published in 1895).

83. Ibid., p. 9.

84. Ibid., p. 7.

85. Ibid., p. xxxi.

86. Ibid., p. 14.

87. Ibid., p. 34.

88. Ibid., p. 117.

89. Ibid., p. 63.

90. Ibid., p. 131.

91. Ibid., p. 137.

92. Ibid., p. 157.

93. S. Freud, *Origins of Psychoanalysis,* ed. by M. Bonaparte, A. Freud, and E. Kris (New York: Basic Books, 1954).

94. S. Freud, "Inhibitions, Symptoms and Anxiety," vol. XX, *Standard Edition*, p. 166.

95. A. Compton, "Psychoanalytic Theories of Anxiety," *Journal of American Psychoanalytic Association* (1972) 20(2):341–94.

96. S. Freud, *Studies on Hysteria,* vol. II, in *Standard Edition,* (London: Hogarth Press, 1955; originally published 1895), p. 33.

97. Ibid., p. 40.

98. Freud, "Inhibitions, Symptoms and Anxiety," vol. XX, *Standard Edition*, p. 130.

99. M. Klein, "A Contribution of the Theory of Anxiety and Guilt," *International Journal of Psychoanalysis* (1948) 29:114–23.

100. O. Fenichel, *The Psychoanalytic Theory of the Psychoneuroses* (New York: Norton, 1945).

101. R. Waelder, *Basic Theory of Psychoanalysis* (New York: International Universities Press, 1960).

102. R. Greenson, *The Technique and Practice of Psychoanalysis* (New York: International Universities Press, 1967).

103. S. Freud, *The Ego and the Id,* vol. XIX, *Standard Edition* (London: Hogarth Press, 1961; originally published in 1923), p. 57.

104. Ibid., p. 58ff.

105. S. Freud, *Beyond the Pleasure Principle,* vol. XVIII in *Standard Edition* (London: Hogarth Press, 1955; originally published 1920), pp. 1–64.

106. Freud, "Thoughts for the Times," vol. XIV, *Standard Edition*, p. 299.

107. E. Jones, *The Life and Work of Sigmund Freud,* vol. I (New York: Basic Books, 1953), p. 40.

108. Ibid., p. 41.
109. Ibid., p. 45.
110. N. Brown, *Life Against Death* (New York: Vintage Books, 1959).
111. S. Freud, "Thoughts for the Times," vol. XIV in *Standard Edition,* pp. 273–300.
112. S. Freud, "The Theme of Three Caskets," vol. XII in *Standard Edition* (London: Hogarth Press, 1966; originally published 1913), pp. 289–302.
113. E. Jones, *The Life and Work of Sigmund Freud,* vols. I, II, III (New York: Basic Books, 1953, 1955, 1957).
114. I. Stone, *Passions of the Mind* (New York: Doubleday, 1971).
115. For example, J. Wortis, *Fragments of an Analysis with Freud* (New York: Simon & Schuster, 1954).
116. For example, S. Freud, *Origins of Psychoanalysis,* eds. M. Bonaparte, A. Freud, and E. Kris (New York: Basic Books, 1954); H. Abraham and E. Freud, eds., *A Psycho-Analytic Dialogue: The Letters of Sigmund Freud and Karl Abraham 1907–1926,* trans. B. Marsa and C. Abraham (New York: Basic Books; London: Hogarth Press and Institute of Psycho-Analysis, 1965); E. Freud and H. Meng, eds., *Psycho-Analysis and Faith: The Letters of Sigmund Freud and Oskar Pfister,* trans. E. Mosbacher (New York: Basic Books; London: Hogarth Press and Institute of Psycho-Analysis, 1963); and E. Pfeiffer, ed., *Sigmund Freud and Lou Andreas-Salomé: Letters,* trans. William and Elaine Robson-Scott (New York: Harcourt Brace Jovanovich; London: Hogarth Press and Institute of Psycho-Analysis, 1972.)
117. Jones, vol. I, p. 4.
118. Ibid., p. 20.
119. Ibid.
120. Ibid., p. xii.
121. Ibid., p. 78.
122. Freud, *Origins of Psychoanalysis,* p. 217.
123. Ibid., p. 129.

Chapter 3

1. S. Anthony, *The Discovery of Death in Childhood and After* (New York: Basic Books, 1972).
2. E. Becker, *The Denial of Death* (New York: Free Press, 1973), p. 36.
3. Anthony, *Discovery of Death,* p. 155.
4. Ibid., pp. 155–56
5. Ibid., p. 157.
6. F. Moellenkoff, "Ideas of Children about Death," *Bulletin of the Menninger Clinic* (1939) 3:148–56.
7. E. Erikson, *Childhood and Society* (New York: W. W. Norton, 1963).
8. Anthony, *Discovery of Death,* pp. 78ff.
9. R. Kastenbaum & R. Aisenberg, *Psychology of Death* (New York: Springer, 1972), p. 9.
10. S. Freud, *The Interpretation of Dreams,* vol. IV in *Standard Edition* (London: Hogarth Press, 1964; originally published 1900), pp. 254–55.
11. R. Lapouse and M. Monk, "Fears and Worries in a Representative Sample of Children," *American Journal of Orthopsychiatry* (1959) 29:803–18.
12. S. Harrison, C. Davenport, and J. McDermott, "Children's Reactions to Bereavement," *Archives of General Psychiatry* (1967) 17:593–97.
13. Anthony, *Discovery of Death;* M. Nagy, "The Child's View of Death," *Journal of Genetic Psychology,* (1948) 73:3–27; P. Schilder & D. Wechsler, "The Attitudes of Children toward Death," *Journal of Genetic Psychology* (1934) 45:406–51; G. Koocher, "Talking with Children about Death," *American Journal of Orthopsychiatry* (1974) 44:404–11; M. MacIntire, C. Angle, and L. Struempler, "The Concept of Death in Mid-Western Children and Youth," *American Journal of Disease of Children* (1972) 123:527–32.
14. Nagy, "Child's View of Death."
15. Anthony, *Discovery of Death,* p. 47–77.
16. Schilder and Wechsler, "Attitudes of Children."
17. Anthony, *Discovery of Death,* p. 158.

18. E. Furman, *A Child's Parent Dies* (New Haven, Conn.: Yale University Press, 1974), p. 5.

19. Anthony, *Discovery of Death*, p. 255.

20. J. Sully, cited in Anthony, *Discovery of Death*, p. 269.

21. J. Piaget, cited in Anthony, *Discovery of Death*, p. 56.

22. Anthony, *Discovery of Death*, p. 59.

23. Kastenbaum and Aisenberg, *Psychology of Death*, p. 9.

24. Kastenbaum and Aisenberg, *Psychology of Death*, p. 12f.

25. S. Brant, cited in Kastenbaum and Aisenberg, *Psychology of Death*, p. 14.

26. Kastenbaum and Aisenberg, *Psychology of Death*, p. 14.

27. G. Rochlin, *Griefs and Discontents: The Focus of Change* (Boston: Little, Brown, 1965), p. 67.

28. G. Rochlin, "How Younger Children View Death and Themselves," in *Explaining Death to Children*," ed. E. Grollman (New York: Beacon Press, 1967).

29. M. Scheler, cited in J. Choron, *Death and Western Thought* (New York: Collier Books, 1963), p. 17.

30. Rochlin, "How Younger Children," p. 56.

31. Ibid., pp. 84–85.

32. M. Klein, "A Contribution to the Theory of Anxiety and Guilt," *International Journal of Psychoanalysis* (1948) 29:114–23.

33. K. Eissler, *The Psychiatrist and the Dying Patient* (New York: International Universities Press, 1959), pp. 57–58.

34. A. Freud, "Discussion of John Bowlby's Paper," *Psychoanalytic Study of the Child* (1960) 15:53–62.

35. Furman, *A Child's Parent Dies*, p. 51.

36. Anthony, *Discovery of Death*, p. 139.

37. Ibid., pp. 157–58.

38. A. Maurer, "Maturation of Concepts of Death," *British Journal of Medical Psychology* (1964) 39:35–41.

39. M. Stern, "Pavor Nocturnis," *International Journal of Psychoanalysis* (1951) 32:302.

40. R. White, "Motivation Reconsidered: The Concept of Competence," *Psychological Review* (1959) 66:297–333.

41. Maurer, "Maturation."

42. Kastenbaum and Aisenberg, *Psychology of Death*, p. 29.

43. Maurer, "Maturation."

44. MacIntire, Angle, and Struempler, "The Concept of Death."

45. I. Alexander and A. Adlerstein, "Affective Responses to the Concept of Death in a Population of Children and Early Adolescents," *Journal of Genetic Psychology* (1958) 93:167–77.

46. Nagy, "Child's View of Death."

47. S. Hostler, "The Development of the Child's Concept of Death," in *The Child and Death*, ed. O. J. Sahler (St. Louis, Mo.: C. V. Mosby, 1978), p. 9.

48. E. Jaques, "Death and the Mid-Life Crisis," *International Journal of Psychoanalysis* (1968) 46:502–13.

49. J. Masserman, *The Practice of Dynamic Psychiatry* (Philadelphia and London: W. B. Saunders, 1955), p. 467.

50. V. Frankl, oral communication, 1974.

51. Anthony, *Discovery of Death*, p. 154.

52. Ibid., p. 155.

53. Schilder and Wechsler, "Attitudes of Children."

54. Anthony, *Discovery of Death*, p. 155.

55. Ibid., p. 257.

56. Schilder and Wechsler, "Attitudes of Children."

57. Nagy, "Child's View of Death."

58. Koocher, "Talking with Children."

59. I. Opie, *The Love and Language of School Children* (Oxford: Clarendon Press, 1959).

60. Maurer, "Maturation."

61. J. Bowlby, *Attachment and Loss*, vol. II: *Separation* (New York: Basic Books, 1973).

62. A. Jersild and F. Holmes, *Children's Fears* (New York: Teachers College, Columbia University, 1935); and A. Jersild, "Studies of Children's Fears," in *Child Behavior and De-*

velopment, eds., R. Barker, J. Kounin, and H. Wright (New York, London: McGraw-Hill, 1943).

63. Bowlby, *Attachment and Loss*, pp. 105–18.

64. R. May, *The Meaning of Anxiety* (New York: W. W. Norton, 1977) pp. 105–9.

65. Ibid., pp. 107–8

66. Klein, "A Contribution"; and D. Winnicott, *The Maturational Process and the Facilitating Environment* (New York: International Universities Press, 1965), p. 41.

67. A. Freud, "Discussion."

68. Anthony, *Discovery of Death*, p. 161.

69. C. Wahl, "The Fear of Death," in *The Meaning of Death*, ed. H. Feifel (New York: McGraw-Hill, 1959), pp. 214–23.

70. S. Freud, *An Outline of Psycho-Analysis*, vol. XXIII, in *Standard Edition* (London: Hogarth Press, 1964; originally published 1940), p. 185.

71. S. Rosenzweig, and D. Bray, "Sibling Death in Anamneses of Schizophrenic Patients," *Psychoanalytic Review* (1942) 49:71–92; and S. Rosenzweig, "Sibling Death as a Psychological Experience with Special Reference to Schizophrenia," *Psychoanalytic Review* (1943) 30:177–86.

72. Rosensweig, "Sibling Death."

73. Ibid.

74. H. Searles, "Schizophrenia and the Inevitability of Death," *Psychiatric Quarterly* (1961) 35:631–55.

75. J. Hilgard, M. Newman, and F. Fisk, "Strength of Adult Ego Following Childhood Bereavement," *American Journal of Orthopsychiatry* (1960) 30:788–98.

76. Furman, *A Child's Parent Dies*; Bowlby, *Attachment and Loss*; R. Furman, "Death and the Young Child," *Psychoanalytic Study of the Child* (1964) 29:321–33; and R. Zeligs, *Children's Experience with Death* (Springfield, Ill.: C. C. Thomas, 1974), pp. 1–49.

77. Maurer, "Maturation."

78. MacIntire, Angle, and Struempler, "The Concept of Death"; F. Brown, "Depression and Childhood Bereavement," *Journal of Mental Science* (1961) 107:754–77; I. Gregory, "Studies in Parental Deprivation in Psychiatric Patients," *American Journal of Psychiatry* (1958) 115:432–42; G. Pollack, "Childhood Parent and Sibling Loss in Adult Patients," *Archives of General Psychiatry* (October 1962) 7:295–305; and H. Barry and E. Lindeman, "Critical Ages for Maternal Bereavement in Psychoneuroses," *Psychosomatic Medicine* (1960) 22:166–81.

79. J. Hilgard and M. Newman, "Evidence for Functional Genesis in Mental Illness: Schizophrenia, Depressive Psychoses and Psychoneurosis," *Journal of Nervous and Mental Disease* (1961) 132:3–6.

80. M. Breckenridge and E. Vincent, *Child Development*, ed. W. B. Saunders, 4th ed. (Philadelphia, Pa.: W. B. Saunders 1960), p. 138.

81. E. Kübler-Ross, address at Stanford Medical School, May 1978.

82. S. Ferenczi, cited in Anthony, *Discovery of Death*, p. 157.

83. Anthony, *Discovery of Death*, p. 159.

84. J. Bruner, cited in H. Galen, "A Matter of Life and Death," *Young Children* (August 1972) 27:351–56.

85. Galen, "A Matter of Life."

86. Rochlin, "How Younger Children," p. 63.

Chapter 4

1. S. Kierkegaard, cited in E. Becker, *The Denial of Death* (New York: Free Press, 1973), p. 70.

2. O. Rank, *Will Therapy and Truth and Reality* (New York: Alfred A. Knopf, 1945), p. 126.

3. P. Tillich, *The Courage to Be* (New Haven and London: Yale University Press, 1952), p. 66.

4. Becker, *Denial of Death*, p. 66.

5. R. Lifton, "The Sense of Immortality: On Death and the Continuity of Life," in *Ex-*

plorations of Psychohistory, eds. R. Lifton and E. Olson (New York: Simon & Schuster, 1974), p. 282

6. L. Loesser and T. Bry, "The Role of Death Fears in the Etiology of Phobic Anxiety," *International Journal of Group Psychotherapy* (1960) 10:287–97.

7. Rank, *Will Therapy*, p. 124.

8. E. Fromm, *Escape from Freedom* (New York: Holt, Rinehart & Winston, 1941), p. 6

9. L. Tolstoy, *The Death of Ivan Ilych and Other Stories* (New York: Signet Classics, 1960), pp. 131–32.

10. R. Frost, *In the Clearing* (New York; Holt, Rinehart & Winston, 1962), p. 39.

11. N. Kazantzakis, *Report to Greco*, trans. P. A. Bien (New York: Simon & Schuster, 1965), p. 457.

12. N. Kazantzakis, *The Odyssey: A Modern Sequel*, trans. Kimon Friar (New York: Simon & Schuster, 1958).

13. C. Baker, *Ernest Hemingway: A Life Story* (New York: Charles Scribner, 1969), p. 5.

14. E. Hemingway, *The Old Man and the Sea* (New York: Charles Scribner, 1961).

15. C. Wahl, "Suicide as a Magical Act," *Bulletin of Menninger Clinic*, (May 1957) 21:91–98.

16. F. Kluckholm and F. Stroedbeck, *Variations in Value Orientations* (New York: Harper & Row, 1961), p. 15.

17. J. M. Keynes, cited in Norman Brown, *Life Against Death* (New York: Vintage Books, 1959), p. 107.

18. L. Tolstoy, *Anna Karenina* (New York: Modern Library, 1950), p. 168.

19. H. Feifel, *Taboo Topics*, ed. Norman Forberow (New York: Atherton Press, 1963), p. 15.

20. Rank, *Will Therapy*, p. 130.

21. H. Ibsen, cited in Rank, *Will Therapy*, p. 131.

22. S. Freud, *Some Character Types Met with in Psychoanalytic Work*, vol. XIV in *Standard Edition* (London: Hogarth Press, 1957; originally published in 1916), pp. 316–31.

23. Rank, *Will Therapy*, p. 119.

24. A. Maslow, *The Further Reaches of Human Nature* (New York: Viking, 1971), p. 35.

25. Becker, *Denial of Death*, pp. 35–39.

26. Fromm, *Escape from Freedom*, (New York: Holt, Rinehart & Winston, 1941), pp. 174–79.

27. J. Masserman, *The Practice of Dynamic Psychiatry* (London: W. B. Saunders, 1955), pp. 476–81.

28. L. Tolstoy, *War and Peace* (New York: Modern Library, 1931), p. 231.

29. S. Kierkegaard, cited in Rollo May, *The Meaning of Anxiety*, rev. ed. (New York: W. W. Norton, 1977), p. 38.

30. M. Heidegger, *Being and Time* (New York: Harper & Row, 1962), p. 105.

31. S. Arieti, "Psychotherapy of Severe Depression," *American Journal of Psychiatry* (1977), 134(8):864–68.

32. Ibid.

33. I. Yalom and G. Elkins, *Everyday Gets a Little Closer* (New York: Basic Books, 1974).

34. Rank, *Will Therapy*, pp. 119–34.

35. W. Tietz, "School Phobia and the Fear of Death," *Mental Hygiene* (1970) 54:565–68.

36. Oral communication, May 1979.

37. E. Greenberger, "Fantasies of Women Confronting Death," *Journal of Consulting Psychology* (1965) 29:252–60.

38. M. Mahler, F. Pine, and A. Bergman, *The Psychological Birth of the Infant* (New York: Basic Books, 1975).

39. Rank, *Will Therapy*, p. 126.

40. S. Kierkegaard, *Fear and Trembling and the Sickness unto Death* (New York: Doubleday Anchor Books, 1953), pp. 182–200.

41. Tillich, *The Courage to Be*, p. 52.

42. Rank, *Will Therapy*, p. 149.

43. H. Searles, "Schizophrenia and the Inevitability of Death," *Psychiatric Quarterly* (1961) 35:631–55.

44. Ibid.

45. Ibid.

46. Ibid.

47. Ibid.

48. N. Brown, *Life Against Death* (New York: Vintage Books, 1959), p. 107.

49. H. Witkin, *Psychological Differentiation* (New York: John Wiley, 1962).

50. H. Witkin, "Psychological Differentiation and Forms of Pathology," *Journal of Abnormal Psychology* (1965) 70(5):317–36.

51. J. Rotter, "Generalized Expectancies for Internal vs. External Control of Reinforcement," *Psychological Monographs* (1966) 80 (1, whole #609).

52. E. Phares, *Locus of Control in Personality* (Morristown, N.J.: General Learning Press, 1976).

53. J. Rotter, "Some Implications of Social Learning Theory for the Prediction of Goal Directed Behavior from Testing Procedures," *Psychology Review* (1960) 67:301–16.

54. W. Mischel, R. Zeiss, and A. Zeiss, "Internal-External Control and Persistence," *Journal of Personality and Social Psychology* (1974) 29:265–78.

55. Phares, *Locus of Control* p. 7.

56. Ibid., pp. 144–56.

57. Ibid., p. 149.

58. P. Duz, "Comparison of the Effects of Behaviorally Oriented Action and Psychotherapy Reeducation of Intraversion-Extraversion, Emotionality, and Internal-External Control," *Journal of Counseling Psychology* (1970) 17:567–72.

59. Witkin, "Psychological Differentiation," Rotter, "Some Implications," and Phares, *Locus of Control.*

60. R. Ryckman and M. Sherman, "Relationship between Self Esteem and Internal-External Locus of Control," *Psychological Reports* (1973) 32:1106; and B. Fish and S. Karabenick, "Relationship between Self Esteem and Locus of Control," *Psychological Reports* (1971) 29:784.

61. D. Kilpatrick, W. Dubin, and D. Marcotte, "Personality, Stress of the Medical Education Process and Changes in Affective Mood State," *Psychology Reports* (1974) 3:1215–23.

62. F. Melges and A. Weisz, "The Personal Future and Suicidal Ideation," *Journal of Nervous and Mental Disease* (1971) 153:244–50; and H. Lefcourt, *Locus of Control* (Hillsdale, N.J.: Lawrence Erlbaum, 1976), p. 148.

63. J. Shybutt, "Time Perspective, Internal vs. External Control and Severity of Psychological Disturbance," *Journal of Clinical Psychology* (1968) 24:312–15; and C. Smith, M. Peyer, and M. Distefano, "Internal-External Control and Severity Emotional Impairment," *Journal of Clinical Psychology* (1971) 27:449–50.

64. M. Harrow and A. Ferrante, "Locus of Control in Psychiatric Patients," *Journal of Consulting and Clinical Psychology* (1969) 33:582–89; and R. Cromwell, "Description of Parental Behavior in Schizophrenic and Normal Subjects," *Journal of Personality* (1961) 29:363–79.

65. C. Fersten, "A Functional Analysis of Depression," *American Psychologist* (1973) 28:857–70; P. Lewinsohn, cited in Lefcourt, *Aspects of Depression;* W. Miller and M. Seligman, "Depression and the Perception of Reinforcement," *Journal of Abnormal Psychology* (1973) 82:62–73; and L. Abramson and H. Sackeim, "A Paradox in Depression: Uncontrollability and Self-Blame," *Psychology Bulletin* (1977) 84:838–52.

66. A. Tolor and M. Reznikoff, "Relation between Insight, Repression-Sensitization, Internal-External Control and Death Anxiety," *Journal of Abnormal Psychology* (1967) 72:426–31.

67. A. Berman and J. Hays, "Relation between Death Anxiety, Belief in Afterlife, and Locus of Control," *Journal of Consulting and Clinical Psychology* (1973) 41:318.

Chapter 5

1. N. Kazantzakis, *The Odyssey: A Modern Sequel,* trans. Kimon Friar (New York: Simon & Schuster, 1958).

2. S. Kierkegaard, cited in R. May, *The Meaning of Anxiety,* rev. ed. (New York: W. W. Norton, 1977), p. 37.

3. M. Heidegger, *Being and Time* (New York: Harper & Row, 1962), p. 294.

4. F. Nietzsche, *The Gay Science*, trans. W. Kaufman (New York: Random House, Vintage, 1974), p. 37.

5. M. Montaigne, *The Complete Essays of Montaigne*, trans. D. Frame (Stanford, Calif.: Stanford University Press, 1945), p. 65.

6. G. Santayana, cited in K. Fisher, "Ultimate Goals in Psychotherapy," *Journal of Existentialism* (Winter 1966–67) 7:215–32.

7. R. Assagioli, *Psychosynthesis* (New York: Viking Press, 1971), p. 116.

8. P. Landsburg, cited in J. Choron, *Death and Western Thought* (New York: Collier Books, 1963), p. 16.

9. J. Donne, *Complete Poetry and Selected Prose* (New York: Modern Library, 1952), p. 332.

10. R. Gardner, "The Guilt Reaction of Parents of Children with Severe Physical Disease," *American Journal of Psychiatry* (1969), 126:82–90.

11. Heidegger, *Being and Time*, p. 105.

12. S. Golburgh and C. Rotman, "The Terror of Life: A Latent Adolescent Nightmare," *Adolescence* (1973), 8:569–74.

13. E. Jaques, "Death and the Mid-Life Crisis," *International Journal of Psychoanalysis* (1965), 46:502–513.

14. C. Jung, cited in D. Levinson, *The Seasons of a Man's Life* (New York: Alfred A. Knopf, 1978), p. 4.

15. D. Krantz, *Radical Career Change: Life Beyond Work* (New York: Free Press, 1978).

16. R. Noyes, "Attitude Changes Following Near-Death Experiences," *Psychiatry*, in press.

17. Montaigne, *Complete Essays*, p. 62.

18. A. Kurland, et al. "Psychedelic Therapy Utilizing LSD in the Treatment of the Alcoholic Patient," *American Journal of Psychiatry* (1967) 123(10):1202–9.

19. I. Silbermann, The Psychical Experience during the Shocks in Shock-Therapy," *International Journal of Psychoanalysis* (1940) 21:179–200.

20. P. Koestenbaum, *Is There an Answer to Death?* (Englewood Cliffs, N.J.: Prentice-Hall, 1976), pp. 31–41, 65–74.

21. E. Aronson, oral communication, 1977.

22. J. Laube, "Death and Dying Workshop for Nurses: Its Effects on Their Death Anxiety Level," *International Journal of Nursing Students* (1977) 14:111–120; P. Murray, "Death Education and Its Effects on the Death Anxiety Level of Nurses," *Psychological Reports* (1974) 35:1250; J. Bugental, "Confronting the Existential Meaning of My Death Through Group Exercises," *Interpersonal Development* (1973) 4:1948–63; and W. Whelan and W. Warren, "A Death Awareness Workshop: Theory Application and Results," unpublished manuscript, 1977.

23. Whelan and Warren, "Death Awareness Workshop."

24. J. Fowles, *Daniel Martin* (Boston: Little, Brown, 1977), p. 177.

25. I. Yalom, et al. "The Written Summary as a Group Psychotherapy Technique," *Archives of General Psychiatry* (1975) 32:605–13.

26. G. Zilboorg, "Fear of Death," *Psychoanalytic Quarterly* (1943) 12:465–75.

27. S. Freud, *Three Essays on the Theory of Sexuality*, vol. VII in *Standard Edition* (London: Hogarth Press, 1957; originally published, 1905), pp. 125–231.

28. M. Stern, "Fear of Death and Neurosis," *Journal of American Psychoanalytic Association* (May 1966), pp. 3–31.

29. Dante Alighieri, *La Divina Commedia* (Florence, Italy: Casa Editrice Nerbini, n. d.); translation by John Freccero, 1980.

30. Jaques, "Death and the Mid-Life Crisis."

31. H. Rosenberg, "The Fear of Death as an Indispensable Factor in Psychotherapy," *American Journal of Psychotherapy* (1963) 17:619–30.

32. J. Breuer and S. Freud, *Studies on Hysteria*, vol. II in *Standard Edition* (London: Hogarth Press, 1964; originally published, 1895), p. 268.

33. M. Eliade, *Shamanism: Archaic Techniques of Ecstasy* (Princeton, N.J.: Princeton University Press, 1964), p. 43.

34. Ibid., p. 45.

35. Stern, "Fear of Death."

36. J. Bugental, *The Search for Authenticity* (New York: Holt, Rinehart & Winston, 1965), p. 167.

37. J. Hinton, "The Influence of Previous Personality on Reactions to Having Terminal Cancer," *Omega* (1975) 6:95–111.

38. F. Nietzsche, cited in N. Brown, *Life Against Death* (New York: Vintage Books, 1959), p. 107.

39. H. Searles, "Schizophrenia and the Inevitability of Death," *Psychiatric Quarterly* (1961) 35:631–55.

40. Montaigne, *Complete Essays,* p. 268.

41. Whelan and Warren, "Death Awareness Workshop."

42. D. Kaller, "An Evaluation of a Self-Instructional Program Designed to Reduce Anxiety and Fear about Death and of the Relation of That Program to Sixteen Personal History Variables," *Dissertation Abstracts* (May 1975) 35(11):7125–A.

43. E. Pratt, "A Death Education Laboratory as a Medium for Influencing Feelings Toward Death," *Dissertation Abstracts* (1974) 4026(B).

44. Laube, "Death and Dying Workshop."

45. Murray, "Death Education."

Chapter 6

1. J. Sartre, *Being and Nothingness,* trans. Hazel Barnes (New York: Philosophical Library, 1956), p. 633.

2. J. Sartre, *Nausea,* trans. Hazel Barnes (New York: New Directions, 1964), pp. 126–130.

3. *The Encyclopedia of Philosophy,* ed. P. Edwards, vol. IV (New York: Macmillan and Free Press, 1967), p. 308.

4. J. Russel, "Sartre, Therapy, and Expanding the Concept of Responsibility," *American Journal of Psychoanalysis* (1978) 38:259–69.

5. Sartre, *Being and Nothingness,* p. 566.

6. Sartre, cited in D. Follesdal, "Sartre on Freedom," in *Library of Living Philosophers,* ed. Paul Schilpp (Evanston: Northwestern University Press), forthcoming.

7. *Encyclopedia of Philosophy,* vol. V, pp. 416–19.

8. E. Fromm, *Escape from Freedom* (New York: Holt, Rinehart & Winston, 1941).

9. R. Kogod, oral communication, 1974.

10. V. M. Gatch and M. Temerlin, "Belief in Psychic Determinism and the Behavior of the Psychotherapist," *Review of Existential Psychology and Psychiatry* (1965) 5:16–35.

11. M. Mazer, "The Therapeutic Function of the Belief in Will," *Psychiatry* (1960) 23:45–52.

12. F. Perls, cited in J. Russel, "Sartre, Therapy."

13. F. Perls and P. Baumgardner, *Legacy from Fritz* (Palo Alto, Calif.: Science and Behavior Books, 1975), pp. 45–46.

14. A. Levitsky and F. Perls, "The Rules and Games of Gestalt Therapy," in *Gestalt Therapy Now,* ed. J. Fagan and Irma Lee Shepherd (Palo Alto: Science and Behavior Books, Inc., 1973), p. 143.

15. Ibid., p. 98.

16. F. Perls, *Gestalt Therapy Verbatim* (New York: Bantam Books, 1969), p. 80.

17. V. Frankl, *The Will to Meaning* (Cleveland, O.: New American Library, 1969), pp. 101–7.

18. J. Haley, *Uncommon Therapy: The Psychiatric Techniques of Milton Erickson* (New York: W. W. Norton, 1973); and P. Watzlawick, J. Beavin, and D. Jackson, *Pragmatics of Human Communication* (New York: W. W. Norton, 1967).

19. Perls and Baumgardner, *Legacy from Fritz,* p. 117.

20. F. Perls, *Gestalt Therapy Verbatim,* p. 79.

21. Ibid., pp. 69–70.

22. Perls and Baumgardner, *Legacy from Fritz,* p. 44.

23. Ibid., p. 44–45.

24. Perls, *Gestalt Therapy Verbatim,* p. 79.

25. R. Drye, R. Goulding, and M. Goulding, "No Suicide Decision: Patient Monitoring of Suicidal Risk," *American Journal of Psychiatry* (1973) 130:171–74.

26. H. Kaiser, *Effective Psychotherapy: The Contribution of Hellmuth Kaiser*, ed. L. Fierman (New York: Free Press, 1965).

27. Ibid., p. 135.

28. Ibid., p. 126.

29. Ibid., p. 129.

30. H. Kaiser, "The Problem of Responsibility in Psychotherapy," *Psychiatry* (1955) 18:205–11.

31. Kaiser, *Effective Psychotherapy: The Contribution of Hellmuth Kaiser*, pp. 159ff.

32. Ibid., pp. 172–202.

33. W. Dyer, *Your Erroneous Zones* (New York: Avon Books, 1977).

34. Ibid., p. 14.

35. W. Dyer, *Pulling Your Own Strings* (New York: Funk & Wagnalls, 1978).

36. G. Weinberg, *Self-Creation* (New York: Avon Books, 1978).

37. Dyer, *Your Erroneous Zones*, pp. 194–196.

38. Ibid., pp. 214–15.

39. A. Lazarus and A. Fay, *I Can If I Want To* (New York: William Morrow, 1975).

40. N. Lande, *Mindstyles Lifestyles* (Los Angeles: Price, Stern, Sloan, 1976), pp. 135–46.

41. A. Bry, *EST—60 Hours That Transform Your Life* (New York: Harper & Row, 1976), pp. 49–50.

42. Ibid., p. 53.

43. L. Rhinehart, *The Book of EST* (New York: Holt, Rinehart & Winston, 1976), pp. 142–44.

44. Bry, *EST*, p. 59.

45. Rhinehart, *The Book of EST*, pp. 144–45.

46. Bry, *EST*, p. 61.

47. Ibid., pp. 71.

48. Ibid., p. 72–73.

49. Ibid., p. 73.

50. Ibid., p. 72.

51. Ibid., p. 76.

52. Ibid., pp. 72–73.

53. Ibid., p. 128.

54. Ibid., p. 129.

55. S. Fenwick, *Getting It: The Psychology of EST* (New York: J. P. Lippincott., 1976), p. 181.

56. R. Ryckman and M. Sherman, "Relationship between Self-Esteem and Internal-External Locus of Control," *Psychological Report* (1973) 32:1106; and B. Fish and S. Karabenich, "Relationships between Self-Esteem and Locus of Control," *Psychological Reports* (1971) 29:784–87.

57. D. Kilpatrick, W. Dubin, and D. Marcotte, "Personality, Stress of the Medical Education Process and Changes in Affect Mood State," *Psychological Reports* (1974) 3:1215–23.

58. F. Melgas and A. Weisz, "The Personal Future and Suicidal Ideation," *Journal of Nervous and Mental Disease* (1971) 153:244–50; and H. Lefcourt, *Locus of Control* (New Jersey: Lawrence Erlbaum 1976), p. 148.

59. J. Rotter, "Generalized Expectancies for Internal vs. External Control of Reinforcement," *Psychological Monographs* (1966) 80(1, whole #609) 7, 61, 166.

60. J. Easterbrook, *The Determinants of Free Will* (New York: Academic Press, 1978), p. 26.

61. M. Harrow and A. Ferrante, "Locus of Control in Psychiatric Patients," *Journal of Consulting and Clinical Psychology* (1969) 33:582–89; and R. Cromwell, "Description of Parental Behavior in Schizophrenic and Normal Subjects," *Journal of Personality* (1961) 29:363–79.

62. J. Shybutt, "Time Perspective, Internal vs. External Control and Severity of Psychological Disturbance," *Journal of Clinical Psychology* (1968) 24:312–15; and C. Smith, M. Pryer, and M. Distefano, "Internal-External Control and Severity Emotional Impairment," *Journal of Clinical Psychology* (1971) 27:449–50.

63. C. Fersten, "A Functional Analysis of Depression," *American Psychologist* (1973) 28:857–70; P. Lewinsohn, cited in Lefcourt, *Locus of Control*; W. Miller and M. Seligman, "Depression and the Perception of Reinforcement," *Journal of Abnormal Psychology* (1973) 82:62–73; and L. Abramson and H. Sackeim, "A Paradox in Depression: Uncontrollability and Self-Blame," *Psychological Bulletin* (1977) 84:838–52.

64. M. Seligman, *Helplessness: On Depression, Development and Death* (San Francisco: W. H. Freeman, 1975).

65. M. Seligman and S. Maier, "Failure of Escape Traumatic Shock," *Journal of Experimental Psychology* (1967) 74:1–9; and J. Overmier and M. Seligman, "Effects of Inescapable Shock upon Subsequent Escape," *Journal of Comparative and Physiological Psychology* (1967) 63:23–33.

66. D. Hiroto, "Locus of Control and Learned Helplessness," *Journal of Experimental Psychology* (1974) 102:187–93.

67. D. Hiroto and M. Seligman, "Generality of Learned Helplessness in Man," *Journal of Personality of Social Psychology* (1975) 31:311–27.

68. D. Klein and M. Seligman, "Reversal of Performance Deficits and Perceptual Deficits in Learned Helplessness and Depression," *Journal of Abnormal Psychology* (1976) 85:11–26.

69. W. Miller and M. Seligman, "Depression and the Perception of Reinforcement," *Journal of Abnormal Psychology* (1973) 82:62–73.

70. Abramson and Sackeim, "A Paradox."

71. A. Beck, *Depression: Clinical, Experimental and Theoretical Aspects* (New York: Harper & Row, 1967).

72. Abramson and Sackeim, "A Paradox."

73. Lefcourt, *Locus of Control*, pp. 96–109; and J. Phares, *Locus of Control in Personality* (Morristown, N.J.: General Learning Press, 1976), pp. 144–56.

74. Phares, *Locus of Control*; and C. Crandall, W. Katkovsky, and V. Crandall, "Children's Beliefs in Their Own Control of Reinforcement in Intellectual-Academic Situations," *Child Development* (1965) 36:91–109.

75. J. Gillis and R. Jessor, "Effects of Brief Psychotherapy on Belief in Internal Control," *Psychotherapy: Research and Practice* (1970) 7:135–37.

76. P. Dua, "Comparison of the Effects of Behaviorally Oriented Action and Psychotherapy Reeducation on Intraversion-Extraversion, Emotionality, and Internal vs. External Control," *Journal of Counseling Psychology* (1970) 17:567–72.

77. S. Nowick and J. Bernes, "Effects of a Structured Camp Experience on Locus of Control," *Journal of Genetic Psychology* (1973) 122:247–52.

78. M. Foulds, "Change in Locus of Internal-External Control," *Comparative Group Studies* (1971) 2:293–300; M. Foulds, J. Guinan, and R. Warehine, "Marathon Group: Change in Perceived Locus of Control," *Journal of College Student Personnel* (1974) 15:8–11; and M. Dianard and J. Shapiro, "Change in Locus of Control as a Function of Encounter Group Experiences," *Journal of Abnormal Psychology* (1973) 82:514–18.

79. I. Yalom, *Theory and Practice of Group Psychotherapy* (New York: Basic Books, 1975), pp. 77–98.

80. D. York and C. Eisman, unpublished study.

81. J. Dreyer, University of West Virginia, unpublished study.

82. M. Lieberman, N. Solow, G. Bond, and J. Reibstein, "The Psychotherapeutic Impact of Women's Consciousness-raising Groups," *Archives of General Psychology* (1979) 36:161–68.

83. L. Horowitz, "On the Cognitive Structure of Interpersonal Problems Treated in Psychotherapy," *Journal of Consulting and Clinical Psychology* (1979) 47:5–15.

84. G. Helweg, cited in J. Phares, *Locus of Control*, p. 169.

85. R. Jacobsen, cited in Phares, *Locus of Control*, p. 169.

86. K. Wilson, cited in Phares, *Locus of Control*, pp. 169–70.

87. M. Lieberman, I. Yalom, and M. Miles, *Encounter Groups: First Facts* (New York: Basic Books, 1973).

88. B. Skinner, cited in A. Bandura, *Social Learning Theory* (Englewood Cliffs, N.J.; Prentice Hall, 1977), p. 203.

89. L. Binswanger, *Sigmund Freud: Reminiscences of a Friendship*, trans. N. Guterman, (New York: Grune & Stratton, 1957) p. 90.

90. A. Bandura, "Presidential Address," delivered at the meeting of the American Psychological Association, New Orleans, August 1974.

91. Ibid.; and A. Bandura, "The Self System in Reciprocal Determinism," *American Psychologist* (1978) 33(4):344–58.

92. Bandura, "Presidential Address," p. 633.

93. Epictetus, cited in H. Arendt, *Willing—The Life of the Mind*, vol. II (New York: Harcourt Brace Jovanovich, 1978) p. 29.

94. Sartre, *Being and Nothingness,* p. 629.

95. S. Freud, *The Psychopathology of Everyday Life,* vol. VI in *Standard Edition* (London: Hogarth Press, 1960; originally published 1901), pp. 178–88.

96. O. Simonton, S. Matthews-Simonton, and J. Crieghton, *Getting Well Again* (Los Angeles: J. P. Tarcher, 1978).

97. I. Yalom and C. Greaves, "Group Therapy with the Terminally Ill," *American Journal of Psychiatry,* (1977) 134(4):396–400; and D. Spiegel and I. Yalom, "Cancer Group," *International Journal of Group Psychotherapy* (1978) 28(2):233–45.

98. I. Janis, *Psychological Stress* (New York: John Wiley, 1958).

99. V. Frankl, oral communication, 1972.

100. Yalom and Greaves, "Group Therapy"; and Spiegel and Yalom, "Cancer Group."

101. S. Freud, "New Introductory Lectures on Psychoanalysis," vol. XXII in *Standard Edition* (London: Hogarth Press, 1964; originally published 1933), p. 66.

102. M. Buber, "Guilt and Guilt Feelings," *Psychiatry* (1957) 20:114–29.

103. M. Heidegger, *Being and Time,* trans. J. Macquarrie and E. Robinson (New York: Harper & Row, 1962), p. 327.

104. Ibid., p. 329.

105. Ibid., p. 330.

106. P. Tillich, *The Courage to Be* (New Haven, Conn.: Yale University Press, 1952), p. 52.

107. S. Kierkegaard, *The Sickness Unto Death* (New York: Doubleday, 1941), pp. 186–87.

108. M. Friedman, introduction to M. Buber, *Between Man and Man* (New York: Macmillan, 1965), p. xix.

109. O. Rank, *Will Therapy and Truth and Reality* (New York: Alfred A. Knopf, 1945).

110. R. May, ed., *Existential Psychology* (New York: Random House, 1969), p. 19.

111. R. May, *Art of Counseling* (Nashville, Tenn.: Abingdon Press, Apex Books, 1967), p. 70.

112. R. May, E. Angel, and H. Ellenberger, eds., *Existence* (New York: Basic Books, 1958), p. 52.

113. A. Maslow, *Toward a Psychology of Being* (Princeton, N.J.: D. Van Nostrand, 1962), p. 5.

114. M. Buber, *The Knowledge of Man* (New York: Harper & Row, 1965), pp. 121–48.

115. G. Murphy, *Human Potentialities* (New York: Basic Books, 1958).

116. E. Fromm, *Man for Himself* (New York: Rinehart, 1947).

117. C. Buhler, "Maturation and Motivation," *Dialectica* (1951) 5:312–61.

118. G. Allport, *Becoming* (New Haven, Conn.: Yale University Press, 1955).

119. C. Rogers, *On Becoming a Person* (Boston: Houghton Mifflin, 1961).

120. C. Jung, *Modern Man in Search of a Soul* (New York: Harcourt, 1933).

121. Maslow, *Psychology of Being,* pp. 19–41.

122. K. Horney, *Neurosis and Human Growth* (New York: W. W. Norton, 1950).

123. Ibid., p. 17.

124. Maslow, *Psychology of Being,* pp. 3–4.

125. J. S. Mill, cited in Arendt, *Willing,* p. 9.

126. St. Augustine, cited in Arendt, *Willing,* p. 98.

127. F. Kafka, *Tagebucher 1910-1923* (Germany: S. Fischer Verlag; New York: Schocken, 1948), p. 350.

128. F. Kafka, *The Trial* (New York: Modern Library, Random House, 1956), pp. 247–78.

129. J. Heuscher, "Inauthenticity, Flight from Freedom, Despair," *American Journal of Psychoanalysis* (1976) 36:331–7.

130. Kafka, *The Trial,* p. 266.

131. Kafka, cited in M. Buber, *The Knowledge of Man* (New York: Harper & Row, 1965) p. 143.

132. Buber, *Knowledge of Man,* p. 143.

133. Heuscher, "Inauthenticity."

134. Ibid.

135. S. Kierkegaard, cited in R. May, *The Meaning of Anxiety,* rev. ed. (New York: W. W. Norton, 1977) p. 40.

Chapter 7

1. A. Wheelis, "The Place of Action in Personality Change," *Psychiatry* (1950) 13:135–48.

2. A. Wheelis, "Will and Psychoanalysis," *Journal of Psychoanalytic Association* (1956) 4:285–303.

3. Ibid.

4. E. Jones, *The Life and Work of Sigmund Freud*, vol. I (New York: Basic Books, 1953), p. 41.

5. S. Freud, cited in R. May, *Love and Will* (New York: W. W. Norton, 1969), p. 183.

6. May, *Love and Will*, p. 183.

7. S. Freud, *The Ego and the Id*, vol. XIX in *Standard Edition* (London: Hogarth Press, 1961, originally published in 1923), p. 50.

8. May, *Love and Will*, p. 198.

9. T. Hobbes, cited in H. Arendt, *Willing*, vol. II in *The Life of Mind* (New York: Harcourt Brace Jovanovich, 1978), p. 23.

10. B. Spinoza, *The Chief Works*, ed. R. H. Elwes, vol. II (New York: Dover, 1951), p. 390.

11. May, *Love and Will*, pp. 197–98.

12. Aristotle, cited in Arendt, *Willing*, pp. 15–18.

13. Arendt, *Willing*, p. 32.

14. I. Kant, cited in Arendt, *Willing*, p. 6.

15. L. Farber, *The Ways of the Will* (New York: Basic Books, 1966), p. 27.

16. Wheelis, "Will and Psychoanalysis."

17. S. Arieti, *The Will to Be Human* (New York: Quadrangle Books, 1972), p. 2.

18. Wheelis, "Will and Psychoanalysis."

19. Arendt, *Willing*, p. 15.

20. A. Schopenhauer, *The World as Will and Representation* (Indian Hills, Col.: Falcon's Wing Press, 1958).

21. F. Nietzsche, cited in Arendt, *Willing*, p. 161.

22. Aristotle, cited in Arendt, *Willing*, p. 16.

23. Arendt, *Willing*, p. 13; and May, *Love and Will*, p. 243.

24. W. James, *Psychology* (Greenwich, Conn.: Fawcett, 1963), pp. 376–80.

25. E. Becker, *Denial of Death* (New York: Free Press, 1973).

26. O. Rank, *Will Therapy and Truth and Reality* trans. J. Taft, (New York: Alfred A. Knopf, 1945).

27. Ibid., p. 111.

28. Ibid., p. 24.

29. Ibid., p. 28.

30. O. Rank, "The Training of the Will and Emotional Development," *Journal of Otto Rank Associates*, (December 1967) 3:51–74.

31. Ibid., p. 68.

32. Ibid., p. 68.

33. Ibid., p. 69.

34. Rank, *Will Therapy*, p. 230.

35. Ibid., p. 7.

36. Ibid., p. 9.

37. Ibid., p. 12.

38. Ibid., p. 8.

39. Ibid., p. 11.

40. S. Tomkins, cited in R. May, *Love and Will* (New York: W. W. Norton, 1969), p. 194.

41. Wheelis, "Will and Psychoanalysis."

42. Rank, *Will Therapy*, p. 16.

43. Ibid, p. 56.

44. L. Farber, *The Ways of the Will* (New York: Basic Books, 1966).

45. Ibid., p. 8.

46. Ibid., p. 15.

47. May, *Love and Will*, p. 197.

48. Ibid., p. 211.

49. Ibid., p. 243.

50. Ibid., p. 211.

51. S. Freud, *Interpretation of Dreams*, vol. V in *Standard Edition* (London: Hogarth Press, 1953; originally published in 1900), pp. 565–70.

52. Ibid., pp. 550–572.

53. May, *Love and Will*, p. 210.

54. Ibid., p. 211.

55. Ibid., p. 218.

56. Ibid.

57. Rank, *Will Therapy*, p. 12.

58. H. Arendt, *Willing*, p. 158.

59. E. Keen, cited in May, *Love and Will*, p. 268.

60. May, *Love and Will*, p. 165.

61. J. Nemiah, "Alexithymia and Psychosomatic Illness," *Journal of Continuing Education and Psychiatry* (October 1978) pp. 25–38.

62. S. Freud, *Studies on Hysteria*, vol. II in *Standard Edition* (London: Hogarth Press, 1955; originally published, 1895).

63. I. Yalom, *Theory and Practice of Group Psychotherapy* (New York: Basic Books, 1975), pp. 77–79.

64. S. Rose, "Intense Feeling Therapy," in *Emotional Flooding*, ed. P. Olsen (New York: Penguin Books, 1977), pp. 80–96.

65. T. Stampfl and D. Lewis, "Essentials of Implosive Therapy," *Journal of Abnormal Psychology* (1967) 6:496–503.

66. A. Lowen, *Bioenergetics* (N.Y.: Coward, McCann & Geoghegan, 1975).

67. P. Olsen, *Emotional Flooding*, p. 77.

68. A. Janov, *The Primal Scream* (New York: G. P. Putnam, 1970).

69. J. P. Sartre, *The Age of Reason* (New York: Alfred A. Knopf, 1952), p. 144.

70. I. Yalom, Bloch, et al., "The Impact of a Weekend Group Experience on Individual Therapy," *Archives of General Psychiatry* (1977) 34:399–415.

71. D. Hamburg, oral communication, 1968.

72. F. Alexander and T. French, *Psychoanalytic Theory: Principles and Applications* (New York: Ronald Press, 1946).

73. F. Perls, *The Gestalt Approach and Eye-Witness to Therapy* (Palo Alto, Calif.: Science and Behavior Books, 1973), p. 63.

74. Ibid., pp. 63–64.

75. Ibid., p. 68.

76. Ibid., pp. 73–74.

77. Ibid., p. 78.

78. F. Perls, *Gestalt Therapy Verbatim* (Toronto, New York and London: Bantam Books, 1971), p. 1.

79. E. Pohlster and M. Pohlster, *Gestalt Therapy Integrated* (New York: Brunner Mazel, 1973), p. 229.

80. May, *Love and Will*, p. 216.

81. J. Bugental, "Intentionality and Ambivalence," in *William James: Unfinished Business*, ed. R. MacLeod (Washington, D.C.: American Psychological Association, 1969), pp. 93–98.

82. Ibid.

83. M. Heidegger, *Being and Time*, trans. J. Macquarrie and E. Robinson (New York: Harper & Row, 1962), p. 158.

84. A. Camus, *The Fall and Exile in the Kingdom* (New York: Modern Library, 1965), p. 63.

85. S. Beckett, *En Attendant Godot* (Paris: Les Editions de Minuit, 1952); my translation.

86. W. James, *Principles of Psychology* (Greenwich, Conn.: Fawcett, 1963), chap. 26, pp. 365–401.

87. R. Goulding, "New Directions in Transactional Analysis: Creating an Environment for Redecision and Change," in *Progress in Group and Family Therapy*, eds. C. Sager and H. Kaplan (New York: Brunner Mazel, 1972), pp. 105–34.

88. J. Dusay and C. Steiner, "Transactional Analysis in Groups," in *Comprehensive Group Therapy*, eds. H. Kaplan and B. Sadock (Baltimore: Williams & Wilkins, 1971), pp. 198–240.

89. Goulding, "New Directions," pp. 110–112.

90. E. Erikson, *Childhood and Society*, 2nd ed. (New York: W. W. Norton, 1963).

91. J. Gardner, *Grendel* (New York: Ballantine Books, 1971), p. 115.

92. F. Estess, oral communication, 1977.

93. Heidegger, *Being and Time*, p. 310.

94. Wheelis, "Will and Psychoanalysis."

95. *Encyclopedia of Philosophy*, vol. I, p. 428.

96. E. Menaker, "Will and the Problem of Masochism," *Journal of Contemporary Psychotherapy* (1969), 1:186–226.

97. E. Jones and H. Gerard, *Foundations of Social Psychology* (New York: John Wiley, 1967), pp. 186–226.

98. L. Festinger, *A Theory of Cognitive Dissonance* (Evanston, Ill.: Row, Peterson, 1957).

99. Jones and Gerard, *Social Psychology*, pp. 193–94.

100. L. Rhinehart, *The Dice Man* (New York: William Morrow, 1971).

101. J. Bugental, "Someone Needs to Worry: The Existential Anxiety of Responsibility and Decision," *Journal of Contemporary Psychotherapy* (1967) 2:41–53.

102. R. White, "Motivation Reconsidered," *The Psychological Review* (1959) 66:297–333.

103. K. Horney, *Neurosis and Human Growth* (New York: W. W. Norton, 1950).

104. Ibid., p. 17.

105. H. Greenwald, *Decision Therapy* (New York: Peter Wyden, 1973), p. 154.

106. Farber, *Ways of the Will*, p. 450.

107. Greenwald, *Decision Therapy*, p. 22.

108. Ibid., p. 38.

109. May, *Love and Will*, pp. 236–37.

110. J. Frank, "Emotional Reaction of American Soldiers to an Unfamiliar Disease," *Archives of General Psychiatry* (1967) 17:416–427.

111. M. Leiberman, I. Yalom, and M. Miles, *Encounter Groups: First Facts* (New York: Basic Books, 1973), pp. 365–67.

112. R. Nisbett and T. Wilson, "Telling More Than We Can Know: Verbal Reports on Mental Process," *Psychological Reviews* (1977) 84:231–58.

113. Yalom, *Group Psychotherapy*, pp. 440–45.

114. S. Freud, "Constructions in Analysis," vol. XXIII in *Standard Edition* (London: Hogarth Press, 1964; originally published in 1937), p. 259.

115. Ibid., 266.

116. Rank, *Will Therapy*, p. 44.

117. M. Gatch and M. Temerlin, "Belief in Psychic Determinism and the Behavior of the Psychotherapist," *Review of Existential Psychology and Psychiatry*, (1965) 5:16–35.

118. Rank, *Will Therapy*, p. 36.

119. E. Goffman, "The Moral Career of the Mental Patient," *Psychiatry* (1959) 22:123–42.

120. C. Rycroft, *Psychoanalysis Observed* (London: Constable, 1966), p. 18.

Chapter 8

1. M. Heidegger, *Being and Time*, trans. J. Macquarrie and E. Robinson (New York: Harper & Row, 1962), p. 57.

2. S. Freud, "Inhibitions, Symptoms and Anxiety," vol. XX in *Standard Edition* (London: Hogarth Press, 1959; originally published in 1929), pp. 119–23.

3. P. Mullahy, *Psychoanalysis and Interpersonal Psychiatry: The Contribution of Harry Stack Sullivan* (New York: Science House, 1970), p. 137.

4. C. Rogers, "The Loneliness of Contemporary Man as Seen in the Case of Ellen West," in *Review of Existential Psychology and Psychiatry* (1961) 1:94–101.

5. I. Yalom, *Theory and Practice of Group Psychotherapy*, 2nd ed. (New York: Basic Books, 1975), p. 80.

6. Rogers, "Loneliness of Contemporary Man"; F. Fromm-Reichman, "Loneliness," *Psychiatry* (1959) 22:1–16; H. Leiderman, "Intervention," *Psychiatry Clinics* [1969] 6:155–74; E. Josephson and M. Josephson, *Man Alone* (New York: Dell Books, 1962); J. Rubins, "On the Psychopathology of Loneliness," *American Journal of Psychoanalysis* (1964) 24:153–65; D. Reisman, R. Denny, and N. Glaser, *The Lonely Crowd* (New Haven, Conn.: Yale University Press, 1950); G. Moustakas, *Loneliness* (New York: Prentice-Hall, 1961); M. Wood,

Paths of Loneliness (New York: Columbia University Press, 1953); A. Wenkert, "Regaining Identity through Relatedness," *American Journal of Psychoanalysis* (1961) 22:227–33; and W. Willig, "Discussion of A. Wenker paper," *American Journal of Psychoanalysis* (1961) 22:236–39.

7. T. Wolfe, *Look Homeward, Angel* (New York: Charles Scribner, 1929), p. 31.

8. Heidegger, *Being and Time*, p. 284.

9. M. Abrams et al., eds., Everyman, in *The Norton Anthology of English Literature*, vol. I (New York: W. W. Norton, 1962), pp. 281–303.

10. E. Fromm, *The Art of Loving*, (New York: Bantam Books, 1956), p. 7.

11. A. Camus, "La Mort dans l'âme," in *L'Envers et l'endroit* (Paris: Librairie Gallimard, 1937), pp. 87–88; passage translated by Marilyn Yalom.

12. R. Frost, "Desert Places," in *Complete Poems of Robert Frost* (New York: Henry Holt, 1949), p. 386.

13. K. Reinhardt, *The Existential Revolt* (New York: Frederick Ungar, 1952), p. 235.

14. Heidegger, *Being and Time*, p. 233.

15. Ibid., p. 393.

16. H. Drefuss, "Commentary on Being and Time," unpublished manuscript, 1977.

17. F. Nietzsche, cited in M. Heidegger, *An Introduction to Metaphysics* (New York: Anchor Books, 1961), p. 29.

18. L. Fierman, ed., *Effective Psychotherapy: The Contributions of Hellmuth Kaiser* (New York: Free Press, 1965), p. 126.

19. E. Fromm, *Escape From Freedom* (New York: Holt, Rinehart & Winston, 1941), p. 29.

20. O. Rank, *Will Therapy and Truth and Reality*, trans. J. Taft (New York: Alfred A. Knopf, 1945), p. 123.

21. J. Bugental, *The Search for Authenticity* (New York: Holt, Rinehart & Winston, 1965), p. 309.

22. M. Buber, *Between Man and Man* (New York: Macmillan, 1965), p. 11.

23. Ibid., p. 175.

24. M. Buber, *I and Thou* (New York: Charles Scribner, 1970), p. 69.

25. Ibid., pp. 76–79.

26. Buber, *Between Man and Man*, p. xx.

27. Buber, *I and Thou*, p. 54.

28. Ibid., p. 58.

29. Ibid., p. 62.

30. Buber, *Between Man and Man*, p. 22–23.

31. Ibid., p. 19.

32. Ibid., p. 23.

33. V. Frankl, "Encounter: The Concept and Its Vulgarization," *Journal of the American Academy of Psychoanalysis* (1973) 1:73–83.

34. Buber, *Between Man and Man*, p. 19.

35. Ibid., pp. 13–14.

36. Buber, *I and Thou*, pp. 84–85.

37. Hillel, cited in Buber, *I and Thou*, p. 85 n.

38. M. Buber, *Between Man and Man*, pp. 1–2.

39. A. Maslow, *Toward A Psychology of Being* (New York: D. Van Nostrand, 1968), pp. 21–22.

40. Ibid., p. 35.

41. Ibid., p. 36.

42. Ibid., pp. 42–43.

43. E. Fromm, *Art of Loving* (New York: Bantam Books, 1963).

44. Ibid., p. 7.

45. Ibid., p. 15.

46. Ibid., p. 17.

47. Ibid., p. 34.

48. Ibid., p. 18.

49. E. Fromm, *Man for Himself* (New York: Fawcett World Library, 1969), pp. 68–122.

50. Fromm, *Art of Loving*, pp. 21–22.

51. Buber, *I and Thou*, p. 67.

52. Fromm, *Art of Loving*, p. 61.

53. Ibid., p. 39.

54. S. Kierkegaard, *Fear and Trembling/The Sickness unto Death*, trans. W. Lowrie (Garden City, N.Y.: Doubleday, Anchor, 1954), p. 177.

55. L. Carroll, cited in J. Solomon, "Alice and the Red King," *International Journal of Psychoanalysis* (1963) 44:64–73.

56. I. Yalom, *Theory and Practice of Group Therapy* (New York: Basic Books, 1975), pp. 440–45.

57. S. Arieti, "Psychotherapy of Severe Depression," *American Journal of Psychiatry* (1977) 134:864–68.

58. L. Fierman, ed., *Effective Psychotherapy: The Contribution of Hellmuth Kaiser*, op. cit., p. 131.

59. Ibid., p. 110.

60. K. Bach, *Exit-Existentialism* (Belmont, Calif.: Wadsworth, 1973), p. 28.

61. S. Kierkegaard, *Fear and Trembling/The Sickness unto Death*, p. 175.

62. Fierman, *Effective Psychotherapy*, p. 120.

63. Fromm, *Escape from Freedom*, p. 158.

64. S. Freud, *The Psychopathology of Everyday Life*, vol. VI in *Standard Edition* (London: Hogarth Press, 1960; originally published 1901), p. 158.

65. E. Greenspan, "Fantasies of Women Confronting Death," *Journal of Consulting Psychology* (1975) 29:252–60.

66. V. Soloviev, cited in E. Becker, *Angel in Armor* (New York: George Braziller, 1969), p. 5.

67. S. Kierkegaard, *Either/Or*, vol. I., trans. D. Swanson and L. Swanson (Princeton, N.J.: Princeton University Press, 1944), pp. 297–443.

68. Buber, *Between Man and Man*, pp. 29–30.

69. M. Buber, *The Knowledge of Man* (New York: Harper Torchbook, 1965), p. 77.

70. A. Camus, *A Happy Death* (New York: Alfred A. Knopf, 1972), pp. 81–82.

Chapter 9

1. B. Russell, *The Autobiography of Bertrand Russell* (London: Allen & Unwin, 1975), p. 209.

2. Ibid., p. 146.

3. I. Yalom, *Theory and Practice of Group Psychotherapy* (New York: Basic Books, 1975), pp. 78–83.

4. A. Whitehead, *Religion in the Making* (London: Cambridge University Press, 1962), p. 16.

5. E. Fromm, *The Art Of Loving* (New York: Bantam Books, 1963), p. 94.

6. Moustakas, *Loneliness* (New York: Prentice-Hall, 1961), p. 47.

7. A. Camus, cited in M. Charlesworth, *The Existentialists and Jean-Paul Sartre* (Brisbane, Australia: University of Queensland Press, 1975), p. 5.

8. R. Hobson, "Loneliness," *Journal of Analytic Psychology* (1974) 19:71–89.

9. R. Bollendorf, unpublished doctoral dissertation, Northern Illinois University, 1976.

10. O. Will, oral communication, child psychiatry grand rounds, Stanford University, Department of Psychiatry, 1978.

11. L. Sherby, "The Use of Isolation in Ongoing Psychotherapy," *Psychotherapy: Theory, Research and Practice*, (1975) 12:173–74.

12. I. Yalom, et al., "The Impact of a Weekend Group Experience on Individual Therapy," *Archives of General Psychiatry* (1977) 34:399–415.

13. C. Truax and K. Mitchell, "Research on Certain Therapist Interpersonal Skills in Relation to Process and Outcome," in *Handbook of Psychotherapy*, A. Bergin and S. Garfield, eds. (New York: John Wiley, 1971), pp. 299–344; C. Rogers, "Empathic: An Unappreciated Way of Being," *Counseling Psychologist* (1975) 5(2):2–10; C. Truax and R. Carkhuff, *Toward Effective Counseling and Psychotherapy: Training and Practice* (Chicago: Aldine, 1967); G. Barrett-Lennard, "Dimensions of Therapist Response as Causal Factors in Thera-

peutic Change," *Psychological Monographs* 76, no. 43 (whole no. 562), 1962; E. Fieder, "A Comparison of Therapeutic Relationships in Psychoanalytic, Non-Directive and Adlerian Therapy," *Journal of Consulting Psychology* (1950) 14:436–45; A. Bergin and L. Jasper, "Correlates of Empathy in Psychotherapy: A Replication," *Journal of Abnormal Psychology* (1969) 74:477–81; and A. Bergin and S. Solomon, "Personality and Performance Correlates of Empathic Understanding in Psychotherapy," in J. Hart and T. Tomlinson, eds., *New Directions in Client-Centered Therapy* (Boston: Houghton Mifflin, 1970), pp. 223–36.

14. S. Standal and R. Corsini, eds., *Critical Incidents in Psychotherapy* (Englewood Cliffs, N. J.: Prentice Hall, 1959).

15. Ibid., p. 3.

16. Ibid., p. 41.

17. Ibid., p. 67.

18. Ibid., p. 90.

19. Ibid., p. 158.

20. Ibid., p. 178.

21. S. Freud, *Studies on Hysteria,* vol. II in *Standard Edition* (London: Hogarth Press, 1964, originally published in 1895).

22. M. Buber, *The Knowledge of Man,* trans. M. Friedman and R. Smith (New York: Harper Torchbooks, 1965), p. 81.

23. Ibid., p. 82.

24. I. Yalom and G. Elkin, *Every Day Gets a Little Closer: A Twice-Told Therapy* (New York: Basic Books, 1974).

25. H. Kaiser, *Effective Psychotherapy: The Contribution of Hellmuth Kaiser,* ed. L. Fierman (New York: Free Press, 1965), p. 152.

26. K. Fisher, "Ultimate Goals in Therapy," *Journal of Existentialism: The International Quarterly of Existential Thought* (1967) 7:215–32.

27. M. Buber, *The Knowledge of Man* (New York: Harper Torchbooks, 1965), pp. 171–72.

28. C. Sequin, *Love and Psychotherapy* (New York: Libra, 1965), p. 113.

29. Ibid., p. 121.

30. Buber, *Knowledge of Man,* p. 82.

31. M. Buber, *I and Thou,* p. 179.

32. Sequin, *Love and Psychotherapy* p. 123.

33. M. Heidegger, *Being and Time,* (New York: Harper & Row, 1962), p. 158.

34. Buber, *Knowledge of Man,* pp. 166–84.

35. D. Rosenhan, "On Being Sane in Insane Places," *Science* (1973) 179:250–58.

36. S. Freud, *Observations on Transference-Love,* vol. XII in *Standard Edition* (London: Hogarth Press, 1958; originally published in 1915), p. 169.

37. Ibid., p. 165.

38. S. Ferenczi, cited in S. Foulkes, "A Memorandum on Group Therapy," British Military Memorandum, ADM, July 1945.

39. R. Greenson and M. Wexler, "The Non-Transference Relationship in the Psychoanalytic Situation," *International Journal of Psychoanalysis* (1969) 50:27–39.

40. A. Freud, "The Widening Scope of Indications for Psychoanalysis," discussion, *Journal of American Psychoanalytic Association* (1954) 2:607–20.

41. Greenson and Wexler, "Non-Transference Relationship."

42. Ibid.

43. Buber, *I and Thou,* pp. 84–85.

Chapter 10

1. Anonymous, cited in H. Cantril and C. Bumstead, *Reflections on the Human Venture* (New York: New York University Press, 1960), p. 308.

2. L. Tolstoy, *My Confession, My Religion, The Gospel in Brief* (New York: Charles Scribner, 1929), p. 12.

3. Ibid., p. 13.

4. Ibid., p. 14.

5. Ibid.

6. Ibid., p. 20.

7. A. Camus, cited in A. Jaffe, *The Myth of Meaning in the Work of C. J. Jung* (London: Hodden & Stoughton, 1970), title page.

8. C. Jung, cited in Jaffe, *Myth of Meaning*, p. 130.

9. C. Jung, *Collected Works: The Practice of Psychotherapy*, vol. XVI (New York: Pantheon, Bollingen Series, 1966), p. 83.

10. V. Frankl, "The Feeling of Meaninglessness: A Challenge to Psychotherapy," *American Journal of Psychoanalysis* (1972) 32:85–89; V. Frankl, *The Will to Meaning* (New York: World, 1969), p. 90; and V. Frankl, *The Doctor and the Soul* (New York: Alfred A. Knopf, 1965), p. xi.

11. S. Maddi, "The Search for Meaning," in *The Nebraska Symposium on Motivation—1970*, ed. W. Arnold and M. Page (Lincoln: University of Nebraska Press, 1970), pp. 137–86.

12. S. Maddi, "The Existential Neurosis," *Journal of Abnormal Psychology* (1967) 72:311–25.

13. B. Wolman, "Principles of International Psychotherapy" in *Psychotherapy: Theory, Research and Practice* (1975) 12:149–59.

14. N. Hobbs, "Sources of Gain in Psychotherapy," *American Psychologist* (1962) 17:742–48.

15. *The Encyclopedia of Philosophy*, vol. IV, ed. P. Edwards, et al. (New York: Macmillan and Free Press, 1967), pp. 467–78.

16. B. Pascal, cited in V. Frankl, *The Doctor and the Soul*, 2nd ed. (New York: Alfred A. Knopf, 1965), p. 31.

17. V. Frankl, *Man's Search for Meaning* (Boston: Beacon Press, 1963), pp. 186–87.

18. M. Maimonides, *The Guide of the Perplexed*, vol. II (Chicago, London: University of Chicago Press, 1963), pp. 634–36.

19. Jung, cited in Jaffe, *Myth of Meaning*, p. 130.

20. C. Jung, *Memories, Dreams, Reflections* (New York: Pantheon Books, 1961), pp. 255–56.

21. G. Hegel, cited in Jaffe, *Myth of Meaning*, p. 145.

22. R. Rilke, *Ausgewahlte Werke*, vol. I (Leipzig: Iminsel-Verlag, 1930), p. 28; translation by Marilyn Yalom.

23. T. Mann, cited in Jaffe, *Myth of Meaning*, p. 140.

24. Teilhard de Chardin, *The Phenomenon of Man* (New York: Harper, 1959).

25. C. Merchant, *The Death of Nature: Women, Ecology and Scientific Revolution* (San Francisco: Harper & Row, 1980).

26. A. Pope, *The Selected Poetry of Pope*, ed. M. Price (New York: New American Library, 1978), p. 133.

27. T. Dobzhansky, *The Biology of Ultimate Concern* (New York: New American Library, 1967), p. 132.

28. P. Teilhard de Chardin, cited in Dobzhansky, *Biology of Ultimate Concern*, p. 137.

29. A. Camus, *The Myth of Sisyphus and Other Essays* (New York: Alfred A. Knopf, 1955).

30. A. Camus, *A Happy Death* (New York: Alfred A. Knopf, 1972).

31. A. Camus, *The Stranger* (New York: Alfred A. Knopf, 1946).

32. Camus, *Myth of Sisyphus*, p. 90.

33. A. Camus, *The Plague* (New York: Modern Library, 1948).

34. J. P. Sartre, cited in R. Hepburn, "Questions about the Meaning of Life," *Religious Studies* (1965) 1:125–40.

35. J. P. Sartre, *No Exit and Three Other Plays* (New York: Vintage Books, 1955).

36. Ibid., p. 91.

37. Ibid., p. 92.

38. Ibid.

39. Ibid., p. 94.

40. Ibid., p. 94.

41. Ibid., p. 105.

42. Ibid., p. 108.

43. Ibid., p. 121–122.

44. Ibid., p. 123.

45. Ibid., p. 124.

46. G. Allport, cited in V. Frankl, *Will to Meaning*, p. 66.

47. C. Jung, cited in Jaffe, *Myth of Meaning*, p. 146.

48. K. Jaspers, cited in Frankl, *Will to Meaning*, p. 38.

49. W. Durant, *On the Meaning of Life* (New York: Ray Long and Richard R. Smith, 1932), pp. 128–29.

50. Ibid., p. 129.

51. I. Taylor, cited in S. Maddi, "The Strenuousness of the Creative Life," in I. A. Taylor and J. W. Getzels, eds., *Perspectives in Creativity* (Chicago: Aldine, 1975), pp. 173–90.

52. L. Beethoven, cited in M. Von Andics, *Suicide and the Meaning of Life* (London: William Hodge, 1947), p. 178.

53. A. Roe, "Changes in Scientific Activities with Age," *Science* (1965) 150:313–18.

54. M. Crosby, oral communication, 1979.

55. P. Koestenbaum, *Is There an Answer to Death?* (New York: Prentice-Hall, 1976), pp. 37–38.

56. J. Brennecke and R. Amick, *The Struggle for Significance*, 2nd ed. (Beverly Hills, Calif.: Clencoe Press, 1975), pp. 9–10.

57. A. Maslow, *Toward a Psychology of Being* (N.J.: Van Nostrand, 1962), p. 147.

58. M. Buber, "The Way of Man According to the Teachings of Hasidism," in *Religion from Tolstoy to Camus*, ed. W. Kaufman (New York: Harper Torchbooks, 1961), pp. 425–41.

59. Ibid., p. 437.

60. E. Erikson, *Childhood and Society*, 2nd ed. (New York: W. W. Norton, 1963), pp. 247–74.

61. G. Vaillant, *Adaptation to Life* (Boston: Little, Brown, 1977); R. Gould, "The Phases of Adult Life: A Study in Developmental Psychology," *American Journal of Psychiatry* (1972) 129:521–31; and D. Levinson, *The Seasons of A Man's Life* (New York: Alfred A. Knopf, 1978).

62. Erikson, *Childhood*, p. 267.

63. G. Vaillant, *Adaptation*, p. 228.

64. Ibid., p. 232.

65. Ibid., p. 343.

66. N. Haan and J. Block, cited in G. Vaillant, op. cit., p. 330.

67. V. Frankl, *Man's Search for Meaning: An Introduction to Logotherapy* (New York: Pocket Books, 1963).

68. V. Frankl, oral communication, 1971.

69. Frankl, *Will to Meaning*, p. 21.

70. V. Frankl, "Self-transcendence as a Human Phenomenon," *Journal of Humanistic Psychology* (1966) 6:97–107.

71. C. Buhler, "The Human Course of Life in Its Goal Aspects," *Journal of Humanistic Psychology*, (1964) 4:1–17.

72. G. Allport, *Becoming: Basic Considerations for a Psychology of Personality* (New Haven, Conn.: Yale University Press, 1955).

73. Frankl, *Man's Search*, p. 166.

74. Frankl, "Self-transcendence."

75. W. Frankena, *Ethics* (New York: Prentice-Hall, 1973) p. 86.

76. A. Watts, *The Meaning of Happiness* (New York: Perennial Library, Harper & Row, 1940), p. vi.

77. Frankl, *Man's Search for Meaning*, p. 154.

78. A. Ungersma, *The Search for Meaning* (Philadelphia, Pa.: Westminister Press, 1961), pp. 27f.

79. Frankl, "Self-transcendence."

80. Frankl, *Man's Search for Meaning*, p. 155.

81. Ibid., p. 154.

82. Frankl, *Will to Meaning*, p. 70.

83. V. Frankl, cited in J. Fabry, *The Pursuit of Meaning* (Boston: Beacon Press, 1968), p. 40.

84. Ibid., p. 44.

85. Frankl, *Will to Meaning*, p. 21.

86. S. Bloch et al., "Outcome in Psychotherapy Evaluated by Independent Judges,"

British Journal of Psychiatry (1977) 131:410–14; and G. Bond, et al., "The Evaluation of the 'Target Problem' Approach to Outcome Measures," *Psychotherapy: Theory, Research and Practice* (1979) 16(1): 48–54.

87. J. Gardner, doctoral dissertation, University of Chicago, 1977.

88. S. Freud, cited in Edwards, "Meaning and Value," p. 477.

89. Frankl, *Will to Meaning*, p. 84.

90. J. Crumbaugh, "Frankl's Logotherapy: A New Orientation in Counseling," *Journal of Religion and Health* (1971) 10:373–86.

91. Ing. Alois Habinger, cited in V. Frankl, "The Feeling of Meaninglessness: A Challenge to Psychotherapy," *American Journal of Psychoanalysis* (1972) 32:85–89.

92. Maddi, "Search for Meaning"; Maddi, "Existential Neurosis"; and S. Kobasa and S. Maddi, "Existential Personality Theory," in *Current Personality Theory*, ed. R. Corsini (Itasca, Ill.: Peacock Books, 1979).

93. S. Maddi, oral communications, 1979.

94. S. Maddi, S. Kobasa, and M. Hoover, "The Alienation Test," *Journal of Humanistic Psychology* (1979) 19(4): 73–76.

95. Maddi, "Search for Meaning."

96. J. Pike, *Beyond Anxiety* (New York: Charles Scribner, 1953).

97. J. Crumbaugh and L. Maholick, "An Experimental Study in Existentialism: The Approach to Frankl's Concept of Noogenic Neurosis," *Journal of Clinical Psychology* (1964) 20:200–207.

98. J. Braun and G. Dolmino, "The Purpose in Life Test," in *The Seventh Mental Measurements Yearbook*, ed. O. K. Buros (Highland Park, N.J.: Gryphon Press, 1978), p. 656.

99. Ibid.

100. Ibid.

101. J. Battista and R. Almond, "The Development of Meaning in Life," *Psychiatry* (1973) 36:409–27.

102. C. Garfield, "A Psychometric and Clinical Investigation of Frankl's Concept of Existential Vacuum and of Anomie," *Psychiatry* (1973) 36:396–408.

103. Braun and Domino, "Purpose in Life Test."

104. Ibid.

105. J. Crumbaugh, "Cross-Validation of Purpose in Life Test," *Journal of Individual Psychology*, (1968) 24:74–81.

106. M. Familetti, "A Comparison of the Meaning and Purpose in Life of Delinquent and Non-delinquent High School Boys," United States International University, *Dissertation Abstracts International* Sept. 1975 vol. 36(3–A), 1825.

107. B. Padelford, "Relationship between Drug Involvement and Purpose in Life," San Diego State University, *Journal of Clinical Psychology* (1974) 30(3):303–5.

108. Crumbaugh, "Cross-Validation."

109. Ibid.

110. Crumbaugh, "Frankl's Logotherapy."

111. R. Jacobson, D. Ritter, and L. Mueller, "Purpose in Life and Personal Values among Adult Alcoholics," *Journal of Clinical Psychology* (1977) 33(1)314–16.

112. B. Sheffield and P. Pearson, "Purpose in Life in a Sample of British Psychiatric Outpatients," *Journal of Clinical Psychology* (1974) 30(4)459.

113. D. Sallee and J. Casciani, "Relationship between Sex Drive and Sexual Frustration and Purpose in Life," *Journal of Clinical Psychology* (1967) 32(2) 273–75.

114. J. Thomas and E. Weiner, "Psychological Differences among Groups of Critically Ill Hospitalized Patients, Noncritically Ill Hospitalized Patients and Well Controls," *Journal of Consulting and Clinical Psychology* (1974) 42(2) 274–79.

115. J. Crandall and R. Rasmussen, "Purpose in Life as Related to Specific Values," *Journal of Clinical Psychology* (1975) 31(3) 483–85.

116. Ibid.; and D. Soderstrom and E. Wright, "Religious Orientation and Meaning in Life," *Journal of Clinical Psychology* (1977) 33(1) 65–68.

117. J. McCarthy, "Death Anxiety, Intrinsicness of Religion and Purpose in Life among Nuns and Roman Catholic Female Undergraduates," *Dissertation Abstracts International* (1975) vol. 35(11–B) 5646.

118. P. Pearson and B. Sheffield, "Purpose in Life and Social Attitudes in Psychiatric Patients," *Journal of Clinical Psychology* (1975) 31(2) 330–32.

119. J. Crumbaugh, Sister Mary Raphael, and R. Shrader, "Frankl's Will to Meaning in a Religious Order," *Journal of Clinical Psychology* (1970) 21(2) 206–7.

120. McCarthy, op. cit.; and J. Blazer, "The Relationship between Meaning in Life and Fear of Death," *Psychology* (1973) 10(2) 33–34.

121. L. Doerries, "Purpose in Life and Social Participation," *Journal of Individual Psychology*, (1970) 26(1):50–53; and R. Matteson, "Purpose in Life as Related to Involvement in Organized Groups and Certain Sociocultural Variables," *Dissertation Abstracts International* (1975) vol. 35(8–BO) 4147–48.

122. Matteson, "Purpose in Life."

123. A. Butler and L. Carr, "Purpose in Life through Social Action," *Journal of Social Psychology* (1968) 74(2) 243–50.

124. D. Sharpe and L. Viney, "Weltanschauung and the Purpose in Life Test," *Journal of Clinical Psychology* (1973) 29(4) 489–91.

125. Matteson, "Purpose in Life."

126. G. Sargent, "Motivation and Meaning: Frankl's Logotherapy in the Work Situation," *Dissertation Abstracts International* (1973) vol. 34(4-B), 1785.

127. Garfield, "Psychometric and Clinical Investigation."

128. Padelford, "Drug Involvement and Purpose in Life."

129. Crumbaugh, "Cross-Validation."

130. Sheffield and Pearson, "Purpose in Life and Social Attitudes."

131. Battista and Almond, "Development of Meaning."

132. M. Carney and B. Sheffield, "The Effects of Pulse ECT in Neurotic and Endogenous Depression," *British Journal of Psychiatry* (1974) 125:91–94.

Chapter 11

1. V. Frankl, "What Is Meant by Meaning," *Journal of Existentialism* (1966) 7:21–28.

2. Ibid.

3. C. Kluckholm, "Values and Value-Orientation in the Theory of Action," in *Toward A General Theory of Action*, ed. T. Parsons and E. Shils (Cambridge, Mass.; Harvard University Press, 1951), p. 396.

4. Ibid., pp. 388–434.

5. L. Tolstoy, *My Confession, My Religion, The Gospel in Brief* (New York: Charles Scribner, 1929), p. 20.

6. Ibid., p. 185.

7. B. Russell, *A Free Man's Worship* (Portland, Me.; T. B. Mosher, 1927).

8. E. Becker, *Escape from Evil* (New York: Free Press, 1975), p. 3.

9. V. Frankl, *Man's Search for Meaning: An Introduction to Logotherapy* (New York: Pocket Books, 1963), p. 192.

10. D. Hume, cited in A. Flew, "Tolstoi and the Meaning of Life," *Ethics* (1963) 73:110–18.

11. B. Wolman, "Principles of Interactional Psychotherapy," *Psychotherapy: Theory, Research and Practice* (1975) 12:149–59.

12. Frankl, *Man's Search*, p. 176.

13. E. Fromm, *Escape From Freedom* (New York: Holt, Rinehart & Winston, 1941), p. 13.

14. D. Suzuki, "East and West," in E. Fromm, D. Suzuki, and R. DeMartino, *Zen Buddhism and Psychoanalysis* (New York: Harper & Row, 1960), pp. 1–10.

15. Matthew 6:26 (King James' Version).

16. Luke 12:27 (King James' Version).

17. J. Brennecke and R. Amick, *The Struggle for Significance* (Beverly Hills, Calif.: Glencoe Press, 1975), p. 143.

18. W. B. Yeats, cited in R. Hepburn, "Questions about the Meaning of Life," *Religious Studies* (1965) 1:125–40.

19. Hepburn, "Questions."

20. B. Rajneesh, cited in B. Gunther, *Dying for Enlightenment* (New York: Harper & Row, 1979).

21. V. Frankl, "Fragments from the Logotherapeutic Treatment of Four Cases," in *Modern Psychotherapeutic Practice,* ed. A. Burton (Palo Alto, Calif.: Science and Behavior Books, 1965), pp. 365–67.

22. Personal communication, 1970.

23. Frankl, *Man's Search,* pp. 143–44.

24. Ibid., pp. 368–70.

25. T. Zuehlke and J. Watkins, "The Use of Logotherapy with Dying Patients: An Exploratory Study," *Journal of Clinical Psychology* (1975) 31:729–32.

26. C. Jung, *Memories, Dreams, Reflections* (New York: Pantheon Books, 1961), pp. 139–40.

27. P. Koestenbaum, *Is There an Answer to Death* (Englewood Cliffs, N. J.: Prentice-Hall, 1976), p. 81.

28. A. Ungersma, *The Search for Meaning* (Philadelphia: Westminister Press, 1961), p. 27f.; J. Fabry, *The Pursuit of Meaning* (Boston: Beacon Press, 1969); and J. Crumbaugh, *Everything to Gain* (Chicago: Nelson Hall, 1973).

29. V. Frankl, *The Doctor and the Soul* (New York: Alfred A. Knopf, 1965), pp. 221–53.

30. M. Erickson, "The Use of Symptoms as an Integral Part of Hypnotherapy," *American Journal of Clinical Hypnosis* (1965) 8:57–65; J. Haley, *Uncommon Therapy: The Psychiatric Techniques of Milton Erickson* (New York: W. W. Norton, 1973); and P. Watzlawick, J. Beavin, and D. Jackson, *Pragmatics of Human Communication* (New York: W. W. Norton, 1967).

31. J. Crumbaugh, "Frankl's Logotherapy: A New Orientation in Counseling," *Journal of Religion and Health* (1970) 10:373–86.

32. D. Follesdal, oral communication, 1979.

33. T. Nagel, *Mortal Questions* (London: Cambridge University Press, 1979), p. 21.

34. K. Bach, *Exit-Existentialism: A Philosophy of Self-Awareness* (Belmont, Calif.: Wadsworth, 1973), p. 6.

35. A. Schopenhauer, cited in *The Encyclopedia of Philosophy,* vol. IV, ed. P. Edwards, et al. (New York: Macmillan, 1967), p. 468.

36. Nagel, *Mortal Questions,* p. 22.

37. Bach, *Exit-Existentialism,* p. 7.

38. Hume, cited in Nagel, *Mortal Questions,* p. 20.

39. Tolstoy, *My Confession,* p. 16.

40. L. Wittgenstein, *Tractatus Logico-Philosophicus,* trans. D. Pears and B. McGuinness (London and Henley: Routledge & Kegan Paul, 1961), p. 73.

INDEX

abandonment: Freud on, 61, 62, 64

Abramson, Lynn, 264*n*

abreaction, 60

academic community, 21–26

accident proneness, 273

accountability, 277

action: decision in, 314; responsibility, willing and, 286–93; values as blueprint for, 464; wishing and choosing in, 302

active styles of therapy, 242–43, 267; Perls's 246–50

Adler, Alfred, 66, 74, 316; Frankl on, 444; Rank on, 296, 298

Adlerstein, Arthur, 91

adolescence: death awareness during, 91

adventurousness (crusadism), 450

adversity, 272–73

affect: blocking of, 306–11

aged people: children's conceptions of death in, 97–98; death anxiety in, 51–53

aggression: as form of specialness, 127

aging, 172–73; death anxiety and fears of, 199, 201

Aisenberg, Ruth, 50, 84

Albee, Edward, 451

alcoholism: death anxiety in, 38, 197, 198, 213; isolation and, 394; logotherapy used for, 477–78; Purpose in Life Test and, 458

Alexander, Franz, 308

Alexander, Irving, 91

alexithymia, 304, 305

Alice (case history), 321–22

Allen, Woody, 70

Allport, Gordon, 18, 279*n*, 431, 444

Almond, Richard, 459

alternatives: avoidance of renunciation of, 322–23; in decisions, 318

altruism, 431–34; creativity and, 436; life cycles and, 441

ambivalence, 312–13

American Association of Humanistic Psychology, 18–19

Anastasia (case history), 475

Angle, Carol, 91

Anna (case history; Yalom), 395–96

Anna O. (case history; S. Freud and Breuer), 59, 62–64

anniversary reaction, 106–7

Anthony, Sylvia, 76–78, 81–83, 108; on omission of death anxiety from research, 103

Antonioni, Michelangelo, 360, 451

anxiety, 9, 10; death and, 29–74; death as primary source of, 187–203; decisional, 315; disidentification and, 163–64; in existential psychotherapeutic model, 484; of groundlessness, 221–22; guilt and, 280; Heidegger on, 360*n*; isolation, 393, 399; isolation as source of, 357–58, 370; psychopathology as method for coping with, 110; secondary forms of, 112; separation, 101–3; Tillich on, 277–278; *see also* death anxiety

Aquinas, Thomas (saint), 292

Arendt, Hannah, 289, 291, 302

Arieti, Silvano, 133–34, 290, 378

Aristotle, 332; on cosmic meaning, 424; on decision, 318; on entelechy, 279; on teleological causation, 437; on will, 289, 290

Aronson, Elliot, 175

art, 435, 436, 470

Arthur (alcoholic; case history), 38

articulated cognitive style, 154

Assagioli, Roberto, 164

attachment-separation, 362

attitudes: love as, 372, 377

Auden, W. H., 298

Augustine (saint), 30, 280, 302

authoritarianism: in est, 259–61; negatively correlated with death anxiety, 50

autonomous behavior: avoidance of, 229–30

avoidance: of autonomous behavior, 229–30; of decisions, 321–28; of responsibility, mental health and, 262–64

Bach, Kent, 380, 480

Bally, G., 17

Bandura, Albert, 270–71

Barry (case history), 386–88

Basho, 467, 468

Battista, John, 459

Beatrice (case history), 329–31, 334

Beck, Aaron, 264*n*

Becker, Ernest, 20, 42, 74; on death anxiety, 111; on meaning in life, 465; Rank and, 293; on success neurosis, 128

Beckett, Samuel, 314

Index

Index

Index

Index

Index